SOFTWARE SAFETY AND SECURITY

NATO Science for Peace and Security Series

This Series presents the results of scientific meetings supported under the NATO Programme: Science for Peace and Security (SPS).

The NATO SPS Programme supports meetings in the following Key Priority areas: (1) Defence Against Terrorism; (2) Countering other Threats to Security and (3) NATO, Partner and Mediterranean Dialogue Country Priorities. The types of meeting supported are generally "Advanced Study Institutes" and "Advanced Research Workshops". The NATO SPS Series collects together the results of these meetings. The meetings are co-organized by scientists from NATO countries and scientists from NATO's "Partner" or "Mediterranean Dialogue" countries. The observations and recommendations made at the meetings, as well as the contents of the volumes in the Series, reflect those of participants and contributors only; they should not necessarily be regarded as reflecting NATO views or policy.

Advanced Study Institutes (ASI) are high-level tutorial courses to convey the latest developments in a subject to an advanced-level audience.

Advanced Research Workshops (ARW) are expert meetings where an intense but informal exchange of views at the frontiers of a subject aims at identifying directions for future action.

Following a transformation of the programme in 2006 the Series has been re-named and re-organised. Recent volumes on topics not related to security, which result from meetings supported under the programme earlier, may be found in the NATO Science Series.

The Series is published by IOS Press, Amsterdam, and Springer Science and Business Media, Dordrecht, in conjunction with the NATO Emerging Security Challenges Division.

Sub-Series

A.	Chemistry and Biology	Springer Science and Business Media
B.	Physics and Biophysics	Springer Science and Business Media
C.	Environmental Security	Springer Science and Business Media
D.	Information and Communication Security	IOS Press
E.	Human and Societal Dynamics	IOS Press

http://www.nato.int/science
http://www.springer.com
http://www.iospress.nl

Sub-Series D: Information and Communication Security – Vol. 33
ISSN 1874-6268 (print)
ISSN 1879-8292 (online)

Software Safety and Security

Tools for Analysis and Verification

Edited by

Tobias Nipkow
Technische Universität München, Germany

Orna Grumberg
Technion–Israel Institute of Technology, Haifa, Israel

and

Benedikt Hauptmann
Technische Universität München, Germany

IOS Press

Amsterdam • Berlin • Tokyo • Washington, DC
Published in cooperation with NATO Emerging Security Challenges Division

Proceedings of the NATO Advanced Study Institute on Tools for Analysis and Verification of Software Safety and Security
Bayrischzell, Germany
2-14 August 2011

ISBN 978-1-61499-027-7 (print)
ISBN 978-1-61499-028-4 (online)
Library of Congress Control Number: 2012937823

Publisher
IOS Press BV
Nieuwe Hemweg 6B
1013 BG Amsterdam
Netherlands
fax: +31 20 687 0019
e-mail: order@iospress.nl

Distributor in the USA and Canada
IOS Press, Inc.
4502 Rachael Manor Drive
Fairfax, VA 22032
USA
fax: +1 703 323 3668
e-mail: iosbooks@iospress.com

Software Safety and Security
T. Nipkow et al. (Eds.)
IOS Press, 2012

Preface

Over the last decade, we have seen amazing advances in methods and tools for checking the safety and security of software systems. Automatic tools can now detect security flaws not only in programs of the order of a million lines of code, but also in high-level protocol descriptions. Full functional correctness is more difficult, but we have also seen much progress here, for example in the area of operating system verification, where only last year an OS kernel of 10,000 lines was proved correct; something of a breakthrough. The Summer School Marktoberdorf 2011 showed the wide range of computer science, with its foundations, methods and tools, to present the state-of-the-art in research and scientific practice of this challenging, future-oriented and key-topic in computer science. We assembled leading international experts who presented their in-depth knowledge and their experience in the overarching subject matter.

Conceptually, the courses of this NATO ADVANCED STUDY INSTITUTE ON TOOLS FOR ANALYSIS AND VERIFICATION OF SOFTWARE SAFETY AND SECURITY in 2011 were divided into 3 integrated modules:

Foundations of Safety and Security, lectured by Orna Grumberg, Marta Kwiatkowska, Tobias Nipkow, Peter O'Hearn, Helmut Seidl
Applications of Safety Analysis, taught by Gerwin Klein, Rustan Leino, Rupak Majumdar, Sharad Malik
Security Analysis, delivered by Bruno Blanchet, Hubert Comon-Lundh, Andrei Sabelfeld.

In his course, **Mechanized Game-Based Proofs of Security Protocols**, BRUNO BLANCHET presented techniques for automating proofs of security protocols in the computational model. He focused in particular on the automatic computationally sound prover CryptoVerif. CryptoVerif produces proofs presented as sequences of games, similar to the manual proofs of cryptographers. It provides a generic method for specifying the security properties of many cryptographic primitives, proves secrecy and authentication properties, and produces proofs valid for a number of sessions polynomial in the security parameter. Blanchet illustrated CryptoVerif on two simple examples: the encrypt-then-MAC scheme and the Full Domain Hash (FDH) signature scheme.

HUBERT COMMON-LUNDH lectured on **Formal Security Proofs**. The goal of his lecture was to present aspects of formal security proofs of protocols. This is a wide area, and there was the lecture (by B. Blanchet) on related topics. The idea was therefore to explain one particular technique, relying on deducibility constraints, in depth. In short: a deducibility constraint is a sequence of proofs in which some parts are unknown (and formalized with variables) and possibly reused in other constraints. An instance of such constraints yields an attacker's strategy. He explained how to solve such constraints in a particular setting of a few cryptographic primitives.

Model Checking was the topic explored by ORNA GRUMBERG. Computerized systems dominate almost every aspect of our lives and their correct behavior is essential. Model checking is an automated verification technique for checking whether a given system satisfies a desired property. In the lectures, different model checking techniques, which can improve model checking applicability in different ways, were surveyed. Grumberg started from the old-fashioned techniques of BDD-based Symbolic Model Checking and SAT based Bounded Model Checking. She then proceeded to using interpolation and interpolation sequence for SAT-based model checking.

The lecture **Interactive Proof: Applications to Semantics** by GERWIN KLEIN built on the previous introduction to interactive proofs and demonstrated a specific application of interactive proof assistants: the semantics of programming languages. In particular, he showed how to formalize imperative programming languages in the theorem prover Isabelle/HOL, how to define its semantics in different variations, and how to prove properties about the languages in the theorem prover. The emphasis of the lecture was not on formalizing a complex language in depth, but to teach a number of formalization techniques and proof strategies using simple examples. To this purpose, he covered big and small step semantics, typing and type safety, as well as a small machine language with a compiler and compiler correctness proof.

MARTA KWIATKOWSKA delivered a lecture on **Advances in Probabilistic Model Checking**, which is a formal verification technique for the analysis of systems that exhibit stochastic behavior, such as security and communication protocols. It enables a range of quantitative analyses of probabilistic models against specifications such as the worst-case probability of intrusion within 10 seconds or the minimum expected power consumption over all possible scheduling. In recent years, increasing interest in the topic of probabilistic verification has led to significant advances in the applicability and efficiency of these techniques, as well as the discovery of interesting and anomalous behavior in a wide range of real-life case studies.

With **Using and Building an Automatic Program Verifier**, RUSTAN LEINO offered a taste of what current technology can do for program correctness. One of the aims in these lectures was to teach the concepts needed to use a program verifier, and to give students some experience with a program verifier (the language and verifier Dafny). The message which the students took home was to remember verification and verification tools the next time a program is not entirely obvious. The second aim of these lectures was to teach the theoretical foundations of this shared infrastructure, described in terms of an intermediate verification language (the language and verification engine Boogie). The message here was: don't build your plumbing from scratch, leverage an intermediate verification language.

Software Model Checking was the topic of RUPAK MAJUMDAR. Software model checking is the algorithmic analysis of programs to prove properties of their executions. One major goal of software model checking research today is to expand the scope of automated techniques for program reasoning, both in the scale of programs handled and in the richness of properties that can be checked, reducing the burden on the expert human programmer. Majumdar presented some algorithmic advances from the last few decades that have made this possible, at least in certain domains.

Boolean Satisfiability Solvers: Techniques and Extensions was delivered by SHARAD MALIK. Boolean Satisfiability (SAT) is the problem of checking whether a propositional logic formula can ever evaluate to true. SAT manifests itself in several important application domains such as the design and verification of hardware and software systems. Several relatively recent research developments have enabled us to tackle instances with millions of variables and constraints – enabling SAT solvers to be effectively deployed in practical applications including in the analysis and verification of software systems. In the first part of this series of lectures, Malik covered the techniques used in modern SAT solvers. In the second part, he considered extensions of these solvers which have proved useful in analysis and verification.

In his course, **Interactive Proof: Hands-on Introduction**, TOBIAS NIPKOW introduced interactive proving with the Isabelle/HOL system. This involves 3 steps: verified functional programming, predicate logic and structured proofs. The course assumed basic familiarity with some functional programming language of the ML or Haskell family, in particular with recursive data types and pattern matching. No specific background in logic was necessary beyond the ability to read predicate logic formulas.

PETER O'HEARN gave **Lectures on Separation Logic**. Separation logic is an extension of Hoare's logic for reasoning about programs that mutate data held in computer memory. After a section covering the basics, O'Hearn delivered a lecture on semantic foundations. Using a model theoretic perspective, he attempted to describe the extent to which separation logic's 'benefits' do and do not depend on its language of assertions. The later lectures moved on to cover concurrency and mechanized verification, in particular the use of the logic in proof via symbolic execution and static program analysis.

ANDREI SABELFELD lectured on **Information-Flow Security**. He discussed a principled approach to web application security through tracking information flow. Sabelfeld showed that there are some fundamental challenges and tradeoffs which determine the possibilities and limitations of automatically securing web applications. He addressed challenges related to mutual distrust on the policy side (as in web mashups) and tracking information flow in dynamic web programming languages (such as JavaScript) to provide a foundation for practical web application security.

The first part of HELMUT SEIDL's lecture on **Precise Fixpoint Computation through Strategy Iteration and Optimization** considered the numerical properties of integer variables. Here he showed how a generalization of the Bellman-Ford algorithm allows the construction of a precise interval analysis. The second part of his lecture considered the numerical properties of variables holding fractional values – Bellman-Ford is no longer applicable. He succeeded in constructing a precise interval analysis by replacing that algorithm with techniques from linear programming.

As was demonstrated in the Summer School Marktoberdorf series, such presentations, as well as working and learning together, are essential for future scientific results in computer science, and consequently for the development of large-scale reliable and secure software systems. Once more it was proved that, over the years, this NATO Advanced Study Institute has facilitated the strengthening of such connections and applications, and influenced the quality of future research as well as the potential to transfer research into practice. The Summer School provided two weeks of learning, discussion and development of new ideas, and was a productive and beneficial event, at both the professional and social level.

We would like to take this opportunity to thank all the lecturers, the staff, and our hosts in Bayrischzell. Special thanks goes to: Dr. Katharina Spies, Silke Müller, and Katjana Stark for their invaluable support.

The Marktoberdorf Summer School was arranged as an Advanced Study Institute of the *NATO Science for Peace and Security Programme* with support from *Deutscher Akademischer Austausch Dienst (DAAD)* and *Microsoft Research*. We would also like to thank all the authorities involved.

THE EDITORS

Contents

Software Safety and Security
T. Nipkow et al. (Eds.)
IOS Press, 2012
doi:10.3233/978-1-61499-028-4-1

1

Mechanizing Game-Based Proofs of Security Protocols

Bruno BLANCHET [1]

INRIA, École Normale Supérieure, CNRS, Paris, France

Abstract. After a short introduction to the field of security protocol verification, we present the automatic protocol verifier CryptoVerif. In contrast to most previous protocol verifiers, CryptoVerif does not rely on the Dolev-Yao model, but on the computational model. It produces proofs presented as sequences of games, like those manually done by cryptographers; these games are formalized in a probabilistic process calculus. CryptoVerif provides a generic method for specifying security properties of the cryptographic primitives. It can prove secrecy and correspondence properties (including authentication). It produces proofs valid for any number of sessions, in the presence of an active adversary. It also provides an explicit formula for the probability of success of an attack against the protocol, as a function of the probability of breaking each primitive and of the number of sessions.

Keywords. Security protocols; computational model; automatic proof; sequences of games; process calculi.

Introduction

A security protocol is a program that guarantees security properties, such as the secrecy of some piece of data, by relying on cryptographic primitives, such as encryption or signatures. Security protocols make it possible to securely exchange data on insecure networks such as Internet. The design of security protocols is well-known to be error-prone. This can be illustrated by the attack against the Needham-Schroeder public-key protocol [49] found by Lowe [46] 17 years after its publication. Errors in security protocols can have serious consequences, such as loss of money in e-commerce. Furthermore, security errors cannot be detected by testing, since they appear only in the presence of a malicious adversary. Therefore, one aims at proving that security protocols are correct. Manual proofs are complex and error-prone, so formal methods can play an important role by providing tools for proving security protocols correct or for finding attacks.

There exist two main models for analyzing security protocols:

- In the symbolic model, often called *Dolev-Yao* model [37], cryptographic primitives are considered as perfect blackboxes, modeled by function symbols in an algebra of terms, possibly with equations. Messages are terms on these primitives and the adversary can compute only using these primitives.

---

[1] Corresponding Author: Bruno Blanchet, École Normale Supérieure, DI, 45 rue d'Ulm, 75005 Paris, France; E-mail: blanchet@di.ens.fr

- In contrast, in the *computational* model, messages are bitstrings, cryptographic primitives are functions from bitstrings to bitstrings, and the adversary is any probabilistic Turing machine.

The computational model is close to the real execution of protocols, but the proofs are usually manual and informal. The Dolev-Yao model is an abstract model that makes it easier to build automatic verification tools, and many such tools exist: AVISPA [5], FDR [46], and ProVerif [20], for instance. Hubert Comon-Lundh's course will deal with the verification of security protocols in this model. However, security proofs in the Dolev-Yao model in general do not imply security in the computational model.

In order to mechanize proofs in the computational model, several approaches have been considered.

- In the indirect approach, following the seminal paper by Abadi and Rogaway [1], one shows the soundness of the Dolev-Yao model with respect to the computational model, that is, one proves that the security of a protocol in the Dolev-Yao model implies its security in the computational model, modulo additional assumptions. Combining such a result with a Dolev-Yao automatic verifier, one obtains automatic proofs of protocols in the computational model. This approach received much interest [6, 8, 29, 31, 39, 47] and a tool [30] was developed based on [31] to obtain computational proofs using the Dolev-Yao verifier AVISPA, for protocols that rely on public-key encryption and signatures. However, this approach has limitations: since the computational and Dolev-Yao models do not correspond exactly, soundness requires additional hypotheses. (For example, key cycles have to be excluded, or a specific security definition of encryption is needed [3].)

  In a related approach, Backes, Pfitzmann, and Waidner [9–11] have designed an abstract cryptographic library including symmetric and public-key encryption, message authentication codes, signatures, and nonces and shown its soundness with respect to computational primitives, under arbitrary active attacks. This framework has been used for a computationally-sound machine-checked proof of the Needham-Schroeder-Lowe protocol [54].

  Canetti [27] introduced the notion of universal composability. With Herzog [28], they show how a Dolev-Yao-style symbolic analysis can be used to prove security properties of protocols within the framework of universal composability, for a restricted class of protocols using public-key encryption as only cryptographic primitive. Then, they use the automatic Dolev-Yao verification tool Proverif [21] for verifying protocols in this framework.

- Techniques used previously in the Dolev-Yao model have also been adapted in order to obtain proofs in the computational model.

  For instance, Datta, Derek, Mitchell, Shmatikov, and Turuani [35, 36] have adapted the logic PCL (Protocol Composition Logic), first designed for proving protocols in the Dolev-Yao model, to the computational model. Other computationally sound logics include CIL (Computational Indistinguishability Logic) [12] and a specialized Hoare logic designed for proving asymmetric encryption schemes in the random oracle model [32, 33].

  Similarly, type systems [34, 43, 45, 53] can provide computational security guarantees. For instance, [43] handles shared-key and public-key encryption, with an unbounded number of sessions. This system relies on the Backes-Pfitzmann-Waidner library. A type inference algorithm is given in [7].

- In the direct approach, one aims at mechanizing proofs in the computational model, without using a Dolev-Yao protocol verifier. Computational proofs made by cryptographers are typically presented as sequences of games [18,52]: the initial game represents the protocol to prove; the goal is to show that the probability of breaking a certain security property is negligible in this game. Intermediate games are obtained each from the previous one by transformations such that the difference of probability between consecutive games is negligible. The final game is such that the desired probability is obviously negligible from the form of the game. The desired probability is then negligible in the initial game. Halevi [38] suggested to use tools for mechanizing these proofs, and several techniques have been used for reaching this goal.

  CryptoVerif [22–25], which will be the main topic of this course, is such a tool. It generates proofs by sequences of games automatically or with little user interaction. The games are formalized in a probabilistic process calculus. CryptoVerif provides a generic method for specifying security properties of many cryptographic primitives. It proves secrecy and authentication properties. It also provides a bound on the probability of success of an attack. It considerably extends early works by Laud [41,42] which were limited either to passive adversaries or to a single session of the protocol. More recently, Tšahhirov and Laud [44,55] developed a tool similar to CryptoVerif but that represents games by dependency graphs; it handles only public-key and shared-key encryption and proves secrecy properties.

  The tool CertiCrypt [13, 15, 16, 26] enables the machine-checked construction and verification of cryptographic proofs by sequences of games. It relies on the general-purpose proof assistant Coq, which is widely believed to be correct. Easy-Crypt [14] generates CertiCrypt proofs from proof sketches that formally represent the sequence of games and hints, which makes the tool easier to use. Nowak *et al.* [4,50,51] follow a similar idea by providing Coq proofs for several basic cryptographic primitives.

In the tool CryptoVerif, games are represented in a process calculus inspired by the pi-calculus and by the calculi of [48] and of [43]. In this calculus, messages are bitstrings, and cryptographic primitives are functions from bitstrings to bitstrings. The calculus has a probabilistic semantics. The main tool for specifying security assumptions is observational equivalence: Q is observationally equivalent to Q' up to probability p, $Q \approx_p Q'$, when the adversary has probability at most p of distinguishing Q from Q'. With respect to previous calculi mentioned above, our calculus introduces an important novelty which is key for the automatic proof of security protocols: the values of all variables during the execution of a process are stored in arrays. For instance, $x[i]$ is the value of x in the i-th copy of the process that defines x. Arrays replace lists often used by cryptographers in their manual proofs of protocols. For example, consider the standard security assumption on a message authentication code (MAC). Informally, this assumption says that the adversary has a negligible probability of forging a MAC, that is, that all correct MACs have been computed by calling the MAC oracle (*i.e.*, function). So, in cryptographic proofs, one defines a list containing the arguments of calls to the MAC oracle, and when verifying a MAC of a message m, one can additionally check that m is in this list, with a negligible change in probability. In our calculus, the arguments of the MAC oracle are stored in arrays, and we perform a lookup in these arrays in order to find the message

m. Arrays make it easier to automate proofs since they are always present in the calculus: one does not need to add explicit instructions to insert values in them, in contrast to the lists used in manual proofs. Therefore, many trivially sound but difficult to automate syntactic transformations disappear. Furthermore, relations between elements of arrays can easily be expressed by equalities, possibly involving computations on array indices.

CryptoVerif relies on a collection of game transformations, in order to transform the initial protocol into a game on which the desired security property is obvious. The most important kind of transformations exploits the security assumptions on cryptographic primitives in order to obtain a simpler game. As described in Section 2.2, these transformations can be specified in a generic way: we represent the security assumption of each cryptographic primitive by an observational equivalence $L \approx_p R$, where the processes L and R encode oracles: they input the arguments of the oracle and send its result back. Then, the prover can automatically transform a process Q that calls the oracles of L (more precisely, contains as subterms terms that perform the same computations as oracles of L) into a process Q' that calls the oracles of R instead. We have used this technique to specify several variants of shared-key and public-key encryption, signature, message authentication codes, hash functions, Diffie-Hellman key agreement, simply by giving the appropriate equivalence $L \approx_p R$ to the prover. Other game transformations are syntactic transformations, used in order to be able to apply an assumption on a cryptographic primitive, or to simplify the game obtained after applying such an assumption.

In order to prove protocols, these game transformations are organized using a proof strategy based on advice: when a transformation fails, it suggests other transformations that should be applied before, in order to enable the desired transformation. Thanks to this strategy, protocols can often be proved in a fully automatic way. For delicate cases, CryptoVerif has an interactive mode, in which the user can manually specify the transformations to apply. It is usually sufficient to specify a few transformations coming from the security assumptions of primitives, by indicating the concerned cryptographic primitive and the concerned secret key if any; the prover infers the intermediate syntactic transformations by the advice strategy. This mode is helpful for proving some public-key protocols, in which several security assumptions on primitives can be applied, but only one leads to a proof of the protocol. Importantly, CryptoVerif is always sound: whatever indications the user gives, when the prover shows a security property of the protocol, the property indeed holds assuming the given assumptions on the cryptographic primitives.

CryptoVerif has been implemented in Ocaml (29800 lines of code for version 1.12 of CryptoVerif) and is available at http://www.cryptoverif.ens.fr/.

Outline   The next section presents the process calculus for representing games. Section 2 describes the game transformations that serve for proving protocols. Section 3 gives criteria for proving secrecy properties of protocols. Section 4 explains how the prover chooses which transformation to apply at each point. Section 5 presents applications of CryptoVerif and Section 6 concludes.

Notations   We recall the following standard notations. We denote by $\{M_1/x_1, \ldots, M_m/x_m\}$ the substitution that replaces x_j with M_j for each $j \leq m$. The cardinal of a set or multiset S is denoted by $|S|$. If S is a finite set, $x \xleftarrow{R} S$ chooses a random element uniformly in S and assigns it to x. If $\mathcal{A}$ is a probabilistic algorithm, $x \leftarrow \mathcal{A}(x_1, \ldots, x_m)$ denotes the experiment of choosing random coins r and assigning to x the result of running $\mathcal{A}(x_1, \ldots, x_m)$ with coins r. Otherwise, $x \leftarrow M$ is a simple assignment statement.

$$M, N ::= \qquad\qquad\qquad\qquad\qquad\qquad\qquad\qquad \text{terms}$$

i replication index

$x[M_1, \ldots, M_m]$ variable access

$f(M_1, \ldots, M_m)$ function application

$$Q ::= \qquad\qquad\qquad\qquad\qquad\qquad\qquad\qquad\qquad \text{input process}$$

0 nil

$Q \mid Q'$ parallel composition

$!^{i \le n} Q$ replication n times

newChannel $c; Q$ channel restriction

$c[M_1, \ldots, M_l](x_1[\widetilde{i}] : T_1, \ldots, x_k[\widetilde{i}] : T_k); P$ input

$$P ::= \qquad\qquad\qquad\qquad\qquad\qquad\qquad\qquad\qquad \text{output process}$$

$\overline{c[M_1, \ldots, M_l]}\langle N_1, \ldots, N_k \rangle; Q$ output

new $x[i_1, \ldots, i_m] : T; P$ random number

let $x[i_1, \ldots, i_m] : T = M$ in P assignment

if defined$(M_1, \ldots, M_l) \wedge M$ then P else P' conditional

find $(\bigoplus_{j=1}^{m} u_{j1}[\widetilde{i}] \le n_{j1}, \ldots, u_{jm_j}[\widetilde{i}] \le n_{jm_j}$ suchthat

     defined$(M_{j1}, \ldots, M_{jl_j}) \wedge M_j$ then P_j) else P array lookup

event $e(M_1, \ldots, M_l); P$ event

Figure 1. Syntax of the process calculus

1. A Calculus for Games

1.1. Syntax and Informal Semantics

CryptoVerif represents games in the syntax of Figure 1. This calculus assumes a countable set of channel names, denoted by c. It uses parameters, denoted by n, which are integers that bound the number of executions of processes. It also uses types, denoted by T, which are subsets of $bitstring_\perp = bitstring \cup \{\perp\}$ where $bitstring$ is the set of all bitstrings and $\perp$ is a special symbol. Let *fixed-length* types be types that consist of the set of all bitstrings of a certain length. Particular types are predefined: $bool = \{\text{true}, \text{false}\}$, where false is 0 and true is 1; $bitstring$; $bitstring_\perp$; $[1, n]$ where n is a parameter. (We consider integers as bitstrings without leading zeroes.)

The calculus also uses function symbols f. Each function symbol comes with a type declaration $f : T_1 \times \ldots \times T_m \to T$, and represents an efficiently computable, deterministic function that maps each tuple in $T_1 \times \ldots \times T_m$ to an element of T. Particular functions are predefined, and some of them use the infix notation: $M = N$ for the equality test, $M \ne N$ for the inequality test (both taking two values of the same type T and returning a value of type $bool$), $M \vee N$ for the boolean or, $M \wedge N$ for the boolean and, $\neg M$ for the boolean negation (taking and returning values of type $bool$).

In this calculus, terms represent computations on bitstrings. The replication index i is an integer which serves in distinguishing different copies of a replicated process $!^{i \le n}$. (Replication indices are typically used as array indices.) The variable access $x[M_1, \ldots, M_m]$ returns the content of the cell of indices $M_1, \ldots, M_m$ of the m-dimensional array variable x. We use x, y, z, u as variable names. The function application $f(M_1, \ldots, M_m)$ returns the result of applying function f to $M_1, \ldots, M_m$.

The calculus distinguishes two kinds of processes: input processes Q are ready to receive a message on a channel; output processes P output a message on a channel after executing some internal computations. The input process 0 does nothing; $Q \mid Q'$ is the parallel composition of Q and Q'; $!^{i \leq n}Q$ represents n copies of Q in parallel, each with a different value of $i \in [1, n]$; newChannel $c; Q$ creates a new private channel c and executes Q; the semantics of the input $c[M_1, \ldots, M_l](x_1[\tilde{i}] : T_1, \ldots, x_k[\tilde{i}] : T_k); P$ will be explained below together with the semantics of the output.

The output process new $x[i_1, \ldots, i_m] : T; P$ chooses a new random number uniformly in T, stores it in $x[i_1, \ldots, i_m]$, and executes P. (The type T must be a fixed-length type, because probabilistic Turing machines can choose random numbers uniformly only in such types.) Function symbols represent deterministic functions, so all random numbers must be chosen by new $x[i_1, \ldots, i_m] : T$. Deterministic functions make automatic syntactic manipulations easier: we can duplicate a term without changing its value. The process let $x[i_1, \ldots, i_m] : T = M$ in P stores the bitstring value of M (which must be in T) in $x[i_1, \ldots, i_m]$ and executes P. The process event $e(M_1, \ldots, M_l); P$ executes the event $e(M_1, \ldots, M_l)$, then runs P. This event records that a certain program point has been reached with certain values of $M_1, \ldots, M_l$, but otherwise does not affect the execution of the process. Next, we explain the process find $(\bigoplus_{j=1}^m u_{j1}[\tilde{i}] \leq n_{j1}, \ldots, u_{jm_j}[\tilde{i}] \leq n_{jm_j}$ suchthat defined$(M_{j1}, \ldots, M_{jl_j}) \wedge M_j$ then $P_j)$ else P, where $\tilde{i}$ denotes a tuple $i_1, \ldots, i_{m'}$. The order and array indices on tuples are taken component-wise, so for instance, $u_{j1}[\tilde{i}] \leq n_{j1}, \ldots, u_{jm_j}[\tilde{i}] \leq n_{jm_j}$ can be further abbreviated $\widetilde{u_j}[\tilde{i}] \leq \widetilde{n_j}$. A simple example is the following: find $u \leq n$ suchthat defined$(x[u]) \wedge x[u] = a$ then P' else P tries to find an index u such that $x[u]$ is defined and $x[u] = a$, and when such a u is found, it executes P' with that value of u; otherwise, it executes P. In other words, this find construct looks for the value a in the array x, and when a is found, it stores in u an index such that $x[u] = a$. Therefore, the find construct allows us to access arrays, which is key for our purpose. More generally, find $u_1[\tilde{i}] \leq n_1, \ldots, u_m[\tilde{i}] \leq n_m$ suchthat defined$(M_1, \ldots, M_l) \wedge M$ then P' else P tries to find values of $u_1, \ldots, u_m$ for which $M_1, \ldots, M_l$ are defined and M is true. In case of success, it executes P'. In case of failure, it executes P. This is further generalized to m branches: find $(\bigoplus_{j=1}^m u_{j1}[\tilde{i}] \leq n_{j1}, \ldots, u_{jm_j}[\tilde{i}] \leq n_{jm_j}$ suchthat defined$(M_{j1}, \ldots, M_{jl_j}) \wedge M_j$ then $P_j)$ else P tries to find a branch j in $[1, m]$ such that there are values of $u_{j1}, \ldots, u_{jm_j}$ for which $M_{j1}, \ldots, M_{jl_j}$ are defined and M_j is true. In case of success, it executes P_j. In case of failure for all branches, it executes P. More formally, it evaluates the conditions defined$(M_{j1}, \ldots, M_{jl_j}) \wedge M_j$ for each j and each value of $u_{j1}[\tilde{i}], \ldots, u_{jm_j}[\tilde{i}]$ in $[1, n_{j1}] \times \ldots \times [1, n_{jm_j}]$. If none of these conditions is true, it executes P. Otherwise, it chooses randomly with uniform[2] probability one j and one value of $u_{j1}[\tilde{i}], \ldots, u_{jm_j}[\tilde{i}]$ such that the corresponding condition is true and executes P_j. The conditional if defined$(M_1, \ldots, M_l) \wedge M$ then P else P' executes P if $M_1, \ldots, M_l$ are defined and M evaluates to true. Otherwise, it executes P'. This conditional is equivalent to find suchthat defined$(M_1, \ldots, M_l) \wedge M$ then P else P'. The

---

[2] A probabilistic Turing machine can choose a random number uniformly in a set of cardinal m only when m is a power of 2. When m is not a power of 2, there exist approximate algorithms: for example, in order to obtain a random integer in $[0, m-1]$, we can choose a random integer r uniformly among $[0, 2^k - 1]$ for a certain k large enough and return $r \mod m$. The distribution can be made as close as we wish to the uniform distribution by choosing k large enough.

conjunct defined$(M_1, \ldots, M_l)$ can be omitted when $l = 0$ and M can be omitted when it is true.

Finally, let us explain the output $\overline{c[M_1, \ldots, M_l]}\langle N_1, \ldots, N_k \rangle; Q$. A channel $c[M_1, \ldots, M_l]$ consists of both a channel name c and a tuple of terms $M_1, \ldots, M_l$. Channel names c can be declared private by newChannel c; the adversary can never have access to channel $c[M_1, \ldots, M_l]$ when c is private. (This is useful in the proofs, although all channels of protocols are often public.) Terms $M_1, \ldots, M_l$ are intuitively analogous to IP addresses and ports, which are numbers that the adversary may guess. A semantic configuration always consists of a single output process (the process currently being executed) and several input processes. When the output process executes $\overline{c[M_1, \ldots, M_l]}\langle N_1, \ldots, N_k \rangle; Q$, one looks for an input on channel $c[M'_l \ldots, M'_l]$, where $M'_1, \ldots, M'_l$ evaluate to the same bitstrings as $M_1, \ldots, M_l$, and with the same arity k, in the available input processes. If no such input process is found, the process blocks. Otherwise, one such input process $c[M'_1, \ldots, M'_l](x_1[\widetilde{i}] : T_1, \ldots, x_k[\widetilde{i}] : T_k); P$ is chosen randomly with uniform probability. The communication is then executed: for each $j \leq k$, the output message N_j is evaluated and stored in $x_j[\widetilde{i}]$ if it is in T_j (otherwise the process blocks). Finally, the output process P that follows the input is executed. The input process Q that follows the output is stored in the available input processes for future execution. The syntax requires an output to be followed by an input process, as in [43]. If one needs to output several messages consecutively, one can simply insert fictitious inputs between the outputs. The adversary can then schedule the outputs by sending messages to these inputs.

Using different channels for each input and output allows the adversary to control the network. For instance, we may write $!^{i \leq n} c[i](x[i] : T) \ldots \overline{c'[i]}\langle M \rangle \ldots$ The adversary can then decide which copy of the replicated process receives its message, simply by sending it on $c[i]$ for the appropriate value of i.

An else branch of find or if may be omitted when it is else $\overline{yield\langle\rangle}; 0$. (Note that "else 0" would not be syntactically correct.) Similarly, $\overline{yield\langle\rangle}; 0$ may be omitted after an event or a restriction. A trailing 0 after an output may be omitted.

The *current replication indices* at a certain program point in a process are $i_1, \ldots, i_m$ where the replications above the considered program point are $!^{i_1 \leq n_1} \ldots !^{i_m \leq n_m}$. We often abbreviate $x[i_1, \ldots, i_m]$ by x when $i_1, \ldots, i_m$ are the current replication indices, but it should be kept in mind that this is only an abbreviation. Variables x defined under a replication must be arrays with indices the current replication indices at the definition of x: for example, $!^{i_1 \leq n_1} \ldots !^{i_m \leq n_m}$ let $x[i_1, \ldots, i_m] : T = M$ in $\ldots$ More formally, we require the following invariant:

Invariant 1 (Single definition) The process Q_0 satisfies Invariant 1 if and only if

1. in every definition of $x[i_1, \ldots, i_m]$ in Q_0, the indices $i_1, \ldots, i_m$ of x are the current replication indices at that definition, and
2. two different definitions of the same variable x in Q_0 are in different branches of a find (or if).

Invariant 1 guarantees that each variable is assigned at most once for each value of its indices. (Indeed, item 2 shows that only one definition of each variable can be executed for given indices in each trace.)

Invariant 2 (Defined variables) The process Q_0 satisfies Invariant 2 if and only if every occurrence of a variable access $x[M_1, \ldots, M_m]$ in Q_0 is either

- syntactically under the definition of $x[M_1, \ldots, M_m]$ (in which case $M_1, \ldots, M_m$ are in fact the current replication indices at the definition of x);
- or in a defined condition in a find process;
- or in M'_j or P_j in a process of the form find $(\bigoplus_{j=1}^{m''} \widetilde{u}_j[\widetilde{i}] \leq \widetilde{n}_j$ suchthat defined$(M'_{j1}, \ldots, M'_{jl_j}) \wedge M'_j$ then $P_j)$ else P where for some $k \leq l_j$, $x[M_1, \ldots, M_m]$ is a subterm of M'_{jk}.

Invariant 2 guarantees that variables can be accessed only when they have been initialized. It checks that the definition of the variable access is either in scope (first item) or checked by a find (last item).

We use a type system, detailed in [23, Appendix A], to check that bitstrings of the proper type are given to each function and that array indices are used correctly.

Invariant 3 (Typing) The process Q_0 satisfies Invariant 3 if and only if it is well-typed.

We require the adversary to be well-typed. This requirement does not restrict its computing power, because it can always define type-cast functions $f : T \to T'$ to bypass the type system. Similarly, the type system does not restrict the class of protocols that we consider, since the protocol may contain type-cast functions. The type system just makes explicit which set of bitstrings may appear at each point of the protocol. The three invariants are checked by the prover for the initial game and preserved by all game transformations.

The formal semantics is defined by a probabilistic reduction relation [23, Appendix B]. Our semantics is such that all processes can be simulated by probabilistic Turing machines, and conversely.

We say that a function $f : T_1 \times \ldots \times T_m \to T$ is *poly-injective* when it is injective and its inverses are efficiently computable, that is, there exist functions $f_j^{-1} : T \to T_j$ $(1 \leq j \leq m)$ such that $f_j^{-1}(f(x_1, \ldots, x_m)) = x_j$ and f_j^{-1} is efficiently computable. When f is poly-injective, we define a pattern matching construct let $f(x_1, \ldots, x_m) = M$ in P else Q as an abbreviation for let $y : T = M$ in let $x_1 : T_1 = f_1^{-1}(y)$ in $\ldots$ let $x_m : T_m = f_m^{-1}(y)$ in if $f(x_1, \ldots, x_m) = y$ then P else Q. We naturally generalize this construct to let $N = M$ in P else Q where N is built from poly-injective functions and variables.

We denote by $\text{var}(Q)$ the set of variables that occur in Q.

1.2. Example

Let us introduce two cryptographic primitives that we use below.

Definition 1 Let T_{mr}, T_{mk}, and T_{ms} be types that correspond intuitively to random seeds, keys, and message authentication codes, respectively; T_{mr} is a fixed-length type. A message authentication code scheme MAC [17] consists of three function symbols:

- mkgen : $T_{mr} \to T_{mk}$ is the key generation algorithm taking as argument a random bitstring and returning a key. (Usually, mkgen is a randomized algorithm; here, since we separate the choice of random numbers from computation, mkgen takes an additional argument representing the random coins.)

- mac : $bitstring \times T_{mk} \rightarrow T_{ms}$ is the MAC algorithm taking as arguments a message and a key, and returning the corresponding tag. (We assume here that mac is deterministic; we could easily encode a randomized mac by adding an additional argument as for mkgen.)
- verify : $bitstring \times T_{mk} \times T_{ms} \rightarrow bool$ is a verification algorithm such that $\mathrm{verify}(m, k, t) = \mathrm{true}$ if and only if t is a valid MAC of message m under key k. (Since mac is deterministic, $\mathrm{verify}(m, k, t)$ is typically $\mathrm{mac}(m, k) = t$.)

We have $\forall m \in bitstring, \forall r \in T_{mr}, \mathrm{verify}(m, \mathrm{mkgen}(r), \mathrm{mac}(m, \mathrm{mkgen}(r))) = \mathrm{true}$.

The advantage of an adversary against unforgeability under chosen message attacks (UF-CMA) is

$$
\mathrm{Succ}_{\mathrm{MAC}}^{\mathrm{uf-cma}}(t, q_m, q_v, l) = \max_{\mathcal{A}} \Pr \left[\begin{array}{l} r \xleftarrow{R} T_{mr}; k \leftarrow \mathrm{mkgen}(r); \\ (m, s) \leftarrow \mathcal{A}^{\mathrm{mac}(.,k),\mathrm{verify}(.,k,.)} : \mathrm{verify}(m, k, s) \\ \wedge\ m \text{ was never queried to the oracle } \mathrm{mac}(., k) \end{array} \right]
$$

where the adversary $\mathcal{A}$ is any probabilistic Turing machine that runs in time at most t, calls $\mathrm{mac}(., k)$ at most q_m times with messages of length at most l, and calls $\mathrm{verify}(., k, .)$ at most q_v times with messages of length at most l.

$\mathrm{Succ}_{\mathrm{MAC}}^{\mathrm{uf-cma}}(t, q_m, q_v, l)$ is the probability that an adversary forges a MAC, that is, returns a pair (m, s) where s is a correct MAC for m, without having queried the MAC oracle $\mathrm{mac}(., k)$ on m. Intuitively, when the MAC is secure, this probability is small: the adversary has little chance of forging a MAC. Hence, the MAC guarantees the integrity of the MACed message because one cannot compute the MAC without the secret key.

Two frameworks exist for expressing security properties. In the asymptotic framework, used in [22, 23], the length of keys is determined by a security parameter η, and a MAC is UF-CMA when $\mathrm{Succ}_{\mathrm{MAC}}^{\mathrm{uf-cma}}(t, q_m, q_v, l)$ is a negligible function of η when t is polynomial in η. ($f(\eta)$ is *negligible* when for all polynomials q, there exists $\eta_o \in \mathbb{N}$ such that for all $\eta > \eta_0$, $f(\eta) \leq \frac{1}{q(\eta)}$.) The assumption that functions are efficiently computable means that they are computable in time polynomial in η and in the length of their arguments. The goal is to show that the probability of success of an attack against the protocol is negligible, assuming the parameters n are polynomial in η and the network messages are of length polynomial in η. In contrast, in the exact security framework, on which we focus in this course, one computes the probability of success of an attack against the protocol as a function of the probability of breaking the primitives such as $\mathrm{Succ}_{\mathrm{MAC}}^{\mathrm{uf-cma}}(t, q_m, q_v, l)$, of the runtime of functions, of the parameters n, and of the length of messages, thus providing a more precise security result. Intuitively, the probability $\mathrm{Succ}_{\mathrm{MAC}}^{\mathrm{uf-cma}}(t, q_m, q_v, l)$ is assumed to be small (otherwise, the computed probability of attack will be large), but no formal assumption on this probability is needed to establish the security theorem.

Definition 2 Let T_r and T'_r be fixed-length types representing random coins; let T_k and T_e be types for keys and ciphertexts respectively. A symmetric encryption scheme SE [17] consists of three function symbols:

- kgen : $T_r \rightarrow T_k$ is the key generation algorithm taking as argument random coins and returning a key,

- enc : $bitstring \times T_k \times T'_r \to T_e$ is the encryption algorithm taking as arguments the cleartext, the key, and random coins, and returning the ciphertext,
- dec : $T_e \times T_k \to bitstring_\perp$ is the decryption algorithm taking as arguments the ciphertext and the key, and returning either the cleartext when decryption succeeds or $\perp$ when decryption fails,

such that $\forall m \in bitstring, \forall r \in T_r, \forall r' \in T'_r, \mathrm{dec}(\mathrm{enc}(m, \mathrm{kgen}(r), r'), \mathrm{kgen}(r)) = m$.

Let $LR(x, y, b) = x$ if $b = 0$ and $LR(x, y, b) = y$ if $b = 1$, defined only when x and y are bitstrings of the same length. The advantage of an adversary against indistinguishability under chosen plaintext attacks (IND-CPA) is

$$\mathsf{Succ}_{\mathsf{SE}}^{\mathsf{ind-cpa}}(t, q_e, l) = \max_{\mathcal{A}} 2\Pr\left[\begin{matrix} b \xleftarrow{R} \{0,1\}; r \xleftarrow{R} T_r; k \leftarrow \mathrm{kgen}(r); \\ b' \leftarrow \mathcal{A}^{r' \xleftarrow{R} T'_r; \mathrm{enc}(LR(.,.,b),k,r')} : b' = b \end{matrix}\right] - 1$$

where $\mathcal{A}$ is any probabilistic Turing machine that runs in time at most t and calls $r' \xleftarrow{R} T'_r; enc(LR(.,.,b), k, r')$ at most q_e times on messages of length at most l.

Given two bitstrings a_0 and a_1 of the same length, the left-right encryption oracle $r' \xleftarrow{R} T'_r; enc(LR(.,.,b), k, r')$ returns $r' \xleftarrow{R} T'_r; enc(LR(a_0, a_1, b), k, r')$, that is, encrypts a_0 when $b = 0$ and a_1 when $b = 1$. $\mathsf{Succ}_{\mathsf{SE}}^{\mathsf{ind-cpa}}(t, q_e, l)$ is the probability that the adversary distinguishes the encryption of the messages a_0 given as first arguments to the left-right encryption oracle from the encryption of the messages a_1 given as second arguments. Intuitively, when the encryption scheme is IND-CPA secure, this probability is small: the ciphertext gives almost no information what the cleartext is (one cannot determine whether it is a_0 or a_1 without having the secret key).

Example 1 Let us consider the following trivial protocol:

$$A \to B : e, \mathrm{mac}(e, x_{mk}) \quad \text{where } e = \mathrm{enc}(x'_k, x_k, x'_r)$$

$$\text{and } x'_r, x'_k \text{ are fresh random numbers}$$

A and B are assumed to share a key x_k for a symmetric encryption scheme and a key x_{mk} for a message authentication code. A creates a fresh key x'_k and sends it encrypted under x_k to B. A MAC is appended to the message, in order to guarantee integrity. In other words, the protocol sends the key x'_k encrypted using an encrypt-then-MAC scheme [17]. The goal of the protocol is that x'_k should be a secret key shared between A and B. This protocol can be modeled in our calculus by the following process Q_0:

$$Q_0 = start(); \mathsf{new}\ x_r : T_r; \mathsf{let}\ x_k : T_k = \mathrm{kgen}(x_r)\ \mathsf{in}$$

$$\mathsf{new}\ x_{mr} : T_{mr}; \mathsf{let}\ x_{mk} : T_{mk} = \mathrm{mkgen}(x_{mr})\ \mathsf{in}\ \overline{c}\langle\rangle; (Q_A \mid Q_B)$$

$$Q_A = !^{i \le n} c_A[i](); \mathsf{new}\ x'_k : T_k; \mathsf{new}\ x'_r : T'_r;$$

$$\mathsf{let}\ x_m : bitstring = \mathrm{enc}(\mathrm{k2b}(x'_k), x_k, x'_r)\ \mathsf{in}\ \overline{c_A[i]}\langle x_m, \mathrm{mac}(x_m, x_{mk})\rangle$$

$$Q_B = !^{i' \le n} c_B[i'](x'_m, x_{ma}); \mathsf{if}\ \mathrm{verify}(x'_m, x_{mk}, x_{ma})\ \mathsf{then}$$

$$\mathsf{let}\ i_\perp(\mathrm{k2b}(x''_k)) = \mathrm{dec}(x'_m, x_k)\ \mathsf{in}\ \overline{c_B[i']}\langle\rangle$$

When Q_0 receives a message on channel $start$, it begins execution: it generates the keys x_k and x_{mk} by choosing random coins x_r and $x_{r'}$ and applying the appropriate key generation algorithms. Then it yields control to the adversary, by outputting on channel c. After this output, n copies of processes for A and B are ready to be executed, when the adversary outputs on channels $c_A[i]$ or $c_B[i]$ respectively. In a session that runs as expected, the adversary first sends a message on $c_A[i]$. Then Q_A creates a fresh key x'_k (T_k is assumed to be a fixed-length type), encrypts it under x_k with random coins x'_r, computes the MAC under x_{mk} of the ciphertext, and sends the ciphertext and the MAC on $c_A[i]$. The function k2b : $T_k \rightarrow bitstring$ is the natural injection k2b$(x) = x$; it is needed only for type conversion. The adversary is then expected to forward this message on $c_B[i]$. When Q_B receives this message, it verifies the MAC, decrypts, and stores the obtained key in x''_k. (The function $i_\perp : bitstring \rightarrow bitstring_\perp$ is the natural injection; it is useful to check that decryption succeeded.) This key x''_k should be secret.

The adversary is responsible for forwarding messages from A to B. It can send messages in unexpected ways in order to mount an attack.

This very small example is sufficient to illustrate the main features of CryptoVerif. Section 5 presents results obtained on more realistic protocols.

1.3. Observational Equivalence

Let us now formally define game indistinguishability, which we name observational equivalence by analogy with that notion in the Dolev-Yao model. A context is a process containing a hole $[\,]$. An evaluation context C is a context built from $[\,]$, newChannel $c; C$, $Q \mid C$, and $C \mid Q$. We use an evaluation context to represent the adversary. We denote by $C[Q]$ the process obtained by replacing the hole $[\,]$ in the context C with the process Q. The executed events can be used to distinguish games, so we introduce an additional algorithm, a *distinguisher* D that takes as input a sequence of events $\mathcal{E}$ and returns true or false. An example of distinguisher is D_e defined by $D_e(\mathcal{E}) =$ true if and only if $e \in \mathcal{E}$: this distinguisher detects the execution of event e. More generally, distinguishers can detect various properties of the sequence of events $\mathcal{E}$ executed by the game. We denote by $\Pr[Q \rightsquigarrow D]$ the probability that Q executes a sequence of events $\mathcal{E}$ such that $D(\mathcal{E})$ returns true.

Definition 3 (Observational equivalence) Let Q and Q' be two processes and V a set of variables. Assume that Q and Q' satisfy Invariants 1, 2, and 3 and the variables of V are defined in Q and Q', with the same types.

An evaluation context is said to be *acceptable* for Q with public variables V if and only if var$(C) \cap$ var$(Q) \subseteq V$ and $C[Q]$ satisfies Invariants 1, 2, and 3.

We say that Q and Q' are *observationally equivalent* up to probability p with public variables V, written $Q \approx_p^V Q'$, when for all evaluation contexts C acceptable for Q and Q' with public variables V, for all distinguishers D, $|\Pr[C[Q] \rightsquigarrow D] - \Pr[C[Q'] \rightsquigarrow D]| \leq p(C, D)$.

This definition formalizes that algorithms C and D distinguish Q and Q' with probability at most $p(C, D)$. The probability p typically depends on the runtime of C and D, but may also depend on other parameters, such as the number of messages sent by C to each replicated process. That is why p takes as arguments C and D themselves.

The unusual requirement on variables of C comes from the presence of arrays and of the associated find construct which gives C direct access to variables of Q and Q': the context C is allowed to access variables of Q and Q' only when they are in V. (In more standard settings, the calculus does not have constructs that allow the context to access variables of Q and Q'.) When V is empty, we write $Q \approx_p Q'$ instead of $Q \approx_p^V Q'$.

The following result is not difficult to prove:

Lemma 1   1. *Reflexivity:* $Q \approx_0^V Q$.
   2. *Symmetry: if* $Q \approx_p^V Q'$, *then* $Q' \approx_p^V Q$.
   3. *Transitivity: if* $Q \approx_p^V Q'$ *and* $Q' \approx_{p'}^V Q''$, *then* $Q \approx_{p+p'}^V Q''$.
   4. *If* $Q \approx_p^V Q'$ *and* C *is an evaluation context acceptable for Q and Q' with public*
      variables V, then $C[Q] \approx_{p'}^{V'} C[Q']$, *where* $p'(C', D) = p(C'[C], D)$ *and* $V' \subseteq$
      $V \cup \mathrm{var}(C)$.

Proofs by sequences of games consist of a sequence of observationally equivalent games $Q_0 \approx_{p_1}^V Q_1 \approx_{p_2}^V \ldots \approx_{p_n}^V Q_n$. By transitivity, $Q_0 \approx_{p_1+\ldots+p_n}^V Q_n$, so by definition of observational equivalence, $\Pr[C[Q_0] \rightsquigarrow D] \leq \Pr[C[Q_n] \rightsquigarrow D] + (p_1 + \ldots + p_n)(C, D)$.

2. Game Transformations

In this section, we describe the game transformations that allow us to transform the process that represents the initial protocol into a process on which the desired security property can be proved directly, by criteria given in Section 3. These transformations are parameterized by the set V of variables that the context can access. As we shall see in Section 3, V contains variables that we would like to prove secret. (The context will contain test queries that access these variables.) These transformations transform a process Q_0 into a process Q_0' such that $Q_0 \approx_p^V Q_0'$; CryptoVerif evaluates the probability p.

2.1. Syntactic Transformations

RemoveAssign(x): When x is defined by an assignment let $x[i_1, \ldots, i_l] : T = M$ in P and x does not occur in M (non-cyclic assignment), we replace x with its value. When x has several definitions, we simply replace $x[i_1, \ldots, i_l]$ with M in P. (For accesses to x guarded by find, we do not know which definition of x is actually used.) When x has a single definition, we replace everywhere in the game $x[M_1, \ldots, M_l]$ with $M\{M_1/i_1, \ldots, M_l/i_l\}$. We additionally update the defined conditions of find to preserve Invariant 2 and to make sure that, if a condition of find guarantees that $x[M_1, \ldots, M_l]$ is defined in the initial game, then so does the corresponding condition of find in the transformed game. When $x \in V$, its definition is kept unchanged. Otherwise, when x is not referred to at all after the transformation, we remove the definition of x. When x is referred to only at the root of defined tests, we replace its definition with a constant. (The definition point of x is important, but not its value.)

Example 2 In the process of Example 1, the transformation **RemoveAssign(x_{mk})** substitutes $\mathrm{mkgen}(x_{mr})$ for x_{mk} in the whole process and removes the assignment let $x_{mk} : T_{mk} = \mathrm{mkgen}(x_{mr})$. After substitution, $\mathrm{mac}(x_m, x_{mk})$ becomes $\mathrm{mac}(x_m, \mathrm{mkgen}(x_{mr}))$ and $\mathrm{verify}(x'_m, x_{mk}, x_{ma})$ becomes $\mathrm{verify}(x'_m, \mathrm{mkgen}(x_{mr}), x_{ma})$, thus exhibiting terms required in Section 2.2. The situation is similar for **RemoveAssign(x_k)**.

SArename(x): The transformation **SArename** (single assignment rename) aims at renaming variables so that each variable has a single definition in the game; this is useful for distinguishing cases depending on which definition of x has set $x[\widetilde{i}]$. This transformation can be applied only when $x \notin V$. When x has $m > 1$ definitions, we rename each definition of x to a different variable $x_1, \ldots, x_m$. Terms $x[\widetilde{i}]$ under a definition of $x_j[\widetilde{i}]$ are then replaced with $x_j[\widetilde{i}]$. Each branch of find $FB = \widetilde{u}[\widetilde{i}] \leq \widetilde{n}$ suchthat defined($M_1, \ldots, M_l$) $\wedge M$ then P where $x[\widetilde{M}]$ is a subterm of some M_k for $k \leq l$ is replaced with m branches $FB\{x_j[\widetilde{M}]/x[\widetilde{M}]\}$ for $1 \leq j \leq m$.

Simplify: The prover uses a simplification algorithm, based on an equational prover, using an algorithm similar to the Knuth-Bendix completion [40]. This equational prover uses:

- User-defined equations, of the form $\forall x_1 : T_1, \ldots, \forall x_m : T_m, M$ which mean that for all values of x_1 in $T_1, \ldots, x_m$ in T_m, M evaluates to true. For example, considering MAC and encryption schemes as in Definitions 1 and 2 respectively, we have:

$$\forall r : T_{mr}, \forall m : bitstring, \text{verify}(m, \text{mkgen}(r), \text{mac}(m, \text{mkgen}(r))) = \text{true} \tag{mac}$$

$$\forall m : bitstring; \forall r : T_r, \forall r' : T_r', \text{dec}(\text{enc}(m, \text{kgen}(r), r'), \text{kgen}(r)) = \text{i}_\perp(m) \tag{enc}$$

We express the poly-injectivity of the function k2b of Example 1 by

$$\forall x : T_k, \forall y : T_k, (\text{k2b}(x) = \text{k2b}(y)) = (x = y)$$
$$\forall x : T_k, \text{k2b}^{-1}(\text{k2b}(x)) = x \tag{k2b}$$

where k2b^{-1} is a function symbol that denotes the inverse of k2b. We have similar formulas for $\text{i}_\perp$.

- Equations that come from the process. For example, in the process if M then P else P', we have $M = \text{true}$ in P and $M = \text{false}$ in P'.
- The low probability of collision between random values. For example, when x is defined by new $x : T$ under replications bounded by $n_1, \ldots, n_m$, $x[M_1, \ldots, M_m] = x[M_1', \ldots, M_m']$ implies $M_1 = M_1', \ldots, M_m = M_m'$ up to probability $p = \frac{(n_1 \ldots n_m)^2}{2|T|}$ (probability that two distinct cells of the array x are equal). This transformation is performed when the type T is *large*, which means that $|T|$ is large enough so that the probability p can be considered small.
  Similarly, when 1) x is defined by new $x : T$ and T is a large type, 2) for each value of M_1, there is at most one value of x (or of a part of x of a large type) that can yield that value of M_1, and 3) M_2 does not depend on x, then $M_1 \neq M_2$ up to a small probability. The fact that M_2 does not depend on x is proved using a dependency analysis.

The prover combines these properties to simplify terms, and uses simplified forms of terms to simplify processes. For example, if M simplifies to true, then if M then P else P' simplifies to P. Similarly, a branch of find is removed when the associated condition simplifies to false.

Details on the simplification procedure can be found in [23, Appendix C]. The asymptotic version of the following proposition is proved in [23, Appendix E.1].

Proposition 1 *Let Q_0 be a process that satisfies Invariants 1, 2, and 3 and Q'_0 the process obtained from Q_0 by one of the transformations above. Then Q'_0 satisfies Invariants 1, 2, and 3, and $Q_0 \approx^V_p Q'_0$, where $p = 0$ for the transformations* **RemoveAssign** *and* **SArename***, and p is the probability of eliminated collisions for* **Simplify***.*

2.2. Applying the Security Assumptions on Primitives

The security of cryptographic primitives is defined using observational equivalences given as axioms. Importantly, this formalism allows us to specify many different primitives in a generic way. Such equivalences are then used by the prover in order to transform a game into another, observationally equivalent game, as explained below.

The primitives are specified using equivalences of the form $(G_1, \ldots, G_m) \approx_p$ $(G'_1, \ldots, G'_m)$ where G is defined by the following grammar, with $l \geq 0$ and $m \geq 1$:

$G ::=$ group of oracles
  $!^{i \leq n} \text{new } y_1 : T_1; \ldots; \text{new } y_l : T_l; (G_1, \ldots, G_m)$ replication, restrictions
  $O(x_1 : T_1, \ldots, x_l : T_l) := OP$ oracle

$OP ::=$ oracle processes
  M term
  $\text{new } x[\widetilde{i}] : T; OP$ random number
  $\text{let } x[\widetilde{i}] : T = M \text{ in } OP$ assignment
  $\text{find } (\bigoplus_{j=1}^m \widetilde{u}_j[\widetilde{i}] \leq \widetilde{n}_j \text{ suchthat}$
    $\text{defined}(M_{j1}, \ldots, M_{jl_j}) \wedge M_j \text{ then } OP_j) \text{ else } OP$ array lookup

Intuitively, $O(x_1 : T_1, \ldots, x_l : T_l) := OP$ represents an oracle O that takes as argument values $x_1, \ldots, x_l$ of types $T_1, \ldots, T_l$ respectively and returns a result computed by OP. The observational equivalence $(G_1, \ldots, G_m) \approx_p (G'_1, \ldots, G'_m)$ expresses that the adversary has probability at most p of distinguishing oracles in the left-hand side from corresponding oracles in the right-hand side. Formally, oracles can be encoded as processes that input their arguments and output their result on a channel, as detailed in [23]. Denoting by $[[(G_1, \ldots, G_m)]]$ the encoding of $(G_1, \ldots, G_m)$ as a process, the observational equivalence $(G_1, \ldots, G_m) \approx_p (G'_1, \ldots, G'_m)$ is then an abbreviation for $[[(G_1, \ldots, G_m)]] \approx_p [[(G'_1, \ldots, G'_m)]]$.

For example, the security of a MAC (Definition 1) is represented by the equivalence $L \approx_{p_{\text{mac}}} R$ where:

$$L = !^{i'' \leq n''} \text{new } r : T_{mr}; ($$

$$!^{i \leq n} Omac(x : bitstring) := \text{mac}(x, \text{mkgen}(r)),$$

$$!^{i' \leq n'} Overify(m : bitstring, ma : T_{ms}) := \text{verify}(m, \text{mkgen}(r), ma))$$

$$R = \ !^{i'' \leq n''} \text{new } r : T_{mr}; \ ($$

$$!^{i \leq n} Omac(x : bitstring) := \text{mac}'(x, \text{mkgen}'(r)),$$

$$!^{i' \leq n'} Overify(m : bitstring, ma : T_{ms}) :=$$

$$\text{find } u \leq n \text{ suchthat defined}(x[u]) \wedge (m = x[u])$$

$$\wedge \text{ verify}'(m, \text{mkgen}'(r), ma) \text{ then true else false})$$

$$p_{\text{mac}}(C, D) = n'' \, \text{Succ}_{\text{MAC}}^{\text{uf−cma}}(t_C + (n'' − 1)(\text{time}(\text{mkgen}) + n \, \text{time}(\text{mac}, \text{maxl}(x))$$

$$+ \, n' \, \text{time}(\text{verify}, \text{maxl}(m)), n, n', \max(\text{maxl}(x), \text{maxl}(m))) \tag{mac_{eq}}$$

where mac′, verify′, and mkgen′ are function symbols with the same types as mac, verify, and mkgen respectively. (We use different function symbols on the left- and right-hand sides, just to prevent a repeated application of the transformation induced by this equivalence. Since we add these function symbols, we also add the equation

$$\forall r : T_{mr}, \forall m : bitstring, \text{verify}'(m, \text{mkgen}'(r), \text{mac}'(m, \text{mkgen}'(r))) = \text{true} \tag{mac'}$$

which restates (mac) for mac′, verify′, and mkgen′.) Intuitively, the equivalence $L \approx_{p_{\text{mac}}} R$ leaves MAC computations unchanged (except for the use of primed function symbols in R), and allows one to replace a MAC verification $\text{verify}(m, \text{mkgen}(r), ma)$ with a lookup in the array x of messages whose mac has been computed with key $\text{mkgen}(r)$: if m is found in the array x and $\text{verify}(m, \text{mkgen}(r), ma)$, we return true; otherwise, the verification fails (up to negligible probability), so we return false. (If the verification succeeds with m not in the array x, then the adversary has forged a MAC.) Obviously, the form of L requires that r is used only to compute or verify MACs, for the equivalence to be correct. In the probability $p_{\text{mac}}(C, D)$, t_C is the runtime of context C; n'' is the maximum number of considered MAC keys; n' and n'' are respectively the maximum number of calls to $Omac$ and $Overify$ for each MAC key (n, n', n'' are in fact functions of C); $\text{time}(f, l_1, \ldots, l_k)$ is the maximum runtime of f, called with arguments of length at most $l_1, \ldots, l_k$ (the lengths $l_1, \ldots, l_k$ are omitted when the type of the argument already bounds its length); $\text{maxl}(x)$ is the maximum length of x. Formally, the following result shows the correctness of our modeling. It is a fairly easy consequence of Definition 1, and its asymptotic version is proved in [23, Appendix E.3].

Proposition 2 *If* (mkgen, mac, verify) *is a UF-CMA message authentication code and the symbols* mkgen′, *mac′, and* verify′ *represent the same functions as* mkgen, mac, *and* verify *respectively, then* $[\![L]\!] \approx_{p_{\text{mac}}} [\![R]\!]$.

Similarly, if (kgen, enc, dec) is an IND-CPA symmetric encryption scheme (Definition 2), then we have the following equivalence:

$$!^{i' \leq n'} \text{new } r : T_r; !^{i \leq n} Oenc(x : bitstring) := \text{new } r' : T_r'; \text{enc}(x, \text{kgen}(r), r')$$

$$\approx_{p_{\text{enc}}} !^{i' \leq n'} \text{new } r : T_r; !^{i \leq n} Oenc(x : bitstring) := \text{new } r' : T_r'; \text{enc}'(Z(x), \text{kgen}'(r), r') \tag{enc_{eq}}$$

where $p_{enc}(C, D) = n' \, \text{Succ}_{SE}^{ind-cpa}(t_C + t_D + (n' - 1)(\text{time}(\text{kgen}) + n \, \text{time}(\text{enc},$ $\text{maxl}(x)) + n \, \text{time}(Z, \text{maxl}(x))), n, \text{maxl}(x))$, enc$'$ and kgen$'$ are function symbols with the same types as enc and kgen respectively, and $Z : bitstring \to bitstring$ is the function that returns a bitstring of the same length as its argument, consisting only of zeroes. Using equations such as $\forall x : T, Z(\text{T2b}(x)) = Z_T$, we can prove that $Z(\text{T2b}(x))$ does not depend on x when x is of a fixed-length type T and $\text{T2b} : T \to bitstring$ is the natural injection. The representation of other primitives can be found in [23, Appendix D.3]. The equivalences that formalize the security assumptions on primitives are designed and proved correct by hand from security assumptions in a more standard form, as in the MAC example. Importantly, these manual proofs are done only once for each primitive, and the obtained equivalence can be reused for proving many different protocols automatically.

Assuming $L \approx_p R$, Lemma 1 yields $C[[L]] \approx_{p'}^V C[[R]]$ with $p'(C', D) = p(C'[C], D)$, for all evaluation contexts C acceptable for $[L]$ and $[R]$ with no public variables, so we can transform a process Q_0 such that $Q_0 \approx_0^V C[[L]]$ into a process Q_0' such that $Q_0 \approx_0^V C[[L]] \approx_{p'}^V C[[R]] \approx_0^V Q_0'$. In order to check that $Q_0 \approx_0^V C[[L]]$, the prover uses syntactic conditions detailed in [23, Appendix D.1] and sketched in Example 3 below. The following proposition shows the soundness of the transformation; its asymptotic version is proved in [23, Appendix E.4].

Proposition 3 *Let Q_0 be a process that satisfies Invariants 1, 2, and 3 and Q_0' the process obtained from Q_0 by the above transformation. Then Q_0' satisfies Invariants 1, 2, and 3 and, if $[L] \approx_p [R]$, then $Q_0 \approx_{p'}^V Q_0'$ where $p'(C', D) = p(C'[C], D)$ and C is an evaluation context such that $Q_0 \approx_0^V C[[L]] \approx_{p'}^V C[[R]] \approx_0^V Q_0'$.*

Example 3 In order to treat Example 1, the prover is given as input the indication that T_{mr}, T_r, T_r', and T_k are fixed-length types; the type declarations for the functions mkgen, mkgen$'$: $T_{mr} \to T_{mk}$, mac, mac$'$: $bitstring \times T_{mk} \to T_{ms}$, verify, verify$'$: $bitstring \times T_{mk} \times T_{ms} \to bool$, kgen, kgen$'$: $T_r \to T_k$, enc, enc$'$: $bitstring \times T_k \times T_r' \to T_e$, dec : $T_e \times T_k \to bitstring_\perp$, k2b : $T_k \to bitstring$, i$_\perp$: $bitstring \to bitstring_\perp$, Z : $bitstring \to bitstring$, and the constant Z_k : $bitstring$; the equations (mac), (mac$'$), (enc), and $\forall x : T_k, Z(\text{k2b}(x)) = Z_k$ (which expresses that all keys have the same length); the indication that k2b and i$_\perp$ are poly-injective (which generates the equations (k2b) and similar equations for i$_\perp$); equivalences $L \approx_p R$ for MAC (mac_{eq}) and encryption (enc_{eq}); and the process Q_0 of Example 1. Let $V = \{x_k''\}$.

The prover first applies **RemoveAssign**(x_{mk}) to the process Q_0 of Example 1, as described in Example 2, yielding Q_1. The process can then be transformed using the security of the MAC. In the equivalence $L \approx_{p_{mac}} R$ (mac_{eq}) that expresses the security of the MAC, L is an abbreviation for the process:

$$[L] = \,!^{i'' \leq n''} c_{mkgen}[i''](); \text{new } r : T_{mr}; \overline{c_{mkgen}[i'']}\langle\rangle; ($$

$$!^{i \leq n} c_{mac}[i'', i](x : bitstring); \overline{c_{mac}[i'', i]}\langle\text{mac}(x, \text{mkgen}(r))\rangle \mid$$

$$!^{i' \leq n'} c_{verify}[i'', i'](m : bitstring, ma : T_{ms}); \overline{c_{verify}[i'', i']}\langle\text{verify}(m, \text{mkgen}(r), ma)\rangle)$$

The process Q_1 can be written under the form $C[[L]]$, $Q_1 \approx_0^V C[[L]]$, for the following context C:

$C = \mathsf{newChannel}\ c_{\mathrm{mkgen}}; \mathsf{newChannel}\ c_{\mathrm{mac}}; \mathsf{newChannel}\ c_{\mathrm{verify}}; ([]\ |\ start());$

$\quad \mathsf{new}\ x_r : T_r; \mathsf{let}\ x_k : T_k = \mathrm{kgen}(x_r)\ \mathsf{in}\ \overline{c_{\mathrm{mkgen}}[1]}\langle\rangle; c_{\mathrm{mkgen}}[1](); \overline{c}\langle\rangle; (Q_{CA}\ |\ Q_{CB}))$

$Q_{CA} = !^{i \le n} c_A[i](); \mathsf{new}\ x'_k : T_k; \mathsf{new}\ x'_r : T'_r;$

$\quad \mathsf{let}\ x_m : bitstring = \mathrm{enc}(\mathrm{k2b}(x'_k), x_k, x'_r)\ \mathsf{in}$

$\quad \overline{c_{\mathrm{mac}}[1, i]}\langle x_m\rangle; c_{\mathrm{mac}}[1, i](x_{ma}); \overline{c_A[i]}\langle x_m, x_{ma}\rangle$

$Q_{CB} = !^{i' \le n} c_B[i'](x'_m, x_{ma}); \overline{c_{\mathrm{verify}}[1, i']}\langle x'_m, x_{ma}\rangle; c_{\mathrm{verify}}[1, i'](b); \mathsf{if}\ b\ \mathsf{then}$

$\quad \mathsf{let}\ \mathrm{i}_\perp(\mathrm{k2b}(x''_k)) = \mathrm{dec}(x'_m, x_k)\ \mathsf{in}\ \overline{c_B[i']}\langle\rangle$

Instead of generating the coins x_{mr} for the MAC key itself, this context sends a message on channel $c_{\mathrm{mkgen}}[1]$, which is received by $[\![L]\!]$, so that $[\![L]\!]$ generates these coins. Similarly, instead of computing the MAC, the context C sends the message to MAC on channel $c_{\mathrm{mac}}[1, i]$, so that $[\![L]\!]$ computes the MAC and sends it back on $c_{\mathrm{mac}}[1, i]$. Instead of verifying the MAC, C sends the message and the candidate MAC on channel $c_{\mathrm{verify}}[1, i']$, so that $[\![L]\!]$ verifies the MAC and sends the result back on $c_{\mathrm{verify}}[1, i']$. The channels c_{mkgen}, c_{mac} and c_{verify} are declared private by newChannel, so that the adversary cannot directly access $[\![L]\!]$.

Informally, the conditions verified by CryptoVerif to prove that $Q_1 \approx_0^V C[[\![L]\!]]$ show that there is a correspondence between the variables of L and terms or variables of Q_1. In the example, $r[1]$ in L corresponds to x_{mr} in Q_1, $x[1, a]$ to $x_m[a]$, $m[1, a']$ to $x'_m[a']$, and $ma[1, a']$ to $x_{ma}[a']$. This correspondence must be such that

- A variable $x[\widetilde{a}]$ bound by new $x : T$ in L must correspond to a variable $z[\widetilde{a''}]$ bound by new $z : T$ in Q_1, and the relation that associates $z[\widetilde{a''}]$ to $x[\widetilde{a'}]$ must be an injective function (so that independent random numbers in L correspond to independent random numbers in Q_1).
- An oracle argument $x[\widetilde{a}]$ in L must correspond to a term of the same type as x, and when two terms correspond to the same $x[\widetilde{a}]$, they must evaluate to the same value.
- If L contains an oracle $O(x_1 : T_1, \ldots, x_l : T_l) := M$, the term obtained by replacing the variables of M with their corresponding terms or variables of Q_1 is a term of Q_1. The variables z of Q_1 corresponding to variables x bound by new $x : T$ in L occur only in such terms, at occurrences corresponding to occurrences of x in L. These variables z do not belong to V. In the example, $\mathrm{mac}(x[1, a], \mathrm{mkgen}(r[1]))$ in L corresponds to $\mathrm{mac}(x_m[a], \mathrm{mkgen}(x_{mr}))$ in Q_1 and $\mathrm{verify}(m[1, a'], \mathrm{mkgen}(r[1]), ma[1, a'])$ corresponds to $\mathrm{verify}(x'_m[a'], \mathrm{mkgen}(x_{mr}), x_{ma}[a'])$. The variable x_{mr} does not occur anywhere else in Q_1 and $x_{mr} \notin V$.

CryptoVerif then transforms Q_1 into $C[[\![R]\!]]$, which after some syntactic reorganizations yields the following process Q_2:

$Q_2 = start(); \mathsf{new}\ x_r : T_r; \mathsf{let}\ x_k : T_k = \mathrm{kgen}(x_r)\ \mathsf{in}\ \mathsf{new}\ x_{mr} : T_{mr}; \overline{c}\langle\rangle; (Q_{2A}\ |\ Q_{2B})$

$Q_{2A} = !^{i \le n} c_A[i](); \mathsf{new}\ x'_k : T_k; \mathsf{new}\ x'_r : T'_r;$

$\quad \mathsf{let}\ x_m : bitstring = \mathrm{enc}(\mathrm{k2b}(x'_k), x_k, x'_r)\ \mathsf{in}\ \overline{c_A[i]}\langle x_m, \mathrm{mac}'(x_m, \mathrm{mkgen}'(x_{mr}))\rangle$

$Q_{2B} = !^{i' \leq n} c_B[i'](x'_m, x_{ma});$

find $u \leq n$ suchthat defined$(x_m[u]) \wedge x'_m = x_m[u] \wedge$

$\quad$ verify$'(x'_m, \text{mkgen}'(x_{mr}), x_{ma})$

then (if true then let $i_\perp(\text{k2b}(x''_k)) = \text{dec}(x'_m, x_k)$ in $\overline{c_B[i']}\langle\rangle$)

else (if false then let $i_\perp(\text{k2b}(x''_k)) = \text{dec}(x'_m, x_k)$ in $\overline{c_B[i']}\langle\rangle$)

The initial definition of x_{mr} is removed and replaced with a new definition, which we still call x_{mr}. The term $\text{mac}(x_m, \text{mkgen}(x_{mr}))$ is replaced with $\text{mac}'(x_m, \text{mkgen}'(x_{mr}))$. The term verify$(x'_m, \text{mkgen}(x_{mr}), x_{ma})$ becomes find $u \leq n$ suchthat defined$(x_m[u])$ $\wedge x'_m = x_m[u] \wedge$ verify$'(x'_m, \text{mkgen}'(x_{mr}), x_{ma})$ then true else false, which yields Q_{2B} after transformation of oracle processes into processes. The process looks up the message x'_m in the array x_m, which contains the messages whose MAC has been computed with key $\text{mkgen}(x_{mr})$. If the MAC of x'_m has never been computed, the verification always fails (it returns false) by the security assumption on the MAC. Otherwise, it returns true when verify$'(x'_m, \text{mkgen}'(x_{mr}), x_{ma})$. By instantiating the probability formula given in (mac$_{eq}$), $Q_1 \approx_{p'_{mac}} Q_2$ where $p'_{mac}(C, D) = p_{mac}(C[C'], D) = \text{Succ}_{\text{MAC}}^{\text{uf-cma}}(t_C + \text{time}(\text{kgen}) + n\,\text{time}(\text{enc}, \text{length}(T_k)) + n\,\text{time}(\text{dec}, \text{maxl}(x'_m)), n, n, \max(\text{maxl}(x'_m), \text{maxl}(x_m)))$ since we use one MAC key ($n'' = 1$), there are at most n calls to mac and verify for that key ($n' = n$), and the runtime of the adversary against (mac$_{eq}$) is $t_{C[C']} = t_C + \text{time}(\text{kgen}) + n\,\text{time}(\text{enc}, \text{length}(T_k)) + n\,\text{time}(\text{dec}, \text{maxl}(x'_m))$.

$\quad$ Applying **Simplify** yields a game Q_3: Q_{2A} is unchanged and Q_{2B} becomes

$$Q_{3B} = !^{i' \leq n} c_B[i'](x'_m, x_{ma});$$

$\quad\quad$ find $u \leq n$ suchthat defined$(x_m[u], x'_k[u]) \wedge x'_m = x_m[u] \wedge$

$\quad\quad\quad$ verify$'(x'_m, \text{mkgen}'(x_{mr}), x_{ma})$ then

$\quad\quad$ let $x''_k : T_k = x'_k[u]$ in $\overline{c_B[i']}\langle\rangle$

First, the tests if true then ... and if false then ... are simplified. The term $\text{dec}(x'_m, x_k)$ is simplified knowing $x'_m = x_m[u]$ by the find condition, $x_m[u] = \text{enc}(\text{k2b}(x'_k[u]), x_k,$ $x'_r[u])$ by the assignment that defines x_m, $x_k = \text{kgen}(x_r)$ by the assignment that defines x_k, and $\text{dec}(\text{enc}(m, \text{kgen}(r), r'), \text{kgen}(r)) = i_\perp(m)$ by (enc). So we have $\text{dec}(x'_m,$ $x_k) = \text{dec}(x_m[u], x_k) = \text{dec}(\text{enc}(\text{k2b}(x'_k[u]), x_k, x'_r[u]), x_k) = i_\perp(\text{k2b}(x'_k[u]))$. By injectivity of $i_\perp$ and k2b, the assignment to x''_k simply becomes $x''_k = x'_k[u]$, using the equations $\forall x : bitstring, i_\perp^{-1}(i_\perp(x)) = x$ and $\forall x : T_k, \text{k2b}^{-1}(\text{k2b}(x)) = x$.

$\quad$ After applying **RemoveAssign**(x_k), which yields Q_4, we use the security of encryption, yielding Q_5: $\text{enc}(\text{k2b}(x'_k), \text{kgen}(x_r), x'_r)$ becomes $\text{enc}'(Z(\text{k2b}(x'_k)), \text{kgen}'(x_r),$ $x'_r)$. We have $Q_4 \approx_{p'_{enc}} Q_5$ where $p'_{enc}(C, D) = p_{enc}(C[C''], D) = \text{Succ}_{\text{SE}}^{\text{ind-cpa}}(t_C + t_D + (n + n^2)\text{time}(\text{mkgen}) + n\,\text{time}(\text{mac}, \text{maxl}(m)) + n^2\,\text{time}(\text{verify}, \text{maxl}(m')) + n^2\,\text{time}(=bitstring, \text{maxl}(m'), \text{maxl}(m)), n, \text{length}(T_k))$. (The evaluation of the runtime of the context C'' is rather naive since we consider that $\text{mkgen}(x_{mr})$ is computed once in each execution of Q_{4A} and once for each find test in Q_{4B}, and similarly verify is computed once for each find test in Q_{4B}. By noticing that it is enough to compute $\text{mkgen}(x_{mr})$ once, and verify once in each execution of Q_{4B}, one would obtain $\mathsf{Succ}_{\mathsf{SE}}^{\mathsf{ind-cpa}}(t_C + t_D + \mathrm{time}(\mathrm{mkgen}) + n\,\mathrm{time}(\mathrm{mac}, \mathrm{maxl}(m)) + n\,\mathrm{time}(\mathrm{verify}, \mathrm{maxl}(m')) + n^2\,\mathrm{time}(= bitstring, \mathrm{maxl}(m'), \mathrm{maxl}(m)), n, \mathrm{length}(T_k)).)$ After **Simplify**, $\mathrm{enc}'(Z(\mathrm{k2b}(x_k')), \mathrm{kgen}'(x_r), x_r')$ becomes $\mathrm{enc}'(Z_k, \mathrm{kgen}'(x_r), x_r')$, using $\forall x$: $T_k, Z(\mathrm{k2b}(x)) = Z_k$ (which expresses that all keys have the same length).

So we obtain the following game:

$Q_6 = start(); \mathsf{new}\ x_r : T_r; \mathsf{new}\ x_{mr} : T_{mr}; \overline{c}\langle\rangle; (Q_{6A} \mid Q_{6B})$

$Q_{6A} = !^{i \leq n} c_A[i](); \mathsf{new}\ x_k' : T_k; \mathsf{new}\ x_r' : T_r';$

$\quad \mathsf{let}\ x_m : bitstring = \mathrm{enc}'(Z_k, \mathrm{kgen}'(x_r), x_r')\ \mathsf{in}\ \overline{c_A[i]}\langle x_m, \mathrm{mac}'(x_m, \mathrm{mkgen}'(x_{mr}))\rangle$

$Q_{6B} = Q_{3B}$

By transitivity of $\approx$ (Lemma 1), $Q_0 \approx_{p'_{\mathrm{mac}} + p'_{\mathrm{enc}}}^{V} Q_6$ since the probability is 0 for steps other than applying the security of MAC and encryption.

Using lists instead of arrays simplifies games transformations: we do not need to add instructions that insert values in the list, since all variables are always implicitly arrays. Moreover, if there are several occurrences of $\mathrm{mac}(x_i, k)$ with the same key in the initial process, each $\mathrm{verify}(m_j, k, ma_j)$ is replaced with a find with one branch for each occurrence of mac. Therefore, the prover distinguishes automatically the cases in which the verified MAC ma_j comes from each occurrence of mac, that is, it distinguishes cases depending on the value of i such that $m_j = x_i$. Typically, distinguishing these cases is useful in the following steps of the proof of the protocol. (A similar situation arises for other cryptographic primitives specified using find.)

3. Criteria for Proving Secrecy Properties

Let us now define syntactic criteria that allow us to prove secrecy properties of protocols. The proofs of asymptotic versions of these results can be found in [23, Appendix E.5].

Definition 4 (One-session secrecy) Suppose that the variable x of type T is defined in Q under a single $!^{i \leq n}$. Q *preserves the one-session secrecy of* x *up to probability* p *when, for all evaluation contexts* C *acceptable for* $Q \mid Q_x$ *without public variables that do not contain* S, $2 \Pr[C[Q \mid Q_x] \rightsquigarrow D_{\mathsf{S}}] - 1 \leq p(C)$ *where* $D_{\mathsf{S}}(\mathcal{E}) = (\mathsf{S} \in \mathcal{E})$,

$\quad Q_x = c_0(); \mathsf{new}\ b : bool; \overline{c_0}\langle\rangle;$

$\qquad (c(u : [1, n]); \mathsf{if}\ \mathrm{defined}(x[u])\ \mathsf{then}\ \mathsf{if}\ b\ \mathsf{then}\ \overline{c}\langle x[u]\rangle\ \mathsf{else}\ \mathsf{new}\ y : T; \overline{c}\langle y\rangle$

$\qquad \mid c'(b' : bool); \mathsf{if}\ b = b'\ \mathsf{then}\ \mathsf{event}\ \mathsf{S})$

c_0, c, c', b, b', u, y, and S do not occur in Q.

Intuitively, the adversary C distinguishes the value of each secret $x[u]$ from a random number with probability at most $p(C)$. The adversary performs a single test query on $x[u]$, modeled by sending u on channel c in Q_x. This test query returns $x[u]$ when the random bit b is true and a random number otherwise. The adversary then tries to guess b, by sending its guess b' on channel c'. When the guess is correct, event S is executed.

Proposition 4 (One-session secrecy) *Consider a process Q such that there exists a set of variables S such that 1) the definitions of x are either restrictions* new $x[\widetilde{i}] : T$ *and $x \in S$, or assignments* let $x[\widetilde{i}] : T = z[M_1, \dots, M_l]$ *where z is defined by restrictions* new $z[i'_1, \dots, i'_l] : T$, *and $z \in S$, and 2) all accesses to variables $y \in S$ in Q are of the form "*let $y'[\widetilde{i}] : T' = y[M_1, \dots, M_l]$*" with $y' \in S$. Then Q preserves the one-session secrecy of x up to probability 0.*

Intuitively, only the variables in S depend on the restriction that defines x; the sent messages and the control flow of the process are independent of x, so the adversary obtains no information on x. In the implementation, the set S is computed by fixpoint iteration, starting from x or z and adding variables y' defined by "let $y'[\widetilde{i}] : T' = y[M_1, \dots, M_l]$" when $y \in S$.

Definition 5 (Secrecy) Assume that the variable x of type T is defined in Q under a single $!^{i \le n}$. Q *preserves the secrecy of x up to probability p* when, for all evaluation contexts C acceptable for $Q \mid R_x$ without public variables that do not contain S, $2 \Pr[C[Q \mid R_x] \rightsquigarrow D_S] - 1 \le p(C)$ where $D_S(\mathcal{E}) = (S \in \mathcal{E})$,

$$R_x = c_0(); \text{new } b : bool; \overline{c_0}\langle\rangle;$$

$$(!^{i \le n'} c(u : [1, n]); \text{if defined}(x[u]) \text{ then if } b \text{ then } \overline{c}\langle x[u]\rangle \text{ else}$$

$$\text{find } u' \le n' \text{ suchthat defined}(y[u'], u[u']) \wedge u[u'] = u \text{ then } \overline{c}\langle y[u']\rangle$$

$$\text{else new } y : T; \overline{c}\langle y\rangle$$

$$\mid c'(b' : bool); \text{if } b = b' \text{ then event } S)$$

$c_0, c, c', b, b', u, u', y$, and S do not occur in Q, and $n' \ge n$.

Intuitively, the adversary C distinguishes the secret array x from an array of independent random numbers with probability at most $p(C)$. In this definition, the adversary can perform several test queries, modeled by R_x, which all return the value of x if b is true and a random number if b is false. This corresponds to the "real-or-random" definition of security [2]. (As shown in [2], this notion is stronger than the more standard approach in which the adversary can perform a single test query and some reveal queries, which always reveal $x[u]$.)

Proposition 5 (Secrecy) *Assume that Q satisfies the hypothesis of Proposition 4.*

If $\mathcal{T}$ is a trace of $C[Q]$ for some evaluation context C, we define defRestr$_{\mathcal{T}}(x[\widetilde{a}])$, *the defining restriction of $x[\widetilde{a}]$ in trace $\mathcal{T}$, as follows: if $x[\widetilde{a}]$ is defined by* new $x[\widetilde{a}] : T$ *in $\mathcal{T}$,* defRestr$_{\mathcal{T}}(x[\widetilde{a}]) = x[\widetilde{a}]$; *if $x[\widetilde{a}]$ is defined by* let $x[\widetilde{a}] : T = z[M_1, \dots, M_l]$, defRestr$_{\mathcal{T}}(x[\widetilde{a}]) = z[a'_1, \dots, a'_l]$ *where, for all $k \le l$, M_k evaluates to a'_k in the trace $\mathcal{T}$ at the definition of $x[\widetilde{a}]$.*

For all evaluation contexts C acceptable for Q with public variables $\{x\}$, let $p(C) = \Pr[\exists(\mathcal{T}, \widetilde{a}, \widetilde{a}'), C[Q]$ reduces according to $\mathcal{T} \wedge \widetilde{a} \ne \widetilde{a}' \wedge$ defRestr$_{\mathcal{T}}(x[\widetilde{a}]) =$ defRestr$_{\mathcal{T}}(x[\widetilde{a}'])]$. *Then Q preserves the secrecy of x up to probability $2p$.*

The collisions defRestr$_{\mathcal{T}}(x[\widetilde{a}]) =$ defRestr$_{\mathcal{T}}(x[\widetilde{a}'])$ are eliminated using the same equational prover as for **Simplify** in Section 2.1, which yields a bound on $p(C)$. Intuitively, when $\widetilde{a} \neq \widetilde{a}'$, we have $\mathrm{defRestr}_{\mathcal{T}}(x[\widetilde{a}]) \neq \mathrm{defRestr}_{\mathcal{T}}(x[\widetilde{a}'])$ (except in cases of probability $p(C)$), so $x[\widetilde{a}]$ and $x[\widetilde{a}']$ are defined by different restrictions, so they are independent random numbers.

As we show in [22], secrecy composed with correspondence assertions [56] can be used to prove security of a key exchange. (Correspondence assertions are properties of the form "if some event $e(\widetilde{M})$ has been executed then some events $e_i(\widetilde{M_i})$ for $i \leq m$ have been executed". The verification of correspondence assertions in CryptoVerif in presented in [22].)

Lemma 2 *If $Q \approx_p^{\{x\}} Q'$ and Q preserves the one-session secrecy of x up to probability p' then Q' preserves the one-session secrecy of x up to probability $p''(C) = p'(C) + 2p(C[[] \mid Q_x], D_S)$. A similar result holds for secrecy.*

We can then apply the following technique. When we want to prove that Q_0 preserves the (one-session) secrecy of x, we transform Q_0 by the transformations described in Section 2 with $V = \{x\}$. By Propositions 1 and 3, we obtain a process Q'_0 such that $Q_0 \approx_p^V Q'_0$. We use Propositions 4 or 5 to show that Q'_0 preserves the (one-session) secrecy of x and finally conclude that Q_0 also preserves the (one-session) secrecy of x up to a certain probability by Lemma 2.

Example 4 After the transformations of Example 3, the only variable access to x'_k in the considered process is let $x''_k : T_k = x'_k[u]$ and x''_k is not used in the considered process. So by Proposition 4, the considered process preserves the one-session secrecy of x''_k (with $S = \{x'_k, x''_k\}$). By Lemma 2, the process of Example 1 also preserves the one-session secrecy of x''_k up to probability $2(p'_{\mathrm{mac}} + p'_{\mathrm{enc}})(C[[] \mid Q_x], D_S)$. (The runtimes of Q_x and D_S can be neglected inside this formula.) However, this process does not preserve the secrecy of x''_k, because the adversary can force several sessions of B to use the same key x''_k, by replaying the message sent by A. Accordingly, the hypothesis of Proposition 5 is not satisfied.

The criteria given in this section might seem restrictive, but in fact, they should be sufficient for all protocols, provided the previous transformation steps are powerful enough to transform the protocol into a simpler protocol, on which these criteria can then be applied.

4. Proof Strategy

Up to now, we have described the available game transformations. Next, we explain how we organize these transformations in order to prove protocols.

At the beginning of the proof and after each successful cryptographic transformation (that is, a transformation of Section 2.2), the prover executes **Simplify** and tests whether the desired security properties are proved, as described in Section 3. If so, it stops.

In order to perform the cryptographic transformations and the other syntactic transformations, our proof strategy relies of the idea of advice. Precisely, the prover tries to execute each available cryptographic transformation in turn. When such a cryptographic transformation fails, it returns some syntactic transformations that could make the desired transformation work. (These are the advised transformations.) Then the prover tries to perform these syntactic transformations. If they fail, they may also suggest other advised transformations, which are then executed. When the syntactic transformations finally succeed, we retry the desired cryptographic transformation, which may succeed or fail, perhaps with new advised transformations, and so on.

Examples of advised transformations include:

- Assume that we try to execute a cryptographic transformation, and need to recognize a certain term M of L, but we find in Q_0 only part of M, the other parts being variable accesses $x[\ldots]$ while we expect function applications. In this case, we advise **RemoveAssign**(x). For example, if Q_0 contains $\text{enc}(M', x_k, x'_r)$ and we look for $\text{enc}(x_m, \text{kgen}(x_r), x'_r)$, we advise **RemoveAssign**(x_k). If Q_0 contains let $x_k = \text{mkgen}(x_r)$ and we look for $\text{mac}(x_m, \text{mkgen}(x_r))$, we also advise **RemoveAssign**(x_k). (The transformation of Example 2 is advised for this reason.)
- When we try to execute **RemoveAssign**(x), x has several definitions, and there are accesses to variable x guarded by find in Q_0, we advise **SArename**(x).
- When we want to prove that x is secret or one-session secret, we have an assignment let $x[\widetilde{i}] : T = y[\widetilde{M}]$ in P, and there is at least one assignment defining y, we advise **RemoveAssign**(y).

  When we want to prove that x is secret or one-session secret, we have an assignment let $x[\widetilde{i}] : T = y[\widetilde{M}]$ in P, y is defined by restrictions, y has several definitions, and some variable accesses to y are not of the form let $y'[\widetilde{i'}] : T = y[\widetilde{M'}]$ in P', we advise **SArename**(y).

5. Experimental Results

CryptoVerif has been tested on a number of protocols given in the literature. We proved secrecy of keys for the Otway-Rees and Yahalom protocols as well as original and corrected versions of the Needham-Schroeder shared-key and public-key and Denning-Sacco public-key protocols, as reported in [23]. We proved authentication properties for these protocols as well as for original and corrected versions of the Woo-Lam shared-key and public-key protocols [22]. The proof succeeded in most cases (it failed for only 3 properties that in fact hold). For some proofs, for public-key protocols, we needed to provide manual indications of the game transformations to perform, mainly because several game transformations are sometimes applicable, and the proof succeeds only for a particular choice of the applied game transformation.

For each proof, the prover outputs the sequence of games it has built, a succinct explanation of the transformation performed between consecutive games, and an indication of whether the proof succeeded or failed. When the proof fails, the prover still outputs a sequence of games, but the last game of this sequence does not show the desired property and cannot be transformed further by the prover. Manual inspection of this game often makes it possible to understand why the proof failed: because there is an attack (if there is an attack on the last game), because of a limitation of the prover (if it should in fact be able to prove the property or to transform the game further), for other reasons (such as the protocol cannot be proved from the given assumptions; this situation may not lead immediately to a practical attack in the computational model).

CryptoVerif can also be used for proving cryptographic schemes, such as the FDH signature scheme [25]. It has been used for studying more complex protocols: the Kerberos protocol, with and without its public-key extension PKINIT [24], as well as parts of the record protocol and of the handshake protocol of TLS [19].

6. Conclusion

CryptoVerif produces proofs by sequences of games, in the computational model. The security assumptions on primitives are given as observational equivalences, which are proved once for each primitive and can be reused for proving many different protocols. The protocol or cryptographic scheme to prove is specified in a process calculus. CryptoVerif provides the sequence of games that leads to the proof and a bound on the probability of success of an attack. The user is allowed, but does not have, to provide manual indications on the game transformations to perform.

The essential idea of simulating proofs by sequences of games in an automatic tool can be applied to any protocol or cryptographic scheme. However, CryptoVerif applies in a fairly direct way the security assumptions on the primitives and cannot perform deep mathematical reasoning. Therefore, it is best suited for proving security protocols that use rather high-level primitives such as encryption and signatures. It is more limited for proving the security of such primitives from lower-level primitives, since more subtle mathematical arguments are often needed.

Future work includes adding support for more primitives, for example associativity for exclusive or and primitives with internal state. Improvements in the proof strategy and the possibility to give more precise manual hints would also be useful. Future case studies will certainly suggest additional extensions. In the long term, it would be interesting to certify CryptoVerif, possibly to combine it with the Coq-based framework CertiCrypt [15]. Grand challenges include the proof of protocol implementations in the computational model, by analyzing them (as started in [19] for instance) or by generating them from specifications, and taking into account side-channel attacks.

Acknowledgments I warmly thank David Pointcheval for his advice and explanations of the computational proofs of protocols. This project would not have been possible without him. I also thank Jacques Stern for initiating this work. This work was partly supported by the ANR ProSe project (decision ANR 2010-VERS-004).

References

[1] M. Abadi and P. Rogaway. Reconciling two views of cryptography (the computational soundness of formal encryption). *Journal of Cryptology*, 15(2):103–127, 2002.

[2] M. Abdalla, P.-A. Fouque, and D. Pointcheval. Password-based authenticated key exchange in the three-party setting. *IEE Proceedings Information Security*, 153(1):27–39, Mar. 2006.

[3] P. Adão, G. Bana, J. Herzog, and A. Scedrov. Soundness of formal encryption in the presence of key-cycles. In *ESORICS 2005*, volume 3679 of *LNCS*, pages 374–396. Springer, Sept. 2005.

[4] R. Affeldt, D. Nowak, and K. Yamada. Certifying assembly with formal cryptographic proofs: the case of BBS. In *AVoCS'09*, volume 23 of *Electronic Communications of the EASST*, Sept. 2009.

[5] A. Armando et al. The AVISPA tool for automated validation of Internet security protocols and applications. In *CAV 2005*, volume 3576 of *LNCS*, pages 281–285. Springer, July 2005.

[6] M. Backes, D. Hofheinz, and D. Unruh. CoSP: A general framework for computational soundness proofs. In *CCS'09*, pages 66–78. ACM, Nov. 2009.

[7] M. Backes and P. Laud. Computationally sound secrecy proofs by mechanized flow analysis. In *CCS'06*, pages 370–379. ACM, Nov. 2006.

[8] M. Backes, M. Maffei, and D. Unruh. Computationally sound verification of source code. In *CCS'10*, pages 387–398. ACM Press, Oct. 2010.

[9] M. Backes and B. Pfitzmann. Symmetric encryption in a simulatable Dolev-Yao style cryptographic library. In *CSFW'04*, pages 204–218. IEEE, June 2004.

[10] M. Backes and B. Pfitzmann. Relating symbolic and cryptographic secrecy. *IEEE Transactions on Dependable and Secure Computing*, 2(2):109–123, Apr. 2005.

[11] M. Backes, B. Pfitzmann, and M. Waidner. A composable cryptographic library with nested operations. In *CCS'03*, pages 220–230. ACM, Oct. 2003.

[12] G. Barthe, M. Daubignard, B. Kapron, and Y. Lakhnech. Computational indistinguishability logic. In *CCS'10*, pages 375–386. ACM Press, Oct. 2010.

[13] G. Barthe, B. Grégoire, S. Z. Béguelin, and Y. Lakhnech. Beyond provable security. Verifiable IND-CCA security of OAEP. In *CT-RSA 2011*, volume 6558 of *LNCS*, pages 180–196. Springer, Feb. 2011.

[14] G. Barthe, B. Grégoire, S. Heraud, and S. Z. Béguelin. Computer-aided security proofs for the working cryptographer. In *CRYPTO 2011*, volume 6841 of *LNCS*, pages 71–90. Springer, Aug. 2011.

[15] G. Barthe, B. Grégoire, and S. Zanella. Formal certification of code-based cryptographic proofs. In *POPL'09*, pages 90–101. ACM, Jan. 2009.

[16] S. Z. Béguelin, G. Barthe, S. Heraud, B. Grégoire, and D. Hedin. A machine-checked formalization of sigma-protocols. In *CSF'10*, pages 246–260. IEEE, July 2010.

[17] M. Bellare and C. Namprempre. Authenticated encryption: Relations among notions and analysis of the generic composition paradigm. In *Advances in Cryptology – ASIACRYPT'00*, volume 1976 of *LNCS*, pages 531–545. Springer, Dec. 2000.

[18] M. Bellare and P. Rogaway. The security of triple encryption and a framework for code-based game-playing proofs. In *Eurocrypt 2006*, volume 4004 of *LNCS*, pages 409–426. Springer, May 2006. Extended version available at http://eprint.iacr.org/2004/331.

[19] K. Bhargavan, R. Corin, C. Fournet, and E. Zălinescu. Cryptographically verified implementations for TLS. In *CCS'08*, pages 459–468. ACM, Oct. 2008.

[20] B. Blanchet. An efficient cryptographic protocol verifier based on Prolog rules. In *CSFW-14*, pages 82–96. IEEE, June 2001.

[21] B. Blanchet. Automatic proof of strong secrecy for security protocols. In *IEEE Symposium on Security and Privacy*, pages 86–100, May 2004.

[22] B. Blanchet. Computationally sound mechanized proofs of correspondence assertions. In *CSF'07*, pages 97–111. IEEE, July 2007. Extended version available as ePrint Report 2007/128, http://eprint.iacr.org/2007/128.

[23] B. Blanchet. A computationally sound mechanized prover for security protocols. *IEEE Transactions on Dependable and Secure Computing*, 5(4):193–207, Oct.–Dec. 2008. Updated version available at http://eprint.iacr.org/2005/401.

[24] B. Blanchet, A. D. Jaggard, A. Scedrov, and J.-K. Tsay. Computationally sound mechanized proofs for basic and public-key Kerberos. In *ASIACCS'08*, pages 87–99. ACM, Mar. 2008.

[25] B. Blanchet and D. Pointcheval. Automated security proofs with sequences of games. In *CRYPTO 2006*, volume 4117 of *LNCS*, pages 537–554. Springer, Aug. 2006.

[26] S. Z. Béguelin, B. Grégoire, G. Barthe, and F. Olmedo. Formally certifying the security of digital signature schemes. In *IEEE Symposium on Security and Privacy*, pages 237–250. IEEE, May 2009.

[27] R. Canetti. Universally composable security: A new paradigm for cryptographic protocols. In *FOCS'01*, pages 136–145. IEEE, Oct. 2001. An updated version is available at Cryptology ePrint Archive, http://eprint.iacr.org/2000/067.

[28] R. Canetti and J. Herzog. Universally composable symbolic analysis of mutual authentication and key exchange protocols. In *TCC'06*, volume 3876 of *LNCS*, pages 380–403. Springer, Mar. 2006. Extended version available at http://eprint.iacr.org/2004/334.

[29] H. Comon-Lundh and V. Cortier. Computational soundness of observational equivalence. In *CCS'08*, pages 109–118. ACM, Oct. 2008.

[30] V. Cortier, H. Hördegen, and B. Warinschi. Explicit randomness is not necessary when modeling probabilistic encryption. In *ICS 2006*, volume 186 of *ENTCS*, pages 49–65. Elsevier, Sept. 2006.

[31] V. Cortier and B. Warinschi. Computationally sound, automated proofs for security protocols. In *ESOP'05*, volume 3444 of *LNCS*, pages 157–171. Springer, Apr. 2005.

[32] J. Courant, M. Daubignard, C. Ene, P. Lafourcade, and Y. Lakhnech. Towards automated proofs for asymmetric encryption schemes in the random oracle model. In *CCS'08*, pages 371–380. ACM, Oct. 2008.

[33] J. Courant, M. Daubignard, C. Ene, P. Lafourcade, and Y. Lakhnech. Automated proofs for asymmetric encryption. In *Concurrency, Compositionality, and Correctness*, volume 5930 of *LNCS*, pages 300–321. Springer, 2010.

[34] J. Courant, C. Ene, and Y. Lakhnech. Computationally sound typing for non-interference: The case of deterministic encryption. In *FSTTCS'07*, volume 4855 of *LNCS*, pages 364–375. Springer, Dec. 2007.

[35] A. Datta, A. Derek, J. C. Mitchell, V. Shmatikov, and M. Turuani. Probabilistic polynomial-time semantics for a protocol security logic. In *ICALP'05*, volume 3580 of *LNCS*, pages 16–29. Springer, July 2005.

[36] A. Datta, A. Derek, J. C. Mitchell, and B. Warinschi. Computationally sound compositional logic for key exchange protocols. In *CSFW'06*, pages 321–334. IEEE, July 2006.

[37] D. Dolev and A. C. Yao. On the security of public key protocols. *IEEE Transactions on Information Theory*, IT-29(12):198–208, Mar. 1983.

[38] S. Halevi. A plausible approach to computer-aided cryptographic proofs. Cryptology ePrint Archive, Report 2005/181, June 2005. Available at `http://eprint.iacr.org/2005/181`.

[39] R. Janvier, Y. Lakhnech, and L. Mazaré. Completing the picture: Soundness of formal encryption in the presence of active adversaries. In *ESOP'05*, volume 3444 of *LNCS*, pages 172–185. Springer, Apr. 2005.

[40] D. E. Knuth and P. B. Bendix. Simple word problems in universal algebras. In *Computational Problems in Abstract Algebra*, pages 263–297. Pergamon Press, 1970.

[41] P. Laud. Handling encryption in an analysis for secure information flow. In *ESOP'03*, volume 2618 of *LNCS*, pages 159–173. Springer, Apr. 2003.

[42] P. Laud. Symmetric encryption in automatic analyses for confidentiality against active adversaries. In *IEEE Symposium on Security and Privacy*, pages 71–85, May 2004.

[43] P. Laud. Secrecy types for a simulatable cryptographic library. In *CCS'05*, pages 26–35. ACM, Nov. 2005.

[44] P. Laud and I. Tšahhirov. A user interface for a game-based protocol verification tool. In *FAST2009*, volume 5983 of *LNCS*, pages 263–278. Springer, Nov. 2009.

[45] P. Laud and V. Vene. A type system for computationally secure information flow. In *FCT'05*, volume 3623 of *LNCS*, pages 365–377. Springer, Aug. 2005.

[46] G. Lowe. Breaking and fixing the Needham-Schroeder public-key protocol using FDR. In *TACAS'96*, volume 1055 of *LNCS*, pages 147–166. Springer, 1996.

[47] D. Micciancio and B. Warinschi. Soundness of formal encryption in the presence of active adversaries. In *TCC'04*, volume 2951 of *LNCS*, pages 133–151. Springer, Feb. 2004.

[48] J. C. Mitchell, A. Ramanathan, A. Scedrov, and V. Teague. A probabilistic polynomial-time calculus for the analysis of cryptographic protocols. *Theoretical Computer Science*, 353(1–3):118–164, Mar. 2006.

[49] R. M. Needham and M. D. Schroeder. Using encryption for authentication in large networks of computers. *Commun. ACM*, 21(12):993–999, Dec. 1978.

[50] D. Nowak. A framework for game-based security proofs. In *ICICS 2007*, volume 4861 of *LNCS*, pages 319–333. Springer, Dec. 2007.

[51] D. Nowak. On formal verification of arithmetic-based cryptographic primitives. In *ICISC 2008*, volume 5461 of *LNCS*, pages 368–382. Springer, Dec. 2008.

[52] V. Shoup. Sequences of games: a tool for taming complexity in security proofs. Cryptology ePrint Archive, Report 2004/332, Nov. 2004. Available at `http://eprint.iacr.org/2004/332`.

[53] G. Smith and R. Alpízar. Secure information flow with random assignment and encryption. In *FMSE'06*, pages 33–43, Nov. 2006.

[54] C. Sprenger, M. Backes, D. Basin, B. Pfitzmann, and M. Waidner. Cryptographically sound theorem proving. In *CSFW'06*, pages 153–166. IEEE, July 2006.

[55] I. Tšahhirov and P. Laud. Application of dependency graphs to security protocol analysis. In *TGC'07*, volume 4912 of *LNCS*, pages 294–311. Springer, Nov. 2007.

[56] T. Y. C. Woo and S. S. Lam. A semantic model for authentication protocols. In *IEEE Symposium on Research in Security and Privacy*, pages 178–194, May 1993.

Software Safety and Security
T. Nipkow et al. (Eds.)
IOS Press, 2012
doi:10.3233/978-1-61499-028-4-26

Formal Security Proofs

Hubert Comon-Lundh and Stéphanie Delaune

Abstract. The goal of the lecture is to present some aspects of formal security proofs of protocols. This is a wide area, and there is another lecture (by B. Banchet) on related topics. The idea is therefore to explain in depth one particular technique, that relies on *deducibility constraints*. We rely mainly on two introductory documents [8,14]. Actually, the current notes are the beginning of [8].

Here is a roadmap:

1. We introduce the problem with examples and touch a little the question of the validity of the security models (section 1).
   We describe then a small process algebra, that will serve as a model for the protocols, as well as a few security properties (section 2).
2. The core of the lecture is here: we introduce the attacker model, as a deduction system, and show how to represent any execution in the hostile environment as *deducibility constraints*. In short, a deducibility constraint is a sequence of proofs, in which some parts are unknown (and formalized with variables) and possibly re-used in other constraints. An instance of such a constraints yields an attacker's strategy.
   We explain how to solve such constraints in a particular setting of a few cryptographic primitives. This is more or less what is described in the first part of [12] and is detailed in the section 3.

Though the lecture aims at being self-contained, it assumes some familiarity with inference rules/ formal proofs (or SOS for programming languages) and terms/ substitutions/ unification. Similarly, a knowledge on concurrency is not required, but will make easier the understanding of the model.

Keywords. Security, formal methods, models of concurrency, symbolic constraints, protocols

1. An introductory example

We start with the well-known example of the so-called "Needham-Schroeder public-key protocol" [23], that has been designed in 1978 and for which an attack was found in 1996 by G. Lowe [18], using formal methods.

1.1. An Informal Description

The protocol is a so-called "mutual authentication protocol". Two parties A and B wish to agree on some value, *e.g.* they wish to establish a shared secret that they will use later for fast confidential communication. The parties A and B only use a public communication channel (for instance a postal service, Internet or a mobile phone). The transport of the messages on such channels is insecure. Indeed, a malicious agent might intercept the letter (resp. message) look at its content and possibly replace it with another message or even simply destroy it.

In order to secure their communication, the agents use lockers (or encryption). We consider here public-key encryption: the lockers can be reproduced and distributed, but the key to open them is owned by a single person. Encrypting a message m with the public key of A is written $\{m\}_{\mathsf{pk}(A)}$ whereas concatenating two messages m_1 and m_2 is written $\langle m_1, m_2 \rangle$. An informal description of the protocol in the so-called Alice-Bob notation is given in Figure 1.

$$1.\ A \to B :\ \{\langle A, N_A \rangle\}_{\mathsf{pk}(B)}$$
$$2.\ B \to A :\ \{\langle N_A, N_B \rangle\}_{\mathsf{pk}(A)}$$
$$3.\ A \to B :\ \{N_B\}_{\mathsf{pk}(B)}$$

Figure 1. Informal description of the Needham-Schroeder public key protocol

Description. First the agent A encrypts a nonce N_A, *i.e.* a random number freshly generated, and her identity with the public key of B and sends it on the public channel (message 1). Only the agent B, who owes the corresponding private key can open this message. Upon reception, he gets N_A, generates his own nonce N_B and sends back the pair encrypted with the public key of A (message 2). Only the agent A is able to open this message. Furthermore, since only B was able to get N_A, inserting N_A in the plaintext is a witness that it comes from the agent B. Finally, A, after decrypting, checks that the first component is N_A and retrieves the second component N_B. As an acknowledgement, she sends back N_B encrypted by the public key of B (message 3). When B receives this message, he checks that the content is N_B. If this succeeds, it is claimed that, if the agents A and B are honest, then both parties agreed on the nonces N_A and N_B (they share these values). Moreover, these values are secret: they are only known by the agents A and B.

Attack. Actually, an attack was found in 1996 by G. Lowe [18] on the Needham-Schroeder public-key protocol. The attack described in Figure 2 relies on the fact that the protocol can be used by several parties. Moreover, we have to assume that an honest agent A starts a session of the protocol with a dishonest agent D (message 1). Then D, impersonating A, sends a message to B, starting another instance of the protocol (message 1'). When B receives this message, supposedly coming from A, he answers (messages 2' & 2). The agent A believes this reply comes from C, hence she continues the protocol (message 3). Now, the dishonest agent D decrypts the ciphertext and learn the nonce N_B. Finally, D is able to send the expected reply to B (message 3'). At this stage, two instances of the protocol have been completed with success. In the second instance B believes that he is communicating with A: contrarily to what is expected, A and B do not agree on N_B. Moreover, N_B is not a secret shared only between A and B.

Fixed version of the protocol. It has been proposed to fix the protocol by including the respondent's identity in the response (see Figure 3).

The attack described above cannot be mounted in the corrected version of the protocol. Actually, it is reported in [18] that the technique that permitted to find the Lowe attack on the Needham-Schroeder public key protocol found no attack on this protocol.

1. $A \rightarrow D : \{\langle A, N_A \rangle\}_{\mathsf{pk}(D)}$

$1'. \; D(A) \rightarrow B : \{\langle A, N_A \rangle\}_{\mathsf{pk}(B)}$
$2'. \; B \rightarrow A : \quad\;\; \{\langle N_A, N_B \rangle\}_{\mathsf{pk}(A)}$

2. $B \rightarrow A : \{\langle N_A, N_B \rangle\}_{\mathsf{pk}(A)}$
3. $A \rightarrow D : \{N_B\}_{\mathsf{pk}(D)}$

$3'. \; D(A) \rightarrow B : \{N_B\}_{\mathsf{pk}(B)}$

Figure 2. Attack on the Needham-Schroeder public key protocol

1. $A \rightarrow B : \{\langle A, N_A \rangle\}_{\mathsf{pk}(B)}$
2. $B \rightarrow A : \{\langle \langle N_A, N_B \rangle, B \rangle\}_{\mathsf{pk}(A)}$
3. $A \rightarrow B : \{N_B\}_{\mathsf{pk}(B)}$

Figure 3. Description of the Needham-Schroeder-Lowe protocol

1.2. A More Formal Analysis

The Alice-Bob notation is a semi-formal notation that specifies the conversation between the agents. We have to make more precise the view of each agent. This amounts specifying the concurrent programs that are executed by each party. One has also to be precise when specifying how a message is processed by an agent. In particular, what parts of a received message are checked by the agent? What are the actions performed by the agent to compute the answer?

A classical way to model protocols is to use a process algebra. However, in order to model the messages that are exchanged, we need a process algebra that allows processes to send first-order terms build over a signature, names and variables. These terms model messages that are exchanged during a protocol.

Example 1 *Consider for example the signature* $\Sigma = \{\{\_\}\_, \mathsf{pk}(\_), \mathsf{sk}(\_), \mathsf{dec}, \langle\_,\_\rangle,$ $\mathsf{proj}_1, \mathsf{proj}_2\}$ *which contains three binary function symbols modelling asymmetric encryption, decryption, and pairing, and four unary function symbols modelling projections, public key and private key. The signature is equipped with an equational theory and we interpret equality up to this theory. For instance the theory*

$$\mathsf{dec}(\{x\}_{\mathsf{pk}(y)}, \mathsf{sk}(y)) = x, \;\; \mathsf{proj}_1(\langle x_1, x_2 \rangle) = x_1, \;\; \textit{and} \;\; \mathsf{proj}_2(\langle x_1, x_2 \rangle) = x_2.$$

models that decryption and encryption cancel out whenever suitable keys are used. One can also retrieves the first (resp. second) component of a pair.

Processes $P, Q, R, \ldots$ are constructed as follows. The process new $N.P$ restricts the name N in P and can for instance be used to model that N is a fresh random number. $\mathsf{in}(c, x).P$ models the input of a term on a channel c, which is then substituted for x in process P. $\mathsf{out}(c, t)$ outputs a term t on a channel c. The conditional if $M = N$ then P else Q behaves as P when M and N are equal modulo the equational theory and behaves as Q otherwise.

The program (or process) that is executed by an agent, say a, who wants to initiate a session of the Needham-Schroeder protocol with another agent b is as follows:

$A(a, b) \hat{=}$ new N_a.	a generates a fresh message N_a
$\quad$ out$(c, \{a, N_a\}_{\mathsf{pk}(b)})$.	the message is sent on the channel c
$\quad$ in(c, x).	a is waiting for an input on c
$\quad$ let $x_0 = \mathsf{dec}(x, \mathsf{sk}(a))$ in	a tries to decrypt the message
$\quad$ if $\mathsf{proj}_1(x_0) = N_a$ then	a checks that
	the first component is N_a
$\quad$ let $x_1 = \mathsf{proj}_2(x_0)$ in	a retrieves the second component
$\quad$ out$(c, \{x_1\}_{\mathsf{pk}(b)})$	a sends her answer on c

Note that we use variables for the unknown components of messages. These variables can be (a priori) replaced by any message, provided that the attacker can build it and that it is accepted by the agent. In the program described above, if the decryption fails or if the first component of the message received by a is not equal to N_a, then a will abort the protocol.

Similarly, we have to write the program that is executed by an agent, say b, who has to answer to the messages sent by the initiator of the protocol. This program may look like this:

$B(a, b) \hat{=}$ in(c, y).	b is waiting for an input on c
$\quad$ let $(a, y_0) = \mathsf{dec}(y, \mathsf{sk}(b))$ in	b tries to decrypt it and then
	retrieves the second component
	of the plaintext
$\quad$ new N_b.	b generates a random number N_b
$\quad$ out$(c, \{y_0, N_b\}_{\mathsf{pk}(a)})$.	b sends a reply on the channel c
$\quad$ in(c, y').	b is waiting for an input on c
$\quad$ if $\mathsf{dec}(y', \mathsf{sk}(b)) = N_b$ then Ok.	b tries to decrypt the message
	and checks whether its content
	is N_b or not

The (weak) secrecy property states for instance that, if a, b are honest (their secret keys are unknown to the environment), then, when the process $B(a, b)$ reaches the Ok state, N_b is unknown to the environment. We will also see later how to formalise agreement properties. The "environment knowledge" is actually a component of the description of the global state of the network. Basically, all messages that can be built from the public data and the messages that have been sent are in the knowledge of the environment.

Any number of copies of A and B (with any parameter values) are running concurrently in a hostile environment. Such a hostile environment is modelled by any process that may receive and emit on public channels. We also assume that such an environment owes as many public/private key pairs as it wishes (compromised agents), an agent may also generate new values when needed. The only restrictions on the environment is on the way it may construct new messages: the encryption and decryption functions, as well as public keys are assumed to be known from the environment. However no private key (besides those that it generates) is known. We exhibit now a process that will yield the attack, assuming that the agent d is a dishonest (or compromised) agent who leaked his secret key:

$P \doteq \mathsf{in}(c, z_1).$ `d receives a message (from a)`
     $\mathsf{let}\ \langle a, z_1' \rangle = \mathsf{dec}(z_1, \mathsf{sk}(d))\ \mathsf{in}$ `d decrypts it`
     $\mathsf{out}(c, \{\langle a, z_1' \rangle\}_{\mathsf{pk}(b)}).$ `d sends the plaintext encrypted`
                                    `with` $\mathsf{pk}(b)$

     $\mathsf{in}(c, z_2).\mathsf{out}(c, z_2).$ `d forwards to a the answer`
                                      `he obtained from b`

     $\mathsf{in}(c, z_3).$ `d receives the answer from a`
     $\mathsf{let}\ z_3' = \mathsf{dec}(z_3, \mathsf{sk}(d))\ \mathsf{in}$ `d decrypts it and learn` N_b
     $\mathsf{out}(c, \{z_3'\}_{\mathsf{pk}(b)}).$ `d sends the expected message`
                                    $\{N_b\}_{\mathsf{pk}(b)}$ `to` $b.$

The Needham-Schroeder-Lowe protocol has been proved secure in several formal models close to the one we have sketched in this section [9,6].

1.3. Further Readings

A survey by Clark and Jacob [10] describes several authentication protocols and outlines also the methods that have been used to analyse them. In addition, it provides a summary of the ways in which protocols have been found to fail. The purpose of the SPORE web page [1] is to continue on-line the seminal work of Clark and Jacob, updating their base of security protocols.

As you have seen, some protocols (or some attacks) rely on some algebraic properties of cryptographic primitives. In [15], a list of some relevant algebraic properties of cryptographic operators is given, and for each of them, some examples of protocols or attacks using these properties are provided. The survey also gives an overview of the existing methods in formal approaches for analysing cryptographic protocols.

1.4. Exercises

Exercice 1 $(\star)$
Consider the following protocol:

$$A \to B : \langle A, \{K\}_{\mathsf{pk}(B)} \rangle$$
$$B \to A : \langle B, \{K\}_{\mathsf{pk}(A)} \rangle$$

First, A generates a fresh key K and sends it encrypted with the public key of B. Only B will be able to decrypt this message. In this way, B learns K and B also knows that this message comes from A as indicated in the first part of the message he received. Hence, B answers to A by sending again the key, this time encrypted with the public key of A.

Show that an attacker can learn the key K generated by an honest agent A to another honest agent B.

Exercice 2 ($\star$)

The previous protocol is corrected as in the Needham-Schroeder protocol, *i.e.* we add the identity of the agent inside each encryption.

$$A \to B : \{\langle A, K \rangle\}_{\mathsf{pk}(B)}$$
$$B \to A : \{\langle B, K \rangle\}_{\mathsf{pk}(A)}$$

1. Check that the previous attack does not exist anymore. Do you think that the secrecy property stated in Exercise 1 holds?
2. Two agents want to use this protocol to establish a session key. Show that there is an attack.

Exercice 3 ($\star\star$)

For double security, all messages in the previous protocol are encrypted twice:

$$A \to B : \{\langle A, \{K\}_{\mathsf{pk}(B)} \rangle\}_{\mathsf{pk}(B)}$$
$$B \to A : \{\langle B, \{K\}_{\mathsf{pk}(A)} \rangle\}_{\mathsf{pk}(A)}$$

Show that the protocol then becomes insecure in the sense that an attacker can learn the key K generated by an honest agent A to another honest agent B.

Exercice 4 ($\star\star\star$)

We consider a variant of the Needham-Schroeder-Lowe protocol. This protocol is as follows:

$$1.\ A \to B :\ \{\langle A, N_A \rangle\}_{\mathsf{pk}(B)}$$
$$2.\ B \to A :\ \{\langle N_A, \langle N_B, B \rangle \rangle\}_{\mathsf{pk}(A)}$$
$$3.\ A \to B :\ \{N_B\}_{\mathsf{pk}(B)}$$

1. Check that the 'man-in-the-middle' attack described in Figure 2 does not exist.
2. Show that there is an attack on the secrecy of the nonce N_b.
   hint: type confusion
3. Do you think that this attack is realistic? Why?

1.5. An Attack on the Fixed Version of the Protocol

In this section, we show that we must be cautious with the use of formal methods, and in particular with the assumptions on the implementation of the security primitives. The issue, that is raised here is covered by the *soundness* results that show under which condition the formal model is fully abstract with respect to the computational one. Discussing soundness results would be the subject of another lecture...

Up to now, the encryption is a black-box: nothing can be learnt on a plaintext from a ciphertext and two ciphertexts are unrelated.

Consider however a simple El-Gamal encryption scheme. Roughly (we skip here the group choice for instance), the encryption scheme is given by a cyclic group G of order q and generator g; these parameters are public. Each agent a may choose randomly a secret key $\mathsf{sk}(a)$ and publish the corresponding public key $\mathsf{pk}(a) = g^{\mathsf{sk}(a)}$. Given a message m (assume for simplicity that it is an element $g^{m'}$ of the group), encrypting m with the public key $\mathsf{pk}(a)$ consists in drawing a random number r and letting $\{m\}_{\mathsf{pk}(a)} =$

1. $a \rightarrow d : \{\langle a, N_a \rangle\}_{\mathsf{pk}(d)}$

  $1'. d(a) \rightarrow b : \{\langle a, N_a \rangle\}_{\mathsf{pk}(b)}$

  $2'. b \rightarrow a : \{\langle\langle N_a, N_b \rangle, b \rangle\}_{\mathsf{pk}(a)} = (g^{N_a + 2^{\alpha} \times N_b + 2^{2\alpha} \times b} \times \mathsf{pk}(a)^r, g^r)$

d intercepts this message, and computes

$[g^{N_a + 2^{\alpha} \times N_b + 2^{2\alpha} \times b} \times \mathsf{pk}(a)^r] \times g^{-2^{2\alpha} \times b} \times g^{2^{2\alpha} \times d} = g^{N_a + 2^{\alpha} \times N_b + 2^{2\alpha} \times d} \times \mathsf{pk}(a)^r$

2. $d \rightarrow a : \{\langle\langle N_a, N_b \rangle, d \rangle\}_{\mathsf{pk}(a)} = (g^{N_a + 2^{\alpha} \times N_b + 2^{2\alpha} \times d} \times \mathsf{pk}(a)^r, g^r)$
3. $a \rightarrow d : \{N_b\}_{\mathsf{pk}(d)}$

  $3'. d \rightarrow b : \{N_b\}_{\mathsf{pk}(d)}$

Figure 4. Attack on the Needham-Schroeder-Lowe protocol with El-Gamal encryption.

$(\mathsf{pk}(a)^r \times g^{m'}, g^r)$. Decrypting the message consists in raising g^r to the power $\mathsf{sk}(a)$ and dividing the first component of the pair by $g^{r \times \mathsf{sk}(a)}$. We have that:

$$[\mathsf{pk}(a)^r \times g^{m'}]/(g^r)^{\mathsf{sk}(a)} = [(g^{\mathsf{sk}(a)})^r \times g^{m'}]/(g^r)^{\mathsf{sk}(a)} = g^{m'} = m.$$

This means that this encryption scheme satisfies the equation $\mathsf{dec}(\{x\}_{\mathsf{pk}(y)}, \mathsf{sk}(y)) = x$. However, as we will see, this encryption scheme also satisfies some other properties that are not taken into account in our previous formal analysis.

Attack.   Assume now that we are using such an encryption scheme in the Needham-Schroeder-Lowe protocol and that pairing two group elements $m_1 = g^{m'_1}$ and $m_2 = g^{m'_2}$ is performed in a naive way: $\langle m_1, m_2 \rangle$ is mapped to $g^{m'_1 + 2^{|m'_1|} \times m'_2}$ (*i.e.* concatenating the binary representations of the messages m'_1 and m'_2). In such a case, an attack can be mounted on the protocol (see Figure 4).

Actually, the attack starts as before. We assume that the honest agent a is starting a session with a dishonest party d. Then d decrypts the message and re-encrypt it with the public key of b. The honest party b replies sending the expected message $\{\langle\langle N_a, N_b \rangle, b \rangle\}_{\mathsf{pk}(a)}$. The attacker intercepts this message. Note that the attacker can not simply forward it to a since it does not have the expected form. The attacker intercepts $\{\langle\langle N_a, N_b \rangle, b \rangle\}_{\mathsf{pk}(a)}$, *i.e.* $(\mathsf{pk}(a)^r \times g^{N_a + 2^{\alpha} \times N_b + 2^{2\alpha} \times b}, g^r)$ where α is the length of a nonce. The attacker knows g, α, b, hence he can compute $g^{-2^{2\alpha} \times b} \times g^{2^{2\alpha} \times d}$ and multiply the first component, yielding $\{\langle\langle N_a, N_b \rangle, d \rangle\}_{\mathsf{pk}(a)}$. Then the attack can go on as before: a replies by sending $\{N_b\}_{\mathsf{pk}(d)}$ and the attacker sends $\{N_b\}_{\mathsf{pk}(b)}$ to b, impersonating a.

This example is however a toy example since pairing could be implemented in another way. In [26] there is a real attack that is only based on weaknesses of the El Gamal encryption scheme. In particular, the attack does not dependent on how pairing is implemented.

This shows that the formal analysis only proves the security in a formal model, that might not be faithful. Here, the formal analysis assumed a model in which it is not possible to forge a ciphertext from another ciphertext, without decrypting/encrypting. This property is known as *non-malleability*, which is not satisfied by the El Gamal encryption scheme.

2. A small process calculus

We now define our cryptographic process calculus for describing protocols. This calculus is inspired by the applied pi calculus [3] which is the calculus used by the PROVERIF tool [9]. The applied pi calculus is a language for describing concurrent processes and their interactions. It is an extension of the pi calculus [22] with cryptographic primitives. It is designed for describing and analysing a variety of security protocols, such as authentication protocols (*e.g.* [17]), key establishment protocols (*e.g.* [5]), e-voting protocols (*e.g.* [16]), ... These protocols try to achieve various security goals, such as secrecy, authentication, privacy, ...

In this chapter, we present a simplified version that is sufficient for our purpose and we explain how to formalise security properties in such a calculus.

2.1. Preliminaries

The applied pi calculus is similar to the spi calculus [2]. The key difference between the two formalisms concerns the way that cryptographic primitives are handled. The spi calculus has a fixed set of primitives built-in (symmetric and public key encryption), while the applied pi calculus allows one to define less usual primitives by means of an equational theory. This flexibility is particularly useful to model the new protocols that are emerging and which rely on new cryptographic primitives.

2.1.1. Messages

To describe processes, one starts with an infinite set of *names* $\mathcal{N}$ (which are used to represent atomic data, such as keys, nonces, ...), an infinite set of *variables* $\mathcal{X}$, and a *signature* $\mathcal{F}$ which consists of the *function symbols* which will be used to define *terms*. Each function symbol has an associated integer, its *arity*. In the case of security protocols, typical function symbols will include a binary function symbol senc for symmetric encryption, which takes plaintext and a key and returns the corresponding ciphertext, and a binary function symbol sdec for decryption, taking ciphertext and a key and returning the plaintext. Variables are used to consider messages containing unknown (unspecified) pieces.

Terms are defined as names, variables, and function symbols applied to other terms. Terms and function symbols may be sorted, and in such a case, function symbol application must respect sorts and arities. We denote by $\mathcal{T}(\Sigma)$ the set of terms built on the symbols in Σ. We denote by $fv(M)$ (resp. $fn(M)$) the set of variables (resp. names) that occur in M. A term M that does not contain any variable is a *ground term*. The set of positions of a term T is written $pos(T) \subseteq \mathbb{N}^*$, and its set of subterms $\mathsf{St}(T)$. The subterm of T at position $p \in pos(T)$ is written $T|_p$. The term obtained by replacing $T|_p$ with a term U in T is denoted $T[U]_p$.

We split the function symbols between *private* and *public* symbols, *i.e.* $\mathcal{F} = \mathcal{F}_{\mathsf{pub}} \uplus \mathcal{F}_{\mathsf{priv}}$. Private function symbols are used to model algorithms or data that are not available to the attacker. Moreover, sometimes, we also split the function symbols into *constructors* and *destructors*, *i.e.* $\mathcal{F} = \mathcal{D} \uplus \mathcal{C}$. Destructors are used to model the fact that some operations fail. A typical destructor symbol could be the symbol sdec if we want to model a decryption algorithm that fails when we try to decrypt a ciphertext with a wrong key. A *constructor term* is a term in $\mathcal{T}(\mathcal{C} \cup \mathcal{N} \cup \mathcal{X})$.

By the means of a convergent term rewriting system $\mathcal{R}$, we describe the equations which hold on terms built from the signature. A *term rewriting system* (TRS) is a set of *rewrite rules* $l \rightarrow r$ where $l \in \mathcal{T}(\mathcal{F} \cup \mathcal{X})$ and $r \in \mathcal{T}(\mathcal{F} \cup fv(l))$. A term $S \in \mathcal{T}(\mathcal{F} \cup \mathcal{N} \cup \mathcal{X})$ rewrites to T by $\mathcal{R}$, denoted $S \rightarrow_{\mathcal{R}} T$, if there is $l \rightarrow r$ in $\mathcal{R}$, $p \in pos(S)$ and a substitution σ such that $S|_p = l\sigma$ and $T = S[r\sigma]_p$. Moreover, we assume that $\{x\sigma \mid x \in \mathsf{Dom}(\sigma)\}$ are constructor terms. We denote by $\rightarrow_{\mathcal{R}}^*$ the reflexive and transitive closure of $\rightarrow_{\mathcal{R}}$, and by $=_{\mathcal{R}}$ the symmetric, reflexive and transitive closure of $\rightarrow_{\mathcal{R}}$. A TRS $\mathcal{R}$ is *convergent* if it is:

- *terminating*, i.e. there is no infinite chain $T_1 \rightarrow_{\mathcal{R}} T_2 \rightarrow_{\mathcal{R}} \ldots$; and
- *confluent*, i.e. for all terms S, T such that $S =_{\mathcal{R}} T$, there exists U such that $S \rightarrow_{\mathcal{R}}^* U$ and $T \rightarrow_{\mathcal{R}}^* U$.

A term T is $\mathcal{R}$-*reduced* if there is no term S such that $T \rightarrow_{\mathcal{R}} S$. If $T \rightarrow_{\mathcal{R}}^* S$ and S is $\mathcal{R}$-reduced then S is *a $\mathcal{R}$-reduced form* of T. When this reduced form is unique (in particular if $\mathcal{R}$ is convergent), we write $S = T\downarrow_{\mathcal{R}}$ (or simply $T\downarrow$ when $\mathcal{R}$ is clear from the context). In the following, we will only consider convergent rewriting system. Hence, we have that $M =_{\mathcal{R}} N$, if and only if, $M\downarrow = N\downarrow$. A ground constructor term in normal form is also called a *message*.

Example 2 *In order to model the handshake protocol that we will present later on, we introduce the signature:*

$$\mathcal{F}_{\mathsf{senc}} = \{\mathsf{senc}/2, \, \textit{sdec}/2, \, \mathsf{f}/1\}$$

together with the term rewriting system $\mathcal{R}_{\mathsf{senc}} = \{\textit{sdec}(\mathsf{senc}(x, y), y) \rightarrow x\}$. We will assume that $\mathcal{F}_{\mathsf{senc}}$ only contains constructor symbols. This represents a decryption algorithm that always succeeds. If we decrypt the ciphertext $\mathsf{senc}(n, k)$ with a key $k' \neq k$, the decryption algorithm will return the message $\textit{sdec}(\mathsf{senc}(n, k), k')$.

Here, we have that $\textit{sdec}(\mathsf{senc}(n', \textit{sdec}(n, n)), \textit{sdec}(n, n)) =_{\mathcal{R}} n'$. Indeed, we have that $\textit{sdec}(\mathsf{senc}(n', \textit{sdec}(n, n)), \textit{sdec}(n, n))$ rewrites in one step to n' (with $p = \epsilon$, and $\sigma = \{x \mapsto n', \, y \mapsto \textit{sdec}(n, n)\}$).

Example 3 *In order to model the Needham-Schroeder protocol, we will consider the following signature:*

$$\mathcal{F}_{\mathsf{aenc}} = \{\langle \_, \_ \rangle, \, \mathsf{proj}_1/1, \, \mathsf{proj}_2/1, \, \mathsf{aenc}/2, \, \textit{pk}(/)1, \, \mathsf{sk}/1, \, \mathsf{adec}/2\}$$

together with the term rewriting system $\mathcal{R}_{\mathsf{aenc}}$:

$$\mathsf{proj}_1(\langle x, y \rangle) \rightarrow x \qquad \mathsf{proj}_2(\langle x, y \rangle) \rightarrow y \qquad \mathsf{adec}(\mathsf{aenc}(x, \textit{pk}(y)), \textit{sk}(y)) \rightarrow x$$

This will allow us to model asymmetric encryption and pairing. We will assume that proj_1, proj_2, and adec are destructors symbols. The only private non-constant symbol is the symbol sk. Note that $\mathsf{proj}_1(\langle n, \mathsf{adec}(n, n)\rangle) \neq_{\mathcal{R}} n$. Indeed, the terms $\mathsf{proj}_1(\langle n, \mathsf{adec}(n, n)\rangle)$ and n are both irreducible and not syntactically equal.

2.1.2. Assembling Terms into Frames

At some moment, while engaging in one or more sessions of one or more protocols, an attacker may have observed a sequence of messages $M_1, \ldots, M_\ell$, *i.e.* a set of ground constructor terms in normal form. We want to represent this knowledge of the attacker. It is not enough for us to say that the attacker knows the *set* of terms $\{M_1, \ldots, M_\ell\}$ since he also knows the order that he observed them in. Furthermore, we should distinguish those names that the attacker knows from those that were freshly generated by others and which remain secret from the attacker; both kinds of names may appear in the terms. We use the concept of *frame* from the applied pi calculus [3] to represent the knowledge of the attacker. A *frame* $\phi = $ new $\overline{n}.\sigma$ consists of a finite set $\overline{n} \subseteq \mathcal{N}$ of *restricted* names (those that the attacker does not know), and a substitution σ of the form:

$$\{ {}^{M_1}/_{x_1}, \ldots, {}^{M_\ell}/_{x_\ell} \}.$$

The variables enable us to refer to each message M_i. We always assume that the terms M_i are ground term in normal form that do not contain destructor symbols. The names $\overline{n}$ are bound and can be renamed. We denote by $=_\alpha$ the α-renaming relation on frames. The *domain* of the frame ϕ, written $\mathsf{Dom}(\phi)$, is defined as $\{x_1, \ldots, x_\ell\}$.

2.1.3. Deduction

Given a frame ϕ that represents the information available to an attacker, we may ask whether a given ground constructor term M may be deduced from ϕ. Given a convergent rewriting system $\mathcal{R}$ on $\mathcal{F}$, this relation is written $\phi \vdash_\mathcal{R} M$ and is formally defined below.

Definition 2.1 (Deduction) *Let M be a ground term and $\phi = $ new $\overline{n}.\sigma$ be a frame. We have that new $\overline{n}.\sigma \vdash_\mathcal{R} M$ if, and only if, there exists a term $N \in \mathcal{T}(\mathcal{F}_{\mathsf{pub}} \cup \mathcal{N} \cup \mathsf{Dom}(\phi))$ such that $\mathsf{fn}(N) \cap \overline{n} = \emptyset$ and $N\sigma =_\mathcal{R} M$. Such a term N is a recipe of the term M.*

Intuitively, the deducible messages are the messages of ϕ and the names that are not protected in ϕ, closed by rewriting with $\mathcal{R}$ and closed by application of public function symbols. When new $\overline{n}.\sigma \vdash_\mathcal{R} M$, any occurrence of names from $\overline{n}$ in M is bound by new $\overline{n}$. So new $\overline{n}.\sigma \vdash_\mathcal{R} M$ could be formally written new $\overline{n}.(\sigma \vdash_\mathcal{R} M)$.

Example 4 *Consider the theory $\mathcal{R}_{\mathsf{senc}}$ given in Example 2 and the following frame:*

$$\phi = \text{new } k, s_1.\{ {}^{\mathsf{senc}(\langle s_1, s_2 \rangle, k)}/_{x_1}, {}^{k}/_{x_2} \}.$$

We have that $\phi \vdash_{\mathcal{R}_{\mathsf{senc}}} k$, $\phi \vdash_{\mathcal{R}_{\mathsf{senc}}} s_1$ and $\phi \vdash_{\mathcal{R}_{\mathsf{senc}}} s_2$. Indeed x_2, $\mathsf{proj}_1(\mathsf{sdec}(x_1, x_2))$ and s_2 are recipes of the terms k, s_1 and s_2 respectively.

The relation new $\overline{n}.\sigma \vdash_\mathcal{R} M$ can be axiomatized by the following rules:

$$\frac{}{\text{new } \overline{n}.\sigma \vdash_\mathcal{R} M} \text{ if } \exists x \in dom(\sigma) \text{ such that } x\sigma = M \qquad \frac{}{\text{new } \overline{n}.\sigma \vdash_\mathcal{R} s} \; s \in \mathcal{N} \setminus \overline{n}$$

$$\frac{\phi \vdash_\mathcal{R} M_1 \quad \cdots \quad \phi \vdash_\mathcal{R} M_\ell}{\phi \vdash_\mathcal{R} \mathsf{f}(M_1, \ldots, M_\ell)} \; \mathsf{f} \in \mathcal{F}_{\mathsf{pub}} \qquad \frac{\phi \vdash_\mathcal{R} M}{\phi \vdash_\mathcal{R} M'} \; M =_\mathcal{R} M'$$

Since we only consider convergent rewriting systems, it is easy to prove that the two definitions coincide.

2.1.4. Static Equivalence

The frames we have introduced are too fine-grained as representations of the attacker's knowledge. For example, $\nu k.\{^{\mathsf{senc}(s_0,k)}/_x\}$ and $\nu k.\{^{\mathsf{senc}(s_1,k)}/_x\}$ represent a situation in which the encryption of the public name s_0 (resp. s_1) by a randomly-chosen key has been observed. Since the attacker cannot detect the difference between these two situations, the frames should be considered equivalent. To formalise this, we note that if two recipes M, N on the frame ϕ produce the same constructor term, we say they are equal in the frame, and write $(M =_{\mathcal{R}} N)\phi$. Thus, the knowledge of the attacker can be thought of as his ability to distinguish such recipes. If two frames have identical distinguishing power, then we say that they are *statically equivalent*.

Definition 2.2 (static equivalence) *We say that two terms M and N in $\mathcal{T}(\mathcal{F}_{\mathsf{pub}} \cup \mathcal{N} \cup \mathcal{X})$ are equal in the frame ϕ, and write $(M =_{\mathcal{R}} N)\phi$, if there exists $\overline{n}$ and a substitution σ such that $\phi =_\alpha \nu\overline{n}.\sigma$, $\overline{n} \cap (\mathsf{fn}(M) \cup \mathsf{fn}(N)) = \emptyset$, and $M\sigma{\downarrow}$ and $N\sigma{\downarrow}$ are both constructor terms that are equal, i.e. $M\sigma{\downarrow} = N\sigma{\downarrow}$.*

We say that two frames $\phi_1 = \overline{n_1}.\sigma_1$ and $\phi_2 = \overline{n_2}.\sigma_2$ are statically equivalent, and write $\phi_1 \sim_{\mathcal{R}} \phi_2$, when:

- $\mathsf{Dom}(\phi_1) = \mathsf{Dom}(\phi_2)$,
- *for all term $M \in \mathcal{T}(\mathcal{F}_{\mathsf{pub}} \cup \mathcal{N} \cup \mathcal{X})$ such that $\mathsf{fn}(M) \cap (\overline{n_1} \cup \overline{n_2}) = \emptyset$, we have that: $M\sigma_1{\downarrow}$ is constructor term $\Leftrightarrow$ $M\sigma_2{\downarrow}$ is a constructor term.*
- *for all terms M, N in $\mathcal{T}(\mathcal{F}_{\mathsf{pub}} \cup \mathcal{N} \cup \mathcal{X})$ we have that: $(M =_{\mathcal{R}} N)\phi_1 \Leftrightarrow (M =_{\mathcal{R}} N)\phi_2$.*

Note that by definition of $\sim$, we have that $\phi_1 \sim \phi_2$ when $\phi_1 =_\alpha \phi_2$ and we have also that new $n.\phi \sim \phi$ when n does not occur in ϕ.

Example 5 *Consider the rewriting system $\mathcal{R}_{\mathsf{senc}}$ provided in Example 2. Consider the frames $\phi = $ new $k.\{^{\mathsf{senc}(s_0,k)}/_{x_1}, {}^k/_{x_2}\}$, and $\phi' = $ new $k.\{^{\mathsf{senc}(s_1,k)}/_{x_1}, {}^k/_{x_2}\}$. Intuitively, s_0 and s_1 could be the two possible (public) values of a vote. We have $(\mathsf{sdec}(x_1, x_2) =_{\mathcal{R}_{\mathsf{senc}}} s_0)\phi$ whereas $(\mathsf{sdec}(x_1, x_2) \neq_{\mathcal{R}_{\mathsf{senc}}} s_0)\phi'$. Therefore we have that $\phi \not\sim \phi'$. However, we have that:*

$$\text{new } k.\{^{\mathsf{senc}(s_0,k)}/_{x_1}\} \sim \text{new } k.\{^{\mathsf{senc}(s_1,k)}/_{x_1}\}.$$

Example 6 *Consider again the rewriting system $\mathcal{R}_{\mathsf{senc}}$ provided in Example 2. We have that:*

$$\text{new } k.\{^{\mathsf{senc}(0,k)}/_x\} \sim \text{new } k.\{^{\mathsf{senc}(1,k)}/_x\}$$

$$\{^{\mathsf{senc}(0,k)}/_x, {}^{\langle 0,k\rangle}/_y\} \not\sim \text{new } k.\{^{\mathsf{senc}(1,k)}/_x, {}^{\langle 0,k\rangle}/_y\} \quad (\mathsf{sdec}(x, \mathsf{proj}_2(y)) \overset{?}{=} 0)$$

$$\text{new } a.\{^a/_x\} \sim \text{new } b.\{^b/_x\}$$

$$\text{new } a.\{^a/_x\} \not\sim \text{new } b.\{^b/_y\} \quad (\textit{different domains})$$

$$\{^a/_x\} \not\sim \{^b/_x\} \quad (x \overset{?}{=} a)$$

2.2. Protocols

We now described our cryptographic process calculus for describing protocols. For sake of simplicity, we only consider public channels, *i.e.* under the control of the attacker.

2.2.1. Protocol Language

The grammar for *processes* is given below. One has *plain processes* P, Q, R and *extended processes* A, B, C.

Plain processes. Plain processes are formed from the following grammar

$$
\begin{array}{ll}
P, Q, R \; \hat{=} \; \text{plain processes} & \\
\quad 0 & \text{null process} \\
\quad P \parallel Q & \text{parallel composition} \\
\quad \text{in}(c, M_i).P & \text{message input} \\
\quad \text{out}(c, M_o).P & \text{message output} \\
\quad \text{if } M = N \text{ then } P \text{ else } Q & \text{conditional} \\
\quad \text{new } n.P & \text{restriction} \\
\quad !P & \text{replication}
\end{array}
$$

such that a variable x appears in a term only if the term is in the scope of an input $\text{in}(c, M_i)$ with $x \in fv(M_i)$. The null process 0 does nothing; $P \parallel Q$ is the parallel composition of P and Q. The replication $!P$ behaves as an infinite number of copies of P running in parallel. The conditional construction if $M = N$ then P else Q is standard. We omit else Q when Q is 0. The process $\text{in}(c, M_i).P$ is ready to input on the public channel c, then to run P where the variables of M_i are bound by the actual input message. The term M_i is a constructor term with variables. $\text{out}(c, M_o).P$ is ready to output M_o (it may contains some destructors), then to run P. Again, we omit P when P is 0.

In this definition, we consider both pattern inputs and conditionals, which is redundant in some situations: for any executable process, the patterns can be replaced with conditionals. However, we keep both possibilities, in order to keep some flexibility in writing down the protocols.

Example 7 *We illustrate our syntax with the well-known handshake protocol that can be informally described as follows:*

$$
\begin{array}{rl}
A \;\rightarrow\; B : & \text{senc}(n, w) \\
B \;\rightarrow\; A : & \text{senc}(\text{f}(n), w)
\end{array}
$$

We rely on the signature given in Example 2. The goal of this protocol is to authenticate B from A's point of view, provided that they share an initial secret w. This is done by a simple challenge-response transaction: A sends a random number (a nonce) encrypted with the shared secret key w. Then, B decrypts this message, applies a given function (for instance $\text{f}(n) = n + 1$) to it, and sends the result back, also encrypted with w. Finally, the agent A checks the validity of the result by decrypting the message and checking the decryption against $\text{f}(n)$. In our calculus, we can model the protocol as new $w.(P_A \parallel P_B)$ *where*

- $P_A(w) = $ new $n.$ *out*$(c, \text{senc}(n, w))$. *in*(c, x). if *sdec*$(x, w) = \text{f}(n)$ then P
- $P_B(w) = $ *in*(c, y). *out*$(c, \text{senc}(\text{f}(\textbf{\textit{sdec}}(y, w)), w))$.

where P models an application that is executed when P_B has been successfully authenticated. Here, we use the formalism with explicit destructors but we could also used pattern inputs.

Example 8 *Coming back to the Needham-Schroeder public key protocol described in Section 1 and considering the signature given in Example 3, we have:*

$$P_A(a,b) \mathrel{\hat=} out(c, \mathsf{aenc}(\langle a, N_a\rangle, \mathsf{pk}(b))). \qquad P_B(a,b) \mathrel{\hat=} in(c, \mathsf{aenc}(\langle a, y\rangle, \mathsf{pk}(b))).$$
$$in(c, \mathsf{aenc}(\langle N_a, x\rangle, \mathsf{pk}(a))). \qquad\qquad out(c, \mathsf{aenc}(\langle y, N_b\rangle, \mathsf{pk}(a))).$$
$$out(c, \mathsf{aenc}(x, \mathsf{pk}(b))) \qquad\qquad\qquad in(c, \mathsf{aenc}(N_b, \mathsf{pk}(b)))$$

Here, we have used pattern inputs. We could also have used the alternative formalism of explicit destructors. With pattern inputs, we do not need in general to used destructors to describe the outputs.

Note that all the processes that can be written in this syntax (in particular the one with pattern inputs) are not necessary meaningful. Some of them will not be executable.

Continuing with the Needham-Schroeder protocol, we may define several execution scenarii:

Example 9 (Scenario 1) *The following specifies a copy of the role of Alice, played by a, with d and a copy of the role of Bob, played by b, with a, as well as the fact that d is dishonest, hence his secret key is leaked.*

$$P_1 \mathrel{\hat=} (\text{new } N_a.\ P_A(a,d)) \parallel (\text{new } N_b.\ P_B(a,b)) \parallel out(c, sk(d))$$

Example 10 (Scenario 2) *Assume that we wish a to execute the role of the initiator, however with any other party, which is specified here by letting the environment give the identity of such another party: the process first receives x_b, that might be bound to any value. The other role is specified in the same way.*

$$P_2 \mathrel{\hat=} (\text{new } N_a.\ in(c, x_b).\ P_A(a, x_b)) \parallel (\text{new } N_b.\ in(c, x_a).\ P_B(x_a, b)) \parallel out(c, sk(d))$$

Example 11 (Scenario 3) *In Example 9 and Example 10, a was only able to engage the protocol once (and b was only able to engage once in a response). We may wish a (resp. b) be able to execute any number of instances of the role of the initiator (resp. responder).*

$$P_3 \mathrel{\hat=} !(\text{new } N_a.\ in(c, x_b).\ P_A(a, x_b)) \parallel !(\text{new} N_b.\ in(c, x_a).\ P_B(x_a, b)) \parallel out(c, sk(d))$$

Example 12 (Scenario 4) *Finally, in general, the role of the initiator could be executed by any agent, including b and the role of the responder could be executed by any number of agents as well. We specify an unbounded number of parties, engaging in an unbounded number of sessions by:*

$$P_4 \mathrel{\hat=} \begin{cases} !(\text{new } N_a.\ in(c, x_a).\ in(c, x_b).\ P_A(x_a, x_b)) \ \parallel \\ !(\text{new } N_b.\ in(c, x_a).\ in(c, x_b).\ P_B(x_a, x_b)) \ \parallel \ out(c, sk(d)) \end{cases}$$

We can imagine other scenarios as well. Verifying security will only be relative to a given scenario.

Extended Processes. Further, we extend processes with active substitutions and restrictions:

$$A, B, C := P \mid A \parallel B \mid \text{new } n.A \mid \{^M/_x\}$$

where M is a ground constructor term in normal form. As usual, names and variables have scopes, which are delimited by restrictions and by inputs. We write $fv(A)$, $bv(A)$, $fn(A)$, $bn(A)$ for the sets of free and bound variables (resp. names). Moreover, we require processes to be *name and variable distinct*, meaning that $bn(A) \cap fn(A) = \emptyset$, $bv(A) \cap fv(A) = \emptyset$, and also that any name and variable is bound at most once in A. Note that the only free variables are introduced by active substitutions (the x in $\{^M/_x\}$). Lastly, in an extended process, we require that there is at most one substitution for each variable. An *evaluation context* is an extended process with a hole instead of an extended process.

Extended processes built up from the null process, active substitutions using parallel composition and restriction are called *frames* (extending the notion of frame introduced in Section 2.1.2). Given an extended process A we denote by $\phi(A)$ the frame obtained by replacing any embedded plain processes in it with 0.

Example 13 *Consider the following process:*

$$A = \text{new } s, k_1.(\textit{out}(c, a) \parallel \{^{\text{senc}(s,k_1)}/_x\} \parallel \text{new } k_2.\textit{out}(c, \text{senc}(s, k_2))).$$

We have that $\phi(A) = \text{new } s, k_1.(0 \parallel \{^{\text{senc}(s,k_1)}/_x\} \parallel \text{new } k_2.0).$

2.2.2. Operational Semantics

To formally define the operational semantics of our calculus, we have to introduce three relations, namely *structural equivalence*, *internal reduction*, and *labelled transition*.

Structural Equivalence. Informally, two processes are *structurally equivalent* if they model the same thing, even if the grammar permits different encodings. For example, to describe a pair of processes P_A and P_B running in parallel, we have to write either $P_A \parallel P_B$, or $P_B \parallel P_A$. These two processes are said to be structurally equivalent. More formally, structural equivalence is the smallest equivalence relation closed by application of evaluation contexts and such that:

PAR-0	$A \parallel 0 \equiv A$	
PAR-C	$A \parallel B \equiv B \parallel A$	
PAR-A	$(A \parallel B) \parallel C \equiv A \parallel (B \parallel C)$	
NEW-PAR	$A \parallel \text{new } n.B \equiv \text{new } n.(A \parallel B)$	$n \notin fn(A)$
NEW-C	$\text{new } n_1.\text{new } n_2.A \equiv \text{new } n_2.\text{new } n_1.A$	

Note that the side condition of the rule NEW-PAR is always true on processes that are name and variable distinct. Using structural equivalence, every extended process A can be rewritten to consist of a substitution and a plain process with some restricted names, *i.e.*

$$A \equiv \text{new } \overline{n}.(\{{}^{M_1}\!/_{x_1}\} \parallel \cdots \parallel \{{}^{M_k}\!/_{x_k}\} \parallel P).$$

In particular, any frame can be rewritten as new $\overline{n}.\sigma$ matching the notion of frame introduced in Section 2.1.2. We note that unlike in the original applied pi calculus, active substitutions cannot "interact" with the extended processes. As we will see in the following, active substitutions record the outputs of a process to the environment. The notion of frames will be particularly useful to define equivalence based security properties such as resistance against guessing attacks and privacy type properties.

Internal Reduction.   A process can be executed without contact with its environment, *e.g.* execution of conditionals, or internal communications between processes in parallel. Formally, *internal reduction* is the smallest relation on processes closed under structural equivalence and application of evaluation contexts such that:

REPL $!P \xrightarrow{\tau} P' \parallel !P$ where P' is a fresh renaming of P

THEN if $M = N$ then P else $Q \xrightarrow{\tau} P$ where $M\!\downarrow = N\!\downarrow$ and $M\!\downarrow$ is a message

ELSE if $M = N$ then P else $Q \xrightarrow{\tau} Q$ where $M\!\downarrow \neq N\!\downarrow$ and $M\!\downarrow, N\!\downarrow$ are messages

COMM out$(c, M_1).P_1 \parallel$ in$(c, M_2).P_2 \xrightarrow{\tau} P_1 \parallel P_2\theta$ where θ is such that
$\qquad\qquad\qquad\qquad\qquad\qquad$ Dom$(\theta) = \mathcal{V}(M_2)$, $M_2\theta\!\downarrow = M_1\!\downarrow$, and $M_1\!\downarrow$ is a message.

We write $\rightarrow^*$ for the reflexive and transitive closure of $\xrightarrow{\tau}$. Note that, in some situations, a process of the form if $M = N$ then P else Q may block. This happens when $M\!\downarrow$ (resp. $N\!\downarrow$) contains some destructors.

Labelled Transition.   Communications are synchronous, but (as long as there is no private channel) we can assume that they occur with the environment. We sketch here a labelled transition semantics. The semantics given previously allow us to reason about protocols with an adversary represented by a context. In order to prove that security properties hold for all adversaries, quantification over all contexts is typically required, which can be difficult in practise. The *labelled semantics* aim to eliminate universal quantification of the context. We have two main rules:

IN   in$(c, x).P \xrightarrow{\text{in}(c,M)}_{\ell} P\{{}^{M}\!/_{x}\}$ $\qquad\qquad$ where M is a message

OUT out$(c, M).P \xrightarrow{\text{out}(c,M\downarrow)}_{\ell} P \parallel \{{}^{M\downarrow}\!/_{x}\}$ where x is a fresh variable and $M\!\downarrow$ is a message

The labelled operational semantics is closed by structural equivalence and under some evaluation contexts. Actually, we have that:

$$\frac{A \equiv A' \quad A' \xrightarrow{\alpha}_{\ell} B' \quad B' \equiv B}{A \xrightarrow{\alpha}_{\ell} B} \qquad\qquad \frac{A \xrightarrow{\alpha}_{\ell} B}{C[A] \xrightarrow{\alpha}_{\ell} C[B]}$$

where C is an evaluation context, and in case of an input, *i.e.* $\alpha = $ in(c, M), we have that $\phi(C[A]) \vdash_{\mathcal{R}} M$.

We write $\rightarrow_\ell$ to denote $\xrightarrow{\tau} \cup \xrightarrow{\alpha}_\ell$ and $\rightarrow_\ell^*$ to denote the reflexive and transitive closure of $\rightarrow_\ell$.

Example 14 *Going back to the handshake protocol described in Example 7, the derivation described below represents a normal execution of the protocol. For simplicity of this example we suppose that $x \notin fv(P)$.*

new $w.(P_A(w) \parallel P_B(w))$
$\xrightarrow{out(c,\mathsf{senc}(n,w))}_\ell$
new $w, n.(P_B(w) \parallel \{\mathsf{senc}(n,w)/_{x_1}\} \parallel in(c,x).$ if $\mathsf{sdec}(x,w) = \mathsf{f}(n)$ then $P)$
$\xrightarrow{in(c,\mathsf{senc}(n,w))}_\ell$
new $w, n.(out(c, M) \parallel \{\mathsf{senc}(n,w)/_{x_1}\} \parallel in(c,x).$ if $\mathsf{sdec}(x,w) = \mathsf{f}(n)$ then $P)$
$\xrightarrow{out(c,M\downarrow)}_\ell$
new $w, n.(\{\mathsf{senc}(n,w)/_{x_1}\} \parallel \{M\downarrow/_{x_2}\} \parallel in(c,x).$ if $\mathsf{sdec}(x,w) = \mathsf{f}(n)$ then $P)$
$\xrightarrow{in(c,\mathsf{senc}(\mathsf{f}(n),w))}_\ell$
new $w, n.(\{\mathsf{senc}(n,w)/_{x_1}\} \parallel \{M\downarrow/_{x_2}\} \parallel$ if $\mathsf{sdec}(\mathsf{senc}(\mathsf{f}(n),w),w) = \mathsf{f}(n)$ then $P)$
$\xrightarrow{\tau}$
new $w, n.(\{\mathsf{senc}(n,w)/_{x_1}\} \parallel \{M\downarrow/_{x_2}\} \parallel P)$

where $M = \mathsf{senc}(\mathsf{f}(\mathsf{sdec}(\mathsf{senc}(n,w),w)),w) \rightarrow_{\mathcal{R}_{\mathsf{senc}}} \mathsf{senc}(\mathsf{f}(n),w)$.

Example 15 *Continuing Example 8 we develop some transitions from*

$$P_1 = (\text{new } N_a.\ P_A(a,d)) \parallel (\text{new } N_b.\ P_B(a,b)) \parallel out(c, \mathsf{sk}(d))$$

For convenience, the names N_a and N_b are pushed out. We obtain another process that is structurally equivalent.
Case 1: *The process P_A may move first, yielding*

$P_1 \xrightarrow{out(c,\mathsf{aenc}(\langle a,N_a\rangle,\mathsf{pk}(d)))}_\ell$ new $N_a.$new $N_b.$ (
$\{\mathsf{aenc}(\langle a,N_a\rangle,\mathsf{pk}(d))/_{x_1}\}$
$\parallel (in(c, \mathsf{aenc}(\langle N_a, x\rangle, \mathsf{pk}(a))).\ out(c, \mathsf{aenc}(x, \mathsf{pk}(b)))$
$\parallel P_B(a,b)$
$\parallel out(c, \mathsf{sk}(d)) \ )$

Case 2: *The process P_B may also move first, and the resulting process depends on an input M_1 such that new $N_a, N_b.(\sigma \vdash \mathsf{aenc}(\langle a, M_1\rangle, \mathsf{pk}(b)))$ where $\mathsf{Dom}(\sigma) = \emptyset$.*

$P_1 \xrightarrow{in(c,M_1)}_\ell=$ new $N_a,$ new $N_b.$ ($P_A(a,d)$
$\parallel out(c, \mathsf{aenc}(\langle M_1, N_b\rangle, \mathsf{pk}(a))).in(c, \mathsf{aenc}(N_b, \mathsf{pk}(b)))$
$\parallel out(c, \mathsf{sk}(d)) \ )$

Case 3: *The last process may also move first, yielding*

$$P_1 \xrightarrow{out(c,sk(d))}_\ell \text{new } N_a, \text{new } N_b. \ (\ \{sk(d)/x_1\} \ \| \ P_A(a,d) \ \| \ P_B(a,b) \ )$$

From the resulting processes, there are again several possible transitions. We do not continue here the full transition sequence, which is too large to be displayed.

In the above example, we see that the transition system might actually be infinite. Indeed, the term M_1 is an arbitrary message that satisfies some deducibility conditions. Such deducibility conditions can be simplified (and decided). This will be the subject of Chapter 3 on bounded process verification.

2.3. Security Properties

This section presents mainly through examples how to formalise definitions of the most standard security properties. To prove that security properties hold for all adversaries, quantification over all contexts is required. However, in order to consider realistic adversary, we have to consider processes that are built using public function symbols only and we have to ensure that these processes are executable.

In practise, it may be difficult to reason with the quantification over all contexts. The labelled transition semantics aim to eliminate universal quantification of the context and is easier to manipulate. In this section, we rely on this semantics. Since our small process calculus does not allow us to model private channels, we do not have to consider the rule COMM. The attacker controls the entire network and can eavesdrop, block, intercept, and inject messages.

2.4. Secrecy

Intuitively, a protocol preserves the secrecy of some message M if an adversary cannot obtain M by constructing it from the outputs of the protocol. We can formalise the adversary as a process running in parallel with the protocol, that after constructing M outputs it on a public channel. The adversary process does not have any of the secrets of the protocol. As explained in introduction of this section, another possibility is to rely on the labelled semantics and to simply ask that in any reachable extended process, M can not be deduced from the frame. Below, you illustrate this property through several examples based on the Needham-Schroeder protocol.

Example 16 (Scenario 1) *Consider again the following process defined in Example 8 :*

$$P_1 = (\text{new } N_a. \ P_A(a,d)) \ \| \ (\text{new } N_b. \ P_B(a,b)) \ \| \ out(c, sk(d)).$$

We typically wish to ensure the secrecy of the nonce N_b. For this, we have to show that, for any extended process B such that $P_1 \to_\ell^* B$, we have that $\phi(B) \nvdash N_b$. Actually, this secrecy property does not hold because of the attack described in Chapter 1. Note that, in this scenario, it is not reasonable to require the secrecy of N_a since N_a is generated by an honest agent for a dishonest one.

We may also want to express the secrecy of the nonce N_a received by $P_B(a,b)$. This means that we want that the value of y (this is the variable that represents the nonce N_a in the process $P_B(a,b)$ is not known by the attacker in any possible executions. For this, *we have to show that for each process B such that $P_1 \rightarrow^*_\ell B$ and in which the variable y has been instantiated by some message M, we have that $\phi(B) \not\vdash M$.*

Example 17 (Scenario 2) *Consider now*

$$P_2 = (\text{new } N_a.\ \text{in}(c, x_b).\ P_A(a, x_b)) \ \| \ (\text{new } N_b.\ \text{in}(c, x_a).\ P_B(x_a, b)) \ \| \ \text{out}(c, \text{sk}(d))$$

In such a situation, neither N_a nor N_b can be required to remain secret: this depends on the inputs x_a and x_b. In this case, to express the secrecy of N_b, we can ask that for each process B such that $P_1 \rightarrow^*_\ell B$ and in which the variable x_a has been instantiated by an honest agent (i.e. *not d), we have that $\phi(B) \not\vdash N_b$.*

To express secrecy of a nonce in the scope of a replication, we need extra material. Consider the following scenario

$$P_3 = !(\text{new } N_a.\ \text{in}(c, x_b).\ P_A(a, x_b)) \ \| \ !(\text{new } N_b.\ \text{in}(c, x_a).\ P_B(x_a, b)) \ \| \ \text{out}(c, \text{sk}(d)).$$

Intuitively, we wish that, in any copy of the process, in which $x_b \neq d$, then N_a is secret. Be careful that x_b is actually a local variable of the process and should actually be renamed in each copy. Similarly, N_a and N_b are renamed in each instance.

There are again several ways of specifying the desired properties For instance, we may split the processes in those for which x_b is bound to a honest party and those in which $x_b = d$ and then forget about the different copies in the specification. We may also enrich the calculus with status events. These status events are also very useful to express correspondence properties explained in the following section.

2.5. Correspondence Properties

Correspondence properties are used to capture relationships between events that can be expressed in the form "if an event e has been executed then event e has been previously executed." Moreover, these events may contain arguments. This will allows one to express agreement properties. To reason with correspondence properties, we have to annotate processes with events. These events will mark the different control points reached by the protocol.

We say that an extended process A has reached an event $\text{event}(M_1, \ldots, M_n)$ if, and only if, there exist an evaluation context C, a plain process P and an extended process B such that $A \equiv C[\text{event}(M_1, \ldots, M_n).P \ \| \ B]$.

Aliveness. This property is the weakest form of authentication in Lowe's hierarchy [19].

A protocol satisfies *aliveness* if, whenever an honest agent completes a run of the protocol, apparently with another honest agent B, then B has previously run the protocol.

Note that B may not necessarily believe that he was running the protocol with A. Also, the agent B may not have run the protocol *recently*. The aliveness of principal B to initiator A can be specified in our formalism. First, we have to consider two status events start and end. We insert them at the beginning and at the end of each role respectively. For instance, in $P_A(a, d)$, we insert start(a) at the beginning and end(a, d) at the end. This expresses the fact that the role is executed by a with d. We insert start(b) and end(b, a) in $P_B(a, b)$. Now, the aliveness property from the point of view of b can be specified as follows:

For any trace execution such that $P_1 \rightarrow_\ell A_1 \rightarrow_\ell \ldots \rightarrow_\ell A_n$ such that A_n has reached end(M_1, M_2) with $M_1 \neq d$ and $M_2 \neq d$, there exists i such that A_i has reached start(M_2). This corresponds to the fact that the property "if end(x, y) has been executed then start(y) has been previously executed when x and y are both honest agents." For the Needham-Schroeder public key protocol (*e.g.* Scenario 1) the aliveness property is satisfied.

Weak agreement. Weak agreement is slightly stronger than aliveness.

A protocol guarantees *weak agreement* if, whenever an honest agent completes a run of the protocol, apparently with another honest agent B, then B has previously been running the protocol, apparently with A.

The weak agreement property can also been expressed in our formalism. We have again to add status events start and end in our specification. However, the predicate start will have also two parameters: start(a, d) expresses the fact that a has started a session with d. Now, the weak agreement property can be specified as follows:

For any trace execution such that $P_1 \rightarrow_\ell A_1 \rightarrow_\ell \ldots \rightarrow_\ell A_n$ such that A_n has reached end(M_1, M_2) with $M_1 \neq d$ and $M_2 \neq d$, there exists i such that A_i has reached start(M_2, M_1). For the Needham-Schroeder public key protocol, it is well-known that this property is not satisfied: b can complete a session apparently with a whereas a has never started a session with b. The property is already falsified on Scenario 1.

We can also express some refinements of these properties by distinguishing the case where an agent starts a session as an initiator or as a responder. Moreover, we can also express the fact that the two agents agreed on some message M, *e.g.* the value of a nonce or a key. This allows us to express the non-injective agreement security property. There are also stronger agreement properties, that would require the mapping from end to start to be injective.

2.6. Guessing Attacks

Guessing attacks are a kind of dictionary attack in which the password is supposed to be weak, *i.e.* part of a dictionary for which a brute force attack is feasible. A guessing attack works in two phases. In a first phase the attacker eavesdrops and interacts with one or several protocol sessions. In a second *offline* phase, the attacker tries each of the possible passwords on the data collected during the first phase. To resist against a guessing attack, the protocol must be designed such that the attacker cannot discover on the basis of the data collected whether his current guess of the password is the actual password or not.

The idea behind the definition is the following. Suppose the frame ϕ represents the information gained by the attacker by eavesdropping one or more sessions and let w

be the weak password. Then, we can represent resistance against guessing attacks by checking whether the attacker can distinguish a situation in which he guesses the correct password w and a situation in which he guesses an incorrect one, say w'. We model these two situations by adding $\{^w/_x\}$ (resp. $\{^{w'}/_x\}$) to the frame. We use static equivalence to capture the notion of indistinguishability. This definition is due to M. Baudet [7], inspired from the one of [13]. In our definition, we allow multiple shared secrets, and write $\overline{w}$ for a sequence of such secrets.

Definition 2.3 *Let* $\phi \equiv$ *new* $\overline{w}.\phi'$ *be a frame. We say that the frame* ϕ *is resistant to guessing attacks* against $\overline{w}$ *if*

$$\text{new } \overline{w}.(\phi' \parallel \{^{\overline{w}}/_{\overline{x}}\}) \sim \text{new } \overline{w}'.\text{new } \overline{w}.(\phi' \parallel \{^{\overline{w}'}/_{\overline{x}}\})$$

where $\overline{w}'$ *is a sequence of fresh names and* $\overline{x}$ *a sequence of variables such that* $\overline{x} \cap \text{Dom}(\phi) = \emptyset$.

Note that this definition is general w.r.t. to the equational theory and the number of guessable data items. Now, we can define what it means for a protocol to be resistant against guessing attacks.

Definition 2.4 *Let* A *be a process and* $\overline{w} \subseteq \text{bn}(A)$. *We say that* A *is resistant to guessing attacks* against $\overline{w}$ *if, for every process* B *such that* $A \rightarrow_\ell^* B$, *we have that the frame* $\phi(B)$ *is resistant to guessing attacks against* $\overline{w}$.

Example 18 *Consider the handshake protocol described in Example 7. An interesting problem arises if the shared key* w *is a weak secret, i.e. vulnerable to brute-force off-line testing. In such a case, the protocol has a guessing attack against* w. *Indeed, we have that*

$$\text{new } w.(P_A(w) \parallel P_B(w)) \rightarrow_\ell^* D$$

with $\phi(D) = \text{new } w.\text{new } n.(\{^{\text{senc}(n,w)}/_{x_1}\} \parallel \{^{\text{senc}(\text{f}(n),w)}/_{x_2}\})$. *The frame* $\phi(D)$ *is not resistant to guessing attacks against* w. *The test* $\text{f}(\textit{sdec}(x_1, x)) \overset{?}{=} \textit{sdec}(x_2, x)$ *allows us to distinguish the two associated frames:*

- *new* $w.\text{new } n.(\{^{\text{senc}(n,w)}/_{x_1}\} \parallel \{^{\text{senc}(\text{f}(n),w)}/_{x_2}\} \parallel \{^w/_x\})$, *and*
- *new* $w'.\text{new } w.\text{new } n.(\{^{\text{senc}(n,w)}/_{x_1}\} \parallel \{^{\text{senc}(\text{f}(n),w)}/_{x_2}\} \parallel \{^{w'}/_x\})$.

Hence, the process new $w.(P_A \parallel P_B)$ *is not resistant to guessing attacks against* w.

2.7. Equivalence Properties

The notion of indistinguishability is a powerful concept which allows us to reason about complex properties that cannot be expressed as secrecy or correspondence properties. Intuitively, two processes are said to be equivalent if an observer has no way to tell them apart. While static equivalence models indistinguishability of sequences of terms, it is also possible to lift it to an observational equivalence, *i.e.* indistinguishability of processes that interact with an arbitrary adversary. We define this observational equivalence by the means of a labelled bisimulation. The processes may perform different computations, but they have to look the same to an external observer. This notion allows us to define strong notions of secrecy and also privacy properties.

Before we formalise this notion of equivalence, we have to adapt the labelled semantics provided in Section 2.2.2. Indeed, we will now assume that the attacker can observe the interactions with the environment and we have to capture the fact that the attacker performs the same experiment on both processes. Intuitively, we want that, for any experiment s (sequence of labels) such that $A \xrightarrow{s}^*_\ell A'$, there exists B' such that $B \xrightarrow{s}^*_\ell B'$ and $\phi(A') \sim \phi(B')$. However, our labels are too fine grained.

Let $A = $ new $n.\text{out}(c, n)$ and $B = $ new $n, k.\text{out}(c, \text{senc}(n, k))$. The only transitions that can be performed by A and B are as follows:

- $A \xrightarrow{\text{out}(c,n)}_\ell$ new $n.\{^n/_x\}$, and
- $B \xrightarrow{\text{out}(c,\text{senc}(n,k))}_\ell$ new $n, k.\{^{\text{senc}(n,k)}/_x\}$.

However, in reality an attacker has no way to distinguish these two processes since he will not see any difference between a fresh nonce and an encryption (he does not know the key). The same situation also occurs with the two processes $A = $ new $n.\text{in}(c, y)$ and $B = $ new $n'.\text{in}(c, y)$. We have that $A \xrightarrow{\text{in}(c,n')}$ 0 and B can not mimic this step. B is not allowed to use the name n' since it is restricted. Our labels contains too much information. We modify the IN and OUT rules as follows:

IN $\text{in}(c, x).P \xrightarrow{\text{in}(c,M)}_\ell P\{^M/_x\}$ where M is a message

OUT $\text{out}(c, M).P \xrightarrow{\text{out}(c,x)}_\ell P \parallel \{^{M\downarrow}/_x\}$ where x is a fresh variable and $M\downarrow$ is a message

The labelled operational semantics is closed by structural equivalence and under some evaluation contexts. Actually, we have that:

$$\frac{A \equiv A' \quad A' \xrightarrow{\alpha}_\ell B' \quad B' \equiv B}{A \xrightarrow{\alpha}_\ell B} \qquad \frac{A \xrightarrow{\alpha}_\ell B}{C[A] \xrightarrow{\alpha'}_\ell C[B]}$$

where C is an evaluation context, and in case of an input, *i.e.* $\alpha = \text{in}(c, M)$, we have that $\phi(C[A]) \vdash_\mathcal{R} M$ and $\alpha' = \text{in}(c, M')$ where M' is a recipe witnessing the fact that $\phi(C[A]) \vdash_\mathcal{R} M$.

Moreover, we now consider that structural equivalence is closed under α-renaming.

Example 19 *Going back to the handshake protocol described in Example 7, the derivation described below represents a normal execution of the protocol in the new labelled semantics.*

$\qquad$ new $w.(P_A(w) \parallel P_B(w))$

$\xrightarrow{out(c,x_1)}_{\ell}$ new $w, n.(P_B(w) \parallel \{^{senc(n,w)}/_{x_1}\} \parallel in(c,x).$ if $\textbf{\textit{sdec}}(x,w) = f(n)$ then $P)$

$\xrightarrow{in(c,x_1)}_{\ell}$ new $w, n.(\textbf{\textit{out}}(c, M) \parallel \{^{senc(n,w)}/_{x_1}\} \parallel in(c,x).$ if $\textbf{\textit{sdec}}(x,w) = f(n)$ then $P)$

$\xrightarrow{out(c,x_2)}_{\ell}$ new $w, n.(\{^{senc(n,w)}/_{x_1}\} \parallel \{^{M\downarrow}/_{x_2}\} \parallel in(c,x).$ if $\textbf{\textit{sdec}}(x,w) = f(n)$ then $P)$

$\xrightarrow{in(c,x_2)}_{\ell}$ new $w, n.(\{^{senc(n,w)}/_{x_1}\} \parallel \{^{M\downarrow}/_{x_2}\} \parallel$ if $\textbf{\textit{sdec}}(senc(f(n),w),w) = f(n)$ then $P)$

$\xrightarrow{\tau}$ $\qquad$ new $w, n.(\{^{senc(n,w)}/_{x_1}\} \parallel \{^{M\downarrow}/_{x_2}\} \parallel P)$

where $M = senc(f(\textbf{\textit{sdec}}(senc(n,w),w)),w) \to_{\mathcal{R}_{senc}} senc(f(n),w).$

For every closed extended process A we define its set of traces, each trace consisting in a sequence of visible actions (*i.e.* different from τ) together with the sequence of sent messages:

$$\textsf{trace}(A) = \{(s, \phi(B)) \mid A \xrightarrow{s}_{\ell} B \text{ for some } B\}.$$

Note that, in the new versions of our labelled semantics, the sent messages are exclusively stored in the frame and not in the sequence s (the outputs are made by "reference").

Definition 2.5 (trace equivalence $\approx_t$) *Let A and B be two closed extended processes, $A \sqsubseteq_t B$ if for every $(s, \varphi) \in \textsf{trace}(A)$, there exists $(s', \varphi') \in \textsf{trace}(B)$ such that $s = s'$ and $\varphi \sim \varphi'$. The extended processes A and B are trace equivalent, denoted by $A \approx_t B$, if $A \sqsubseteq_t B$ and $B \sqsubseteq_t A$.*

Example 20 *Consider the equational theory described in Example 2.*

new $s, k.\textbf{\textit{out}}(c, senc(s,k)).in(c,x).$ if $x = s$ then $\textbf{\textit{out}}(c,a)$
$\qquad\qquad\qquad\qquad\qquad \approx_t$ new $s, k.\textbf{\textit{out}}(c, senc(s,k)).in(c,x)$

new $s.\textbf{\textit{out}}(c, senc(s,k)).in(c,x).$ if $x = s$ then $\textbf{\textit{out}}(c,a)$
$\qquad\qquad\qquad\qquad\qquad \not\approx_t$ new $s.\textbf{\textit{out}}(c, senc(s,k)).in(c,x)$

$\qquad\qquad \textbf{\textit{out}}(c,a).\textbf{\textit{out}}(c,a) \approx_t \textbf{\textit{out}}(c,a) \parallel \textbf{\textit{out}}(c,a)$

$\qquad\qquad \textbf{\textit{out}}(c_1,a).\textbf{\textit{out}}(c_2,a) \not\approx_t \textbf{\textit{out}}(c_1,a) \parallel \textbf{\textit{out}}(c_2,a)$

$\qquad\qquad \textbf{\textit{out}}(c,a); \textbf{\textit{out}}(c,b) \not\approx_t \textbf{\textit{out}}(c,a) \parallel \textbf{\textit{out}}(c,b)$

Now, we develop an example to illustrate how this notion of equivalence can be used to formalise anonymity.

Example 21 *We consider a slightly simplified version of a protocol given in [4] designed for transmitting a secret without revealing its identity to other participants. In this protocol, A is willing to engage in communication with B and wants to reveal its identity to B. However, A does not want to compromise its privacy by revealing its identity or the identity of B more broadly. The participants A and B proceed as follows:*

$$A \to B \; : \; \mathsf{aenc}(\langle N_a, \mathsf{pk}(A)\rangle, \mathsf{pk}(B))$$

$$B \to A \; : \; \mathsf{aenc}(\langle N_a, \langle N_b, \mathsf{pk}(B)\rangle\rangle, \mathsf{pk}(A))$$

First A sends to B a nonce N_a and its public key encrypted with the public key of B. If the message is of the expected form then B sends to A the nonce N_a, a freshly generated nonce N_b and its public key, all of this being encrypted with the public key of A. Otherwise, B sends out a "decoy" message: $\mathsf{aenc}(N_b, \mathsf{pk}(B))$. *This message should basically look like B's other message from the point of view of an outsider. This is important since the protocol is supposed to protect the identity of the participants.*

A session of role A played by agent a with b can be modelled by the following basic process where $M = \mathsf{dec}(x, \mathsf{sk}(a))$.

$$A(a, b) \;\hat{=}\;$$
$$\mathbf{\textit{out}}(c, \mathsf{aenc}(\langle N_a, \mathsf{pk}(a)\rangle, \mathsf{pk}(b))).$$
$$\mathbf{\textit{in}}(c, x).$$
$$\text{if } \langle \mathsf{proj}_1(M), \mathsf{proj}_2(\mathsf{proj}_2(M))\rangle = \langle N_a, \mathsf{pk}(b)\rangle \text{ then } 0$$

Similarly, a session of role B played by agent b with a can be modelled by the basic process $B(b, a)$ where $N = \mathsf{dec}(y, \mathsf{sk}(b))$.

$$B(b, a) \;\hat{=}\; \mathbf{\textit{in}}(c, y).$$
$$\text{if } \mathsf{proj}_2(N) = \mathsf{pk}(a) \text{ then } \mathbf{\textit{out}}(c, \mathsf{aenc}(\langle \mathsf{proj}_1(N), \langle N_b, \mathsf{pk}(b)\rangle\rangle, \mathsf{pk}(a)))$$
$$\text{else } \mathbf{\textit{out}}(c, \mathsf{aenc}(N_b, \mathsf{pk}(b))).$$

Intuitively, this protocol preserves anonymity if an attacker cannot distinguish whether b is willing to talk to a (represented by the process $B(b, a)$) or willing to talk to a' (represented by the process $B(b, a')$), provided a, a' and b are honest participants. For illustration purposes, we also consider the process $B'(b, a)$ obtained from $B(b, a)$ by replacing the else branch by else 0. We will see that the "decoy" message plays a crucial role to ensure privacy.

We can ask whether the two following processes P_{ex} and P'_{ex} are in equivalence:

- $P_{\mathsf{ex}} = \mathsf{new}\ N_a.\mathsf{new}\ N_b.[\, A(a, b) \parallel B(b, a) \parallel K(a, a', b)\,]$, *and*
- $P'_{\mathsf{ex}} = \mathsf{new}\ N_a.\mathsf{new}\ N_b.[\, A(a', b) \parallel B(b, a') \parallel K(a, a', b)\,]$.

where $K(a, a', b) = \mathbf{\textit{out}}(c, \mathsf{pk}(a)).\mathbf{\textit{out}}(c, \mathsf{pk}(a')).\mathbf{\textit{out}}(c, \mathsf{pk}(b))$.

Actually, the 'decoy' message is crucial to have this equivalence, and thus anonymity. We have that $P_{\mathsf{ex}} \approx_t P'_{\mathsf{ex}}$ whereas:

$$\mathsf{new}\ N_a, N_b.[\, A(a, b) \parallel B'(b, a) \parallel K(a, a', b)\,]$$
$$\not\approx_t \ \mathsf{new}\ N_a, N_b.[\, A(a', b) \parallel B'(b, a') \parallel K(a, a', b)\,].$$

Another notion of equivalence that has been quite well-studied is the notion of *observationally equivalent*. However, proofs of observational equivalences are difficult because of the universal quantification over all contexts. In the context of the applied pi calculus, it has been shown that observational equivalence coincides with labelled bisimilarity [3]. This should also hold in the calculus presented here.

Definition 2.6 (labelled bisimilarity $\approx_\ell$) Labeled bisimilarity *is the largest symmetric relation $\mathcal{R}$ on closed extended processes such that $A \mathcal{R} B$ implies*

1. $\phi(A) \sim \phi(B)$,
2. *if $A \xrightarrow{\tau} A'$, then $B \rightarrow^* B'$ and $A' \mathcal{R} B'$ for some B',*
3. *if $A \xrightarrow{\alpha}_\ell A'$ then $B \rightarrow^* \xrightarrow{\alpha}_\ell \rightarrow^* B'$ and $A' \mathcal{R} B'$ for some B'.*

It is easy to see that observational equivalence (or labelled bisimilarity) implies trace equivalence while the converse is false in general (see Example 22).

Lemma 2.7 *Let A and B be two extended processes: $A \approx_\ell B$ implies $A \approx_t B$.*

Example 22 *For convenience we introduce for this example a non-deterministic choice operator $+$ and extend the internal reduction by the rule $A + B \rightarrow A$ and structural equivalence by associativity and commutativity of $+$. Consider the two following processes:*

$$A = (out(c, a).out(c, b_1)) + (out(c, a).out(c, b_2))$$

$$B = out(c, a).(out(c, b_1) + out(c, b_2))$$

We have that $A \approx_t B$ whereas $A \not\approx_\ell B$. Intuitively, after B's first move, B still has the choice of emitting b_1 or b_2, while A, trying to follow B's first move, is forced to choose between two states from which she can only emit one of the two.

The notion of labelled bisimilarity is quite strong but is also used to express privacy type properties. It is more or less a matter of taste to define anonymity w.r.t. trace equivalence or w.r.t. the stronger version with labelled bisimilarity.

2.8. Further Readings

The calculus presented in this chapter is very close to the applied pi calculus [3]. A presentation of this calculus in a tutorial style is also available [25]. Another calculus that is very close to the applied pi calculus and for which there exists a tutorial presentation is the spi-calculus [2].

2.9. Exercises

Exercice 5 ($\star$)
Consider the signature described in Example 2. Let

$$\phi = \mathsf{new}\ s, k_1.\{^{\mathsf{senc}(s, \langle k_1, k_2 \rangle)}/_{x_1},\ ^{\mathsf{senc}(k_1, k_2)}/_{x_2}\}.$$

1. Is s deducible fom ϕ?
2. Could you enumerate the subterms of ϕ? Among these subterms, give those that are deducible.
3. Give a term that is deducible from ϕ and that is not a subterm.

Exercice 6 ($\star$)

Give a reasonable formalisation of the following protocol:

$$A \to B : \langle A, \{K\}_{\mathsf{pk}(B)} \rangle$$
$$B \to A : \langle B, \{K\}_{\mathsf{pk}(A)} \rangle$$

First, A generates a fresh key K and sends it encrypted with the public key of B. Only B will be able to decrypt this message. In this way, B learns K and B also knows that this message comes from A as indicated in the first part of the message he received. Hence, B answers to A by sending again the key, this time encrypted with the public key of A.

Exercice 7 ($\star$)

Consider the formalisation of the Needham-Schroeder protocol as described in Example 8, and the following scenario (see Example 16).

$$(\mathsf{new}\ N_a.\ P_A(a, d))\ \|\ (\mathsf{new}\ N_b.\ P_B(a, b))\ \|\ \mathsf{out}(c, \mathsf{sk}(d)).$$

Give the complete transition sequence that yields the attack on the secrecy of the nonce N_b.

Exercice 8 ($\star\star$)

Give a reasonable formalisation of the handshake protocol without using the conditional (if then else). Give a trace that exists in the model presented in 7 and that does not exist in this new formalisation.

3. Deducibility Constraints

In this chapter, we present the NP-complete decision procedure for a bounded number of sessions by H. Comon-Lundh *et al.* [12]. In this setting (*i.e.* finite number of sessions), deducibility constraint systems have become the standard model for verifying security properties, with a special focus on secrecy. Starting with a paper by J. Millen and V. Shmatikov [21], many results (*e.g.* [11,7]) have been obtained within this framework.

Here, we consider only symmetric/asymmetric encryptions, and pairing. We show that any deducibility constraint system can be transformed in (possibly several) much simpler deducibility constraint systems that are called solved forms, preserving all solutions of the original system, and not only its satisfiability. In other words, the deducibility constraint system represents in a symbolic way all the possible sequences of messages that are produced, following the protocol rules, whatever are the intruder's actions. This set of symbolic traces is infinite in general. Solved forms are a simple (and finite) representation of such traces. The procedure preserves all solutions. Hence, we can represent for instance, all attacks on the secrecy and not only decide if there exists one. Moreover, presenting the decision procedure using a small set of simplification rules yields more flexibility for further extensions and modifications.

3.1. Intruder Deduction problem

3.1.1. Preliminaries

An *inference rule* is a rule of the form $\dfrac{u_1 \; \ldots \; u_n}{u_0}$ where $u_0, u_1, \ldots, u_n$ are terms (with variables). An *inference system* is a set of inference rules.

Example 23 *The following inference system* $\mathcal{I}_{\text{DY}}$ *represents the deduction capabilities of an attacker. We consider the signature* $\mathcal{F} = \{\text{senc}, \text{aenc}, \langle \_, \_ \rangle, \text{sk}\}$ *and the underlying rewriting system* $\mathcal{R}$ *is empty. There are several possible ways of defining the intruder capabilities, we choose here the "implicit destructors" formulation, in which the destructors do not appear. This leads to an inference system that is slightly different from the one proposed in Section 2.1.3. For sake of simplicity, we make a confusion between the identity of an agent and his public key.*

$$\frac{x \quad y}{\langle x, y \rangle}\;\text{P} \qquad\qquad \frac{x \quad y}{\text{aenc}(x, y)}\;\text{PKE} \qquad\qquad \frac{x \quad y}{\text{senc}(x, y)}\;\text{SE}$$

$$\frac{\langle x, y \rangle}{x}\;\text{Left} \quad \frac{\langle x, y \rangle}{y}\;\text{Right} \quad \frac{\text{aenc}(x, y) \quad \text{sk}(y)}{x}\;\text{PKD} \quad \frac{\text{senc}(x, y) \quad y}{x}\;\text{SD}$$

The rules P, SE, *and* PKE *are composition rules whereas the rules* Left, Right, SD, *and* PKD *are decomposition rules.*

Definition 3.1 (proof) *Let* $\mathcal{I}$ *be an inference system. A proof* Π *of* $T \vdash u$ *in* $\mathcal{I}$ *is a tree such that:*

- *every leaf of* Π *is labelled with a term* v *such that* $v \in T$,
- *for every node labelled with* v_0 *having* n *sons labelled with* $v_1, \ldots, v_n$, *there is an instance of an inference rule with conclusion* v_0 *and hypotheses* $v_1, \ldots, v_n$. *We say that* Π *ends with this instance if the node is the root of* Π,
- *the root is labelled with* u.

We denote by $\text{Hyp}(\Pi)$ the set of labels of the leaves of a proof Π and $\text{Conc}(\Pi)$ is the label of the root of Π. $\text{Steps}(\Pi)$ is the set of labels of all nodes of Π. The *size* of a proof Π is the number of nodes in it. A proof Π of $T \vdash u$ is *minimal* if it does not exist any proof Π' of $T \vdash u$ having a size strictly smaller than the size of Π.

Example 24 *Let* $\phi = \text{new } a, b, s. \; \{^{\langle \text{senc}(s, \langle a, b \rangle), a \rangle}/_{x_1}, \; ^{\text{senc}(b, a)}/_{x_2}\}$. *We may ask whether* s *is deducible from* ϕ, *i.e. does there exist a proof of*

$$\langle \text{senc}(s, \langle a, b \rangle), a \rangle, \; \text{senc}(b, a) \vdash s.$$

Such a proof is given below:

$$\cfrac{\cfrac{\langle \mathsf{senc}(s, \langle a, b\rangle), a\rangle}{\mathsf{senc}(s, \langle a, b\rangle)} \quad \cfrac{\cfrac{\langle \mathsf{senc}(s, \langle a, b\rangle), a\rangle}{a} \quad \cfrac{\cfrac{\langle \mathsf{senc}(s, \langle a, b\rangle), a\rangle}{\mathsf{senc}(b, a)} \quad a}{b}}{\langle a, b\rangle}}{s}$$

The problem whether an intruder can gain certain information s from a set of knowledge T, *i.e.* whether there is a proof of $T \vdash s$ is called the *intruder deduction problem*.

Intruder deduction problem (for a fixed inference system $\mathcal{I}$)

INPUT: a finite set of terms T, and a term s (the secret).
OUTPUT: Does there exist a proof of $T \vdash s$?

This definition is in-line with the concept of deduction introduced in Section 2.1.3. Here, we do not explicitly rely on the concept of frame. Note that for deduction, the ordering in which the messages have been sent is not relevant. Moreover, restriction on names are not necessary. It is assumed that each name is restricted.

3.1.2. Decidability via Locality

To show that the intruder deduction problem is decidable (in PTIME) for an inference system $\mathcal{I}$, we use the notion of *locality* introduced by D. McAllester [20].

Definition 3.2 (locality) *Let $\mathcal{I}$ be an inference system. The system $\mathcal{I}$ is* local *if whenever $T \vdash u$ in $\mathcal{I}$, there exists a proof Π of $T \vdash u$ such that* $\mathsf{Steps}(\Pi) \subseteq \mathsf{St}(T \cup \{u\})$.

Given an inference system $\mathcal{I}$, to establish that the intruder deduction problem is decidable, it is actually sufficient to prove that:

1. *a locality result* for the inference system $\mathcal{I}$: checking the existence of a proof of $T \vdash u$ amounts to checking the existence of a local proof that only contains subterms of u and T (there is a polynomial number of subterms),
2. *a one-step-deducibility result* to ensure that we can test (in PTIME) whether a term is deducible in one step from a set of terms by using an instance of one of the inference rules. This result trivially holds for the inference system presented in Example 23.

Then, the existence of a local proof of $T \vdash u$ can be checked in polynomial time by saturation of T with terms deducible in one-step. Thanks to locality, the number of iteration to obtain a saturated set is bounded by the number of terms that can be involved in a local proof. This yields a PTIME algorithm.

Lemma 3.3 (locality) *Let T be a set of terms and u be a term. A minimal proof Π of $T \vdash u$ only contains terms in $\mathsf{St}(T \cup \{u\})$, i.e. $\mathsf{Steps}(\Pi) \subseteq \mathsf{St}(T \cup \{u\})$. Moreover, if Π is reduced to a leaf or ends with a decomposition rule, then we have that $\mathsf{Steps}(\Pi) \subseteq \mathsf{St}(T)$.*

Proof: Let Π be a minimal proof of $T \vdash u$. We prove the result by induction on the size of the proof Π.

Base case: In such a case, the proof Π is reduced to a leaf and we easily conclude.
Induction step: We have that:

$$\Pi = \left\{ \begin{array}{c} \Pi_1 \qquad \Pi_n \\ \dfrac{u_1 \quad \cdots \quad u_n}{u} \; \mathsf{R} \end{array} \right.$$

We distinguish several cases depending on the last inference rule of Π.

- If R is a composition rule, then $u_1, \ldots, u_n$ are subterms of u and we easily conclude by relying on our induction hypothesis.
- If R is a projection rule (say proj_1), then $u_1 = \langle u, v \rangle$ for some v. In such a case, by minimality of Π, we know that Π_1 does not end with a composition rule. Hence, by relying on our induction hypothesis, we have that $\mathsf{Steps}(\Pi_1) \subseteq \mathsf{St}(T)$, and thus $u_1 \in \mathsf{St}(T)$. Moreover, we have that $u \in \mathsf{St}(u_1)$, and thus $u \in \mathsf{St}(T)$. This allows us to conclude that $\mathsf{Steps}(\Pi) \subseteq \mathsf{St}(T)$.

The cases where Π ends with a decryption rule (symmetric and asymmetric) can be done in a similar way. $\qquad\qquad \square \qquad\qquad\qquad\qquad \square$

Proposition 3.1 *The intruder deduction problem is decidable in PTIME for $\mathcal{I}_{\mathsf{DY}}$. Actually, this problem is PTIME complete.*

The PTIME-hardness can be proved by a reduction from HORNSAT.

The concept of locality has been used to establish decidability of several inference systems. For instance, we may want to model digital signature, exclusive or operator, commutative encryption, ...

3.2. Deducibility constraints

Assume processes without replication. Then the transition system is finite in depth but might be infinitely branching, as we saw in Example 15. The idea then is to represent in a simple symbolic way the set of terms that satisfy the required conditions. This is what we formalise now.

Definition 3.4 *A* Deducibility constraint system *is either $\bot$ or a conjunction of deducibility constraints of the form:*

$$T_1 \overset{?}{\vdash} u_1 \wedge \ldots \wedge T_n \overset{?}{\vdash} u_n$$

in which $T_1, \ldots, T_n$ are finite sets of terms, $u_1, \ldots, u_n$ are terms. Moreover, we assume that the constraints can be ordered in such a way that:

- *monotonicity:* $\emptyset \neq T_1 \subseteq T_2 \cdots \subseteq T_n$

- *origination: for every i, we have that $\mathcal{V}(T_i) \subseteq \mathcal{V}(u_1, \ldots, u_{i-1})$*

Intuitively, the sets T_i correspond to messages that have been sent on the network, while $u_1, \ldots, u_n$ are the messages that are expected by the processes, hence have to be constructed by the environment. The first condition, called *monotonicity* reflects the fact that the set of messages that have been sent on the network can only increase. In other words, the ordering on the atomic deducibility constraints is a temporal ordering of actions. The second condition (called *origination*) reflects the properties of our processes: variables that occur in a message sent on the network must appear before in messages received from the network.

Definition 3.5 (T_x) *Let $\mathcal{C} = T_1 \overset{?}{\vdash} u_1 \wedge \ldots \wedge T_n \overset{?}{\vdash} u_n$ be a deducibility constraint system and x be a variable that occurs in $\mathcal{C}$. T_x is the minimal set (w.r.t. inclusion) among the sets $T_1, \ldots, T_n$ such that $T \overset{?}{\vdash} u \in \mathcal{C}$ and $x \in \mathcal{V}(u)$.*

Thanks to the monotonicity and the origination properties, for any $x \in \mathcal{V}(\mathcal{C})$, the set T_x exists and is uniquely defined.

Such constraint systems may be enriched with equations/disequations between terms or other constraints, that correspond to the conditions in the process calculus. We consider (for now) only these simple constraints.

Definition 3.6 (solution) *Let $\mathcal{I}$ be an inference system. A substitution σ is a solution of a deducibility constraint system $\mathcal{C} = T_1 \overset{?}{\vdash} u_1 \wedge \ldots \wedge T_n \overset{?}{\vdash} u_n$ if there exists a proof of $T_i\sigma \vdash u_i\sigma$ in $\mathcal{I}$ for every $i \in \{1, \ldots, n\}$.*

Example 25 *Consider the constraints corresponding to one of the possible Needham-Schroeder symbolic trace. We give explicitly the free names to the attacker and assume that all names that are not explicitly given are (supposedly) secret:*

$$\mathcal{C} \hat{=} \begin{cases} a, \ b, \ d, \ \mathsf{sk}(d), \ \mathsf{aenc}(\langle a, N_a \rangle, d) \overset{?}{\vdash} \mathsf{aenc}(\langle a, x \rangle, b) \\ a, \ b, \ d, \ \mathsf{sk}(d), \ \mathsf{aenc}(\langle a, N_a \rangle, d), \ \mathsf{aenc}(\langle x, N_b \rangle, a) \overset{?}{\vdash} \mathsf{aenc}(\langle N_a, y \rangle, a) \end{cases}$$

The failure of the secrecy of N_b (for this scenario) is given by the additional constraint:

$$a, \ b, \ d, \mathsf{sk}(d), \mathsf{aenc}(\langle a, N_a \rangle, d), \ \mathsf{aenc}(\langle x, N_b \rangle, a), \ \mathsf{aenc}(y, d) \overset{?}{\vdash} N_b$$

A solution of $\mathcal{C}$ in $\mathcal{I}_{\mathsf{DY}}$ is $\sigma = \{x \mapsto N_a, y \mapsto N_b\}$.

3.3. Decision Procedure

We describe here a non-deterministic simplification procedure. It can be simplified in many respects, but we will see that the problem of deciding whether a constraint system has at least one solution is NP-complete anyway (for the $\mathcal{I}_{\mathsf{DY}}$ inference system given in Example 23). Many parts of this section, including the set of simplification rules, are borrowed from [12].

3.3.1. Simplification Rules

We prove that any deducibility constraint system can be transformed into simpler ones, called *solved*. Such simplified constraints are then used to decide the security properties.

R_1 $\quad \mathcal{C} \wedge T \overset{?}{\vdash} u \rightsquigarrow \mathcal{C}$ $\qquad\qquad$ if $T \cup \{x \mid (T' \overset{?}{\vdash} x) \in \mathcal{C}, T' \subsetneq T\} \vdash u$

R_2 $\quad \mathcal{C} \wedge T \overset{?}{\vdash} u \rightsquigarrow_\sigma \mathcal{C}\sigma \wedge T\sigma \overset{?}{\vdash} u\sigma$ $\qquad$ if $t \in \mathsf{St}(T), \sigma = \mathsf{mgu}(t, u), t \neq u$
$\qquad\qquad\qquad\qquad\qquad\qquad\qquad\qquad\qquad\qquad\qquad\quad$ t, u not variables

R_3 $\quad \mathcal{C} \wedge T \overset{?}{\vdash} u \rightsquigarrow_\sigma \mathcal{C}\sigma \wedge T\sigma \overset{?}{\vdash} u\sigma$ $\qquad$ if $t_1, t_2 \in \mathsf{St}(T), \sigma = \mathsf{mgu}(t_1, t_2)$,
$\qquad\qquad\qquad\qquad\qquad\qquad\qquad\qquad\qquad\qquad\qquad\qquad$ and $t_1 \neq t_2$

R_4 $\quad \mathcal{C} \wedge T \overset{?}{\vdash} u \rightsquigarrow \perp$ $\qquad\qquad\qquad$ if $\mathcal{V}(T \cup \{u\}) = \emptyset$ and $T \not\vdash u$

R_f $\quad \mathcal{C} \wedge T \overset{?}{\vdash} f(u, v) \rightsquigarrow \mathcal{C} \wedge T \overset{?}{\vdash} u \wedge T \overset{?}{\vdash} v$ $\quad$ for $f \in \{\langle \,, \rangle, \mathsf{senc}, \mathsf{aenc}\}$

Figure 5. Simplification rules.

All the rules are indexed by a substitution (when there is no index then the identity substitution is assumed). We write $\mathcal{C} \rightsquigarrow_\sigma^* \mathcal{C}'$ if there are constraint systems $\mathcal{C}_1, \ldots, \mathcal{C}_n$ such that $\mathcal{C} \rightsquigarrow_{\sigma_0} \mathcal{C}_1 \rightsquigarrow_{\sigma_1} \ldots \rightsquigarrow_{\sigma_n} \mathcal{C}'$ and $\sigma = \sigma_0 \sigma_1 \ldots \sigma_n$. We denote by $\sigma = \mathsf{mgu}(u, v)$ a most general unifier of u and v, such that $\mathcal{V}(v\sigma, u\sigma) \subseteq \mathcal{V}(v, u)$.

A constraint system is called *solved* if it is different from $\perp$ and if each of its constraints is of the form $T \overset{?}{\vdash} x$, where x is a variable. Note that the empty constraint system is solved. Solved constraint systems are particularly simple since they always have a solution. Indeed, let T_1 be the smallest (w.r.t. inclusion) left-hand side of a constraint. From the definition of a constraint system we have that $T_1 \neq \emptyset$ and has no variable. Then the substitution τ defined by $x\tau = t_1$ where $t_1 \in T_1$ for every variable x, is a solution since $T \vdash x\theta$ for any constraint $T \overset{?}{\vdash} x$ of the solved constraint system.

Given a constraint system $\mathcal{C}$, we say that T_i is a *minimal unsolved left-hand side* of $\mathcal{C}$ if T_i is a left-hand side of $\mathcal{C}$ and for all $T \overset{?}{\vdash} u \in \mathcal{C}$ such that $T \subsetneq T_i$, we have that u is a variable.

Lemma 3.7 *The simplification rules transform a deducibility constraint system into a deducibility constraint system.*

Theorem 3.8 *Let $\mathcal{C}$ be an unsolved constraint system.*

1. *(Termination) There is no infinite chain $\mathcal{C} \rightsquigarrow_{\sigma_1} \mathcal{C}_1 \ldots \rightsquigarrow_{\sigma_n} \mathcal{C}_n$.*
2. *(Correctness) If $\mathcal{C} \rightsquigarrow_\sigma^* \mathcal{C}'$ for some constraint system $\mathcal{C}'$ and some substitution σ and if θ is a solution of $\mathcal{C}'$ then $\sigma\theta$ is a solution of $\mathcal{C}$.*
3. *(Completeness) If θ is a solution of $\mathcal{C}$, then there exist a solved constraint system $\mathcal{C}'$ and substitutions σ, θ' such that $\theta = \sigma\theta'$, $\mathcal{C} \rightsquigarrow_\sigma^* \mathcal{C}'$ and θ' is a solution of $\mathcal{C}'$.*

Termination and correctness are quite easy to show. For termination, it is easy to see that the number of variables is non-increasing. Furthermore, this number strictly decreases by the rules R_2 and R_3. Any other rule strictly reduces the total size of the right hand sides of the constraint (here, the "size" is the number of symbols in the term). Completeness is more involved and its proof is detailed in Section 3.3.2. Getting a polynomial bound on the length of simplification sequences requires to consider a particular strategy.

3.3.2. Completeness

First, we show that proofs considered in solutions of constraints can be narrowed to so-called *simple proofs*. Let $T_1 \subseteq T_2 \subseteq \ldots \subseteq T_n$. We say that a proof Π of $T_i \vdash u$ is *left minimal* if, whenever there is a proof of $T_j \vdash u$ for some $j < i$, then Π is also a proof of $T_j \vdash u$. In other words, the left-minimal proofs are those that can be performed in a minimal T_j . We say that a proof is *simple* if all its subproofs are left minimal and there is no repeated label on any branch. Note that a subproof of a simple proof is simple.

Lemma 3.9 *Let $T_1 \subseteq T_2 \subseteq \ldots \subseteq T_n$ be a sequence of sets of terms and u be a term such that $T_i \vdash u$. There exists a simple proof Π of $T_i \vdash u$.*

Proof: Let i be a minimal index for which there is a proof of $T_i \vdash u$. Thanks to Lemma 3.3, there is a local proof Π_0 of $T_i \vdash u$. We prove the lemma by induction on the size of Π_0.

Base case: Π_0 is reduced to a leaf. In such a case, Π_0 is a simple proof.
Induction step: Consider the last rule in the proof of u:

$$\Pi_0 = \left\{ \begin{array}{c} \dfrac{\begin{array}{ccc} \Pi_1 & \cdots & \Pi_n \\ u_1 & & u_n \end{array}}{u} \ R \end{array} \right.$$

For every $j = 1, \ldots, n$, we have that Π_j is a proof of $T_i \vdash u_j$. By induction hypothesis, there are simple proofs Π'_j of u_j. If u appears as a node in some of these proofs, let Π be the corresponding subproof and we get the desired result. Otherwise, let

$$\Pi = \left\{ \begin{array}{c} \dfrac{\begin{array}{ccc} \Pi'_1 & \cdots & \Pi'_n \\ u_1 & & u_n \end{array}}{u} \ R \end{array} \right.$$

The proof Π is a simple proof of u. □ □

Lemma 3.10 *Let C be an unsolved constraint system, θ be a solution of C and $T_i \overset{?}{\vdash} u_i$ be a minimal unsolved constraint of C. Let u be a term. If there is a simple proof of $T_i\theta \vdash u$ having the last rule an axiom or a decomposition then there is $t \in St(T_i) \setminus \mathcal{X}$ such that $t\theta = u$.*

Proof: Let Π be a simple proof of $T_i\theta \vdash u$ such that its last rule is an axiom or a decomposition. Let j be the minimal indice such that $T_j\theta \vdash u$. Note that $j \leq i$ and by definition of a simple proof, we have that Π is also a simple proof of $T_j\theta \vdash u$.

- The last rule is an axiom. Then $u \in T_j\theta$. There is $t \in T_j$ (thus $t \in \mathsf{St}(T_j)$) such that $t\theta \overset{?}{=} u$. If t is a variable then $T_t \vdash t$ is a constraint in $\mathcal{C}$ with $T_t \subsetneq T_j$ (see the definition of a constraint system). Hence $T_t\theta \vdash t\theta$, that is $T_t\theta \vdash u$, which contradicts the minimality of j. Thus, as required, t is not a variable.
- The last rule is a decomposition. Suppose that it is a symmetric decryption. That is, there is w such that $T_j\theta \vdash \mathsf{senc}(u, w)$, and $T_j\theta \vdash w$. By simplicity of the proof, the last rule applied when obtaining $\mathsf{senc}(u, w)$ is an axiom or a decomposition, otherwise the same node would appear twice. Then, applying the induction hypothesis we have that there is $t \in \mathsf{St}(T_j) \setminus \mathcal{X}$ such that $t\theta = \mathsf{senc}(u, w)$. It follows that $t = \mathsf{senc}(t', t'')$ with $t'\theta = u$. If t' is a variable then $T_{t'}\theta \vdash t'\theta$. That is $T_{t'}\theta \vdash u$, which again contradicts the minimality of j. Hence t' is not variable, as required.

For the other decomposition rules the same reasoning holds. □ □

Lemma 3.11 *Let* $\mathcal{C} = T_0 \overset{?}{\vdash} x_0, \ldots, T_{i-1} \overset{?}{\vdash} x_{i-1}, T_i \overset{?}{\vdash} u, \ldots$ *be a constraint system and* σ *be a solution of* $\mathcal{C}$ *such that*

1. T_i *does not contain two distinct subterms* t_1, t_2 *with* $t_1\sigma = t_2\sigma$,
2. u *is a non-variable subterm of* T_i.

Then $T_i' \vdash u$, *where* $T_i' = T_i \cup \{x \mid (T \overset{?}{\vdash} x) \in \mathcal{C}, T \subsetneq T_i\}$.

Proof: Let j be minimal such that $T_j\sigma \vdash u\sigma$. Thus $j \leq i$ and $T_j \subseteq T_i$. Consider a simple proof Π of $T_j\sigma \vdash u\sigma$. We reason by induction on the depth of Π.

Base case: Π is reduced to a leaf. Then there is $t \in T_j$ such that $t\sigma = u\sigma$. By hypothesis 1, we deduce that $t = u$. Hence, we have that $u \in T_j$ and thus $T_i' \vdash u$, as required.

Induction step: We analyse the different cases, depending on the last rule R of Π:

- *Case* R is a composition rule. Assume for example that R $=$ SE. In such a case, we have that:

$$\Pi = \left\{ \frac{\begin{array}{cc} \Pi_1 & \Pi_2 \\ v_1 & v_2 \end{array}}{\mathsf{senc}(v_1, v_2)} \right.$$

with $u\sigma = \mathsf{senc}(v_1, v_2)$. Since u is not a variable, $u = \mathsf{senc}(u_1, u_2)$, $u_1\sigma = v_1$, and $u_2\sigma = v_2$. If u_1 (resp. u_2) is a variable then u_1 (resp. u_2) belongs to $\mathcal{V}(T_i)$ since $u \in \mathsf{St}(T_i)$. Again, this implies $u_1 \in T_i'$ (resp. $u_2 \in T_i'$). Otherwise, u_1 (resp. u_2) is not a variable. Then, by induction hypothesis, $T_i' \vdash u_1$ (resp. $T_i' \vdash u_2$). Hence in both cases we have that $T_i' \vdash u_1$ and $T_i' \vdash u_2$. This allows us to conclude that $T_i' \vdash u$.
- *Case* R $=$ SD. In such a case, there is w such that $T_j\sigma \vdash \mathsf{senc}(u\sigma, w)$, and $T_j\sigma \vdash w$:

$$\Pi = \begin{cases} \quad \Pi_1 \qquad \Pi_2 \\ \dfrac{\mathsf{senc}(u\sigma, w) \quad w}{u\sigma} \end{cases}$$

By simplicity, the last rule of the proof Π_1 is a decomposition or an axiom. By Lemma 3.10, there is $t \in \mathsf{St}(T_j) \smallsetminus \mathcal{X}$ such that $t\sigma = \mathsf{senc}(u\sigma, w)$. Let $t = \mathsf{senc}(t_1, t_2)$ with $t_1\sigma = u\sigma$, and $t_2\sigma = w$. By induction hypothesis, $T_i' \vdash t$. Since $t_1\sigma = u\sigma$, by hypothesis 1, we have that $t_1 = u$.

Now, if t_2 is a variable, and since $t_2 \in \mathcal{V}(T_i)$, we have that $T_{t_2} \subsetneq T_i$ and thus $t_2 \in T_i'$. If t_2 is not a variable, then, from $T_j\sigma \vdash t_2\sigma$ and by induction hypothesis, $T_i' \vdash t_2$. So, in any case, $T_i' \vdash t_2$.

Hence, we have both that $T_i' \vdash \mathsf{senc}(u, t_2)$ and $T_i' \vdash t_2$, from which we conclude that $T_i' \vdash u$, by symmetric decryption.

- *Case* R = PKD. In such a case, there is w such that $T_j\sigma \vdash \mathsf{sk}(w)$ and $T_j\sigma \vdash \mathsf{aenc}(u\sigma, w)$. As in the previous case, there is $t \in \mathsf{St}(T_j) \smallsetminus \mathcal{X}$ such that $t\sigma = \mathsf{aenc}(u\sigma, w)$. By induction hypothesis, $T_i' \vdash t$. Let $t = \mathsf{aenc}(t_1, t_2)$. As in the previous case, we have that $t_1\sigma = u\sigma$, and thus $t_1 = u$ (thanks to hypothesis 1). The last rule in the proof of $T_j\sigma \vdash \mathsf{sk}(w)$ is a decomposition (no composition rule can yield a term headed with $\mathsf{sk}(\_)$). Then, by Lemma 3.10 (T_j satisfies the hypotheses of the lemma since $T_j \subseteq T_i$), there is a non-variable subterm $w_1 \in \mathsf{St}(T_j)$ such that $w_1\sigma = \mathsf{sk}(w)$. Let $w_1 = \mathsf{sk}(w_2)$. By induction hypothesis, $T_j' \vdash \mathsf{sk}(w_2)$. Moreover, since $w_2\sigma = t_2\sigma$, by hypothesis 2, we have that $w_2 = t_2$. Finally, from $T_i' \vdash \mathsf{aenc}(u, w_2)$ and $T_i' \vdash \mathsf{sk}(w_2)$, we conclude that $T_i' \vdash u$.

The proof is similar for the other decomposition rules.   □   □

Proposition 3.2 (Completeness for one step) *If $\mathcal{C}$ is an unsolved deducibility constraint system and σ is a solution of $\mathcal{C}$, then there is a deducibility constraint system $\mathcal{C}'$, a substitution τ, and a solution σ' of $\mathcal{C}'$ such that $\mathcal{C} \rightsquigarrow_\tau \mathcal{C}'$ and $\sigma = \tau\sigma'$.*

Proof: Let $\mathcal{C}$ be an unsolved constraint system and σ be a solution of $\mathcal{C}$. We show that there is a constraint system $\mathcal{C}'$ and a solution σ' of $\mathcal{C}'$ such that $\mathcal{C} \rightsquigarrow_\tau \mathcal{C}'$ and $\sigma = \tau\sigma'$.

Consider a minimal unsolved constraint $T_i \overset{?}{\vdash} u_i$ such that u_i is not a variable. We have that $T_i\sigma \vdash u_i\sigma$. Consider a simple proof Π of $T_i\sigma \vdash u_i\sigma$. We analyse the different cases depending on the last rule of Π.

1. *The last rule is a composition.* Suppose that it is the pairing rule. That is, there are w_1, w_2 such that $T_i\theta \vdash w_1$, $T_i\theta \vdash w_2$ and $\langle w_1, w_2 \rangle = u_i\theta$. Since u_i is not a variable there exists u', u'' such that $u_i = \langle u', u'' \rangle$. Hence we can apply the simplification rule $\mathsf{R_f}$ in order to obtain $\mathcal{C}'$. Since $u'\theta = w_1$ and $u''\theta = w_2$, the substitution θ is also a solution to $\mathcal{C}'$. For the other composition rules the same reasoning holds.

2. *The last rule is an axiom or a decomposition.* Applying Lemma 3.10 we obtain that there is $t \in \mathsf{St}(T_i) \smallsetminus \mathcal{X}$ such that $t\theta = u_i\theta$. We can have the following two possibilities:

   (a) If $t \neq u_i$ then we apply the simplification rule $\mathsf{R_2}$.

(b) Otherwise, if $t = u_i$, then $u_i \in \mathsf{St}(T_i)$ and we already know that u_i is not a variable. We consider two cases:

    i. There are two distinct terms $t_1, t_2 \in \mathsf{St}(T)$ such that $t_1\theta = t_2\theta$. Then we apply the simplification rule R$_3$.

    ii. Otherwise, the simplification rule R$_1$ can be applied (Lemma 3.11).   □

            □

3.3.3. Complexity

The termination stated in Theorem 3.8 does not provide with tight complexity bounds. In fact, applying the simplification rules may lead to branches of exponential length in the size of the constraint system [12]. Inspecting the completeness proof, there is still some room for choosing a strategy to ensure that the length of each branch is polynomially bounded in $\mathcal{C}$ (while keeping completeness). Note that correctness is independent of the order of the rules application.

Moreover, for any suitable representation of terms, we have that $|u\sigma, v\sigma| < |u, v|$ where $\sigma = \mathsf{mgu}(u, v)$. Hence, if we use a DAG representation of terms, when $\mathcal{C} \leadsto_\sigma^* \mathcal{C}'$, we have that the size of $\mathcal{C}'$ is polynomially bounded in the size of $\mathcal{C}$. As a consequence, the security problem is in co-NP and it is actually co-NP-complete [24]. The NP-hardness can be established with a reduction from 3-SAT.

3.4. Further Readings

Many parts of this section are borrowed from [12]. Hence, more details can be found in this paper. Another decision procedure based on constraint simplification rules has been proposed by J. Millen and V. Shmatikov [21]. Many results (*e.g.* [11,7]) have been obtained within this framework. In particular, this framework has been extended by several authors to deal with algebraic properties of cryptographic primitives.

3.5. Exercises

Exercice 9 (⋆)
Consider the following inference system:

$$\frac{x \quad y}{\langle x, y\rangle} \qquad \frac{\langle x, y\rangle}{x} \qquad \frac{\langle x, y\rangle}{y} \qquad \frac{x \quad y}{\mathsf{senc}(x, y)} \qquad \frac{\mathsf{senc}(x, y) \quad y}{x}$$

Let $T = \{\mathsf{senc}(s, \langle k_1, k_2\rangle), \ \mathsf{senc}(k_1, k_3), \ k_3, \ k_2\}$.

1. Enumerate all the subterms of T.
2. The term s is deducible from T. Give a derivation witnessing this fact.
3. Among the subterms of T, give those that are deducible.
4. Give a term u that is not a subterm of T and such that $T \vdash u$.

Exercice 10 (⋆ ⋆ ⋆)
Consider the following inference system:

$$\frac{x \quad y}{\langle x, y \rangle} \qquad \frac{\langle x, y \rangle}{x} \qquad \frac{\langle x, y \rangle}{y} \qquad \frac{x \quad y}{\mathsf{senc}(x, y)} \qquad \frac{\mathsf{senc}(x, y) \quad y}{x}$$

In order to decide whether a term s is deducible from a set of terms T in the inference system described above, we propose the following algorithm:

Algorithm:

1. Apply as much as possible the decryption and the projection rules. This leads to a set of terms called $\mathsf{analz}(T)$.
2. Check whether s can be obtained by applying the encryption and the pairing rules. The (infinite) set of terms obtained by applying the composition rules is denoted $\mathsf{synth}(\mathsf{analz}(T))$.

If $s \in \mathsf{synth}(\mathsf{analz}(T))$ then the algorithm return *yes*. Otherwise, it returns *no*.

1. Show that this algorithm terminates.
2. Show that this algorithm is sound, *i.e.* if the algorithm returns yes then $T \vdash s$.
3. The algorithm is not complete, *i.e.* there exist T and s such that $T \vdash s$, and for which the algorithm returns no. Find an example illustrating this fact.
4. Give an hypothesis on T that allows one to restore completeness.
5. Show that the algorithm is complete when this hypothesis is fulfilled.

Exercice 11 (⋆)
We consider the following inference system allowing us to model asymmetric encryption.

$$\frac{x \quad y}{\mathsf{aenc}(x, y)} \qquad \frac{\mathsf{aenc}(x, \mathsf{pk}(z)) \quad \mathsf{sk}(z)}{x} \qquad \frac{z}{\mathsf{pk}(z)}$$

Is this inference system local, or not? If so, give a proof. If not, give a derivation witnessing this fact.

Exercice 12 (⋆⋆)
Consider the following inference system allowing us to model digital signature.

$$\frac{x \quad \mathsf{sk}(z)}{\mathsf{sign}(x, \mathsf{sk}(z))} \qquad \frac{\mathsf{sign}(x, \mathsf{sk}(z)) \quad \mathsf{vk}(z)}{x} \qquad \frac{z}{\mathsf{vk}(z)}$$

1. This inference system is not local according to Definition 3.2. Give an example witnessing this fact.
2. Show that the intruder deduction problem is decidable.
   You can use the technique described in this chapter and extend the notion of subterm to restore the locality property.

Exercice 13 ($\star$)

We consider the signature and the inference system given in Example 23. Let $T_0 =$ $\{a,\ b,\ c,\ \mathsf{sk}(c),\ \mathsf{aenc}(\langle a, \mathsf{aenc}(s, b)\rangle, b)\}$ and $\mathcal{C} = \{T_0 \overset{?}{\vdash} \mathsf{aenc}(\langle a, \mathsf{aenc}(x_1, b)\rangle, b)\}$. What are the solutions of $\mathcal{C}$?

Exercice 14 ($\star\star$)

Consider the following protocol (defined informally):

$$A \to B : \langle \mathsf{aenc}(k_1, \mathsf{pk}(b)), \mathsf{aenc}(k_2, \mathsf{pk}(b)) \rangle$$
$$B \to A : \mathsf{senc}(k_1, k_2)$$

Here k_1 and k_2 represent two keys that are freshly generated by A at the beginning of each session.

1. Write formally the processes corresponding to an instance of the role A played by two honest agents a,b and an instance of the role B with the same two honest agents
2. Give a deduction constraint system corresponding to the only relevant symbolic trace for the processes of the previous question.
3. Apply the simplification rules to this constraint system and derive all possible attacks on the secrecy of k_1 (resp. k_2) for this scenario.

Exercice 15 ($\star$)

Give an example showing that the rule R_3 is necessary for the completeness of the procedure. More precisely, this example has to show that Proposition 3.2 will be wrong without this rule.

Exercice 16 ($\star\star$)

We consider the following variant of the rule R_3

$$\mathsf{R}_3' : \quad \mathcal{C} \wedge T \overset{?}{\vdash} u \ \leadsto_\sigma \ \mathcal{C}\sigma \wedge T\sigma \overset{?}{\vdash} u\sigma \ \text{ if } t_1, t_2 \in \mathsf{St}(T) \setminus \mathcal{X}, \sigma = \mathsf{mgu}(t_1, t_2), \text{ and } t_1 \neq t_2$$

1. Show that R_3' is not sufficient to restore completeness, *i.e.* give an example witnessing the fact that Proposition 3.2 is wrong if we use the rule R_3' instead of R_3.
2. Consider the set of simplification rules R_1, R_2, R_3', R_f. Show that this set of rules is complete if we consider symmetric encryption/decryption and pairing/projection (no asymmetric encryption).

Ackowledgements

Bruno Blanchet, Steve Kremer and David Pointcheval contributed to these notes and we warmly thank them for their help.

References

[1] Spore, the security protocol open repository. //www.lsv.ens-cachan.fr/spore.

[2] M. Abadi and A.D. Gordon. A calculus for cryptographic protocols: the spi calculus. *Information and Computation*, 148(1), 1999.

[3] Martín Abadi and Cédric Fournet. Mobile values, new names, and secure communication. In *Proc. 28th Symposium on Principles of Programming Languages (POPL'01)*, pages 104–115. ACM Press, 2001.

[4] Martín Abadi and Cédric Fournet. Private authentication. *Theoretical Computer Science*, 322(3):427–476, 2004.

[5] Martín Abadi, Bruno Blanchet, and Cédric Fournet. Just fast keying in the pi calculus. *ACM Transactions on Information and System Security (TISSEC)*, 10(3):1–59, 2007.

[6] Alessandro Armando, David A. Basin, Yohan Boichut, Yannick Chevalier, Luca Compagna, Jorge Cuéllar, Paul Hankes Drielsma, Pierre-Cyrille Héam, Olga Kouchnarenko, Jacopo Mantovani, Sebastian Mödersheim, David von Oheimb, Michaël Rusinowitch, Judson Santiago, Mathieu Turuani, Luca Viganò, and Laurent Vigneron. The avispa tool for the automated validation of internet security protocols and applications. In *Computer Aided Verification*, volume 3576 of *Lecture Notes in Computer Science*. Springer, 2005.

[7] Mathieu Baudet. Deciding security of protocols against off-line guessing attacks. In *Proc. 12th Conference on Computer and Communications Security*, pages 16–25. ACM Press, 2005.

[8] B. Blanchet, H. Comon-Lundh, S. Delaune, C. Fournet, S. Kremer, and D. Pointcheval. Cryptographic protocols: formal and computational proofs of security. Lecture Notes of the Parisian Master of Research in Computer Science (MPRI), 2011. Available on the MPRI web pages.

[9] Bruno Blanchet. An efficient cryptographic protocol verifier based on Prolog rules. In *Computer Security Foundations Workshop (CSFW'01)*, 2001.

[10] J. Clark and J. Jacob. A survey of authentication protocol literature. http://www.cs.york.ac.uk/~jac/papers/drareviewps.ps, 1997.

[11] H. Comon-Lundh and V. Shmatikov. Intruder deductions, constraint solving and insecurity decision in preence of exclusive or. In P. Kolaitis, editor, *Eighteenth Annual IEEE Symposium on Logic in Computer Science*, Ottawa, Canada, June 2003. IEEE Computer Society.

[12] Hubert Comon-Lundh, Véronique Cortier, and Eugen Zlinescu. Deciding security properties of cryptographic protocols. application to key cycles. *Transaction on Computational Logic*, 11(2), 2010.

[13] Ricardo Corin, Jeroen Doumen, and Sandro Etalle. Analysing password protocol security against off-line dictionary attacks. *ENTCS*, 121:47–63, 2005.

[14] V. Cortier and S. Kremer, editors. *Formal Models and Techniques for Analyzing Security Protocols*. IOS Press, 2011.

[15] Véronique Cortier, Stéphanie Delaune, and Pascal Lafourcade. A survey of algebraic properties used in cryptographic protocols. *Journal of Computer Security*, 14(1):1–43, 2006.

[16] Stéphanie Delaune, Steve Kremer, and Mark D. Ryan. Verifying privacy-type properties of electronic voting protocols. *Journal of Computer Security*, 17(4):435–487, July 2009.

[17] Cédric Fournet and Martín Abadi. Hiding names: Private authentication in the applied pi calculus. In *Proc. International Symposium on Software Security (ISSS'02)*, volume 2609 of *Lecture Notes in Computer Science*, pages 317–338. Springer, 2003.

[18] Gavin Lowe. An attack on the needham-schroeder public-key authentication protocol. *Information Processing Letters*, 56(3):131–133, 1996.

[19] Gavin Lowe. A hierarchy of authentication specification. In *10th Computer Security Foundations Workshop (CSFW '97), June 10-12, 1997, Rockport, Massachusetts, USA*, pages 31–44. IEEE Computer Society, 1997.

[20] David McAllester. Automatic recognition of tractability in inference relations. *Journal of the ACM*, 40(2), 1993.

[21] J. Millen and V. Shmatikov. Constraint solving for bounded-process cryptographic protocol analysis. In *Proc. 8th ACM Conference on Computer and Communications Security*, 2001.

[22] Robin Milner, Joachim Parrow, and David Walker. A calculus of mobile processes, i & ii. *Inf. Comput.*, 100(1):1–77, 1992.

[23] R. Needham and M. Schroeder. Using encryption for authentification in large networks of computers. *Communications of the ACM*, 21(12):993–999, 1978.

[24] Michael Rusinowitch and Mathieu Turuani. Protocol insecurity with finite number of sessions is np-complete. In *Proc.14th IEEE Computer Security Foundations Workshop*, Cape Breton, Nova Scotia,

June 2001.

[25] M. Ryan and B. Smyth. Applied pi calculus. In V. Cortier and S. Kremer, editors, *Formal Models and Techniques for Analyzing Security Protocols*. IOS Press, To appear.

[26] Bogdan Warinschi. A computational analysis of the needham-schroeder protocol. In *16th Computer security foundation workshop (CSFW)*, pages 248–262. IEEE, 2003.

Software Safety and Security
T. Nipkow et al. (Eds.)
IOS Press, 2012
doi:10.3233/978-1-61499-028-4-64

Model Checking:
From BDDs to Interpolation

Orna GRUMBERG

Computer Science Department, Technion,
Haifa, Israel

Abstract. In this paper we describe the development of model checking from BDD-based verification, through SAT-based bug finding, to Interpolation-based verification.

Model checking is an automatic approach to formally verifying that a given system satisfies a given specification. BDD-based *Symbolic Model Checking* (SMC) was the first to enable model checking of real-life designs with a few hundreds of state elements. Currently, SAT-based model checking is the most widely used method for verifying industrial designs. This is due to its ability to handle designs with thousands of state elements and more. Its main drawback, however, is its orientation towards "bug-hunting" rather than full verification.

In this paper we present two SAT-based approaches to full verification. The approaches combine BMC with *interpolation* or *interpolation-sequence* in order to compute an over-approximated set of the system's reachable states while checking that the specification is not violated. We compare the two methods both algorithmically and experimentally and conclude that they are incomparable.

Keywords. Model Checking, BDD-based Symbolic Model Checking (SMC), SAT-based Model Checking, Interpolation, Interpolation Sequence, Bounded Model Checking (BMC)

1. Introduction

Computerized systems dominate almost every aspect of our lives and their correct behavior is essential. *Model checking* [15] is an automated verification technique for checking whether a given system satisfies a desired property. Unlike testing or simulation based verification, model checking tools are exhaustive in the sense that they traverse *all* behaviors of the system, and either confirm that the system behaves correctly or present a *counterexample.*

Model checking has been successfully applied to verifying hardware and software systems. However, with the rapid increase in size and complexity of computerized systems, there is a constant need for a similar increase in verification capabilities.

In this paper we will survey several model checking techniques which can improve model checking applicability and scalability. We will start with the "old fashion" techniques of BDD-based Symbolic Model Checking (SMC) [9] and SAT-based Bounded Model Checking (BMC) [7]. We will then proceed to using inter-polation and interpolation-sequence for SAT-based model checking.

One of the main limitations of model checking is the *state explosion problem* which arises due to the huge state space of the checked systems. The size of the model induces high memory and time requirements that may make model check-ing infeasible. Traditionally, BDD-based methods are known to suffer from high memory requirements while SAT-based methods have high time requirements. Much research efforts have been invested along the years in trying to solve this problem.

The first significant solution was the introduction of BDDs [8] into model checking. BDD-based *Symbolic Model Checking* (SMC) [9] enabled model checking of real-life hardware designs with a few hundreds of state elements. However, current design blocks with well-defined functionality typically have thousands of state elements and more. To handle designs of that scale, SAT-based *Bounded Model Checking* (BMC) [7] has been developed. BMC is currently the most widely used method for formal verification of industrial designs. Its main drawback, however, is its orientation towards "bug-hunting" rather than full verification.

Several works extend BMC for full verification. [6] defines a *Reachability Di-ameter*, which sets a bound on the number of BMC iterations needed for full ver-ification. This bound, however, is usually hard to compute. Moreover, the bound is often very large and therefore the resulting formulas are too large for a SAT solver to handle.

[35] suggests to use *Induction* for full verification. This method uses the BMC check as the induction base. Then, the induction step is determined by checking a second formula. The induction method works automatically mainly for simple local properties. For complex properties, the user has to come up with a good inductive invariant. A completely different approach is the *Proof-Based Abstraction* [32] which exploits BMC to determine an abstract model on which BDD-based model checking can be applied.

In this paper we present two SAT-based approaches to full verification which combine BMC with *interpolation* [17] or *interpolation-sequence* [24,31]. The pro-posed methods compute an over-approximated set of the system's reachable states while checking that the specification is not violated. The process terminates with either a counterexample produced by BMC, or by reaching a fixpoint, indicating that no more reachable states will be found. In the latter case, since no violation of the formula has been encountered so far, it is guaranteed that the property holds.

The two approaches result in different traversals of the sets of reachable states, thus their convergence may differ. We compare them both on the algorithmic level and by running experiments. As is often the case with model checking techniques and tools, none is overall superior to the other.

In order to compare the methods experimentally we implemented them within Intel's verification tool. All experiments were conducted on models from Intel's Sandy Bridge micro-architecture. The checked properties are real specifications, used to verify those designs. The experiments compare various parameters of the two methods. In all our experiments, when a fixpoint could be reached only at a high bound, the interpolation-sequence based (ISB) algorithm performed better than the interpolation based (IB) algorithm. The IB algorithm, on the other hand, performed better when a fixpoint could be reached at a low bound. Falsified properties always favored the ISB algorithm.

When describing the two methods we assume a safety property of the form AGq, where q is a propositional formula. This, however, does not restrict their generality since model checking of liveness properties can be reduced to handling safety properties [4]. Further, model checking of safety properties can be reduced to handling properties of the form AGq [25].

2. Model Checking

Temporal logic model checking [15] is an automatic approach to formally verifying that a given system satisfies a given specification. The system is often modelled by a finite state transition graph called *Kripke structure* and the specification is written in a *temporal logic*. Determining whether a model satisfies a given specification is often based on an exploration of the model's state space in a search for violations of the specification.

Definition 2.1. Given a set of atomic propositions AP, a *Kripke structure* M is the quadruple $M = (S, INIT, TR, L)$ where S is a finite set of states, $INIT \subseteq S$ is a set of initial states and $TR \subseteq S \times S$ is a *total* transition relation. That is, for every $s \in S$ there exists $s' \in S$ such that $(s, s') \in TR$. Additionally, $L : S \to \mathcal{P}(AP)$ is the labeling function which associates with every state $s \in S$ the set $L(s)$ of atomic propositions true in s.

A *path* in a Kripke structure M is a sequence of states $\pi = (s_0, s_1, \ldots)$ such that for all $i \geq 0$, $s_i \in S$ and $(s_i, s_{i+1}) \in TR$. The length of a path is denoted by $|\pi|$. If π is infinite then $|\pi| = \infty$. If $\pi = (s_0, s_1, \ldots, s_n)$ then $|\pi| = n$. A path is an *initial path* when $s_0 \in INIT$. We sometimes refer to a prefix of a path as a path as well.

A formula in *Linear Temporal Logic* (LTL) [15,34] is of the form $\mathbf{A}f$ where f is a path formula. A model M satisfies an LTL property $\mathbf{A}f$ if all infinite initial paths in M satisfy f. If there exists an infinite initial path not satisfying f, this path is defined to be a *counterexample*.

In this paper we consider a subset of LTL formulas of the form $\mathbf{AG}\,q$, where q is a propositional formula. As mentioned before, this does not restrict the generality of the suggested methods since model checking of liveness properties can be reduced to handling safety properties [4]. Further, model checking of safety properties can be reduced to handling properties of the form $\mathbf{AG}\,q$ [25].

The *model checking problem* is the problem of determining whether a given model satisfies a given property. Let M be a model, *Reach* be the set of reachable states in M, and $f = \mathbf{AG}\,q$ be a property. If for every $s \in Reach$, $L(s) \models q$ then the property holds in M. On the other hand, if there exists a state $s \in Reach$ such that $L(s) \models \neg q$ then there exists an initial path $\pi = s_0, s_1, \ldots, s_n$ such that $s_n = s$. The path π is a *counterexample* for the property f.

We would sometimes like to represent a Kripke structure by means of propositional formulas (or, equivalently, Boolean functions). In order to do so, we define a set of *Boolean state variables*, denoted V. When $|V| = n$, a state $s \in S$ is represented by a vector in the set $\{0,1\}^n$. Thus, s is a valuation of the state variables in V. A set of states S' can be represented by a formula η over V, where the satisfying assignments of η represent the states in S'. By abuse of notation we will refer to a formula η over V as a set of states and use the notion $s \in \eta$ for states represented by η. For some variable v, v' is used to denote the value of v after one time unit. The set of these variables is denoted by V'. In the general case V^i is used to denote the variables in V after i time units (thus, $V^0 \equiv V$). Let η be a formula over V^i, the formula $\eta[V^i \leftarrow V^j]$ is identical to η except that for each variable $v \in V$, v^i is replaced with v^j.

Model checking has been successfully applied in hardware verification, and is emerging as an industrial standard tool for hardware design . A partial list of tools for hardware verification includes SMV [28] and NuSMV [13], FormalCheck [21], RuleBase [2], and Forecast [19]. In recent years, several tools for model checking of software have been developed and applied to non-trivial examples. A partial list consists of SPIN [23], Bandera [16], Java PathFinder [22], SLAM, Bebop, and Zing [1], Blast [3], Magic [11], and CBMC [14]. An extensive overview of model checking algorithms can be found in [15].

The main technical challenge in model checking is the *state explosion* problem which occurs if the system is a composition of several components or if the system variables range over large domains.

An explicit state model checker is a program which performs model checking directly on a Kripke structure. SPIN [23] is an example of a successful tool of that kind. Large models are often handled implicitly, based on a symbolic representation of the Kripke structure by means of Boolean functions or propositional formulas. Two widely used such approaches are the BDD-based model checking [10,28] and the SAT-based bounded model checking [5], described in the following sections.

3. BDD-Based Model Checking

Ordered Binary Decision Diagrams (BDDs) [8] are canonical representations of Boolean functions. They are often concise in their memory requirements. Furthermore, most operations needed for model checking can be defined in terms of Boolean operations on Boolean functions and can be implemented efficiently with BDDs.

In BDD-based (also called *symbolic*) model checking (SMC) sets of states are represented by Boolean functions over the set of Boolean state variables V, as explained in the previous section. Those functions are represented by BDDs. The transition relation of the Kripke structure is also represented by a Boolean function (and thus by a BDD), over the sets V and V' of variables representing current and next states, respectively.

BDDs are sometimes, but not always, exponentially smaller than explicit representation of the corresponding Boolean functions. In such cases, symbolic verification is successful.

Since BDDs are particularly suitable for representing set of states, BDD-based algorithms are based on operations on sets, which are implemented by means of operations on BDDs (or the corresponding Boolean function). For example, union and intersection of sets correspond to disjunction and conjunction of the BDDs representing those sets.

Two special operations are central to model checking. Given a set of states Q, the *image computation* computes the set of successors of states in Q:

$$Image(Q) := \{t \mid \exists s[TR(s,t) \ \wedge \ Q(s)]\}.$$

The *preimage computation* computes the set of the predecessors of states in Q:

$$Preimage(Q) := \{s \mid \exists t[TR(s,t) \ \wedge \ Q(t)]\}.$$

Unfortunately, in contrast to pure Boolean operations, these operations are not efficiently computable [28], and their computation is a major bottleneck in symbolic model checking.

We conclude this section by demonstrating a BDD-based algorithm for model checking the property $\mathbf{AG}\, q$, for some atomic proposition q. The algorithm manipulates sets of states represented as BDDs. It checks whether $M \models \mathbf{AG}\, q$ by computing the set of reachable states starting from the set of initial states. It iteratively applies the image computation in order to find the set of successors of the current set of states. If a reachable state that does not satisfy q is found, then the procedure returns "$M \not\models \mathbf{AG}\, q$". Otherwise, when all reachable states have been found, the procedure returns "$M \models \mathbf{AG}\, q$". We assume that the structure M is given by the following BDDs: $TR(V, V')$ is the BDD representing the transition relation, $INIT(V)$ represents the set of initial states, and for each $p \in AP$, $S_p(V)$ represents the set of states in M that satisfy p. Figure 1 presents the algorithm.

```
 1: procedure CHECKAG(S_q)
 2:      Reach := INIT
 3:      New := INIT
 4:      while New ≠ ∅ do
 5:          if New ∩ S̄_q ≠ ∅ then return "M ⊭ AG q"     // New ⊄ S_q
 6:          end if
 7:          New := Image(New)
 8:          New := New \ Reach
 9:          Reach := Reach ∪ New
10:      end while
11:      return "M ⊨ AG q"
12: end procedure
```

Figure 1. The procedure CheckAG for checking the formula $f = \mathbf{AG}\, q$

4. Bounded Model Checking

Many problems, including some versions of model checking, can naturally be translated into the *satisfiability* problem of the propositional calculus. The satisfiability problem is known to be NP-complete. Nevertheless, modern SAT-solvers, developed in recent years, can handle formulas with several thousands of variables within a few seconds. SAT-solvers such as Grasp [26], Prover [36], Chaff [33], Min-iSAT [18], and many others, are based on sophisticated learning techniques and data structures that accelerate the search for a satisfying assignment, if exists.

A SAT solver is a complete decision procedure that given a propositional formula, determines whether the formula is *satisfiable* or *unsatisfiable*. Most SAT solvers assume a formula in *Conjunctive Normal Form* (CNF), consisting of a conjunction of a set of clauses, each of which is a disjunction of propositional variables or their negation. A CNF formula is satisfiable if there exists a *satisfying assignment* for which every clause in the set is evaluated to $\top$. If the clause set is satisfiable then the SAT solver returns a satisfying assignment for it. If it is not satisfiable (unsatisfiable), meaning, it has no satisfying assignment, then modern SAT solvers produce a *proof of unsatisfiability* [32,39]. The proof of unsatisfiability has many useful applications. We will introduce one of them in the next section.

Below we describe a simple way to exploit satisfiability for bounded model checking of properties of the form **AG** q, where q is a Boolean formula.

Bounded model checking (BMC) [7] is an iterative process for checking properties of a given structure up to a given bound. Let M be a Kripke structure and $f = AGq$ be the property to be verified. Given a bound k, BMC either finds a counterexample of length k or less for f in M, or concludes that there is no such counterexample. In order to search for a counterexample of length k the following propositional formula is built:

Formula 1. $\varphi_M^k(f) = INIT(V^0) \wedge TR(V^0, V^1) \wedge TR(V^1, V^2) \wedge \ldots \wedge TR(V^{k-1}, V^k) \wedge (\neg q(V^k))$

$\varphi_M^k(f)$ is then passed to a SAT solver which searches for a satisfying assignment. If there exists a satisfying assignment for $\varphi_M^k(f)$ then the property is violated, since there exists a path of M of length k violating the property. In order to conclude that there is no counterexample of length k or less, BMC iterates all lengths from 0 up to the given bound k. At each iteration a SAT procedure is invoked.

When M and f are obvious from the context we omit them from the formula $\varphi_M^k(f)$ denoting it as φ^k. The BMC algorithm is described in Figure 2.

The main drawback of this approach is its incompleteness. It can only guarantee that there is no counterexample of size smaller or equal to k. It cannot guarantee that there is no counterexample of size greater than k.

Thus, this method is mainly suitable for refutation. Verification is obtained only if the bound k exceeds the length of the longest path among all shortest paths from an initial state to some state in M. In practice, it is hard to compute this bound and even when known, it is often too large to handle. Several methods for full verification with SAT have been suggested, such as induction [35], ALL-SAT [12,20,29], and interpolation [27,30,38]. In the rest of the paper we will focus on SAT-based verification with interpolation.

```
1: function BMC(M,f,k)
2:     i := 0
3:     while i ≤ k do
4:         build φ^i_M(f)
5:         result = SAT(φ^i_M(f))
6:         if result = true then
7:             return cex       // returning the counterexample
8:         else
9:             i = i + 1
10:        end if
11:    end while
12:    return No cex for bound k
13: end function
```

Figure 2. Bounded model checking

5. Interpolation

In this section we introduce two notions, *interpolation* [17] and *interpolation-sequence* [24] that, when combined with BMC can provide full program verification.

Throughout the paper we denote the value *false* as $\perp$ and the value *true* as $\top$. For a formula X, $\mathcal{L}(X)$ is the set of variables appearing in X. For a set of formulas $\{X_1, \ldots, X_n\}$ we will use $\mathcal{L}(X_1, \ldots, X_n)$ to denote the variables appearing in $X_1, \ldots, X_n$. That is, $\mathcal{L}(X_1, \ldots, X_n) = \mathcal{L}(X_1) \cup \ldots \cup \mathcal{L}(X_n)$.

Definition 5.1. Let (A, B) be a pair of formulas such that $A \wedge B \equiv \perp$. The *interpolant* for (A, B) is a formula I such that:

- $A \Rightarrow I$.
- $I \wedge B \equiv \perp$.
- $\mathcal{L}(I) \subseteq \mathcal{L}(A) \cap \mathcal{L}(B)$.

The interpolant can be viewed as the part of A that is sufficient to contradict B. As mentioned above, modern SAT solvers produce a *proof of unsatisfiability* if the checked formula is unsatisfiable. An interpolant can be extracted from a proof of unsatisfiability [30], where different proofs yield different interpolants.

A similar notion can be defined when we have a sequence of formulas whose conjunction is unsatisfiable.

Definition 5.2. Let $\Gamma = \{A_1, A_2, \ldots, A_n\}$ be a set of formulas such that $\bigwedge \Gamma \equiv \perp$. That is $\bigwedge \Gamma = A_1 \wedge \ldots \wedge A_n$ is unsatisfiable. An *interpolation-sequence* for Γ is a set $\{\mathcal{I}_0, \mathcal{I}_1, \ldots, \mathcal{I}_n\}$ such that:

1. $\mathcal{I}_0 \equiv \top$ and $\mathcal{I}_n \equiv \perp$
2. For every $0 \leq j < n$ it holds that $\mathcal{I}_j \wedge A_{j+1} \Rightarrow \mathcal{I}_{j+1}$
3. For every $0 < j < n$ it holds that $\mathcal{L}(\mathcal{I}_j) \subseteq \mathcal{L}(A_1, \ldots, A_j) \cap \mathcal{L}(A_{j+1}, \ldots, A_n)$

Computing an interpolation-sequence for a sequence of formulas is done in the following way: for each $\mathcal{I}_i$, $0 < i < n$, the sequence of formulas is partitioned

in a different way such that $\mathcal{I}_i$ is the interpolant for the formulas $A(i) = \bigwedge\limits_{j=1}^{i} A_j$
and $B(i) = \bigwedge\limits_{j=i+1}^{n} A_j$. In fact, all interpolants $\mathcal{I}_i$ in the sequence can be computed efficiently at once, by a single traversal of a given proof of unsatisfiability [38].

Theorem 5.3. *Let* $\Gamma = \{A_1, A_2, \ldots, A_n\}$ *be a set of formulas such that* $\bigwedge \Gamma \equiv \bot$ *and let* Π *be a proof of unsatisfiability for* $\bigwedge \Gamma$. *For every* $1 \leq i < n$ *let us define* $A(i) = A_1 \wedge \ldots \wedge A_i$ *and* $B(i) = A_{i+1} \wedge \ldots \wedge A_n$. *Let* $\mathcal{I}_i$ *be the interpolant for the pair* $(A(i), B(i))$ *extracted using* Π *then the set* $\{\top, \mathcal{I}_1, \mathcal{I}_2, \ldots, \mathcal{I}_{n-1}, \bot\}$ *is an interpolant sequence for* Γ.

6. Exploiting Interpolation-Sequence in Model Checking

In this section we present a SAT-based algorithm for full verification (sometimes also called *unbounded model checking* (UMC)), which combines BMC and interpolation-sequence [38]. BMC is used to search for counterexamples while the interpolation-sequence is used to produce over-approximated sets of reachable states and to check for termination.

Interpolation-sequence has been introduced and used in [24] and [31]. In [24] it is used for computing an abstract model based on predicate abstraction for software model checking. In [31] interpolation-sequence is used for software model checking and lazy abstraction and is applied to individual execution paths in the control flow graph. The method presented in this section exploits interpolation-sequence in a different manner. In particular, it is applied to the whole model for imitating SMC.

From this point and on, we will use M to denote the Kripke structure representing the model and $f = AGq$ for a propositional formula q, as the property to be verified.

In order to better understand the algorithm and the motivation behind it, we first review some basic concepts of symbolic model checking (SMC).

6.1. Revisiting Symbolic Reachability Analysis

SMC performs *forward reachability analysis* by computing sets of reachable states S_j where j is the number of transitions needed to reach a state in S_j when starting from the initial states. Further, for every $j \geq 1$, $S_j(V) \wedge TR(V, V') \equiv S_{j+1}(V')$. Once S_j is computed, if it contains states violating q, a counterexample of length i is found and returned. Otherwise, if $S_j \subseteq \bigcup\limits_{i=1}^{j-1} S_i$ then a *fixpoint* has been reached, meaning that all reachable states have been found already. If no reachable state violates the property then the algorithm concludes that $M \models f$.

6.2. Interpolation-Sequence Based Model Checking (ISB)

The method presented in this section demonstrates how over-approximated sets, similar to S_i in their characteristics, can be extracted from BMC, based on interpolation-sequences.

Informally, we will use the notion of *fixpoint* when we can conclude that all *reachable* states in the model have been visited[1].

Note that, the interpolation-sequence exists for a bound N only when there is no counterexample of length N. In case a counterexample exists, BMC returns a counterexample and the interpolation-sequence is not needed.

Definition 6.1. A *BMC-partitioning* for φ^N is the set $\Gamma = \{A_1, A_2, \dots, A_{N+1}\}$ of formulas such that $A_1 = INIT(V^0) \wedge TR(V^0, V^1)$, for every $2 \leq i \leq N$ $A_i = TR(V^{i-1}, V^i)$ and $A_{N+1} = \neg q(V^N)$. Note that $\varphi^N = \bigwedge_{i=1}^{N+1} A_i \; (= \bigwedge \Gamma)$.

For a bound N, consider a BMC formula φ^N and its BMC-partitioning Γ. In case φ^N is unsatisfiable, its interpolation-sequence is denoted by $\bar{I}^N = (I_0^N, I_1^N, \dots, I_{N+1}^N)$. Note that the BMC-partitioning for φ^N contains $N + 1$ elements and therefore the interpolation-sequence contains $N + 2$ elements where the first element and the last one are always $\top$ and $\bot$, respectively.

Next, we intuitively explain our method. We start with $N = 1$. Consider the formula φ^1 and its BMC-partitioning: $\{A_1, A_2\}$. In case φ^1 is unsatisfiable, there exists an interpolation-sequence of the form $\bar{I}^1 = (I_0^1 = \top, I_1^1, I_2^1 = \bot)$. By Definition 5.2, $S_1 \subseteq I_1^1$, where S_1 is the set of states reachable from the initial states in one transition. This is because $\top \wedge A_1 \Rightarrow I_1^1$ where $A_1 = INIT(V^0) \wedge TR(V^0, V^1)$. Also, $I_1^1 \wedge \neg q(V^1)$ is unsatisfiable, since $I_1^1 \wedge A_2 \Rightarrow \bot$, where $A_2 = \neg q(V^1)$. Therefore, $I_1^1 \models q$.

In the next BMC iteration, for $N = 2$, consider φ^2 and its BMC-partitioning $\{A_1, A_2, A_3\}$. In case φ^2 is unsatisfiable, we get $\bar{I}^2 = (\top, I_1^2, I_2^2, \bot)$. Here too, $S_1 \subseteq I_1^2$ and the states reachable from it in one transition are a subset of I_2^2 since $I_1^2 \wedge A_2 \Rightarrow I_2^2$. Also, $S_2 \subseteq I_2^2$ and $I_2^2 \models q$. Let us define the sets $I_1 = I_1^1 \wedge I_1^2$ and $I_2 = I_2^2$. These sets have the following properties, $S_1 \subseteq I_1$, $S_2 \subseteq I_2$, $I_1 \models q$ and $I_2 \models q$. Moreover, $I_1[V^1 \leftarrow V] \wedge TR(V, V') \Rightarrow I_2[V^2 \leftarrow V']$.

In the general case if φ^N is unsatisfiable then for every $1 \leq j \leq N$, $S_j \subseteq I_j^N$. If we now define $I_j = \bigwedge_{k=j}^{N} I_j^k$ then for every $1 \leq j \leq N$ we get:

- $I_j \models q$ since $I_j^j \models q$.
- $I_j \wedge TR(V, V') \Rightarrow I_{j+1}$ since $I_j^k \wedge TR(V^j, V^{j+1}) \Rightarrow I_{j+1}^k$ for every $1 \leq k \leq N$
- $S_j \subseteq I_j$ since $S_j \subseteq I_j^k$ for every $1 \leq k \leq N$.

As a result, the sets $I_1, I_2, \dots, I_N$ can be used to determine if $M \models f$. Intuitively, the sets I_j are similar to the sets S_j computed by SMC except that they are over-approximations of S_j. Therefore, these sets can be used to imitate the forward reachability analysis of the model's state-space by means of an over-approximation. This is done in the following manner. BMC runs as usual with one extension. After checking bound N, if a counterexample is found, the algorithm terminates. Otherwise, the interpolation-sequence $\bar{I}^N$ is extracted and the sets I_j

---

[1]Since we compute over-approximated sets of reachable states, the computed sets are not monotonic. Therefore, we cannot define a monotonic function g for which the existence of a fixpoint is guaranteed.

for $1 \le j \le N$ are updated. If $I_j \Rightarrow \bigvee_{i=1}^{j-1} I_i$ for some $1 \le j \le N$, then we conclude that a fixpoint has been reached and all reachable states have been visited. Thus, $M \models f$. If no fixpoint is found, the bound N is increased and the computation is repeated for $N + 1$.

Next, we explain why the ISB algorithm uses $I_j = \bigwedge_{k=j}^{N} I_j^k$ rather than I_j^N in its Nth iteration. Informally, the following facts are needed in order to guarantee the correctness of the algorithm. For every $1 \le j \le N$ we need:

1. I_j should satisfy q.
2. $I_j(V) \wedge TR(V, V') \Rightarrow I_{j+1}(V')$ for $j \ne N$.
3. $S_j \subseteq I_j$.

This means that the algorithm cannot be implemented using the extracted interpolation sequence $\bar{I}^N$ alone. This is because $\bar{I}^N$ does not satisfy condition (1): while $I_N^N \models q$, I_j^N for $j \ne N$, does not necessarily satisfy q. This can be remedied by conjuncting each I_j^N with I_j^j. However, now condition (2) no longer holds. Taking $I_j = \bigwedge_{k=j}^{N} I_j^k$ results in a set with all three properties.

Definition 6.2. If no counterexample of length N or less exists in M, then $I_j = \bigwedge_{k=j}^{N} I_j^k[V^j \leftarrow V]$ where I_j^k is the j-th element in the interpolation-sequence extracted for the BMC-partitioning of φ^k. The *reachability vector* is defined to be $\bar{I} = (I_1, I_2, \ldots, I_N)$.

The algorithms for updating the reachablility vector and checking for a fixpoint are described in Figure 3 and Figure 4, respectively. The complete model checking algorithm using the method described above is given in Figure 5.

It is important to note that a call to UPDATEREACHABILITY changes all elements of the reachability vector. Therefore, the function FIXPOINTREACHED cannot count on inclusion checks done in previous iterations and needs to search for a fixpoint at every point in $\bar{I}$. Moreover, it is not sufficient to check for inclusion of only the last element I_N of $\bar{I}$. Indeed, if for any $j \le N$, $I_j \Rightarrow \bigvee_{i=1}^{j-1} I_i$ then all reachable states have been found already. However, the implication $I_N \Rightarrow \bigvee_{i=1}^{N-1} I_i$ might not hold due to additional *unreachable* states in I_N. This is because for all $1 \le j < N$, I_{j+1} is an over-approximation of the states reachable from I_j and not the exact image (That is, $I_j \wedge TR(V, V') \Rightarrow I_{j+1}[V \leftarrow V']$ rather than $I_j \wedge TR(V, V') \equiv I_{j+1}[V \leftarrow V']$).

6.3. Correctness of the ISB algorithm

The following lemmas and definition formalize the above explanation and prove the correctness of the algorithm.

```
1: function UPDATEREACHABLE($\bar{I}, \bar{I}^k$)
2:     $j = 1$
3:     while ($j < k$) do
4:         $I_j = I_j \wedge I_j^k$
5:         $\bar{I}[j] = I_j$
6:         $j = j + 1$
7:     end while
8:     $\bar{I}[k] = I_k^k$
9: end function
```

Figure 3. Updating the reachability vector

```
1: function FIXPOINTREACHED($\bar{I}$)
2:     $j = 2$
3:     while ($j \leq \bar{I}.length$) do
4:         $R = \bigvee_{k=1}^{j-1} I_k$
5:         $\varphi = I_j \wedge \neg R$ // Negation of $I_j \Rightarrow R$
6:         if (SAT($\varphi$) == false) then return true
7:         end if
8:         $j = j + 1$
9:     end while
10:    return false
11: end function
```

Figure 4. Checking if a fixpoint has been reached

Lemma 6.3. *If M does not have a counterexample of length N, then $S_j \subseteq I_j^N[V^j \leftarrow V]$ for every $1 \leq j \leq N$ and $I_N^N \models q$.*

Proof. M does not have a counterexample of length N. Therefore, the formula φ^N is unsatisfiable. Let $\bar{I}^N$ be the interpolation-sequence for the BMC-partitioning of φ^N. By Definitions 5.2 and 6.1, for $j = 1$, $\top \wedge INIT(V^0) \wedge TR(V^0, V^1) \Rightarrow I_1^1$. For each $2 \leq j \leq N$, $I_j^N \wedge TR(V^j, V^{j+1}) \Rightarrow I_{j+1}^N$. Hence, $S_j \subseteq I_j^N$. Definition 5.2 also state that $I_N^N \wedge \neg q(V^N) \Rightarrow \bot$ and therefore $I_N^N \models q$. $\qquad\square$

Lemma 6.4. *If M does not have a counterexample of length N or less, then $S_j \subseteq I_j$ and $I_j \models q$ for every $1 \leq j \leq N$.*

Proof. For every $j \leq k \leq N$ by Lemma 6.3 $S_j \subseteq I_j^k$ and $I_j^j \models q$. Since I_j is the conjunction of I_j^k for every $j \leq k \leq N$, $S_j \subseteq I_j$ and $I_j \models q$. $\qquad\square$

Lemma 6.5. *Let $\bar{I} = (I_1, I_2, \ldots, I_N)$ be the reachability vector. For every $1 \leq j < N$, $I_j \wedge TR(V, V') \Rightarrow I_{j+1}[V \leftarrow V']$.*

Proof. Definition 6.2 and 5.2 imply that $I_j = \bigwedge_{k=j}^{N} I_j^k[V^j \leftarrow V]$ and that for every $j \leq k \leq N$, $I_{j-1}^k \wedge TR(V^{j-1}, V^j) \Rightarrow I_j^k$. We get $I_j \wedge TR(V, V') \Rightarrow I_{j+1}[V \leftarrow V']$. $\qquad\square$

```
 1: function ISB(M,f)
 2:     k := 0
 3:     result = BMC(M, f, 0)
 4:     if (result == cex) then
 5:         return cex
 6:     end if
 7:     Ī = ∅        // the reachability vector
 8:     while (true) do
 9:         k = k + 1
10:         result = BMC(M, f, k)
11:         if (result == cex) then
12:             return cex
13:         end if
14:         Īᵏ = (⊤, I₁ᵏ, . . . , Iₖᵏ, ⊥)
15:         UPDATEREACHABLE(Ī,Īᵏ)
16:         if (FIXPOINTREACHED(Ī) == true) then
17:             return true
18:         end if
19:     end while
20: end function
```

Figure 5. The ISB Algorithm

Theorem 6.6. *Assume there is no path of length N or less violating f in M. If there exist $1 < j \leq N$ such that $I_j \Rightarrow \bigvee_{i=1}^{j-1} I_i$, then $M \models f$.*

Proof. By assumption, there is no path in M of length N or less that violates f. We now show that given $I_j \Rightarrow \bigvee_{i=1}^{j-1} I_i$ we can conclude that there is no path of any length violating f. Let $R = \bigvee_{i=1}^{j-1} I_i$. By assumption, $I_j \Rightarrow R$ and by Lemma 6.5, for every $1 \leq i < j$, $I_i \wedge TR(V^i, V^{i+1}) \Rightarrow I_{i+1}$. Thus, $R(V) \wedge TR(V, V') \Rightarrow R(V')$ (1). Moreover, for every $1 \leq i \leq j$ the formula $I_i \wedge \neg q$ is unsatisfiable (since $I_i \models q$ by Lemma 6.4). Hence, $R \wedge \neg q$ is unsatisfiable (2).

We can show by induction that all reachable states are in $R^* = R \vee INIT$. The base case handles initial states. This holds trivially by the definition of R^*. Now let us assume it holds for all states reachable in k steps. It should be proved for states reachable in $k+1$ steps. Let s_{k+1} be a state reachable in $k+1$ steps from an initial state. Let $\pi = s_0, s_1, \ldots, s_k, s_{k+1}$ be an initial path to s_{k+1}. By the induction hypothesis $s_k \in R^*$. From (1) we know that $R[V \leftarrow V^k] \wedge TR(V^k, V^{k+1}) \Rightarrow R[V \leftarrow V^{k+1}]$. Therefore, $s_{k+1} \in R^*$.

By assumption, $INIT \models q$ since there is no path of length N or less violating f. By that and (2), $R^* \models q$. Thus, the set of reachable states satisfy q which implies that $M \models f$.

□

Lemma 6.7. *Suppose* $M \models f$ *then there exists a bound* N *such that* $\bar{I} = (I_1, I_2, \ldots, I_N)$ *and there exists an index* $1 < j \leq N$ *such that* $I_j \Rightarrow \bigvee\limits_{i=1}^{j-1} I_i$.

Proof. The set of states S is finite. Let us define $N = j = |S| + 1$. $M \models f$ hence for every $0 \leq k \leq N$, φ^k is unsatisfiable. Thus, the interpolation-sequence $\bar{I}^k$ exists for every $0 \leq k \leq N$ and by that the reachability vector $\bar{I} = (I_1, I_2, \ldots, I_N)$ exists. Since $|S| < \infty$ we get $I_j \Rightarrow \bigvee\limits_{i=1}^{j-1} I_i$. $\qquad \square$

Theorem 6.8. *There exists a path* π *of length* N *such that* π *violates* f *if and only if ISB terminates and returns cex.*

Proof. Assume that the minimal violating path is of length N. For $N - 1$ there is no path in M violating f. By Theorem 6.6 we get that for every j such that $1 \leq j < N$, $I_j \Rightarrow \bigvee\limits_{i=1}^{j-1} I_i$ does not hold. Therefore, the algorithm cannot terminate by returning *true* in the first $N - 1$ iterations. When the algorithm reaches the N-th iteration, $BMC(M, f, N)$ will return a counterexample and the algorithm terminates. The other direction is immediate. $\qquad \square$

Theorem 6.9. *For every model* M *and a property* $f = AGq$ *there exists* N *such that ISB terminates.*

Proof. If $M \models f$ it follows by Lemma 6.7 that the algorithm terminates and returns *true*. If there is a path in M that violates f, it follows by Theorem 6.8 that the algorithm terminates and returns *cex*. $\qquad \square$

7. Interpolation Based Model Checking (IB)

In [30], *interpolation* has been suggested for the first time in order to obtain a SAT-based model checking algorithm for full verification.

The algorithm combines BMC and Craig's Interpolation [17]. Similarly to the ISB algorithm presented in the previous section, the interpolant is used to compute an over-approximation of the set of reachable states. However, the computation is done differently. As before, the algorithm concludes that the property holds when a fixpoint is reached during the computation of the reachable states and none of the computed state violates the property.

The following definition is useful in explaining the interpolation based algorithm. Recall that the verified property is of the form $f = AGq$.

Definition 7.1. For a set of states T, T is a S_j-*approximation* w.r.t N, where $1 \leq j \leq N$, if the following two conditions hold: $S_j \subseteq T$ and there is no path of length $(N - j)$ or less violating q, starting from a state $s \in T$. We write $S_j \preceq_N T$ to denote that T is a S_j-approximation w.r.t N.

The formula φ^k is used in BMC to represent a counterexample of length exactly k. This formula can be modified to represent a counterexample of length

function CHECKREACHABLE(M,f,k)
    $R = M.INIT$ // Initialize R - initial states of M
    if $(BMC(M, f, 1, k) == cex)$ **then**
        return cex
    end if
    $M' = M$
    repeat
        $A = J(V^0) \wedge TR(V^0, V^1)$
        $B = TR(V^1, V^2) \wedge \ldots \wedge TR(V^{k-1}, V^k) \wedge (\bigvee_{j=1}^{k} \neg q(V^j))$
        $J = SAT.getInterpolant(A, B)$
        if $J \subseteq R$ **then**
            return $fixpoint$
        end if
        $R = R \cup J$
        $M'.INIT = J$
    until $(BMC(M', f, 1, k) == cex)$
    return $abort$
end function

Figure 6. Computing reachable states using interpolation and BMC with a specific bound k

l for $1 \le l \le k$. We denote this formula by $\varphi^{1,k}$ and write $BMC(M, f, 1, k)$ when BMC runs on $\varphi^{1,k}$.

Formula 2. $\varphi^{1,k} = INIT(V^0) \wedge TR(V^0, V^1) \wedge TR(V^1, V^2) \wedge \ldots \wedge TR(V^{k-1}, V^k) \wedge$
$(\bigvee_{j=1}^{k} \neg q(V^j))$

Consider the following partitioning for $\varphi^{1,k}$:

- $A = INIT(V^0) \wedge TR(V^0, V^1)$
- $B = \bigwedge_{i=1}^{k-1} TR(V^i, V^{i+1}) \wedge (\bigvee_{j=1}^{k} \neg q(V^j))$.

Clearly $\varphi^{1,k} \equiv A \wedge B$. Assume that $\varphi^{1,k}$ is unsatisfiable. By the interpolation theorem [17], there exists an interpolant J_1^k which, by Definition 5.1, has the following properties:

- J_1^k is defined over the variables of $\mathcal{L}(A) \cap \mathcal{L}(B)$, namely, V^1.
- $A \Rightarrow J_1^k$. Hence, $S_1 \subseteq J_1^k$.
- $J_1^k(V_1) \wedge B$ is unsatisfiable. This means that there is no path of length $k - 1$ or less, starting from J_1^k, which violates q.

By the above we get that $S_1 \preceq_k J_1^k$. We can now proceed by replacing the initial states of M with the computed interpolant J_1^k. BMC is reinvoked with the same bound k and with the modified model $M' = (S, J_1^k[V^1 \leftarrow V], TR, L)$ in which the initial states are J_1^k. A new interpolant J_2^k is then extracted. J_2^k satisfies $S_2 \preceq_{k+1} J_2^k$. It is important to notice that J_1^k now satisfies $S_1 \preceq_{k+1} J_1^k$

since the BMC run on M' did not find a counterexample of length k starting from a state in J_1^k. In the general case we replace *INIT* with J_i^k and get J_{i+1}^k.

Figure 6 presents, for a given bound k, the computation of an over-approximated set of reachable states. Note that after L iterations of the main loop in CHECKREACHABLE we get L interpolants and for every $1 \leq i \leq L$, $S_i \preceq_{k+L} J_i^k$. All computed states are collected in R. If at any iteration, the interpolant J is contained in R, then all reachable states have been found with no violation of f. CHECKREACHABLE then returns *"fixpoint"*.

On the other hand, if a counterexample is found on a modified model, then CHECKREACHABLE(M,f,k) is aborted and CHECKREACHABLE($M,f,k+1$) is initiated. Recall that the counterexample has been obtained on an over-approximated set of states and therefore might not represent a real counterexample in the original model. In case a real counterexample exists, it will be found during a BMC run on the original model M for a larger bound.

In [37], an optimization for CHECKREACHABLE is suggested. If the current bound is k and at the L-th iteration a counterexample is found, then CHECK-REACHABLE is reinvoked with bound $k + L$ (rather than $k + 1$). This is possible since M is known not to have a counterexample of length $k + L - 1$. The usefulness of this heuristic highly depends on the type of property that is checked. On the one hand, if the property is false, this heuristic indeed results in a better performance. On the other hand, for true properties, this approach may hurt performance since a fixpoint could have been found at a lower bound than $k + L$ (e.g. $k + 1$).

8. Comparing Interpolation-Sequence Based MC to Interpolation Based MC

In the previous sections we presented two model checking algorithms which combine BMC and interpolation: the Interpolation-Sequence Based (*ISB*) [38] and the Interpolation Based (IB) [30]. In this section we analyze the differences between the algorithms. In the next section we compare them experimentally.

Both methods compute an over-approximation of the set of reachable states. However, their state traversal is different. As a result, none is better than the other in all cases. In specific cases, though, one may converge faster.

Several technical details distinguish between ISB and IB. First, the formulas from which the interpolants are extracted are different. For a given bound N, ISB uses the formula φ^N while IB uses $\varphi^{1,N}$.

Second, the approximated sets are computed in different manners. ISB computes the sets I_j incrementally and refines them after each iteration of BMC, as part of the BMC loop. IB, on the other hand, recomputes the interpolants whenever the bound is incrememnted (that is, whenever CHECKREACHABLE is called with a greater bound).

Third, ISB can be viewed as an addition to the BMC loop. At each application of BMC (with a different bound), the addition includes the extraction of an interpolation-sequence and the check if a fixpoint has been reached. Indeed, after N iterations of the BMC loop in ISB, there are N over-approximated sets of states, $I_1, \ldots, I_N$ satisfying, for each $1 \leq j \leq N$, $S_j \preceq_N I_j$.

SMC	ISB	IB
$\{S_1,\dots,S_N\}$	$\{I_1,I_2,\dots,I_N\}$ $S_i \preceq_N I_i$ After checking bounds 1 to N	$\{J_1^1,J_2^1,\dots,J_N^1\}$ $S_i \preceq_N J_i^1$ N iterations at bound 1, if possible
$\{S_1,\dots,S_{N+L}\}$	$\{I_1,\dots,I_L,\dots,I_{N+L}\}$ $S_i \preceq_{N+L} I_i$ After checking bounds 1 to $N+L$	$\{J_1^N,J_2^N,\dots,J_L^N\}$ $S_i \preceq_{N+L} J_i^N,\ (1 \le i \le L)$ L iterations at bound N, if possible

Table 1. The correlation between the interpolants computed by ISB and IB to the sets computed by SMC

On the other hand, IB consists of two nested loops. The outer loop increments the bounds while the inner loop computes over-approximated sets of reachable states. If the outer loop is at some bound $N > 1$ and the inner loop performs L iterations then there are L sets of states $J_1^N,\dots,J_L^N$, each satisfying $S_i \preceq_{N+L} J_i^N$ $(1 \le i \le L)$. Table 1 summarizes the above differences.

In summary, IB can compute, at a given bound N, as many sets as needed as long as no counterexample is found (not necessarily a real counterexample). On the other hand, for bound N, ISB can only compute N sets. However, it does not need recurrent BMC calls for each bound (only one is needed). Thus, we can conclude that in cases IB can compute all the needed sets at a low bound it performs better than ISB. However, for examples where the needed sets can only be computed using higher bounds, ISB has an advantage. This fact is reflected in the experimental results.

As mentioned before, when a counterexample exists the over-approximated sets of reachable states are not needed. If a property is violated then there exists a minimal bound N for which a violating path of length N exists. Both algorithms have to reach this bound in order to find the counterexample. Here, ISB has a clear advantage over IB. This is because after each BMC run on the original model, IB executes at least one additional BMC run on a modified model. Thus, IB invokes at least two BMC runs for each bound from 1 to $N-1$. Clearly, the second BMC run is more demanding than the inclusion check performed by ISB. In all our experiments, this kind of properties always favored ISB.

9. Implementation Details and Experimental Results

9.1. Implementation Details

Both the ISB and the IB algorithms were implemented within Intel's verification system using a SAT-based model checker which is based on Intel's in-house SAT solver *Eureka*. The interpolants are represented by a data-structure similar to an And-Inverter Graph (AIG) and are simplified and optimized using known methods such as constant propagation and sharing of redundant expressions.

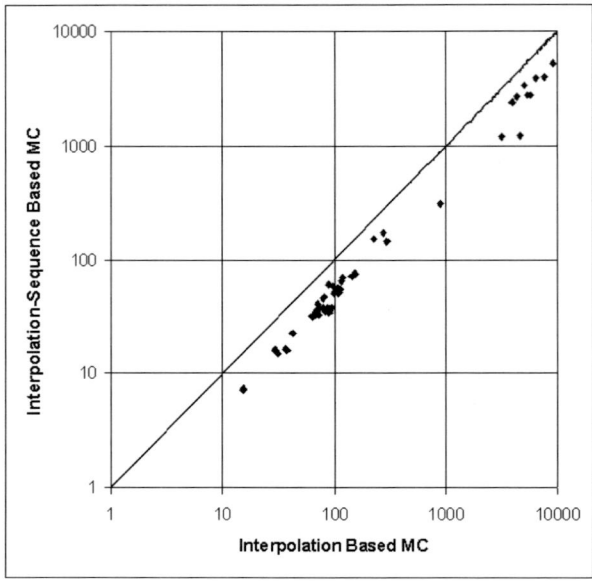

Figure 7. Runtime of falsified properties on Intel's recent micro-architecture.

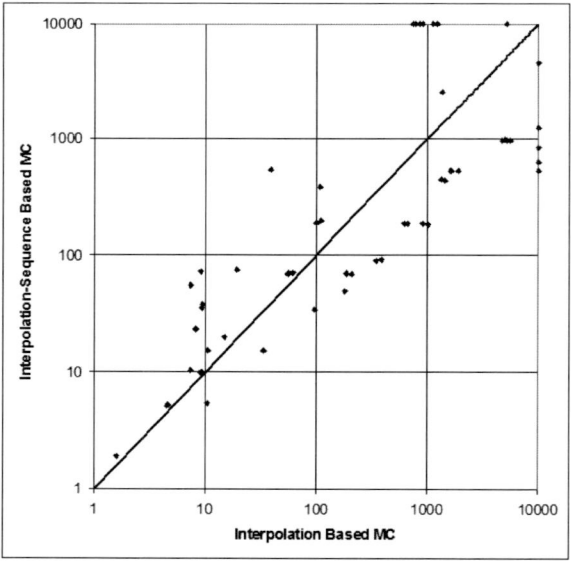

Figure 8. Runtime of verified properties on Intel's recent micro-architecture.

9.2. Experimental Results

The two algorithms have been checked on various models taken from two of Intel's recent CPU designs. The characteristics of the checked models appear in Table 3. The 136 properties chosen for the experiments were all real safety properties used to verify the correctness of the designs. The cone of influence for the properties

Name	♯Vars	B	B_{IB}	♯I	♯I_{IB}	♯BMC	♯BMC$_{IB}$	Time [s]	Time$_{IB}$ [s]
f_1	3406	16	15	136	80	16	80	970	5518
f_2	1753	9	8	45	40	9	40	91	388
f_3	1753	7	6	28	28	7	28	49	179
f_4	1753	16	15	136	94	16	94	473	1901
f_5	3406	6	5	21	13	6	13	68	208
f_6	1761	2	1	3	2	2	2	5	4
f_7	3972	3	1	6	3	3	3	19	14
f_8	2197	3	1	6	3	3	3	10	7
f_9	1629	23	6	276	39	23	39	2544	1340
f_{10}	4894	5	1	15	3	5	3	635	101

Table 2. Verified properties and their running parameters. Unindexed columns refer to the ISB algorithm; columns indexed with IB refer to the IB algorithm. ♯$Vars$ stands for the number of state variables in the cone of influence. B - bound at convergence, ♯I - number of interpolants computed, ♯BMC - number of calls to the BMC algorithm, and $Time[s]$ - the runtime in seconds.

contains thousands of state variables and tens of thousands of gates and signals. The properties vary in that some are *true* and some are *false*. During all checks, a timeout of 10,000 seconds has been set. Experiments were conducted on systems with a dual core Xeon 5160 processors (Core 2 micro-architecture) running at 3.0GHz (4MB L2 cache) with 32GB of main memory. Operating system running on the system is Linux SUSE.

Figure 7 and Figure 8 show the runtime in seconds for the two algorithms. Each point represents a property from the set of chosen properties. The X axis represents runtime for IB while the Y axis represents the runtime using ISB. We can see that the results vary. Figure 7 shows the runtime for the falsified properties. Figure 8 shows the runtime for the verified properties. All falsified properties (total of 67) favor ISB. There are five properties that can be verified by ISB and not by IB (due to timeout) and two properties that can be falsified using ISB while cannot be falsified using IB. On the other hand, there are seven properties that cannot be verified by ISB but can be verified by IB. The rest of the properties (57 total) are all verified by both algorithms.

A more accurate analysis of the algorithms is shown in Table 2 that presents running parameters (number of state variables in the cone of influence, bound at convergence, number of interpolants computed, number of calls to BMC and runtime) on various properties for both IB and ISB. For some cases, even though IB converges at a lower bound, and computes less interpolants than ISB, ISB still converges faster by means of runtime. This is due to the fact that BMC calls are computationally heavier than the extraction of the interpolants. Since IB issues more calls to BMC than ISB in these cases, the influence on its runtime is noticeable. Through all our experiments, when convergence for IB could be achieved only at high bounds, ISB always performed better while for convergence at lower bounds, IB performs better. This result is supported by the analysis presented in the previous section.

Name	♯ Latches	♯ Inputs	♯ Gates
M_1	3611	3	84570
M_2	4968	2079	133255
M_3	12806	402	89392
M_4	1672	459	11195
M_5	19213	305	146717

Table 3. Models used for testing

10. Conclusion

We presented two methods which use interpolation for SAT-based unbounded model checking. The experiments show a clear advantage of ISB when the properties are falsified. In case of verified properties, the results vary: some favor ISB while others favor IB.

Further investigation in needed in order to obtain a better understanding of the difference between the methods and to characterize the type of properties (when the properties are true) suitable for each of the methods.

Acknowledgment

The author would like to thank Yael Meller and Yakir Vizel for careful reading and useful comments.

References

[1] T. Ball and S. Rajamani. Checking temporal properties of software with boolean programs. In *In Proceedings of the Workshop on Advances in VErification (WAVE)*, July 2000.

[2] I. Beer, S. Ben-David, C. Eisner, and A. Landver. RuleBase: an industry-oriented formal verification tool. In *proceedings of the 33rd Design Automation Conference (DAC'96)*, pages 655–660. IEEE Computer Society Press, June 1996.

[3] Dirk Beyer, Thomas A. Henzinger, Ranjit Jhala, and Rupak Majumdar. Checking memory safety with Blast. In *Proceedings of the International Conference on Fundamental Approaches to Software Engineering (FASE)*, volume 3442 of *Lecture Notes in Computer Science*, pages 2–18, 2005.

[4] A. Biere and C. Artho. Liveness checking as safety checking. In *FMICS02*.

[5] A. Biere, A. Cimatti, E. M. Clarke, M. Fujita, and Y. Zhu. Symbolic model checking using SAT procedures instead of BDDs. In *proceedings of the 36rd Design Automation Conference (DAC'99)*. IEEE Computer Society Press, June 1999.

[6] A. Biere, A. Cimatti, E.M. Clarke, O. Strichman, and Y. Zhu. *Bounded Model Checking*, volume 58 of *Advances in Computers*. Elsevier, 2003.

[7] A. Biere, A. Cimatti, E.M. Clarke, and Y. Zhu. Symbolic Model Checking Without BDDs. In *Tools and Algorithms for the Construction and Analysis of Systems (TACAS'99)*, LNCS. Springer.

[8] R. E. Bryant. Graph-based algorithms for boolean function manipulation. *IEEE transactions on Computers*, C-35(8):677–691, 1986.

[9] J. R. Burch, E. M. Clarke, K. L. McMillan, D. L. Dill, and L. J. Hwang. Symbolic model checking: 10^{20} states and beyond. *Information and Computation*, 98(2):142–170, June 1992.

[10] J.R. Burch, E.M. Clarke, K.L. McMillan, D.L. Dill, and L.J. Hwang. Symbolic model checking: 10^{20} states and beyond. *Information and Computation*, 98(2):142–171, June 1992. Special Issue: Selections from 1990 IEEE Symposium on Logic in Computer Science.

[11] S. Chaki, E. Clarke, A. Groce, S. Jha, and H. Veith. Modular verification of software components in C. In *International Conference on Software Engineering (ICSE)*, pages 385–395, 2003.

[12] P. Chauhan, E. M. Clarke, and D. Kroening. Using SAT based image computation for reachability analysis. Technical Report CMU-CS-03-151, Carnegie Mellon University, School of Computer Science, 2003.

[13] A. Cimatti, E. M. Clarke, F. Giunchiglia, and M. Roveri. NUSMV: A new symbolic model checker. *STTT*, 2(4):410–425, 2000.

[14] E. Clarke and D. Kroening. Hardware verification using ANSI-C programs as a reference. In *Proceedings of ASP-DAC 2003*, pages 308–311. IEEE Computer Society Press, January 2003.

[15] E.M. Clarke, O. Grumberg, and D.A. Peled. *Model Checking*. MIT press, December 1999.

[16] J. C. Corbett, M. B. Dwyer, J. Hatcliff, S. Laubach, C. S. Pasareanu, Robby, and H. Zheng. Bandera: extracting finite-state models from java source code. In *International Conference on Software Engineering*, pages 439–448, 2000.

[17] W. Craig. Linear reasoning. a new form of the herbrand-gentzen theorem. *Journal of Symbolic Logic*, 22(3):250–268, 1957.

[18] N. Eén and N. Sörensson. An extensible sat-solver. In *SAT*, pages 502–518, 2003.

[19] R. Fraer, G. Kamhi, Z. Barukh, M.Y. Vardi, and L. Fix. Prioritized traversal: Efficient reachability analysis for verification and falsification. In *12th International Conference on Computer Aided Verification (CAV'00)*, volume 1855 of *LNCS*, Chicago, USA, July 2000.

[20] O. Grumberg, A. Schuster, and A. Yadgar. Reachability Using a Memory-Efficient All-Solutions SAT Solver. In *Fifth Inernation Conference on Formal Methods in Computer-Aided Design (FMCAD'04)*, November 2004.

[21] Z. Har'El and R. P. Kurshan. Software for analytical development of communications protocols. *AT&T Technical Journal*, 69(1):45–59, Jan.–Feb. 1990.

[22] K. Havelund and T. Pressburger. Model checking JAVA programs using JAVA PathFinder. *International Journal on Software Tools for Technology Transfer*, 2(4):366–381, 2000.

[23] G. Holzmann. *Design and Validation of Computer Protocols*. Prentice-Hall International Editors, 1991.

[24] R. Jhala and K.L. McMillan. Interpolant-Based Transition Relation Approximation. In *17th International Conference on Computer Aided Verification (CAV'05)*, LNCS 3576, Edinburgh, July 2005.

[25] O. Kupferman and M.Y. Vardi. Model checking of safety properties. In *Computer-Aided Verification (CAV'99)*, Lecture Notes in Computer Science. Springer-Verlag.

[26] J.P. Marques-Silva and K.A. Sakallah. Conflict analysis in search algorithms for propositional satisfiability. In *IEEE International Conference on Tools with Artificial Intelligence*, 1996.

[27] K. McMillan. Applications of craig interpolation to model checking. In *11th International Conference on Tools and Algorithms for the Construction and Analysis of Systems (TACAS)*, Lecture Notes in Computer Science, pages 1–12, Edinburgh, Scotland, April 2005. Springer.

[28] K. L. McMillan. *Symbolic Model Checking: An Approach to the State Explosion Problem*. Kluwer Academic Publishers, 1993.

[29] Ken L. McMillan. Applying SAT methods in unbounded symbolic model checking. In *Computer Aided Verification*, 2002.

[30] K.L. McMillan. Interpolation and SAT-based Model Checking. In *Proceedings of the 15th International Conference on Computer Aided Verification (CAV'03)*, volume 2725 of *LNCS*, Bolder, Colorado, 2003.

[31] K.L. McMillan. Lazy Abstraction with Interpolants. In *18th International Conference on Computer Aided Verification (CAV'06)*, LNCS 4144, Seattle, August 2006.

[32] K.L. McMillan and N. Amla. Automatic abstraction without counterexamples. In *Conference on Tools and Algorithms for the Construction and Analysis of Systems (TACAS'03)*,

volume 2619 of *LNCS*, pages 331–346, Warsaw, Poland, April 2003.

[33] M.W. Moskewicz, C.F. Madigan, Y. Zhao, L. Zhang, and S. Malik. Chaff: engineering an efficient SAT solver. In *39th Design Aotomation Conference (DAC'01)*, 2001.

[34] A. Pnueli. The temporal logic of programs. In *Proceedings of the Eighteenth Annual Symposium on Foundations of Computer Science (FOCS'77)*, 1977.

[35] M. Sheeran, S. Singh, and G. Staalmarck. Checking safety properties using induction and a SAT-solver. In *Third International Conference on Formal methods in Computer-Aided Design (FMCAD'00)*, Austin, Texas, November 2000.

[36] M. Sheeran and G. Staalmarck. A tutorial on stalmarck's proof procedure for propositional logic. *Formal Methods in System Design*, 16(1), January 2000.

[37] João P. Marques Silva. Improvements to the implementation of interpolant-based model checking. In *Correct Hardware Design and Verification Methods, 13th IFIP WG 10.5 Advanced Research Working Conference (CHARME'05)*, volume 3725 of *Lecture Notes in Computer Science*, pages 367–370, Saarbrücken, Germany, 2005. Springer.

[38] Y. Vizel and O. Grumberg. Interpolation-sequence based model checking. In *Ninth International Conference on Formal methods in Computer-Aided Design (FMCAD'09)*, pages 1–8, Austin, Texas, 2009.

[39] Lintao Zhang and Sharad Malik. Validating sat solvers using an independent resolution-based checker: Practical implementations and other applications. In *2003 Design, Automation and Test in Europe Conference and Exposition (DATE 2003), 3-7 March 2003, Munich, Germany*, pages 10880–10885. IEEE Computer Society, 2003.

Software Safety and Security
T. Nipkow et al. (Eds.)
IOS Press, 2012
doi:10.3233/978-1-61499-028-4-85

Interactive Proof:
Applications to Semantics

Gerwin KLEIN

NICTA and The University of New South Wales, Australia

Abstract. Building on a previous lecture in the summer school, the introduction to interactive proof, this lecture demonstrates a specific application of interactive proof assistants: the semantics of programming languages. In particular, I show how to formalise a small imperative programming language in the theorem prover Isabelle/HOL, how to define its semantics in different variations, and how to prove properties about the language in the theorem prover.

The emphasis of the lecture is not on formalising a complex language deeply, but to teach formalisation techniques and proof strategies using simple examples. To this purpose, we cover big- and small step semantics, typing and type safety, as well as a small machine language with compiler and compiler correctness proof.

Keywords. Isabelle, interactive theorem proving, semantics.

Introduction

The purpose of these lecture notes is to demonstrate a specific application of interactive proof assistants: the semantics of programming languages. The topics cover how to formalise a small imperative programming language, IMP, in the theorem prover Isabelle/HOL, how to define its semantics in different variations, and how to prove properties about the language in the theorem prover. In particular, the material includes big- and small step semantics, typing and type safety, as well as a small machine language with compiler and compiler correctness proof.

The emphasis of the lecture is not on formalising a complex language deeply, but to teach formalisation techniques and proof strategies using simple examples.

The notation is standard Isabelle notation as introduced in the previous lecture of the same summer school on interactive proof. If we use new notation for concepts from the semantics of programming languages, we will introduce this notation when it first occurs, together with how it is declared and defined in the theorem prover.

Formulas in text are typeset as follows: $x = y$. They are produced by Isabelle LaTeX antiquotations such as @{term "x = y"}. A typical definition is typeset as

```
definition successor :: "nat ⇒ nat" where "successor n ≡ n+1"
```

and a typical lemma as follows:

```
lemma successor_is_Suc: "successor n = Suc n"
```

In the remainder of this document, we begin the exposition by choosing a small programming language, by formalising its abstract syntax, and by defining the semantics of its arithmetic and boolean expressions in section 1.

In the following section 2 we define the big-step semantics of the language in Isabelle/HOL, use it to prove that the language is deterministic, and show how to prove semantic equivalence of small program fragments. On this basis, we further introduce an alternative small-step semantics of the language that allows us to more easily talk about termination and that in a more elaborate setting could be used to express properties about concurrent execution. We show how to prove equivalence to the big-step semantics.

Based on the small step semantics, section 3 introduces a formalisation of types and typing rules for the language in Isabelle. We formulate a type soundness theorem and prove that the language is type safe. As an additional application, we present a security type system that is designed to prevent unwanted information flows within a program and show its correctness by proving that is enforces a high-level non-interference property.

The final part, section 4, changes abstraction levels and introduces the formalisation of a small, simplified machine language, including its execution semantics. Again, the purpose is not to accurately model an existing machine, but to introduce a number of basic concepts. This formalisation then allows us to define a very simple, non-optimising compiler for our previous language and prove its correctness.

1. The Language

This section shows how to define the abstract syntax of the language IMP and defines the semantics of expressions.

The constructs we need in IMP for a Turing complete imperative language are variable assignment, sequential composition (semicolon), conditionals (if-then-else), and loops (while-do). We will also include the skip command that does nothing. The right-hand side of variable assignments will have some form of arithmetic expressions, and the conditions in if-then-else and while loops will take boolean expressions. A program is simply one, possibly complex, command in this language.

Again, to keep things simple, the values our language IMP computes on will be mathematical integers and booleans only.

With this in mind, we can now formalise IMP in Isabelle/HOL. We are seeking to define the set of all possible abstract syntax trees. To do this, we use a data type definition in Isabelle with one constructor for each syntactic alternative. We will use the types `com` for commands, `aexp` for arithmetic expressions, and `bexp` for boolean expressions.

The section below shows the corresponding Isabelle definitions. Both, arithmetic and boolean expressions, mention variable names (as does the assignment statement of com) for which we pick the type `string`. Any other type would work as well.

Further to variable names, we will want arithmetic expressions to be able to mention literal values such as numbers. For a more complex language we would invent a datatype with the different value types the language supports. Here, we again keep things simple and pick `int` as the only kind of value arithmetic expressions can return.

The first two type definitions below are the corresponding Isabelle commands for variable names and values.

1.1. Syntax of Expressions and Commands

```
type_synonym  val  = int
type_synonym  name = string

datatype aexp = N val | V name | Plus aexp aexp

datatype bexp =  B bool | Not bexp | And bexp bexp | Less aexp aexp

datatype
  com = SKIP
      | Assign name aexp      ("_ ::= _"  [1000, 61] 61)
      | Semi   com com        ("_; _"   [60, 61] 60)
      | If     bexp com com   ("IF _ THEN _ ELSE _"  [0, 0, 61] 61)
      | While  bexp com       ("WHILE _ DO _"  [0, 61] 61)
```

Next to introducing the abstract syntax, the definition above also adds concrete infix syntax for Isabelle to parse and print such that we can write terms of the language more conveniently. The term `"If b c₁ c₂"` for instance will be printed as `IF b THEN c₁ ELSE c₂`.

1.2. Expression Semantics

With the structure of commands and expressions defined, we can make our first definitions of semantic concepts: the meaning of expressions. Looking over the structure of arithmetic expressions in IMP, the meaning of an expression is simply an integer — the value of the expression. There is only one kind of expression that we cannot determine directly: variables. The value of a variable depends on the current state of the program. In IMP these are the only thing that we need to keep track of in the program state.

We begin by defining an Isabelle type for this state, a function from variable `name` to `val`. In more complex languages, this state space may grow to include a distinction between local variables, global variables, and a memory heap, for instance.

```
type_synonym state = "name ⇒ val"
```

We will write a denotational style semantics for expressions: a function that associates one semantic object with each syntactic entity. In our example, this means taking an arithmetic expression and returning a function from program state to value.

Going through the abstract syntax of arithmetic expressions, this function is easy to write recursively: numbers `N n` are mapped to the function that always returns n, variable lookup `V x` applies the variable name to the state, the addition syntax `Plus e1 e2` maps to the function that adds the semantics of `e1` applied to the state to the semantics of `e2` in the same state. The other operators follow the same pattern.

The definition in Isabelle is the following.

```
primrec aval :: "aexp ⇒ state ⇒ val" where
"aval (N n) _          = n" |
"aval (V x) st         = st x" |
"aval (Plus e1 e2) st  = aval e1 st + aval e2 st"
```

When writing such definitions, it is not uncommon to get them slightly wrong on the first go. It pays off to play with them a little before proceeding to any serious work.

The Isabelle command value is a great tool for evaluating sample terms. Below, we evaluate the expression that might be written as 3 + x in concrete syntax on an example state that maps alls variables to 0, apart from x which will be 7.

```
value "aval (Plus (V ''x'') (N 5)) (%x. if x = ''x'' then 7 else 0)"
```

For large states, we introduce special notation and write terms such as [''x'' → 7, ''y'' → 5] to mean that variable x maps to 7, y to 5 and all others to 0. Our evaluation example now becomes shorter and more readable.

```
value "aval (Plus (V ''x'') (N 5)) [''y'' → 7]"
```

Isabelle evaluates this to the expected 5.

After this syntax side tour, we return to defining the semantics of expressions. The definition for boolean expressions is largely analogous to the arithmetic expression case. The IMP language does not have boolean-valued variables, so the variable lookup equation is missing. Instead we have the comparison operator Less with a different syntactic category, aexp, as parameters. We simply use our arithmetic expression semantics from above to evaluate and combine these.

```
primrec bval :: "bexp ⇒ state ⇒ bool" where
"bval (B b) _          = b" |
"bval (Not b) st       = (¬ bval b st)" |
"bval (And b1 b2) st   = (bval b1 st ∧ bval b2 st)" |
"bval (Less a₁ a₂) st  = (aval a₁ st < aval a₂ st)"
```

As before, we briefly try out our definition using the value command in the same state and get the expected result True.

```
value "bval (Less (V ''y'') (Plus (N 3) (V ''x''))) [''x''→1,''y''→2]"
```

1.3. Optimisation: Simplifying Expressions

Even though we have not even defined the semantics for the whole language yet, we can already prove some first facts about expressions.

As an example, consider the the optimisation *constant folding* that many compiler perform before translating a program to simplify expressions. The idea is to evaluate the constant part of expressions as far as possible at compile time instead of at runtime. The justification is that the values of constant expressions do not depend on the program state. It therefore does not matter when they are evaluated.

We can define constant folding on arithmetic expressions by recursing over the abstract syntax. The interesting cases are binary operators such as `Plus`. For these, we recursively perform constant folding on their operands and then make a case distinction over the result: if both sides fold into constants, we return their sum as a constant result, otherwise, we return a new `Plus` with their partially folded operands. In Isabelle:

```
primrec simp_const :: "aexp ⇒ aexp" where
"simp_const (N n)        = N n" |
"simp_const (V x)        = V x" |
"simp_const (Plus e1 e2) = (case (simp_const e1, simp_const e2) of
    (N n1, N n2) ⇒ N(n1+n2) | (e1',e2') ⇒ Plus e1' e2')"
```

The correctness criterion for this function is that the folded/simplified expression should have the same semantics as the original expression. The point-wise formulation of this statement, both sides applied to the same arbitrary state, is proved by Isabelle with a single line of input.

```
theorem aval_simp_const[simp]: "aval (simp_const a) st = aval a st"
```

The proof follows a general pattern for statements about primitive recursive functions. We start with induction of the parameter that the function recurses over. This case is particularly nice, because both functions `simp_const` and `aval` follow the same recursion pattern. The `auto` proof method in the second part performs a combination of term rewriting and classical logic reasoning on all subgoals that are left by the induction (one for each constructor). The parameter `split: aexp.split` tells `auto` to automatically perform case distinction on case constructs of type `aexp`. We add it, because the `simp_const` contains such case constructs and the proof will have to go through these cases to make progress. Isabelle comes with enough proof setup about arithmetic to complete the rest of the proof automatically.

By declaring the lemma `[simp]`, we directly set up automation for further proofs involving the term pattern `aval (simp_const a) st`, telling the Isabelle simplifier to replace it with the simpler right-hand side of the equation.

A good automation setup is essential for keeping proofs short and manageable. Theorems that are obviously useful as simplification rules should be declared as such. Overusing this feature can quickly lead to frustrating non-terminating automatic proof methods, though, so care is needed.

In a larger development it pays off to come back to the basic definitions and design appropriate normal forms for combinations of functions, and to design sets of simplification rules for reaching these normal forms automatically.

This concludes the section on the syntax of IMP and the semantics of expressions. As is usual in the formal treatment of programming languages, we have focussed on the abstract syntax of the language instead of the concrete syntax. We have used the expression semantics for evaluating sample expressions and for proving the correctness of a simple constant folding algorithm for expressions.

We also definitions of recursive functions together with a common proof schema for simple properties about them. The proofs so far have turned out very simple and automatic. This was because the properties we were interested aligned nicely with the corresponding definitions and induction principles.

All of the definitions so far have been executable operations on executable data types. In principle, we could therefore automatically generate SML, OCaml, or Haskell code from them if we intended to use or validate the semantics in an external tool.

2. Semantics

This section shows two ways to define the semantics of commands in IMP: *big-step* and *small-step* operational semantics. Big-step semantics is also called *natural semantics* and small-step may occur under the name *structural operational semantics* (SOS).

Big-step semantics is simpler to define, with fewer rules and cases to consider in proofs, but it makes it hard to distinguish issues such as termination from undefined execution. Small-step semantics will result in more rules and higher proof effort for some properties, but its finer-grained structure allows us to talk about termination more naturally, and to define the interleaved execution of programs in a concurrent setup.

In the following, we first define the big-step semantics for IMP, use it to prove small language properties such as deterministic execution, define an explicit termination relation, define the small-step semantics for IMP, and finally prove that the two semantics definitions are equivalent. This means, for further properties, we are free to chose whichever representation is more convenient for the proof at hand.

2.1. Big-Step Semantics of Commands

2.1.1. The Definition

In an operational semantics setting, the semantics of a program is captured as a relation. In big-step semantics, the relation is between program, initial state, and final state. Intermediate states during the execution of the program are not visible in the formal construct, the whole program is executed in one big step.

To formalise this concept in the theorem prover, we recall that a relation is simply a set of tuples, and to say that a command c executes in state s to some state s' is to say that the tripe (c, s, s') is an element of this set that defines the semantics of IMP.

Textbook-style semantics formalisations usually introduce concrete syntax to write such judgements in a more intuitive form. We use Isabelle's syntax mechanism to do the same here and will write $(c, s) \Rightarrow s'$ for (c, s, s') is in the `big_step` relation.

We will use an inductive definition to define which triples this relation is made up of. For each syntactic construct we will give a number of rules that enumerate the possible executions for the construct in pattern matching style.

```
inductive
    big_step :: "com × state ⇒ state ⇒ bool" (infix "⇒" 55)
where
    Skip:     "(SKIP, s) ⇒ s"
|   Assign:   "(x ::= a, s) ⇒ s(x := aval a s)"

|   Semi:     "(c1, s1) ⇒ s2    ⟹    (c2, s2) ⇒ s3    ⟹
              (c1; c2,  s1) ⇒ s3"
```

```
| IfTrue:    "bval b s  ⟹   (c1,s) ⇒ s'  ⟹
                (IF b THEN c1 ELSE c2, s) ⇒ s' "
| IfFalse:  "¬bval b s  ⟹   (c2,s) ⇒ s'  ⟹
                (IF b THEN c1 ELSE c2, s) ⇒ s' "

| WhileFalse: "¬bval b s ⟹ (WHILE b DO c,s) ⇒ s"
| WhileTrue:  "bval b s1  ⟹   (c,s1) ⇒ s2  ⟹   (WHILE b DO c, s2) ⇒ s3
                ⟹ (WHILE b DO c, s1) ⇒ s3"
```

This is the full definition of the big-step semantics for IMP.

The rules given in the definition are the introduction rules for the inductive definition big_step. Note that instead of a set, we defined a predicate instead which is isomorphic to the intended set, but slightly more convenient to use. We use a tuple as the left side of our $(\_,\_) \Rightarrow \_$ syntax and only declare the arrow $\Rightarrow$ as new.

Going through each of the named rules, they admit the following executions in IMP.

- If the command is $SKIP$, the initial and final state must be the same.
- If the command is a variable assignment $x ::= a$, and the initial state is s, then the final state is the same state s where the value of variable x is replaced by the evaluation of the expression a in state s.
- If the command is a sequential composition, rule $Semi$ says the combined command $c1;\ c2$ started in $s1$ executes to $s3$ if the the first command executes in $s1$ to some intermediate state $s2$ and $c2$ takes this $s2$ to $s3$.
- The conditional is the first command that has two rules, depending on the value of its boolean expression in the current state s. If that value is $True$, then the $IfTrue$ rule says that the execution ends in the same state s' that the command $c1$ results in if started in s. The $IfFalse$ rule does the same for the command $c2$ in the $False$ case.
- While loops are slightly more interesting. If the condition evaluates to false, the whole loop is skipped, which is expressed in rule $WhileFalse$. If the condition evaluations in state $s1$ to $True$, however, and the body c of the loop takes this state $s1$ to some intermediate state $s3$, *and* if the same while loop, started in $s2$ ends in $s3$, then the entire loop also terminates in $s3$ if started in $s1$.

The rules of the inductive definition above can be directly used as introduction rules in proofs. However, a better way to execute the big-step rules is to use Isabelle's code generator. The following command tells it to generate code for the predicate $op \Rightarrow$ and make thus make the predicate available in the values command.

code_pred big_step .

Functions in general cannot easily be printed, so we need to convert the interesting part of the state to something printable such as a list to make use of the code generator here:

values "{map t [''x'', ''y'']|t. (''x'' ::= N 2, λ_. 0) ⇒ t}"

This has the result $\{[2, 0]\}$.

In semantics text books, inductive definitions are often presented in graphical proof rule form. If the correct package is included, Isabelle antiquotations can produce the same layout in LATEX. For example, the antiquotation @{thm [mode=Rule] Semi} produces the following layout:

$$\frac{(c1, \ s1) \ \Rightarrow \ s2 \qquad (c2, \ s2) \ \Rightarrow \ s3}{(c1; \ c2, \ s1) \ \Rightarrow \ s3}$$

Finding or designing the right set of introduction rules for a language is not necessarily hard. The idea is to have at least one rule per syntactic construct and to add further rules when case distinctions become necessary. For each single rule, you start with the conclusion, for instance *(c1; c2, s)* ⇒ *s'*, and then construct the assumptions of the rule by thinking about which conditions have to be true about *s*, *s'*, and the parameters of the abstract syntax constructor, in the example *c1* and *c2*, for the conclusion to be true. If the assumptions collapse to an equation about *s'* as in the *SKIP* and *x ::= a* case, *s'* can be replaced directly.

Introduction rules are often written for readability and easy intuition, not necessarily for the most efficient automatic proof setup. It often pays off to derive further rules that aid automation in the rest of the formalisation. We do this for the big step rules of IMP below.

2.1.2. Proof and Automation Setup

The most important proof tool for inductive definition is rule induction. After splitting pairs into their components, we get the folllowing rule for our definition:

```
⟦(c, s) ⇒ s'; ⋀s. P SKIP s s; ⋀x a s. P (x ::= a) s (s(x → aval a s));
 ⋀c1 s1 s2 c2 s3.
   ⟦(c1, s1) ⇒ s2; P c1 s1 s2; (c2, s2) ⇒ s3; P c2 s2 s3⟧
   ⟹ P (c1; c2) s1 s3;
 ⋀b s c1 s' c2.
   ⟦bval b s; (c1, s) ⇒ s'; P c1 s s'⟧
   ⟹ P (IF b THEN c1 ELSE c2) s s';
 ⋀b s c2 s' c1.
   ⟦¬ bval b s; (c2, s) ⇒ s'; P c2 s s'⟧
   ⟹ P (IF b THEN c1 ELSE c2) s s';
 ⋀b s c. ¬ bval b s ⟹ P (WHILE b DO c) s s;
 ⋀b s1 c s2 s3.
   ⟦bval b s1; (c, s1) ⇒ s2; P c s1 s2; (WHILE b DO c, s2) ⇒ s3;
   P (WHILE b DO c) s2 s3⟧
   ⟹ P (WHILE b DO c) s1 s3⟧
 ⟹ P c s s'
```

It reads: if we know *(c, s)* ⇒ *s'*, then proving any property *P* about *c*, *s*, and *s'*, can be reduced to proving the same property about each inductive case. The rule *Skip* and *Assign* provide the base cases, the step cases are allowed to assume *P* for their inductive preconditions.

The second common proof principle for inductive definitions are the introduction rules themselves. We tell Isabelle to use all of them as logic introduction rules. For the recursive rules this does risk non-termination and may require backtracking, so we declare them as unsafe using [intro] instead of the more insistent [intro!].

declare *big_step.intros [intro]*

The rules of `big_step` are syntax directed, i.e. each of the syntactic categories is covered by its own distinct set of rules. This means we can easily use the rules in both directions. This technique is called rule inversion. We can tell Isabelle to automatically generate inversion rules for each particular conclusion pattern using the `inductive_cases` command. All of these rules are safe elimination rules for the classical logic reasoner, so we declare them as such and enable it to perform rule inversion for these patterns automatically.

```
inductive_cases skipE [elim!]:    "(SKIP, s) ⇒ s'"
inductive_cases assignE [elim!]:  "(x ::= a, s) ⇒ s'"
inductive_cases semiE [elim!]:    "(c0; c1, s) ⇒ s'"
inductive_cases ifE [elim!]:      "(IF b THEN c0 ELSE c1, s) ⇒ s'"
inductive_cases whileE [elim]:    "(WHILE b DO c, s) ⇒ s'"
```

The rule for assignment for instance says that if the pattern $(x ::= a, s) \Rightarrow s'$ occurs in an assumption, then by rule inversion s' must be $s(x \rightarrow aval\ a\ s)$:

$$[\![(x ::= a, s) \Rightarrow s';\ s' = s(x \rightarrow aval\ a\ s)]\!] \Longrightarrow P$$

The rule $semiE$ shows a recursive case:

$$[\![(c0; c1, s) \Rightarrow s';\ \bigwedge s2.\ [\![(c0, s) \Rightarrow s2;\ (c1, s2) \Rightarrow s']\!]]\!] \Longrightarrow P]\!] \Longrightarrow P$$

Using these elimation rules, we can additionally prove equations for use with Isabelle's simplifier can use. All of these proofs are already automatic, but they make essential use of both the elimination rules and also the potentially unsafe introduction rules. What we have achieved is that the simplifier can now do these steps on its own when just invoked with `simp`. This is gives more fine-grained control and is therefore preferable to the `auto` method that often tries too hard and to does too much.

This concludes our automation setup of the big step semantics. We have tuned the induction principle for the expected application, we have provided automated introduction rules, elimination rules, and finally simplification rules for common cases.

2.1.3. Equivalence of statements

In this section we apply our setup to first define semantic equivalence of commands and then show a number of simple instances of equivalent statements.

We call two statements c and c' equivalent wrt. the big-step semantics when c *started in s terminates in s' iff c' started in the same s also terminates in the same s'.* Formally:

```
definition
  equiv_c :: "com ⇒ com ⇒ bool" (infix "∼" 50) where
  "c ∼ c' = (∀ s s'. (c, s) ⇒ s' ⟷ (c', s) ⇒ s')"
```

Again, we provide proof rules for reasoning about equivalence automatically. The introduction rule is safe, so we declare it as such, the destruction rules depend on which direction to take, so we will supply them manually when needed.

```
lemma equivI [intro!]: "(⋀s s'. (c, s) ⟹ s' = (c', s) ⟹ s') ⟹ c ~ c'"
lemma equivD1: "c ~ c' ⟹ (c, s) ⟹ s' ⟹ (c', s) ⟹ s'"
lemma equivD2: "c ~ c' ⟹ (c', s) ⟹ s' ⟹ (c, s) ⟹ s'"
```

Experimenting with this concept, we see that Isabelle manages to prove many simple equivalences automatically. Such rules could be used for instance to transform source-level programs in a compiler optimisation phase.

```
lemma while_unfold:
  "(WHILE b DO c) ~ (IF b THEN c; WHILE b DO c ELSE SKIP)"
lemma triv_if: "(IF b THEN c ELSE c) ~ c"
lemma commute_if:
  "(IF b2 THEN (IF b1 THEN c11 ELSE c2) ELSE (IF b1 THEN c12 ELSE c2))
   ~
   (IF b1 THEN (IF b2 THEN c11 ELSE c12) ELSE c2)"
```

Note that we have neglected to provide an analogous equivalence definition for expressions. If we intended to reason more deeply about program equivalence, we would need to provide these and we would allow rewriting in expressions as well.

In IMP, loops that are trivially non-terminating, because their loop condition is always true, are indistinguishable in the big step semantics:

```
lemma while_never: "(c, s) ⟹ u ⟹ c ≠ WHILE (B True) DO c1"
lemma equiv_while_True: "(WHILE (B True) DO c1) ~ (WHILE (B True) DO c2)"
```

This property is the first strong indication that big-step semantics, while nice to write and easy to reason about, may not be the right tool for all language properties. The main reason for this is that it does not talk about intermediate states or any intermediate input/output of the program. Many event-based programs have a loop of the form `WHILE B True DO c`, and of course it matters what precisely `c` is. Yet our lemma above says `c` can be replaced arbitrarily without effect. The effect of the replacement is not observable in the final state (which does not exist), but it is observable in intermediate states. If such properties are of interest, the more fine-grained small-step semantics is a better formal analysis tool.

2.1.4. Execution is deterministic

In this section we investigate properties of the language itself. Having defined the semantics of the language as a relation, it is not immediately obvious for instance if execution in this language is deterministic or not. None of the `big_step` introduction rules in isolation would preclude multiple nondeterministic execution. On the other hand, we have not provided any particular rule that would introduce nondeterminism into IMP.

Formally, the language is deterministic if for any two executions of the same statement and we will always arrive in the same terminal state if we start in the same initial state.

With our automation setup for `big_step` this is a one-line proof – almost too easy for Isabelle:

```
theorem deterministic: "⟦ (c, s) ⟹ t; (c, s) ⟹ u ⟧ ⟹ u = t"
```

Note that the automation in this proof is not completely obvious. Using `auto` for instance leads to non-termination, but the backtracking capabilities of `blast` manage to solve each subgoal. To discover that `blast+` works, one would try each case separately and if `blast` works for the interesting cases, attempt `blast+` to cover all.

In lectures about semantics of programming languages the property that IMP is deterministic is often taken as a first simple proof to introduce rule induction and language properties. Solving this proof fully automatically is counterproductive for such a demonstration. Isabelle's Isar language allows us to provide level of readable detail similar to what would be presented in a lecture, but also allows us to hide boring cases by using automation.

The following proof demonstrates this technique. It is not necessary to step through the proof in detail to explain it in a lecture, but often using the tool in a live demonstration makes the material more accessible.

```
theorem
  "(c, s) ⇒ t ⟹ (c, s) ⇒ u ⟹ u = t"
proof (induct arbitrary: u rule: big_step.induct)
    — the simple SKIP case for demonstration:
    fix s u assume "(SKIP, s) ⇒ u"
    thus "u = s" by blast
next
    — and the only really interesting case, WHILE:
    fix b c s s1 s2 u
    assume "IHc": "⋀u. (c, s) ⇒ u ⟹ u = s2"
    assume "IHw": "⋀u. (WHILE b DO c, s2) ⇒ u ⟹ u = s1"

    assume "bval b s" and "(WHILE b DO c, s) ⇒ u"
    then obtain s' where
        c: "(c, s) ⇒ s'" and
        w: "(WHILE b DO c, s') ⇒ u"
      by auto

    from c "IHc" have "s' = s2" by blast
    with w "IHw" show "u = s1" by blast
qed blast+ — prove the rest automatically
```

This concludes the section about deterministic execution and thereby the section on big-step semantics.

In this section, we have defined the big-step semantics of IMPinductively, we have set up Isabelle's automation capabilities for it, and we have explored some first proofs about properties of the language.

2.2. Small-Step Semantics of Commands

2.2.1. The transition relation

This section introduces the small-step semantics of IMP. The big-step semantics gave us the completed execution of a program from its initial state. Short of inspecting the derivation tree of big-step introduction rules, it did not allow us to explicitly observe intermediate execution states. This also made it hard for us to talk about termination.

If we want to observe partial executions, for instance if we would like to talk about the interleaved execution of concurrent programs, we can make them explicit using small-step semantics. The main idea for representing a partial execution is to introduce a concept of how far execution has progressed in the program. Traditionally, for a high-level language like IMP, we modify the type of the big-step judgement from $com \times state \Rightarrow state \Rightarrow bool$ to something like $com \times state \Rightarrow com \times state \Rightarrow bool$. The second $com \times state$ component of the judgement is the result state of one small, atomic execution step together with a modified program statement that represents what still has to be executed.

　　　The idea is easiest to understand by looking at the set of rules. They define one atomic execution step. The execution of a program is a sequence of such steps.

```
inductive
   small_step :: "com * state ⇒ com * state ⇒ bool" (infix "→" 55)
where
Assign:   "(x ::= a, s) → (SKIP, s(x := aval a s))" |

Semi1:    "(SKIP;c₂,s) → (c₂,s)" |
Semi2:    "(c₁,s) → (c₁',s') ⟹ (c₁;c₂,s) → (c₁';c₂,s')" |

IfTrue:   "bval b s ⟹ (IF b THEN c₁ ELSE c₂,s) → (c₁,s)" |
IfFalse:  "¬bval b s ⟹ (IF b THEN c₁ ELSE c₂,s) → (c₂,s)" |

While:    "(WHILE b DO c,s) → (IF b THEN c; WHILE b DO c ELSE SKIP,s)"
```

Going through the rules above we see that variable assignment is an atomic step. We represent the terminated program by $SKIP$. There are two rule for the semicolon: either the first part is fully executed already (signified by $SKIP$), then we can just continue with the second part, or the first part still can be executed further, in which case we perform that execution step and return its result. An if-then-else reduces either to the if-branch or the else-branch, depending on the value of the condition. The final rule is the while loop: we just unroll the loop once. The subsequent execution steps will take care of testing the condition and possibly execution the body.

　　　Had we wanted to observe partial execution of arithmetic or boolean expressions, we could have introduced a small-step semantics for these as well and made the corresponding small-step rules for assignment, if, and while non-atomic in the same style as the semicolon rules.

　　　Before we can define program execution as a sequence of small-step semantics steps, we make a small detour to define the transitive, reflexive closure of binary predicates. Isabelle already comes with such a definition for relations. We briefly re-do it for predicates below to be able to keep big-step and small-step judgements analogous.

```
inductive
   star :: "('a ⇒ 'a ⇒ bool) ⇒ 'a ⇒ 'a ⇒ bool"
for r where
refl:  "star r x x" |
step:  "r x y ⟹ star r y z ⟹ star r x z"
```

The main property we will need is transitivity which is easily shown by rule induction:

```
lemma star_trans: "star r x y ⟹ star r y z ⟹ star r x z"
```

A common case is concluding that if two elements are in the base predicate, they are in the closure. Again this rule is useful for proof search and for simplification. It may require backtracking—not every time we see `star r x y` it is enough to prove `r x y`.

```
lemma step1[simp, intro]: "r x y ⟹ star r x y"
```

Returning from our excursion back to theory `Small_Step`, we can now define the execution of a program as the transitive, reflexive closure of the `small_step` judgement:

```
abbreviation
   small_steps :: "com * state ⇒ com * state ⇒ bool" (infix "→*" 55)
   where "x →* y == star small_step x y"
```

2.2.2. Executability

As with the other relations we have defined, we make the rules available to the code generator for looking at examples. This time, we will get multiple elements in the set returned by the `values` command. They correspond to all partial executions of the program.

```
values "{(c',map t [''x'',''y'',''z''])  |c' t.
    (''x'' ::= V ''z''; ''y'' ::= V ''x'',
    [''x'' → 3, ''y'' → 7, ''z'' → 5]) →* (c',t)}"
```

The result Isabelle displays contains four steps, starting with the original program in the initial state, going through partial execution of the the two assignments, and ending with the final state of the final program *SKIP*: `{ (''x'' ::= V ''z''; ''y'' ::= V ''x'', [3, 7, 5]), (SKIP; ''y'' ::= V ''x'', [5, 7, 5]), (''y'' ::= V ''x'', [5, 7, 5]), (SKIP, [5, 5, 5]) }`

2.2.3. Proof infrastructure

As always, we start the proof part in theory Small_Step with setting up automation and infrastructure.

We make the introduction rules available for the simplifier and for proof search. For the rules with assumptions this is not entirely safe and might lead to non-termination in proof methods, but we take that risk to gain more automation when it works. After including the usual setup for rule inversion using the command `inductive_cases`, we are already done. As a test for the setup, we prove that, as in the big-step case, the rules give us a deterministic language.

```
lemma deterministic:
   "cs → cs' ⟹ cs → cs'' ⟹ cs'' = cs'"
```

The proof is as automatic as the big-step case.

2.2.4. Equivalence with big-step semantics

Having defined and set up an alternative semantics for the same language, the first interesting question is of course if our definitions are equivalent and describe the same executions.

The game plan for this proof is to show both directions separately: if there is a big-step execution, there is an equivalent small-step execution and vice versa.

The proof of the first direction is by rule induction on the big-step judgement. For each case we then construct the equivalent small-step sequence. In the semicolon case, we will need to conclude from the two separate small-step executions of $c1$ and $c2$ that $c1$; $c2$ will terminate in the same result. We extract this into a separate lemma which needs another small helper lemma that allows us to lift an execution of $(c1, s) \rightarrow *$ $(c1', s')$ into a semicolon context.

```
lemma star_semi2: "(c1,s) →∗ (c1',s') ⟹ (c1;c2,s) →∗ (c1';c2,s')"
lemma semi_comp: "⟦ (c1,s1) →∗ (SKIP,s2); (c2,s2) →∗ (SKIP,s3) ⟧
    ⟹ (c1;c2, s1) →∗ (SKIP,s3)"
```

The following proof is now the rule induction on the big-step semantics. The precise lemma statement is that if $(c, s) \Rightarrow t$ then $(c, s) \rightarrow * (SKIP, t)$, that is, there is a sequence of small steps that terminates successfully in $SKIP$ with the same state t. The proof corresponds to one written on the black board where one would construct chains of $\rightarrow$ and $\rightarrow *$ steps.

```
lemma big_to_small:
  "(c,s) ⟹ t ⟹ (c,s) →∗ (SKIP,t)"
proof (induct rule: big_step_induct)
  fix s show "(SKIP,s) →∗ (SKIP,s)" by simp
next
  fix x a s show "(x ::= a,s) →∗ (SKIP, s(x := aval a s))" by auto
next
  fix c1 c2 s1 s2 s3
  assume "(c1,s1) →∗ (SKIP,s2)" and "(c2,s2) →∗ (SKIP,s3)"
  thus "(c1;c2, s1) →∗ (SKIP,s3)" by (rule semi_comp)
next
  fix s::state and b c0 c1 t
  assume "bval b s"
  hence "(IF b THEN c0 ELSE c1,s) → (c0,s)" by simp
  also assume "(c0,s) →∗ (SKIP,t)"
  finally show "(IF b THEN c0 ELSE c1,s) →∗ (SKIP,t)" .  —— = by assumption
next
  fix s::state and b c0 c1 t
  assume "¬bval b s"
  hence "(IF b THEN c0 ELSE c1,s) → (c1,s)" by simp
  also assume "(c1,s) →∗ (SKIP,t)"
  finally show "(IF b THEN c0 ELSE c1,s) →∗ (SKIP,t)" .
next
  fix b c and s::state
  assume b: "¬bval b s"
  let ?if = "IF b THEN c; WHILE b DO c ELSE SKIP"
  have "(WHILE b DO c,s) → (?if, s)" by blast
  also have "(?if,s) → (SKIP, s)" by (simp add: b)
  finally show "(WHILE b DO c,s) →∗ (SKIP,s)" by auto
next
  fix b c s s' t
  let ?w  = "WHILE b DO c"
  let ?if = "IF b THEN c; ?w ELSE SKIP"
  assume w: "(?w,s') →∗ (SKIP,t)"
  assume c: "(c,s) →∗ (SKIP,s')"
```

```
  assume b: "bval b s"
  have "(?w,s) → (?if, s)" by blast
  also have "(?if, s) → (c; ?w, s)" by (simp add: b)
  also have "(c; ?w,s) →* (SKIP,t)" by (rule semi_comp[OF c w])
  finally show "(WHILE b DO c,s) →* (SKIP,t)" by auto
qed
```

Each case of the induction could also be proved automatically.

The other direction of the proof is even shorter. It cannot necessarily be called the easier direction, though, because the proof idea is less obvious. The main statement we want is $(c, s) \to* (SKIP, t) \implies (c, s) \Rightarrow t$. Our first attempt would be rule induction on the derivation of the transitive closure. It quickly becomes clear that the lemma statement is too specialised for this. If we only consider steps that terminate in $SKIP$, we cannot chain them in the induction. The trick, as always, is to suitably generalise the lemma statement.

In this case, if we generalise $SKIP$ to an arbitrary c', the statement does not make sense any more, because the big-step semantics does not have any concept for an intermediate c'. The key observation is that the big-step semantics always executes the program fully and the state (c', s') is just an intermediate state in this execution. That means, executing the 'rest' (c', s') and executing the original (c, s) should give us precisely the same result in the big-step semantics. Formally: $[(c, s) \to* (c', s'); (c', s') \Rightarrow t] \implies (c, s) \Rightarrow t$. If we substitute $SKIP$ for c', we get that s' must be t and we are back to what we where out to show originally.

This new statement can now be proved by induction on the transitive closure. We extract the step case into its own lemma which Isabelle proves automatically after rule induction. It is the same statement, only for a single step in the small-step semantics.

```
lemma small1_big_continue:
  "(c,s) → (c',s') ⟹ (c',s') ⇒ t ⟹ (c,s) ⇒ t"
lemma small_big_continue:
  "(c,s) →* (c',s') ⟹ (c',s') ⇒ t ⟹ (c,s) ⇒ t"
lemma small_to_big: "(c,s) →* (SKIP,t) ⟹ (c,s) ⇒ t"
```

Both directions together let us conclude the equivalence we were aiming at.

```
theorem big_iff_small:   "(c,s) ⇒ t = (c,s) →* (SKIP,t)"
```

3. Types

3.1. A Typed Language

3.1.1. A New Language

In this section we show a very basic static type system as a typical application the formal definition of language semantics.

The idea is to define the type system formally and to use the semantics for stating and proving its soundness.

The IMP language we have used so far is not well-suited for this proof, because it has only one type of values. This is not enough for even a simple type system. To make things at least slightly non-trivial, we invent a new language that computes on reals as well as integers. This means our value type now has two alternatives:

```
datatype val = Iv int | Rv real
```

Variable names and state are as before:

```
type_synonym name = string
type_synonym state = "name ⇒ val"
```

and arithmetic expressions now have two kinds of constants: `int` and `real`.

```
datatype aexp =  Ic int | Rc real | V name | Plus aexp aexp
```

In contrast to vanilla IMP, we can now write arithmetic expressions that make no sense and have no semantics. The expression `Plus (Ic 1) (Rc 3)` for example is trying to add an integer to a real number. Assuming for a moment that these are fundamentally incompatible types that cannot possibly be reconciled in an addition, we would like to express in our semantics that this is not a defined program. One alternative would be a denotational style as before that returns `val option` with `None` for the undefined cases, but that would mean we would have to explicitly consider all undefined cases. Instead, we write an operational semantics judgement for arithmetic expressions. Since we are not interested in intermediate executions at this point, we are happy with a big-step style.

The judgement relates an expression, the state it is evaluated in, and the value it is evaluated to. We refrain from introducing additional syntax and call this judgement `taval` for *typed arithmetic value* of an expression.

```
inductive taval :: "aexp ⇒ state ⇒ val ⇒ bool" where
"taval (Ic i) s (Iv i)" |
"taval (Rc r) s (Rv r)" |
"taval (V x) s (s x)" |
"taval a1 s (Iv i1) ⟹ taval a2 s (Iv i2) ⟹
   taval (Plus a1 a2) s (Iv(i1+i2))" |
"taval a₁ s (Rv r1) ⟹ taval a2 s (Rv r2) ⟹
   taval (Plus a1 a2) s (Rv(r1+r2))"
```

The definition is straight forward. The interesting cases are the ones that are not there. For instance, there is no rule to add a `real` to an `int`. We only needed to provide rules for the cases that make sense and we have implicitly defined what the error cases are.

The syntax for boolean expressions remains unchanged wrt. IMP. The evaluation, however, of boolean expressions is different to IMP. If we want to make use of the operational semantics for arithmetic expressions that we just defined, we need to use the same style for boolean expressions. Even though the case distinction for boolean expressions is complete, i.e. the rules cover everything and there are no error cases left, we have implicitly correctly propagated the evaluation errors from arithmetic expressions: if there is no execution for an arithmetic expression in state s, there is no execution for a boolean expression that mentions it in the same state.

```
inductive tbval :: "bexp ⇒ state ⇒ bool ⇒ bool" where
```

```
"tbval (B bv) s bv" |
"tbval b s bv ⟹ tbval (Not b) s (¬ bv)" |
"tbval b1 s bv1 ⟹ tbval b2 s bv2 ⟹ tbval (And b1 b2) s (bv1 & bv2)" |
"taval a1 s (Iv i1) ⟹ taval a2 s (Iv i2) ⟹
  tbval (Less a1 a2) s (i1 < i2)" |
"taval a1 s (Rv r1) ⟹ taval a2 s (Rv r2) ⟹
  tbval (Less a1 a2) s (r1 < r2)"
```

The syntax for commands is again unchanged. The definition of the small-step semantics for commands is almost unchanged as well. It merely refers to the new judgements for arithmetic and boolean expressions.

Small-step semantics are better suited for type soundness proofs, because error states are explicitly visible in intermediate states: if there is an error, the semantics gets stuck in a non-terminal program configuration with no further progress possible.

```
inductive
    small_step :: "(com × state) ⇒ (com × state) ⇒ bool" (infix "→" 55)
where
Assign:   "taval a s v ⟹ (x ::= a, s) → (SKIP, s(x := v))" |

Semi1:    "(SKIP;c,s) → (c,s)" |
Semi2:    "(c1,s) → (c1',s') ⟹ (c1;c2,s) → (c1';c2,s')" |

IfTrue:   "tbval b s True ⟹ (IF b THEN c1 ELSE c2,s) → (c1,s)" |
IfFalse:  "tbval b s False ⟹ (IF b THEN c1 ELSE c2,s) → (c2,s)" |

While:    "(WHILE b DO c,s) → (IF b THEN c; WHILE b DO c ELSE SKIP,s)"
```

As before, the execution of a program is a sequence of small steps.

```
abbreviation
    small_steps :: "com * state ⇒ com * state ⇒ bool" (infix "→*" 55)
    where "x →* y == star small_step x y"
```

3.1.2. The Type System

Having defined the new language and its semantics above in a way such that execution can fail or get stuck, we are now defining a type system that statically determines safe programs, i.e. programs that are guaranteed not to get into stuck or error states.

The type system we use for this is very rudimentary, it has only two types: int and real, written as the constructors Ity and Rty.

```
datatype ty = Ity | Rty
```

The purpose of the type system is to keep track of the type of each variable and to allow only compatible combinations in expressions. For this purpose, we define a typing environment as a function from variable name to type.

```
type_synonym tyenv = "name ⇒ ty"
```

With this, we can give typing rules for arithmetic expressions. The idea is simple: constants have fixed type, variables have the type the environment Γ prescribes, and $Plus$

can be typed with type τ if both operands have the same type τ. The formalisation is straight forward.

```
inductive atyping :: "tyenv ⇒ aexp ⇒ ty ⇒ bool"
  ("(1_/ ⊢/ (_ :/ _))" [50,0,50] 50)
where
Ic_ty:    "Γ ⊢ Ic i : Ity" |
Rc_ty:    "Γ ⊢ Rc r : Rty" |
V_ty:     "Γ ⊢ V x : Γ x" |
Plus_ty:  "Γ ⊢ a1 : τ ⟹ Γ ⊢ a2 : τ ⟹ Γ ⊢ Plus a1 a2 : τ"
```

The typing rules for booleans are even simpler. We do not need a result type, because it will always be bool. For the most part, we just need to capture that boolean expressions are well-typed if their subexpression are well-typed. The interesting case is the connection to arithmetic expressions in `Less`. Here we demand that both operands have the same type τ.

```
inductive btyping :: "tyenv ⇒ bexp ⇒ bool" (infix "⊢" 50)
where
B_ty: "Γ ⊢ B bv" |
Not_ty: "Γ ⊢ b ⟹ Γ ⊢ Not b" |
And_ty: "Γ ⊢ b1 ⟹ Γ ⊢ b2 ⟹ Γ ⊢ And b1 b2" |
Less_ty: "Γ ⊢ a1 : τ ⟹ Γ ⊢ a2 : τ ⟹ Γ ⊢ Less a1 a2"
```

Similarly, commands are well-typed if their subexpressions are well typed. The only non-regular case here is assignment: we demand that the arithmetic expression has the same type as the variable it is assigned to.

```
inductive ctyping :: "tyenv ⇒ com ⇒ bool" (infix "⊢" 50) where
Skip_ty: "Γ ⊢ SKIP" |
Assign_ty: "Γ ⊢ a : Γ(x) ⟹ Γ ⊢ x ::= a" |
Semi_ty: "Γ ⊢ c1 ⟹ Γ ⊢ c2 ⟹ Γ ⊢ c1;c2" |
If_ty: "Γ ⊢ b ⟹ Γ ⊢ c1 ⟹ Γ ⊢ c2 ⟹ Γ ⊢ IF b THEN c1 ELSE c2" |
While_ty: "Γ ⊢ b ⟹ Γ ⊢ c ⟹ Γ ⊢ WHILE b DO c"
```

This concludes the definition of the type system itself. Type systems can be arbitrarily complex. The one here is intentionally simple to show the structure of a type soundness proof without getting side tracked in interesting type system details.

3.1.3. Well-typed Programs Do Not Get Stuck

In this section we prove that the type system defined above is sound. Robert Milner coined the phrase that "well-typed programs do not go wrong", i.e. that well-typed programs will not exhibit any runtime errors such as segmentation faults or undefined execution. In a small-step semantics, this can be expressed nicely as the formal statement that well-typed programs never get stuck. They either terminate successfully, or they make further well-defined progress.

The main new concept we need to show type safety is that of a well-typed state. We so far have the state assigning values to variables and we have the type system statically assigning types to variables in the program. We connect these two concepts by defining a judgement that determines if a runtime state is compatible with a typing environment for variables. We call such states well-typed, and the judgement *styping* below. We also say that a state *s conforms* to a typing environment Γ.

With this judgement, the type soundness property naturally decomposes into two parts: preservation and progress. Preservation means that well-typed states stay well-typed during execution. Progress means that in a well-typed state, the program either terminates successfully or can make one more step of execution progress.

We start the formalisation by defining a function from values to types. In the IMP world, this is very simple. In more sophisticated type systems, there may be multiple types that can be assigned to a value and we may need a compatibility or sub-type relation between types to define the *styping* judgement. In our case, we merely have to map *Iv* values to *Ity* types and *Rv* values to *Rty* types.

```
fun type :: "val ⇒ ty" where
"type (Iv i) = Ity" |
"type (Rv r) = Rty"
```

The following two equations allow us to infer the value constructor from the result of the *type* function.

```
lemma type_Ity [simp]: "type v = Ity ⟷ (∃i. v = Iv i)"
lemma type_Rty [simp]: "type v = Rty ⟷ (∃r. v = Rv r)"
```

Our *styping* judgement for well-typed states is now very simple: for all variables, the type of the runtime value must be exactly the type predicted in the typing environment.

```
definition styping :: "tyenv ⇒ state ⇒ bool" (infix "⊢" 50)
where "Γ ⊢ s ⟷ (∀x. type (s x) = Γ x)"
```

We now have everything defined to start the soundness proof. The plan is to prove progress and preservation for statements, and to conclude from that the final type soundness statement that an execution started in a well-typed state will never get stuck. To prove progress and preservation for statements, we will need the same properties for arithmetic and boolean expressions.

Preservation for arithmetic expressions means the following: If expression *a* has type τ under environment Γ, if *a* evaluates to *v* in state *s*, and if *s* conforms to Γ, then the type of the result *v* must be τ. The proof is by rule induction on the type derivation Γ ⊢ *a* : τ. Since we have declared rule inversion on *taval* to be used automatically, Isabelle manages the rest automatically if we unfold the definition of *styping*.

```
lemma apreservation:
  "Γ ⊢ a : τ ⟹ taval a s v ⟹ Γ ⊢ s ⟹ type v = τ"
```

The progress lemma is more verbose. It is almost the only place where something interesting is concluded in the soundness proof: there is the potential of something going wrong. If the operands of a *Plus* were of incompatible type, there would be no value *v* the expression evaluates to. Of course, the type system excludes precisely this case.

The progress statement is as standard as the preservation statement for arithmetic expressions: given that *a* has type τ under environment Γ, and given a conforming state *s*, there must exist a result value *v* such that *a* evaluates to *v* in *s*.

The proof is again by rule induction on the typing derivation. The interesting case is `Plus`. The induction hypothesis gives us two values `v1` and `v2` for the subexpressions `a1` and `a2`. If `v1` is an integer, then, by preservation, the type of `a1` must have been `Ity`. The typing rule says the type of `a2` must be the same, so must, again by preservation, the type of `v2`. If the type of `v2` is `Ity` then `v2` must be an `Iv` value and we can conclude using the `taval` introduction rule for `Plus` that the execution has a result. Isabelle completes this reasoning chain automatically if we carefully provide it with the right facts and rules. The case for reals is analogous, and the other typing cases are easily solved automatically.

lemma *aprogress:* "Γ ⊢ a : τ ⟹ Γ ⊢ s ⟹ ∃v. taval a s v"

For boolean expressions, there is no preservation lemma, because the way the rules are written they obviously can only return boolean values. The progress statement makes sense, though, and follows the standard progress statement schema. As always, the proof is by rule induction on the typing derivation. The interesting case is where something could go wrong, namely where we execute arithmetic expressions in `Less`. The proof is very similar to the one for `Plus`: we obtain the values of the subexpressions; we perform a case distinction on one of them to reason about its type; we infer the other has the same type by typing rules and by preservation on arithmetic expressions; and we conclude that execution can therefore progress. Again this case is automatic if written carefully, the other cases are trivial.

lemma *bprogress:* "Γ ⊢ b ⟹ Γ ⊢ s ⟹ ∃v. tbval b s v"

For commands, there are two preservation statements, because our small-step semantics has two return values: program and state. We first show that the program remains well-typed and then that the state does. Both are by induction on the small-step semantics. They could be proved by induction on the typing derivation as well, but that would require us to declare additional rule inversion lemmas for the small-step rules which we have omitted above. Often it is preferable to try induction on the typing derivation first, because the type system typically has fewer cases. On the other hand, depending on the complexity of the language, the more fine grained information that is available in operational semantics might make the more numerous cases easier to prove in the other induction alternative. In both cases it pays off to design the structure of the rules in both systems such that they technically fit together nicely, for instance such that the decompose along the same syntactic lines.

The preservation of program typing is fully automatic in this simple language. The only mildly interesting case where we are not just transforming the program into a subexpression is the while loop. Here we just need to apply the typing rules for if-then-else and sequential composition and are done.

theorem *ctyping_preservation:*
  "(c, s) → (c', s') ⟹ Γ ⊢ c ⟹ Γ ⊢ c' "

The preservation of state well-typedness again composes easily through the induction. The place where something interesting happens is the substitution in the assignment operation. We update the state with a new value. Type preservation on expressions gives us that the new value has the same type, and unfolding the `styping` judgement shows that it is unaffected by substitutions that are type preserving. In more complex languages, there are likely to be a number of such substitution cases and the corresponding substitution lemma is a central piece of type soundness proofs.

theorem *styping_preservation:*
"$(c,s) \rightarrow (c',s') \implies \Gamma \vdash c \implies \Gamma \vdash s \implies \Gamma \vdash s'$ "

The progress lemma for commands is more verbose again. Here, we need to take into account that the program might have fully terminated. If it has not, and we have a well-typed program in a well-typed state, we demand that we can make at least one step.

This time the only induction alternative is on the typing derivation again. The cases with arithmetic and boolean expressions make use of the corresponding progress lemmas to generate the values the small-step rules demand. For *If*, we additionally perform a case distinction for picking the corresponding introduction rule. In the other cases, *SKIP* is trivial, *Semi* just applies the induction hypothesis and makes a case distinction if *c1* is *SKIP* or not, and *While* always trivially makes progress in the small-step semantics.

theorem *progress:*
"$\Gamma \vdash c \implies \Gamma \vdash s \implies c \neq SKIP \implies \exists cs'. (c,s) \rightarrow cs'$ "

All that remains is to assemble the pieces into the final type soundness statement: given any execution of a well-typed program started in a well-typed state, we are not stuck; we have either terminated successfully, or the program can perform another step.

The proof lifts the one-step preservation and progress results to a sequence of steps by induction on the transitive closure.

theorem *type_sound:*
"$(c,s) \rightarrow* (c',s') \implies \Gamma \vdash c \implies \Gamma \vdash s \implies$
$c' = SKIP \lor (\exists cs''. (c',s') \rightarrow cs'')$ "

This concludes the section on typing. We have seen at the example of a very simple type system what a type soundness statement entails, how it interacts with the small-step semantics, and how it is proved. While the proof itself will grow in complexity for more interesting language, the general schema of progress and preservation with a potential substitution lemma usually remains.

For the type soundness theorem to be meaningful, it is important that the failures the type system is supposed to prevent are observable in the semantics so that their absence can be shown. In a framework like the above, the precise definition of the small-step semantics carries the main meaning and strength of the type soundness statement.

3.2. Security Type Systems

In the previous section we have seen a simple static type system with soundness proof. However, type systems can be used for more than the traditional concepts of integers, reals, etc. In theory, type systems can be arbitrarily complex logical systems used to statically predict properties of programs. In the following, we will look at a type system that aims to enforce a security property: the absence of information flows from private data into public channels.

Ensuring such properties based on a programming language analysis such as a type system is also called *language-based security*. An commonly used alternative to language-based security is the use of cryptography to ensure the secrecy of private data. Cryptography only admits probabilistic arguments (one could always guess the key), whereas language-based security allows a more absolute statement.

Note that these absolute statements are always with respect to assumptions on the execution environment. For instance, our proof below will have the implicit assumption that the machine actually behaves as our semantics predicts. There are practical ways in which these assumptions can be broken or circumvented: intentionally introducing hardware-based errors into the computation to deduce private data, direct physical observation of memory contents, deduction of private data by analysis of execution time, and more. These attacks make use of details that are not visible on the abstraction level of the semantic model our proof is based on — they are *covert channels* of information flow.

The field of language-based security is substantial [3], the type system and the soundness statement in the sections below go back to Volpano and Smith [4]. While language-based security had been investigated before Volpano and Smith, they were the first to give a security type system with a soundness proof that expresses the enforced security property in terms of the standard semantics of the language. Formalise their type system and proof in Isabelle, we will see that such non-trivial properties are comfortably within the reach of machine-checked interactive proof.

3.2.1. Security Levels and Expressions

We begin by defining security levels. The idea is that each variable will have an associated security level. The type system will then enforce the policy that variables of 'higher' security level will not leak information to variables of 'lower' security levels.

In the literature, levels are often reduced to just two: high and low. We keep things slightly more general making levels natural numbers. We can then compare security levels by just writing $<$ and we can compute the maximal or minimal security level of two different variables by taking the maximum or minimum respectively. The term $l < l'$ in this system would mean that l is less private or confidential than l', so level $0::'a$ could be equated with 'public'.

It would be easily possible to generalise further and just assume a lattice of security levels with $<$, join, and meet operations.

```
type_synonym level = nat
```

For the type system and security proof below it would be sufficient to merely assume the existence of a HOL constant that maps variables to security levels. This would express that we assume each variable to possess a security level and that this level remains the same during execution of the program.

For the sake of showing examples — the general theory does not rely on it! —, we arbitrarily choose a specific function for this mapping: a variable of length n has security level n:

```
definition sec :: "name ⇒ level" where   "sec n = size n"
```

The kinds of information flows we would like to avoid are exemplified by the following two:

- explicit: `low ::= high`
- implicit: `IF high1 < high2 THEN low ::= 0 ELSE low ::= 1`

The property we are after is called *noninterference*: a variation in the value of high variables should not interfere with the computation or values of low variables. 'High should not interfere with low.'

More formally, a program c guarantees noninterference iff for all states $s1$ and $s2$: If $s1$ and $s2$ agree on low variables (but may differ on high variables!), then the states resulting from executing $(c, s1)$ and $(c, s2)$ must also agree on low variables.

As opposed to our previous type soundness statement, this definition compares the outcome of two executions of the same program in different, but related initial states. It requires again potentially different, but equally related final states.

With this in mind, we can now proceed to define the type system that will enforce this property. We begin by computing the security level of arithmetic and boolean expressions. We are interested in flows from higher to lower variables, so we compute the security level of an expression as the highest level of any variable that occurs in it:

```
fun sec_aexp :: "aexp ⇒ level" where
  "sec_aexp (N n) = 0" |
  "sec_aexp (V x) = sec x" |
  "sec_aexp (Plus a₁ a₂) = max (sec_aexp a₁) (sec_aexp a₂)"

fun sec_bexp :: "bexp ⇒ level" where
  "sec_bexp (B bv) = 0" |
  "sec_bexp (Not b) = sec_bexp b" |
  "sec_bexp (And b₁ b₂) = max (sec_bexp b₁) (sec_bexp b₂)" |
  "sec_bexp (Less a₁ a₂) = max (sec_aexp a₁) (sec_aexp a₂)"
```

A first lemma indicating that we are moving into the right direction will be that if we change the value of only variables with a higher level than `sec_aex a`, the value of `a` should be the same.

To express this property, we introduce notation for two states agreeing on the value of all variables below a certain security level. The concept is light-weight enough that a syntactic abbreviation is sufficient and avoids us having to go through the motions of setting up additional proof infrastructure.

We will need both ≤ and the strict < later on, so we define both here:

```
abbreviation eq_le :: "state ⇒ state ⇒ level ⇒ bool"
  ("(_ = _ '(≤ _'))" [51,51,0] 50) where
  "s = s' (≤ l) == (∀ x. sec x ≤ l ⟶ s x = s' x)"

abbreviation eq_less :: "state ⇒ state ⇒ level ⇒ bool"
  ("(_ = _ '(< _'))" [51,51,0] 50) where
  "s = s' (< l) == (∀ x. sec x < l ⟶ s x = s' x)"
```

With this, the proof of our first two security properties is simple and automatic:

```
lemma aval_eq_if_eq_le:
  "⟦ s₁ = s₂ (≤ l); sec_aexp a ≤ l ⟧ ⟹ aval a s₁ = aval a s₂"
lemma bval_eq_if_eq_le:
  "⟦ s₁ = s₂ (≤ l); sec_bexp b ≤ l ⟧ ⟹ bval b s₁ = bval b s₂"
```

3.2.2. Syntax Directed Typing

As usual in IMP, the typing for expressions was simple. We now define the typing rules for commands. We deviate a little from the standard presentation of Volpano and Smith and instead give an equivalent, syntax-directed form of the rules. This makes the rules directly executable and allows us to run examples. The main idea of the type system is to track the security level of variables that that decisions are made on, and make sure that their level is lower or equal to variables assigned to in that context.

We write $l \vdash c$ to say command c contains only safe flows to variables higher or equal to l.

```
inductive sec_type :: "nat ⇒ com ⇒ bool" ("(_ / ⊢ _)" [0,0] 50) where
Skip:    "l ⊢ SKIP" |
Assign:  "⟦ sec x ≥ sec_aexp a;   sec x ≥ l ⟧ ⟹ l ⊢ x ::= a" |
Semi:    "⟦ l ⊢ c₁;   l ⊢ c₂ ⟧ ⟹ l ⊢ c₁;c₂" |
If:      "⟦ max (sec_bexp b) l ⊢ c₁;   max (sec_bexp b) l ⊢ c₂ ⟧ ⟹
              l ⊢ IF b THEN c₁ ELSE c₂" |
While:   "max (sec_bexp b) l ⊢ c ⟹ l ⊢ WHILE b DO c"
```

Going through the rules in detail, we have defined $SKIP$ to be safe at any level. We have have defined assignment to be safe if the level of x is higher than or equal to the level of the information source a, but lower than or equal to l. For semicolon to conform to a level l, we just recursively demand that both parts conform to the same level l. As previously shown in the motivating example, the IF statement could admit indirect flows. We prevent these by demanding that for if-then-else to conform to l, both $c1$ and $c2$ have to conform to level l or the level of the decision expression, whichever is higher. We can conveniently express this with the maximum operator max. The While case is similar to an If: the body must have at least the level of b and of the whole statement.

Using the max function makes the type system executable if we tell Isabelle to treat the level and the program as input to the predicate.

Testing our intuition about what we have just defined, we execute four examples for various security levels.

```
value "0 ⊢ IF Less (V ''x1'') (V ''x'') THEN ''x1'' ::= N 0 ELSE SKIP"
value "1 ⊢ IF Less (V ''x1'') (V ''x'') THEN ''x''  ::= N 0 ELSE SKIP"
value "2 ⊢ IF Less (V ''x1'') (V ''x'') THEN ''x1'' ::= N 0 ELSE SKIP"
value "3 ⊢ IF Less (V ''x1'') (V ''x'') THEN ''x1'' ::= N 0 ELSE SKIP"
```

We expect the first evaluation to yield $True$: the condition has level 2, the assignment sets a level 2 variable, and the context is 0. The next line has to yield $False$: we are in a level 1 context overall, but since the condition has level 2, we are not allowed to assign to a level 1 variable. The next line is $True$ again, whereas the last line is $False$: while the if-statement itself is fine, the context says we can at most assign to level 3 variables.

As we can already see from these simple examples, the type system is not complete: it will reject some safe programs as unsafe. For instance, if the value of x in the second statement was already 0 in the beginning, the context would not have mattered, we only would have overwritten 0 with 0. As with any type system that can be checked automatically we should not expect otherwise. The best we can hope for is a safe approximation such that the false alarms are hopefully programs that rarely occur in practise or that can be rewritten easily.

It is the case that the Volpano-Smith security type system in its simple form has been criticised as too restrictive. It excludes too many safe programs. This can be addressed by making the type system more refined, more flexible, and more context aware.

For demonstrating the type system and its soundness proof in these notes, we will stick to its simplest form.

3.2.3. Soundness

We introduced the correctness statement for this type system as noninterference: two executions of the same program started in related states end up in related states. The relation in our case is that the values of variables below security level l are the same. Formally, this is the following statement

$$ [\![(c,\ s)\ \Rightarrow\ s';\ (c,\ t)\ \Rightarrow\ t';\ 0 \vdash c;\ s\ =\ t\ (\leq\ l)]\!] \implies s'\ =\ t'\ (\leq\ l) $$

The key lemma in the argument for this proof is *confinement*: an execution that is typed safe in context l can only change variables of level l and above, or conversely, all variables below l will remain unchanged.

An important property in that lemma is the so-called anti-monotonicity of the type system: a command that is typeable in l is also typeable in any level smaller than l. In fact, anti-monotonicity is directly part of the type system as a typing rule in the standard presentation of Volpano-Smith. In exchange, the standard presentation does not need an explicit max calculation. Here, we can derive anti-monotinicity as a lemma by rule induction on the type system:

lemma $anti\_mono:$ $"[\![\ l \vdash c;\ \ l' \leq l\ ]\!] \implies l' \vdash c"$

In this proof, we used the sledgehammer tool extensively after the main proof idea. The automated provers found an answer for each of the subgoals.

We now come to the confinement property mentioned above: if we have an execution of c from s to t, and c is safe in context l, then the states s and t agree on all variables below level l. The first instinct may be to try rule induction on the type system again, but the while-case will only give us an induction hypothesis about the body when we will have to show our goal for the whole loop. Rule induction on the big-step execution on the other hand does get us through. In the if- and while-cases, we make use of anti-monotinicity to instantiate the induction hypothesis. In the if-true-case, for instance, the hypothesis is $l \vdash c1 \implies s\ =\ t\ (<\ l)$, but from the type system we only know max $(sec\_bexp\ b)\ l \vdash c1$. Anti-monotonicity allows us to reason from max to l.

lemma $confinement:$ $"[\![\ (c,s)\ \Rightarrow\ t;\ \ l \vdash c\ ]\!] \implies s\ =\ t\ (<\ l)"$

With these two lemmas, we can start the main noninterference proof.

Similarly to above, we will not get through with induction on the typing derivation, but we do manage with induction on the big-step execution. This time, the proof is a little more involved.

theorem $noninterference:$
$"[\![\ (c,s)\ \Rightarrow\ s';\ (c,t)\ \Rightarrow\ t';\ \ 0 \vdash c;\ \ s\ =\ t\ (\leq\ l)\ ]\!] \implies s'\ =\ t'\ (\leq\ l)"$

The base case of the proof is automatic, as it should be.

The assignment case is already somewhat interesting. First, we note that s' is the usual state update $s(x \rightarrow aval\ a\ s)$ in the first big-step execution. We perform rule inversion for the second execution to get the same update for t. We also perform rule inversion on the typing statement to get the relationship between security levels of x and a. Now we show that the two updated states s' and t' still agree on all variables below l. Isabelle's auto method tells us that it is sufficient to show that the states agree on the new value if the level of x is below l, and that all other variables y below l still agree as before. In the first case, looking at x, we know from above that $sec\_aexp\ a \leq sec$ x. Hence, by transitivity, we have that the a has a level no more than l. This is enough for our noninterference result on expressions to apply, given that we also know $s = t$ $(\leq l)$ from the premises. The case for all other variables below l is simple and follows directly from $s = t$ $(\leq l)$.

In the semicolon case, we merely need to compose the induction hypotheses. This is solved automatically.

If-then-else has two symmetric cases as usual. We will look only at if-true in more detail. We begin the case by noting via rule inversion that both branches are safe to level $sec\_bexp\ b$, since the maximum with 0 is the identity. Then we perform a case distinction: either the level of b is $\leq l$ or it is not. If $sec\_bexp\ b \leq l$, i.e. the if-decision is on a more public level than l, then s and t which agree below l also agree below $sec\_bexp\ b$. That in turn means by our noninterference lemma for expressions that they evaluate to the same result, so $bval\ b\ s = True$ and $bval\ b\ t = True$. We already noted $sec\_bexp\ b \vdash c1$ by rule inversion, and with anti-monotonicity, we get the necessary $0 \vdash c1$ to apply the induction hypothesis and conclude the case. In the other case, if $l < sec\_bexp\ b$, i.e. a condition on a more confidential level than l we do not now that both if-statements will take the same branch. However, we do know that the whole statement is a high-confidentiality computation. It must be safe to level $sec\_bexp\ b$, since the parts are safe to the maximum of this level and l, and we now can apply confinement: everything below $sec\_bexp\ b$ will be preserved — in particular the state of variables up to l. This is true for t to t' as well as s to s'. Together with the initial $s = t$ $(\leq l)$, we can conclude $s' = t'$ $(\leq l)$ which closes the whole if-true case.

The if-false and while-false cases are analogous. Either the conditions evaluate to the same value and we can apply the induction hypothesis, or the security level is high enough such that we can apply confinement.

Even the while-true case is very similar. Here, we have to work slightly harder to apply the induction hypothesis, once for the body and once for the rest of the loop, but the confinement side of the argument stays the same.

3.2.4. The Standard Typing System

The judgement $l \vdash c$ presented above is nicely intuitive and executable. As mentioned, however, the standard formulation is slightly different, replacing the maximum computation by the anti-monotonicity rule. We introduce the standard system now and show equivalence with our formulation.

```
inductive sec_type' :: "nat ⇒ com ⇒ bool" ("(_/ ⊢'' _)" [0,0] 50) where
Skip':    "l ⊢' SKIP" |
```

```
Assign':   "⟦ sec x ≥ sec_aexp a; sec x ≥ 1 ⟧ ⟹ l ⊢' x ::= a" |
Semi':     "⟦ l ⊢' c₁; l ⊢' c₂ ⟧ ⟹ l ⊢' c₁;c₂" |
If':       "⟦ sec_bexp b ≤ l; l ⊢' c₁; l ⊢' c₂ ⟧ ⟹
               l ⊢' IF b THEN c₁ ELSE c₂" |
While':    "⟦ sec_bexp b ≤ l; l ⊢' c ⟧ ⟹ l ⊢' WHILE b DO c" |
anti_mono': "⟦ l ⊢' c; l' ≤ l ⟧ ⟹ l' ⊢' c"
```

The equivalence proof goes by rule induction on the respective type system in each direction separately. We use sledgehammer to automatically find a proof for each subgoal.

```
lemma sec_type_sec_type': "l ⊢ c ⟹ l ⊢' c"
lemma sec_type'_sec_type: "l ⊢' c ⟹ l ⊢ c"
```

4. Compiler

This section presents another application of programming language semantics: proving compiler correctness.

To this end, we will define a small machine language, based on a simple stack machine as it would be found for instance in the Java Virtual Machine. We then write a compiler from IMP and prove that the compiled program has the same semantics as the source program. The compiler will contain a very simple, standard optimisation for boolean expressions, but is otherwise non-optimising.

As in the other sections, the emphasis here is on showing the structure and main setup of such a proof. Our compiler proof shows the core of the argument, but compared to real compilers we make drastic simplifications: our target language is comparatively high-level, we do not consider optimisations, we ignore the compiler front-end, and our source language does not contain any concepts that are particularly hard to translate into machine language.

Two compiler correctness proofs in the literature are for the Java-like language Jinja [1] in a style that is similar to the one presented here, and more recently, the fully realistic, optimising C-compiler CompCert by Leroy et al [2] which compiles to PowerPC, x86, and ARM architectures. Both proofs are naturally more complex than the one presented here, both working with the concept of intermediate languages and multiple compilation stages. This is done to simplify the argument and to concentrate on specific issues on each level.

We begin by defining the instruction set architecture and semantics of our stack machine. Working with proofs on the machine language, we found it convenient for the program counter to admit negative values, i.e. to be of type int instead of the initially more intuitive nat. The effect of this choice is that various decomposition lemmas about machine executions have nicer algebraic properties and less preconditions than their nat counterparts. Such effects are usually discovered during the proof, not a priory.

Because of this choice we make a small detour before we write down the machine semantics.

4.1. List setup

Our machine language will model programs as lists of instructions and our int program counter will need to index into these lists. Isabelle comes with a predefined list index operator *nth*, but it works on *nat*. Instead of constantly converting between *int* and *nat* and dealing with the arising side-conditions in proofs, we define our own *int* version of *nth*. The size of lists is similar, but here the conversion does not present us with side conditions, because we only convert into the easy direction from *nat* to *int*.

abbreviation *"isize xs == int (length xs)"*

primrec
   inth :: *"'a list => int => 'a"* (**infixl** *"!!"* 100) **where**
   inth_Cons: *"(x # xs) !! n = (if n = 0 then x else xs !! (n - 1))"*

The only lemma we need about the new *inth* is indexing over append:

lemma *inth_append [simp]:*
  "0 $\leq$ n $\Longrightarrow$ (xs @ ys) !! n =
               (if n < isize xs then xs !! n else ys !! (n - isize xs))"

4.2. Instructions and Stack Machine

We are now ready to define the machine itself. To keep things simple, we reuse the concepts of values and variable names from the source language. Values pose no problems, but variable names as strings are a little strange in a low-level machine, usually one would have to map such names to address locations first. We skip this complication here. It could be added easily in a separate additional compilation step for instance.

    The instructions in our machine are the following:

datatype *instr =*   *LOADI val | LOAD name*   *| ADD | STORE name |*
                      JMP int   *| JMPLESS int | JMPGE int*

In detail, they are: load immediate value onto the stack, load value of a variable, add the two topmost stack values, store the top of stack into a variable, jump by a relative value, compare the two topmost stack elements and jump if the top is less, compare and jump if the top is greater or equal.

    These are enough to compile IMP programs. A real machine would have significantly more arithmetic and comparison operators, different addressing modes that are useful to implement procedure stacks and pointers, potentially a number of primitive datatypes that the machine understands, and a number of instructions to deal with hardware features such as the memory management subsystem that we ignore completely in this formalisation.

    As with the source language, after defining program instructions or statements, we proceed by defining the state such programs run on followed by the definition of the actual semantics.

    Our state or program configuration consists of an *int* program counter, a variable assignment for which we re-use the type *state* from the source language, and a stack which we model as a list of values.

type_synonym *stack =* *"val list"*
type_synonym *config =* *"int$\times$state$\times$stack"*

We now define the semantics of machine execution in multiple levels. First, we define what effect a single instruction has on a configuration, then we define how an instruction is selected from the program, and finally we take the transitive closure to get full machine program executions.

In the first level, the effect of single instructions, we will need to talk about the second element of a list. The following notations makes this slightly nicer to read:

```
abbreviation "hd2 xs == hd(tl xs)"
abbreviation "tl2 xs == tl(tl xs)"
```

The formal definition for single instructions is a similar judgement to the small-step semantics of the source language, and we introduce similar syntax for it. Each introduction rule implements the effect of the corresponding instruction as described above. The program counter is i, usually incremented by 1, apart from the jump instructions. Variables are loaded from and stored into the variable state s with function application and function update. The stack stk uses standard list constructs $\#$, hd, tl, as well as our new $hd2$ and $tl2$.

```
inductive iexec1 :: "instr ⇒ config ⇒ config ⇒ bool"
    ("(_/ ⊢i (_ →/ _))" [50,0,0] 50)
where
"LOADI n ⊢i (i,s,stk) → (i+1,s, n#stk)" |
"LOAD x  ⊢i (i,s,stk) → (i+1,s, s x # stk)" |
"ADD     ⊢i (i,s,stk) → (i+1,s, (hd2 stk + hd stk) # tl2 stk)" |
"STORE n ⊢i (i,s,stk) → (i+1,s(n := hd stk),tl stk)" |
"JMP n   ⊢i (i,s,stk) → (i+1+n,s,stk)" |
"JMPLESS n ⊢i (i,s,stk) →
    (if hd2 stk < hd stk then i+1+n else i+1,s,tl2 stk)" |
"JMPGE n ⊢i (i,s,stk) →
    (if hd2 stk >= hd stk then i+1+n else i+1,s,tl2 stk)"
```

The next level up, a single execution step of a program, which we model as an abstract list of instructions, selects the instruction the program counter points to and uses the `iexec1` judgment to execute it. For execution to be well-defined, we additionally check if the pc does actually point to a valid location in the list.

Modelling the program as a list of instructions is another abstraction we introduce to a real low-level machine. It corresponds roughly to the level of abstraction of the JVM. A real CPU would implement a von-Neumann machine, which adds fetching and decoding of instructions to the execution cycle. The main difference is that our model would not admit self-modifying programs which is not necessary for IMP.

```
inductive
    exec1 :: "instr list ⇒ config ⇒ config ⇒ bool"
       ("(_/ ⊢ (_ →/ _))" [50,0,0] 50) where
"⟦ P!!i ⊢i (i,s,stk) → c'; 0 ≤ i; i < isize P ⟧ ⟹ P ⊢ (i,s,stk) → c'"
```

The last level is the lifting from single step execution to multiple steps using the standard reflexive, transitive closure definition that we already used for the small-step semantics of the source language.

```
inductive exec :: "instr list ⇒ config ⇒ config ⇒ bool"
```

```
("_/ ⊢ (_ →*/ _)" 50) where
refl: "P ⊢ c →* c" |
step: "P ⊢ c → c' ⟹ P ⊢ c' →* c'' ⟹ P ⊢ c →* c''"
```

This concludes our definition of the machine and its semantics. We can now try out a simple example:

```
values
  "{(i,map t ['' x'',''y''],stk) | i t stk.
    [LOAD ''y'', STORE ''x''] ⊢
    (0, [''x'' → 3, ''y'' → 4], []) →* (i,t,stk)}"
```

The result is the following sequence of machine configurations: $\{(0, [3, 4], []),$ $(1, [3, 4], [4]), (2, [4, 4], [])\}$.

4.3. Verification infrastructure

The compiler proof is more involved than the short proofs we have seen so far. We will need a lot more infrastructure setup and small technical lemmas before we get to the actual problem itself. We have seen enough concepts at this stage that we can present the whole machine semantics in one go in this section instead of splitting it and its setup over multiple sections as we did for the source language.

When constructing such a proof, one usually starts with a reasonably small infrastructure setup and then grows the infrastructure as needed during the proof.

We begin with the constant `iexec1` and will work our way upwards through the 3 semantic layers of the machine. The goal is to be able to execute machine programs symbolically as far as possible using Isabelle's proof tools. We will then use this ability in the compiler proof to assemble the various program parts.

The rules of `iexec1` can easily be transformed into equations. In fact, we could have defined the judgement using `fun` or `definition` instead of an inductive predicate. The reason for using `inductive` was better readability and the fact that it fits more naturally into the general schema we used for other judgment definitions. To derive the equational form, we first set up automatic rule inversion, and then use it to prove the rest automatically.

Large parts of the compiler correctness argument are about the execution of code that is embedded in larger programs. For this purpose we show that execution results are preserved if we append additional code to the left or right of a program.

Appending at the right side is easy to state and solved automatically after rule induction:

```
lemma exec_appendR: "P ⊢ c →* c' ⟹ P@P' ⊢ c →* c'"
```

Appending additional code on the left side requires a moment of thought: the lemma statement will need to update the program counter and shift the execution by `size P'` to the right if we append `P'` on the left.

For this to go through, we need the same statement on the single-instruction level. Formulating this statement we discover that single-instruction execution at `iexec1` is actually independent of the program counter:

```
lemma iexec_shift [simp]:
  "(X ⊢i (n+i,s,stk) → (n+i',s',stk')) =
   (X ⊢i (i,s,stk) → (i',s',stk'))"
```

The result is then easily lifted to the program level, and afterwards by induction to the execution of multiple steps.

```
lemma exec1_appendL:
  "P ⊢ (i,s,stk) → (i',s',stk') ⟹
   P' @ P ⊢ (isize(P')+i,s,stk) → (isize(P')+i',s',stk')"
lemma exec_appendL:
  "P ⊢ (i,s,stk) →* (i',s',stk') ⟹
   P' @ P ⊢ (isize(P')+i,s,stk) →* (isize(P')+i',s',stk')"
```

We then specialise the above lemmas to enable automatic proofs of $P \vdash c \to* c'$ where P is a mixture of concrete instructions and pieces of code of which we already know how they execute (by induction), combined by @ and #. Backward jumps are not supported. For details we refer to the proof scripts.

4.4. Compilation

We are now ready to define the actual compiler. We begin with arithmetic expressions which are very easy to compile into a stack machine. A constant maps to *LOADI*, a variable maps to *LOAD*, and addition maps to *ADD*.

```
fun acomp :: "aexp ⇒ instr list" where
"acomp (N n) = [LOADI n]" |
"acomp (V x) = [LOAD x]" |
"acomp (Plus a1 a2) = acomp a1 @ acomp a2 @ [ADD]"
```

The idea is that the compiled code leaves the result of the computation on the top of the stack and otherwise does not change anything. This is already one direction of the correctness statement for arithmetic expressions and easily written down formally. The proof is by induction on the structure of expressions.

```
lemma acomp_correct[intro]:
  "acomp a ⊢ (0,s,stk) →* (isize(acomp a),s,aval a s#stk)"
```

The form of the lemma is suitable for an introduction rule to use automatically in the following proofs.

Compiling boolean operations has a different correctness statement. These expressions are used in if-then-else and while-statements, and what we expect the compiled code to do is to give us one exit program counter for the *True* case and another for the *False* case and apart from that leave the state and stack unchanged. We chose the pc after the expression code as the first exit and give the expression compiler an additional parameter n for the distance to the jump target that is our the second exit. We add another parameter c that tells us which exit to use in the *True* and *False* case. If c is *False*, then the *True* case will be the first exit.

This enables us to perform a small bit of optimisation: boolean constants do not really need to execute any code, they either compile to nothing or to a jump to the second exit, depending on the value of c. The *Not* case simply inverts c to swap exits. The *And* case performs shortcut evaluation: if *b1* evaluates to *False* we exit the whole expression taking the exit c demands. Otherwise we continue evaluation with *b2*. The *Less* operator uses the *acomp* compiler for *a1* and *a2* and then selects the jmp/compare instruction according to c.

```
fun bcomp :: "bexp ⇒ bool ⇒ int ⇒ instr list" where
"bcomp (B bv) c n = (if bv=c then [JMP n] else [])" |
"bcomp (Not b) c n = bcomp b (¬c) n" |
"bcomp (And b1 b2) c n =
  (let cb2 = bcomp b2 c n;
        m = (if c then isize cb2 else isize cb2+n);
     cb1 = bcomp b1 False m
   in cb1 @ cb2)" |
"bcomp (Less a1 a2) c n =
  acomp a1 @ acomp a2 @ (if c then [JMPLESS n] else [JMPGE n])"
```

This optimisation basically entails a form of primitive constant folding in boolean expressions. The expression *And (B True) (B True)* for instance with c = *False* compiles to the empty list.

A more usual case will translate to a series of load and jump instructions. A test case in Isabelle:

```
value "bcomp (And (Less (V ''x'') (V ''y''))
                  (Not (Less (V ''u'') (V ''v''))))
             False 3"
```

The result of this evaluation is *[LOAD ''x'', LOAD ''y'', JMPGE 6, LOAD ''u'', LOAD ''v'', JMPLESS 3]*.

The correctness statement for boolean expressions encapsulates the intention we had when writing *bcomp*: stack and state remain unchanged and the program counter indicates if the expression evaluated to *True* or *False*. If c = *False* then we end at *isize (bcomp b c n)* in the *True* case and *isize (bcomp b c n) + n* in the *False* case. If c = *True* it is the other way around. This statement only really makes sense for forward jumps, hence the precondition on n. We could generalise slightly and only exclude exits that lead back into the code of *bcomp b c n*, but this form is slightly easier to work with. As for the arithmetic case, we tell Isabelle to use this correctness statement automatically as an introduction rule.

```
lemma bcomp_correct[intro]:
"0 ≤ n ⟹ bcomp b c n ⊢ (0, s, stk) →*
            (isize(bcomp b c n) + (if c = bval b s then n else 0), s, stk)"
```

The proof of this lemma is by structural induction on the expression b. The constant and *Less* cases are solved automatically. For *Not* Isabelle needs some hand-holding by suitably instantiating the induction hypothesis; similarly in the *And* case.

With both kinds of expressions done, we can now proceed to compiling programs. The idea is to generate a program that will perform the same state transformation on the state s as the source, that will result in nothing new on the stack (but may push and consume intermediate values for expressions), and that will always end with program counter `size (ccomp c)`.

Relying on this condition recursively, this is surprisingly straightforward to achieve: `SKIP` compiles to the empty list and assignment compiles the expression, then stores the result into the state. The if-then-else statement compiles into the expression part and jumps to the corresponding branch. Linearising the tree structure of the abstract source syntax, we jump over the compiled `c2` to the end of the code when the `True` branch `c1` has finished executing. While loops compile into the condition followed by the body and a backwards jump to the beginning of the condition. The exit branch of the condition jumps beyond the backward branch directly to the end of the code.

The formal definition in Isabelle follows.

```
fun ccomp :: "com ⇒ instr list" where
"ccomp SKIP = []" |
"ccomp (x ::= a) = acomp a @ [STORE x]" |
"ccomp (c1;c2) = ccomp c1 @ ccomp c2" |
"ccomp (IF b THEN c1 ELSE c2) =
  (let cc1 = ccomp c1;
       cc2 = ccomp c2;
       cb = bcomp b False (isize cc1 + 1)
   in cb @ cc1 @ JMP (isize cc2) # cc2)" |
"ccomp (WHILE b DO c) =
  (let cc = ccomp c; cb = bcomp b False (isize cc + 1)
   in cb @ cc @ [JMP (- (isize cb + isize cc + 1))])"
```

Since everything in this definition is within the executable fragment of Isabelle/HOL, we can inspect the results of compiler runs:

```
value "ccomp (WHILE Less (V ''u'') (N 1)
             DO (''u'' ::= Plus (V ''u'') (N 1)))"
```

evaluates to `[LOAD ''u'', LOADI 1, JMPGE 5, LOAD ''u'', LOADI 1, ADD, STORE ''u'', JMP -8]`.

4.5. Preservation of semantics

Since we had already completed our infrastructure setup before we started the definition of the compiler, we are now ready to state the first direction of the correctness statement and prove it.

The idea of the compiler was to achieve the same state change as the source program, so we formulate that if `(c, s) ⇒ t` we can execute the compiled `c` starting in `0` to its completion at `isize (ccomp c)` and achieve the same state change from `s` to `t`, leaving any existing stack unchanged.

Since we conveniently have a statement about a big-step execution in the assumptions, we can proceed with rule induction on this statement. We will go into the cases into more detail below.

```
lemma ccomp_bigstep:
  "(c,s) ⇒ t ⟹ ccomp c ⊢ (0,s,stk) →* (isize(ccomp c),t,stk)"
```

As mentioned, the main structure of the proof is a rule induction on the big-step judgment. With the correctness statements for expressions used implicitly and our specifically designed composition lemmas, the proof is in large parts automatic. The $SKIP$, while-false, and if-then-else cases are solved fully automatically. The assignment case only needs a little help to align the two function updates that Isabelle manages to derive for both sides.

In the semicolon case, we instantiate the two induction hypotheses for $c1$ and $c2$ appropriately and put both of them into the full $ccomp\ c1\ @\ ccomp\ c2$ context. Transitivity then gives us the execution of the whole statement.

In the while-true case, we begin the proof by observing that if the condition is true, and by induction hypothesis the body c executes from state $s1$ to $s2$, the whole compiled program will execute from pc 0 in $s1$ to the position of the backwards jump instruction and state $s2$. Moreover, we observe that the jump instruction will transport us back to the beginning of the loop in state $s2$. By induction hypothesis again, we know that the loop started in $s2$ and pc 0 will terminate correctly in $s3$. Putting these three steps together by transitivity, we can conclude the case and thereby the whole proof.

This direction of the correctness proof is so convenient, because rule induction on the big-step semantics is such a powerful proof principle and it is easy in our machine to compose smaller executions into larger ones.

The real correctness statement we are after is the if-and-only-if

$$(c,\ s) \Rightarrow t \longleftrightarrow$$
$$ccomp\ c \vdash (0,\ s,\ stk) \rightarrow_* (isize\ (ccomp\ c),\ t,\ stk)$$

and the other direction is much less convenient. So much so that it may be worth thinking about if this direction is really necessary at all. Do we not already know enough? For any execution of the source program we know that the machine will produce the same execution. Unfortunately if we want to transport program correctness statements from the source to the machine level, this is precisely the wrong direction:

If we have proved a standard partial program correctness property of the form $\forall s\ t$. $(c,\ s) \Rightarrow t \longrightarrow P\ s \longrightarrow Q\ t$ as it would come out of a Hoare triple $\{P\}\ c\ \{Q\}$, and we would like a similar Hoare-triple to be true about the compiled program, then we will have to assume a machine execution and show the existence of a corresponding source execution to satisfy the first premise of the implication. This is precisely direction two of our proof!

It is worth pointing out that in a deterministic language like IMP, the second direction reduces to preserving termination: if the machine program terminates, so must the source program. If that was the case, we could conclude that started in s the source must terminate in some t'. Using the first direction of the compiler proof and by determinism of the machine language, we could then conclude that $t' = t$ and that therefore the source execution was already the right one. Unfortunately, showing that machine-level termination implies source-level termination is not much easier than showing the second direction of our compiler proof directly, and so we will not take that path here. Instead, we will prove the second direction directly.

4.6. Compiler Correctness, 2nd direction

In this section, we will prove the second direction of compiler correctness: $ccomp\ c \vdash$ $(0,\ s,\ stk) \to* (isize\ (ccomp\ c),\ t,\ stk') \implies (c,\ s) \Rightarrow t$.

As argued above, this direction is more technically involved than the first one. The main reason for this is the lack of a nice structural induction principle on the machine side. Since rule induction is not applicable, we have only two further induction principles left in the arsenal we have seen so far: structural induction on the command c or induction on the length of the $\to*$ execution. Neither is strong enough on its own. Trying structural induction, we get into the usual problem for the while-case that our induction hypothesis only talks about the execution of the body c, but not the rest of the loop. Induction on the length of the execution is more promising at first, but does not work either. Consider the semicolon case: for $ccomp\ c1$ @ $ccomp2 \vdash (0,\ s,\ stk) \to*$ $(isize\ (ccomp\ (c1;\ c2)),\ t,\ stk')$ the first command $c1$ could be $SKIP$ and $ccomp\ SKIP$ therefore the empty list. This means the statement collapses to $ccomp2 \vdash$ $(0,\ s,\ stk) \to* (isize\ (ccomp\ c2),\ t,\ stk')$ and we have no shorter execution that an induction hypothesis could apply to.

The solution is to do both: an outside structural induction on c which will take care of all cases but $WHILE$, and then a nested, inner induction on the length of the execution for the while-case. This takes care of the general proof structure. We will now merely be left with the problem of decomposing larger machine executions into smaller ones.

Intuitively, this is an easy problem. Consider $cs1$ @ $cs2 \vdash s \to* s'$. It seems obvious that there must be some s'' such that $cs1 \vdash s \to* s''$ and $cs2 \vdash s'' \to*$ s', but this is by far not true for all possible $cs1$ and $cs2$, or even s and s''. For instance, execution may be jumping between $cs1$ and $cs2$ continuously, and neither may make sense in isolation.

A large part of the formalisation below will be concerned with identifying the useful cases where this decomposition is possible and instantiating it suitably to be applied in the main induction that is the compiler proof. The key idea in this part is to identify the possible exit program counters for a given list of instructions. In general, instruction lists may jump anywhere, but it turns out that code produced by the compiler is particularly well behaved. Code compiled from a statement c will always run to $pc\ =\ isize$ $(ccomp\ c)$ and any jump targets will be only inside the generated code, not outside.

The final new concept we will need for the proof is a machine execution of explicit length n. This will enable us to do induction on this n, showing that a property P holds for any n if it holds for any $m\ <\ n$. This saves us from having to splice off single execution steps at a time and gives us more flexibility in decomposing the large execution in the nested induction for the while-case.

In the following sections, we first define the new concepts outlined above, establish their basic properties and main lemmas, and finally put them together in the nested induction over IMP statements and the length of machine executions.

4.6.1. Definitions

An execution of length n is easily defined using primitive recursion. It's role is to replace the transitive closure of $exec1$ that we used before.

```
primrec
    exec_n :: "instr list ⇒ config ⇒ nat ⇒ config ⇒ bool"
    ("_/ ⊢ (_ →^_/ _)" [65,0,55,55] 55)
where
    "P ⊢ c →^0 c' = (c'=c)" |
    "P ⊢ c →^(Suc n) c'' = (∃c'. (P ⊢ c → c') ∧ P ⊢ c' →^n c'')"
```

The next concept is the definition of the possible pc exits of a given instruction sequence. We build up this definition in three steps: first, we define *isuccs*, the possible successor pcs of a given instruction at position *n*, then we lift this to *succs P n* which gives us the successor pcs of an instruction sequence *P* which itself may be embedded in a larger program at position *n*, and finally we subtract the set {0..isize P} from *succs P 0* to arrive at the possible exits of *P*.

The set of possible successors of an instruction at position *n* is usually just the singleton {n + 1}, only for jump instructions we get a different successor, and we get two possibilities for conditional jumps.

```
definition
    "isuccs i n ≡ case i of
        JMP j ⇒ {n + 1 + j}
      | JMPLESS j ⇒ {n + 1 + j, n + 1}
      | JMPGE j ⇒ {n + 1 + j, n + 1}
      | _ ⇒ {n +1}"
```

The possible successors pcs of an instruction list is the union of all instruction successors. The set comprehension below prefers a closed term over a recursion and uses the list indices to provide the position of the instruction to *isuccs*.

```
definition
    "succs P n = {s. ∃i. 0 ≤ i ∧ i < isize P ∧ s ∈ isuccs (P!!i) (n+i)}"
```

With the possible successors defined, the set of possible exits is straightforward.

```
definition "exits P = succs P 0 - {0..< isize P}"
```

4.6.2. Basic properties of exec_n

We begin the property sections by relating our new *exec_n* with the existing judgement *exec* and by setting up some automation for *exec_n*.

The equivalence is proved by induction on *n* in one direction and rule induction in the other.

```
lemma exec_eq_exec_n: "(P ⊢ c →* c') = (∃n. P ⊢ c →^n c')"
```

As in the easy direction of the compiler proof, we design a set of lemmas that we can use to symbolically execute a mixture of concrete instructions and unknown parts of the instruction sequence.

Previously, we designed a set of introduction rules, because we needed to compose smaller executions into larger ones in the conclusion of the goal. Here, we will need to decompose larger executions into smaller ones, reasoning forward from known assumptions. We therefore provide conditional rewrite rules instead, which can be used in both, conclusion and assumptions.

4.6.3. Basic properties of *succs*

With the basic facts about execution set up, we can turn our attention the successor and exit functions. Our goal is to derive lemmas about the possible exits for the results of *acomp*, *bcomp*, and *ccomp*. The main proofs for these results will be by induction on the expression or statement to be compiled. The key lemmas are about the constructor and append case of *succs*.

```
lemma succs_Cons:
  "succs (x#xs) n = isuccs x n ∪ succs xs (1+n)"
lemma succs_append [simp]:
  "succs (xs @ ys) n = succs xs n ∪ succs ys (n + isize xs)"
```

The first of the *succs* lemmas for *acomp*, *bcomp*, and *ccomp* is pleasantly well behaved, because *acomp* does not contain any jumps.

```
lemma acomp_succs [simp]:
  "succs (acomp a) n = {n + 1 .. n + isize (acomp a)}"
```

The *exits* for *acomp* follow easily.

```
lemma exits_acomp [simp]: "exits (acomp a) = {isize (acomp a)}"
```

Compilation for boolean expressions is less well behaved, but still almost automatic. We need to put some care into formulating the statement: Firstly, to exclude trivial spurious cases, the jump target parameter of *bcomp* should lead to a forward jump. As for the compilation, we could try for a more general statement, but we are not going to need it. Secondly, we are not able to provide a nice, short equational form for *bcomp*. The main idea is that *bcomp* has two possible *exits*, one for the true-case, one for the false-case, and therefore corresponding successor pcs. However, the result of *bcomp* may be the empty list, for instance, and therefore statically have no successors (the compilation will always just fall through into the true-case). More generally, the partial constant folding optimisation that *bcomp* performs may statically exclude one or both of the possible exits. Instead of trying to precisely describe each of these cases for stating an equation, we settle for a less precise statement and just provide an upper bound for the possible successors of *bcomp*.

The proof is mostly automatic. Isabelle merely needs some hand holding in the *And*-case where we tell it how to apply the induction hypothesis.

```
lemma bcomp_succs:
  "0 ≤ i ⟹
  succs (bcomp b c i) n ⊆ {n .. n + isize (bcomp b c i)}
                          ∪ {n + i + isize (bcomp b c i)}"
```

Again, we can derive the *exits* directly from the *succs* lemma.

```
lemma bcomp_exits:
```

```
"0 ≤ i ⟹
 exits (bcomp b c i) ⊆ {isize (bcomp b c i), i + isize (bcomp b c i)}"
```

The remaining compilation function is *ccomp*. Our intuition is that the exits are {*isize (ccomp c)*}. Since we can arrive at empty compilations, though, for instance because of *SKIP*, and since we only have an upper bound for boolean expressions, we again only formulate an upper bound for *succs*.

The proof is still largely automatic for each case of the induction, we mainly give some help in how to apply the induction hypothesis.

lemma *ccomp_succs:* "*succs (ccomp c) n ⊆ {n..n + isize (ccomp c)}*"

From *succs*, the *exits* again derive easily.

lemma *ccomp_exits:* "*exits (ccomp c) ⊆ {isize (ccomp c)}*"

4.6.4. Splitting up machine executions

The main purpose of this section is to derive lemmas for decomposing larger executions into smaller ones. There are two main results: The first fully executes a sub-sequence of machine instructions and lifts it out of its execution context. The second result can deal with a partial execution of a sub-sequence, but only drops its left context under the condition that there are no jumps into the left context.

For the first result, we need a connection between our definition of exits and successors and the semantics of machine executions, a correctness statement for *succs* if you want. The idea is that each execution step must yield a new pc that is within the set predicted by *succs*.

lemma *succs_iexec1:*
```
  "P!!i ⊢i (i,s,stk) → c' ⟹ 0 ≤ i ⟹ i < isize P ⟹
   fst c' ∈ succs P 0"
```

For the first decomposition lemma, we assume an execution in the program $P @ c @ P'$ where the initial program counter is within c and the final program counter j is not within c. It must then be the case that there exists an execution of only c without additional context, started in the same state, ending in an intermediate state s'', and ending with a pc in the exits of c. This execution must be able to conclude to the same final state from s'' in the rest of the program, possibly including c again. The lengths of these two executions must add up to the length of the original execution.

The proof is by induction on n.

lemma *exec_n_split:*
```
  shows "⟦ P @ c @ P' ⊢ (isize P + i, s) →^n (j, s');
           0 ≤ i; i < isize c; j ∉ {isize P ..< isize P + isize c} ⟧ ⟹
        ∃s'' i' k m.
                c ⊢ (i, s) →^k (i', s'') ∧
                i' ∈ exits c ∧
                P @ c @ P' ⊢ (isize P + i', s'') →^m (j, s') ∧
                n = k + m"
```

The base case is simple. The step case executes one execution step, and lifts it to the only-c context with an additional lemma. This is possible because we know the program counter to be within c. We then perform a case distinction: either the execution of c is not finished yet ($j0 \in \{0..<isize\ c\}$), then we apply the induction hypothesis; or the execution of c has finished, and therefore the pc is within the exits of c and the rest of the execution from the step case will bring us to the final state.

We can instantiate the general form of this lemma to just drop a right context. This situation occurs frequently in the main proof.

The second decomposition result mentioned above can be used to drop a left context. We can relax the condition from a complete to a partial execution of the right side, but we are adding a restriction on the exits of the executing part that prevents backward jumps out of the code sequence. This tells us that the left context cannot interfere with the execution of the right context. The proof is again by induction on the length of execution.

```
lemma exec_n_drop_left:
  "⟦ P @ P' ⊢ (i, s, stk) →^k (n, s', stk');
     isize P ≤ i; exits P' ⊆ {0..} ⟧ ⟹
     P' ⊢ (i - isize P, s, stk) →^k (n - isize P, s', stk')"
```

The base case is trivial. In the step case, we again start from a single step and the rest of the execution. We lift the single step, compute the new program counter, and using the $exits$ assumption conclude that the program counter is still within $P2$, which means we can apply the induction hypothesis to get the rest of the executio and conclude the lemma.

From this general lemma, we can easily derive the Cons case where we drop an individual instruction from the head of the list, which will again be a frequent case in the compiler proof.

Both lemmas taken together, dropping left and right contexts, can be used to fully decompose an append of two instruction sequences P @ P' into isolated executions, one for P and one for P'. This case is useful for arithmetic expressions, and the semicolon case of $ccomp$, but it only works if the execution of the left side seamlessly leads over into execution of the right, i.e. if the exits of P are just $\{isize\ P\}$. This is true for the results $acomp$ and $ccomp$, and we call such instruction sequences *closed*:

```
definition "closed P ⟷ exits P ⊆ {isize P}"

lemma ccomp_closed [simp, intro!]: "closed (ccomp c)"
lemma acomp_closed [simp, intro!]: "closed (acomp c)"
lemma exec_n_split_full:
  assumes exec: "P @ P' ⊢ (0,s,stk) →^k (j, s', stk')"
  assumes P: "isize P ≤ j"
  assumes closed: "closed P"
  assumes exits: "exits P' ⊆ {0..}"
  shows "∃ k1 k2 s'' stk''.
             P ⊢ (0,s,stk) →^k1 (isize P, s'', stk'') ∧
             P' ⊢ (0,s'',stk'') →^k2 (j - isize P, s', stk')"
```

4.6.5. Correctness theorem

In this section, we prove the main theorem of this part, the second direction of the compiler proof. As before, we work our way up from $acomp$ over $bcomp$ to $ccomp$.

The correctness statement for `acomp` says that any complete execution of an arithmetic expression will leave the result value on the otherwise unchanged stack, and will not change the state of variables.

The proof is by induction on the expression, and most cases are solved automatically using our lemma set for symbolic execution. In the `Plus`-case, we decompose the execution manually, apply the induction hypothesis for the parts, and combine the results symbolically executing the `ADD` instruction.

```
lemma acomp_exec_n [dest!]:
  "acomp a ⊢ (0,s,stk) →^n (isize (acomp a),s',stk') ⟹
  s' = s ∧ stk' = aval a s#stk"
```

The correctness statement for `bcomp` is more verbose than the `acomp` version, because we need to take the two different exits into account. We demand that the expression has been fully executed, i.e. that the exit program counter `i` is not within the compiled expression any more. With the usual exclusion of backward jumps in `bcomp` we can then conclude that the exit program counter corresponds precisely with the value of the evaluation of the source expression. Stack and state remain unchanged.

As in the arithmetic case, we prove the lemma by induction on the expression. The `And` case is the only interesting one. We first split the execution into one for the left operand `b1` and one for the right operand `b1` with our splitting lemmas above. We then determine by induction hypothesis that stack and state did not change for `b1` and that the program counter will either exit directly, in which case we are done, or it will point to the instruction sequence for `b1`, in which case we apply the second induction hypothesis to conclude the case and the lemma.

```
lemma bcomp_exec_n [dest]:
  "⟦ bcomp b c j ⊢ (0, s, stk) →^n (i, s', stk');
    isize (bcomp b c j) ≤ i; 0 ≤ j ⟧ ⟹
  i = isize(bcomp b c j) + (if c = bval b s then j else 0) ∧
  s' = s ∧ stk' = stk"
```

We are now ready to tackle the main lemma. Its statement is what we set out for initially, merely phrased for `exec_n` instead pf `exec`. As was the plan, the main proof is an outer induction on `c`, and a nested induction on `n` for the while-case.

```
lemma ccomp_exec_n:
  "ccomp c ⊢ (0,s,stk) →^n (isize(ccomp c),t,stk')
    ⟹ (c,s) ⇒ t ∧ stk'=stk"
```

The first three cases of the structural induction are automatic with the lemmas that we have built up so far. The if-then-else case is more verbose, but not much more complex. It consists mainly of splitting of the evaluation of the boolean expression, case distinction and applying the induction hypothesis for the statement on `c1` and `c2`.

The while-case unsurprisingly is the most involved. We gain the induction hypothesis that `ccomp c` will execute correctly, but we need the induction on `n` to reason about the rest of the loop. We start with a case distinction on the loop condition. If this is false, we have jumped to the end of the loop and know that state and stack did not change. We can construct the same execution on the source level with the While-False rule.

The case where the loop condition is true is the interesting one. Similarly to if-then-else, we start by splitting of the execution of $bcomp$ b so we can apply the $bcomp$ correctness lemma. Since we already now the condition evaluates to true, the exit program counter must be the start of $ccomp$ c. Now we would like split off the execution of $ccomp$ c to apply the outer induction hypothesis and gain information about the execution of the source-level c. This is only possible if $ccomp$ c is non-empty, so we first perform a case distinction. If it is empty, then evaluation will be trivial (SKIP), and we can symbolically execute the jump instruction to the beginning of the loop, and by induction hypothesis on the now at least one step smaller execution of the rest of the while loop conclude the case. Note that this case is actually vacuous: the loop will not terminate and therefore our main assumption is false. Establishing that contradiction is more difficult than just applying the induction hypothesis, though. The second case, where $ccomp$ c $\neq$ $[]$ goes the more normal route: split off the execution of $ccomp$ c, apply the outer induction hypothesis to get the source-level execution of c, symbolically execute the backwards jump and, because the rest of the execution must be less steps than the whole, get the rest of the source-level while execution by induction hypothesis. Together with the fact that the loop condition was true, we can use the While-True rule from the big-step semantics to put these parts together and conclude the final correctness statement.

Converting $exec\_n$ back into $exec$ we get what we set out to prove:

theorem $ccomp\_exec$:
  "$ccomp$ c $\vdash$ $(0,s,stk)$ $\rightarrow*$ $(isize(ccomp$ $c),t,stk')$ $\implies$ (c,s) $\Rightarrow$ t"

As a corollary, we get final soundness statement of our compiler.

corollary $ccomp\_sound$:
  "$ccomp$ c $\vdash$ $(0,s,stk)$ $\rightarrow*$ $(isize(ccomp$ $c),t,stk)$ $\longleftrightarrow$ (c,s) $\Rightarrow$ t"

5. Summary

These lecture notes have presented the formalisation of a simple programming language in Isabelle/HOL together with a number of increasingly complex applications.

The aim of the presentation was to show that using an interactive theorem prover for programming language semantics brings clear benefits in tool assistance, experimentation, executability, and even readability for presentation in publications.

References

[1] G. Klein and T. Nipkow. A machine-checked model for a Java-like language, virtual machine and compiler. *ACM Trans. Prog. Lang. Syst.*, 28(4):619–695, 2006.
[2] X. Leroy. Formal certification of a compiler back-end or: programming a compiler with a proof assistant. In *Proc. 33rd ACM SIGPLAN-SIGACT Symposium on Principles of Programming Languages*, pages 42–54. ACM, 2006.
[3] A. Sabelfeld and A. Myers. Language-based information-flow security. *Selected Areas in Communications, IEEE Journal on*, 21(1):5–19, 2003.
[4] D. Volpano, C. Irvine, and G. Smith. A sound type system for secure flow analysis. *Journal of computer security*, 4(2/3):167–188, 1996.

Software Safety and Security
T. Nipkow et al. (Eds.)
IOS Press, 2012
doi:10.3233/978-1-61499-028-4-126

Advances in Probabilistic Model Checking

Marta KWIATKOWSKA [a], David PARKER [a]

[a] *Department of Computer Science, University of Oxford, Oxford, UK*

Abstract. Probabilistic model checking is an automated verification method that aims to establish the correctness of probabilistic systems. Probability may arise, for example, due to failures of unreliable components, communication across lossy media, or through the use of randomisation in distributed protocols. Probabilistic model checking enables a range of exhaustive, quantitative analyses of properties such as "the probability of a message being delivered within 5ms is at least 0.89".

In the last ten years, probabilistic model checking has been successfully applied to numerous real-world case studies, and is now a highly active field of research. This tutorial gives an introduction to probabilistic model checking, as well as presenting material on selected recent advances. The first half of the tutorial concerns two classical probabilistic models, discrete-time Markov chains and Markov decision processes, explaining the underlying theory and model checking algorithms for the temporal logic PCTL. The second half discusses two advanced topics: quantitative abstraction refinement and model checking for probabilistic timed automata. We also briefly summarise the functionality of the probabilistic model checker PRISM, the leading tool in the area.

Keywords. Markov models; Probabilistic temporal logics; Probabilistic model checking; Quantitative model checking

1. Introduction

Probabilistic modelling is widely used for the design and analysis of computer systems. Probability is typically employed to quantify unreliable or unpredictable behaviour, for example in fault-tolerant systems and communication protocols, where properties such as component failure and message loss can be expressed probabilistically. In distributed co-ordination algorithms, randomness serves as a symmetry breaker in order to derive efficient algorithms, see e.g. random back-off schemes in IEEE 802.11 or Bluetooth device discovery, and population protocols [4]. Traditionally, probability has also been used as a tool to analyse system performance and Quality of Service.

Probabilistic model checking is an automatic procedure for establishing if a desired property holds in a probabilistic system model. Conventional model checkers input a description of a model, representing a state-transition system, and a specification, typically a formula in some temporal logic, and return "yes" or "no", indicating whether or not the model satisfies the specification. In the latter case, a diagnostic trace, referred to as a counterexample, is returned. In probabilistic model checking, the models are probabilistic (typically variants of Markov

chains), in the sense that they encode the *probability* of making a transition between states instead of simply the existence of such a transition. A probability
space induced on the executions of the system enables calculation of the likelihood
of the occurrence of certain events of interest. This in turn allows *quantitative*
statements to be made about the system's behaviour, expressed as probabilities
or expectations, in addition to the qualitative statements made by conventional
model checking. Probabilities are captured via *probabilistic operators* that extend
conventional (timed or untimed) temporal logics. Models can be additionally annotated with costs and rewards, and the *reward operator* enables the computation
of expectations with respect to the underlying probability space. The extended
logics can express the following *probabilistic* and *reward specifications*:

- for a randomised leader election algorithm: "leader election is eventually
  resolved *with probability* 1";
- for a security protocol: "the chance of intrusion is *at most* 0.0001%";
- for a web service: "what is the probability of a response *within* 5ms?";
- for a wireless communication protocol: "what is the worst-case *expected
  time* for delivering a data packet?";
- for a battery-powered device: "the maximum *expected energy consumption*
  in 24hrs is at most 190J".

Note that answers to the above queries can be truth values, when the specification
simply asks for a comparison to a probability threshold, or quantitative, returning
the actual probability or expectation.

The first algorithms for probabilistic model checking were proposed in the
1980s [36,63,21], originally focussing on *qualitative* probabilistic temporal properties (i.e. those satisfied with probability 1 or 0) but later also introducing *quantitative* properties. These were followed by various extensions [35,14,8] and first
implementations [34,5]. However, the first industrial strength probabilistic model
checkers were developed only in the 2000s [24,40], when the field matured. Probabilistic model checking draws on conventional model checking, since it relies on
reachability analysis of the underlying transition system, and to this end techniques such as symbolic model checking, symmetry reduction, counterexamples
and abstraction refinement have been usefully adapted. This is combined with
appropriate numerical methods, such as linear algebra or linear programming, in
order to provide the calculation of the actual likelihoods and expectations. The
main advantage is that the analysis is exhaustive, resulting in numerically exact
answers to the temporal logic queries (in contrast to approximate analysis methods such as simulation), and is able to express detailed temporal constraints on
the system's executions (in contrast to analytical methods).

Probabilistic model checking has been successfully applied in a multitude of
domains: distributed coordination algorithms, wireless communication protocols,
security, anonymity and quantum cryptographic protocols, nanotechnology designs, power management and modelling of biological processes. Several flaws and
unusual features have been discovered using the techniques; for more information,
see e.g. [50,67]. As more real-world case studies are being analysed, user expectations are growing with regards to the efficiency and accuracy of the results, the de-
gree of automation of the methods, and the range of systems that can be modelled

and analysed. Probabilistic model checking has developed into an exciting and highly active field of research that covers the full spectrum, from theory, through implementation techniques, to applications, and we are pleased to introduce the reader to the main concepts, as well describe some research highlights.

Outline. This tutorial begins with an introduction to probabilistic model checking based on two classical probabilistic models with discrete states and discrete probability distributions – discrete time Markov chains and Markov decision processes – which respectively model fully probabilistic systems and concurrent probabilistic systems. We introduce the probabilistic temporal logic PCTL and its reward extension, which is interpreted over states of the two classical models, and explain the corresponding model checking methods. The second half of the tutorial discusses two advanced topics: quantitative abstraction refinement for Markov decision processes and model checking for probabilistic timed automata. The latter can be viewed as Markov decision processes extended with real-valued clocks, and the former method underpins their model checking, in addition to model checking for real probabilistic software. The models, specification formalisms and techniques introduced here are supported by the probabilistic model checker PRISM [55,67], which is also briefly described.

2. Preliminaries

Let Ω be a *sample set*, the set of possible outcomes of an experiment. A pair $(\Omega, \mathcal{F})$ is said to be a *sample space* if $\mathcal{F}$ is a σ-field of subsets of Ω, often built from *basic cylinders/cones* by closing w.r.t. countable unions and complement. The elements of $\mathcal{F}$ are called *events*. A triple $(\Omega, \mathcal{F}, \mu)$ is a *probability space* if μ is a probability measure over $\mathcal{F}$, i.e. $0 \leqslant \mu(A) \leqslant 1$ for all $A \in \mathcal{F}$; $\mu(\varnothing) = 0$, $\mu(\Omega) = 1$ and $\mu(\bigcup_{k=1}^{\infty} A_k) = \sum_{k=1}^{\infty} \mu(A_k)$ for disjoint A_k.

Let $(\Omega, \mathcal{F}, \mu)$ be a probability space. A measurable function $X : \Omega \to \mathbb{R}_{\geqslant 0}$ is said to be a *random variable*. The *expectation* (or average value) of X with respect to the measure μ is given by the following integral:

$$\mathbb{E}[X] \stackrel{\text{def}}{=} \int_{\omega \in \Omega} X(\omega) \, d\mu \ .$$

For a countable set S, a *discrete probability distribution* on S is a function $\mu : S \to [0, 1]$ such that $\sum_{s \in S} \mu(s) = 1$. The set of all probability distributions over the S is denoted $Dist(S)$.

3. Model Checking for Discrete-time Markov Chains

We begin with the simplest probabilistic model, that of *discrete-time Markov chains (DTMCs)*, which model systems whose behaviour at each point in time can be described by a discrete probabilistic choice over several possible outcomes. This might represent, for example, an electronic coin toss, as used to implement a randomised algorithm, or transmission of a message over an unreliable channel,

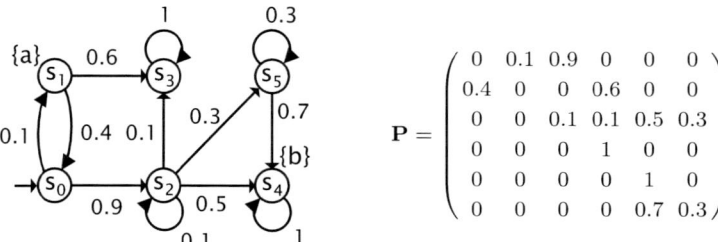

$$\mathbf{P} = \begin{pmatrix} 0 & 0.1 & 0.9 & 0 & 0 & 0 \\ 0.4 & 0 & 0 & 0.6 & 0 & 0 \\ 0 & 0 & 0.1 & 0.1 & 0.5 & 0.3 \\ 0 & 0 & 0 & 1 & 0 & 0 \\ 0 & 0 & 0 & 0 & 1 & 0 \\ 0 & 0 & 0 & 0 & 0.7 & 0.3 \end{pmatrix}$$

Figure 1. An example DTMC and its transition probability matrix $\mathbf{P}$.

which is known to fail with a certain probability. Essentially, a DTMC can be thought of as a labelled state-transition system in which each transition is annotated with a probability value indicating the likelihood of its occurrence. For this model, we introduce PCTL, a probabilistic and reward extension of the branching time logic CTL, and briefly describe the underlying algorithms.

3.1. Discrete-time Markov Chains

A discrete time Markov chain consists of discrete states, representing the configurations of the system, and has transitions governed by (discrete) probability distributions over the target states.

Definition 1 (Discrete-time Markov chain) *A discrete-time Markov chain (DTMC) is a tuple $\mathcal{D} = (S, \bar{s}, \mathbf{P}, L)$ where S is a (countable) set of states, $\bar{s} \in S$ is an initial state, $\mathbf{P} : S \times S \to [0, 1]$ is a transition probability matrix such that $\sum_{s' \in S} \mathbf{P}(s, s') = 1$ for all $s \in S$, and $L : S \to 2^{AP}$ is a labelling function mapping each state to a set of atomic propositions taken from a set AP.*

Each element $\mathbf{P}(s, s')$ of the matrix $\mathbf{P}$ gives the probability of taking a transition from s to s', where the transition is assumed to take a discrete time-step. This means that there is no notion of real time, though reasoning about discrete time is possible through state variables keeping track of time and 'counting' transition steps. Note that there are no deadlocks, and all terminating states are modelled with a self-loop.

We can unfold a DTMC model into a set of paths. A *path* through a DTMC is a non-empty (finite or infinite) sequence of states $\omega = s_0 \, s_1 \, s_2 \ldots$ with $\mathbf{P}(s_i, s_{i+1}) > 0$ for all $i \geqslant 0$. The probability matrix $\mathbf{P}$ induces a probability space on the set of infinite paths $Path_s$, which start in the state s, using the cylinder construction [48] as follows. An observation of a finite path determines a basic event (cylinder). Let $s = s_0$. For $\pi = s_0 s_1 \ldots s_n$, we define the probability measure Pr_s^{fin} for the π-cylinder by putting $Pr_s^{\text{fin}} = 1$ if π consists of a single state, and $Pr_s^{\text{fin}} = \mathbf{P}(s_0, s_1) \cdot \mathbf{P}(s_1, s_2) \cdot \ldots \cdot \mathbf{P}(s_{n-1}, s_n)$ otherwise. This extends to a unique measure Pr_s on the set of infinite paths $Path_s$ [48].

Example 1 *Figure 1 shows an example of a DTMC $\mathsf{D} = (S, \bar{s}, \mathbf{P}, L)$ with 6 states $S = \{s_0, \ldots, s_5\}$ and initial state $\bar{s} = s_0$. The transition probability matrix $\mathbf{P}$ is also shown in Figure 1. The set of atomic propositions AP is $\{a, b\}$ and function L labels s_1 with a and s_4 with b.*

3.2. The Logic PCTL

Specifications for DTMC models can be written in PCTL (Probabilistic Computation Tree Logic) [35], a probabilistic extension of the temporal logic CTL.

Definition 2 (PCTL syntax) *The syntax of PCTL is as follows:*

$$\phi ::= \texttt{true} \mid a \mid \phi \wedge \phi \mid \neg \phi \mid \mathsf{P}_{\bowtie p}[\psi]$$
$$\psi ::= \mathsf{X}\, \phi \mid \phi \,\mathsf{U}\, \phi$$

where a is an atomic proposition, $\bowtie \in \{\leqslant, <, \geqslant, >\}$ and $p \in [0, 1]$.

PCTL formulas are interpreted over the states of a DTMC. PCTL replaces the CTL existential and universal quantification over paths with the *probabilistic operator* $\mathsf{P}_{\bowtie p}[\cdot]$, where $p \in [0, 1]$ is a *probability bound* or *threshold*. Path formulas can occur only within the scope of the probabilistic operator. Intuitively, a state s satisfies $\mathsf{P}_{\bowtie p}[\psi]$ if the probability of taking a path from s that satisfies ψ is in the interval specified by $\bowtie p$. Formally, the meaning of the $\mathsf{P}_{\bowtie p}[\cdot]$ operator is:

$$s \models \mathsf{P}_{\bowtie p}[\psi] \Leftrightarrow Pr_s(\psi) \bowtie p \quad \text{where} \quad Pr_s(\psi) \overset{\text{def}}{=} Pr_s\{\omega \in Paths_s \mid \omega \models \psi\}.$$

We allow standard CTL path formulas ψ, namely *next state* ($\mathsf{X}\,\phi$) and *unbounded until* ($\phi_1 \,\mathsf{U}\, \phi_2$), as well as the usual abbreviations, e.g. $\mathsf{F}\,\phi$ is equivalent to $\texttt{true}\,\mathsf{U}\,\phi$. For simplicity, we omit *bounded until* ($\phi_1 \,\mathsf{U}^{\leqslant k}\, \phi_2$). The formula $\mathsf{X}\,\phi$ is true for a path $\omega \in Paths_s$ if ϕ is satisfied in the next state, and $\phi_1 \,\mathsf{U}\, \phi_2$ is true if ϕ_2 is satisfied at some state along the path and ϕ_1 is true up until that point. The intuition is that the probability measure of the set of ψ-paths is calculated and compared to the probability bound, yielding true or false respectively (that this set is measurable was shown in [63]). The *qualitative* fragment of PCTL comprises the formulas where p is equal to 0 or 1. Note that $\mathsf{P}_{>0}[\phi_1 \,\mathsf{U}\, \phi_2]$ is equivalent to CTL $\exists[\phi_1 \,\mathsf{U}\, \phi_2]$, whereas $\mathsf{P}_{\geqslant 1}[\phi_1 \,\mathsf{U}\, \phi_2]$ is weaker than $\forall[\phi_1 \,\mathsf{U}\, \phi_2]$.

We often use the *quantitative* (numerical) form of PCTL formulas, $\mathsf{P}_{=?}[\cdot]$, omitting the probability bound for the outermost probabilistic operator. Such a formula evaluates to the probability value computed by the PCTL model checking algorithm. It is often useful to study and plot a range of such probability values by varying one or more parameters, either of the model or of the property.

Example 2 *Below are examples of PCTL formulas for the DTMC in Figure 1:*

- $\mathsf{P}_{\leqslant 0.1}[\mathsf{X}\,a]$ - *"the probability that a is true in the next state is at most 0.1";*
- $\mathsf{P}_{=?}[\neg a \,\mathsf{U}\, b]$ - *"what is the probability of reaching a b-labelled state passing only through states that do not satisfy a?"*

3.3. Model Checking for PCTL over DTMCs

The PCTL model checking algorithm [35] takes as inputs a labelled DTMC $\mathsf{D} = (S, \overline{s}, \mathbf{P}, L)$ and a PCTL formula ϕ. The algorithm proceeds, as for CTL [19], by bottom-up traversal of the parse tree for ϕ, recursively computing the set

$Sat(\phi') = \{s \in S \mid s \models \phi'\}$ of states satisfying each subformula ϕ'. Therefore, the algorithm will eventually compute the set of *all* states satisfying ϕ. To establish if a given state s satisfies ϕ, we simply check if $s \in Sat(\phi)$. For the non-probabilistic operators, the algorithm computes as for CTL:

$$Sat(\texttt{true}) = S$$
$$Sat(a) = \{s \in S \mid a \in L(s)\}$$
$$Sat(\neg\phi) = S \setminus Sat(\phi)$$
$$Sat(\phi_1 \wedge \phi_2) = Sat(\phi_1) \cap Sat(\phi_2)\,.$$

For the probabilistic operator $\mathsf{P}_{\bowtie p}[\psi]$, we have:

$$Sat(\mathsf{P}_{\bowtie p}[\psi]) = \{s \in S \mid Pr_s(\psi) \bowtie p\}\,.$$

It is convenient to view the DTMC as the matrix $\mathbf{P}$ and $Sat(\phi)$ as a *column vector* $\underline{\phi} : S \longrightarrow \{0,1\}$ given by $\underline{\phi}(s) = 1$ if $s \models \phi$ and 0 otherwise. Consider the next state operator. The probabilities for all states can then be computed by a single matrix-by-vector multiplication, written in vector notation $\underline{Pr}(\mathsf{X}\,\phi) = \mathbf{P} \cdot \underline{\phi}$.

For the path formula $\phi_1 \,\mathsf{U}\, \phi_2$, the probabilities $Pr_s(\phi_1 \,\mathsf{U}\, \phi_2)$ are obtained as the unique solution of the *linear equation system* in variables $\{x_s \mid s \in S\}$:

$$x_s = \begin{cases} 0 & \text{if } s \in S^{no} \\ 1 & \text{if } s \in S^{yes} \\ \sum_{s' \in S} \mathbf{P}(s,s') \cdot x_{s'} & \text{if } s \in S^{?} \end{cases}$$

where $S^{no} \stackrel{\text{def}}{=} Sat(\mathsf{P}_{\leqslant 0}[\phi_1 \,\mathsf{U}\, \phi_2])$ and $S^{yes} \stackrel{\text{def}}{=} Sat(\mathsf{P}_{\geqslant 1}[\phi_1 \,\mathsf{U}\, \phi_2])$ denote the sets of *all* states that satisfy $\phi_1 \,\mathsf{U}\, \phi_2$ with probability exactly 0 and 1, respectively, and $S^{?} = S \setminus (S^{no} \cup S^{yes})$.

The sets S^{no} and S^{yes} are precomputed using conventional fixed point computations. For example, for S^{no}, we first compute the set of states from which we can reach, with positive probability, a ϕ_2-state passing only through states satisfying ϕ_1, and then subtract this set from S. Since the values for the precomputed states are known (0 or 1), the solution of the resulting linear equation system in $|S^{?}|$ variables can be obtained by any direct method (e.g. Gaussian elimination) or iterative method (e.g. Jacobi, Gauss-Seidel). For qualitative PCTL properties, it suffices to use these precomputation algorithms alone. Note that the precomputation algorithms determine the exact probability in case it is 0 or 1, thus avoiding the problem of round-off errors that are typical for numerical computation.

Example 3 *Consider the DTMC* D *from Example 1 (see Figure 1) and the PCTL formula* $\mathsf{P}_{>0.8}[\neg a \,\mathsf{U}\, b]$. *We have* $S^{no} = \{s_1, s_3\}$ *and* $S^{yes} = \{s_4, s_5\}$. *These sets, and the resulting linear equation system, are shown in Figure 2. This yields the solution* $(0.8, 0, \frac{8}{9}, 0, 1, 1)$, *and we see that* $Sat(\mathsf{P}_{>0.8}[\neg a \,\mathsf{U}\, b]) = \{s_2, s_4, s_5\}$.

3.4. Extending DTMCs and PCTL with Rewards

In this section we introduce *rewards* which can be used to annotate DTMCs with information about resources and their usage, for example the energy consumption

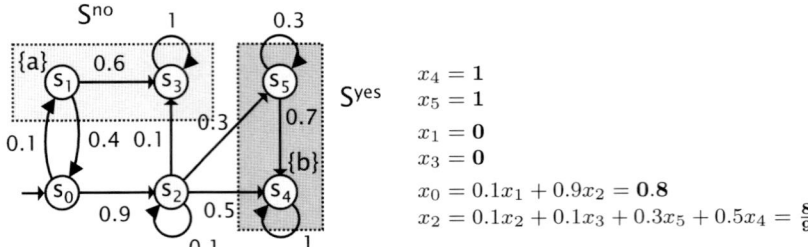

Figure 2. Determining the probabilities $Pr_s(\neg a \cup b)$ for the DTMC D from Example 1.
Left: the DTMC, labelled with the sets S^{no} and S^{yes} from precomputation;
Right: linear equation system to determine probabilities for the remaining states.

or the number of lost messages. We consistently use the terminology *rewards* but,
often, these will be used to model *costs*.

Let $D = (S, \bar{s}, \mathbf{P}, L)$ be a DTMC. A *reward structure* is a pair (r_s, r_t) of
functions: a *state reward* function $r_s : S \to \mathbb{R}_{\geq 0}$ mapping a state to the reward
acquired per time-step, and a *transition reward* function $r_t : S \times S \to \mathbb{R}_{\geq 0}$,
mapping each transition to the reward acquired as the transition is taken. The
rewards can be interpreted in two ways: *instantaneous* (omitted for simplicity) or
cumulated over system execution.

Example 4 *The reward structure "number of messages lost" is defined by r_s equal
to zero and r_t mapping each transition that loses a message to 1. Reward structure
"power consumption" is given by r_s equal to per-time-step energy consumption in
each state and r_t equal to the energy cost of each transition.*

The logic PCTL is extended [53] to allow for the reward properties by the
addition of the *reward operator* $\mathsf{R}_{\bowtie r}[\cdot]$ and the following state formulas:

$$\mathsf{R}_{\bowtie r}[\mathsf{C}^{\leq k}] \mid \mathsf{R}_{\bowtie r}[\mathsf{F}\, \phi]$$

where $\bowtie \in \{<, \leq, \geq, >\}$, $r \in \mathbb{R}_{\geq 0}$, $k \in \mathbb{N}$ and ϕ is a PCTL state formula.
Intuitively, a state s satisfies $\mathsf{R}_{\bowtie r}[\mathsf{C}^{\leq k}]$ (*cumulative* reward) if, from state
s, the expected reward cumulated over k time-steps satisfies $\bowtie r$; and $\mathsf{R}_{\bowtie r}[\mathsf{F}\, \phi]$
(*reachability* reward) is true if, from state s, the expected reward cumulated before
a state satisfying ϕ is reached meets $\bowtie r$. Formally, the semantics of the reward
operator is defined using the expectation of an appropriate random variable:

$$s \models \mathsf{R}_{\bowtie r}[\mathsf{C}^{\leq k}] \quad \Leftrightarrow \quad \mathbb{E}_s(X_{\mathsf{C}^{\leq k}}) \bowtie r$$
$$s \models \mathsf{R}_{\bowtie r}[\mathsf{F}\, \phi] \quad \Leftrightarrow \quad \mathbb{E}_s(X_{\mathsf{F}\, \phi}) \bowtie r$$

for any $s \in S$, $k \in \mathbb{N}$, $r \in \mathbb{R}_{\geq 0}$ and PCTL formula ϕ, and where $\mathbb{E}_s$ denotes
expectation with respect to the probability measure Pr_s. The random variables
$X_{\mathsf{C}^{\leq k}}, X_{\mathsf{F}\, \phi} : Path_s \to \mathbb{R}_{\geq 0}$ corresponding to the two forms of the reward operator
are defined, for any path $\omega = s_0 s_1 s_2 \cdots \in Path_s$, as follows:

$$X_{\mathsf{C}^{\leqslant k}}(\omega) \stackrel{\text{def}}{=} \begin{cases} 0 & \text{if } k = 0 \\ \sum_{i=0}^{k-1} r_s(s_i) + r_t(s_i, s_{i+1}) & \text{otherwise} \end{cases}$$

$$X_{\mathsf{F}\,\phi}(\omega) \stackrel{\text{def}}{=} \begin{cases} 0 & \text{if } s_0 \models \phi \\ \infty & \text{if } \forall i \in \mathbb{N}.\, s_i \not\models \phi \\ \sum_{i=0}^{\min\{j|s_j \models \phi\}-1} r_s(s_i) + r_t(s_i, s_{i+1}) & \text{otherwise.} \end{cases}$$

As for the probabilistic operator, if the outermost operator of a PCTL formula is $\mathsf{R}_{\bowtie r}[\cdot]$, we can omit the bound $\bowtie r$ and compute the expected value instead. This also enables a range of such values to be obtained by varying one or more parameters, either of the model or of the property.

Example 5 *Below are some examples of reward based specifications:*

- $\mathsf{R}_{=?}[\mathsf{C}^{\leqslant 10}]$ - *what is the expected number of messages lost within the first 10 time-steps?;*
- $\mathsf{R}_{\leqslant 5}[\mathsf{F}\ end]$ - *the expected time to termination is at most 5.*

Model checking of the reward operator is similar to computing probabilities for the probabilistic operator, and follows through the solution of recursive equations (for $\mathsf{R}_{\bowtie r}[\mathsf{C}^{\leqslant k}]$) or a system of linear equations (for $\mathsf{R}_{\bowtie r}[\mathsf{F}\,\phi]$). For more details on this, and other aspects of probabilistic model checking for DTMCs, see e.g. [53,9].

3.5. More on Model Checking for DTMCs

The time complexity for PCTL model checking over DTMCs, including the reward operator, is linear in the size of the formula $|\phi|$ (number of logical connectives and temporal operators) and polynomial in the size of the state space $|S|$ [35].

DTMCs can also be verified against LTL properties, but the verification method is quite different. The LTL formula is first translated into a Rabin automaton and then model checking reduces to the computation of probabilistic reachability of bottom strongly connected components on the product of the DTMC and the formula automaton [9]. The overall complexity for LTL is doubly exponential in $|\phi|$ and polynomial in in $|S|$, but can be reduced to a single exponential.

4. Model Checking for Markov Decision Processes

We now explain how to model check *Markov decision processes* (MDPs), which generalise discrete-time Markov chains with the addition of *nondeterminism*. Probability is employed to quantify aspects of system behaviour where probability distributions are known. In contrast, nondeterminism is used to model *unknown environments*, where such distributions are not known. It is also used to model *concurrency*, where it represents the different possible interleavings of multiple components operating in parallel. Alternatively, we can use nondeterminism to capture the possible ways that a *controller* can influence the behaviour of the system, e.g. in planning and robotics.

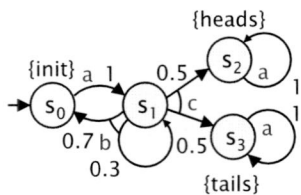

Figure 3. An example MDP.

4.1. Markov Decision Processes

Formally, we define a Markov decision process as follows.

Definition 3 (Markov decision process) *A* Markov decision process *(MDP) is a tuple* $M=(S, \bar{s}, Act, Steps, L)$ *where* S *is a set of states,* $\bar{s} \in S$ *is an initial state, Act is an alphabet of actions, Steps* $: S \times Act \to Dist(S)$ *is a (partial) probabilistic transition function and* $L : S \to 2^{AP}$ *is a labelling function mapping each state to a set of atomic propositions taken from a set* AP.

In an MDP, several *actions* may be available in a given state s, each corresponding to a probability distribution. We denote this set by $A(s) = \{a \in Act \mid Steps(s, a)$ is defined$\}$. As for DTMCs, we disallow deadlocks, and hence assume that $A(s)$ is non-empty for all $s \in S$. The behaviour of an MDP M is as follows. Firstly, a choice between one or more actions from the alphabet Act is made *nondeterministically*. Secondly, for the chosen action a, a successor state s' is chosen randomly, according to the probability distribution $Steps(s, a)$, i.e. the probability that a transition to s' occurs is $Steps(s, a)(s')$.

An *infinite path* through an MDP is a sequence $\omega = s_0 a_0 s_1 a_1 \ldots$ where $s_i \in S$, $a_i \in A(s_i)$ and $Steps(s_i, a_i)(s_{i+1}) > 0$ for all $i \in \mathbb{N}$. A *finite path* $\pi = s_0 a_0 s_1 \ldots s_n$ is a prefix of an infinite path ending in a state. We denote by $Path_s$ and $Path_s^{fin}$ the sets of all infinite and finite paths from state s, respectively, and by $Path$ and $Path^{fin}$ the corresponding sets of paths from any state. For a finite path π, the last state of π is denoted $last(\pi)$.

Example 6 *Figure 3 shows an example MDP* $M = (S, \bar{s}, Act, Steps, L)$ *with states* $S = \{s_0, \ldots, s_3\}$, *initial state* s_0 *and alphabet of actions* $\{a, b, c\}$. *State* s_1, *for example, has a nondeterministic choice between two actions, b and c.*

To reason formally about MDPs, we need a probability space over infinite paths. However, a probability space can only be constructed once all the nondeterminism has been resolved. Each possible resolution of nondeterminism is represented by an *adversary*, also called a *policy*, which is responsible for choosing an action in each state of the MDP, based on the history of its execution so far.

Definition 4 (Adversary) *An* adversary *of an MDP* $M = (S, \bar{s}, Act, Steps, L)$ *is a function* $\sigma : Path^{fin} \to Dist(Act)$ *such that* $\sigma(\pi)(a) > 0$ *only if* $a \in A(last(\pi))$. *An adversary* σ *is* memoryless *if* $\sigma(\pi)$ *depends only on* $last(\pi)$ *and* deterministic *if the distribution* $\sigma(\pi)$ *always selects a single action with probability 1.*

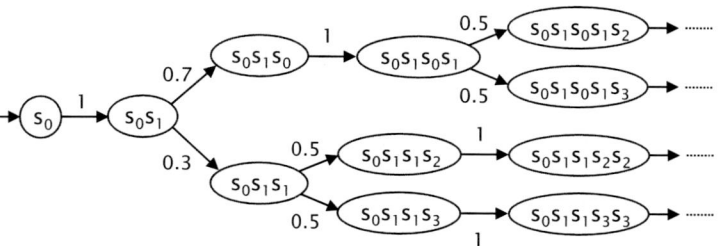

Figure 4. The induced DTMC for an adversary of the MDP in Figure 3.

The set of *all* adversaries of an MDP M is denoted *Adv*. Under a particular adversary $\sigma \in Adv$, the behaviour of M is fully probabilistic and can be captured by an *induced DTMC*, denoted M^σ, each state of which is a finite path of M.

Definition 5 (Induced DTMC) *For an MDP* $\mathsf{M} = (S, \overline{s}, Act, Steps, L)$ *and adversary* σ, *the* induced DTMC *is* $\mathsf{M}^\sigma = (Path^{\mathrm{fin}}, \overline{s}, \mathbf{P}, L')$ *where:*

- *for any* $\pi, \pi' \in Path^{\mathrm{fin}}$:

$$\mathbf{P}(\pi, \pi') = \begin{cases} \sigma(\pi)(a) \cdot Steps(last(\pi), a)(s) & \text{if } \pi' = \pi as, \ a \in A(last(\pi)) \\ 0 & otherwise; \end{cases}$$

- $L'(\pi) = L(last(\pi))$ *for all* $\pi \in Path^{\mathrm{fin}}$.

Notice that there is a one-to-one mapping between the infinite paths of the DTMC M^σ and the infinite paths of MDP M when under the control of adversary σ. This means that the DTMC yields, for a start state s, a probability space, denoted Pr_s^σ over these infinite paths. The induced DTMC M^σ has a (countably) infinite number of states. However, in the case of memoryless adversaries, its state space is isomorphic to S and M^σ can be reduced to an $|S|$-state DTMC.

Example 7 *Consider the MDP* M *from Example 6 (shown in Figure 3) and the (deterministic, but non-memoryless) adversary* σ, *which picks action b the first time that state* s_1 *is reached, and then action c the second time. The induced DTMC* M^σ *is shown in Figure 4.*

4.2. PCTL Model Checking over MDPs

Probabilistic statements about MDPs typically involve quantification over adversaries, so as to establish that some specified event is observed *for all* possible adversaries. The logic PCTL, for example, is defined for MDPs as for DTMCs [14], the key difference being that the semantics of the probabilistic operator contains explicit universal quantification:

$$s \models \mathsf{P}_{\bowtie p}[\psi] \quad \Leftrightarrow \quad Pr_s^\sigma \{\omega \in Path_s \mid \omega \models \psi\} \bowtie p \ \text{ for all } \sigma \in Adv.$$

The algorithm for PCTL model checking proceeds as for DTMCs, except for the probabilistic operator. For $\mathsf{P}_{\rhd p}[\psi]$ where $\rhd \in \{\geqslant, >\}$, this reduces to the calculation of the *minimum probability* $Pr_s^{\min}(\psi)$. The case of $\mathsf{P}_{\lhd p}[\psi]$ for $\lhd \in \{\leqslant, <\}$ is dual, via the *maximum probability* $Pr_s^{\max}(\psi)$:

$$Sat(\mathsf{P}_{\rhd p}[\psi]) = \{s \in S \mid Pr_s^{\min}(\psi) \rhd p\}$$
$$Sat(\mathsf{P}_{\lhd p}[\psi]) = \{s \in S \mid Pr_s^{\max}(\psi) \lhd p\}$$

where $Pr_s^{\min}(\psi) = \inf_{\sigma \in Adv}\{Pr_s^\sigma(\psi)\}$ and $Pr_s^{\max}(\psi) = \sup_{\sigma \in Adv}\{Pr_s^\sigma(\psi)\}$.

To describe the computation of these values, we restrict our attention to the case of minimum probabilities. If $\psi = \mathsf{X}\,\phi$, we have:

$$Pr_s^{\min}(\mathsf{X}\,\phi) = \min_{a \in A(s)}\left[\sum_{s' \in Sat(\phi)} Steps(s,a)(s')\right].$$

For $\psi = \phi_1 \cup \phi_2$, the minimum probabilities are the unique solution of:

$$Pr_s^{\min}(\psi) = \begin{cases} 0 & \text{if } s \in S^{no} \\ 1 & \text{if } s \in S^{yes} \\ \min_{a \in A(s)}\left[\sum_{s' \in S} Steps(s,a)(s') \cdot Pr_{s'}^{\min}(\psi)\right] & \text{if } s \in S^? \end{cases}$$

with S^{no} and S^{yes} denoting the sets of states where the minimum probability is respectively 0 and 1, precomputed in a similar fashion to the DTMC case via a fixpoint (see e.g. [28]). The computation of these probabilities can be performed in several different ways; we detail three such methods below.

Linear programming. The minimum probabilities $Pr_s^{\min}(\phi_1 \cup \phi_2)$ for $s \in S$ can be obtained as the unique solution of the following linear program (LP):

$$\text{maximise } \sum_{s \in S} x_s \text{ subject to the constraints:}$$
$$x_s = 0 \qquad\qquad \text{for all } s \in S^{no}$$
$$x_s = 1 \qquad\qquad \text{for all } s \in S^{yes}$$
$$x_s \leqslant \sum_{s' \in S} Steps(s,a)(s') \cdot x_{s'} \quad \text{for all } s \in S^? \text{ and } a \in A(s).$$

This can be solved using standard techniques such as the simplex, ellipsoid or branch-and-cut methods.

Value iteration. The minimum probabilities can also be approximated iteratively, since $Pr_s^{\min}(\phi_1 \cup \phi_2) = \lim_{n \to \infty} x_s^{(n)}$, as follows:

$$x_s^{(n)} = \begin{cases} 0 & \text{if } s \in S^{no} \\ 1 & \text{if } s \in S^{yes} \\ 0 & \text{if } s \in S^? \text{ and } n = 0 \\ \min_{a \in A(s)}\left\{\sum_{s' \in S} Steps(s,a)(s') \cdot x_{s'}^{(n-1)}\right\} & \text{if } s \in S^? \text{ and } n > 0. \end{cases}$$

In practice, the iterative computation is terminated when the values $x_s^{(n)}$ have converged sufficiently with respect to a given level of precision $\varepsilon > 0$.

Policy iteration. This method iterates over adversaries (i.e. policies), as opposed to probability values. It starts with an arbitrary, memoryless adversary σ and computes the probability p_s^σ of satisfying $\phi_1 \cup \phi_2$ from each state s under σ. This

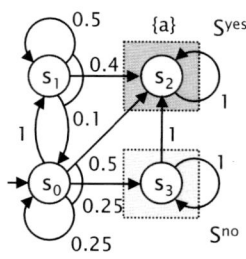

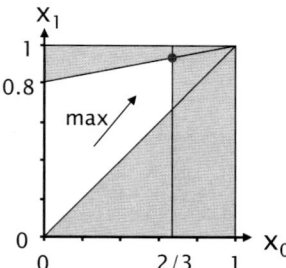

(a) Example MDP, labelled with the sets S^{no} and S^{yes} from precomputation.

(b) Linear programming problem yielding minimum probabilities of reaching a-labelled states.

Figure 5. Determining the probabilities $Pr_s^{min}(\mathsf{F}\,a)$ for an example MDP.

is done on the induced DTMC, e.g., by solving a linear equation system. The adversary σ can be improved to adversary σ' as follows:

$$\sigma'(s) = \arg\min_{a \in A(s)} \sum_{s' \in S} Steps(s,a)(s') \cdot p_{s'}^{\sigma}.$$

The process is repeated until there is no change, and hence the optimal adversary is found. To ensure termination, adversary choices should only be changed when there is a strict improvement in the probability for s.

Example 8 *Consider the MDP in Figure 5(a) and the probabilities $Pr_s^{min}(\mathsf{F}\,a) = Pr_s^{min}(\text{true U } a)$. We have $S^{no} = \{s_3\}$ and $S^{yes} = \{s_2\}$, which are also marked in Figure 5(a). We need to compute the minimum probabilities for the remaining two states in $S^? = \{s_0, s_1\}$. First, we solve a linear program. We have:*

maximise $x_0 + x_1$ subject to the constraints:
$$x_0 \leqslant x_1$$
$$x_0 \leqslant 0.25 \cdot x_0 + 0.5$$
$$x_1 \leqslant 0.1 \cdot x_0 + 0.5 \cdot x_1 + 0.4$$
$$x_2 = 1$$
$$x_3 = 0$$

The optimisation problem (restricted to variables x_0 and x_1) is illustrated graphically in Figure 5(b), with the central white region representing the intersection of the constraints. The required solution is shown by the dot in the top right corner, which is $(x_0, x_1) = (\frac{2}{3}, \frac{14}{15})$, so we have $\underline{Pr}^{min} = (\frac{2}{3}, \frac{14}{15}, 1, 0)$.

Alternatively, we can compute the probabilities using value iteration. Figure 6 (left) shows the values computed for $x_s^{(n)}$, converging after 21 steps when the maximum difference between values in successive iterations drops below $\varepsilon = 10^{-6}$. The right-hand side of Figure 6 shows the same values (for states s_0 and s_1) plotted over the linear program from above.

Finally, we observe that the points $(\frac{2}{3}, \frac{14}{15})$ and $(1,1)$ in the linear program correspond to the two memoryless adversaries obtained by taking the two different choices in state s_0. If policy iteration were applied instead, starting with the second

$$[\quad x_0^{(n)}, \qquad x_1^{(n)}, \quad x_2^{(n)}, x_3^{(n)} \;]$$

$n = 0:$ [0.000000, 0.000000, 1, 0]
$n = 1:$ [0.000000, 0.400000, 1, 0]
$n = 2:$ [0.400000, 0.600000, 1, 0]
$n = 3:$ [0.600000, 0.740000, 1, 0]
$n = 4:$ [0.650000, 0.830000, 1, 0]
$n = 5:$ [0.662500, 0.880000, 1, 0]
$n = 6:$ [0.665625, 0.906250, 1, 0]
$n = 7:$ [0.666406, 0.919688, 1, 0]
$n = 8:$ [0.666602, 0.926484, 1, 0]
$n = 9:$ [0.666650, 0.929902, 1, 0]

$\cdots$

$n = 20:$ [0.666667, 0.933332, 1, 0]
$n = 21:$ [0.666667, 0.933332, 1, 0]

$\approx$ [2/3, 14/15, 1, 0]

Figure 6. Left: Vectors from value iteration on the reachability problem from Figure 5; Right: Value iteration points plotted against the linear program

one (which gives $x_0 = x_1 = 1$), then the first round of improvement of policy iteration would yield the first, optimal adversary.

4.3. Extending MDPs with Rewards

As for DTMCs, we can augment an MDP with rewards, useful for representing quantitative system information such as the energy consumption or the number of packets sent. A *reward structure* for an MDP $\mathsf{M} = (S, \bar{s}, Act, Steps, L)$ is a pair (r_s, r_a) comprising a *state reward* function $r_s : S \to \mathbb{R}_{\geqslant 0}$ and an *action reward* function $r_a : S \times Act \to \mathbb{R}_{\geqslant 0}$.

The logic PCTL is extended, as for DTMCs, with the reward operator $\mathsf{R}_{\bowtie r}[\cdot]$ (and its quantitative form $\mathsf{R}_{\min=?}[\cdot]$ or $\mathsf{R}_{\max=?}[\cdot]$). The difference is that now we compute minimum (or maximum) reward values as expectations.

Example 9 *Below are some examples of reward based specifications:*

- $\mathsf{R}_{\min=?}[\mathsf{C}^{\leqslant 3600}]$ - *the minimum expected energy consumption over one hour;*
- $\mathsf{R}_{\max=?}[\mathsf{F} \; end]$ - *the maximum expected time to termination.*

4.4. More on Model Checking for MDPs

The time complexity for PCTL model checking over an MDP is (again) linear in the size of the formula $|\phi|$ and polynomial in the size of the state space $|S|$. Like for DTMCs, MDPs can also be verified against LTL properties via the construction of the product with a deterministic Rabin automaton for the LTL formula. Model checking reduces to the computation of maximum reachability probabilities of a set of end components of the product MDP. See e.g. [9,28] for details. The overall complexity for LTL is doubly exponential in $|\phi|$ and polynomial in $|S|$; unlike for DTMCs, this *cannot* be reduced to a single exponential.

MDPs can also be verified under *fairness* conditions [10,7]. Fairness is necessary, for example, in the context of parallel composition to ensure progress for each concurrent component whenever possible. For modelling and verification of probabilistic systems comprising multiple components, the closely related model of *probabilistic automata* has been developed, along with rich theories for compositional modelling and analysis [61].

5. Quantitative Abstraction Refinement

The techniques described in the preceding two sections can be used to establish a wide range of useful properties of systems modelled as DTMCs and MDPs. Furthermore, these methods are efficient: typically the time complexity is polynomial in the size of the state space of the model. In practice, though, one of the principal challenges in applying probabilistic model checking to real-life systems is *scalability*: the models that need to be constructed and analysed are often simply too big for the process to be feasible. This phenomenon, commonly called the *state-space explosion problem*, affects all verification approaches that rely on an exhaustive analysis of a model's state space.

In this section, we describe the use of *abstraction* as a mechanism for overcoming the state-space explosion problem. Abstraction techniques work by hiding aspects of the system being modelled that are not relevant to the property currently being verified, resulting in a smaller *abstract model*. Let us refer to the states $s \in S$ of the model that is to be abstracted as *concrete states*. We will define an abstraction of the model based on a partition $\mathcal{A}$ of these concrete states, with each subset in the partition referred to as an *abstract state* $a \in \mathcal{A}$. We then build an abstract model, whose state space is the set of abstract states $\mathcal{A}$.

5.1. Abstracting MDPs as Stochastic Games

In this tutorial, we will focus on the problem of building abstractions for Markov decisions processes (MDPs), since this is the more general of the two models that we have considered. One approach to defining an abstraction of an MDP M, based on a partition $\mathcal{A}$ of its states into abstract states, is to use an *existential abstraction* [22], which takes the form of another MDP $M_{\mathcal{A}}$ with state space $\mathcal{A}$.

The existential abstraction $M_{\mathcal{A}}$ is built by *lifting* each probability distribution μ (over S) in MDP M to a distribution $\mu_{\mathcal{A}}$ over $\mathcal{A}$, i.e. for each $a \in \mathcal{A}$, $\mu_{\mathcal{A}}(a) = \sum_{s \in a} \mu(a)$. For each abstract state a in $M_{\mathcal{A}}$, $Steps(a)$ then contains the distributions $\mu_{\mathcal{A}}$ for all distributions μ from any state s such that $s \in a$.

Example 10 *Figure 7(a) shows a fragment of an MDP M, annotated with a partition $\mathcal{A}$ of its states. Figure 7(b) shows the corresponding fragment of the existential abstraction $M_{\mathcal{A}}$.*

Formally, the MDP M and its abstraction $M_{\mathcal{A}}$ are related through *strong simulation* [62], which means that the abstraction preserves the "safe" fragment of PCTL. Furthermore, $M_{\mathcal{A}}$ yields bounds on the reachability probabilities for M. More precisely, letting t be an atomic proposition labelling a *target* abstract state in $M_{\mathcal{A}}$, we can obtain a lower bound on the minimum probability of reaching t and an upper bound on the maximum probability of reaching it:

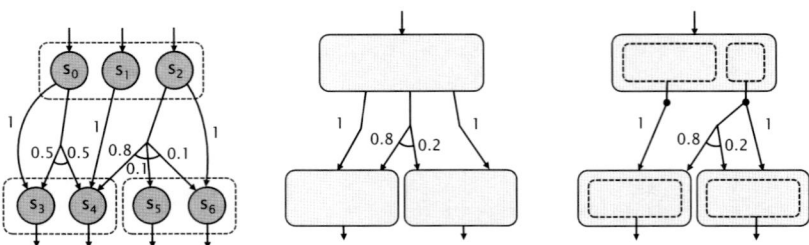

(a) MDP M labelled with partition $\mathcal{A}$ of its states. (b) MDP representing the existential abstraction $M_{\mathcal{A}}$. (c) The stochastic game abstraction $G_{\mathcal{A}}$.

Figure 7. Fragments of an MDP and corresponding abstractions.

$$Pr_{M_{\mathcal{A}}}^{\min}(\mathsf{F}\,t) \leqslant Pr_{M}^{\min}(\mathsf{F}\,t) \quad \text{and} \quad Pr_{M}^{\max}(\mathsf{F}\,t) \leqslant Pr_{M_{\mathcal{A}}}^{\max}(\mathsf{F}\,t)$$

An alternative approach to abstraction was presented in [51], based on the construction of a *stochastic two-player game* $G_{\mathcal{A}}$ to abstract the MDP M using state space partition $\mathcal{A}$. Stochastic two-player games are a generalisation of MDPs that include two distinct forms of nondeterminism, each controlled by a separate player. The key idea behind the stochastic game abstraction is to use player 1 to represent the nondeterminism introduced through the process of abstraction and player 2 to represent nondeterminism from the original MDP M.

Example 11 *Figure 7(c) illustrates the construction of the stochastic game abstraction $G_{\mathcal{A}}$ for the same MDP M used in Example 10 (and shown in Figure 7(a)). Like for existential abstraction, distributions from M are lifted from S to $\mathcal{A}$, except that they are now grouped according to the concrete states of M from which they emanate. For example, the right-hand black dot in Figure 7(c) shows the (lifted) distributions from state s_2 of M. The left-hand dot shows the distributions for states s_0 and s_1, which become identical when lifted to $\mathcal{A}$. The corresponding groups of states for each dot are indicated by the rounded boxes with dashed edges.*

The game is played as follows. The abstract states, shown as rounded boxes with solid edges, are controlled by player 1. He chooses one of the successor player 2 states, represented by the black dots. Player 2 then chooses one of the distributions emanating from the player 2 state. The chosen distribution is used to randomly select the next abstract state.

An important advantage of the stochastic game abstraction over the existential abstraction is that it yields both lower and upper bounds for either minimum or maximum reachability probabilities. From the stochastic game, we can determine the *optimal probabilities* for each player, e.g. the maximum probability of reaching a t-labelled state that player 1 can achieve, assuming that player 2 is trying to minimise it, denoted $Pr_{G_{\mathcal{A}}}^{\max,\min}(\mathsf{F}\,t)$. The dual probability $Pr_{G_{\mathcal{A}}}^{\min,\max}(\mathsf{F}\,t)$ is defined similarly. We can also determine either the minimum or maximum probability of reaching t, assuming that the two players collaborate, denoted $Pr_{G_{\mathcal{A}}}^{\min,\min}(\mathsf{F}\,t)$ and $Pr_{G_{\mathcal{A}}}^{\max,\max}(\mathsf{F}\,t)$, respectively. All four values can be computed (approximately) with an adapted version of the value iteration method described

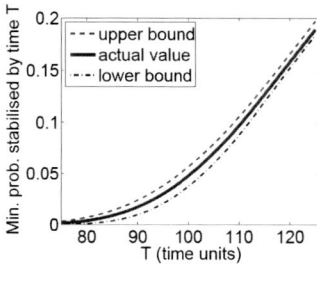

(a) Self-stabilisation protocol.

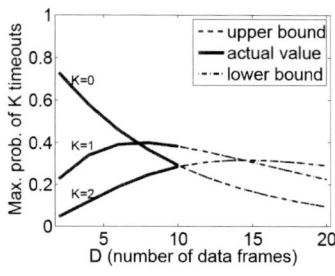

(b) Sliding window protocol.

Figure 8. Graphs illustrating the lower and upper bounds obtained from the stochastic game abstractions of MDPs from two large case studies.

in Section 4.2 for MDPs. The values, when computed for the stochastic game abstraction G_A of an MDP M, yield lower and upper bounds as follows:

$$Pr_{G_A}^{\min,\min}(F\,t) \leqslant Pr_M^{\min}(F\,t) \leqslant Pr_{G_A}^{\max,\min}(F\,t)$$
$$Pr_{G_A}^{\min,\max}(F\,t) \leqslant Pr_M^{\max}(F\,t) \leqslant Pr_{G_A}^{\max,\max}(F\,t)$$

Figure 8 shows some typical examples of these bounds, obtained from real case studies [45]. Part (a) plots results for the "minimum probability of termination within time T" on a model of Israeli & Jalfon's self-stabilisation protocol, for a range of values of T. In this case, the MDP has 1,048,575 states, whereas the stochastic game abstraction has only 627. Part (b) shows results for "the maximum probability of K time-outs" on a model of a sliding window protocol, varying both K and the number frames sent D. In this case, we see that the lower and upper bounds are tight, yielding the exact answers. Also, in this example, the use of *predicate abstraction* allows us to build and analyse abstractions for MDPs that are too large to verify directly. Thus, we see results on the right-hand side of the graph that could not have been obtained without the use of abstraction.

5.2. Quantitative Abstraction Refinement

Although the stochastic game abstractions presented above were constructed and analysed in a fully automated fashion, one crucial part of the process was still performed manually: the specification of the abstract state space A. The practical applicability and usefulness of the abstraction techniques are completely reliant on being able to determine an appropriate partition A of the concrete state space, i.e. one that is coarse enough to yield a small abstract model, but which gives lower and upper bounds that are close enough to provide useful information.

Here, we discuss a way to construct such a partition A in a fully automatic fashion, using *abstraction refinement*. This is inspired by the successful *counterexample-guided abstraction refinement* (CEGAR) approach [20], developed to build abstractions for non-probabilistic model checking. The idea is to start with a simple, coarse partition, build the corresponding abstraction, and then iteratively refine the partition, resulting in increasingly precise abstractions. In CEGAR, the refinement step is driven by counterexamples obtained by model

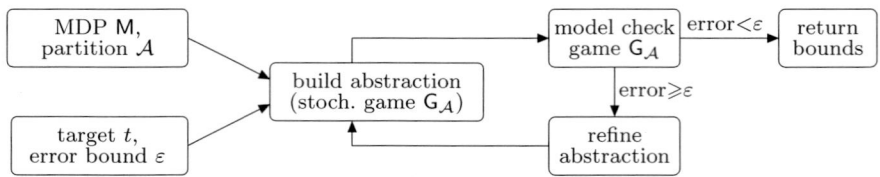

Figure 9. Quantitative abstraction-refinement loop.

checking the abstractions produced at each iteration, and the iterations of refinement are terminated when the current abstraction can be used either to verify or refute the property being verified.

Here, we describe *quantitative abstraction refinement* [47], which can be seen as a quantitative analogue of CEGAR, applied to the stochastic game abstraction approach of [51]. The idea is that the difference between the lower and upper bounds obtained from an abstraction (which we call the "error") *quantifies* the precision of the abstraction. If the error is too high, the abstraction should be refined (i.e. a finer partition A used).

Figure 9 shows a quantitative abstraction-refinement loop used to automatically construct stochastic game abstractions of an MDP M. Starting with an initial (coarse) partition, abstractions are repeatedly constructed, analysed and refined until the difference between the lower and upper bounds obtained for the property of interest (say, the minimum or maximum probability of reaching t-labelled states) falls below some threshold ε.

The applicability of quantitative abstraction refinement was initially demonstrated in [47], on a simple explicit-state implementation, applied to a set of benchmark models. Subsequently, the approach has been successfully applied to the verification of:

- probabilistic real-time systems, modelled using probabilistic timed automata [54] (see the next section for a more in-depth discussion);
- probabilistic software, based on the use of ANSI-C code, augmented with probabilistic commands [46];
- concurrent probabilistic programs, as analysed by the probabilistic abstraction tool PASS [29];
- probabilistic programs over arbitrary abstract domains [27];
- probabilistic hybrid automata [31].

Several other methods for abstraction refinement of probabilistic systems have also been proposed [22,41,25,16]; see e.g. [47] for a discussion of the differences between these approaches.

6. Probabilistic Timed Automata

The two models that we presented in the first half of this tutorial, DTMCs and MDPs, both use a *discrete* model of time, i.e. a system execution is modelled as a sequence of discrete time-steps. In this section, we discuss modelling and verification of probabilistic *real-time* systems, which use a continuous (dense) model of time. These systems will be modelled by *probabilistic timed automata*.

Another popular model incorporating a continuous notion of time is *continuous-time Markov chains* (CTMCs), an extension of DTMCs where the delays between state transitions are represented by exponential distributions. See, for example, [8,53] for overviews of probabilistic model checking techniques for CTMCs.

6.1. Probabilistic Timed Automata

Probabilistic timed automata (PTAs) [42,59] model systems that exhibit probabilistic, nondeterministic and real-time characteristics. They can be seen as an extension of MDPs with *clocks*, real-valued variables whose values increase simultaneously over time. Like in the classic model of timed automata [2], states and transitions of PTAs can be labelled with *invariants* and *guards*, that is, predicates on clocks respectively dictating how long to remain in a state and when transitions can occur. Transitions between states (represented, as in MDPs, by probability distributions) can also reset the values of one or more clocks.

To specify invariants and guards, we use *clock constraints*. Assuming a set of clocks $\mathcal{X}$, the set of allowable clock constraints, denoted $CC(\mathcal{X})$, is defined by the following grammar:

$$\chi ::= \texttt{true} \mid x \leqslant d \mid c \leqslant x \mid x+c \leqslant y+d \mid \neg\chi \mid \chi \wedge \chi$$

where $x, y \in \mathcal{X}$ and $c, d \in \mathbb{N}$. A PTA can then be formally defined as follows.

Definition 6 (Probabilistic timed automaton) *A* probabilistic timed automaton *(PTA) is defined by a tuple* $\mathsf{P}=(Loc, \bar{l}, \mathcal{X}, Act, inv, enab, prob, L)$ *where:*

- *Loc is a finite set of* locations;
- $\bar{l} \in Loc$ *is an* initial location;
- $\mathcal{X}$ *is a finite set of* clocks;
- *Act is a finite set of* actions;
- $inv : Loc \to CC(\mathcal{X})$ *is the* invariant condition;
- $enab : Loc \times Act \to CC(\mathcal{X})$ *is the* enabling condition;
- $prob : Loc \times Act \to Dist(2^{\mathcal{X}} \times Loc)$ *is a (partial)* probabilistic transition function;
- $L : Loc \to 2^{AP}$ *is a* labelling function *mapping each location to a set of atomic propositions taken from a set AP.*

The semantics of a PTA P is given by an infinite-state MDP whose states are of the form $(l, v) \in Loc \times (\mathbb{R}_{\geqslant 0})^{\mathcal{X}}$, where l is a location and v gives a value for each clock in $\mathcal{X}$. For simplicity, we omit a full descriptions of the semantics (see e.g. [58] for details). Intuitively, the behaviour of a PTA is as follows. The initial state is $(l, \mathbf{0})$, where $\mathbf{0}$ denotes a value of 0 for all clocks. For a general state $s = (l, v)$, there is a nondeterministic choice between either: (i) time elapsing, i.e. all clocks increasing in value, subject to the invariant $inv(l)$ staying true; (ii) an action a being taken, such that $prob(l, a)$ is defined and the guard $enab(l, a)$ is satisfied. If the latter, $prob(l, a)$ is a distribution over pairs $(X, l') \in 2^{\mathcal{X}} \times Loc$, giving the probability of moving to location l' and resetting the clocks in X to zero.

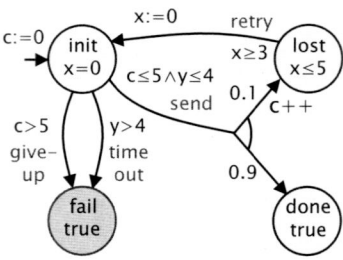

Figure 10. Example PTA.

Example 12 *Figure 10 shows an example of a PTA with locations Loc =
{init, lost, done, fail} and two clocks {x, y}. Locations are labelled with their invariants, under the location name, and transitions are annotated with actions
(from the set Act = {send, retry, giveup, timeout}), guards (e.g. y > 4), clock
resets (e.g. x := 0) and probabilities. For modelling convenience, we also use an
integer variable c, whose value can feature in guards or be set on a transition.*

*The PTA models repeated attempts to transmit a message over a faulty com-
munication channel. Each send happens instantaneously (thanks to the invariant
x = 0 in location init), after which the transmission succeeds with probability 0.9
and fails with probability 0.1. In the case of failure, a delay of between 3 and 5
time units occurs before transmission is re-attempted. The variable c counts the
number of attempts. If either c exceeds 5, or the total time elapsed (stored by clock
y) exceeds 4, then transmission is aborted and the PTA moves to location fail.*

6.2. Model Checking for PTAs

A variety of model checking approaches have been proposed for PTAs. Properties
to be verified are typically expressed in probabilistic temporal logic. One possibility is the logic PTCTL [59], a probabilistic extension of the timed temporal logic
TCTL. In many cases, though, the simpler logic PCTL, discussed earlier in this
tutorial for DTMCs and MDPs, suffices.

The principle hurdle to overcome when developing model checking algorithms
for PTAs is the fact that the models are inherently infinite-state. Fundamental
results about the decidability and complexity of model checking for PTAs can
be obtained through the construction of a *region graph* [59]. This is based on a
division of the PTA's state space into a finite number of *regions*, sets of states
which satisfy exactly the same temporal logic formulas. This reduces the problem
of model checking a PTA to the problem of analysing a finite-state MDP, whose
states are regions. In practice, however the region graph is prohibitively large,
and thus several more efficient methods have been developed for model checking:

- The *digital clocks* method [57] translates *closed* PTAs (those where clock
  constraints contain no strict comparisons) into a finite-state MDP, based
  on the *digitisation* of real-valued to integer-valued clocks. The MDP is then
  analysed in standard fashion. For PTAs whose clock values vary across large
  ranges this approach can become expensive, but it has been successfully
  applied to several large case studies.

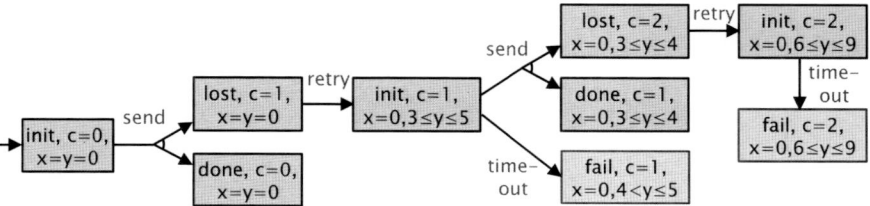

Figure 11. Reachability graph.

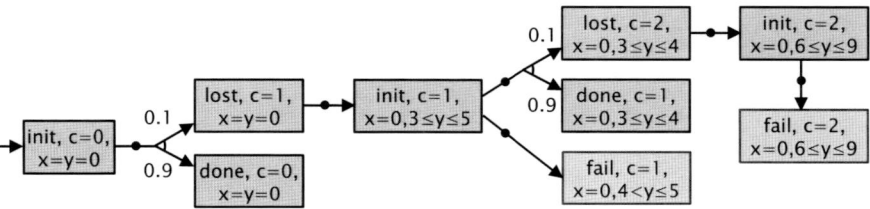

Figure 12. Stochastic game abstraction.

- *Backwards reachability* [60] performs a backwards traversal of the state space of a PTA using efficient data structures to represent and manipulate clock constraints for PTA state sets. As for digital clocks, a finite-state MDP is then built and model checked to obtain results. Although the operations required to implement this approach can be expensive, with appropriate optimisations [13] it has been shown to perform well.

- *Abstraction refinement with stochastic games* [54] uses the quantitative abstraction refinement approach [47] described in Section 5 to verify PTAs. In this instance, abstract states are modelled with clock constraints (zones), represented by difference-bound matrices (DBMs). A sequence of stochastic games are built through successive refinements, finally yielding an exact result for the PTA model checking problem.

Example 13 *We illustrate the third of these approaches, abstraction refinement, using the PTA given previously in Example 12 (see Figure 10). Our aim is to determine the maximum probability of reaching location* fail. *The abstraction refinement approach of [54] works by constructing a* reachability graph, *a connected set of abstract states of the form* (l, ζ) *where* l *is a location and* ζ *a clock constraint. This is constructed based on a forwards traversal of the reachable fragment of the PTA. The reachability graph for the example is shown in Figure 11.*

From the graph, we can construct a stochastic game abstraction, which is then analysed to obtain lower and upper bounds on the required reachability probability, in the manner described in Section 5.1. Figure 12 shows the stochastic game for the reachability graph of Figure 11. In this case, the obtained lower and upper bounds reveal that the maximum probability of reaching location fail *is in the interval* $[0.01, 0.1]$. *From the results of the analysis of the game, we are able to refine the reachability graph, splitting one or more of its abstract states into parts.*

For this example, a single refinement (which splits the clock constraint $x=0 \wedge 3 \leqslant y \leqslant 5$ in abstract state $((\text{init}, c=1), x=0 \wedge 3 \leqslant y \leqslant 5)$ into two, $x=0 \wedge 3 \leqslant y \leqslant 4$ and $x=0 \wedge 4 < y \leqslant 5$) suffices to produce an abstraction which yields the bounds $[0.1, 0.1]$. Thus, the maximum probability of failure is 0.1.

6.3. More on Model Checking for PTAs

As discussed previously for DTMCs and MDPs, we can augment PTAs with *rewards* to capture additional quantitative properties of the models. In fact, these are often used to model *costs* or *prices*. Computation of the (minimum or maximum) expected reward cumulated until a target is reached can be performed using the digital clocks method [57]. Another useful class of reward properties for PTAs is the probability that the cumulative reward exceeds a certain bound. A semi-algorithm for model checking such properties can be found in [12].

7. Probabilistic Model Checking in Practice

We conclude this tutorial with a discussion of some of the practical aspects of probabilistic model checking. As usage of these techniques has become more widespread, a variety of supporting software tools have been developed. The two most widely used are PRISM [55] and MRMC [43]. MRMC's core functionality is model checking of (discrete- and continuous-time) Markov chains, with a particular focus on reward properties. PRISM supports Markov chains, as well as MDPs and PTAs, and is described in more detail below. Other tools providing model checking of MDPs include LiQuor [18] and ProbDiVinE [11]. Software supporting verification of PTAs includes UPPAAL-PRO [66], Fortuna [13] and mcpta [37]. A more detailed list of probabilistic model checking tools can be found at [68].

7.1. PRISM

PRISM [55] is a probabilistic model checker developed at the Universities of Birmingham and Oxford. It is an open-source software tool which accepts probabilistic models written in a textual modelling language based on Reactive Modules, a state-based language using guarded commands. The three main model types discussed in this tutorial, DTMCs, MDPs and PTAs, and their reward (price) extensions are all directly supported by PRISM, as are continuous-time Markov chains (CTMCs). A wide range of properties can be specified and model checked: PRISM admits the logics PCTL, LTL and PCTL*, and additionally CSL (for CTMCs). It also includes the reward operators and quantitative (numerical) properties discussed earlier in this tutorial.

PRISM includes multiple model checking engines, notably several based on *symbolic* implementations (using binary decision diagrams and their extensions). These can enable the probabilistic verification of models of up to 10^{10} states. On average, the tool usually handles models with up to $10^7 - 10^8$ states. PRISM also features explicit-state model checking functionality, as well as a variety of advanced techniques such as abstraction refinement and symmetry reduction. There is also support for approximate/statistical model checking through a discrete-event simulation engine.

PRISM has been applied to numerous case studies, from communication, security and population protocols, power management, embedded control, nanotechnology designs, to biological systems; for more information consult [67].

7.2. Research Directions

Finally, we briefly mention some other directions for the development of probabilistic model checking that have shown promising results.

- *Symbolic model checking* techniques, using data structures based on binary decision diagrams (BDDs) [5,49] offer scalability to large models by exploiting high-level structure and regularities.

- *Model reduction* techniques such as bisimulation minimisation [44], symmetry reduction [52,26] and partial order reduction [23,6] provide ways to reduce the size of probabilistic models, whilst preserving exact model checking results.

- *Compositional probabilistic verification* [61] decomposes the effort required for model checking into separate sub-tasks for each system component; in particular, *assume-guarantee* verification techniques for MDPs [56] have recently proved to provide real practical gains in scalability.

- *Approximate (or statistical) probabilistic model checking* improves scalability by combining Monte Carlo simulation with statistical methods to either generate approximate results to quantitative model checking queries [39] or efficiently check properties featuring probability thresholds [65].

- *Systems biology* is proving to be an exciting and challenging application of probabilistic model checking, for which various novel techniques have been specifically developed [64,38].

- *Probabilistic counterexamples* [32,1,3] provide diagnostic information to the user of a probabilistic model checker if a temporal logic query is found to be false. Typically, this takes the form of a *set* of violating system executions, whose combined probability exceeds some desired threshold.

- *Synthesis* techniques aim to generate correct-by-construction model components or controllers based on quantitative objectives [17,15].

- *Parametric* approaches to probabilistic model checking can be used to synthesise the range of model parameter values that satisfy some specification [33] or to produce model checking results that are symbolic expressions in terms of the parameters [30].

8. Conclusions

This tutorial presented an introduction to probabilistic model checking, covering details of two basic models, Markov chains and Markov decision processes, and two more advanced topics, quantitative abstraction refinement and model checking of probabilistic timed automata. The focus has been on models which feature discrete states, discrete probability distributions and possibly nondeterminism, in conjunction with (in the case of PTAs) dense real-time.

The following tutorial papers provide more comprehensive introductory material for the topics covered here:

- [53] (sections 1–3), for discrete-time Markov chains (DTMCs);
- [28] (sections 1–7), for Markov decision processes (MDPs);
- [58], for probabilistic timed automata (PTAs).

Chapter 10 of [9] is also highly recommended for additional and deeper coverage of model checking for DTMCs and MDPs.

Acknowledgments. The authors are part supported by ERC Advanced Grant VERIWARE, EPSRC grant EP/F001096/1 and EU-FP7 project CONNECT.

References

[1] H. Aljazzar and S. Leue. Directed explicit state-space search in the generation of counterexamples for stochastic model checking. *IEEE Transactions on Software Engineering*, 36(1):37–60, 2010.

[2] R. Alur and D. Dill. A theory of timed automata. *Theoretical Computer Science*, 126:183–235, 1994.

[3] M. Andrés, P. D'Argenio, and P. van Rossum. Significant diagnostic counterexamples in probabilistic model checking. In H. Chockler and A. Hu, editors, *Proc. 4th Int. Haifa Verification Conf. Hardware and Software: Verification and Testing (HVC'08)*, volume 5394 of *LNCS*, pages 129–148. Springer, 2008.

[4] D. Angluin, J. Aspnes, and D. Eisenstat. A simple population protocol for fast robust approximate majority. *Distributed Computing*, 21(2):87–102, 2008.

[5] C. Baier, E. Clarke, V. Hartonas-Garmhausen, M. Kwiatkowska, and M. Ryan. Symbolic model checking for probabilistic processes. In P. Degano, R. Gorrieri, and A. Marchetti-Spaccamela, editors, *Proc. 24th International Colloquium on Automata, Languages and Programming (ICALP'97)*, volume 1256 of *LNCS*, pages 430–440. Springer, 1997.

[6] C. Baier, M. Groesser, and F. Ciesinski. Partial order reduction for probabilistic systems. In *Proc. 1st International Conference on Quantitative Evaluation of Systems (QEST'04)*, pages 230–239. IEEE CS Press, 2004.

[7] C. Baier, M. Größer, and F. Ciesinski. Quantitative analysis under fairness constraints. In *Proc. 7th International Symposium on Automated Technology for Verification and Analysis (ATVA'09)*, volume 5799 of *LNCS*, pages 135–150. Springer, 2009.

[8] C. Baier, B. Haverkort, H. Hermanns, and J.-P. Katoen. Model-checking algorithms for continuous-time Markov chains. *IEEE Transactions on Software Engineering*, 29(6):524–541, 2003.

[9] C. Baier and J.-P. Katoen. *Principles of Model Checking*. MIT Press, 2008.

[10] C. Baier and M. Kwiatkowska. Model checking for a probabilistic branching time logic with fairness. *Distributed Computing*, 11(3):125–155, 1998.

[11] J. Barnat, L. Brim, I. Cerna, M. Ceska, and J. Tumova. ProbDiVinE-MC: Multi-core LTL model checker for probabilistic systems. In *Proc. 5rd International Conference on Quantitative Evaluation of Systems (QEST'08)*, pages 77–78. IEEE CS Press, 2008.

[12] J. Berendsen, D. Jansen, and J.-P. Katoen. Probably on time and within budget – on reachability in priced probabilistic timed automata. In *Proc. 3rd International Conference on Quantitative Evaluation of Systems (QEST'06)*, pages 311–322. IEEE CS Press, 2006.

[13] J. Berendsen, D. Jansen, and F. Vaandrager. Fortuna: Model checking priced probabilistic timed automata. In *Proc. 7th International Conference on Quantitative Evaluation of SysTems (QEST'10)*, pages 273–281, 2010.

[14]   A. Bianco and L. de Alfaro. Model checking of probabilistic and nondeterministic systems. In P. Thiagarajan, editor, *Proc. 15th Conference on Foundations of Software Technology and Theoretical Computer Science (FSTTCS'95)*, volume 1026 of *LNCS*, pages 499–513. Springer, 1995.

[15]   P. Cerný, K. Chatterjee, T. Henzinger, A. Radhakrishna, and R. Singh. Quantitative synthesis for concurrent programs. In G. Gopalakrishnan and S. Qadeer, editors, *Proc. 23rd International Conference on Computer Aided Verification (CAV'11)*, volume 6806 of *LNCS*, pages 243–259. Springer, 2011.

[16]   R. Chadha and M. Viswanathan. A counterexample guided abstraction-refinement framework for Markov decision processes. *ACM Transactions on Computational Logic*, 12(1):1–49, 2010.

[17]   K. Chatterjee, T. Henzinger, B. Jobstmann, and R. Singh. Measuring and synthesizing systems in probabilistic environments. In *Proc. 22nd International Conference on Computer Aided Verification (CAV'10)*, LNCS. Springer, 2010.

[18]   F. Ciesinski and C. Baier. Liquor: A tool for qualitative and quantitative linear time analysis of reactive systems. In *Proc. 3rd International Conference on Quantitative Evaluation of Systems (QEST'06)*, pages 131–132. IEEE CS Press, 2006.

[19]   E. Clarke and A. Emerson. Design and synthesis of synchronization skeletons using branching time temporal logic. In *Proc. Workshop on Logic of Programs*, volume 131 of *LNCS*. Springer, 1981.

[20]   E. Clarke, O. Grumberg, S. Jha, Y. Lu, and H. Veith. Counterexample-guided abstraction refinement. In A. Emerson and A. Sistla, editors, *Proc. 12th Int. Conf. Computer Aided Verification (CAV'00)*, volume 1855 of *Lecture Notes in Computer Science*, pages 154–169. Springer, 2000.

[21]   C. Courcoubetis and M. Yannakakis. Verifying temporal properties of finite state probabilistic programs. In *Proc. 29th Annual Symposium on Foundations of Computer Science (FOCS'88)*, pages 338–345. IEEE Computer Society Press, 1988.

[22]   P. D'Argenio, B. Jeannet, H. Jensen, and K. Larsen. Reachability analysis of probabilistic systems by successive refinements. In L. de Alfaro and S. Gilmore, editors, *Proc. 1st Joint International Workshop on Process Algebra and Probabilistic Methods, Performance Modelling and Verification (PAPM/PROBMIV'01)*, volume 2165 of *LNCS*, pages 39–56. Springer, 2001.

[23]   P. D'Argenio and P. Niebert. Partial order reduction on concurrent probabilistic programs. In *Proc. 1st International Conference on Quantitative Evaluation of Systems (QEST'04)*. IEEE CS Press, 2004.

[24]   L. de Alfaro, M. Kwiatkowska, G. Norman, D. Parker, and R. Segala. Symbolic model checking of probabilistic processes using MTBDDs and the Kronecker representation. In S. Graf and M. Schwartzbach, editors, *Proc. 6th International Conference on Tools and Algorithms for the Construction and Analysis of Systems (TACAS'00)*, volume 1785 of *LNCS*, pages 395–410. Springer, 2000.

[25]   L. de Alfaro and P. Roy. Magnifying-lens abstraction for Markov decision processes. In *Proc. 19th International Conference on Computer Aided Verification (CAV'07)*, volume 4590 of *LNCS*, pages 325–338. Springer, 2007.

[26]   A. Donaldson and A. Miller. Symmetry reduction for probabilistic model checking using generic representatives. In S. Graf and W. Zhang, editors, *Proc. 4th Int. Symp. Automated Technology for Verification and Analysis (ATVA'06)*, volume 4218 of *Lecture Notes in Computer Science*, pages 9–23. Springer, 2006.

[27]   J. Esparza and A. Gaiser. Probabilistic abstractions with arbitrary domains. In *Proc. 18th International Symposium on Static Analysis (SAS'11)*, pages 334–350, 2011.

[28]   V. Forejt, M. Kwiatkowska, G. Norman, and D. Parker. Automated verification techniques for probabilistic systems. In M. Bernardo and V. Issarny, editors, *Formal Methods for Eternal Networked Software Systems (SFM'11)*, volume 6659 of *LNCS*, pages 53–113. Springer, 2011.

[29]   E. M. Hahn, H. Hermanns, B. Wachter, and L. Zhang. PASS: Abstraction refinement for infinite probabilistic models. In J. Esparza and R. Majumdar, editors, *Proc. 16th International Conference on Tools and Algorithms for the Construction and Analysis of*

Systems (TACAS'10), volume 6105 of *LNCS*, pages 353–357. Springer, 2010.

[30] E. M. Hahn, H. Hermanns, and L. Zhang. Probabilistic reachability for parametric Markov models. In C. Pasareanu, editor, *Proc. 16th International SPIN Workshop*, volume 5578 of *LNCS*, pages 88–106. Springer, 2009.

[31] E. M. Hahn, G. Norman, D. Parker, B. Wachter, and L. Zhang. Game-based abstraction and controller synthesis for probabilistic hybrid systems. In *Proc. 8th International Conference on Quantitative Evaluation of SysTems (QEST'11)*, pages 69–78. IEEE CS Press, September 2011.

[32] T. Han, J.-P. Katoen, and B. Damman. Counterexample generation in probabilistic model checking. *IEEE Transactions on Software Engineering*, 35(2):241–257, 2009.

[33] T. Han, J.-P. Katoen, and A. Mereacre. Approximate parameter synthesis for probabilistic time-bounded reachability. In *Proc. IEEE Real-Time Systems Symposium (RTSS 08)*, pages 173–182. IEEE CS Press, 2008.

[34] H. Hansson. *Time and Probability in Formal Design of Distributed Systems*. Elsevier, 1994.

[35] H. Hansson and B. Jonsson. A logic for reasoning about time and reliability. *Formal Aspects of Computing*, 6(5):512–535, 1994.

[36] S. Hart, M. Sharir, and A. Pnueli. Termination of probabilistic concurrent programs. *ACM Transactions on Programming Languages and Systems*, 5(3):356–380, 1983.

[37] A. Hartmanns and H. Hermanns. A modest approach to checking probabilistic timed automata. In *Proc. 6th International Conference on Quantitative Evaluation of Systems (QEST'09)*, 2009. To appear.

[38] T. Henzinger, M. Mateescu, L. Mikeev, and V. Wolf. Hybrid numerical solution of the chemical master equation. In *Proc. 8th International Conference on Computational Methods in Systems Biology (CMSB'10)*, pages 55–65. ACM, 2010.

[39] T. Hérault, R. Lassaigne, F. Magniette, and S. Peyronnet. Approximate probabilistic model checking. In *Proc. 5th International Conference on Verification, Model Checking and Abstract Interpretation (VMCAI'04)*, volume 2937 of *LNCS*. Springer, 2004.

[40] H. Hermanns, J.-P. Katoen, J. Meyer-Kayser, and M. Siegle. A Markov chain model checker. In S. Graf and M. Schwartzbach, editors, *Proc. 6th International Conference on Tools and Algorithms for the Construction and Analysis of Systems (TACAS'00)*, volume 1785 of *LNCS*, pages 347–362. Springer, 2000.

[41] H. Hermanns, B. Wachter, and L. Zhang. Probabilistic CEGAR. In A. Gupta and S. Malik, editors, *Proc. 20th International Conference on Computer Aided Verification (CAV'08)*, volume 5123 of *LNCS*, pages 162–175. Springer, 2008.

[42] H. Jensen. Model checking probabilistic real time systems. In *Proc. 7th Nordic Workshop on Programming Theory*, pages 247–261, 1996.

[43] J.-P. Katoen, E. M. Hahn, H. Hermanns, D. Jansen, and I. Zapreev. The ins and outs of the probabilistic model checker MRMC. In *Proc. 6th International Conference on Quantitative Evaluation of Systems (QEST'09)*, pages 167–176. IEEE CS Press, 2009.

[44] J.-P. Katoen, T. Kemna, I. Zapreev, and D. Jansen. Bisimulation minimisation mostly speeds up probabilistic model checking. In O. Grumberg and M. Huth, editors, *Proc. 13th International Conference on Tools and Algorithms for the Construction and Analysis of Systems (TACAS'07)*, volume 4424 of *LNCS*, pages 87–101. Springer, 2007.

[45] M. Kattenbelt, M. Kwiatkowska, G. Norman, and D. Parker. Game-based probabilistic predicate abstraction in PRISM. In *Proc. 6th Workshop on Quantitative Aspects of Programming Languages (QAPL'08)*, 2008.

[46] M. Kattenbelt, M. Kwiatkowska, G. Norman, and D. Parker. Abstraction refinement for probabilistic software. In N. Jones and M. Muller-Olm, editors, *Proc. 10th International Conference on Verification, Model Checking, and Abstract Interpretation (VMCAI'09)*, volume 5403 of *LNCS*, pages 182–197. Springer, 2009.

[47] M. Kattenbelt, M. Kwiatkowska, G. Norman, and D. Parker. A game-based abstraction-refinement framework for Markov decision processes. *Formal Methods in System Design*, 36(3):246–280, 2010.

[48] J. Kemeny, J. Snell, and A. Knapp. *Denumerable Markov Chains*. Springer-Verlag, 2nd edition, 1976.

[49]   M. Kwiatkowska, G. Norman, and D. Parker. Probabilistic symbolic model checking with PRISM: A hybrid approach. *International Journal on Software Tools for Technology Transfer (STTT)*, 6(2):128–142, 2004.

[50]   M. Kwiatkowska, G. Norman, and D. Parker. Probabilistic model checking in practice: Case studies with PRISM. *ACM SIGMETRICS Performance Evaluation Review*, 32(4):16–21, 2005.

[51]   M. Kwiatkowska, G. Norman, and D. Parker. Game-based abstraction for Markov decision processes. In *Proc. 3rd International Conference on Quantitative Evaluation of Systems (QEST'06)*, pages 157–166. IEEE CS Press, 2006.

[52]   M. Kwiatkowska, G. Norman, and D. Parker. Symmetry reduction for probabilistic model checking. In T. Ball and R. Jones, editors, *Proc. 18th International Conference on Computer Aided Verification (CAV'06)*, volume 4114 of *LNCS*, pages 234–248. Springer, 2006.

[53]   M. Kwiatkowska, G. Norman, and D. Parker. Stochastic model checking. In M. Bernardo and J. Hillston, editors, *Formal Methods for the Design of Computer, Communication and Software Systems: Performance Evaluation (SFM'07)*, volume 4486 of *LNCS (Tutorial Volume)*, pages 220–270. Springer, 2007.

[54]   M. Kwiatkowska, G. Norman, and D. Parker. Stochastic games for verification of probabilistic timed automata. In J. Ouaknine and F. Vaandrager, editors, *Proc. 7th International Conference on Formal Modelling and Analysis of Timed Systems (FORMATS'09)*, volume 5813 of *LNCS*, pages 212–227. Springer, 2009.

[55]   M. Kwiatkowska, G. Norman, and D. Parker. PRISM 4.0: Verification of probabilistic real-time systems. In G. Gopalakrishnan and S. Qadeer, editors, *Proc. 23rd International Conference on Computer Aided Verification (CAV'11)*, volume 6806 of *LNCS*, pages 585–591. Springer, 2011.

[56]   M. Kwiatkowska, G. Norman, D. Parker, and H. Qu. Assume-guarantee verification for probabilistic systems. In J. Esparza and R. Majumdar, editors, *Proc. 16th International Conference on Tools and Algorithms for the Construction and Analysis of Systems (TACAS'10)*, volume 6105 of *LNCS*, pages 23–37. Springer, 2010.

[57]   M. Kwiatkowska, G. Norman, D. Parker, and J. Sproston. Performance analysis of probabilistic timed automata using digital clocks. *Formal Methods in System Design*, 29:33–78, 2006.

[58]   M. Kwiatkowska, G. Norman, D. Parker, and J. Sproston. *Modeling and Verification of Real-Time Systems: Formalisms and Software Tools*, chapter Verification of Real-Time Probabilistic Systems, pages 249–288. John Wiley & Sons, 2008.

[59]   M. Kwiatkowska, G. Norman, R. Segala, and J. Sproston. Automatic verification of real-time systems with discrete probability distributions. *Theoretical Computer Science*, 282:101–150, 2002.

[60]   M. Kwiatkowska, G. Norman, J. Sproston, and F. Wang. Symbolic model checking for probabilistic timed automata. *Information and Computation*, 205(7):1027–1077, 2007.

[61]   R. Segala. *Modelling and Verification of Randomized Distributed Real Time Systems*. PhD thesis, Massachusetts Institute of Technology, 1995.

[62]   R. Segala and N. Lynch. Probabilistic simulations for probabilistic processes. In B. Jonsson and J. Parrow, editors, *Proc. 5th International Conference on Concurrency Theory (CONCUR'94)*, volume 836 of *LNCS*, pages 481–496. Springer, 1994.

[63]   M. Vardi. Automatic verification of probabilistic concurrent finite state programs. In *Proc. 26th Annual Symposium on Foundations of Computer Science (FOCS'85)*, pages 327–338. IEEE Computer Society Press, 1985.

[64]   V. Wolf, R. Goel, M. Mateescu, and T. Henzinger. Solving the chemical master equation using sliding windows. *BMC Systems Biology Journal*, 4(42), 2010.

[65]   H. Younes and R. Simmons. Probabilistic verification of discrete event systems using acceptance sampling. In E. Brinksma and K. Larsen, editors, *Proc. 14th International Conference on Computer Aided Verification (CAV'02)*, volume 2404 of *LNCS*, pages 223–235. Springer, 2002.

[66]   http://www.cs.aau.dk/~arild/uppaal-probabilistic/.

[67]   http://www.prismmodelchecker.org/.

[68]   http://www.prismmodelchecker.org/other-tools.php.

Software Safety and Security
T. Nipkow et al. (Eds.)
IOS Press, 2012
doi:10.3233/978-1-61499-028-4-152

Getting Started with Dafny: A Guide

Jason KOENIG [a] and K. Rustan M. LEINO [b]

[a] *Carnegie Mellon University, Pittsburgh, PA, USA*
[b] *Microsoft Research, Redmond, WA, USA*

Abstract. Common program specification and verification build on concepts like method pre- and postconditions and loop invariants. These lectures notes teach those concepts in the context of the language and verifier Dafny.

Keywords. Automatic program verification, program specification, Dafny, precondition, postcondition, loop invariant, termination specification

0. Introduction

Dafny is a language that is designed to make it easy to write correct code. This means correct in the sense of not having any runtime errors, but also correct in actually doing what the programmer intended it to do. To accomplish this, Dafny relies on high-level annotations to reason about and prove correctness of code. The effect of a piece of code can be given abstractly, using a natural, high-level expression of the desired behavior, which is easier and less error prone to write. Dafny then generates a proof that the code matches the annotations (assuming they are correct, of course!). Dafny lifts the burden of writing bug-free *code* into that of writing bug-free *annotations*. This is often easier than writing the code, because annotations are shorter and more direct. For example, the following fragment of annotation in Dafny says that every element of the array is strictly positive:

```
forall k: int :: 0 <= k < a.Length ==> 0 < a[k]
```

This says that for all integers k that are indices into the array, the value at that index is greater than zero. By writing these annotations, one is confident that the code is correct. Further, the very act of writing the annotations can help one understand what the code is doing at a deeper level.

In addition to proving a correspondence to user supplied annotations, Dafny proves that there are no run time errors, such as index out of bounds, null dereferences, division by zero, etc. This guarantee is a powerful one, and is a strong case in and of itself for the use of Dafny and tools like it. Dafny also proves the termination of code, except in specially designated loops.

These lecture notes give a guide to Dafny, explaining the specification features that get used routinely in all verification tasks. Although the lecture notes focus on Dafny, the concepts explained apply to program specification and verificaton more generally.

The appendix of these lecture notes contains a reference guide to a large subset of the Dafny language. Turn to it if you need to know more about the syntax or constructs available.

The best way to learn from these notes is to try things out yourself. There are three ways to run the Dafny verifier. The slickest way is to run it in the Microsoft Visual Studio integrated development environment, since this continuously runs the verifier in the background and highlights errors in your program as you develop it. Another way is to run Dafny from the command line, which requires a .NET virtual machine (built in on Windows platforms, and provided by Mono on non-Windows platforms). The third way to run Dafny uses any web browser and requires no installation.[0] More information about these options and installation are available from the Dafny homepage.[1]

Let's get started writing some Dafny programs.

1. Methods

In many ways, Dafny is a typical imperative programming language. There are methods, variables, types, loops, if statements, arrays, integers, and more. One of the basic units of any Dafny program is the *method*. A method is a piece of imperative, executable code. In other languages, they might be called procedures, or functions, but in Dafny the term "function" is reserved for a different concept that we will cover later. A method is declared in the following way:

```
method Abs(x: int) returns (r: int)
{
    . . .
}
```

This declares a method called "Abs" which takes a single integer parameter, called "x", and returns a single integer, called "r". Note that the types are required for each parameter and return value, and follow each name after a colon (":"). Also, the return values (out parameters) are named, and there can be multiple return values, as in below:

```
method MultipleReturns(x: int, y: int) returns (more: int, less: int)
{
    . . .
}
```

The method body is the code contained within the braces, which until now has been cleverly represented as " . . . " (which is *not* Dafny syntax). The body consists of a series of *statements*, such as the familiar imperative assignments, **if** statements, loops, other method calls, return statements, etc. For example, the MultipleReturns method may be implemented as:

---

[0] `rise4fun.com`
[1] `research.microsoft.com/dafny`

```
method MultipleReturns(x: int, y: int) returns (more: int, less: int)
{
    more := x + y;
    less := x - y;
    // comments: are not strictly necessary.
    /* unless you want to keep your sanity. */
}
```

Assignments do not use "=", but rather ":=". (In fact, as Dafny uses "==" for equality, there is no use of a single equals sign in Dafny statements and expressions.) Simple statements must be followed by a semicolon, and whitespace and comments are ignored. To return a value from a method, the value is assigned to one of the named return values sometime before the method returns. In fact, the return values act very much like local variables, and can be assigned to more than once. The input parameters, however, are read only. Return statements are used when one wants to return before reaching the end of the body block of the method. Return statements can be just the **return** keyword (where the current value of the out parameters are used), or they can take a list of values to return. There are also compound statements, such as **if** statements. **if** statements require parentheses around the boolean condition, and act as one would expect:

```
method Abs(x: int) returns (r: int)
{
    if (x < 0)
        { return -x; }
    else
        { return x; }
}
```

One caveat is that they always need braces around the branches, even if the branch only contains a single statement (compound or otherwise). Here the **if** statement checks whether x is less than zero, using the familiar comparison operator syntax, and sets r to the absolute value as appropriate. (Other comparison operators are <=, >, >=, !=, and ==, with the expected meaning.) Here we use the implicit return at the end of the function. Regardless of the branch taken, the correct value is put into r, so when we get to the end of the function, the result is returned properly.

2. Pre- and Postconditions

None of what we have seen so far has any annotations: the code could be written in virtually any imperative language (with appropriate considerations for multiple return values). The real power of Dafny comes from the ability to annotate these methods to specify their behavior. For example, one property that we observe with the Abs method is that the result is always greater than or equal to zero, regardless of the input. We could put this observation in a comment, but then we would have no way to know whether the method actually had this property. Further, if someone came along and changed the method, we wouldn't be guaranteed that the comment was changed to match. With annotations, we can have Dafny prove that the property we claim of the method is true. There are several ways to give annotations, but some of the most common, and most basic, are method *pre-* and *postconditions* (see also, *e.g.*, [10,19,20,9,3,1]).

This property of the Abs method, that the result is always non-negative, is an example of a postcondition: it is something that is true after the method returns. Postconditions, declared with the **ensures** keyword, are given as part of the method's declaration, after the return values (if present) and before the method body. The keyword is followed by the boolean expression and a semicolon, which are both required. Like an **if** or **while** condition and most annotations, a postcondition is always a boolean expression: something that can be *false* or *true*. In the case of the Abs method, a reasonable postcondition is the following:

```
method Abs(x: int) returns (y: int)
    ensures 0 <= y;
{
    ...
}
```

You can see here why return values are given names. This makes them easy to refer to in the postcondition of a method. When the expression is true, we say that the postcondition *holds*. The postcondition must hold for every possible invocation of the function, and for every possible return point (including the implicit one at the end of the function body). In this case, the only property we are expressing is that the return value is always at least zero.

Sometimes there are multiple properties that we would like to establish about our code. In this case, we have two options. We can either join the two conditions together with the boolean *and* operator (&&), or we can write multiple **ensures** annotations. The latter is the same as the former, but it helps make distinct properties clearer. For example, the return value names from the MultipleReturns method might lead one to guess the following postconditions:

```
method MultipleReturns(x: int, y: int) returns (more: int, less: int)
    ensures less < x;
    ensures x < more;
{
    more := x + y;
    less := x - y;
}
```

The postcondition can also be written:

```
    ensures less < x && x < more;
```

or even:

```
    ensures less < x < more;
```

because of the *chaining* comparison operator syntax in Dafny. (In general, most of the comparison operators can be chained, but only "in one direction", *i.e.*, not mixing greater than and less than; see Section A.8.)

The first way of expressing the postconditions separates the "less" part from the "more" part, which may be desirable. Another thing to note is that we have included one of the input parameters in the postcondition. This is useful because it allows us to relate the input and output of the method to one another (this works because input parameters are read only, and so are the same at the end as they were at the beginning).

Dafny actually rejects this program, claiming that the first postcondition does not hold (*i.e.*, is not true). This means that Dafny wasn't able to prove that this annotation holds every time the method returns. In general, there are two main causes for Dafny verification errors: annotations that are inconsistent with the code, and situations where it is not "clever" enough to prove the required properties. Differentiating between these two possibilities can be a difficult task, but fortunately, Dafny and the Boogie/Z3 system [0,18,5] on which it is based [14] are pretty smart, and will prove matching code and annotations with a minimum of fuss.

In this situation, Dafny is correct in saying there is an error with the code. The key to the problem is that y is an integer, so it can be negative. If y is negative (or zero), then more can actually be smaller than or equal to x. Our method will not work as intended unless y is strictly larger than zero. This is precisely the idea of a *precondition*. A precondition is similar to a postcondition, except that it is something that must be true *before* a method is called. When you call a method, it is your job to establish (make true) the preconditions, something Dafny will enforce using a proof. Likewise, when you write a method, you get to assume the preconditions, but you must establish the postconditions. The caller of the method then gets to assume that the postconditions hold after the method returns.

Preconditions have their own keyword, **requires**. We can give the necessary precondition to MultipleReturns as below:

```
method MultipleReturns(x: int, y: int) returns (more: int, less: int)
    requires 0 < y;
    ensures less < x < more;
{
    more := x + y;
    less := x - y;
}
```

Like postconditions, multiple preconditions can be written either with the boolean *and* operator (&&), or by multiple **requires** keywords. Traditionally, **requires** annotations precede **ensures** annotations in the source code, though this is not strictly necessary. (The order of the **requires** and **ensures** annotations with respect to others of the same type can sometimes matter, as we will see later.) With the addition of this condition, Dafny now verifies the code as correct, because this assumption is all that is needed to guarantee the code in the method body is correct.

Exercise 0 *Write a method Max that takes two integer parameters and returns their maximum. Add appropriate annotations and make sure your code verifies.*

Not all methods necessarily have preconditions. For example, the Abs method we have already seen is defined for all integers, and so has no preconditions (other than the trivial requirement that its argument is an integer, which is enforced by the type system). Even though it has no need of preconditions, the Abs function as it stands now is not very useful. To investigate why, we need to make use of another kind of annotation, the *assertion*.

3. Assertions

Unlike pre- and postconditions, an assertion is placed somewhere in the middle of a method. Like the previous two annotations, an assertion has a keyword, **assert**, followed by the boolean expression and a semicolon. An assertion says that a particular expression always holds when control reaches that part of the code. For example, the following is a trivial use of an assertion inside a dummy method:

```
method Testing()
{
    assert 2 < 3;
}
```

Dafny proves this method correct, as 2 is always less than 3. Asserts have several uses, but chief among them is checking whether your expectations of what is true at various points is actually true. You can use this to check basic arithmetical facts, as above, but they can also be used in more complex situations. Assertions are a powerful tool for debugging annotations, by checking what Dafny is able to prove about your code. For example, we can use it to investigate what Dafny knows about the Abs function.

To do this, we need one more concept: local variables. Local variables behave exactly as you would expect, except maybe for a few issues with shadowing. Local variables are declared with the **var** keyword, and can optionally have type declarations. Unlike method parameters, where types are required, Dafny can infer the types of local variables in almost all situations. This is an example of an initialized, explicitly typed variable declaration:

```
var x: int := 5;
```

The type annotation can be dropped in this case:

```
var x := 5;
```

Multiple variables can be declared at once:

```
var x, y, z: bool := 1, 2, true;
```

Explicit type declarations apply only to the immediately preceding variable, so here the **bool** declaration applies only to z, and not x or y, which are both inferred to be of type **int**. We needed variables because we want to talk about the return value of the Abs method. We cannot put Abs inside a annotations directly, as the method could change memory state, among other problems. So we capture the return value of a call to Abs as follows:

```
// use definition of Abs() from before.
method Testing()
{
    var v := Abs(3);
    assert 0 <= v;
}
```

This is an example of a situation where we can ask Dafny what it knows about the values in the code, in this case v. We do this by adding assertions, like the one above. Every time Dafny encounters an assertion, it tries to prove that the condition holds for all executions of the code. In this example, there is only one control path through the method, and Dafny is able to prove the annotation easily because it is exactly the postcondition of the Abs method. Abs guarantees that the return value is non-negative, so it trivially follows that v, which is this value, is non-negative after the call to Abs.

Exercise 1 *Write a test method that calls your Max method from Exercise 0 and then asserts something about the result.*

But we know something stronger about the Abs method. In particular, for non-negative x, Abs(x) == x. Specifically, in the above program, the value of v is 3. If we try adding an assertion (or changing the existing one) to say:

```
    assert v == 3;
```

we find that Dafny cannot prove our assertion, and gives an error. The reason this happens is that Dafny "forgets" about the body of every method except the one it is currently working on. This simplifies Dafny's job tremendously, and is one of the reasons it is able to operate at reasonable speeds. It also helps us reason about our programs by breaking them apart and so we can analyze each method in isolation (given the annotations for the other methods). We don't care at all what happens inside each method when we call it, as long as it satisfies its annotations. This works because Dafny will prove that all the methods satisfy their annotations, and refuse to compile our code until they do.

For the Abs method, this means that the only thing Dafny knows in the Testing method about the value returned from Abs is what the postconditions say about it, and *nothing more*. This means that Dafny won't know the nice property about Abs and non-negative integers unless we tell it by putting this in the postcondition of the Abs method. Another way to look at it is to consider the method annotations (along with the type of the parameters and return values) as fixing the behavior of the method. Everywhere the method is used, we assume that it is any conceivable method that satisfies the pre- and postconditions. In the Abs case, we might have written:

```
method Abs(x: int) returns (y: int)
    ensures 0 <= y;
{
    y := 0;
}
```

This method satisfies the postconditions, but clearly the program fragment:

```
var v := Abs(3);
assert v == 3;
```

would not be true in this case. Dafny is considering, in an abstract way, all methods with those annotations. The mathematical absolute value certainly is such a method, but so are all methods that return a positive constant, for example. We need stronger postconditions to eliminate these other possibilities, and "fix" the method down to exactly the one we want. We can partially do this with the following:

```
method Abs(x: int) returns (y: int)
    ensures 0 <= y;
    ensures 0 <= x ==> x == y;
{
    if (x < 0) { y := -x; }
        else { y := x; }
}
```

This expresses exactly the property we discussed before, that the absolute value is the same for non-negative integers. The second **ensures** uses implication operator, ==>, which basically says that the left-hand side implies the right in the mathematical sense (it binds more weakly than boolean *and* and comparisons, so the above says 0 <= x implies x == y). The left and right sides must both be boolean expressions.

The postcondition says that after Abs is called, if the value of x was non-negative, then y is equal to x. One caveat of the implication is that it is still true if the left part (the antecedent) is false. So the second postcondition is trivially true when x is negative. In fact, the only thing that the annotations say when x is negative is that the result, y, is non-negative. But this is still not enough to fix the function, so we must add another postcondition, to make the following complete annotation covering all cases:

```
method Abs(x: int) returns (y: int)
    ensures 0 <= y;
    ensures 0 <= x ==> y == x;
    ensures x < 0 ==> y == -x;
{
    if (x < 0) { y := -x; }
        else { y := x; }
}
```

These annotations are enough to require that our method actually computes the absolute value of x. But we still have an issue: there seems to be a lot of duplication. The body of the method is reflected very closely in the annotations. While this is correct code, we want to eliminate this redundancy. As you might guess, Dafny provides a means of doing this: functions.

Exercise 2 *Using a precondition, change Abs to say it can only be called on negative values. Simplify the body of Abs into just one assignment statement and make sure the method still verifies.*

Exercise 3 *Keeping the postconditions of Abs the same as above, change the body of Abs to y := x + 2;. What precondition do you need to annotate the method with in order for the verification to go through? And what precondition do you need if the body is y := x + 1;? What does that precondition say about calling the method?*

4. Functions

A function in Dafny closely follows the concept of a mathematical function. Unlike methods, a Dafny function cannot write to memory, and consists solely of one expression. They are required to have a single return value, which is unnamed. The declaration looks similar to that of a method:

```
function abs(x: int): int
{
    ...
}
```

This declares a function called abs which takes a single integer, and returns an integer (the second **int**). Unlike a method, which can have all sorts of statements in its body, a function body must consist of exactly one expression, with the correct type. Here our body must be an integer expression. In order to implement the absolute value function, we need to use an *if expression*. An if expression behaves like the ternary operator in other languages.

```
function abs(x: int): int
{
    if x < 0 then -x else x
}
```

Obviously, the condition must be a boolean expression, and the two branches must have the same type. You might wonder why anyone would bother with functions, if they are so limited compared to methods. The power of functions comes from the fact that they can be *used directly in annotations*. So we can write:

```
assert abs(3) == 3;
```

In fact, not only can we write this statement directly without capturing to a local variable, we didn't even need to write all the postconditions that we did with the method (though functions can and do have pre- and postconditions in general). The limitations of functions are precisely what let Dafny do this. Unlike methods, Dafny does not forget the body of a function when considering other functions. So it can expand the definition of abs in the above assertion and determine that the result is actually 3.

Exercise 4 *Write a function max that returns the larger of two given integer parameters. Write a test method that uses an **assert** statement to check some property of the value of max on some arguments (for example, 34 < max(21,55) or max(21,55) == max(55,21)).*

One caveat of functions is that not only can they appear in annotations, they can only appear in annotations. One cannot write:

```
var v := abs(3);
```

as this is not an annotation. Functions are never part of the final compiled program, they are just tools to help us verify our code. Nevertheless, sometimes it is convenient to use a function in real code too, so one can define a **function method**, which *can* be called from real code. Note that there are restrictions on what functions can be function methods.

Exercise 5 *Change the test method in Exercise 4 to put the result of max into a local variable and then use an **assert** statement to check some property of that local variable. Dafny will reject this program, because you're calling max from real code. Fix this problem using a **function method**.*

Exercise 6 *Now that we have an abs function, change the postcondition of method Abs (at the end of Section 3) to make use of abs. After you make sure the method still verifies, change the body of Abs to also use abs. (After doing this, you will also realize there's not much point in having a method that does exactly the same thing as a function method.)*

Unlike methods, functions can appear in expressions. Thus we can do something like implement the mathematical Fibonacci function:

```
function fib(n: nat): nat
{
    if n == 0 then 0 else
    if n == 1 then 1 else
                fib(n - 1) + fib(n - 2)
}
```

Here we use **nat**, the type of natural numbers (non-negative integers), which is often more convenient than annotating everything to be non-negative. It turns out that we could make this function a function method if we wanted to. But executing that function method would be extremely slow, as this version of calculating the Fibonacci numbers has exponential complexity. There are much better ways to calculate the Fibonacci function. But this function is still useful, as we can have Dafny prove that our fast version really matches the mathematical definition. We can get the best of both worlds: the guarantee of correctness and the performance we want.

We can start by defining a method like the following:

```
method ComputeFib(n: nat) returns (b: nat)
    ensures b == fib(n);
{
}
```

We haven't written the body yet, so Dafny will complain that our post condition doesn't hold. We need an algorithm to calculate the nth Fibonacci number. The basic idea is to keep a counter, and repeatedly calculate adjacent pairs of Fibonacci numbers until the desired number is reached. To do this, we need a loop. In Dafny, this is done via a **while** loop:

```
var i := 0;
while (i < n)
{
    i := i + 1;
}
```

This is a trivial loop that just increments i until it reaches n. This will form the core of our loop to calculate Fibonacci numbers.

5. Loop Invariants

Loops present a problem for Dafny. There is no way for Dafny to know in advance how many times the code will go around the loop. But Dafny needs to consider all paths through a program, which could include going around the loop any number of times. To make it possible for Dafny to work with loops, you need to provide *loop invariants*, another kind of annotation.

A loop invariant is an expression that holds upon entering a loop, and after every execution of the loop body. It captures something that is invariant, *i.e.*, does not change, about every step of the loop. Now, obviously we are going to want to change variables, etc. each time around the loop, or we wouldn't need the loop. Like pre- and postconditions, an invariant is a *property* that is preserved for each execution of the loop, expressed using the same boolean expressions we have seen. For example, we see in the above loop that if i starts off positive, then it stays positive. So we can add the invariant, using its own keyword, to the loop:

```
var i := 0;
while (i < n)
    invariant 0 <= i;
{
    i := i + 1;
}
```

When you specify an invariant, Dafny proves two things: the invariant holds upon entering the loop, and it is preserved by the loop. By preserved, we mean that assuming that the invariant holds at the beginning of the loop, we must show that executing the loop body once makes the invariant hold again. Dafny can only know upon analyzing the loop body what the invariants say, in addition to the loop guard (the loop condition). Just as Dafny will not discover properties of a method on its own, it will not know any but the most basic properties of a loop are preserved unless it is told via an invariant.

In our example, the point of the loop is to build up the Fibonacci numbers one (well, two) at a time until we reach the desired number. After we exit the loop, we will have that i == n, because i will stop being incremented when it reaches n. We can use our assertion trick to check to see if Dafny sees this fact as well:

```
var i := 0;
while (i < n)
   invariant 0 <= i;
{
   i := i + 1;
}
assert i == n;
```

We find that this assertion fails. As far as Dafny knows, it is possible that i somehow became much larger than n at some point during the loop. All it knows after the loop exits (*i.e.*, in the code after the loop) is that the loop guard failed, and the invariants hold. In this case, this amounts to n <= i and 0 <= i. But this is not enough to guarantee that i == n, just that n <= i. Somehow we need to eliminate the possibility of i exceeding n. One first guess for solving this problem might be the following:

```
var i := 0;
while (i < n)
   invariant 0 <= i < n;
{
   i := i + 1;
}
```

This does not verify, as Dafny complains that the invariant is not preserved (also known as maintained) by the loop. We want to be able to say that after the loop exits, then all the invariants hold. Our invariant holds for every execution of the loop *except* for the very last one. Because the loop body is executed only when the loop guard holds, in the last iteration i goes from n - 1 to n, but does not increase further, at the loop exits. Thus, we have only omitted exactly one case from our invariant, and repairing it relatively easy:

```
. . .
   invariant 0 <= i <= n;
. . .
```

Now we can say both that n <= i from the loop guard and 0 <= i <= n from the invariant, which allows Dafny to prove the assertion i == n. The challenge is finding a loop invariant that is preserved by the loop, but also that lets you prove what you need after the loop has executed.

Exercise 7 *Change the loop invariant to 0 <= i <= n+2. Does the loop still verify? Does the assertion i == n after the loop still verify?*

Exercise 8 *Once again using the invariant 0 <= i <= n for the loop above, change the loop guard from i < n to i != n. Do the loop and the assertion after the loop still verify?*

In addition to the counter, our algorithm called for a pair of numbers which represent adjacent Fibonacci numbers in the sequence. Unsurprisingly, we will have another invariant or two to relate these numbers to each other and the counter. To find these invariants, we employ a common Dafny trick: working backwards from the postconditions.

Our postcondition for the Fibonacci method is that the return value b is equal to fib(n). But after the loop, we have that i == n, so we need b == fib(i) at the end of the loop. This might make a good invariant, as it relates something to the loop counter. This observation is surprisingly common throughout Dafny programs. Many times a method is just a loop that, when it ends, makes the postcondition true by having a counter reach another number, often an argument or the length of an array or sequence. So we have that the variable b, which is conveniently our out parameter, will be the current Fibonacci number:

```
invariant b == fib(i);
```

We also note that in our algorithm, we can compute any Fibonacci number by keeping track of a pair of numbers, and summing them to get the next number. So we want a way of tracking the previous Fibonacci number, which we will call a. Another invariant will express that number's relation to the loop counter. The invariants are:

```
invariant a == fib(i - 1);
```

At each step of the loop, the two values are summed to get the next leading number, while the trailing number is the old leading number. Using a parallel assignment, we can write a loop that performs this operation:

```
var i := 1;
var a := 0;
b := 1;
while (i < n)
    invariant 0 < i <= n;
    invariant a == fib(i - 1);
    invariant b == fib(i);
{
    a, b := b, a + b;
    i := i + 1;
}
```

Here a is the trailing number, and b is the leading number. The parallel assignment means that the entire right-hand side is calculated before the assignments to the variables are made. Thus a will get the old value of b, and b will get the sum of the two old values, which is precisely the behavior we want.

We also have made a change to the loop counter i. Because we also want to track the trailing number, we can't start the counter at 0, as otherwise we would have to calculate a negative Fibonacci number. The problem with doing this is that the loop counter invariant may not hold when we enter the loop. The only problem is when n is 0. This can be eliminated as a special case, by testing for this condition at the beginning of the loop. The completed Fibonacci method becomes:

```
method ComputeFib(n: nat) returns (b: nat)
   ensures b == fib(n);
{
   if (n == 0) { return 0; }
   var i := 1;
   var a := 0;
   b := 1;
   while (i < n)
      invariant 0 < i <= n;
      invariant a == fib(i - 1);
      invariant b == fib(i);
   {
      a, b := b, a + b;
      i := i + 1;
   }
}
```

Dafny no longer complains about the loop invariant not holding, because if n were 0, it would return before reaching the loop. Dafny is also able to use the loop invariants to prove that after the loop, i == n and b == fib(i), which together imply the postcondition, b == fib(n).

Exercise 9 *The ComputeFib method above is more complicated than necessary. Write a simpler program by not introducing a as the Fibonacci number that precedes b, but instead introducing a variable c that that succeeds b. Verify that your program is correct.*

Exercise 10 *Starting with the final ComputeFib method above, delete the **if** statement and change the initializations to start i at 0, a at 1, and b at 0. Verify this new program by adjusting the loop invariants to match the new behavior.*

One of the problems with using invariants is that it is easy to forget to have the loop *make progress*, *i.e.*, do work at each step. For example, we could have omitted the entire body of the loop in the previous program. The invariants would be correct, because they are still true upon entering the loop, and since the loop doesn't change anything, they would be preserved by the loop. But the crucial step from the loop to the postcondition wouldn't hold. We know that *if* we exit the loop, then we can assume the negation of the guard and the invariants, but this says nothing about what happens if we never exit the loop. Thus we would like to make sure the loop ends at some point, which gives us a much stronger correctness guarantee.

6. Termination

Dafny proves code terminates, *i.e.*, does not loop forever, by using **decreases** annotations. For many things, Dafny is able to guess the right annotations, but sometimes it needs to be made explicit. In fact, for all of the code we have seen so far, Dafny has been able to do this proof on its own, which is why we haven't needed the **decreases** annotation explicitly yet. There are two places Dafny proves termination: loops and recursion. Both of these situations require either an explicit annotation or a correct guess by Dafny.

A **decreases** annotation, as its name suggests, gives Dafny an expression that decreases with every loop iteration or recursive call. There are two conditions that Dafny needs to verify when using a **decreases** expression: that the expression actually gets smaller, and that it is bounded. Many times, an integral value (natural or plain integer) is the quantity that decreases, but other things can be used as well. In the case of integers, the bound is assumed to be zero. For example, the following is a proper use of a **decreases** annotation on a loop:

```
while (0 < i)
    invariant 0 <= i;
    decreases i;
{
    i := i - 1;
}
```

Here Dafny has all the ingredients it needs to prove termination. The variable i gets smaller each loop iteration, and is bounded below by zero. This is fine, except the loop is backwards from most loops, which tend to count up instead of down. In this case, what decreases is not the counter itself, but rather the distance between the counter and the upper bound. A simple trick for dealing with this situation is given below:

```
while (i < n)
    invariant 0 <= i <= n;
    decreases n - i;
{
    i := i + 1;
}
```

This is actually Dafny's guess for this situation, as it sees i < n and assumes that n - i is the quantity that decreases. The upper bound of the loop invariant implies that 0 <= n - i, and gives Dafny a lower bound on the quantity. This also works when the bound n is not constant, such as in the binary search algorithm, where two quantities approach each other.

Exercise 11 *In the loop above, the invariant i <= n and the negation of the loop guard allow us to conclude i == n after the loop (as we checked in Section 5 by writing an* **assert** *statement). Note that if the loop guard were instead written as i != n (as in Exercise 8), then the negation of the guard immediately gives i == n after the loop, regardless of the loop invariant. Change the loop guard to i != n and delete the invariant annotation. Does the program verify?*

The other situation that requires a termination proof is when methods or functions are recursive. Similarly to looping forever, these methods could potentially call themselves forever, never returning to their original caller. When Dafny is not able to guess the termination condition, an explicit **decreases** clause can be given along with pre- and postconditions, as in the unnecessary annotation for the fib function:

```
function fib(n: nat): nat
   decreases n;
{
   ...
}
```

As before, Dafny can guess this condition on its own, but sometimes the decreasing condition is hidden within a field of an object where Dafny cannot find it on its own, and then it requires an explicit annotation.

7. Arrays

All that we have considered is fine for toy functions and little mathematical exercises, but it really isn't helpful for real programs. So far we have only considered a handful of values at a time in local variables. Now we turn our attention to arrays of data. Arrays are a built in part of the language, with their own type, **array**<T>, where T is another type. For now we only consider arrays of integers, **array**<**int**>. Arrays can be **null**, and have a built in length field called Length. Element access uses the standard bracket syntax and are indexed from zero, so a[3] is preceded by the 3 elements a[0], a[1], and a[2], in that order. All array accesses must be proven to be within bounds, which is part of the no-runtime-errors safety guaranteed by Dafny. Because bounds checks are proven at verification time, no runtime checks need to be made. To create a new array, it must be allocated with the **new** keyword, but for now we will only work with methods that take a previously allocated array as an argument.

One of the most basic things we might want to do with an array is search through it for a particular key, and return the index of a place where we can find the key if it exists. We have two outcomes for a search, with a different correctness condition for each. If the algorithm returns an index (*i.e.*, non-negative integer), then the key should be present at that index. This might be expressed as follows:

```
method Find(a: array<int>, int key) returns (index: int)
   requires ...
   ensures 0 <= index ==> index < a.Length && a[index] == key;
{
   ...
}
```

The array index here is safe because the implication operator is *short circuiting*. Short circuiting means if the left part is false, then the implication is already true regardless of the truth value of the second part, and thus it does not need to be evaluated. Using the short circuiting property of the implication operator, along with the boolean *and* (&&), which is also short circuiting, is a common Dafny practice. The condition index < a.Length is necessary because otherwise the method could return a large integer which is not an index into the array. Together, the short circuiting behavior means that by the time control reaches the array access, index must be a valid index.

If the key is not in the array, then we would like the method to return a negative number. In this case, we want to say that the method did not miss an occurrence of the key; in other words, that the key is not in the array. To express this property, we turn to another common Dafny tool: quantifiers.

8. Quantifiers

A quantifier in Dafny most often takes the form of a **forall** expression, also called a universal quantifier. As its name suggests, this expression is true if some property holds for all elements of some set. For now, we will consider the set of integers. An example universal quantifier, wrapped in an assertion, is given below:

```
assert forall k :: k < k + 1;
```

A quantifier introduces a temporary name for each element of the set it is considering. This is called the bound variable, in this case k. The identifier has a type, which is almost always inferred rather than given explicitly and is usually **int** anyway. (In general, one can have any number of bound variables; we will encounter an example in Section 9.) A pair of colons (`::`) separates the bound variable and its optional type from the quantified property (which must be of type **bool**). In this case, the property is that adding 1 to any integer makes a strictly larger integer. Dafny is able to prove this simple property automatically. Generally it is not very useful to quantify over infinite sets, such as all the integers. Instead, quantifiers are typically used to quantify over all elements in an array or data structure. We do this for arrays by using the implication operator to make the quantified property trivially true for values which are not indices:

```
assert forall k :: 0 <= k < a.Length ==> ...a[k]...;
```

This says that some property holds for each element of the array. The implication makes sure that k is actually a valid index into the array before evaluating the second part of the expression. Dafny can use this fact not only to prove that the array is accessed safely, but also to reduce the set of integers it must consider to only those that are indices into the array.

    With a quantifier, saying the key is not in the array is straightforward:

```
forall k :: 0 <= k < a.Length ==> a[k] != key
```

Thus our method becomes (with the addition of the non-nullity requirement on a):

```
method Find(a: array<int>, key: int) returns (index: int)
    requires a != null;
    ensures 0 <= index ==> index < a.Length && a[index] == key;
    ensures index < 0 ==> forall k :: 0 <= k < a.Length ==> a[k] != key;
{
    ...
}
```

We can fill in the body of this method in a number of ways, but perhaps the easiest is a linear search, implemented below:

```
index := 0;
while (index < a.Length)
{
    if (a[index] == key) { return; }
    index := index + 1;
}
index := -1;
```

As you can see, we have omitted the loop invariants on the while loop, so Dafny gives us a verification error on one of the postconditions. The reason we get an error is that Dafny does not know that the loop actually covers all the elements. In order to convince Dafny of this, we have to write an invariant that says that everything before the current index has already been looked at (and is not the key). Just like the postcondition, we can use a quantifier to express this property:

```
invariant forall k :: 0 <= k < index ==> a[k] != key;
```

This says that everything before, but excluding, the current index is not the key. Notice that upon entering the loop, i is 0, so the first part of the implication is always false, and thus the quantified property is always true. This common situation is known as *vacuous truth*: the quantifier holds because it is quantifying over an empty set of objects. This means that it is true when entering the loop. We test the value of the array before we extend the non-key part of the array, so Dafny can prove that this invariant is preserved. One problem arises when we try to add this invariant: Dafny complains about the index being out of range for the array access within the invariant.

This is erroneous because there is no invariant on index, so it could be greater than the length of the array. Then the bound variable, k, could exceed the length of the array. To fix this, we put the standard bounds on index, 0 <= index <= a.Length. Note that because we say k < index, the array access is still protected from error even when index == a.Length. The use of a variable that is one past the end of a growing range is a common pattern when working with arrays, where it is often used to build a property up one element at a time. The complete method is given below:

```
method Find(a: array<int>, key: int) returns (index: int)
    requires a != null;
    ensures 0 <= index ==> index < a.Length && a[index] == key;
    ensures index < 0 ==> forall k :: 0 <= k < a.Length ==> a[k] != key;
{
    index := 0;
    while (index < a.Length)
        invariant 0 <= index <= a.Length;
        invariant forall k :: 0 <= k < index ==> a[k] != key;
    {
        if (a[index] == key) { return; }
        index := index + 1;
    }
    index := -1;
}
```

Exercise 12 *Write a method that takes an integer array, which it requires to have at least one element, and returns an index to the maximum of the array's elements. Annotate the method with pre- and postconditions that state the intent of the method, and annotate its body with loop invariants to verify it.*

A linear search is not very efficient, especially when many queries are made of the same data. If the array is sorted, then we can use the efficient binary search procedure to find the key. But in order for us to be able to prove our implementation correct, we need some way to require that the input array actually is sorted. We could do this directly with a quantifier inside a **requires** clause of our method, but a more modular way to express this is through a *predicate*.

9. Predicates

A predicate is a function that returns a boolean. It is a simple but powerful idea that occurs throughout Dafny programs. For example, preparing the way for the binary search method in Section 11, we define the sorted predicate over arrays of integers as a function that takes an array as an argument, and returns true if that array is sorted in increasing order. The use of predicates makes our code shorter, as we do not need to write out a long property over and over. It can also make our code easier to read by giving a common property a name.

There are a number of ways we could write the sorted predicate, but the easiest is to use a quantifier over the indices of the array. We can write a quantifier that expresses the property, "if x is before y in the array, then x <= y", as a quantifier over two bound variables:

```
forall j, k :: 0 <= j < k < a.Length ==> a[j] <= a[k]
```

Here we have two bound variables, j and k, which are both integers. The comparisons between the two guarantee that they are both valid indices into the array, and that j is before k. Then the second part says that they are ordered properly with respect to one another. The function, along with the standard non-null precondition required for using the array, is thus:

```
function sorted(a: array<int>): bool
    requires a != null;
{
    forall j, k :: 0 <= j < k < a.Length ==> a[j] <= a[k]
}
```

Dafny rejects this code as given, claiming that the function cannot read the elements of a. Dealing with this complaint requires another annotation, the *reads annotation*.

Exercise 13 *To get practice with quantifiers, modify the definition of function* sorted *so that it returns true only when the array is sorted and all its elements are distinct.*

10. Framing

The sorted predicate is not able to access the array because the array was not included in the function's *reading frame*. The reading frame of a function is all the memory locations that the function is allowed to read. The reason we might limit what a function can read is so that when we write to memory, we can be sure that functions that do not read that part of memory yield the same value after the write as they did before the write. For example, we might have two arrays, one of which we know is sorted. If we did not put a reads annotation on the sorted predicate, then when we modify the unsorted array, we cannot immediately determine whether the other array stopped being sorted. While we might be able to give invariants to preserve it in this case, it gets even more complex when manipulating data structures and dealing with recursive functions. In those cases, framing is essential to making the verification process feasible.

To specify a reading frame, we use a reads annotation, again with its own keyword:

```
function sorted(a: array<int>): bool
    . . .
    reads a;
    . . .
```

A **reads** annotation can appear anywhere along with the pre- and postconditions, but it does not give a boolean expression like the other annotations we have seen; instead, it specifies a set of memory locations that the function is allowed to access. The name of an array, like a in the above example, stands for all the elements of that array. One can also specify object fields and sets of objects, but we will not concern ourselves with those topics here. Dafny will check that you do not read any memory location that is not stated in the reading frame. This means that function calls within a function must have reading frames that are a subset of the calling function's reading frame. One thing to note is that parameters to the function are not memory locations, so do not need to be declared.

Frames also affect methods. As you might have guessed, methods are not required to list the things they read, as we have written a method which accesses an array with no reads annotation. Methods are allowed to read whatever memory they like, but they are required to list which parts of memory they modify, with a *modifies annotation*. They are almost identical to their reads cousins, except they say what can be changed. In combination with reads, modification restrictions allow Dafny to prove properties of code that would otherwise be very difficult or impossible. Reads and modifies are two of the tools that allow Dafny to work on one method at a time, because they restrict what would otherwise be arbitrary modifications of memory to something that Dafny can reason about.

11. Binary Search

Predicates are used to make other annotations clearer:

```
method BinarySearch(a: array<int>, key: int) returns (index: int)
    requires a != null && sorted(a);
    ensures 0 <= index ==> index < a.Length && a[index] == key;
```

```
    ensures index < 0 ==> forall k :: 0 <= k < a.Length ==> a[k] != key;
{
    ...
}
```

Exercise 14 *What happens if you remove the precondition* `a != null`*? Change the definition of* `sorted` *so that it allows its argument to be null but returns false if it is.*

We have the same postconditions that we did for the linear search, as the goal is the same. The difference is that now we know the array is sorted. Because Dafny can unwrap functions, inside the body of the method it knows this too. We can then use that property to prove the correctness of the search. The method body is given below:

```
var low, high := 0, a.Length;
while (low < high)
    invariant 0 <= low <= high <= a.Length;
    invariant forall i :: 0 <= i < a.Length && !(low <= i < high)
                            ==> a[i] != key;
{
    var mid := (low + high) / 2;
    if (a[mid] < key) {
        low := mid + 1;
    } else if (key < a[mid]) {
        high := mid;
    } else {
        index := mid;
        return;
    }
}
index := -1;
```

First we declare our range to search over. This can be thought of as the remaining space where the key could possibly be. The first invariant expresses the fact that this range is within the array. The second says that the key is not anywhere outside of this range. In the first two branches of the **if** chain, we find the element in the middle of our range is not the key, and so we move the range to exclude that element and all the other elements on the appropriate side of it. We need the addition of 1 when moving the lower end of the range because it is inclusive. If we do not add this, then the loop may continue forever when `mid == low`, which happens when `low + 1 == high`. We could change this to say that the loop exits when `low` and `high` are one apart, but this would mean we would need an extra check after the loop to determine if the key was found at the one remaining index. In the above formulation, this is unnecessary because when `low == high`, the loop exits. But this means that no elements are left in the search range, so the key was not present. This can be deduced from the loop invariant:

```
invariant forall i :: 0 <= i < a.Length && !(low <= i < high)
                        ==> a[i] != key;
```

When low == high, the negated condition in the first part of the implication is always true (because no i can be both at least and strictly smaller than the same value). Thus the invariant says that all elements in the array are not the key, and the second postcondition holds. As you can see, it is easy to introduce subtle off-by-one errors in this code. With the invariants, not only can Dafny prove the code correct, but we can understand the operation of the code easier ourselves.

Exercise 15 *Change the assignments in the body of* BinarySearch *to set* low *to* mid *or to set* high *to* mid - 1. *In each case, what goes wrong?*

12. Further Study

For advanced uses of specification features in Dafny or other tools, we recommend studying textbooks on program correctness (such as [6,8,7,11]), collections of verified programs (such as [23,4]), or, as have become more prevalent lately, the solutions submitted to verification challenges ([22,16,17]) and verification competitions ([13]).

There are several techniques for specifying programs with dynamic data structures (for a survey, see [10]). For this purpose, Dafny supports a specification idiom based on *dynamic frames* [12,21]. That idiom goes beyond what we have covered in these lecture notes, but see [15,14].

13. Conclusion

We've seen a whirlwind tour of the major features of Dafny, and used it for some interesting, if a little on the small side, examples of what Dafny can do. Even if you do not use Dafny regularly, writing down what it is that your code does, in a precise way, and using this to prove code correct is a useful skill to have. Invariants, pre- and postconditions, and annotations are useful in debugging code, and also as documentation for future developers. When modifying or adding to a codebase, they confirm that the guarantees of existing code are not broken. If annotations are checked at run time, they act as test oracles injected in the code. They also ensure that APIs are used correctly, by formalizing behavior and requirements and enforcing correct usage. Reasoning from invariants, considering pre- and postconditions, and writing assertions to check assumptions are all general computer science skills that will benefit you no matter what language you work in.

References

[0] Mike Barnett, Bor-Yuh Evan Chang, Robert DeLine, Bart Jacobs, and K. Rustan M. Leino. Boogie: A modular reusable verifier for object-oriented programs. In Frank S. de Boer, Marcello M. Bonsangue, Susanne Graf, and Willem-Paul de Roever, editors, *Formal Methods for Components and Objects: 4th International Symposium, FMCO 2005*, volume 4111 of *Lecture Notes in Computer Science*, pages 364–387. Springer, September 2006.

[1] Mike Barnett, Manuel Fähndrich, K. Rustan M. Leino, Peter Müller, Wolfram Schulte, and Herman Venter. Specification and verification: the Spec# experience. *Communications of the ACM*, 54(6):81–91, June 2011.

[2]   Raymond T. Boute. The Euclidian definition of the functions div and mod. *ACM Transactions on Programming Languages and Systems*, 14(2):127–144, April 1992.

[3]   Lilian Burdy, Yoonsik Cheon, David R. Cok, Michael D. Ernst, Joeseph R. Kiniry, Gary T. Leavens, K. Rustan M. Leino, and Erik Poll. An overview of JML tools and applications. *International Journal on Software Tools for Technology Transfer*, 7(3):212–232, June 2005.

[4]   Dafny test suite. Files with extension .dfy in the subdirectories of Test at boogie.codeplex.com.

[5]   Leonardo de Moura and Nikolaj Bjørner. Z3: An efficient SMT solver. In C. R. Ramakrishnan and Jakob Rehof, editors, *Tools and Algorithms for the Construction and Analysis of Systems, 14th International Conference, TACAS 2008*, volume 4963 of *Lecture Notes in Computer Science*, pages 337–340. Springer, March–April 2008.

[6]   Edsger W. Dijkstra. *A Discipline of Programming*. Prentice Hall, Englewood Cliffs, NJ, 1976.

[7]   Edsger W. Dijkstra and W. H. J. Feijen. *A Method of Programming*. Addison-Wesley, July 1988.

[8]   David Gries. *The Science of Programming*. Texts and Monographs in Computer Science. Springer-Verlag, 1981.

[9]   John V. Guttag and James J. Horning, editors. *Larch: Languages and Tools for Formal Specification*. Texts and Monographs in Computer Science. Springer, 1993. With Stephen J. Garland, Kevin D. Jones, Andrés Modet, and Jeannette M. Wing.

[10] John Hatcliff, Gary T. Leavens, K. Rustan M. Leino, Peter Müller, and Matthew Parkinson. Behavioral interface specification languages. Technical Report CS-TR-09-01a, Department of Electrical Engineering and Computer Science, University of Central Florida, October 2010. To appear in *ACM Computing Surveys*.

[11] Anne Kaldewaij. *Programming: The Derivation of Algorithms*. Series in Computer Science. Prentice-Hall International, 1990.

[12] Ioannis T. Kassios. Dynamic frames: Support for framing, dependencies and sharing without restrictions. In Jayadev Misra, Tobias Nipkow, and Emil Sekerinski, editors, *FM 2006: Formal Methods, 14th International Symposium on Formal Methods*, volume 4085 of *Lecture Notes in Computer Science*, pages 268–283. Springer, August 2006.

[13] Vladimir Klebanov, Peter Müller, Natarajan Shankar, Gary T. Leavens, Valentin Wüstholz, Eyad Alkassar, Rob Arthan, Derek Bronish, Rod Chapman, Ernie Cohen, Mark Hillebrand, Bart Jacobs, K. Rustan M. Leino, Rosemary Monahan, Frank Piessens, Nadia Polikarpova, Tom Ridge, Jan Smans, Stephan Tobies, Thomas Tuerk, Mattias Ulbrich, and Benjamin Weiß. The 1st verified software competition: Experience report. In Michael Butler and Wolfram Schulte, editors, *FM 2011: Formal Methods - 17th International Symposium on Formal Methods*, volume 6664 of *Lecture Notes in Computer Science*, pages 154–168. Springer, June 2011.

[14] K. Rustan M. Leino. Specification and verification of object-oriented software. In Manfred Broy, Wassiou Sitou, and Tony Hoare, editors, *Engineering Methods and Tools for Software Safety and Security*, volume 22 of *NATO Science for Peace and Security Series D: Information and Communication Security*, pages 231–266. IOS Press, 2009. Summer School Marktoberdorf 2008 lecture notes.

[15] K. Rustan M. Leino. Dafny: An automatic program verifier for functional correctness. In Edmund M. Clarke and Andrei Voronkov, editors, *LPAR-16*, volume 6355 of *Lecture Notes in Computer Science*, pages 348–370. Springer, April 2010.

[16] K. Rustan M. Leino and Rosemary Monahan. Dafny meets the verification benchmarks challenge. In Gary T. Leavens, Peter W. O'Hearn, and Sriram K. Rajamani, editors, *Verified Software: Theories, Tools, Experiments, Third International Conference, VSTTE 2010*, volume 6217 of *Lecture Notes in Computer Science*, pages 112–126. Springer, August 2010.

[17] K. Rustan M. Leino and Michał Moskal. VACID-0: Verification of ample correctness of invariants of data-structures, edition 0. In *Tools and Experiments workshop at VSTTE 2010*, August 2010.

[18] K. Rustan M. Leino and Philipp Rümmer. A polymorphic intermediate verification language: Design and logical encoding. In Javier Esparza and Rupak Majumdar, editors, *Tools and Algorithms for the Construction and Analysis of Systems, 16th International Conference, TACAS 2010*, volume 6015 of *Lecture Notes in Computer Science*, pages 312–327. Springer, March 2010.

[19] Barbara Liskov and John Guttag. *Abstraction and Specification in Program Development*. MIT Electrical Engineering and Computer Science Series. MIT Press, 1986.

[20] Bertrand Meyer. *Object-oriented Software Construction*. Series in Computer Science. Prentice-Hall International, 1988.

[21] Jan Smans, Bart Jacobs, Frank Piessens, and Wolfram Schulte. Automatic verifier for Java-like programs

based on dynamic frames. In José Luiz Fiadeiro and Paola Inverardi, editors, *Fundamental Approaches to Software Engineering, 11th International Conference, FASE 2008*, volume 4961 of *Lecture Notes in Computer Science*, pages 261–275. Springer, March–April 2008.

[22] Bruce W. Weide, Murali Sitaraman, Heather K. Harton, Bruce Adcock, Paolo Bucci, Derek Bronish, Wayne D. Heym, Jason Kirschenbaum, and David Frazier. Incremental benchmarks for software verification tools and techniques. In Natarajan Shankar and Jim Woodcock, editors, *Verified Software: Theories, Tools, Experiments, Second International Conference, VSTTE 2008*, volume 5295 of *Lecture Notes in Computer Science*, pages 84–98. Springer, October 2008.

[23] Why3 gallery of certified programs. `proval.lri.fr/gallery/why3.en.html`.

A. Dafny Quick Reference

This appendix illustrates many of the most common language features in Dafny.

A.0. Programs

At the top level, a Dafny program (stored as a file with extension `.dfy`) is a set of declarations. The declarations introduce fields, methods, and functions, as well as classes and inductive datatypes, where the order of introduction is irrelevant. A class also contains a set of declarations, introducing fields, methods, and functions. Fields, methods, and functions declared outside a class go into an implicit class called `_default`, giving the appearance of the program having global variables, procedures, and functions. If the program contains a unique parameter-less method called `Main`, then program execution starts there, but it is not necessary to have a main method to do verification.

Comments start with `//` and go to the end of the line, or start with `/*` and end with `*/` and can be nested.

A.1. Fields

A field x of some type T is declared as:

```
var x: T;
```

Unlike for local variables and bound variables, the type is required and will not be inferred. The field can be declared to be a *ghost* field by preceding the declaration with the keyword **ghost**. Ghost entities (fields, variables, functions, methods, code) are not represented at run time; they are only used by the verifier, which treats them as it treats non-ghost entities.

Dafny's types include **bool** for booleans, **int** for mathematical (that is, unbounded) integers, user-defined classes and inductive datatypes, **set**<T> for finite mathematical (immutable) sets of T values (where T is any type), and **seq**<T> for mathematical (immutable) sequences of T values. In addition, there are array types (which are like predefined "class" types) of one and more dimensions, written **array**<T>, **array2**<T>, **array3**<T>, ... The type **object** is a supertype of all class types, that is, an **object** denotes any reference, including **null**. Finally, the type **nat** denotes a subrange of **int**, namely the non-negative integers.

A.2. Methods

A method declaration has the form:

```
method M(a: A, b: B, c: C) returns (x: X, y: Y, z: Y)
    requires Pre;
    modifies Frame;
    ensures Post;
    decreases Rank;
{
    Body
}
```

where a, b, c are the method's in-parameters, x, y, z are the method's out-parameters, Pre is a boolean expression denoting the method's precondition, Frame denotes a set of objects whose fields may be updated by the method, Post is a boolean expression denoting the method's postcondition, Rank is the method's variant function, and Body is a statement that implements the method. Frame can be a list of expressions, each of which is a set of objects or a single object, the latter standing for the singleton set consisting of that one object. The method's frame is the union of these sets, plus the set of objects allocated by the method body. If omitted, the pre- and postconditions default to **true** and Frame defaults to the empty set. The variant function is a list of expressions, denoting the unending lexicographic tuple consisting of the given expressions followed implicitly by "top" elements. If omitted, Dafny will guess a variant function for the method, namely the lexicographic tuple that starts with the list of the method's in-parameters.

A method can be declared as ghost by preceding the declaration with the keyword **ghost**. By default, a method has an implicit receiver parameter, **this**. This parameter can be removed by preceding the method declaration with the keyword **static**. A static method M in a class C can be invoked by C.M(...).

In a class, a method can be declared to be a constructor method by replacing the keyword **method** with the keyword **constructor**. A constructor can only be called at the time an object is allocated (see object-creation examples below), and for a class that contains one or more constructors, object creation must be done in conjunction with a call to a constructor.

A.3. Functions

A function declaration has the form:

```
function F(a: A, b: B, c: C): T
    requires Pre;
    reads Frame;
    ensures Post;
    decreases Rank;
{
    Body
}
```

where a, b, c are the method's parameters, T is the type of the function's result, Pre is a boolean expression denoting the function's precondition, Frame denotes a set of objects whose fields the function body may depend on, Post is a boolean expression denoting the function's postcondition, Rank is the function's variant function, and Body is an expression that defines the function. The precondition allows a function to be partial, that is, the precondition says when the function is defined (and Dafny will verify that every use of the function meets the precondition). The postcondition is usually not needed, since the body of the function gives the full definition. However, the postcondition can be a convenient place to declare properties of the function that may require an inductive proof to establish. For example:

```
function Factorial(n: int): int
   requires 0 <= n;
   ensures 1 <= Factorial(n);
{
   if n == 0 then 1 else Factorial(n-1) * n
}
```

says that the result of Factorial is always positive, which Dafny verifies inductively from the function body. To refer to the function's result in the postcondition, use the function itself, as shown in the example.

By default, a function is ghost, and cannot be called from non-ghost code. To make it non-ghost, replace the keyword **function** with the two keywords **function method**.

By default, a function has an implicit receiver parameter, **this**. This parameter can be removed by preceding the function declaration with the keyword **static**. A static function F in a class C can be invoked by C.F(...). This can give a convenient way to declare a number of helper functions in a separate class.

A.4. Classes

A class is defined as follows:

```
class C {
   // member declarations go here
}
```

where the members of the class (fields, methods, and functions) are defined (as described above) inside the curly braces.

A.5. Datatypes

An inductive datatype is a type whose values are created using a fixed set of constructors. A datatype Tree with constructors Empty and Node is declared as follows:

```
datatype Tree = Empty | Node(Tree, int, Tree);
```

The constructors are separated by vertical bars. Parameter-less constructors need not use parentheses, as is shown here for Empty.

For each constructor Ct, the datatype implicitly declares a boolean member Ct?, which returns **true** for those values that have been constructed using Ct. For example, after the code snippet:

```
var t0 := Empty;
var t1 := Node(t0, 5, t0);
```

the expression t1.Node? evaluates to **true** and t0.Node? evaluates to **false**. Two datatype values are equal if they have been created using the same constructor and equal parameters to that constructor. Therefore, for parameter-less constructors like Empty, t.Empty? gives the same result as t == Empty.

A constructor can optionally declare a destructor for any of its parameters, which is done by introducing a name for the parameter. For example, if Tree were declared as:

```
datatype Tree = Empty | Node(left: Tree, data: int, right: Tree);
```

then t1.data == 5 and t1.left == t0 hold after the code snippet above.

A.6. Generics

Dafny supports generic types. That is, any class, inductive datatype, method, and function can have type parameters. These are declared in angle brackets after the name of what is being declared. For example:

```
class Multiset<T> { /*...*/ }
datatype Tree<T> = Empty | Node(Tree<T>, T, Tree<T>);
method Find<T>(key: T, collection: Tree<T>) { /*...*/ }
function IfThenElse<T>(b: bool, x: T, y: T): T { /*...*/ }
```

A.7. Statements

Here are examples of the most common statements in Dafny.

```
var LocalVariables := ExprList;
Lvalues := ExprList;
assert BoolExpr;
print PrintList;
if (BoolExpr0) {
    Stmts0
} else if (BoolExpr1) {
    Stmts1
} else {
    Stmts2
}
while (BoolExpr)
```

```
    invariant Inv;
    modifies Frame;
    decreases Rank;
{
    Stmts
}
match (Expr) {
    case Empty =>  Stmts0
    case Node(l, d, r) =>  Stmts1
}
break;
return;
```

The **var** statement introduces local variables (which are not allowed to shadow other variables declared inside the same set of most tightly enclosing curly braces). Each variable can optionally be followed by :T for any type T, which explicitly gives the preceding variable the type T (rather than being inferred). The ExprList with initial values is optional. To declare the variables as ghost variables, precede the declaration with the keyword **ghost**.

The assignment statement assigns each right-hand side in ExprList to the corresponding left-hand side in Lvalues. These assignments are performed in parallel, so the left-hand sides must denote distinct L-values. Each right-hand side can be an expression or an object creation of one of the following forms:

```
new T
new T.Init(ExprList)
new T[SizeExpr]
new T[SizeExpr0, SizeExpr1]
```

The first form allocates an object of type T. The second form additionally invokes an initialization method or constructor Init on the newly allocated object. The other forms show examples of array allocations, in particular a one- and a two-dimensional array of T values, respectively.

The entire right-hand side of an assignment can also be a method call, in which case the left-hand sides are the actual out-parameters (omitting the ":=" if there are no out-parameters).

The **assert** statement claims that the given expression evaluates to **true** (which is checked by the verifier).

The **print** statement outputs to standard output the values of the given print expressions. A print expression is either an expression or a string literal (where \n is used to denote a newline character).

The **if** statement is the usual one. The example shows stringing together alternatives using **else if**. The **else** branch is optional, as usual.

The **while** statement is the usual loop, where the **invariant** declaration gives a loop invariant, the **modifies** clause restricts the modification frame of the loop, and the **decreases** clause introduces a variant function for the loop. By default, the loop invariant is **true**, the modification frame is the same as in the enclosing context (usually the **modifies** clause of the enclosing method), and the variant function is guessed from the loop guard.

The **match** statement evaluates the source Expr, an expression whose type is an inductive datatype, and then executes the case corresponding to which constructor was used to create the source datatype value, binding the constructor parameters to the given names.

The **break** statement can be used to exit loops, and the **return** statement can be used to exit a method.

A.8. Expressions

The expressions in Dafny are quite similar to those in Java-like languages. Here are some noteworthy differences.

In addition to the short-circuiting boolean operators && (and) and || (or), Dafny has a short-circuiting implication operator ==> and an if-and-only-if operator <==>. As suggested by their widths, <==> has lower binding power than ==>, which in turn has lower binding power than && and ||. Implication associates to the right.

Dafny comparison expressions can be chaining, which means that comparisons "in the same direction" can be strung together. For example,

```
0 <= i < j <= a.Length == N
```

has the same meaning as:

```
0 <= i && i < j && j <= a.Length && a.Length == N
```

Note that boolean equality can be expressed using both == and <==>. There are two differences between these. First, == has a stronger binding power than <==>. Second, == is chaining while <==> is associative. That is, a == b == c is the same as a == b && b == c, whereas a <==> b <==> c is the same as a <==> (b <==> c), which is also the same as (a <==> b) <==> c.

Operations on integers are the usual ones, except that / (integer division) and % (integer modulo) follow the Euclidean definition, which means that % always results in a non-negative number [2]. (Hence, when the first argument to / or % is negative, the result is different than what you get in C, Java, or C#.)

Dafny expressions include universal and existential quantifiers, which have the form:

```
forall BoundVariables :: Expr
```

and likewise for **exists**, where each bound variable can optionally be followed by an explicit type, as in x: T, and Expr is a boolean expression.

Operations on sets include + (union), * (intersection), and – (set difference), as well as the set comparison operators < (proper subset), <= (subset), their duals > and >=, and !! (disjointness). The expression x **in** S says that x is a member of set S, and x !**in** S is a convenient way of writing !(x **in** S). To make a set from some elements, enclose them in curly braces. For example, {x,y} is the set consisting of x and y (which is a singleton set if x == y), {x} is the singleton set containing x, and {} is the empty set.

Operations on sequences include + (concatenation) and the comparison operators <
(proper prefix) and <= (prefix). Membership can be checked like for sets: x **in** S and
x **!in** S. The length of a sequence S is denoted |S|, and the elements of such a sequence
have indices from 0 to less than |S|. The expression S[j] denotes the element at index j
of sequence S. The expression S[m..n], where 0 <= m <= n <= |S|, returns a sequence
whose elements are the n−m elements of S starting at index m (that is, from S[m], S[m+1],
...to but not including S[n]). The expression S[m..] (often called "drop m") is the same
as S[m..|S|], that is, it returns the sequence whose elements are all but the first m ele-
ments of S. The expression S[..n] (often called "take n") is the same as S[0..n], that is,
it returns the sequence that consists of the first n elements of S. If j is a valid index into
sequence S, then the expression S[j := x] is the sequence that is like S except that it has
x at index j. Finally, to make a sequence from some elements, enclose them in square
brackets. For example, [x,y] is the sequence consisting of the two elements x and y
such that [x,y][0] == x and [x,y][1] == y, [x] is the singleton sequence whose only
element is x, and [] is the empty sequence.

The if-then-else expression has the form:

```
if BoolExpr then Expr0 else Expr1
```

where Expr0 and Expr1 are any expressions of the same type. Unlike the **if** statement,
the if-then-else expression does not require parentheses around the guard expression,
uses the **then** keyword, and must include an explicit **else** branch.

The **match** statement also has an analogous match expression, which has a form like:

```
match Expr
case Empty => Expr0
case Node(l, d, r) => Expr1
```

As with the **if** statement versus the if-then-else expression, note that the **match** expression does not require parentheses around the source expression and does not surround
the cases with curly braces. A **match** expression can only be used in the body of function definitions, where it must either be the entire body or be the entire expression for
a case in an enclosing **match** expression; furthermore, the source expression must be a
parameter of the enclosing function.

Software Safety and Security
T. Nipkow et al. (Eds.)
IOS Press, 2012
© *2012 The authors and IOS Press. All rights reserved.*
doi:10.3233/978-1-61499-028-4-182

Lecture Notes on
Software Model Checking

Rupak MAJUMDAR

Max Planck Institute for Software Systems, Germany; Email: rupak@mpi-sws.org.

Abstract. This article gives an overview of software model checking, with a focus on model checkers using abstraction and refinement. It grew out of notes accompanying my lectures at the Marktoberdorf Summer School in Summer, 2011.

Keywords. Software model checking, verification, abstraction-refinement.

1. Introduction

Software model checking is the algorithmic analysis of programs to prove properties of their executions. It traces its roots to at least three, initially somewhat disconnected, disciplines. First, developments in logic and theorem proving provided the conceptual framework in which to formalize the fundamental questions and introduced decision procedures for the analysis of logical questions. Second, automatic *model checking* techniques introduced finite representations of potentially unbounded structures and efficient techniques to search over these representations. Third, compiler analysis, formalized through *abstract interpretation*, provided connections between exact computations over infinite state spaces and approximate computations of program properties. Throughout the 1980s and 1990s, the three communities developed with only occasional interactions. However, over the last decade, there has been a marked convergence in the research directions. Modern software model checkers are a culmination of ideas that combine and perhaps supersede each area alone. In particular, the term "software model checker" is probably a misnomer, since modern tools simultaneously perform analyses traditionally classified as theorem proving, or model checking, or compiler analysis.

Results on undecidability ruled out the possibility of a sound and complete algorithmic solution for any sufficiently powerful programming model, and even under restrictions (such as finite state spaces), the correctness problem remained computationally intractable. However, just because a problem is hard does not mean it never appears in practice. Also, just because the *general* problem is undecidable does not imply that specific *instances* of the problem will also be hard.

Initially, the focus of program verification research was on manual reasoning. The development of axiomatic semantics and logics for reasoning about programs provided a means to treat programs as logical objects, and to relate program semantics to reasoning in logic. As the size of software systems grew, the burden of providing entire manual proofs became too cumbersome, and brought into questions whether long and laborious proofs of correctness could themselves be trusted. This marked a trend toward automating the more mundane parts, leaving the human to provide guidance to an automatic tool (for example, through loop invariants and function pre- and post-conditions). This trend has continued since: the goal of software model checking research is to expand the scope of automated techniques for program reasoning, both in the scale of programs handled and in the richness of properties that can be checked, reducing the burden on the expert human programmer.

Interest in software model checking was re-kindled to a large extent by the SLAM project at Microsoft Research [8] and the Blast project at UC Berkeley [40]. These projects developed a suite of techniques for the automatic verification of safety properties of actual implementations in C, and implemented these techniques into tools that were quite successful in checking device driver code against OS kernel API specifications. SLAM transitioned to a product (the Static Driver Verifier). Soon, several related projects were initiated, which increased the capabilities of SLAM and Blast in non-trivial ways: to deal with concurrency, to deal with pointers and heap data structures, to deal with liveness properties, and to deal with more expressive language-level constructs such as higher-order functions.

These lecture notes give an outline of the state-of-the-art in software model checking, with a view towards automation. Instead of fixing a specific programming language, we take a more abstract view, focusing on the core algorithmic ideas in software model checking rather than their instantiation in a specific language or tool.

The material covered in the lectures roughly follows the article *Software model checking* by Ranjit Jhala and Rupak Majumdar in ACM Computing Surveys, 2009 [47]. See also the recent overview article [5]. We omit detailed bibliographical references in the lecture notes; they can be found in the survey article.

Acknowledgments. These lecture notes grew out of a series of lectures presented at the Marktoberdorf Summer School in Summer 2011. I thank the organizers for inviting me to the event and for the participants in the summer school for commenting on the material. The presentation of the abstraction-refinement algorithm as inference rules came about through discussions with Amit Goel and Sava Krstić.

2. Transition Systems and Invariants

A transition system $\mathcal{S} = (S, S_0, A)$ consists of a (not necessarily finite) set S of states, a set $S_0 \subseteq S$ of initial states, and a set A of *transitions*. Each transition $a \in A$ is a binary relation on S. We write $s \xrightarrow{a} t$ if $(s, t) \in a$. When S is finite, we say $\mathcal{S}$ is a *finite* transition system. Given a state $s \in S$ and a transition $a \in A$, we call the set $\{t \mid s \xrightarrow{a} t\}$ the *a-successors* of s. For a set $T \subseteq S$ of states and transition $a \in A$, we define the two operations

$$\mathsf{post}(T, a) = \{s \mid \exists s' \in T.s' \xrightarrow{a} s\}$$

which describes the set of states reachable from a set T in one step by executing transition a, and

$$\mathsf{pre}(T, a) = \{s \mid \exists s' \in T.s \xrightarrow{a} s'\}$$

which describes the set of states that can reach T in one step by executing transition a.

A *run* of a transition system is a (possibly infinite) sequence $s_0, s_1, \ldots$ such that $s_0 \in S_0$, and for each $i \geq 0$, there is an $a_i \in A$ such that $s_i \xrightarrow{a_i} s_{i+1}$. A state $s \in S$ is *reachable* if there is a run $s_0, s_1 \ldots, s_k$ such that $s_k = s$. Let Reach denote the set of all reachable states.

For a transition system $\mathcal{S} = (S, S_0, A)$, a set $T \subseteq S$ of states is an *invariant* of $\mathcal{S}$ if every reachable state belongs to T, that is, if Reach $\subseteq T$. The invariant verification problem asks, given a transition system $\mathcal{S}$ and a set of states T, whether T is an invariant of $\mathcal{S}$. Invariant verification is a fundamental problem in system verification, and it can be shown that any safety property of the system (intuitively, properties that assert that nothing bad happens) can be reduced to invariant verification.

Example: Programs and Control Flow Graphs We model sequential programs using control flow graph representations. A *program* P $= (x, \text{locs}, \ell_0, \mathcal{T})$ consists of a set x of variables, a set locs of *control locations*, an initial location $\ell_0 \in$ locs, and a set $\mathcal{T}$ of *transitions*. Each transition $\tau \in \mathcal{T}$ is a tuple (ℓ, ρ, ℓ') where $\ell, \ell' \in$ locs are control flow locations, and ρ is a constraint over free variables from $x \cup x'$, where the variables from x' denote the values of the variables from x in the next state.

As concrete examples of the relation ρ, consider an imperative programming language with assignment operations $y := exp$ and conditionals $\texttt{assume}(bexp)$, for expressions exp and predicates $bexp$. The relation ρ for the assignment statement is

$$y' = exp \wedge \bigwedge_{z \in x, z \neq y} z' = z$$

and for the conditional statement is

$$bexp \wedge \bigwedge_{y \in x} y' = y$$

A program defines a transition system in the following way. A state of the program P consists of its location $\ell \in$ locs and a valuation of the variables from x. The set of initial states consist of the initial location ℓ_0 and an arbitrary valuation to the variables. Each edge $e = (\ell, \rho, \ell')$ in the control flow graph gives rise a transition $(\ell, v) \xrightarrow{e} (\ell', v')$ where $\rho(v, v')$ holds.

Enumerative Reachability One way to check if T is invariant is to explicitly compute the set Reach of reachable states and check that each reachable state belongs to T. In case $\mathcal{S}$ is finite, one can compute Reach by a graph reachability algorithm. Figure 1 gives a simple description of such an algorithm.

The graph reachability algorithm maintains two data structures: a set data structure Reachable to store the set of states already found to be reachable, and a multiset data structure Frontier to store the states that need to be explored. Initially, Frontier contains all the initial states from S_0 and Reachable is empty. The reachability algorithm is a loop that runs while Frontier is not empty. The algorithm maintains the property that every state in Reachable as well as every state in Frontier is reachable. In each iteration, the algorithm removes a state s from Frontier and checks if $s \in T$. If not, T cannot be an invariant. Otherwise, it checks if s is already known to be reachable (i.e., if $s \in$ Reachable). If so, it proceeds to the next iteration. Otherwise, if $s \notin$ Reachable, the

---

Algorithm 1 Enumerative reachability algorithm

Input: transition system $S = (S, S_0, A)$, set of states $T \subseteq S$
Output: "yes" if T is an invariant, "no" otherwise

 1: **set** Reachable, **multiset** Frontier
 2: Reachable $= \emptyset$;
 3: Frontier $= S_0$
 4: **while** Frontier $\neq \emptyset$ **do**
 5:     choose s from Frontier; Frontier $=$ Frontier $\setminus \{s\}$
 6:     **if** $s \notin T$ **then**
 7:         **return** "no"
 8:     **end if**
 9:     **if** $s \notin$ Reachable **then**
10:         Reachable $=$ Reachable $\cup \{s\}$
11:         **foreach** $a \in A$, add all $t \in S$ such that $s \xrightarrow{a} t$ to Frontier
12:     **end if**
13: **end while**
14: **return** "yes"'

---

algorithm adds s to Reachable and for all $a \in A$, adds all a-successors of s to Frontier. On termination, Reachable consists of the set of reachable states, and since the check $s \notin T$ never failed, all these states are known to be a subset of T. Different implementations of the data structures gives graph traversal strategies such as depth-first search (Frontier maintained as a stack) or breadth-first search (Frontier maintained as a queue).

The graph reachability algorithm runs in linear time in the size of the graph. Of course, if the transition system is not finite, then there is no guarantee that graph reachability will terminate (it terminates in the simple case when the set of reachable states is finite). Even when the transition system is finite, going over the states one at a time can be extremely time consuming. This motivates the use of *symbolic techniques* which look at *sets* of states at a time.

Symbolic Reachability   The core idea of *symbolic* techniques is to represent sets of states of a transition system using formulas in some logic, and performing operations on sets of states by manipulating logical formulas.

We define symbolic transition systems using a set of predicates and functions coming from a *state vocabulary* S and a fixed set $\mathcal{D}$ on which the vocabulary will be interpreted. A *state formula* is a formula over the state vocabulary. For a state vocabulary S, we write S' for the vocabulary in which each symbol x from S is given a new name x'. We extend the priming notation to formulas: the S'-formula φ' is obtained from the S-formula φ by substitution each symbol $x \in S$ by the primed version x'.

A *symbolic transition system* $S_\star = (\langle S, \mathcal{D} \rangle, \text{Init}, A)$ consists of a state vocabulary S and a set $\mathcal{D}$, a state formula Init (called the *initial condition*), and a set A of *(symbolic) actions*. Each symbolic action $a \in A$ is a formula over the vocabulary $S \cup S'$.

A symbolic transition system represents a transition system (S, S_0, A) in the following way. The set S of states consists of all interpretations to the vocabulary S in the set $\mathcal{D}$. A state is initial if it satisfies the initial condition Init. The set of actions A consists of the binary relations induced by the formulas a in A. That is, for two states s, t and an action $a \in A$, we have $s \xrightarrow{a} t$ if $\langle s, t \rangle$ satisfies the $S \cup S'$-formula a, where t' is an interpretation of all symbols in $\mathcal{S}'$ obtained by assigning the value $t(x)$ to each symbol $x' \in \mathcal{S}'$ on a copy of $\mathcal{D}$. Under this interpretation, state formulas define sets of states of the underlying transition system; for a state formula ψ, we write $[\![\psi]\!]$ to denote this set of states.

We write $\varphi \models \psi$ to denote the set of states represented by φ is a subset of the set of states represented by ψ, and we use standard logical connectives. For a state formula φ and action $a \in \mathcal{A}$, we define $\mathsf{post}(\varphi, a)$ and $\mathsf{pre}(\varphi, a)$ as the state formulas

$$\mathsf{post}(\varphi, a) \equiv (\exists \mathcal{S}.\varphi \wedge a)[\mathcal{S}/\mathcal{S}']$$

$$\mathsf{pre}(\varphi, a) \equiv \exists \mathcal{S}'.a \wedge \varphi'$$

where the existential quantifer "$\exists \mathcal{S}$" quantifies out all symbols in $\mathcal{S}$, and the substitution "$[\mathcal{S}/\mathcal{S}']$" substitutes all symbols in $\mathcal{S}'$ with their unprimed version from $\mathcal{S}$. Semantically, $[\![\mathsf{post}(\varphi, a)]\!] = \mathsf{Post}([\![\varphi]\!], a)$ and $[\![\mathsf{pre}(\varphi, a)]\!] = \mathsf{Pre}([\![\varphi]\!], a)$. We write $\varphi\langle a\rangle\psi$ as shorthand for $\mathsf{post}(\varphi, a) \models \psi$, or equivalently, $\varphi \wedge a \models \psi'$.

A state formula φ is an invariant if every reachable state of the underlying transition system satisfies φ. The *invariant verification problem* asks, given a symbolic transition system $\mathcal{S}_\star$ and a state formula ψ, if ψ is an invariant of $\mathcal{S}_\star$.

Given a symbolic transition system, one can compute the set of reachable states as follows, assuming decision procedures for the underlying logic. The set of states reachable in at most 0 steps, Reach_0, is just the set of initial states. So we define $\mathsf{Reach}_0 = \mathsf{Init}$. Having defined Reach_i, we define the set of states reachable in at most $i + 1$ steps as $\mathsf{Reach}_{i+1} = \mathsf{Reach}_i \vee \bigvee_{a \in \mathcal{A}} \mathsf{post}(\mathsf{Reach}_i, a)$. If for some N, we find that $\mathsf{Reach}_{N+1} \models \mathsf{Reach}_N$, then we have reached a fixed point in the iteration, and $\mathsf{Reach} = \mathsf{Reach}_N$. For a state formula ψ, we have that ψ is an invariant iff $\mathsf{Reach} \models \psi$.

Reachability analysis defined using the post operator is called *forward* analysis, as it starts with the initial states and explores the transition graph "forward." An analogous *backward* analysis can be defined as follows. We define $\mathsf{Breach}_0 = \neg\psi$, the set of "bad" regions, and iterate $\mathsf{Breach}_{i+1} = \mathsf{Breach}_i \vee \bigvee_{a \in \mathcal{A}} \mathsf{pre}(\mathsf{Breach}_i, a)$. To ensure that ψ is an invariant, we check that the fixed point of the iteration does not intersect the initial states; i.e., ψ is an invariant iff $\cup_{i \in \mathbb{N}}\mathsf{Breach}_i \cap \mathsf{Init}$ is not satisfiable.

Instead of full reachability analysis, which checks if there is a path of some length, sometimes one is interested in checking if a path of length exactly $k \geq 0$ can reach a state not in ψ. This problem can be reduced to the satisfiability problem for the underlying logic in the following way. Let $T(\mathcal{S}, \mathcal{S}') = \bigvee\{a(\mathcal{S}, \mathcal{S}') \mid a \in \mathcal{A}\}$, where we have explicitly indicated the vocabulary $\mathcal{S} \cup \mathcal{S}'$ in the formula. We introduce the *priming notation*: the vocabulary $\mathcal{S}'^{(n)}$ is a disjoint copy of the vocabulary $\mathcal{S}$ with n primes attached to each non-logical symbol. We can construct the formula

$$\mathsf{Init}(\mathcal{S}) \wedge T(\mathcal{S}, \mathcal{S}') \wedge \ldots \wedge T(\mathcal{S}'^{(k-1)}, \mathcal{S}'^{(k)}) \wedge \neg\psi[\mathcal{S}'^{(k)}/\mathcal{S}] \qquad (1)$$

and ask if it is satisfiable (over the vocabulary $\mathcal{S} \cup \ldots \mathcal{S}'^{(k)}$). The above formula unrolls the transition relation for k steps, and checks if the last state along the run is outside ψ. This idea of reducing the search for bad paths to satisfiability of formulas is called *bounded model checking*, and has been very successfully applied to bug finding in hardware and software [12].

It can happen that each Reach$_i$ is representable in the logic, but their (infinite) union, the set of reachable states, is not. In that case, the iterations can continue forever. This is not surprising, since reachability analysis for most models is undecidable, even if the k-step reachability relation is decidable.

2.1. Examples of Symbolic Transition Systems

Boolean Systems and BDDs Let X be a set of Boolean variables. A transition system whose states consist in valuations to variables in X can be encoded symbolically using propositional formulas and using satisfiability procedures for propositional logic. The encoding of symbolic transition systems using propositional logic represented using binary decision diagrams (BDDs) [14] was a key step in the industrialization of model checking, and in fact, symbolic model checking was synonymous with model checking Boolean symbolic transition systems using BDDs [15,51]. For bounded model checking, one can use propositional satisfiability checkers to check if the formula in Equation (1) is satisfiable.

Timed Automata Timed automata [3] are models of timed systems that incorporate discrete automata with real-valued clocks. At each location of the automaton, the clocks increase in value at a constant rate. Based on the values of the clocks, discrete edges can be taken to new locations, and on taking a discrete edge, some clocks can be reset. A symbolic representation for clock values of timed systems can be given using *difference constraints* of the form $x - y \sim c$, where x, y are real-valued variables, c is a constant, and $\sim \in \{\leq, <, =, >, \geq\}$. A set of states is then represented as a list of pairs, the first part of the pair is the discrete location and the second part is a conjunction of difference constraints over the clock variables.

2.2. Termination and Well-Structured Systems

For finite-state systems, invariant verification is decidable of course. In some infinite models, reachability (or related relations such as coverability) remains decidable. The most common techniques to show decidability of reachability are the following.

Bisimulation Relation of Finite Index Let S be a transition system and T a set of states. Two states s and t are related by a bisimulation relation if the following conditions hold: (a) either both $s \in T$ and $t \in T$ or both $s \notin T$ and $t \notin T$, (b) for each s' such that $s \to s'$ there is a t' such that $t \to t'$ and s' and t' are related by a bisimulation relation, and (c) for each t' such that $t \to t'$ there is a s' such that $s \to s'$ and s' and t' are related by a bisimulation relation. It is easy to see that bisimulation is an equivalence relation.

Suppose that S has a bisimulation relation with a finite number of equivalence classes. Then, one can perform reachability analysis on the (finite state) *quotient* whose states are equivalence classes of the bisimulation relation, and which has an edge between two equivalence classes if there is a state s in the first and a state t in the second such that $s \to t$. It can be shown that the equivalence class of T is reachable in the quotient iff T is reachable in the original transition system.

The existence of bisimulation relations of a finite index is used to prove that backward reachability analysis terminates for timed automata [3,42,41].

Well-quasi Orderings   A reflexive and transitive binary relation $\preceq \subseteq S \times S$ is a *well-quasi-order* (wqo) if for every infinite sequence

$$s_0 s_1 s_2 \ldots$$

of elements from S, one can always find an i and a j with $i < j$ and $s_i \preceq s_j$. For example, consider the set $\mathbb{N}^k$ of k-vectors of natural numbers. The pointwise comparison ordering ($u \leq v$ if for each $i \in \{1, \ldots, k\}$ we have $u_i \leq v_i$) is a well-quasi-order. Consider the relation $\leq$ on strings where $u \leq v$ if u is a substring of v. Then $\leq$ is a well-quasi-order.

Now let S be a transition system with a well-quasi-ordering $\preceq$ defined on its set of states, and assume that S has the following monotonicity property: $s \preceq s'$ and $s \to t$ implies there exists a t' such that $t \preceq t'$ and $s' \to t'$. Call a set U *upward closed* if whenever $u \in U$ and $u \preceq v$ we have $v \in U$. First note that for monotonic transition systems and upward closed sets U, we have pre(U) is upward closed.

If S is a monotonic transition system with respect to a wqo $\preceq$, and U an upward closed set of states of S, then the sequence of iterations $U_0 = U$, $U_{i+1} = U_i \cup \text{pre}(U_i)$ stabilizes in a finite number of steps. The reason is that each set U_i in the sequence is upward-closed, and if the sequence did not terminate, we could construct an infinite sequence of elements violating the well-quasi-ordering assumption on $\preceq$.

In general, forward reachability need not terminate even if backward reachability terminates. Moreover, the bound on the number of iterations of backward reachability can be extremely bad (non-primitive recursive).

The existence of well-quasi-orderings is, in some sense, a canonical requirement for reachability analysis to terminate. For example, from the existence of a bisimulation relation of finite index, one can define a well-quasi-ordering on the state space, and more generally, from the termination of a backward reachability procedure, one can define a suitable well-quasi-ordering on the state space that demonstrates the termination of the reachability analysis.

The power of well-quasi-orderings comes from a large number of *natural* models of computation on which (simple) well-quasi-orderings can be defined [2,28]. For example, Petri nets, lossy channel systems, broadcast protocols, asynchronous programs, etc. all define well-structure transition systems.

2.3. Inductive Invariants and Abstract Reachability Graphs

In general, reachability does not terminate for programs (indeed, just two integer valued variables is enough for undecidability [53]). Hence, we turn to heuristics that, while incomplete in general, work well in practice.

First, notice that computing the set of reachable states is often overkill to solve the invariant verification problem. Instead of computing the exact set of reachable states, and checking that this set is contained in ψ, one can prove that ψ is an invariant by devising an *inductive invariant* ϕ and checking the following conditions:

     (I1: Initiation) Init $\models \phi$;
     (I2: Inductiveness) for each $a \in A$, we have $\phi \langle a \rangle \phi$; and
     (I3: Safety) $\phi \models \psi$.

By induction, it is easy to show that for any ϕ satisfying (I1) and (I2), we have that Reach $\models \phi$. Together with condition (I3), this entails that ψ is an invariant.

Given a candidate inductive invariant ϕ, the checks (I1)-(I3) can be discharged using a decision procedure for the underlying logic. The *invariant synthesis* problem is to construct a suitable inductive invariant. We introduce abstract reachability graphs as a first step toward invariant synthesis.

Let $\mathcal{S}_\star = (\langle \mathcal{S}, \mathcal{D} \rangle, \mathsf{Init}, \mathcal{A})$ be a symbolic transition system and let ψ be a state formula. An *abstract reachability graph* (ARG) $G = \langle V, E, \mathsf{r}, \Phi \rangle$ is a rooted, directed, labeled graph with a set V of nodes, a set of *transition edges* $E \subseteq V \times \mathcal{A} \times V$, a special root node $\mathsf{r} \in V$, and a node-labeling function Φ mapping each node in V to a state formula.

We write $\mathsf{n} \xrightarrow{a} \mathsf{n}_1$ for $(\mathsf{n}, a, \mathsf{n}_1) \in E$. For a node $\mathsf{n} \in V$, we say n is *reachable from* r and write $\mathsf{r} \xrightarrow{*} \mathsf{n}$ if there is some $\ell \geq 0$ and a path $\mathsf{r} \xrightarrow{a_1} \mathsf{n}_1 \xrightarrow{a_2} \ldots \xrightarrow{a_\ell} \mathsf{n}$ of E-edges from r to n.

An ARG is *well-labeled* if the following conditions hold:

WL$_1$ $\mathsf{Init} \models \Phi(\mathsf{r})$;
WL$_2$ For each edge $\mathsf{n} \xrightarrow{a} \mathsf{n}_1$ in E, $\Phi(\mathsf{n})\langle a \rangle \Phi(\mathsf{n}_1)$; and
WL$_3$ For each n such that $\mathsf{r} \xrightarrow{*} \mathsf{n}$, we have $\Phi(\mathsf{n}) \models \psi$.

An ARG is *complete* if for each node $\mathsf{n} \in V$ such that $\mathsf{r} \xrightarrow{*} \mathsf{n}$ and for each transition $a \in \mathcal{A}$, there is a $\mathsf{n}_1 \in V$ such that $\mathsf{n} \xrightarrow{a} \mathsf{n}_1$ is in E.

Theorem 1 *Let $\mathcal{S}_\star$ be a symbolic transition system and ψ a state formula. If there exists a well-labeled and complete ARG for $\mathcal{S}_\star$ and ψ, then ψ is an invariant of $\mathcal{S}_\star$.*

PROOF. We claim that

$$\bigvee \{\Phi(\mathsf{n}) \mid \mathsf{n} \in V, \mathsf{r} \xrightarrow{*} \mathsf{n}\}$$

satisfies conditions I_1, I_2, and I_3. Condition I_1 holds because $\mathsf{Init} \models \Phi(\mathsf{r})$ by the well-labeling condition. Condition I_2 holds because (by well-labeling) $\Phi(\mathsf{n})\langle a \rangle \Phi(\mathsf{n}_1)$ holds for each edge $\mathsf{n} \xrightarrow{a} \mathsf{n}_1$ for each n reachable from r, and moreover, by completeness, each node reachable from the root node has an outgoing edge for each $a \in \mathcal{A}$. Condition I_3 holds because $\Phi(\mathsf{n}) \models \psi$ for each n reachable from r by the well-labeling condition. $\square$

2.4. Abstraction

The key observation that makes the ARG useful is that for any edge $\mathsf{n} \xrightarrow{a} \mathsf{n}_1$, the label $\Phi(\mathsf{n}_1)$ need not be *exactly* $\mathsf{post}(\Phi(\mathsf{n}), a)$, but should *contain* $\mathsf{post}(\Phi(\mathsf{n}), a)$. This opens up the possibility of *approximate*, or abstract, computations of reachable sets. As long as the abstractions do not lose too much precision, in the sense of condition WL$_3$, one can use the approximations to check if ψ is an invariant.

We now give an algorithm to construct ARGs through a non-deterministic algorithm, Algorithm AbstractSafety. Its inputs are a symbolic transition system $\mathcal{S}_\star$ and a state formula ψ. We assume that $\mathsf{Init} \models \psi$ (otherwise, we stop immediately and return that ψ is not an invariant).

Initially, the algorithm starts with an ARG with one node: the root node r labeled Init. Initially, there are no edges, i.e., $E = \emptyset$. This graph is well-labeled, but not complete if $A \neq \emptyset$.

In each step, it picks a node n in the ARG and a transition $a \in \mathcal{A}$ such that n has no outgoing edge labeled with a. It picks a state predicate ϕ such that $\Phi(\mathsf{n})\langle a \rangle \phi$ holds. If $\phi \wedge \neg \psi$ is satisfiable, the algorithm stops with an error.

Otherwise, if there is already a node n_1 in the ARG labeled ϕ, the algorithm adds the edge $\mathsf{n} \xrightarrow{a} \mathsf{n}_1$ to E. Otherwise, if there is no such node, it adds a new node n_2 to the ARG and labels it with ϕ.

Each step of the algorithm makes the graph "more complete." The algorithm terminates, and states ψ is an invariant, if there is no node n and action a such that node n has no outgoing a-edge in E.

Theorem 1 *[Soundness] If Algorithm* AbstractSafety, *on input* $\mathcal{S}_\star$ *and* ψ, *terminates and states* ψ *is an invariant, then* ψ *is an invariant of* $\mathcal{S}_\star$.

The proof of the proposition follows by checking the properties WL$_1$-WL$_3$ of the ARG at the end of the computation. When the algorithm returns an error, we can additionally produce a *possible counterexample*: a list of transitions labeling the path from the root node until the node at which error was raised, together with the transition for which the error was raised. Note that a possible counterexample need not be a "real" counterexample of the system: the process of choosing ϕs introduces approximations, and the counterexample produced by the algorithm may not be feasible in $\mathcal{S}_\star$.

We must answer two key steps to implement the algorithm: what strategy should we use to expand nodes, and how do we choose ϕ? The first question is technically not very deep (choose any graph traversal strategy), but can have practical consequences on the efficiency and scalability of the algorithm.

The theory of abstract interpretation [22] formalizes the second question in terms of fixing abstract domains and computing "best" approximations relative to the abstract domains. Instead of giving the general theory, we give two examples.

Polyhedral Abstraction   In *polyhedral abstraction*, we look for state formulas defined by linear constraints over constants in the vocabulary, that is, polyhedral sets in the n-dimensional space of program variables. Using efficient algorithms for polyhedral manipulation, one can implement the logical operations effectively: the conjunction operation is polyhedral intersection, the disjunction operation either keeps an explicit list of polyhedra or, to make the algorithm efficient, takes the convex hull of the operands, and satisfiability checking determines if a polyhedron is non-empty. If the transition relations are defined by linear constraints, then one can compute the pre and post operations using intersections and projections of polyhedra.

Polyhedral abstractions have been successfully used to verify properties of programs, such as array bounds checks or error bounds in numerical computations. Notice that the ARG construction need not terminate when using a polyhedral abstraction. To ensure termination, a *widening* operation, that guarantees syntactically that increasing chains stabilize in a finite number of steps, is used.

Faster, but less expressive, abstract domains that can represent a subclass of polyhedra, such as intervals (of the form $c_1 \leq x \leq c_2$), difference constraints (of the form $x - y \leq c$), or octagons (of the form $x \pm y \leq c$) have been used as well.

Predicate Abstraction In *predicate abstraction*, we fix a finite set Π of first order formulas over the vocabulary S and consider of the lattice of Boolean formulas over Π ordered by implication. The predicate abstraction of a state formula ψ with respect to the set Π of predicates is the smallest (in the implication ordering) state formula $\text{Abs}(\psi, \Pi)$ which contains ψ and is representable as a Boolean combination of predicates from Π:

$$\text{Abs}(\psi, \Pi) \;=\; \bigwedge \{\phi \mid \phi \text{ is a Boolean formula over } \Pi \wedge \psi \Rightarrow \phi\}$$

The region $\text{Abs}(\psi, \Pi)$ can be computed by recursively splitting as follows [23]:

$$\text{Abs}(\psi, \Pi) = \begin{cases} true & \text{if } \Pi = \emptyset \text{ and } \psi \text{ satisfiable} \\ false & \text{if } \Pi = \emptyset \text{ and } \psi \text{ unsatisfiable} \\ (p \wedge \text{Abs}(\psi \wedge p, \Pi')) & \\ \qquad\qquad \vee & \text{if } \Pi = \{p\} \cup \Pi' \\ (\neg p \wedge \text{Abs}(\psi \wedge \neg p, \Pi')) & \end{cases}$$

The satisfiability checks can be discharged by a decision procedure [54,26,24]. In the worst case, the computation is exponential in the number of predicates, and several heuristics with better performance in practice have been proposed [61,30].

Using incremental decision procedures, the predicate abstraction $\text{Abs}(\psi, \Pi)$ can be computed as follows. For each predicate $p \in \Pi$, introduce a Boolean variable b_p, and consider the formula

$$\psi \wedge \bigwedge_{p \in \Pi} b_p \leftrightarrow p \qquad\qquad (2)$$

If the formula is not satisfiable, then the predicate abstraction is *false*. Otherwise, consider a satisfying assignment to the formula (2), and project the satisfying assignment to the Boolean variables $\{b_p \mid p \in \Pi\}$. By replacing b_p with p in the assignment, we get a minterm in the predicate abstraction. We can now conjoin the complement of the assignment to the formula (2) and ask for a different satisfying assignment, until there are no more. Incremental decision procedures based on conflict clauses can implement the sequence of queries efficiently. The predicate abstraction is the disjunction of all the satisfying assignments found in this way.

Many implementations of predicate-based software model checkers implement an over-approximation of the predicate abstraction that can be computed efficiently in order to avoid the exponential cost. *Cartesian* predicate abstraction is one such precision-efficiency tradeoff: it can be computed more efficiently than full predicate abstraction but can be quite imprecise in the worst case. Cartesian abstraction formalizes the idea of ignoring relations between components of tuples, and approximates a set of tuples by the smallest Cartesian product containing the set [7]. Formally, the cartesian abstraction of ψ with respect to the set Π of predicates is the smallest (in the implication ordering) region $\text{CartAbs}(\psi, \Pi)$ which contains ψ and is representable as a *conjunction* of predicates from Π. The region $\text{CartAbs}(\psi, \Pi)$ can be computed as:

$$\text{CartAbs}(\psi, \Pi) = \begin{cases} true & \text{if } \Pi = \emptyset \\ p \wedge \text{CartAbs}(\psi, \Pi') & \text{if } \Pi = \{p\} \cup \Pi' \text{ and } (\psi \wedge \neg p) \text{ unsatisfiable} \end{cases}$$

Cartesian predicate abstraction was implemented for C programs as part of SLAM in a tool called c2bp [6], and since then in other software verifiers. While it is sufficient for checking state-machine like properties, it is usually too imprecise in the presence of data structure reasoning.

2.5. Abstraction Refinement

Algorithm AbstractSafety is sound — if it claims ψ is an invariant, then ψ is indeed an invariant — but can produce spurious counterexamples. That is, it can stop with an error even though ψ is an invariant. This can happen if the choice of ϕ in the expansion step is too coarse (so that $\phi \cap \neg\psi$ is satisfiable). As a trivial example, we can always choose *true* as a candidate ϕ. The idea of an *abstraction refinement* algorithm is to start with some abstraction, and then analyze the counterexamples produced by the abstract model checker to see whether they can be replayed on the concrete system, or if not, to devise a new abstraction that rules out this counterexample (and ideally many more).

We modify the ARG construction in the following way. We augment an ARG with an additional node-labeling function Cex, called the *counterexample labeling*, mapping each node in V to a formula representing, intuitively, the subset of $\Phi(n)$ from which a path to some state not satisfying ψ is possible.

Initially, the ARG consists of two nodes: a root node r with $\Phi(r) = $ Init and Cex(r) = *false*, and a "top" node top with $\Phi(\text{top}) = true$ and Cex(top) = $\neg\psi$.

The construction algorithm has two kinds of steps. First, as before, an *expansion* step adds a-successors of nodes for transitions $a \in A$ (making the graph "more complete"), In addition, a *refinement* step refines the labelings Φ and Cex on nodes (creating new nodes if necessary) to establish, if possible, the condition that all nodes reachable from the root satisfy condition (WL$_2$) and have a counterexample label *false*.

The refinement step considers *bad edges* n $\xrightarrow{\cdot}$ n$_1$ in E, for which n is reachable from r, Cex(n) $\equiv$ *false*, but Cex(n$_1$) $\not\equiv$ *false*.

We give a non-deterministic description of the algorithm using a set of inference rules shown in Figure 1. The algorithm builds an ARG (V, E, Φ) by application of the inference rules (we omit mentioning the graph explicitly in the rules in Figure 1). The algorithm non-deterministically applies the expansion and refinement steps until they are not applicable or until the root node gets a non-empty counterexample label (i.e., Cex(r) $\not\equiv$ *false*).

The expansion step is implemented using the rule (Expand) which expands existing nodes with unexplored transitions. The (Error) rule raises an error if the root node gets a non-empty counterexample label.

The refinement step is implemented by the rules (Switch), (Back), and (Refine). These rules take a bad edge and try to fix the labeling to either establish that all nodes n reachable from r have Cex(n) = *false* or to "push" the counterexamples toward the root.

The applicability of the (Back) rule and the (Switch) and (Refine) rules are complementary. Let n $\xrightarrow{a}$ n$_1$ be a bad edge, and consider the formula $\Phi(n) \wedge a \wedge$ Cex(n$_1$). If this formula is satisfiable, then (Back) applies. If not, then either (Switch) or (Refine) —or possibly both— applies.

The (Back) rule propagates a counterexample label Cex(n$_1$) up to its predecessor. If a counterexample can be pushed up to the root, then the (Error) rule raises an error. The (Switch) rule replaces a bad edge out of a node n with a good edge out of n to an

EXPAND

$$\frac{\text{pick } n \in V, a \in \mathcal{A}, r \xrightarrow{*} n \qquad n \text{ has no outgoing } a\text{-edge in } E \qquad \mathsf{Cex}(n) = false}{\text{add } n \xrightarrow{a} \text{top to } E}$$

ERROR

$$\frac{\mathsf{Cex}(r) \neq false}{\textbf{raise } \text{Error}}$$

BACK

$$\frac{\text{pick bad edge } n \xrightarrow{a} n_1 \text{ in } E \qquad \text{pick formula } \beta \text{ s.t. } \beta \models \Phi(n) \text{ and } \beta \langle a \rangle \mathsf{Cex}(n_1)}{\text{update } \mathsf{Cex}(n) \text{ to } \beta}$$

SWITCH

$$\frac{\text{pick bad edge } n \xrightarrow{a} n_1 \text{ in } E, n_2 \in V \qquad}{\mathsf{Cex}(n_2) \equiv false \qquad \Phi(n_2) \models \Phi(n_1) \qquad \Phi(n) \langle a \rangle \Phi(n_2)}$$
$$\frac{}{\text{Remove } n \xrightarrow{a} n_1 \text{ from } E, \text{ add } n \xrightarrow{a} n_2 \text{ to } E}$$

REFINE

$$\frac{\text{pick bad edge } n \xrightarrow{a} n_1 \text{ in } E, \text{ formula } \alpha \qquad \Phi(n) \langle a \rangle \alpha \qquad \alpha \models \neg \mathsf{Cex}(n_1)}{\text{create fresh node } n_2 \text{ in } V, \text{ set } \Phi(n_2) = \Phi(n_1) \wedge \alpha, \mathsf{Cex}(n_2) = false}$$
$$\text{remove } n \xrightarrow{a} n_1 \text{ from } E, \text{ add } n \xrightarrow{a} n_2 \text{ to } E$$

Figure 1. Rules for a non-deterministic model checking algorithm

existing node. The (Refine) rule adds a new node n_2 to the graph whose label $\Phi(n_2)$ is stronger than $\Phi(n_1)$ such that $\mathsf{Cex}(n_2) \equiv false$. The (Back) and (Refine) rules require the discovery of formulas β and α, respectively.

The algorithm NonDetSafety, on input $\mathcal{S}_\star$ and ψ, non-deterministically applies the rules until either **error** is produced or no rule is applicable or the algorithm goes on forever. During its execution, it builds an ARG (additionally labeled with counterexample labelings).

Theorem 2   1. **[Soundness]** *On input $\mathcal{S}_\star$ and ψ, if Algorithm NonDetSafety terminates because no rules are applicable, then ψ is an invariant of $\mathcal{S}_\star$.*

2. **[Validity of Counterexamples]** *If Algorithm NonDetSafety terminates with "error" then ψ is not an invariant of $\mathcal{S}_\star$.*

PROOF. In the first case, we show that the ARG (V, E, Φ) computed by the algorithm is well-labeled and complete for $\mathcal{S}_\star$ and ψ. We use the invariant that for each edge $n_1 \xrightarrow{a} n_2$, if $r \xrightarrow{*} r$ and $\mathsf{Cex}(n_2) \equiv false$ then $\Phi(n_1)\langle a \rangle \Phi(n_2)$. If no rules are applicable, then every node n reachable from r has $\mathsf{Cex}(n) \equiv false$ (otherwise, either (Back) or (Switch) or (Refine) is applicable). Further, the graph must be complete (otherwise, the (Expand) rule should be applicable at some node).

In the second case, we argue that there is a path from some initial state to a state not in ψ: consider the path in the ARG from the root to top, such that for each node n along the path, $\mathsf{Cex}(n)$ is not empty. By the property of (Back), for each edge $n_i \xrightarrow{a} n_{i+1}$

along this path, we have that every state in $\mathsf{Cex}(n_i)$ has an a-successor to some state in $\mathsf{Cex}(n_{i+1})$. $\square$

Since invariant verification is undecidable in general, the algorithm is not guaranteed to terminate. For finite-state systems, the algorithm is guaranteed to terminate on each run in which we prioritize (Switch) over (Refine), that is, if we apply (Refine) only when (Switch) is not applicable. We refer to the instance of Algorithm NonDetSafety that prioritizes (Switch) over (Refine) as Algorithm SRSafety.

We now make some concrete choices in the ARG construction, leading to some well-known algorithms.

Implementation: Lazy Abstraction In lazy abstraction [40], the expansion and refinement steps use predicate abstraction in the following way. The algorithm maintains a global set of predicates Π and performs predicate abstraction w.r.t. predicates in Π. It maintains the invariant that the labels of each node can be represented as a Boolean combination of predicates from Π.

For $n \in V$ and $a \in \mathcal{A}$, the (Expand) and (Switch) steps are combined in the following way. First, the algorithm computes $\mathsf{Abs}(\mathsf{post}(\Phi(n), a), \Pi)$. If there is already a node $n_1 \in V$ such that $\mathsf{Abs}(\mathsf{post}(\Phi(n), a), \Pi) \models \Phi(n_1)$ and $\mathsf{Cex}(n_1) \equiv \mathit{false}$, it adds $n \xrightarrow{a} n_1$ to E. Otherwise, it introduces a new node n_2 and sets $\Phi(n_2)$ to $\mathsf{Abs}(\mathsf{post}(\Phi(n), a), \Pi)$ and $\mathsf{Cex}(n_2)$ to $\mathsf{Abs}(\mathsf{post}(\Phi(n), a), \Pi) \wedge \neg\psi$.

The β in the (Back) rule is computed as $\mathsf{pre}(\mathsf{Cex}(n_1), a)$ (without any abstraction).

The (Refine) procedure introduces new predicates to Π through the use of *interpolants*. Let φ_1 and φ_2 be first-order formulas such that $\varphi_1 \wedge \varphi_2$ is unsatisfiable. A formula ψ is called an *interpolant* for (φ_1, φ_2) if (a) $\varphi_1 \Rightarrow \psi$, (b) $\psi \wedge \varphi_2$ is unsatisfiable, and (c) ψ is over the common language of φ_1 and φ_2. Interpolants always exist for first-order logic (extended with recursively enumerable theories), and can be computed from first-order proofs of unsatisfiability (e.g., in a resolution-based proof system).

The (Refine) rule computes an interpolant α' between $\Phi(n) \wedge a$ and $\neg\mathsf{Cex}(n_1)'$, and adds all (unprimed) atomic formulas from α' to Π. It then removes the edge $n \xrightarrow{a} n_1$ and adds a new node n_2 labeled with $\mathsf{Abs}(\mathsf{post}(\Phi(n), a), \Pi)$ (with the updated Π) and $\mathsf{Cex}(n_2) = \mathit{false}$.

The *lazy interpolation* algorithm of McMillan [52] dispenses with the predicate abstraction, and solely uses interpolants in the node labelings. That is, it computes α' as the interpolant between $\Phi(n) \wedge a$ and $\neg\mathsf{Cex}(n_1)'$ and uses α as the new label.

Tools based on Abstraction Refinement Several academic and industrial tools have been developed using the ideas of abstraction refinement. We have already mentioned SLAM [5], which pioneered much of the research in the area. SLAM was closely followed by Blast [40], a tool that introduced several ideas such as on-the-fly construction of abstract state spaces and interpolation-based refinement. The tool F-Soft [45] developed at NEC research combined abstraction refinement ideas with bounded model checking.

2.6. Some Open Problems

We conclude this section with some open problems in abstraction refinement for software verification.

First, refinement based on one counterexample at a time may not be adequate for the verification of many programs, and the refinement loop can go on forever. The problem is that we would like a "good" refinement to rule out a large family of counterexamples, rather than just the one. Recognizing good generalizations from counterexamples is quite open, see [11] for some initial ideas.

Second, while software model checking tools based on abstraction refinement have successfully verified control-flow properties of programs, such as locks are acquired and released in alternation, or that a device driver calls the kernel API according to a state machine, their application to data intensive programs require more work. Over the past decade, there has been a slew of work in modeling properties of the heap using specialized analyses (shape analysis) and logics (separation logic). A tool combining predicate abstraction refinement and separation logic-based reasoning would be very useful.

In the same spirit, we expect to see more robust tools combining abstraction refinement techniques with more expressive programming formalisms (concurrency, higher-order functions, asynchronous calls). In recent years, the theory for these tools have been developed, and tool development is also under way. A very interesting line of work is the marriage of refinement types and predicate abstraction [60].

Techniques arising out of symbolic model checking and abstraction have found their way into testing practice, and conversely, ideas from testing have influenced new model checking algorithms. A very interesting example of this confluence is *dynamic* symbolic execution, in which a program is run simultaneously with concrete as well as symbolic inputs. Dynamic symbolic execution has been quite successful in test case generation and bug finding of large-scale software systems [35,16]. On the other hand, it has led to more efficient implementations of abstraction refinement algorithms [37,36]. For concurrent programs, a similar combination is demonstrated by *context-bounded* verification, a generalization of bounded model checking to concurrent recursive programs [58]. We expect to see further confluence between testing and verification.

3. Recursive Procedures

So far, our model of programs has ignored recursion. Transition systems can be used as a model for recursive programs as well, by explicitly encoding the program stack in the state. As the stack can be unbounded, the resulting transition systems are not going to be finite-state in general, even if we interpret the vocabulary over a finite structure, and a "generic" reachability algorithm may not terminate. Instead, we now show how one can get a reachability algorithm by modeling a recursive program as a context-free process (and using algorithms for context free grammars).

We represent programs using control flow graphs, one for each procedure. The set of procedure names is denoted Σ. For each $\sigma \in \Sigma$, the control flow graph for σ is a labeled, directed graph (V_σ, E_σ), together with a unique entry node $v_\sigma^e \in V_\sigma$ and a unique exit node $v_\sigma^x \in V_\sigma$. We assume the program has (global) variables from some set Y of variables and that each variable $y \in Y$ ranges over a finite domain. Each edge in E_σ is labeled with either a constraint ρ over the free variables $Y \cup Y'$ or a procedure call to a procedure $\sigma' \in \Sigma$ (which can be σ itself). The nodes of the control flow graph correspond to control locations of the program, the entry and exit nodes represent, respectively, where execution of a procedure starts and returns. We assume that each node

$v \in V_\sigma$ is reachable from v_σ^e and can reach v_σ^x, and that execution of the program begins at the entry node v_{main}^e of a special procedure main $\in \Sigma$.

The program representation defines a context-free grammar $G = (V, \Sigma \cup \text{stmts}, \mathcal{P}, v_{\text{main}}^e)$, where $V = \uplus \{V_\sigma \mid \sigma \in \Sigma\}$ is the disjoint union of all control flow nodes, stmts is the set of constraints labeling program edges, and the set of productions $\mathcal{P}$ is the smallest set such that

- $(X \to \rho Y) \in \mathcal{P}$ if the edge (X, Y) in the control flow graph is labeled with the operation ρ,
- $(X \to v_\sigma^e Y) \in \mathcal{P}$ if the edge (X, Y) in the control flow graph is labeled with a call to procedure $\sigma \in \Sigma$, and
- $(v_\sigma^x \to \epsilon) \in \mathcal{P}$ for each $\sigma \in \Sigma$.

To capture the effect of constraints on program edges on the program variables, we define an NFA $R = (D, d_0, \text{stmts}, \delta)$ where D is the set of valuations to variables in Y, d_0 is the initial valuation, and $\delta = \{(d, \rho, d') \mid d, d' \in D, (d, d') \models \rho\}$. (For the moment, we omit the final states.)

Intuitively, a leftmost derivation of the grammar G starting from v_{main}^e defines an interprocedurally valid path in the program. A possible global state of the program is given by a state in D obtained by executing the NFA R along the path (note that the constraints can be non-deterministic, and there can be several global states).

We can take a product of the grammar G with the NFA R to construct a grammar G_R in the following way. The grammar $G_R = (V_R, \emptyset, \mathcal{P}_R)$, where $V_R = \{[dvd'] \mid d, d' \in D, v \in V\}$ and $\mathcal{P}_R$ is the least set such that:

- if $(X \to \epsilon) \in \mathcal{P}$ then $([dXd] \to \epsilon) \in \mathcal{P}_R$,
- if $(X \to \rho Y) \in \mathcal{P}$, $(d, \rho, d') \in \delta$, and $d'' \in D$, then $([dXd''] \to [d'Yd'']) \in \mathcal{P}_R$, and
- if $(X \to v_\sigma^e Y) \in \mathcal{P}$, and $d_0, d_1, d_2 \in D$, then $([d_0 X d_2] \to [d_0 v_\sigma^e d_1][d_1 Y d_2]) \in \mathcal{P}_R$.

The product construction ensures the following invariant: if $[dXd'] \to^* \epsilon$ then there exists $w \in \text{stmts}^*$ such that $d \xrightarrow{w} d'$ in R and $X \to^* w$ in G, and conversely, if $d \xrightarrow{w} d'$ in R and $X \to^* w$ in G then $[dXd'] \to^* \epsilon$ in G_R.

Without loss of generality, we can reduce the invariant verification problem to checking if the program has an execution leading to a special state $d_\star \in D$ when the control location is at v_{main}^x. This reduces to the question if $[d v_{\text{main}}^e d_\star] \to^* \epsilon$, which can be checked using a "marking algorithm" for context-free language emptiness. Moreover, the algorithm can be made symbolic by keeping track of sets of data values, and manipulating them symbolically. We omit the details of the algorithm, see [59,9].

4. Checking Liveness

4.1. Safety and Liveness Properties

So far, we have focused on *safety* properties, which intuitively, state that "nothing bad happens." We now describe how we can check for *liveness* properties, that state "something good" happens. To understand the difference between safety and liveness, consider the design of a mutual exclusion protocol. A "bad state" for the protocol is that two processes are in the critical section at the same time, and a safety property can state that the protocol never gets into this bad state. However, simply ensuring the safety property is not enough: it is easy to design a protocol that prevents *all* requrests to go to the critical section, thus ensuring the safety property trivially. Thus, we want the design to additionally satisfy the liveness property that if a process wants to enter the critical section, then it is able to do so no matter how other processes behave.

Let $S = (S, S_0, A)$ be a transition system. Formally, properties are sets of infinite sequences from S^ω. An infinite run $s_0 s_1 \ldots$ satisfies a property Π if $s_0 s_1 \ldots \in \Pi$. A *safety property* Π is a set of infinite traces such that for every infinite sequences $\sigma \notin \Pi$, there is a finite prefix $\sigma' \in S^*$ of σ such that no extension of σ' satisfies Π. (Safety properties have finite counterexamples.)

A *liveness property* Π on the other hand, is such that for every finite sequence $\sigma \in \Sigma^*$, there is an extension $\alpha \in S^\omega$ such that $\sigma \cdot \alpha$ satisfies Π. That is, every finite run can be extended to one that can satisfy the liveness property.

It is known that every safety verification problem can be reduced to checking invariants (over a larger state space). Similarly, every liveness property can be reduced to checking *termination*, the property that a transition system has no infinite runs.

For many systems, termination may only be proved only under certain assumptions about the non-deterministic choices made during program execution. A common strategy in modeling systems is to abstract "irrelevant" details using non-determinism, with an implicit assumption that the non-deterministic choices are resolved in a "fair" manner over any infinite execution. For example, one can model a scheduler as non-deterministically providing a resource to one or other process, with the assumption that both processes are picked infinitely often. Similarly, to model asynchronous processes without exact details of their relative speeds, one can use non-deterministic "stutter" steps, together with the assumption that each process makes progress infinitely often. When the implicit fairness assumptions are not considered, the non-deterministic choices can lead to certain undesirable behaviors, such as one in which a scheduler always picks one process, or an asynchronous system in which only one process ever executes transitions. The standard way to rule out these undesirable infinite behaviors from the scope of verification is through *fairness conditions* [31]. Typically, a fairness condition can be translated to an automaton on infinite words [64]. *Fair termination* is the property that every run of a transition system either terminates or violates the fairness requirements.

In the following, we first focus on checking termination. The techniques for checking termination can be extended to checking fair termination using an automata-theoretic construction.

4.2. Checking Termination

Let $S = (S, S_0, A)$ be a transition system. We say the transition system *terminates* if every run $s_0 s_1 \ldots s_n$ is finite.

The main tool to prove termination is *well-foundedness*. Let X be a set. A binary relation $\rho \subseteq X \times X$ is *well-founded* if there is no infinite sequence $x_0, x_1, \ldots$ such that for each $i \geq 0$, we have $\rho(x_i, x_{i+1})$. We call (X, ρ) a well-founded set. For example, the relation $>$ on natural numbers is well-founded: there is no infinite decreasing sequence of natural numbers. However, the relation $>$ on integers is not well-founded.

Define the transition relation $\rightarrow \subseteq S \times S$ as $s \rightarrow t$ iff there exists $a \in A$ such that $s \xrightarrow{a} t$. The *reachable transition relation* is the restriction of the transition relation to the set of reachable states: $\rightarrow \cap (\text{Reach} \times \text{Reach})$. The transition system $\mathcal{S}$ terminates iff the reachable transition relation is well-founded. It is important to restrict attention to the reachable states: a terminating system can have unreachable loops.

Thus, checking termination reduces to the following problems. First, compute the reachable transition relation, the restriction of the transition relation to the reachable states. Second, show that it is well-founded.

As we have seen in the case of invariants, an exact computation of the reachable transition relation may not be possible. Instead, we compute a *transition invariant*, a binary relation on states that contains the reachable transition relation, and check that the transition invariant is well-founded. The problem of computing a transition invariant can be reduced to computing a (state) invariant in the following way.

Let $\mathcal{S} = (S, S_0, A)$ be a transition system. Define the extension $\mathcal{S}^2 = (S \times S, \{(s_0, s_0) \mid s_0 \in S_0\}, A')$ whose set of states consist of pairs of states from S, whose initial states are pairs of initial states, and whose set of transitions are defined as follows. For each $a \in A$, there is a transition $a' \in A'$ such that $(s_1, s_2) \xrightarrow{a'} (s_2, t)$ where $s_2 \xrightarrow{a} t$. Intuitively, the states of $\mathcal{S}^2$ maintain a one-step "history" of the execution in the first part of the pair. Each transition updates the second part, and copies the current second part to the first part of the successor.

With this transformation, it is easy to show that a relation $R \subseteq S \times S$ is a transition invariant of $\mathcal{S}$ iff it is a state invariant of $\mathcal{S}^2$. We can now use the machinery of invariant verification developed in the previous section to the problem of computing transition invariants.

A further development in checking termination of systems is the use of *disjunctively well-founded relations* [57,20]. It is often hard to find a single well-founded relation into which a transition invariant can be embedded, but easier to find several well-founded relations whose union "covers" it. One has to be careful though: if there are well-founded relations T_1 and T_2 such that $R \subseteq T_1 \cup T_2$, then R need not be well-founded. Consider $X = \{a, b\}$, $R = \{(a, b), (b, a)\}$, $T_1 = \{(a, b)\}$, and $T_2 = \{(b, a)\}$. However, the following can be shown. Define R^+ to be the irreflexive transitive closure of the relation R.

Theorem 2 *Let X be a set. Let T_1 and T_2 be well-founded relations on X, and R a binary relation on X. If $R^+ \subseteq T_1 \cup T_2$ then R is well-founded.*

The idea of disjunctive well-foundedness, like that of well-quasi-orderings, seems to be a frequently rediscovered phenomenon.

We give a proof based on case analysis, apparently due to Dieter Hofbauer (see [33], pg. 31). Suppose toward a contradiction that R is not well-founded, and let $x_0 x_1 \ldots$ be such that for each $i \geq 0$, we have $R(x_i, x_{i+1})$. Consider the subsequence $x_{i_1} x_{i_2} \ldots$ of the elements of this sequence such that for each x_{i_j} in the subsequence, there is no k such that $i_j < k$ and $T_1(x_{i_j}, x_k)$.

If this subsequence is finite, then there is an N (the maximal position in this subsequence) such that for all $i \geq N$, there is a $j > i$ such that $T_1(x_i, x_j)$. This contradicts T_1 is well-founded.

On the other hand, if the subsequence is infinite, then each pair $(x_{i_j}, x_{i_{j+1}})$ in the sequence, which are all in R^+, must be related by T_2. But this is a contradiction to T_2 being well-founded.

The argument can be extended to a finite number of well-founded relations covering R^+. An alternate proof, based on the infinite Ramsey's theorem, can be found in [57].

The idea of computing the irreflexive transitive closure of the reachable transition relation, end finding a finite number of well-founded relations covering it has been implemented in a termination checker for C programs called Terminator [20].

Finally, we show how the computation of an over-approximation of the irreflexive transitive closure of the reachable transition relation, $\to^+ \cap \text{Reach} \times \text{Reach}$, can be reduced to computing a (state) invariant.

Let $\mathcal{S} = (S, S_0, A)$ be a transition system, and define the extension $\mathcal{S}^2 = (S \times S, \{(s_0, s_0) \mid s_0 \in S_0\}, A')$ whose set of states consist of pairs of states from S, whose initial states are pairs of initial states, and whose set of transitions are defined as follows. For each $a \in A$, there is a transition $a' \in A'$ such that $(s_1, s_2) \xrightarrow{a'} (s_2, t)$, where $s_2 \xrightarrow{a} t$. Intuitively, the states of $\mathcal{S}^2$ maintain a "history" of the last state of the execution in the first part of the pair. Each transition updates the second part, copies the the current state to the history (the first part of the pair in the successor state). With this transformation, it is easy to show that R is a transition invariant of $\mathcal{S}$ iff it is a state invariant of $\mathcal{S}^2$. We can now use the machinery of invariant verification developed in the previous section to the problem of computing transition invariants.

Now suppose we are given a binary relation $R \subseteq S \times S$ on states. How can we show it is well-founded? The general technique is to find a *rank function*. Suppose (X, ρ) is a well-founded set and that we can find a mapping $r : S \to X$ (the rank) such that for every $t \in S$ such that $R(s, t)$, we have $\rho(r(s), r(t))$. Then we can conclude R is well-founded: each "decrease" along R decreases along ρ, and since ρ is well-founded, we cannot have infinitely many decreases. More formally, the relation R is well-founded if it can be embedded in a well-founded set. The set X and the ordering ρ can be taken without loss of generality to be the ordinals and the (well-founded) inclusion ordering on ordinals.

Of course, finding a rank function is not easy. For special cases, such as relations defined by linear constraints, one can give relatively complete techniques: if there is rank function of a certain form, the algorithm is guaranteed to find one [56,13].

5. Concurrency

Some of the biggest successes in model checking came from the discovery of subtle bugs in concurrent systems. Our model of transition systems is naturally concurrent (each transition $a \in A$ denotes an atomic action). However, a direct implementation of concurrent exploration for multi-threaded software does not work well for the following reasons. First, the state space of the system grows exponentially with the number of components. If a program has n threads, and each thread has just one action, there are already $n!$ transition sequences, and the state space grows exponentially with the number of threads. Second, if the threads are recursive, we cannot apply the summarization algorithm from Section 3. One cannot hope to modify the summarization procedure: the reachability problem for multi-threaded recursive programs is undecidable (it is equivalent to the emptiness problem for the intersection of context free languages).

We point out a few interesting research directions in the analysis of concurrent software.

Partial Order Reduction   Partial-order reduction [63,49,34] is a classical technique for reducing the state space to be explored in model checking. It exploits the independence between parallel threads of execution on unrelated parts of the state. That is, if two transitions a_1 and a_2 in parallel threads of execution access independent sets of variables, the final state reached after executing a_1 and a_2 in that order is the same as that reached after executing first a_2 and then a_1. An algorithm based on partial order reduction chooses to explore one candidate interleaving among independent transitions rather than all of them.

A related technique is *symmetry reduction* [19,27,44,62]. Symmetry reduction determines symmetries in the program, and explores one element from each symmetry class. In general, identifying symmetries in the state space may be difficult, and in practice, the syntax of the programming language is used to identify symmetries. In many examples, such as parameterized protocols, symmetry-based techniques can yield dramatic reductions in the state space [44].

Both partial order reduction and symmetry reduction have been very successful in enumerative model checking, and implemented in flagship enumerative model checkers Spin and Murϕ. A combination of these reduction techniques with abstraction refinement is a fruitful direction, and some initial results are very promising [17,25].

Thread Modular Analysis   In thread-modular analysis, the analysis of a multi-threaded program is decomposed to the analysis of a single thread running concurrently with a state-machine abstracting the behavior of all the other threads. The idea of thread-modular reasoning for controlling state space explosion of multi-threaded programs goes back to Owicki-Gries rules extending Hoare logic to multi-threaded programs [55] and rely-guarantee reasoning [48]. To check a 2-threaded program $T_1 || T_2$, the programmer specifies suitable abstractions G_1 and G_2 for the transition relations T_1 of thread 1 and T_2 of thread 2, and then separately analyzes $T_1 || G_2$ and $G_1 || T_2$. This reasoning is "thread-modular" if the abstractions G_1 and G_2 constrain only the shared variables, and consequently the analyzed systems $T_1 || G_2$ and $G_1 || T_2$ each depend on the private variables of at most one thread. The abstraction G_2 is an environment assumption for thread 1, and G_1 constrains the environment of thread 2. Thread-modular reasoning, therefore, is a form of assume-guarantee reasoning [1,4], which is sound for safety properties:

> If no error states are reachable in $T_1 || G_2$ nor in $G_1 || T_2$, and $T_1 || G_2 \subseteq G_1$ and $G_1 || T_2 \subseteq G_2$, then no error states are reachable in $T_1 || T_2$.

While thread-modular reasoning is not complete for safety properties [55], it suffices for establishing the safety of many concurrency-control mechanisms commonly used in multithreaded programming [29].

One problem in applying thread-modular reasoning is the annotation burden involved in specifying the environment assumptions G_1 and G_2. However, thread-modular reasoning can be combined with abstraction refinement to automatically generate environment assumptions [39,43,18,38].

Thread-modular analysis has also been used to prove liveness properties of concurrent programs [21]: one constructs as before a suitable well-founded transition invariant and shows that environment steps do not increase the rank.

Asynchronous Programs *Asynchronous programming* is a common systems programming idiom in which the programmer can make asynchronous procedure calls which are stored in a task buffer pending for later execution, instead of being executed right away. In addition, the programmer can also make the usual *synchronous* procedure calls where the caller blocks until the callee finishes. A co-operative *scheduler* repeatedly picks *pending handler instances* from the task buffer and executes them atomically to completion. Execution of the handler instance can lead to further handler being *posted*. The posting of a handler is done using the asynchronous call mechanism. The interleaving of different picks-and-executes of pending handler instances (a pick-and-execute is often referred to as a *dispatch*) hides latency in the system.

Asynchronous programming has been used to build fast servers and routers, embedded systems and sensor networks, and forms the basis of web programming using Ajax. It is known that multi-threaded programming and asynchronous programming are *duals*: a concurrent program can be written in either style [50]. Asynchronous programs have the advantage of requiring fewer resources, but pushes resource management to the programmer, making the job of writing correct and efficient asynchronous programs hard.

There is a close connection between asynchronous programs (over finite data) and Petri nets: each asynchronous program can be simulated by a Petri net such that safety and liveness properties on the asynchronous program reduces to corresponding problems on the Petri net. Conversely, coverability and reachability problems on Petri nets can be reduced to safety and liveness problems on an asynchronous program. This correspondence can be used to show that safety and liveness problems are decidable for asynchronous programs, albeit with a high complexity (EXPSPACE-complete for safety properties, and equivalent to Petri net reachability — for which the best algorithms use non-primitive recursive space — for liveness) [32]. While the worst-case complexities are bad, there is hope that well-engineered analysis tools for Petri nets should be sufficient for many practical examples. For example, "simple" abstractions based on abstract counters are often sufficient to prove interesting properties of such programs. In [46], the abstraction refinement idea was extended to asynchronous programs with a 0, 1, ω abstraction which tracked whether 0, 1, or arbitrarily many instances of a handler are pending, and ideas combining abstractions and counters have since been explored [10]. It is likely that similar abstractions will work well for liveness properties as well, but there have not yet been good tools for the analysis of asynchronous programs.

6. Conclusions

The past two decades have seen enormous progress in techniques for automatic invariant synthesis. However, safety and liveness verification of industrial-scale software systems is still very much an open problem. One immediate direction is a better synthesis of various independently developed techniques, and a better understanding of their relative performance in specific application domains. A second direction is to develop more expressive logics for "native" reasoning about systems. Third, the proof of the pudding is in the eating: we would like to see robust tools coming out of research in software verification that is applicable to "real" codebases, at least in some restricted context.

References

[1] M. Abadi and L. Lamport. Conjoining specifications. *ACM Transactions on Programming Languages and Systems*, 17(3):507–534, 1995.

[2] P. A. Abdulla, K. Čerāns, B. Jonsson, and Y.-K. Tsay. General decidability theorems for infinite-state systems. In *Proceedings of the Eleventh Annual Symposium on Logic in Computer Science*, pages 313–321. IEEE Computer Society Press, 1996.

[3] R. Alur and D. Dill. A theory of timed automata. *Theoretical Computer Science*, 126:183–235, 1994.

[4] R. Alur and T. Henzinger. Reactive modules. *Formal Methods in System Design*, 15(1):7–48, 1999.

[5] T. Ball, V. Levin, and S. Rajamani. A decade of software model checking with SLAM. *Commun. ACM*, 54(7):68–76, 2011.

[6] T. Ball, R. Majumdar, T. Millstein, and S. K. Rajamani. Automatic predicate abstraction of C programs. In *PLDI 01: Programming Languages Design and Implementation*, pages 203–213. ACM, 2001.

[7] T. Ball, A. Podelski, and S. K. Rajamani. Boolean and Cartesian abstractions for model checking C programs. In *TACAS 01: Tools and Algorithms for Construction and Analysis of Systems*, Lecture Notes in Computer Science 2031, pages 268–283. Springer-Verlag, 2001.

[8] T. Ball and S. Rajamani. The SLAM project: debugging system software via static analysis. In *POPL 02: Principles of Programming Languages*, pages 1–3. ACM, 2002.

[9] T. Ball and S. K. Rajamani. Bebop: A symbolic model checker for Boolean programs. In *SPIN 00: SPIN Workshop*, Lecture Notes in Computer Science 1885, pages 113–130. Springer-Verlag, 2000.

[10] G. Basler, M. Mazzucchi, T. Wahl, and D. Kroening. Symbolic counter abstraction for concurrent software. In *CAV*, volume 5643 of *Lecture Notes in Computer Science*, pages 64–78. Springer, 2009.

[11] D. Beyer, T. Henzinger, R. Majumdar, and A. Rybalchenko. Path invariants. In *PLDI 07: Programming Language Design and Implementation*, pages 300–309. ACM, 2007.

[12] A. Biere, A. Cimatti, E. Clarke, and Y. Zhu. Symbolic model checking without BDDs. In *TACAS 99: Tools and Algorithms for the Construction and Analysis of Systems*, Lecture Notes in Computer Science 1579, pages 193–207. Springer-Verlag, 1999.

[13] A. Bradley, Z. Manna, and H. Sipma. The polyranking principle. In *ICALP 05: International Colloquium on Automata, Languages, and Programming*, Lecture Notes in Computer Science 3580, pages 1349–1361. Springer-Verlag, 2005.

[14] R. Bryant. Graph-based algorithms for Boolean function manipulation. *IEEE Transactions on Computers*, C-35(8):677–691, 1986.

[15] J. Burch, E. Clarke, K. McMillan, D. Dill, and L. Hwang. Symbolic model checking: 10^{20} states and beyond. *Information and Computation*, 98(2):142–170, 1992.

[16] C. Cadar, V. Ganesh, P. Pawlowski, D. Dill, and D. Engler. EXE: automatically generating inputs of death. In *CCS 02: Conference on Computer and Communications Security*. ACM, 2006.

[17] A. Cimatti, I. Narasamdya, and M. Roveri. Boosting lazy abstraction for SystemC with partial order reduction. In *TACAS '11*, volume 6605 of *Lecture Notes in Computer Science*, pages 341–356. Springer, 2011.

[18] E. Clarke, M. Talupur, and H. Veith. Proving Ptolemy right: The environment abstraction framework for model checking concurrent systems. In *TACAS '08*, volume 4963 of *Lecture Notes in Computer Science*, pages 33–47. Springer, 2008.

[19] E. M. Clarke, T. Filkorn, and S. Jha. Exploiting symmetry in temporal logic model checking. In *CAV 93: Computer Aided Verification*, Lecture Notes in Computer Science 697, pages 450–462. Springer-Verlag, 1993.

[20] B. Cook, A. Podelski, and A. Rybalchenko. Termination proofs for systems code. In *PLDI 06: Programming Languages Design and Implementation*, pages 415–426. ACM, 2006.

[21] B. Cook, A. Podelski, and A. Rybalchenko. Proving thread termination. In *PLDI '07*, pages 320–330. ACM, 2007.

[22] P. Cousot and R. Cousot. Abstract interpretation: a unified lattice model for the static analysis of programs. In *POPL 77: Principles of Programming Languages*, pages 238–252. ACM, 1977.

[23] S. Das, D. L. Dill, and S. Park. Experience with predicate abstraction. In *CAV 99: Computer-Aided Verification*, Lecture Notes in Computer Science 1633, pages 160–171. Springer-Verlag, 1999.

[24] L. de Moura and N. Bjørner. Z3: An efficient SMT solver. In *TACAS 08: Tools and Algorithms for the Construction and Analysis of Systems*, Lecture Notes in Computer Science 4963, pages 337–340. Springer-Verlag, 2008.

[25] A. Donaldson, A. Kaiser, D. Kroening, and T. Wahl. Symmetry-aware predicate abstraction for shared-variable concurrent programs. In *CAV '11*, volume 6806 of *LNCS*, pages 356–371. Springer, 2011.

[26] B. Dutertre and L. de Moura. Yices SMT solver. http://yices.csl.sri.com/.

[27] E. Emerson and A. Sistla. Symmetry and model checking. *Formal Methods in System Design*, 9:105–131, 1996.

[28] A. Finkel and P. Schnoebelen. Well-structured transition systems everywhere. Technical Report LSV-98-4, Laboratoire Spécification et Vérification, 1998.

[29] C. Flanagan, S. Freund, and S. Qadeer. Thread-modular verification for shared-memory programs. In *ESOP 02: European Symposium on Programming*, Lecture Notes in Computer Science 2305, pages 262–277. Springer-Verlag, 2002.

[30] C. Flanagan and S. Qadeer. Predicate abstraction for software verification. In *POPL 02: Principles of Programming Languages*, pages 191–202. ACM, 2002.

[31] N. Francez. *Fairness*. Springer-Verlag, 1986.

[32] P. Ganty and R. Majumdar. Algorithmic verification of asynchronous programs. *CORR*, abs/1011.0551, 2010.

[33] A. Geser. *Relative termination*. PhD thesis, University of Passau, 1990.

[34] P. Godefroid. *Partial-Order Methods for the Verification of Concurrent Systems – An Approach to the State-Explosion Problem*. Lecture Notes in Computer Science 1032. Springer-Verlag, 1996.

[35] P. Godefroid, N. Klarlund, and K. Sen. DART: directed automated random testing. In *PLDI 05: Programming Language Design and Implementation*, pages 213–223. ACM, 2005.

[36] P. Godefroid, A. Nori, S. Rajamani, and S. Tetali. Compositional may-must program analysis: unleashing the power of alternation. In *POPL '10*, pages 43–56. ACM, 2010.

[37] B. Gulavani, T. A. Henzinger, Y. Kannan, A. Nori, and S. Rajamani. SYNERGY: a new algorithm for property checking. In *SIGSOFT FSE*, pages 117–127. ACM, 2006.

[38] A. Gupta, C. Popeea, and A. Rybalchenko. Predicate abstraction and refinement for verifying multi-threaded programs. In *POPL '11*, pages 331–344. ACM, 2011.

[39] T. Henzinger, R. Jhala, R. Majumdar, and S. Qadeer. Thread-modular abstraction refinement. In *CAV 03: Computer-Aided Verification*, Lecture Notes in Computer Science. Springer-Verlag, 2003.

[40] T. Henzinger, R. Jhala, R. Majumdar, and G. Sutre. Lazy abstraction. In *POPL 02: Principles of Programming Languages*, pages 58–70. ACM, 2002.

[41] T. Henzinger, R. Majumdar, and J.-F. Raskin. A classification of symbolic transition systems. *ACM Transactions on Computational Logic*, 6:1–32, 2005.

[42] T. Henzinger, X. Nicollin, J. Sifakis, and S. Yovine. Symbolic model checking for real-time systems. *Information and Computation*, 111(2):193–244, 1994.

[43] T. A. Henzinger, R. Jhala, and R. Majumdar. Race checking by context inference. In *PLDI 2004: Programming Languages Design and Implementation*, pages 1–12. ACM, 2004.

[44] C. Ip and D. Dill. Better verification through symmetry. *Formal Methods in System Design*, 9:41–75, 1996.

[45] F. Ivancic, Z. Yang, M. K. Ganai, A. Gupta, and P. Ashar. Efficient SAT-based bounded model checking for software verification. *Theoretical Computer Science*, 404(3):256–274, 2008.

[46] R. Jhala and R. Majumdar. Interprocedural analysis of asynchronous programs. In *POPL '07: Principles of Programming Languages*. ACM, 2007.

[47] R. Jhala and R. Majumdar. Software model checking. *ACM Computing Surveys*, 2009.

[48] C. Jones. Tentative steps toward a development method for interfering programs. *ACM Transactions on Programming Languages and Systems*, 5(4):596–619, 1983.

[49] S. Katz and D. Peled. Verification of distributed programs using representative interleaving sequences. *Distributed Computing*, 6(2):107–120, 1992.

[50] H. Lauer and R. Needham. On the duality of operating system structures. *Operating Systems Review*, 13(2):3–19, 1979.

[51] K. McMillan. *Symbolic Model Checking: An Approach to the State-Explosion Problem*. Kluwer Academic Publishers, 1993.

[52] K. L. McMillan. Lazy abstraction with interpolants. In *CAV 2006*, Lecture Notes in Computer Science, pages 123–136. Springer-Verlag, 2006.

[53] M. Minsky. *Finite and infinite machines*. Prentice-Hall, 1967.

[54] G. Nelson. Techniques for program verification. Technical Report CSL81-10, Xerox Palo Alto Research Center, 1981.

[55]　S. Owicki and D. Gries. An axiomatic proof technique for parallel programs. *Acta Informatica*, 6(4):319–340, 1976.

[56]　A. Podelski and A. Rybalchenko. A complete method for the synthesis of linear ranking functions. In *VMCAI*, pages 239–251, 2004.

[57]　A. Podelski and A. Rybalchenko. Transition invariants. In *LICS 04: Logic in Computer Science*. IEEE, 2004.

[58]　S. Qadeer and J. Rehof. Context-bounded model checking of concurrent software. In *TACAS*, pages 93–107, 2005.

[59]　T. Reps, S. Horwitz, and M. Sagiv. Precise interprocedural dataflow analysis via graph reachability. In *POPL 95: Principles of Programming Languages*, pages 49–61. ACM, 1995.

[60]　P. Rondon, M. Kawaguchi, and R. Jhala. Liquid types. In *PLDI*, pages 158–169, 2008.

[61]　H. Saïdi and N. Shankar. Abstract and model check while you prove. In *CAV 99: Computer-aided Verification*, Lecture Notes in Computer Science 1633, pages 443–454. Springer-Verlag, 1999.

[62]　A. Sistla, V. Gyuris, and E. Emerson. SMC: A symmetry-based model checker for verification of safety and liveness properties. *ACM Transactions on Software Engineering Methodology*, 9:133–166, 2000.

[63]　A. Valmari. A stubborn attack on state explosion. *Formal Methods in System Design*, 1(4):297–322, 1992.

[64]　M. Vardi. An automata-theoretic approach to linear temporal logic. In *Logics for Concurrency - Structure versus Automata (8th Banff Higher Order Workshop Proceedings)*, volume 1043 of *Lecture Notes in Computer Science*, pages 238–266. Springer-Verlag, 1995.

Software Safety and Security
T. Nipkow et al. (Eds.)
IOS Press, 2012
© *2012 The authors and IOS Press. All rights reserved.*
doi:10.3233/978-1-61499-028-4-205

205

Boolean Satisfiability Solvers:
Techniques and Extensions

Georg WEISSENBACHER [a] and Sharad MALIK [a]

[a] *Princeton University*

Abstract. Contemporary satisfiability solvers are the corner-stone of many successful applications in domains such as automated verification and artificial intelligence. The impressive advances of SAT solvers, achieved by clever engineering and sophisticated algorithms, enable us to tackle *Boolean Satisfiability* (SAT) problem instances with millions of variables – which was previously conceived as a hopeless problem. We provide an introduction to contemporary SAT-solving algorithms, covering the fundamental techniques that made this revolution possible. Further, we present a number of extensions of the SAT problem, such as the enumeration of *all satisfying assignments* (ALL-SAT) and determining the *maximum number of clauses that can be satisfied by an assignment* (MAX-SAT). We demonstrate how SAT solvers can be leveraged to solve these problems. We conclude the chapter with an overview of applications of SAT solvers and their extensions in automated verification.

Keywords. Satisfiability solving, Propositional logic, Automated decision procedures

1. Introduction

Boolean Satisfibility (SAT) is the problem of checking if a propositional logic formula can ever evaluate to true. This problem has long enjoyed a special status in computer science. On the theoretical side, it was the first problem to be classified as being NP-complete. NP-complete problems are notorious for being hard to solve; in particular, in the worst case, the computation time of any known solution for a problem in this class increases exponentially with the size of the problem instance. On the practical side, SAT manifests itself in several important application domains such as the design and verification of hardware and software systems, as well as applications in artificial intelligence. Thus, there is strong motivation to develop practically useful SAT solvers.

However, the NP-completeness is cause for pessimism, since it is unlikely that we will be able to scale the solutions to large practical instances. While attempts to develop practically useful SAT solvers have persisted for almost half a century, for the longest time it was a largely academic exercise with little hope of seeing practical use. Fortunately, several relatively recent research developments have enabled us to tackle instances with millions of variables and constraints – enabling SAT solvers to be effectively deployed in practical applications including in the analysis and verification of software.

This chapter provides an introduction to contemporary SAT-solving techniques and is organised as follows: Section 2 introduces the syntax and semantics of propositional logic. The remaining chapter is split into three parts: The first part (Section 3) covers the techniques used in modern SAT solvers. Further, it covers basic extensions such as the constructions of unsatisfiability proofs. For instances that are unsatisfiable, the proofs of unsatisfiability have been used to derive an unsatisfiable subset of constraints of the formula, referred to as the UNSAT core. The UNSAT core has seen successful applications in model checking. The second part (Section 4) considers extensions of these solvers that have proved to be useful in analysis and verification. Related to the UNSAT core are the concepts of minimal correction sets and maximally satisfiable subsets. A maximally satisfiable subset of an unsatisfiable instance is a maximal subset of constraints that is satisfiable, and a minimal correction set is a minimal subset of constraints that needs to be dropped to make the formula satisfiable. Section 4 discusses how these concepts are related and covers algorithms to derive them. The third part (Section 5) discusses applications of the techniques presented in the Sections 3 and 4 in the field of automated verification. These applications include automated test case generation, bounded model checking and equivalence checking, and fault localisation. Finally, Appendix A provides a number of exercises and their solutions.

2. Preliminaries

This section establishes the notation and syntax we employ throughout this chapter and the meaning (semantics) that is assigned to it.

2.1. Propositional Logic

Propositional logic is a formalism that enables us to make statements about *propositions* (or variables). While propositions may have some underlying meaning associated with them (e.g., the implicit meaning of x_1 being true may be that "it is raining outside"), we do not concern ourselves with such interpretations, but merely require that each proposition can have exactly one of two truth values (true or false).

2.1.1. Notation

Let V be a set of n propositional logic variables and let 0 and 1 denote the elements of the Boolean domain $\mathbb{B}$ representing false and true, respectively. Every Boolean function f $\mathbb{B}^n \to \mathbb{B}$ can be expressed as a propositional logic formula F in n variables $x_1, \ldots, x_n \in V$. The syntax of propositional logic formulae is provided in Figure 1.

The interpretation of the logical connectives $\{-, +, \cdot, \to, \leftrightarrow, \oplus\}$ is provided in Table 1. We use $\equiv$ to denote logical equivalence. For brevity, we may omit $\cdot$ in conjunctions (e.g., $x_1 \bar{x}_3$). An assignment $\mathcal{A}$ is a mapping from V to $\mathbb{B}$, and $\mathcal{A}(x)$ denotes the value that $\mathcal{A}$ assigns to x. We call $\mathcal{A}$ a *total* assignment if $\mathcal{A}$ is a total function. Otherwise, $\mathcal{A}$ is a partial assignment. $\mathcal{A}$ *satisfies* a formula $F(x_1, \ldots x_n)$ iff $F(\mathcal{A}(x_1), \ldots, \mathcal{A}(x_n))$ is defined and evaluates to 1 (denoted by $\mathcal{A} \models F$). A formula F is satisfiable iff $\exists \mathcal{A} . \mathcal{A} \models F$, and unsatisfiable (inconsistent, respectively) otherwise. We use $\#\mathcal{A}_F$ to denote the number of satisfying total assignments of a formula F and drop the subscript if F is clear from the context. A formula F *holds* iff $\mathcal{A} \models F$ for all total assignments $\mathcal{A}$.

We use $\text{Lit}_V = \{x, \bar{x} \mid x \in V\}$ to denote the set of literals over V, where $\bar{x}$ is the negation of x. Given a literal $\ell \in \text{Lit}_V$, we write $\text{var}(\ell)$ to denote the variable occuring in ℓ. A *cube* over V is a product of literals $\ell_1 \ldots \ell_m$ such that $\ell_i \in \text{Lit}_V$ and

x	y	$\overline{x}$	$x \cdot y$	$x + y$	$x \rightarrow y$	$x \leftrightarrow y$	$x \oplus y$
0	0	1	0	0	1	1	0
0	1	1	0	1	1	0	1
1	0	0	0	1	0	0	1
1	1	0	1	1	1	1	0

Table 1. Definition of Propositional Logic Operators

formula	::=	formula · formula | formula + formula |
		formula → formula | formula ↔ formula |
		formula ⊕ formula | $\overline{formula}$ | (formula) | atom
atom	::=	propositional identifier | constant
constant	::=	1 | 0

Figure 1. Syntax of Propositional Logic

formula	::=	formula · (clause) | (clause)
clause	::=	clause + literal | literal
literal	::=	atom | $\overline{atom}$
atom	::=	propositional identifier

Figure 2. Syntax of Propositional Logic in Conjunctive Normal Form

$\text{var}(\ell_i) \neq \text{var}(\ell_j)$ for all $i, j \in \{1..m\}$ with $i \neq j$. We write $\ell \in C$ to indicate that the literal ℓ occurs in a cube C. Given an assignment $\mathcal{A}$, we use $C_{\mathcal{A}}$ to denote the cube $\prod_{i=1}^{n} \ell_i$ where $\ell_i = x_i$ if $\mathcal{A}(x_i) = 1$ and $\ell_i = \overline{x}_i$ otherwise.

2.1.2. Conjunctive Normal Form

The Conjunctive Normal Form (CNF) of a formula is a restricted form of propositional logic formulae. Figure 2 shows the syntax of propositional logic formulae in CNF. A formula in CNF is product of sums (a conjunction of clauses, respectively). Note that the empty clause (denoted by □) corresponds to the logical value 0.

The formula $\overline{x}_1 \cdot (x_1 + \overline{x}_2) \cdot (\overline{x}_1 + x_2) \cdot x_1$ is in CNF, for instance. A commonly used alternative (and more compact) representation of this formula is $(\overline{x}_1) (x_1 \overline{x}_2) (\overline{x}_1 x_2) (x_1)$, i.e., the logical connectives · and + are dropped, since they are clear from the context.

Clauses are commonly regarded as *sets of literals*. While we stick to the notation defined in Figure 2, we will implicitly assume that clauses have the properties of sets of literals. Accordingly, $(\overline{x}_1 x_2 x_2)$ and $(x_1 x_2)$ are indistinguishable from their logically equivalent counterparts $(\overline{x}_1 x_2)$ and $(x_2 x_1)$, respectively. Therefore, a formula in CNF is a set of sets of literals. Note that this representation implicitly incorporates *factoring* (i.e., merging of unifiable literals).

Each formula F in propositional logic can be transformed into CNF. Unfortunately, the resulting formula may be exponentially larger than F. It is, however, possible to construct a formula G in CNF such that F and G are *equi-satisfiable* (i.e., $(\exists \mathcal{A} . \mathcal{A} \models F) \leftrightarrow (\exists \mathcal{A} . \mathcal{A} \models G))$ and the size of G is polynomial in the size of the original formula F. Such an equi-satisfiable formula can be obtained by means of Tseitin's transformation [Tse83]. Given a formula F in propositional logic (as defined in Figure 1), this transformation involves the following steps:

1. Recursively replace each sub-formula $(F_1 \triangleright F_2)$ of the original formula F (where $\triangleright \in \{-, +, \cdot, \rightarrow, \leftrightarrow, \oplus\}$) with a fresh propositional identifier x and add the constraint $x \leftrightarrow (F_1 \triangleright F_2)$.
2. Rewrite the resulting formula into CNF by using the rules presented in Table 2.

Example 2.1 *We demonstrate Tseitin's transformation by converting the formula $(y \leftrightarrow z)$ into conjunctive normal form.*

1. *The first step is to replace $(y \leftrightarrow z)$ with a fresh propositional identifier x_1. After adding the corresponding constraint, we obtain $\overline{x}_1 \cdot (x_1 \leftrightarrow (y \leftrightarrow z))$*
2. *In the next step, we replace $\overline{x}_1$ with x_2. This step is optional, since $(\overline{x}_1)$ is already in clausal form. This transformation step yields the formula*

$$x_2 \cdot (x_2 \leftrightarrow \overline{x}_1) \cdot (x_1 \leftrightarrow (y \leftrightarrow z)) \ .$$

3. *This formula can be rewritten according to Table 2:*

$$x_2 \cdot \underbrace{(x_2 \leftrightarrow \overline{x}_1)}_{(\overline{x_1}+\overline{x}_2)\cdot(x_1+x_2)} \cdot \underbrace{(x_1 \leftrightarrow (y \leftrightarrow z))}_{(\overline{x}_1+\overline{y}+z)\cdot(\overline{x}_1+\overline{z}+y)\cdot(\overline{y}+\overline{z}+x_1)\cdot(y+z+x_1)}$$

4. *We obtain an equi-satisfiable formula in CNF:*

$$x_2 \cdot (\overline{x_1} + \overline{x}_2) \cdot (x_1 + x_2) \cdot (\overline{x}_1 + \overline{y} + z) \cdot (\overline{x}_1 + \overline{z} + y) \cdot (\overline{y} + \overline{z} + x_1) \cdot (y + z + x_1)$$

We also encourage the reader to solve the Exercises 1 and 2 in Section A.

3. Boolean Satisfiability Checking: Techniques

In this section, we formally introduce the problem of Boolean satisfiability (SAT) and present a number of techniques to tackle it.

3.1. Problem Definition

Definition 3.1 (Boolean Satisfiability Problem) *Given a propositional logic formula F, determine whether F is satisfiable.*

The Boolean Satisfiability Problem, usually referred to as SAT, is a prototypical NP-complete problem [Coo71], i.e., there is no known algorithm that efficiently solves all instances of SAT. While Definition 3.1 refers to formulae in propositional logic in general, the problem can be easily reduced to formulae in CNF: Using Tseitin's transformation (c.f. Section 2.1.2), any arbitrary propositional formula can be transformed into an equi-satisfiable formula in clausal form. It is therefore sufficient to focus on formulae in conjunctive normal form.

Negation:
$$x \leftrightarrow \overline{y} \equiv (x \rightarrow \overline{y}) \cdot (\overline{y} \rightarrow x)$$
$$\equiv (\overline{x} + \overline{y}) \cdot (y + x)$$

Disjunction:
$$x \leftrightarrow (y + z) \equiv (y \rightarrow x) \cdot (z \rightarrow x) \cdot (x \rightarrow (y + z))$$
$$\equiv (\overline{y} + x) \cdot (\overline{z} + x) \cdot (\overline{x} + y + z)$$

Conjunction:
$$x \leftrightarrow (y \cdot z) \equiv (x \rightarrow y) \cdot (x \rightarrow z) \cdot ((y \cdot z) \rightarrow x)$$
$$\equiv (\overline{x} + y) \cdot (\overline{x} + z) \cdot (\overline{(y \cdot z)} + x)$$
$$\equiv (\overline{x} + y) \cdot (\overline{x} + z) \cdot (\overline{y} + \overline{z} + x)$$

Equivalence:
$$x \leftrightarrow (y \leftrightarrow z) \equiv (x \rightarrow (y \leftrightarrow z)) \cdot ((y \leftrightarrow z) \rightarrow x)$$
$$\equiv (x \rightarrow ((y \rightarrow z) \cdot (z \rightarrow y)) \cdot ((y \leftrightarrow z) \rightarrow x)$$
$$\equiv (x \rightarrow (y \rightarrow z)) \cdot (x \rightarrow (z \rightarrow y)) \cdot ((y \leftrightarrow z) \rightarrow x)$$
$$\equiv (\overline{x} + \overline{y} + z) \cdot (\overline{x} + \overline{z} + y) \cdot ((y \leftrightarrow z) \rightarrow x)$$
$$\equiv (\overline{x} + \overline{y} + z) \cdot (\overline{x} + \overline{z} + y) \cdot (((y \cdot z) + (\overline{y} \cdot \overline{z})) \rightarrow x)$$
$$\equiv (\overline{x} + \overline{y} + z) \cdot (\overline{x} + \overline{z} + y) \cdot ((y \cdot z) \rightarrow x) \cdot ((\overline{y} \cdot \overline{z}) \rightarrow x)$$
$$\equiv (\overline{x} + \overline{y} + z) \cdot (\overline{x} + \overline{z} + y) \cdot (\overline{y} + \overline{z} + x) \cdot (y + z + x)$$

Table 2. Tseitin transformation [Tse83] for standard Boolean connectives

There are two important sub-classes of SAT:

- *2-SAT.* Each clause of the formula contains at most 2 literals. The satisfiability of such 2-CNF formulae can be decided in polynomial time [Kro67]: each clause $(\ell_1 \ell_2)$ can be rewritten as an implication $\overline{\ell}_1 \rightarrow \ell_2$ (or $1 \rightarrow \ell_1$ and $\overline{\ell}_1 \rightarrow 0$ in case of a clause (ℓ_1) with only one literal). The formula is satisfiable if the transitive closure of the implications does not yield 0. This approach effectively amounts to resolution (see Section 3.2).
- *3-SAT.* Each clause of the formula contains at most 3 literals. This form is relevant because any arbitrary formula in CNF can be reduced to an equi-satisfiable 3-CNF formula by means of Tseitin's transformation (Section 2.1.2).

3.2. Resolution Proofs

The *resolution principle* states that an assignment satisfying the clauses $C + x$ and $D + \overline{x}$ also satisfies $C + D$. The clauses $C + x$ and $D + \overline{x}$ are the *antecedents*, x is the *pivot*, and $C + D$ is the *resolvent*. Let Res(C, D, x) denote the resolvent of the clauses C and D with the pivot x. The corresponding resolution rule is formally described below.

$$\frac{C + x \qquad D + \overline{x}}{C + D} \quad \text{Res}$$

Resolution corresponds to existential quantification of the pivot and subsequent quantifier elimination, as demonstrated by the following sequence of logical transformation steps (where $F_{(x \leftarrow e)}$ denotes the substitution of all free occurrences of x in F with the expression e):

$$\exists x \,.\, (C + x) \cdot (D + \overline{x})$$
$$\equiv ((C + x) \cdot (D + \overline{x}))_{(x \leftarrow 1)} + ((C + x) \cdot (D + \overline{x}))_{(x \leftarrow 0)}$$
$$\equiv \underbrace{(C + 1)}_{1} \cdot \underbrace{(D + \overline{1})}_{D} + \underbrace{(C + 0)}_{C} \cdot \underbrace{(D + \overline{0})}_{1}$$
$$\equiv C + D$$

The repeated application of the resolution rule results in a resolution proof.

Definition 3.2 *A resolution proof R is a directed acyclic graph $(V_R, E_R, piv_R, \lambda_R, s_R)$, where V_R is a set of vertices, E_R is a set of edges, piv_R is a pivot function, λ_R is the clause function, and $s_R \in V_R$ is the sink vertex. An initial vertex has in-degree 0. All other vertices are internal and have in-degree 2. The sink has out-degree 0. The pivot function maps internal vertices to pivot variables of the respective resolution step. For each internal vertex v and $(v_1, v), (v_2, v) \in E_R$, $\lambda_R(v) = \mathrm{Res}(\lambda_R(v_1), \lambda_R(v_2), piv_R(v))$.*

A resolution proof R is a refutation if $\lambda_R(s_R) = \square$. A refutation R is a refutation for a formula F (in CNF) if the label of each initial vertex of R is a clause of F.

Example 3.1 (Unit Propagation and Resolution) *Figure 3 shows an example of a resolution proof for the formula*

$$(\overline{x}_1) \cdot (x_1 + \overline{x}_2) \cdot (\overline{x}_1 + x_2) \cdot (x_1) \,. \tag{1}$$

In Figure 3, each node v is represented by its label $\lambda(v)$ (the parentheses around the literals are dropped since each node is associated with exactly one clause and there is no risk of ambiguity). Moreover, Figure 3 does not show the pivot variables explicitly, since they are uniquely determined by the clauses labelling a node and its predecessors and therefore clear from the context.

Note that this formula is a 2-CNF formula and can therefore be solved by means of transitive closure of the corresponding implications. Equivalently, the unsatisfiability of Formula (1) can be established by repeated application of the unit-resolution rule:

$$\frac{\ell \qquad D + \overline{\ell}}{D} \quad \text{URes}$$

Here, ℓ denotes a literal over the pivot variable.

3.3. The Davis-Putnam Procedure

The resolution rule is sufficient to devise a complete algorithm for deciding the satisfiability of a CNF formula [Rob65].

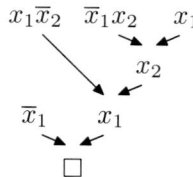

Figure 3. Resolution proof

Theorem 3.1 (Completeness of Propositional Resolution) *If F is an inconsistent formula in CNF, then there is a resolution refutation for F.*

Proof sketch.   By induction over the number of variables in F (c.f. [Bus98]). In the base case, where no variables appear in F, the formula must contain the empty clause $\square$. For the induction step, let x be a fixed variable in F, and let F_1 to be the formula defined as follows:

1. For all clauses $(C + x)$ and $(D + \overline{x})$ in F, the resolvent $\text{Res}((C + x), (D + \overline{x}), x)$ is in F_1.
2. Every clause C in F which contains neither x nor $\overline{x}$ is in F_1.

It is clear that x does not occur in F_1 unless F contains trivial clauses C for which $\{x, \overline{x}\} \subseteq C$. W.l.o.g., such tautological clauses can be dropped. Then, F_1 is satisfiable if and only if F is, from whence the theorem follows by the induction hypothesis.

Remark   Resolution is merely *refutation-complete*, i.e., while it is always possible to derive $\square$ from an inconsistent formula, it does not enable us to derive all valid implications: we cannot deduce $(x + y)$ from (x) by means of resolution, for instance, even though the latter obviously entails the former.

The constructive proof sketch above is interesting for two reasons:

- It demonstrates that propositional resolution is refutation-complete even if we fix the order of pivots along each path in the proof, and
- it outlines a decision procedure which is known as Davis-Putnam procedure [DP60].

We refer to the algorithm presented in [DP60] as "Davis-Putnam" procedure or simply DP. The Davis-Putnam procedure comprises three rules:

1. *1-literal rule.* Whenever one of the clauses in F is a *unit clause*, i.e., contains only a single literal ℓ, then we obtain a new formula F_1 by

    (a) removing any instances of $\overline{\ell}$ from the other clauses, and
    (b) removing any clause containing ℓ, including the unit clause itself.

    This rule obviously subsumes unit-resolution (see Example 3.1).
2. *The affirmative-negative rule.* If any literal ℓ occurs *only positively* or *only negatively* in F, then remove all clauses containing ℓ. This transformation obviously preserves satisfiability.
3. *The rule for eliminating atomic formulae.* For all clauses $(C + x)$ and $(D + \overline{x})$ in F, where neither C nor D contain x or $\overline{x}$, the resolvent $\text{Res}((C + x), (D + \overline{x}), x)$ is in F_1. Moreover, every clause C in F which contains neither x nor $\overline{x}$ is in F_1.

The last rule can make the formula increase in size significantly. However, it completely eliminates all occurrences of the atom x. The correctness of the transformation is justified by the resolution principle (see Section 3.2).

In practice, the resolution rule should only be applied *after* the 1-literal rule and affirmative-negative rule. The 1-literal rule is also known as *unit propagation* and lends itself to efficient implementations.

Once this option is exhausted, we face a choice of which pivot variable x to resolve on. While there is no "wrong" choice that forfeits completeness (as established in the proof of Theorem 3.1), a "bad" choice of a pivot may result in a significant blowup of the formula, and therefore retard the performance of the solver. We postpone the discussion of selection strategies to Section 3.7.

3.4. The Davis-Putnam-Logeman-Loveland Procedure

For realistic problems, the number of clauses generated by the DP procedure grows quickly. To avoid this explosion, Davis, Logemann, and Loveland [DLL62] suggested to replace the resolution rule with a case split. This modified algorithm is commonly referred to as DPLL procedure. It is based on the identity known as Shannon's expansion [Sha49]:

$$F \equiv x \cdot F_{(x \leftarrow 1)} + \overline{x} \cdot F_{(x \leftarrow 0)} \tag{2}$$

Accordingly, checking the satisfiability of a formula F can be reduced to testing $F \cdot x$ and $F \cdot \overline{x}$ separately. The subsequent application of unit propagation (the 1-literal rule, respectively) can reduce the size of these formulae significantly. This transformation, applied recursively, yields a complete decision procedure.

In practice, this split is not implemented by means of recursion but in an iterative manner (using tail recursion, respectively). We keep track of the recursive case-splits and their implications using an explicit trail. Each entry in this trail represents an assignment to a variable of F imposed by either a case split or by unit propagation. We refer to the former kind of entries as *guessed* and to the latter as *implied* assignments.

Definition 3.3 (Clauses under Partial Assignments) *A* trail *represents a* partial assignment $\mathcal{A}$ *to the variables* $\mathcal{V}$ *of F.*

- *A clause C is* satisfied *if one or more of its literals evaluates to 1 under the partial assignment* $\mathcal{A}$.
- *A clause C is* conflicting *if all of its literals are assigned and C evaluates to 0 under* $\mathcal{A}$.
- *A clause C becomes* unit *under a partial assignment if all but one of its literals are assigned but C is not satisfied. As such, C gives rise to an implied assignment. In this case, we say that C is the* antecedent *of the implied assignment.*
- *In all other cases, we say that the clause C is* unresolved.

Example 3.2 *Consider the clauses*

$$C_1 \equiv (\overline{x}_1 \, \overline{x}_4 \, x_3) \qquad \text{and} \qquad C_2 \equiv (\overline{x}_3 \, \overline{x}_2) \,.$$

Level	Partial Assignment	Clauses	Trail
0	–	$(\overline{x}_1\,\overline{x}_4\,x_3)(\overline{x}_3\overline{x}_2)$	
1	$\{x_1 \mapsto 1\}$	$(\overline{x}_1\,\overline{x}_4\,x_3)(\overline{x}_3\overline{x}_2)$	x_1, guessed
2	$\{x_1 \mapsto 1, x_4 \mapsto 1\}$	$(\overline{x}_1\,\overline{x}_4\,x_3)(\overline{x}_3\overline{x}_2)$	x_4, guessed
	$\{x_1 \mapsto 1, x_4 \mapsto 1, x_3 \mapsto 1\}$	$(x_3)(\overline{x}_3\overline{x}_2)$	x_3, implied
	$\{x_1 \mapsto 1, x_4 \mapsto 1, x_3 \mapsto 1, x_2 \mapsto 0\}$	$(\overline{x}_2)$	$\overline{x}_2$, implied

Table 3. Assignment trail for Example 3.2

Table 3 shows a possible trail for this instance. Initially, neither of the clauses is unit, forcing us to guess *an assignment for one of the variables and thus to introduce a new decision. We choose to explore the branch in which x_1 is assigned 1 first. The first entry in the trail, the literal x_1, represents this decision. Neither of the clauses is unit under this assignment; we decide to assign x_4. The clause C_1 is unit under the partial assignment $\{x_1 \mapsto 1, x_4 \mapsto 1\}$ and implies the assignment $x_3 \mapsto 1$ (note that we mark the assignment as "implied" in the trail). This assignment, in turn, makes C_2 unit, imposing the assignment $x_2 \mapsto 0$. The resulting assignment satisfies C_1 as well as C_2.*

A trail may lead to a dead end, i.e., result in a conflicting clause, in which case we have to explore the alternative branch of one of the case splits previously made. This corresponds to reverting one of the decisions or *backtracking*, respectively.

Example 3.3 (Backtracking) *Consider the set of clauses*

$$C_1 \equiv (x_2\,x_3) \quad C_2 \equiv (\overline{x}_1\overline{x}_4) \quad C_3 \equiv (\overline{x}_2 x_4) \quad C_4 \equiv (\overline{x}_1 x_2\overline{x}_3)\,.$$

Figure 4(a) shows a trail that leads to a conflict (assignments are represented as literals, c.f. Section 2.1.1). Clause C_4 is conflicting under the given assignment. The last (and only) guessed assignment on the given trail is $x_1 \mapsto 1$. Accordingly, we backtrack *to this most recent decision (dropping all implications made after this point) and revert it to $x_1 \mapsto 0$ (see Figure 4(b)). We tag the assignment $x_1 \mapsto 0$ as* implied, *since $x_1 \mapsto 1$ led to a conflict. Thus, we prevent that this assignment is reverted back to $x_1 \mapsto 1$ at a later point in time, which would lead to a non-terminating loop.*

When backtracking enough times, the search algorithm always yields a conflicting clause or a satisfying assignment and eventually exhausts all branches. However, always reverting the last decision made is not necessarily the best strategy, as the following example from [Har09] shows.

Example 3.4 *Consider the clauses $C_1 \equiv (\overline{x}_1\,\overline{x}_n\,x_{n+1})$ and $C_2 \equiv (\overline{x}_1\,\overline{x}_n\,\overline{x}_{n+1})$ as part of an unsatisfiable formula F. Exploring the trail $x_1\,x_2\cdots x_{n-1}\,x_n$ leads to a conflict forcing us to backtrack and explore the trail $x_1\,x_2\cdots x_{n-1}\overline{x}_n$. Since F is unsatisfiable, we are eventually (perhaps after further case-splits) forced to backtrack. Unfortunately, each time we change one of the assignments to $x_2, \ldots, x_{n-1}$, we will unnecessarily explore the case in which x_n is 1 again, since the solver is "unaware" of the fact that $x_1 \rightarrow \overline{x}_n$ (which follows from $\mathrm{Res}(C_1, C_2, x_{n+1})$).*

The next section introduces *conflict clauses* as a means to prevent the repeated exploration of infeasible assignments.

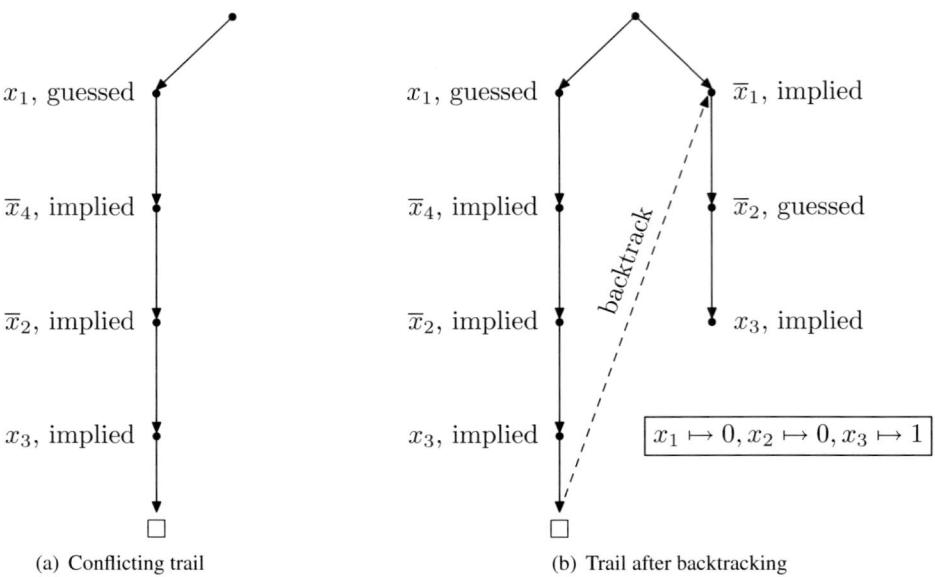

(a) Conflicting trail   (b) Trail after backtracking

Figure 4. Backtracking

3.5. *Conflict-Driven Clause Learning*

In their solvers GRASP and RELSAT, João Marques-Silva and Karen Sakallah [MSS96], and Roberto Bayardo and Robert Schrag [JS97], respectively, introduced a novel mechanism to analyse the conflicts encountered during the search for a satisfying assignment.

First, they partition trails into decision levels according to recursion depth of the case-splits performed.

Definition 3.4 (Decision Levels) *Each recursive application of the splitting rule gives rise to a new* decision level. *If a variable x is assigned 1 (owing to either a case split or unit propagation) at decision level n, we write $x@n$. Conversely, $\overline{x}@n$ denotes an assignment of 0 to x at decision level n.*

Secondly, the implications in a trail are represented using an *implication graph*.

Definition 3.5 (Implication Graph) *An implication graph is a labelled directed acyclic graph $G(V, E)$.*

- *The nodes V represent assignments to variables. Each $\upsilon \in V$ is labelled with a literal and its corresponding decision level.*
- *Each edge in an implication graph represents an implication deriving from a clause that is unit under the current partial assignment. Edges are labelled with the respective antecedent clauses of the assignment the edge points to.*
- *An implication graph may contain a single* conflict node *(indicated by the symbol $\Box$), whose incoming edges are labelled with the corresponding conflicting clause.*

Example 3.5 (Implication Graph for Example 3.2) *Figure 5 shows the implication graph for the trail presented in Example 3.2.*

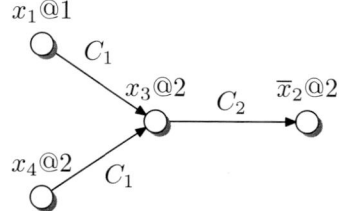

Figure 5. An implication graph for the trail in Table 3

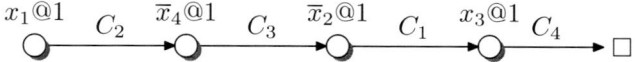

Figure 6. An implication graph with a conflict

If the implication graph contains a conflict, we can use it to determine the decisions that led to this conflict. Moreover, it enables us to derive a *conflict clause*, which, if added to the original formula, prevents the algorithm from repeating the decision(s) that led to the conflict.

Example 3.6 (Implication Graph with Conflict) *Figure 6 shows an implication graph for a trail emanating from the decision* $x_1 \mapsto 1$ *for the clauses*

$$C_1 \equiv (x_2\,x_3), \quad C_2 \equiv (\overline{x}_1\overline{x}_4), \quad C_3 \equiv (\overline{x}_2 x_4), \quad C_4 \equiv (\overline{x}_1 x_2 \overline{x}_3).$$

The final node in the graph represents a conflict. The initial node of the graph is labelled with the decision that causes the conflict. Adding the unit clause $(\overline{x}_1)$ *to the original clauses guarantees that the decision* x_1 *will never be repeated.*

Example 3.7 *Figure 7 shows a partial implication graph for the clauses*

$$C_1 \equiv (\overline{x}_1 x_3 x_5), \quad C_2 \equiv (\overline{x}_1 x_2), \quad C_3 \equiv (\overline{x}_2 x_4), \quad and \quad C_4 \equiv (\overline{x}_3 \overline{x}_4)$$

and the decisions $x_1@5$ *and* $\overline{x}_5@2$. *Using the implication graph, the decisions responsible for the conflict can be easily determined. Adding the conflict clause* $(\overline{x}_1 + x_5)$ *to the original formula rules out that this very combination of assignments is explored again.*

The advantage of *conflict clauses* over simple backtracking becomes clear when we revisit Example 3.4. Using an implication graph, we can quickly determine the assignments $x_1@1$ and $x_n@m$ which caused a conflict for either $C_1 \equiv (\overline{x}_1\,\overline{x}_n\,x_{n+1})$ or $C_2 \equiv (\overline{x}_1\,\overline{x}_n\,\overline{x}_{n+1})$. The conflict clause $(\overline{x}_1 + \overline{x}_n)$ eliminates this combination, pruning a large fraction of the search space which simple backtracking would have otherwise explored.

After adding a conflict clause, at least some of the decisions involved in the conflict need to be reverted (otherwise, the trail remains inconsistent with the clauses). Changing an assignment in the trail might invalidate all subsequently made decisions. Therefore, if we *backtrack* to a certain decision level n, we discard all decisions made at a level higher than n. It is clear that, of all decisions contributing to the conflict clause, we have to at least revert the one associated with the *current* decision level ($x_1@5$ in Example 3.7, for

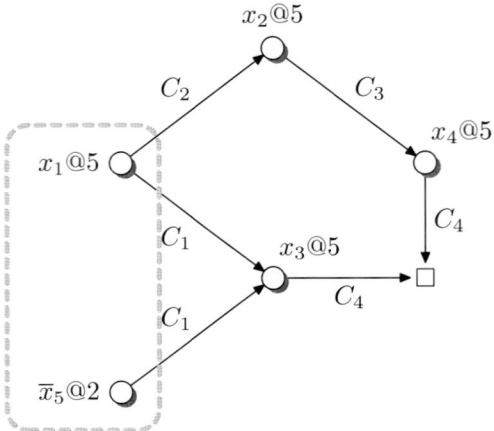

Figure 7. An implication graph for Example 3.7

instance). The *conflict-driven backtracking strategy* suggests to backtrack to the *second most recent decision level in the conflict clause* [MZM$^+$01] (level 2 in Example 3.7). This strategy has a compelling advantage: The conflict clause is *unit* (or *assertive*) under the resulting partial assignment. For instance, $(\overline{x}_1 + x_5)$ in Example 3.7 immediately implies $\overline{x}_1$ in this scenario.

3.6. Conflict Clauses and Resolution

Clause learning with conflict analysis does not impair the completeness of the search algorithm: even if the learnt clauses are dropped at a later point during the search, the trail guarantees that the solver never repeatedly enters a decision level with the same partial assignment.

   We show the correctness of clause learning by demonstrating that each conflict clause is implied by the original formula. The following example is based on [KS08].

Example 3.8 (Conflict Clauses and Resolution) *Figure 8 shows a partial implication graph for the clauses*

$$C_1 \equiv (\overline{x}_4\, x_{10}\, x_6) \quad C_2 \equiv (\overline{x}_4\, x_2\, x_5) \quad C_3 \equiv (\overline{x}_5\, \overline{x}_6\, \overline{x}_7) \quad C_4 \equiv (\overline{x}_6\, x_7)\,.$$

The conflicting clause in this example is C_4. The immediate cause for the conflict are assignments $x_6@6$ and $\overline{x}_7@6$ to the literals $\overline{x}_6$ and x_7 of the clause C_4. These literals are implied by the clauses C_3 and C_1, respectively. Clearly, C_3 and C_4 (and C_1 and C_4) do not agree on the assignment of x_7 (and x_6, respectively). Accordingly, if we construct the resolvent of C_3 and C_4 for the pivot x_7, we obtain a clause C_5:

$$C_5 \quad \equiv \quad \text{Res}(C_4, C_3, x_7) \quad \equiv \quad (\overline{x}_5\, \overline{x}_6)$$

While C_5 is certainly conflicting under the current partial assignment, we will not use it as a conflict clause: both x_5 and x_6 are assigned at decision level 6 and therefore C_5 is not assertive after backtracking.

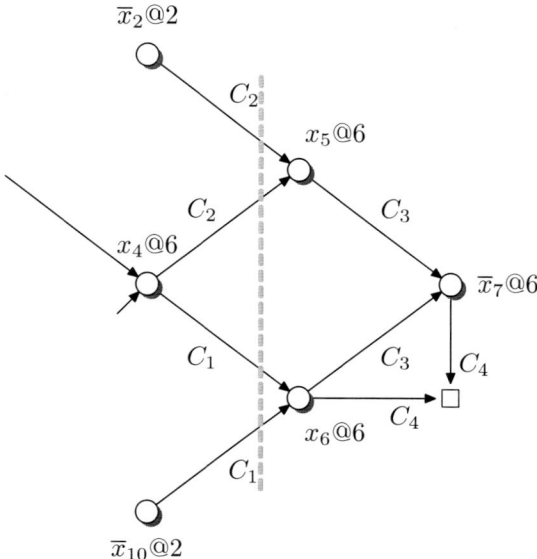

Figure 8. Conflict analysis and resolution

As previously mentioned, C_1 is the antecedent of x_6, and by a similar resolution step as before we obtain

$$C_6 \quad \equiv \quad \text{Res}(C_5, C_1, x_6) \quad \equiv \quad (\overline{x}_4\, \overline{x}_5\, x_{10}) \,.$$

Again, x_4 as well as x_5 are assigned at decision level 5. The clause C_2 is the antecedent of x_5, and we execute a final resolution step:

$$C_7 \quad \equiv \quad \text{Res}(C_6, C_2, x_5) \quad \equiv \quad (x_2\, \overline{x}_4\, x_{10})$$

The resulting clause $(x_2\, \overline{x}_4\, x_{10})$ has the virtue of containing only one literal which is assigned at decision level 6 while still conflicting with the current partial assignment. Accordingly, if we backtrack to a decision level below 6, C_7 becomes assertive, forcing the solver to flip x_4. Therefore, we choose C_7 as conflict clause. Note that this clause corresponds to a cut (shown in Figure 8) that separates the (implied and guessed) decisions causing the conflict from the conflicting node.

We observe in Example 3.8 that it is possible to derive a conflict clause from the antecedents in the implication graph by means of resolution. These antecedents might in turn be conflict clauses. However, by induction, each conflict clause is implied by the original formula. Formal arguments establishing the completeness and correctness of clause learning and conflict analysis are provided in [MS95,MS99,Zha03]. The following example (based on the example presented in [MSS96]) demonstrates that, in general, there is a choice of assertive conflict clauses.

Example 3.9 *Consider the partial implication graph in Figure 9. Figure 10 shows three possible cuts that separate the decisions causing the conflict from the conflicting node. This results in three candidates for conflict clauses:*

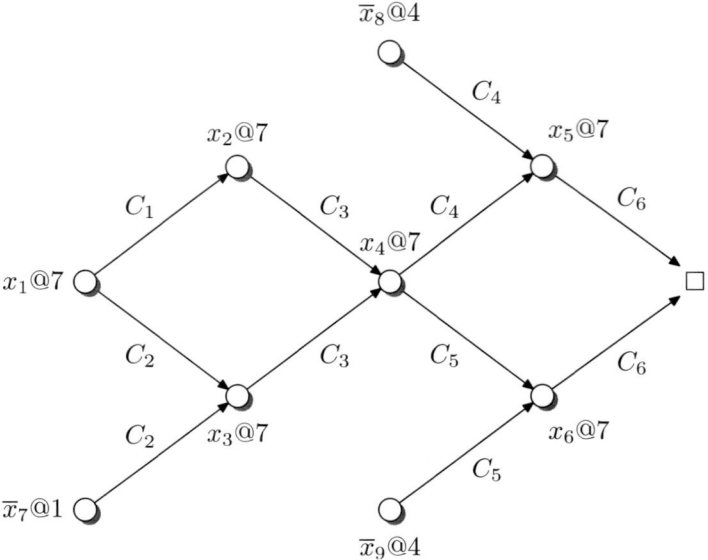

Figure 9. An implication graph with two *unique implication points*

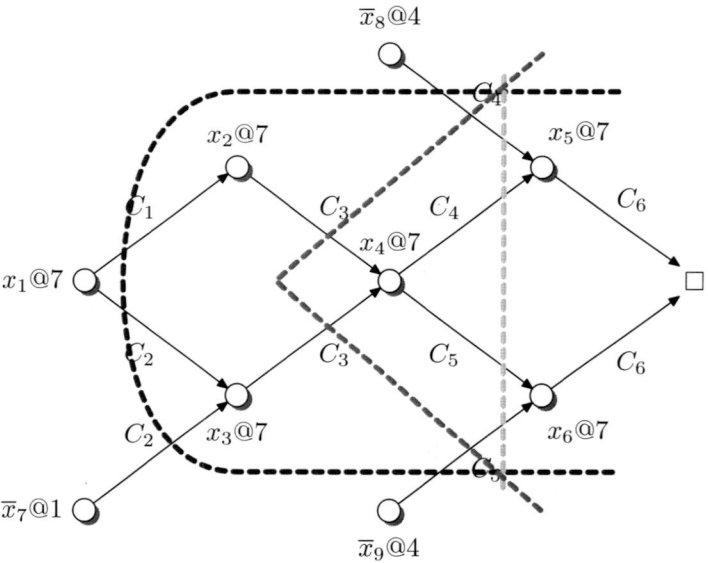

Figure 10. Possible cuts separating decision variables from the conflicting clause

1. $C_7 \equiv (x_8\, \overline{x}_1\, x_7\, x_9)$
2. $C_8 \equiv (x_8\, \overline{x}_4\, x_9)$
3. $C_9 \equiv (x_8\, \overline{x}_2\, \overline{x}_3\, x_9)$

We can dismiss the last clause, since it fails to be assertive after backtracking. The clauses $(x_8\, \overline{x}_1\, x_7\, x_9)$ and $(x_8\, \overline{x}_4\, x_9)$, however, are viable candidates for a conflict clause.

> ① If conflict at decision level 0 → UNSAT
> ② Repeat:
>
> ❶ if all variables assigned return SAT
> ❷ Make decision
> ❸ Propagate constraints
> ❹ No conflict? Go to ❶
> ❺ If decision level = 0 return UNSAT
> ❻ Analyse conflict
> ❼ Add conflict clause
> ❽ Backtrack and go to ❸

Figure 11. The DPLL algorithm with clause learning

The distinguishing property of clauses C_7 and C_8 when compared to clause C_9 in Example 3.9 is that the former two clauses contain only one literal assigned at the current decision level. This literal corresponds to a *unique implication point* (UIP).

Definition 3.6 (Unique Implication Point) *A unique implication point is any node (other than the conflict node) in the partial conflict graph which is on* all paths *from the decision node*[1] *to the conflict node of the current decision level.*

Accordingly, we can stop searching for a conflict clause (which is done by means of resolution) once we reach a unique implication point. But which UIP should we choose? We will base our choice on the following property of the conflict clause corresponding to the UIP *closest* to the conflict (referred to as the *first* UIP): by construction, the conflict clause induced by the first UIP *subsumes* any other conflict clause except for the asserting literal. For instance, in Example 3.9, $C_7 \equiv (x_8\,\overline{x}_1\,x_7\,x_9)$ contains all literals that occur in $C_8 \equiv (x_8\,\overline{x}_4\,x_9)$, except for the literal $\overline{x}_4$ which was assigned at decision level 6. Therefore, choosing C_8 as conflict clause has the following advantages:

1. The conflict clause C_8 is smaller than C_7, making it a more likely candidate for unit implications at a later point in the search algorithm.
2. Stopping at the first UIP has the lowest computational cost.
3. The second most recent decision level in the clause C_8 is at least as low as in any other conflict clause, which forces the solver to backtrack to a lower decision level.

The "first UIP" strategy is implemented in CHAFF [ZMMM01], whereas GRASP [MSS96], in contrast, learns clauses at all UIPs.

Figure 11 shows the complete DPLL algorithm with clause learning.

3.7. Decisions and Decision Heuristics

Step ②.❷ of the algorithm Figure 11 leaves the question of which variable to assign open. As we know from Section 3.3, this choice has no impact on the completeness of the search algorithm. It has, however, a significant impact on the performance of the solver, since this choice is instrumental in pruning the search space.

---

[1]The decision node of the current decision level is a unique implication point by definition.

3.7.1. 2 Literal Watching for Unit Propagation

The choice is clear as long as there are clauses that are unit under the current assignment. The book-keeping required to detect when a clause becomes unit can involve a high computational overhead if implemented naïvely, though. The authors of the CHAFF solver [MZM$^+$01] observed that it is sufficient to *watch* in each clause *any two* literals that have not been assigned, yet: a clause with m literals can only be unit (or conflicting) after at least $m - 1$ of its literals have been set to 0. Assignments to the non-watched literals can be safely ignored. When a variable is assigned 1, the solver only needs to visit clauses where the corresponding watched literal is negated. Each time one of the watched literals is assigned 0 the solver chooses one of the remaining unassigned literals to watch. If this is not possible, the clause is necessarily unit under the current partial assignment: any sequence of assignments that makes a clause unit will include an assignment of one of the watched literals. The computational overhead of this strategy is relatively low: in a formula with n clauses and m variables, $2 \cdot n$ literals need to be watched, and n/m clauses are visited per assignment on average. One of the key advantages of this approach is that the watched literals do not need to be updated upon backtracking. This is in contrast to the solver SATO [Zha97], for instance, which uses head and tail pointers that need to be updated whenever decisions are reverted.

In the case that no clauses are unit under the current partial assignment, however, it is necessary to choose a decision variable in step ②.❷ in Figure 11. In the following, we will discuss only a few such selection strategies; we refer the reader to [MS99] and [KS08] for a more complete overview over heuristics for choosing decision variables.

3.7.2. Dynamic Largest Individual Sum

It is conventional wisdom that it is advantageous to assign the most tightly constrained variables, i.e., variables that occur in a large number of clauses. On representative of such a selection strategy is known as the *dynamic largest individual sum* (DLIS) heuristic. At each decision point, it chooses the assignment that satisfies the most unsatisfied clauses. Formally, let p_x be the number of unresolved clauses containing x and n_x be the number of unresolved clauses containing $\overline{x}$. Moreover, let let x be variable for which p_x is maximal, and let y be variable for which n_y is maximal. If $p_x > n_y$, choose 1 as the value for x. Otherwise, choose $y \mapsto 0$. The disadvantage of this strategy is that the computational overhead is high: the algorithm needs to visit *all* clauses that contain a literal that has been set to true in order to update the values p_x and n_x for all variables contained in these clauses. Moreover, the process needs to be reversed upon backtracking.

3.7.3. Variable State Independent Decaying Sum

A heuristic commonly used in contemporary SAT solvers favours literals in recently added conflict clauses. Each literal is associated with a counter, which is initialised to zero. Whenever a (conflict) clause is added, its literals are *boosted*, i.e., the respective counters are increased. Periodically, all counters divided by constant, resulting in a decay causing a bias towards *recent* conflicts. At each decision point, the solver then chooses the unassigned literal with the highest counter (where ties are broken randomly by default). This approach, known as the *variable state independent decaying sum* (VSIDS) heuristics, was first implemented in the CHAFF solver [MZM$^+$01]. CHAFF maintains a list of unassigned literals sorted by counter. This list is only updated when conflict clauses are added, resulting in a very low overhead. Decisions can be made in constant time.

The emphasis on variables that are involved in recent conflicts leads to a *locality* based search, effectively focusing on sub-spaces [MZ09]. The sub-spaces induced by this decision strategy tend to coalesce, resulting in more opportunities for resolution of conflict clauses, since most of the variables are common.

Representing the counter using integer variables leads to a large number of ties. MINISAT avoids this problem by using a floating point number to represent the weight [ES04a]. Another possible (but significantly more complex) strategy is to concentrate *only* on unresolved conflicts by maintaining a stack of conflict clauses [GN02].

3.8. Unsatisfiable Cores

Given an unsatisfiable instance F, we can use the techniques described in Section 3.6 to construct a resolution refutation (see Definition 3.2 in Section 3.2). Intuitively, such a refutation identifies a *reason* for the inconsistency of the clauses in F. The clauses at the leaves of a resolution refutation are a subset of the clauses of F. By construction, the conjunction of these clauses is unsatisfiable.

Definition 3.7 (Unsatisfiable Core) *Given an unsatisfiable formula $F \equiv C_1 \cdot C_2 \cdots C_n$, any unsatisfiable subset of the set of clauses of F is an unsatisfiable core.*

Resolution proofs and unsatisfiable cores have applications in hardware verification [McM03]. Note that a formula typically does not have a unique unsatisfiable core. The following example demonstrates how we can use a SAT solver to construct an unsatisfiable core.

Example 3.10 (Constructing Unsatisfiable Cores) *Consider the following formula in conjunctive normal form:*

$$(\overline{x} + y) \cdot (\overline{x} + \overline{y}) \cdot (x + z) \cdot (x + \overline{z}) \cdot (z + y + \overline{x})$$

The problem instance does not contain unit literals, so the satisfiability solver is forced to make a decision. The VSIDS heuristic (see Section 3.7) assigns the highest priority to the literal $\overline{x}$. Accordingly, the solver assigns $x \mapsto 0$. This decision immediately yields a conflict, as depicted in Figure 12(a). Accordingly, the solver derives a conflict clause (x) – the justifying resolution step is shown in Figure 12(b). The conflict clause (x) forces the solver to assign $x \mapsto 1$ at decision level zero $(x@0)$. Again, this leads to a conflict (see Figure 12(c)). The corresponding conflict clause is $(\overline{x})$ (see Figure 12(d)). This time, however, the conflict occurs at decision level zero and the satisfiability solver determines that the instance is unsatisfiable. The SAT solver finalises the resolution proof by resolving $(\overline{x})$ and (x) (see Figure 12(e)).
The unsatisfiable core

$$\{ \quad (\overline{x} + y), \ (\overline{x} + \overline{y}), \ (x + z), \ (x + \overline{z}) \quad \}$$

can be easily extracted from the resolution proof in Figure 12(e). The clause $(z + y + \overline{x})$ did not contribute to the contradiction and is therefore not contained in the core.

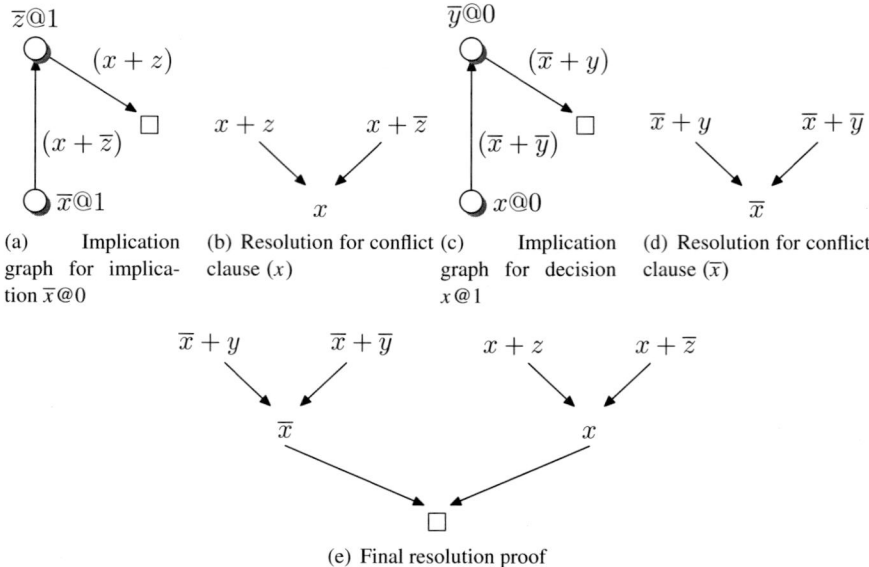

Figure 12. Construction of a resolution proof

An unsatisfiable core is minimal if removing any clause from the core makes the remaining set of clauses satisfiable.

Definition 3.8 (Minimal and Minimum Unsatisfiable Cores) *Let UC be an unsatisfiable core of the formula F (i.e., a set of clauses $UC \subseteq F$ such that $C_1 \cdot C_2 \cdots C_n \to 0$ if $C_i \in UC$ for $1 \le i \le n$). The unsatisfiable core UC is* minimal *if removing any one of its clauses C_i leaves the conjunction of the remaining clauses $UC \setminus C_i$ satisfiable. An unsatisfiable core is* minimum *if the original formula does not contain an unsatisfiable core UC_2 such that $|UC_2| < |UC|$.*

3.9. Incremental Satisfiability Solving

Many applications of SAT solvers require solving a sequence of similar instances which share a large number of clauses. Incremental satisfiability solvers [Str01,KSW01] support the reuse of learnt clauses in subsequent calls to the SAT solver when only a fraction of the clauses of the original problem have changed. To this end, an incremental solver drops all learnt clauses and reverts all decisions that derive from clauses that are part of the original instance but not of the subsequent related problem.

Example 3.11 *Recall the formula from Example 3.3:*

$$(x_2 + x_3) \cdot (\overline{x}_1 + \overline{x}_4) \cdot (\overline{x}_2 + x_4) \cdot (\overline{x}_1 + x_2 + \overline{x}_3)$$

Assume that the SAT solver derives the initial satisfying assignment

$$\{x_1 \mapsto 0, x_2 \mapsto 0, x_3 \mapsto 1, x_4 \mapsto 0\}$$

for this formula, which can be represented as the cube $\overline{x}_1 \cdot \overline{x}_2 \cdot x_3 \cdot \overline{x}_4$. Note that at this point the SAT solver has learnt the clause $(\overline{x}_1)$ (c.f. Figure 4).

Assume that in the next step we want to add the clause $(x_1 + x_2 + \overline{x}_3 + x_4)$ (which happens to be the negation of $\overline{x}_1 \cdot \overline{x}_2 \cdot x_3 \cdot \overline{x}_4$) to the current set of clauses:

$$(x_2 + x_3) \cdot (\overline{x}_1 + \overline{x}_4) \cdot (\overline{x}_2 + x_4) \cdot (\overline{x}_1 + x_2 + \overline{x}_3) \cdot \underbrace{(\overline{x}_1)}_{learnt} \cdot \underbrace{(x_1 + x_2 + \overline{x}_3 + x_4)}_{new\ clause}$$

Note that, while we have to revert the decisions made during the first run of the SAT solver, we are allowed to retain the learnt clause $(\overline{x}_1)$, since it is a logical consequence of the original formula (i.e., at decision level 0). The SAT solver can now proceed to find a new satisfying assignment (e.g., $\{x_1 \mapsto 0, x_2 \mapsto 1, x_3 \mapsto 1, x_4 \mapsto 1\}$). In this example, the new clause $(x_1 + x_2 + \overline{x}_3 + x_4)$ guarantees that this assignment differs from the previous one.

3.10. Pre-processing Formulae

This section covers pre-processing techniques presented in [EB05] which enable us to reduce the size of the formula either before passing it to a satisfiability checker or during the search process.

3.10.1. Subsumption

A clause C_1 is said to subsume a clause C_2 if $C_1 \subseteq C_2$, i.e., all literals in C_1 also occur in C_2. If formula in CNF contains two clauses C_1 and C_2 such that C_1 subsumes C_2, then C_2 can be discarded. This is justified by the fact that, given a resolution proof, we can replace any occurrence of a clause C_2 by a clause C_1 which subsumes C_2 without invalidating the correctness of the proof. In fact, such a modification typically enables a reduction of the size of the proof [BIFH+11].

3.10.2. Self-subsuming Resolution

Even though initial instance does not necessarily contain clauses subsuming others, such clauses may materialise during the search process. Eén and Biere [EB05] observes that formulae in CNF often contain clauses $(x + C_1)$ which *almost* subsume clauses $(\overline{x} + C_2)$ (where $C_1 \subseteq C_2$). After one resolution step we obtain the clause $\mathrm{Res}((x + C_1), (\overline{x} + C_2), x) = C_2$, which subsumes $(\overline{x}+C_2)$. Accordingly, the clause $(\overline{x}+C_2)$ can be dropped after resolution. Eén and Biere dubbed this simplification rule *self-subsuming resolution*.

Efficient data structures for implementing (self-)subsumption are presented in [EB05].

3.10.3. Variable Elimination by Substitution

Formulae that are encoded in CNF using the transformation introduced in Section 2.1.2 (or a similar approach) typically contain a large number of *functionally dependent* variables, namely the fresh variables introduced to represent terms (or gate outputs, respectively). In the following formula, for instance, the value of the variable x is completely determined by the values of y and z (c.f. Example 2.1):

$$\underbrace{(x \leftrightarrow (y \leftrightarrow z))}_{(\overline{x}+\overline{y}+z)\cdot(\overline{x}+\overline{z}+y)\cdot(\overline{y}+\overline{z}+x)\cdot(y+z+x)}$$

The algorithms previously presented are oblivious to this structural property and therefore fail to exploit it.Eén and Biere [EB05] presents an approach that eliminates dependent variables by substitution in an attempt to reduce the size of the resulting formula. First, note that the auxiliary variable x can be eliminated using the *rule for eliminating atomic formulae* introduced in Section 3.3. The application of this rule amounts to variable elimination by means of resolution. In general, given a set S of clauses all of which contain x, we can partition S into clauses containing x and clauses containing $\overline{x}$. Let $S_x \overset{\text{def}}{=} \{C \mid C \in S, x \in C\}$ and $S_{\overline{x}} \overset{\text{def}}{=} \{C \mid C \in S, \overline{x} \in C\}$. Abusing the notation we introduced in Section 3.2, we define

$$\text{Res}(S_x, S_{\overline{x}}, x) \overset{\text{def}}{=} \{\text{Res}(C_x, C_{\overline{x}}, x) \mid C_x \in S_x, C_{\overline{x}} \in S_{\overline{x}}\}.$$

A clause is trivial if it contains a literal and its negation. We observe that the pairwise resolution of the clauses corresponding to a definition of x introduced by the Tseitin transformation (see Table 2) yields *only* trivial clauses. We demonstrate this for the definition $x \leftrightarrow (y \leftrightarrow z)$ introduced in Example 2.1. Let

$$G \overset{\text{def}}{=} \{(\overline{x} + \overline{y} + z), (\overline{x} + \overline{z} + y), (\overline{y} + \overline{z} + x), (y + z + x)\}$$

denote the set of clauses introduced by the transformation. Splitting G as suggested above yields

$$G_{\overline{x}} = \{(\overline{x} + \overline{y} + z), (\overline{x} + \overline{z} + y)\} \qquad G_x = \{(\overline{y} + \overline{z} + x), (y + z + x)\},$$

and we obtain

$$\text{Res}(G_x, G_{\overline{x}}, x) = \{(\overline{y} + z + \overline{z}), (\overline{y} + z + y), (\overline{z} + y + \overline{y}), (\overline{z} + y + z)\}.$$

The reader may verify that this holds for all transformations presented in Table 2. Accordingly, given a set of clauses S (all of which contain x) and the definition $G \subseteq S$ of x, we can safely omit the resolution steps $\text{Res}(G_x, G_{\overline{x}}, x)$. Let $R = S \setminus G$ be the *remaining* clauses that are not part of the definition of x. Then one can partition $\text{Res}(S_x, S_{\overline{x}}, x)$ into

$$\underbrace{\text{Res}(R_x, G_{\overline{x}}, x) \cdot \text{Res}(G_x, R_{\overline{x}}, x)}_{S''} \cdot \underbrace{\text{Res}(G_x, G_{\overline{x}}, x)}_{G'} \cdot \underbrace{\text{Res}(R_x, R_{\overline{x}}, x)}_{R'}.$$

In our example, G_x and $G_{\overline{x}}$ encode $x + \overline{(y \leftrightarrow z)}$ (i.e., $\overline{x} \rightarrow \overline{(y \leftrightarrow z)}$) and $\overline{x} + (y \leftrightarrow z)$, respectively. Accordingly, $\text{Res}(R_x, G_{\overline{x}}, x)$ can be interpreted as *substitution* of $(y \leftrightarrow z)$ for x in R_x (and similarly for $\text{Res}(G_x, R_{\overline{x}}, x)$). As a consequence, R' can be derived from S'' in a single hyper-resolution step (or a sequence of resolution steps) [GOMS04]. It is therefore admissible to replace S with S''.

Example 3.12 *Consider the CNF instance*

$$\underbrace{(x_1 + u)}_{R_{x_1}} \cdot \underbrace{(\overline{x}_1 + v)}_{R_{\overline{x}_1}} \cdot \underbrace{(\overline{x}_1 + \overline{y} + z) \cdot (\overline{x}_1 + \overline{z} + y)}_{G_{\overline{x}_1}} \cdot \underbrace{(\overline{y} + \overline{z} + x_1) \cdot (y + z + x_1)}_{G_{x_1}}.$$

We obtain

$$S'' \equiv (u + \overline{y} + z) \cdot (u + \overline{z} + y) \cdot (v + \overline{y} + \overline{z}) \cdot (v + y + z),$$

allowing us to reduce the size of the original formula by two clauses.

A more elaborate example for this approach is provided in Exercise 10 in Appendix A.

4. Boolean Satisfiability Checking: Extensions

After covering contemporary techniques to generate satisfying assignments or refutation proofs for propositional formulae in Section 3, we address a number of extensions of the SAT problem (Definition 3.1). As we will see, an in-depth understanding of the internals of SAT solvers is crucial to the techniques discussed in this section – the naïvely applying a SAT solver as a black box may result in a suboptimal performance of the resulting algorithm.

4.1. All-SAT

Given a satisfiable formula, the algorithms presented in Section 3 provide a single satisfying assignment. Some applications, however, require us to enumerate *all* satisfiable assignments of a formula [McM02]. It is easy to see that solving this problem is at least as hard as the Boolean satisfiability problem (Definition 3.1). In fact, the problem of determining the number of satisfying assignments of a formula is a prominent representative of the complexity class #P (see, for instance, [AB09]).

In practice, the problem can be tractable for certain instances, even though no polynomial algorithm is known. We can force the SAT solver to enumerate all satisfying assignments by subsequently *blocking* all assignments previously found. As explained in Section 2.1.1, any satisfying assignment $\mathcal{A}$ of a formula F can be represented as a *cube* over the variables of F. The negation of such a cube is a clause (by De Morgan's theorem). Adding this clause C to F effectively *blocks* the assignment, since C is clearly in conflict with the current assignment. C is therefore called a *blocking clause*. In fact, this approach has already been demonstrated in Example 3.11. To obtain all satisfying assignments, the process in Example 3.11 is repeated until the formula becomes unsatisfiable.

While we can take advantage of incremental satisfiability checking algorithms (c.f. Section 3.9), the size of the formula augmented with blocking clauses grows quickly. Moreover, blocking clauses which contain *all* variables of the original instance are less likely to become unit. Therefore, it is desirable to reduce the size of the blocking clause [McM02], i.e., to construct a smaller clause which still blocks the assignment $\mathcal{A}$. One possibility is to block the *decisions* that led to the current assignment (this information can be extracted from the trail described in Section 3.4). Let D be the cube representing these decisions. Clearly, $F \cdot D \leftrightarrow C_{\mathcal{A}}$, i.e., the decisions, in conjunction with the original formula, imply the single and unique assignment $\mathcal{A}$ (and *vice versa*). Moreover, $\overline{D} \to \overline{C_{\mathcal{A}}}$. Therefore $\overline{D}$ is a viable candidate for blocking $\mathcal{A}$.

An example application of All-SAT is presented in Example 4.7.

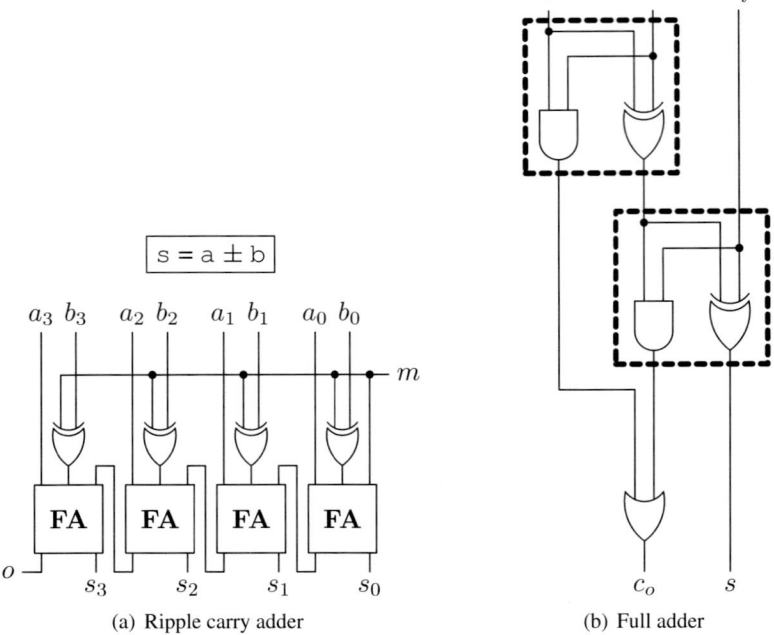

(a) Ripple carry adder   (b) Full adder

Figure 13. Encoding addition and subtraction in propositional logic

4.2. Cardinality Constraints

Satisfiability solvers are designed to work in the Boolean domain and do not support numeric reasoning *per se*. There is a number of applications for which it is desirable, however, to have at least rudimentary support for arithmetic over bounded domains. A common approach is to represent binary numbers using the two's complement system and to encode arithmetic operations using their corresponding circuit representation. Figure 13 shows the encoding of addition/subtraction as a ripple-carry-adder (Figure 13(a)), implemented as a chain of full adders (Figure 13(b)). This technique is known as eager bit-flattening. We refer the reader to [KS08] for a more detailed treatment of this topic.

Cardinality constraints are a common application of numerical constraints. Given a set $\{\ell_1, \ldots, \ell_n\}$ of literals, a cardinality constraint $((\sum_i \ell_i) \leq k)$ rules out all assignments in which more than k of these literals evaluate to 1 (here, $\sum$ denotes the arithmetic sum and not the logical "or" operator). This constraint can technically be encoded by constructing a circuit that computes $k - (\sum_i \ell_i)$ (using a tree of adder-subtractors depicted in Figure 13) and checking for arithmetic underflow. Such an encoding, however, introduces chains of exclusive-or gates. Note that exclusive-or is a non-monotonic operator (c.f. Table 1): a change of the value of a single variable occurring in a long chain of exclusive-or gates may propagate and necessitate an alteration of the values of a large number of subsequent variables in the chain (forced by unit-propagation), thus posing a challenge to contemporary satisfiability checkers.

Figure 14 shows a *sorting network* for two literals, an alternative way of encoding the constraint $((\sum_i \ell_i) \leq k)$ (where $i = 2$ in Figure 14). Intuitively, a sorting network shuffles all input values that are 1 "to the left", i.e., if m of the inputs of an n-bit sort-

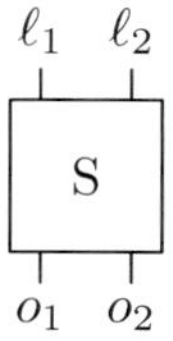

ℓ_1	ℓ_2	o_1	o_2
0	0	0	0
0	1	1	0
1	0	1	0
1	1	1	1

$$o_1 \stackrel{\text{def}}{=} \ell_1 + \ell_2$$

$$o_2 \stackrel{\text{def}}{=} \ell_1 \cdot \ell_2$$

Figure 14. A sorting network for two literals

ing network (where $m \leq n$) are 1, then the output is a sequence of m ones followed by $n - m$ trailing zeroes. To encode an "at most k" constraint it is therefore sufficient to constrain the $(k + 1)^{\text{th}}$ output signal to 0. The advantage of this construction over the previously discussed encoding is that sorting networks can be built entirely from (monotone) and-gates and or-gates (by cascading the circuit shown in Figure 14), thus avoiding the exclusive-or gates (and the associated snowball effect caused by unit-propagation, as described above) that retard the performance of the SAT solver. Sorting networks for n bits can be implemented using $O(n \cdot (\log n)^2)$ (see, for instance, [Par92]) or even $O(n \cdot \log n)$ gates [AKS83].

4.3. Maximum Satisfiability Problem (MAX-SAT)

Even if a formula F is unsatisfiable, there might still be assignments which satisfy a large number of its clauses. The *maximum satisfiability problem* (MAX-SAT) is concerned with finding the largest number of clauses that can be satisfied by some assignment.

Definition 4.1 (Maximum Satisfiability Problem) *Given a formula F in conjunctive normal form, determine the maximum number of clauses of F that can be satisfied by some assignment.*

If (and only if) the formula F is satisfiable, then there is an assignment that satisfies *all* of its clauses. Accordingly, the MAX-SAT problem is NP-hard. If, however, F is unsatisfiable, one needs to determine the largest subset of the clauses of F which, if conjoined, are still satisfiable. Equivalently, one can compute the smallest set of clauses that need to be dropped from the original instance to make it satisfiable.

Example 4.1 *Consider the unsatisfiable formula*

$$(\bar{r} + \bar{s} + t) \cdot (\bar{r} + s) \cdot (r) \cdot (\bar{t}) \cdot (s). \tag{3}$$

Dropping the clause $(\bar{t})$ makes the instance satisfiable. Note that the largest set of satisfiable clauses is not unique: dropping the clause (r) also results in a satisfiable formula with four clauses as well.

The *partial* MAX-SAT problem is a generalisation of the MAX-SAT problem, in which some of the clauses are tagged as *hard* and must not be dropped.

Definition 4.2 (Partial Maximum Satisfiability Problem) *Given a formula F and a set $\{C_1, \ldots, C_m\} \subseteq F$ of hard clauses, determine the maximum number of clauses of F that can be satisfied by some assignment $\mathcal{A} \models C_1 \cdot C_2 \cdots C_m$.*

We refer to clauses of a partial MAX-SAT instance that are not hard as *soft* clauses.

Example 4.2 *We revisit Example 4.1, but require that the clauses* (r) *and* $(\bar{t})$ *of Formula (3) must not be dropped this time. In this scenario, dropping* $(\bar{r}+\bar{s}+t)$ *makes the formula satisfiable. Note that dropping either* $(\bar{r}+s)$ *or* (s) *does not yield a satisfiable instance.*

4.3.1. Relaxation Literals

The satisfiability checking techniques covered in Section 3 lack the ability to drop clauses. Contemporary satisfiability solvers such as MINISAT [ES04a], however, do at least provide the option to specify a partial assignment, which can be reverted in a subsequent call to the solver without sacrificing the learnt clauses that do not depend on this assignment.

As it turns out, this mechanism is sufficient to exclude clauses from the search process if we augment these clauses with so called *relaxation literals*. A relaxation literal is a literal over a variable v that does not occur in the original formula. If we replace a clause C_i that is part of the original formula with the *relaxed* clause $(v_i + C_i)$, the literal v_i acts as a switch which enables us to activate the clause C_i by setting v_i to 0. Conversely, the solver will ignore $(v_i + C_i)$ if v_i is set to 1 (by virtue of the *affirmative-negative rule* introduced in Section 3.3).

Example 4.3 *We continue working in the setting of Example 4.2. The following formula resembles Formula 3, except for the fact that the* soft *clauses have been augmented with the relaxation literals u, v, and w, respectively:*

$$(u + \bar{r} + \bar{s} + t) \cdot (v + \bar{r} + s) \cdot (r) \cdot (\bar{t}) \cdot (w + s). \tag{4}$$

Now, any satisfiability solver can be used to determine that Formula 4 is satisfiable. The resulting satisfying assignment to u, v, and w determines which clauses were "dropped" by the solver.

Unfortunately, the technique outlined in Example 4.3 gives us no control over *which*, and more importantly, *how many* clauses the solver drops. Unless we modify the decision procedure, minimality is not guaranteed.

We can, however, restrict the number of dropped clauses by adding *cardinality constraints* (Section 4.2) to the relaxed formula. The corresponding constraint for the formula in Example 4.3, $(u + v + w) \le 1$, instructs the SAT solver to drop *at most one* clause. Moreover, we already know that the solver has to drop *at least one* clause, since the original formula is unsatisfiable [MPLMS08]. In the case of Example 4.3, the SAT solver will find a satisfying solution. The rather restrictive cardinality constraint, however, does not account for (partial) MAX-SAT solutions that require the relaxation of more than one clause.

Example 4.4 *Consider the unsatisfiable formula*

$$(s) \cdot (\bar{s}) \cdot (t) \cdot (\bar{t}).$$

Note that this formula has two disjoint *unsatisfiable cores (c.f. Section 3.8). Accordingly, the formula*

$$(u + s) \cdot (v + \bar{s}) \cdot (w + t) \cdot (x + \bar{t}) \cdot (\sum \{u, v, w, x\} \le 1)$$

is still *unsatisfiable.*

The formula in Example 4.4 requires the solver drop at least two clauses. This can be achieved by *replacing* the cardinality constraint with the slightly modified constraint $\sum \{u, v, w, x\} \le 2$. As outlined in Section 4.2, this can be easily achieved by modifying a *single unit clause* as long as we use sorting networks to encode the constraint. Moreover, such a modification does not necessarily require us to restart the search from scratch, as mentioned in the first paragraph of Section 4.3.1. Incremental satisfiability solvers (see Section 3.9) are able to retain at least some of the clauses learnt from the first instance.

Accordingly, it is possible to successively relax the cardinality constraint in an efficient manner. If we follow this scheme, we obtain an algorithm to solve the partial MAX-SAT problem. If we successively increase the numeric parameter of the cardinality constraint (by forcing one single assignment of a literal of the sorting network), starting with one, we have a solution of the partial MAX-SAT problem readily at hand as soon as the SAT solver finds a satisfying assignment.

4.3.2. Core-Guided MAX-SAT

Example 4.5 *Consider the unsatisfiable formula*

$$(r + t) \cdot (r + s) \cdot (s) \cdot (\bar{s}) \cdot (t) \cdot (\bar{t}) ,$$

which resembles the formula in Example 4.4, except for the two clauses $(r + t)$ and $(r + s)$. Neither of these clauses influences the satisfiability of the formula. Accordingly, instrumenting these clauses with relaxation literals unnecessarily introduces additional variables and increases the size of the sorting network.

It is possible to avoid this unnecessary overhead in Example 4.5 by excluding the clauses $(r + t)$ and $(r + s)$ from the set of clauses the solver considers for removal (relaxation, respectively). However, how can we know that this is sound? The exclusion of a random clause may result in an invalid answer to the MAX-SAT problem.

The answer lies in the *minimal* unsatisfiable cores (Definition 3.8 in Section 3.8) of the formula. A clause C that is not contained in *any* (minimal) unsatisfiable core of F has no impact on the satisfiability of F. Accordingly, it is not necessary to instrument C with a relaxation literal. It is therefore possible to use cores to *guide* the selection of clauses to be relaxed [FM06] as demonstrated in the following example.

Example 4.6 *We continue working in the setting of Example 4.5. Following the method presented in Example 3.10, we obtain an initial core $\{(s), (\bar{s})\}$. Similar to Example 4.4, we instrument the clauses occurring this core with fresh relaxation literals and impose a cardinality constraint on these literals:*

$$(r + t) \cdot (r + s) \cdot (u + s) \cdot (v + \bar{s}) \cdot (t) \cdot (\bar{t}) \cdot (\sum \{u, v\} \le 1) \qquad (5)$$

This relaxation "deactivates" the core (and also overlapping non-minimal cores, which demonstrates that the core guiding our instrumentation is not required to be minimal).

① While instance unsatisfiable, repeat:

❶ Obtain unsatisfiable core UC
❷ If UC contains no soft clauses, return UNSAT
❸ For all *soft* clauses $\{C_1, \dots, C_n\} \subseteq UC$

  * introduce fresh relaxation variable v_i
  * $C_i = C_i \cup \{v_i\}$

❹ Add constraint $\left(\sum_{i=1}^{n} v_i\right) \leq 1$

② Obtain satisfying assignment $\mathcal{A}$
③ Return number of relaxation literals v_i with $\mathcal{A}(v_i) = 1$

Figure 15. A core-guided MAX-SAT algorithm

The modified formula (5), however, is still not satisfiable. It contains a second core, namely $\{(t), (\bar{t})\}$. Defusing this core in a similar manner as the previous one yields

$$(r+t) \cdot (r+s) \cdot (u+s) \cdot (v+\bar{s}) \cdot (w+t) \cdot (x+\bar{t}) \cdot \left(\sum\{u, v\} \leq 1\right) \cdot \left(\sum\{w, x\} \leq 1\right)$$

A final run of the satisfiability solver yields a satisfying assignment which indicates that we need to relax two clauses. Note that it was not necessary to instrument the clauses $(r+t)$ and $(r+s)$ – this is a crucial advantage when it comes to large problem instances.

Figure 15 shows the pseudo-code of the core-guided MAX-SAT algorithm outlined in Example 4.6. Note that the introduction of relaxation literals complicates the use of incremental SAT algorithms (c.f. Section 3.9). At least the clauses learnt from hard constraints, however, can be retained across all instances.

4.4. Minimal Correction Sets (MCS)

In the previous section, the focus gradually shifted from clauses that can be satisfied simultaneously to clauses that need to be dropped to obtain a satisfiable formula. A set of clauses that has the latter property is also known as *minimal correction set* (MCS). The complement of each maxim*al* set of satisfiable clauses is an MCS. Accordingly, minimal correction sets are a generalisation of the MAX-SAT problem [LS09] – as the name indicates, we merely require minimality, i.e., in general, an MCS is not minim*um*.

Given this close relationship between the MAX-SAT problem and MCSes, it seems natural to extend the algorithm from Figure 15 to compute correction sets. Indeed, the algorithm readily provides one MCS (whose size, in fact, is minimum). But what if we desire to compute more than one, or even *all* MCSes? The technique presented in [LS09] is based on the algorithm in Section 4.3.2 and relies on blocking clauses (see Section 4.1) to exhaustively enumerate *all* minimal correction sets.

The algorithm in Figure 16 uses several auxiliary helper functions which implement techniques we have encountered in the previous sections.

- The procedure INSTRUMENT adds relaxation literals to clauses of the formula provided as parameter. If no second parameter is provided, the procedure instruments *all* clauses. Otherwise, the procedure only instruments clauses contained

---

① $k = 1$
② $\text{MCSes} = \emptyset$
③ $\text{UC}_k = $ unsatisfiable core of F
④ While ($\text{INSTRUMENT}(F) \cdot (\text{BLOCK}(\text{MCSes}))$ is satisfiable

   ❶ Instrument clauses in UC_k with relaxation literal:
      $F_k = \text{INSTRUMENT}(F, \text{UC}_k) \cdot \text{ATMOST}(k, \text{UC}_k)$
   ❷ Enumerate satisfying assignments to relaxation variables:
      $\text{MCSes} = \text{MCSes} \cup \text{ALLSAT}(F_k \cdot \text{BLOCK}(MCSes))$
   ❸ $\text{UC}_{k+1} = \text{UC}_k \cup $ core of $F_k \cdot \text{BLOCK}(MCSes)$
      (projected to clauses of F)
   ❹ $k = k + 1$

⑤ return MCSes

Figure 16. A core-guided algorithm to compute MCSes

in the set of clauses provided as second parameter. This process is outlined in Example 4.3.

- The procedure BLOCK adds blocking clauses that rule out the minimal correction sets provided as parameter. To this end, BLOCK adds one blocking clause for each MCS and assures thus that at least one clause of each MCS provided as parameter is *not* dropped.

- ATMOST generates a cardinality constraint which states that at most k clauses are dropped from the set of clauses provided as second parameter. (Cardinality constraints are discussed in Section 4.2.) Note that, unlike in the algorithm in Figure 15, which introduces one cardinality constraint per core, the algorithm in Figure 16 introduces only a single constraint. This improvement over [FM06] was first presented in [MSP08] and subsequently used in [LS09].

- ALLSAT enumerates all satisfying assignments to the relaxation literals contained in the formula provided as parameter. In our context, each of these assignments represents a minimal correction set. The respective techniques are covered in Section 4.1.

At the core of the algorithm in Figure 16 lies the MAX-SAT algorithm from Figure 15. In particular, the first intermediate result of the algorithm in Figure 16 is the set of all minim*um* correction sets, obtained by means of computing all solutions to the MAX-SAT problem. Subsequently, the algorithm gradually relaxes the cardinality constraint, allowing for correction sets of a larger cardinality while blocking MCSes found in previous iterations. In each iteration, the algorithm enumerates *all* correction sets of cardinality k. By induction, this guarantees the completeness of the algorithm; a formal argument is given in [LS09].

Example 4.7 *We recall the Formula 3 presented in Example 4.1:*

$$(\bar{r} + \bar{s} + t) \cdot (\bar{r} + s) \cdot (r) \cdot (\bar{t}) \cdot (s)$$

We simulate the algorithm in Figure 16 on this example. Since MCSes $= \emptyset$ in the initial iteration of the algorithm, the relaxed formula in line ④ is satisfiable. If we follow the *algorithm presented in Section 3.8, the satisfiability solver returns the unsatisfiable core* $\{(\bar{r} + \bar{s} + t), (r), (\bar{t}), (s)\}$. *Accordingly, the algorithm constructs the formula*

$$(u + \bar{r} + \bar{s} + t) \cdot (\bar{r} + s) \cdot (v + r) \cdot (w + \bar{t}) \cdot (x + s) \cdot \left(\sum \{u, v, w, x\} \leq 1\right)$$

Then, it incrementally *constructs all satisfying assignments to* $\{u, v, w, x\}$ *that are consistent with this formula. We obtain the partial assignments*

$$\{u \mapsto 1, v \mapsto 0, w \mapsto 0, x \mapsto 0\},$$

$$\{u \mapsto 0, v \mapsto 1, w \mapsto 0, x \mapsto 0\}, \text{ and}$$

$$\{u \mapsto 0, v \mapsto 0, w \mapsto 1, x \mapsto 0\}.$$

and the corresponding blocking clauses $(\bar{u})$, $(\bar{v})$, *and* $(\bar{w})$. *The respective MCSes of cardinality one are* $\{(\bar{r} + \bar{s} + t)\}$, $\{r\}$, *and* $\{\bar{t}\}$. *Note that the partial assignment* $\{u \mapsto 0, v \mapsto 0, w \mapsto 0, x \mapsto 1\}$ *is not a satisfying assignment, since dropping the clause* (s) *does not make the formula satisfiable – the unit clause* (s) *can be inferred from* $(\bar{r} + s)$ *and* (r). *After blocking all MCSes (controlled by the variables* $\{u, v, w, x\}$*), we end up with the formula*

$$(u + \bar{r} + \bar{s} + t) \cdot (\bar{r} + s) \cdot (v + r) \cdot (w + \bar{t}) \cdot (x + s)$$

$$\cdot \left(\sum \{u, v, w, x\} \leq 1\right) \cdot (\bar{u}) \cdot (\bar{v}) \cdot (\bar{w}).$$

In step ❸*, the algorithm constructs the core of this formula, replaces the instrumented clauses with their original counterparts, and drops the cardinality constraint and the blocking clauses from the core. We obtain the new core*

$$\{(\bar{r} + \bar{s} + t), (\bar{r} + s), (r), (\bar{t})\}.$$

Note that, since the blocking clauses do not prevent (s) *from being dropped, the clause* $(\bar{r} + s)$ *must be contained in this core.*

   In the next step, the algorithm increases k. Now, all clauses have to be instrumented (since the union of both cores computed so far happens to be the set of all clauses of the original formula), and all MCSes computed so far need to be blocked. In combination with the new cardinality constraint, we obtain

$$(u + \bar{r} + \bar{s} + t) \cdot (y + \bar{r} + s) \cdot (v + r) \cdot (w + \bar{t}) \cdot (x + s) \cdot (\bar{u}) \cdot (\bar{v}) \cdot (\bar{w})$$

$$\cdot \left(\sum \{u, v, w, x, y\} \leq 2\right).$$

Since neither dropping (s) *nor dropping* $(\bar{r} + s)$ *from the original instance makes the formula satisfiable, the algorithm determines the satisfying assignment* $\{u \mapsto 0, y \mapsto 1, v \mapsto 0, w \mapsto 0, x \mapsto 1\}$. *This assignment is in fact the only satisfying partial assignment to the variables* $\{u, v, w, x, y\}$ *for the given formula. The corresponding blocking clause is* $(\bar{x} + \bar{y})$.

   We leave it to the reader to verify that INSTRUMENT$(F) \cdot (\bar{u}) \cdot (\bar{v}) \cdot (\bar{w}) \cdot (\bar{x} + \bar{y})$ *in line* ④ *is now unsatisfiable, and that the algorithm therefore terminates reporting the MCSes*

$$\{(\bar{r} + \bar{s} + t)\}, \quad \{(r)\}, \quad \{(\bar{t})\}, \quad \text{and} \quad \{(s), (\bar{r} + s)\}.$$

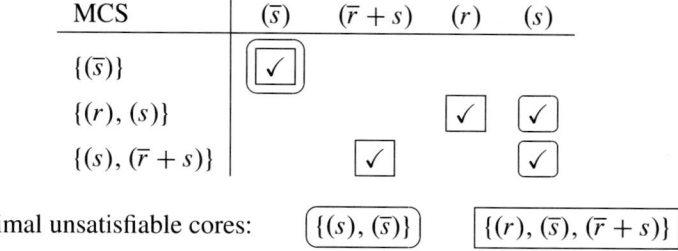

Figure 17. MCSes are hitting sets of minimal unsatisfiable cores, and vice versa

4.5. Minimal Unsatisfiable Cores

We observed in Section 4.4 that a minimal correction set comprises clauses that need to be dropped to "defuse" all unsatisfiable cores of a formula. Conversely, choosing at least one clause from each minimal correction set of a formula yields an unsatisfiable core. The following definition enables us to formalise this observation.

Definition 4.3 (Hitting Set) *Given a set of sets S, a hitting set of S is a set H such that*

$$\forall S \in \mathcal{S} . H \cap S \neq \emptyset$$

Minimal correction sets and unsatisfiable cores are dual [LS08] in the following sense:

- Let S be the set of all MCSes of an unsatisfiable formula F. Then each (minimal) hitting set of S is a (minimal) unsatisfiable core (see Section 3.8).
- Let S be the set of all minimal unsatisfiable cores of an unsatisfiable formula F. Then each (minimal) hitting set of S is a (minimal) correction set for F.

The following example illustrates this duality.

Example 4.8 *The leftmost column in Figure 17 shows the set of all minimal correction sets $\{\{(\bar{s})\}, \{(r),(s)\}, \{(s),(\bar{r}+s)\}\}$ for the unsatisfiable formula*

$$F \quad \equiv \quad (\bar{s}) \cdot (\bar{r}+s) \cdot (r) \cdot (s) .$$

The check-marks in the table indicate the occurrences of the clauses of F in the respective MCS. By choosing a subset of clauses of F which "hit" all MCSes, we obtain a minimal unsatisfiable core. The formula F has two minimal unsatisfiable cores, namely $\{(s),(\bar{s})\}$ and $\{(r),(\bar{s}),(\bar{r}+s)\}$. The choice of appropriate "hitting" clauses is indicated in Figure 17 by oval and rectangular boxes, respectively.

The problem of deciding whether a given set of sets has a hitting set of size k (or smaller) is NP-complete ([Kar72] in [LS08]). An algorithm optimised for the purpose of extracting cores from sets of MCSes can be found in [LS08].

Instead of presenting the algorithm suggested in [LS08], we draw the readers attention to the fact that after the final iteration of the algorithm in Figure 16, the set of clauses (BLOCK(MCSes)) in step ③ is a *symbolic* representation of all minimal correction sets. Essentially, we are looking for assignments that satisfy the CNF formula (BLOCK(MCSes)). Note that the phase of all literals in (BLOCK(MCSes)) is negative, since the respective clauses block assignments of 1 to relaxation variables. Accordingly, in order to find minimal unsatisfiable cores, we need to minimise the number of variables set to 0 in the satisfying assignment to (BLOCK(MCSes)). Again, this can be achieved by means of gradually relaxed cardinality constraints.

Example 4.9 *In Example 4.7, we ended up with the blocking clause*

$$(\overline{u}) \cdot (\overline{v}) \cdot (\overline{w}) \cdot (\overline{x} + \overline{y}),$$

where the relaxation literals u, v, w, x, and y correspond to the clauses $(\overline{r}+\overline{s}+t)$, (r), $(\overline{t})$, (s), and $(\overline{r}+s)$, respectively. Each of the clauses is satisfied if at least one of its literals evaluates to 1 (and the corresponding variable evaluates to 0, respectively). In order to find a minimal hitting set, we constrain the literals using a cardinality constraint:

$$(\overline{u}) \cdot (\overline{v}) \cdot (\overline{w}) \cdot (\overline{x} + \overline{y}) \cdot \left(\sum\{\overline{u}, \overline{v}, \overline{w}, \overline{x}, \overline{y}\} \leq k\right)$$

Note that k has to be at least four, since there are four clauses which do not share any literals. This threshold can be obtained using a syntactical analysis of the formula or simply by incrementally increasing k until it is sufficiently large.

If we generate all minimal satisfying assignments to the constrained formula (using blocking clauses in a way similar to Example 4.7) we obtain the following assignments for $k = 4$:

$$\{\overline{u} \mapsto 1, \overline{v} \mapsto 1, \overline{w} \mapsto 1, \overline{x} \mapsto 1, \overline{y} \mapsto 0\} \text{ and}$$

$$\{\overline{u} \mapsto 1, \overline{v} \mapsto 1, \overline{w} \mapsto 1, \overline{x} \mapsto 0, \overline{y} \mapsto 1\}$$

These assignments correspond to the minimal unsatisfiable cores

$$\{(\overline{r} + \overline{s} + t), (r), (\overline{t}), (s)\}$$

$$\{(\overline{r} + \overline{s} + t), (r), (\overline{t}), (\overline{r} + s)\}.$$

The hitting set problem is equivalent to the set cover problem, an NP-complete problem that has been extensively studied in complexity theory. We do not claim that the technique in Example 4.9 is competitive compared to other algorithms such as the one presented in [LS08] – the purpose of the example is to gain a deeper understanding of hitting sets.

The following section discusses examples of applications of the techniques presented in Sections 3 and 4.

5. Applications in Automated Verification

Contemporary SAT solvers are the enabling technology for a number of successful verification techniques. Bounded Model Checking, for instance, owes its existence to a large extent to the impressive advances of satisfiability solvers. This section presents – without claiming completeness in any way – a number of examples of how SAT solvers are applied in contemporary verification tools. After discussing how propositional logic can be used to represent circuits and software programs (Section 5.1), we discuss automated test-case generation (Section 5.2), Bounded Model Checking (Section 5.3), and fault localisation (Section 5.4).

5.1. Encoding Circuits and Programs

There is a natural correspondence between combinational circuits, such as the full-adder in Figure 13(b), and propositional logic formulae. Accordingly, the encoding of the circuit in Figure 13(b) is straight forward:

$$(o_1 \leftrightarrow (a \cdot b)) \cdot (o_2 \leftrightarrow (a \oplus b)) \cdot (o_3 \leftrightarrow (o_2 \cdot c_i)) \cdot$$
$$(s \leftrightarrow (o_2 \oplus c_i)) \cdot (c_o \leftrightarrow (o_1 + o_3)) \tag{6}$$

As described in the first step of Tseitin's encoding (presented in Section 2.1.2), the encoding introduces fresh variables o_1, o_2, o_3 that represent the inner signals and wires of the circuit that do not correspond to inputs or outputs. Based on Formula 6, we can construct a relation R which maps valuations to the input signals to the corresponding output signals:

$$R(\underbrace{a, b,}_{\text{inputs}} \underbrace{s, c_o}_{\text{outputs}}) \stackrel{\text{def}}{=} \exists o_1\, o_2\, o_3 . \left(\begin{array}{c} (o_1 \leftrightarrow (a \cdot b)) \cdot (o_2 \leftrightarrow (a \oplus b)) \cdot (o_3 \leftrightarrow (o_2 \cdot c_i)) \cdot \\ (s \leftrightarrow (o_2 \oplus c_i)) \cdot (c_o \leftrightarrow (o_1 + o_3)) \end{array} \right) \tag{7}$$

Any satisfying assignment to this relation R (or to Formula 6, respectively) represents a possible combination of input/output signals, e.g.,

$$a \mapsto 0,\ b \mapsto 1,\ c_i \mapsto 1, s \mapsto 0, c_o \mapsto 1$$

corresponds to the case in which the full-adder yields a sum of zero and a set carry-out bit for an input of 0 and 1 and a carry-in bit of value 1. The *transition* relation R (7) is a symbolic encoding of *all* possible input/output pairs of the full-adder.

In a sequential circuit (see Figure 18(a)), the relation R encodes *one* execution cycle of the circuit. It is possible to extend this representation to a fixed number of k execution cycles by *replicating* (or *unfolding*) the combinational part of the circuit k times. The unfolding yields an *iterative logic array* [ABF90] (as illustrated in Figure 18(b) for two cycles). For each time-frame t, we introduce a fresh set of variables (as indicated by the super-script t). The initial state of the circuit imposes no constraints on the internal signals: their value can be either 1 or 0 (indicated by $\star$ in Figure 18(b)).

Figure 18 shows a simple example of such an unfolding. The sequential circuit in Figure 19(a) has two input signals i_1 and i_2 and one output signal o. In the corresponding 2-cycle unfolding in Figure 19(b) we introduce a fresh variable for each of these signals in each execution cycle (e.g., i_1^1, i_1^2, ...).

By means of Tseitin's transformation (Section 2.1.2) we obtain the propositional representation in Figure 20 of the unfolded circuit in Figure 19(b) in conjunctive normal

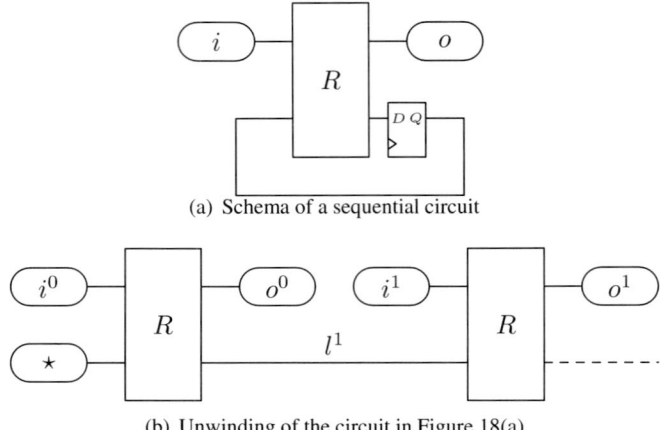

(a) Schema of a sequential circuit

(b) Unwinding of the circuit in Figure 18(a)

Figure 18. Unwinding circuits

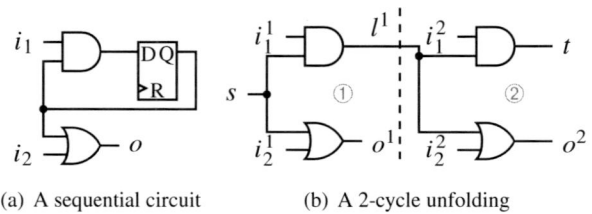

(a) A sequential circuit   (b) A 2-cycle unfolding

Figure 19. A simple example of an unfolded circuit

$$
\begin{array}{lll}
& \mathrel{\rlap{\raise.5ex\hbox{$\mathsf D$}}} & \mathrel{\rlap{\raise.5ex\hbox{$\mathsf D$}}} \\
\text{cycle } \textcircled{1} & (\overline{l^1}\, i^1_1)\, (\overline{l^1}\, s)\, (i^1_1\, \overline{s}\, l^1) & (\overline{i^1_2}\, o^1)\, (\overline{s}\, o^1)\, (\overline{o^1}\, i^1_2\, s) \\
\text{cycle } \textcircled{2} & (\overline{t}\, i^2_1)\, (\overline{t}\, l^1)\, (\overline{i^2_1}\, \overline{l^1}\, t) & (\overline{i^2_2}\, o^2)\, (\overline{l^1}\, o^2)\, (\overline{o^2}\, i^2_2\, l^1)
\end{array}
$$

Figure 20. Propositional encoding of the unwound circuit in Figure 19(b)

form. The clauses in Figure 20 are grouped with respect to the gates and cycles by which they are contributed.

Each satisfying assignment of this formula represents a feasible execution of two cycles of the sequential circuit in Figure 19(a). In general, k cycles are encoded by k instances of the relation R:

$$
R(\vec{i}^1, \vec{o}^1) \cdot R(\vec{i}^2, \vec{o}^2) \cdots R(\vec{i}^k, \vec{o}^k) \tag{8}
$$

(where $\vec{i}^t, \vec{o}^t$ represents the input and output variables of time-frame t).

Software programs can be encoded in a similar manner. The semantics of each instruction of a program is determined by the hardware implementation of the operators that occur in the instruction. The addition of two 4-bit variables a and b, for instance, can be encoded using the ripple-carry adder in Figure 13(a). Accordingly, each n-bit variable a in the program is encoded using n propositional variables representing the n bits of a;

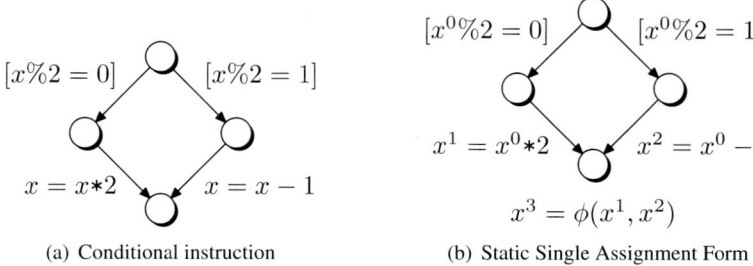

(a) Conditional instruction   (b) Static Single Assignment Form

Figure 21. Encoding the control flow of software programs

this technique is known as *bit-flattening* or *bit-blasting*. We refer the reader to [KS08] for a detailed treatment of various operators of common imperative programming languages such as ANSI-C or Java.

Accordingly, an instruction at the program location ℓ of the given program can be represented using a propositional relation $R_\ell(\vec{v}^i, \vec{v}^j)$, where $\vec{v}^i$ refers to the propositional variables representing the program state *before* the execution of the instruction and $\vec{v}^j$ refers to the variables representing the state *after* the execution. To avoid notational clutter, we refrain from using the bit-level representation of program instructions and will deploy a more abstract notation for transition relations (such as $R_\ell(x^i, x^j) \stackrel{\text{def}}{=} (x^j = x^i + 1)$ for the instruction x++ at location ℓ).

Unlike circuits, which are executed in a *synchronous* manner, software programs typically have a control flow structure which determines which instruction is executed at which point in time. Figure 21(a), for instance, illustrates the control flow graph (CFG) of the conditional instruction `if (x%2) {x=x*2;}else{x--;}`. Accordingly, it is not sufficient to simply encode all instructions as propositional relations; one also has to take the control flow of the program into account.

In Figure 21(a), the variable x is assigned in two different branches of the conditional statement. We cannot simply use the same propositional variables to represent the value of x in each branch, since this would result in an unsatisfiable formula (x cannot take two values at the same time). Therefore, we need to guarantee, that different *versions* of the variables are used in each branch. This can be achieved by transforming the program into the *static single assignment* (SSA) form [CFR+91]. The SSA form of a program is an intermediate representation used in compiler construction which guarantees that each variable is assigned exactly once. This property is achieved by replacing existing variables in the original program with fresh variables such that the right-hand side of each assignment in the program gets its own version of the assigned variable. The SSA form of the program fragment in Figure 21(a) is shown in Figure 21(b). In the SSA form, the assignment $x^3 = \phi(x^1, x^2)$ indicates a *join* of two branches of the program. At this point the variable x^3 needs to be assigned the value of either x^1 or x^2, depending on which branch was executed. It is, however, impossible to determine *statically* which branch modifies x. Therefore, we encode the control flow dependency into the transition relation as follows:

$$(x^1 = x^0*2) \cdot (x^2 = x^0 - 1) \cdot \left((x^0\%2 = 0) \cdot (x^3 = x^1) + (x^0\%2 = 1) \cdot (x^3 = x^2)\right)$$

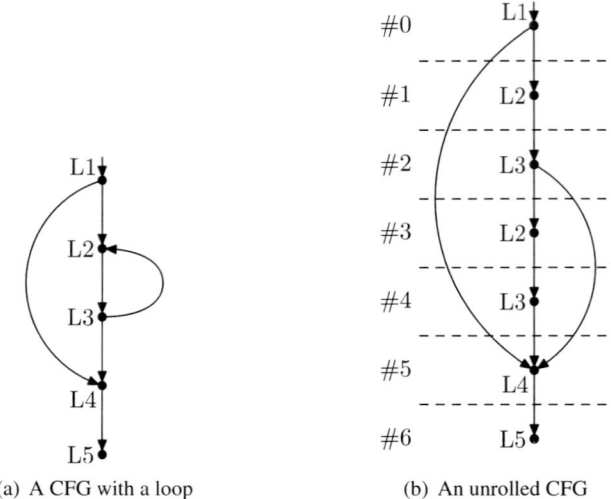

(a) A CFG with a loop   (b) An unrolled CFG

Figure 22. Unwinding loops in software programs

```
                           if ( x )  {
  while ( x )                  BODY;
     BODY;          ⟶       if ( x )
                                BODY;
                           else
                                exit ( );
                        }
```

Figure 23. An unrolling of a **while** loop. The exit statement terminates paths of depth greater than 2 .

In this formula, the value of x^3 depends on the value of x^0, the version of the variable x representing the value of x before the execution of the conditional statement.

Repetitive constructs (such as loops) can be treated similar to the encoding of execution cycles of a hardware circuit. However, instead of unwinding the entire transition relation of the program, each loop is unwound separately up to a pre-determined bound. Syntactically, this corresponds to a replication the loop body and the appropriate guard (Figure 23). The unwinding is illustrated in Figure 22. The CFG on the left side (Figure 22(a)) represents a simple program with a single loop. The graph on the right side (Figure 22(b)) illustrates the structure resulting from unwinding the loop body between the program locations L3 and L4 twice. The size of the resulting unwound program is linear in the size of the original program and the depth of the unwinding. Alternative unwinding techniques are discussed in the survey [DKW08]. After transforming the resulting unwound program into SSA, the bounded instance can be encoded as a propositional formula as before. The resulting formula effectively *simulates* all possible executions up to the pre-determined unwinding depth of the loops in the program. Accordingly, this technique is also known as *symbolic simulation* [Kin70].

5.2. Test-Case Generation

The fact that a bounded unwinding of a circuit design or a program symbolically encodes all possible executions up to a certain depth k makes it an ideal tool for automated test-case generation: each satisfying assignment generated by a SAT solver corresponds to a test scenario. In this setting, the circuit design or program takes the role of a specification; the resulting test-cases are used to verify the actual integrated circuit or a compiled version of the program. There is one subtle pitfall: a test-case extracted from the source code of the actual program (or chip design) under test must necessarily succeed if the compiler (or synthesis tool) is correct. It is therefore common practice to extract test-cases for the implementation from a *model* or abstract specification of the artifact under test. With the rise of model-based development (MBD) methodologies such models are available increasingly often. In [BHM$^+$10], for instance, test-cases are extracted from Simulink models. In combination with an incremental SAT solver it is possible to generate an entire suite of test-cases which satisfies certain coverage criteria such as path coverage or modified condition/decision coverage (MC/DC): the coverage criteria are simply encoded as constraints, and previously generated test-cases are barred by means of blocking clauses [HSTV08,HSTV09].

The test-case generator described in [BHM$^+$10], for instance, deploys *mutations* as a coverage criterion. A mutation is a small modification – such as using a wrong operator or variable name – to the original design or source code. A test suite which does not detect the injected fault is considered insufficient. Instead of using mutations to evaluate a given test-suite, however, [BHM$^+$10] uses mutations as a catalyst to generate a test-suite which, by construction, covers all injected faults. To this end, the test-generation algorithm contrasts the unwound transition relation of the *mutated* source code with the original unwound transition relation. Let R_m^k (R^k, respectively) denote the relation encoding k unwindings of the mutated (original) transition relation, respectively. The test-case generator then constructs the following formula:

$$R^k(\vec{i}^1, \vec{o}^k) \cdot R_m^k(\vec{i}^1, \vec{m}^k) \cdot \underbrace{\left((o_1^k \oplus m_1^k) + (o_2^k \oplus m_2^k) + \cdots + (o_n^k \oplus m_n^k)\right)}_{\text{miter}}. \qquad (9)$$

Observe that the *input* variables for both the original as well as the mutated transition relations are the same. A so called *miter* enforces that Formula 9 is only satisfiable if the valuation to the input variables yields output values $\vec{o}^k$ and $\vec{m}^k$ for the two different transition relations which disagree on at least one value. This approach (which is based on equivalence checking) guarantees that the resulting test case detects the faults injected in R_m^k.

Example 5.1 *Consider the mutated version (depicted in Figure 24) of the circuit in Figure 19(b). Note that the "and"-gate in the first cycle has been replaced with an "or"-gate, and that all output and internal signals were renamed. The input signals i_1^1, i_2^1, i_1^2, i_2^2, and the signal s representing the initial state of the latch remain unchanged.*

We obtain the following encoding in conjunctive normal form:

$$\begin{array}{lll}
cycle~① & (r^1\,\overline{i_1^1})\,(r^1\,\overline{s})\,(i_1^1\,s\,\overline{r^1}) & (\overline{i_2^1}\,m^1)\,(\overline{s}\,m^1)\,(\overline{m^1}\,i_2^1\,s) \\
cycle~② & (\overline{u}\,i_1^2)\,(\overline{u}\,r^1)\,(i_1^2\,\overline{r^1}\,t) & (i_2^2\,m^2)\,(\overline{l^1}\,m^2)\,(\overline{m^2}\,i_2^2\,r^1)
\end{array}$$

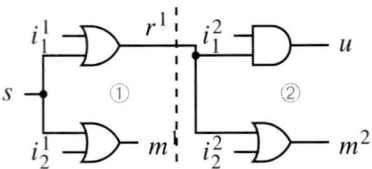

Figure 24. A mutated version of the circuit in Figure 19(b)

The miter $(o^1 \oplus m^1) + (o^2 \oplus m^2)$ enforces that any assignment satisfying the conjunction of the formula representing the original circuit and the formula representing the mutated circuit yields different values for at least one output. The reader may verify that o^2 and m^2 must take different values in any extension of the partial assignment

$$s \mapsto 0 \quad i_1^1 \mapsto 1 \quad i_2^1 \mapsto 0 \quad i_1^2 \mapsto 0 \quad i_2^2 \mapsto 0$$

to a total assignment. Accordingly, the corresponding test-case detects the incorrect "or"-gate.

5.3. Bounded Model Checking

Model checking [CGP99] is a technique that explores all reachable states of a model to check whether a given property is satisfied. Unlike testing, model checking performs an exhaustive search of the state space and provides a correctness guarantee that is rarely achieved by means of testing. Moreover, if the specification is violated, model checking tools are able to provide a *counterexample*, i.e., a witness demonstrating how the property in question can be violated.

Bounded model checking (BMC) [BCCZ99] is a variation of model checking which restricts the exploration to execution traces up to a certain (user-defined) length k. BMC either provides a guarantee that the first k execution steps of the model satisfy the property P or a counterexample of length at most k. This setting should sound familiar to the reader: Section 5.1 describes how all execution traces up to depth k can be encoded in a propositional formula. Given such an encoding, it is sufficient to augment each execution cycle with a formula encoding the negation of the property P. This is indicated in the following diagram (here, I denotes a constraint encoding the valid initial states of the model):

$$\frac{I \;\cdot\; R}{P \;+\; P} \xrightarrow{\quad} \frac{R}{P} \xrightarrow{\quad} \frac{R}{P} \;\cdots\; \frac{R}{P} \xrightarrow{\quad} \frac{R}{P}$$

Any assignment satisfying the resulting formula represents a counterexample to the claim that P holds. If the formula is unsatisfiable, on the other hand, then the claim holds in the first k execution steps. An example for a bounded model checking tool for programs written in the ANSI-C language is CBMC [CKL04].

5.4. Fault Localisation

The techniques discussed in Section 5.2 and Section 5.3 are aimed at discovering bugs in software and hardware designs. Finding a bug, however, is just the first step. Localising and understanding the underlying fault is often a much more daunting task.

Accordingly, automated support for fault localisation is highly desirable. In this section, we discuss how MAX-SAT and minimal correction sets can be applied to localise bugs. This approach, also known as *consistency-based diagnosis*, has been successfully applied to localise faults in hardware designs (see, for instance, [SMV$^+$07,SFBD08, FSBD08,CSVMS09,CSMSV10,ZWM11]) as well as in software [JM11].

Consistency-based diagnoses aims at identifying the fractions of the hardware design or the source code of the software that are *inconsistent* with an observed (or expected) behaviour. We distinguish two scenarios:

1. The transition relation R (obtained from the source code or hardware design) represents the *implementation* of the artifact under test and an observed behaviour of this implementation contradicts the specification (e.g., the requirements document or a use case scenario). This setting is addressed in [SMV$^+$07,SFBD08,FSBD08,CSVMS09,CSMSV10,JM11], for instance.
2. The transition relation R represents the *specification* of the artifact under test. The observed behaviour (e.g., a test run of a manufactured integrated circuit) is inconsistent with R. This scenario is addressed in [ZWM11].

In the first case we assume that the specification is given as a set of constraints or an assignment to the input and output variables of the transition relation R. In the second case we assume that the observed test scenario is provided as an assignment to the variables of R. While the two scenarios are in a sense dual, the objective in both cases is to identify the "elements" of the transition relation R that are inconsistent with the observed (or expected) behaviour. In both cases, we have to specify what we mean by "elements" – this is determined by the underlying *fault model*. The notion of a fault model is similar to the concept of a mutation, discussed in Section 5.2. A fault model determines which and how components of the transition relation can possibly fail. A gate in an integrated circuit, for instance, may malfunction and constantly yield an output value of 1 – this fault is known as *stuck-at-constant*. In a program, the developer may accidentally use the instruction y=x++ instead of y=++x, which results in an incorrect value of the variable y. The faulty element is the respective gate in the first case and the respective line of code in the second case. In both cases, we would like to automatically pinpoint the location of the fault.

In the following, we consider only a rather simplistic fault model for hardware as well as for software: we assume that the output of a gate or the result of an assignment may be an *arbitrary* value. The motivation is that this fault model can be easily encoded in the transition relation R by means of *relaxation literals* (c.f. Section 4.3.1). By relaxing the set of clauses that encode the output value o_i of a gate or an assignment of an SSA variable x_i we effectively cut the signal or variable loose. The following two examples illustrate how minimal correction sets enable us to locate faults in this setting.

Example 5.2 *We work in scenario 1 described above. The code fragment in SSA in Figure 25 represents the implementation of a program. We assume that the specification of the software states that the value of y must be even after the execution of the conditional statement. This requirement is represented by the constraint $(y^3 \% 2 = 0)$ and obviously violated if x^0 is odd. Assume that the test engineer reports that the requirement does not hold for $x^0 = 1$. By combining the constraint and the assignment with the encoding of the program we obtain the formula*

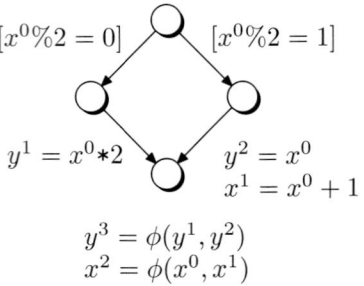

Figure 25. A conditional statement with a faulty branch

$$(y^1 = x^0 * 2) \cdot (y^2 = x^0) \cdot (x^1 = x^0 + 1)$$

$$\cdot \left((x^0 \% 2 = 0) \cdot (x^2 = x^0) \cdot (y^3 = y^1) + (x^0 \% 2 = 1) \cdot (x^2 = x^1) \cdot (y^3 = y^2) \right)$$

$$\cdot (x^0 = 1) \cdot (y^3 \% 2 = 0) \, .$$

Notably, this formula is unsatisfiable; for the given input the transition relation does not satisfy the requirement. In order to fix the bug, the developer needs to locate the fault. In accordance with the simplistic fault model suggested above, we assume that one of the assignments $y = x * 2$ or $y = x{+}{+}$ (represented by the expressions $(y^1 = x^0 * 2)$ and $(y^2 = x^0) \cdot (x^1 = x^0 + 1))$ are at fault. In order to locate the fault, we mark the propositional clauses encoding these expressions as soft clauses *and compute all minimal correction sets for the resulting formula. Note that, in accordance with our fault model, the conditions $(x^0 \% 2 = 0)$ and $(x^0 \% 2 = 1)$ are represented by hard clauses and may not be dropped. Moreover, the constraints $(x^0 = 1) \cdot (y^3 \% 2 = 0)$ representing the test scenario and the requirement must not be relaxed, either, since changing the test scenario or the requirements is an undesired solution to the problem.*

Using the algorithm described in Section 4.4, we can now compute the minimal correction sets for the problem instance described above. The $(y^2 = x^0)$ is identified as the culprit and helps the developer to narrow down the fault location to the instruction $y = x{+}{+}$.

Example 5.3 *In Scenario 2, the behaviour of the test artifact does not comply with the specification represented by R. This situation may arise in the context of* post-silicon validation, *for instance: the manufacturing process may introduce a fault in the prototype of a chip, resulting in a discrepancy of the behaviour of the integrated circuit and its design. Debugging an integrated circuit is non-trivial, since unlike in software debugging, its internal signals can not be easily observed.*

Consider the sequential circuit in Figure 19(a). After resetting the latch, we expect the output o to remain 0 as long as the input signal i_2 is constantly 0. Assume, however, that we observe an output value of 1 after two cycles when executing the described scenario on the chip. Figure 19(b) depicts a two-cycle unfolding of the circuit. Figure 20 shows the corresponding CNF encoding. Assume that we observe and record the values $o^1 \mapsto 0$ and $o^2 \mapsto 1$ during a test-run with the initial state $s \mapsto 0$ and the stimuli $i_2^1 \mapsto 0$, and $i_2^2 \mapsto 0$. Note that we have no information about the signal l^1. These observations contribute the hard constraint $\overline{o^1} \cdot o^2 \cdot \overline{s} \cdot \overline{i_2^1} \cdot \overline{i_2^2}$, which is not satisfiable in *conjunction with the formula in 20. Using a* MAX-SAT *solver, we can derive that the conjunction becomes satisfiable if we drop either* $(\overline{l^1}\,s)$ *or* $(\overline{o^2}\,i_2^2\,l^1)$ *(both of which are an MCS) from 20. Accordingly, either the "and"-gate in cycle one or the "or"-gate in cycle two must have defaulted. Notably, our fault localisation technique managed to narrow down the set of possibly faulty gates* without *knowledge about the internal signals of the physical circuit. Fault localisation in silicon debug is addressed in more detail in [ZWM11].*

6. Conclusion

The advances of contemporary SAT solvers have transformed the way we think about NP complete problems. They have shown that, while these problems are still unmanageable in the worst case, many instances can be successfully tackled. In Section 3, we discussed the main contributions and techniques that made this paradigm shift possible. Section 4 covers a number of natural extensions to the SAT problem, such as the enumeration all satisfying assignments (ALL-SAT) and determining the maximum number of clauses that can be satisfied by an assignment (MAX-SAT). SAT solvers and their extensions have immediate applications in domains such as automated verification, as discussed in Section 5. In fact, many successful verification techniques such as Bounded Model Checking owe their existence to the impressive advances of modern SAT solvers. While SAT solvers can easily be used as a black box, the realisation of many of these applications relies on internal features of SAT solvers and requires an in-dept understanding of the underlying algorithms.

    SAT solvers are still improving at an impressive rate (as demonstrated by the results of the annual SAT solver competition – http://www.satcompetition.org/) and novel applications are conceived and published on a regular basis.

7. Acknowledgements

The authors are indebted to Matthias Schlaipfer and the attendees of the Summer School Marktoberdorf 2011 for their comments on this tutorial.

A. Exercises

Exercise 1 *Use Tseitin's transformation to convert $x + (y \cdot (\bar{z} \oplus x))$ into CNF.*

Solution   By introducing the following fresh variables

$$x + (y \cdot (\underbrace{\overbrace{(\underbrace{\overbrace{\bar{z} \cdot \bar{x}}^{p} + \overbrace{z \cdot x}^{q}}_{u}})}_{v}}^{w}))$$

we obtain the formula

$$w \cdot (q \leftrightarrow (z \cdot x)) \cdot (p \leftrightarrow (\bar{z} \cdot \bar{x})) \cdot (u \leftrightarrow (p + q)) \cdot (v \leftrightarrow (y \cdot u)) \cdot (w \leftrightarrow (x + v))$$

We can now apply the rules

$$a \leftrightarrow (b + c) \equiv (\bar{b} + a) \cdot (\bar{c} + a) \cdot (\bar{a} + b + c) \tag{10}$$

$$a \leftrightarrow (b \cdot c) \equiv (\bar{a} + b) \cdot (\bar{a} + c) \cdot (\bar{b} + \bar{c} + a) \tag{11}$$

and get

$$w \cdot (\bar{q} + z) \cdot (\bar{q} + x) \cdot (\bar{z} + \bar{x} + q) \cdot (\bar{p} + \bar{z}) \cdot (\bar{p} + \bar{x}) \cdot (z + x + p) \cdot$$
$$(\bar{p} + u) \cdot (\bar{q} + u) \cdot (\bar{u} + p + q) \cdot (\bar{y} + v) \cdot (\bar{u} + v) \cdot (\bar{v} + y + u) \cdot$$
$$(\bar{x} + w) \cdot (\bar{v} + w) \cdot (\bar{w} + x + v)$$

Exercise 2 *Follow the scheme in Table 2 in Section 2.1.2 to derive the Tseitin clauses that characterise the n-ary Boolean formulas $(y_1 + y_2 + \cdots + y_n)$ and $(y_1 \cdot y_2 \cdot \cdots \cdot y_n)$.*

Solution

- Disjunction:

$$x \leftrightarrow (y_1 + y_2 + \cdots + y_n)$$
$$\equiv (x \rightarrow (y_1 + y_2 + \cdots + y_n)) \cdot ((y_1 + y_2 + \cdots + y_n) \rightarrow x)$$
$$\equiv (\bar{x} + y_1 + y_2 + \cdots + y_n) \cdot ((y_1 \rightarrow x) \cdot (y_2 \rightarrow x) \cdots (y_n \rightarrow x))$$
$$\equiv (\bar{x} + y_1 + y_2 + \cdots + y_n) \cdot (\bar{y}_1 + x) \cdot (\bar{y}_2 + x) \cdots (\bar{y}_n + x)$$

- Conjunction:

$$x \leftrightarrow (y_1 \cdot y_2 \cdot \cdots \cdot + y_n)$$
$$\equiv (x \rightarrow (y_1 \cdot y_2 \cdot \cdots \cdot y_n)) \cdot ((y_1 \cdot y_2 \cdot \cdots \cdot y_n) \rightarrow x)$$
$$\equiv ((\bar{x} + y_1) \cdot (\bar{x} + y_2) \cdot \cdots \cdot (\bar{x} + y_n)) \cdot \left((\overline{y_1 \cdot y_2 \cdot \cdots \cdot y_n}) + x \right)$$
$$\equiv ((\bar{x} + y_1) \cdot (\bar{x} + y_2) \cdot \cdots \cdot (\bar{x} + y_n)) \cdot (\bar{y}_1 + \bar{y}_2 + \cdots + \bar{y}_n + x)$$

Exercise 3 *Which of the Boolean formulae below are satisfiable, and which ones are unsatisfiable?*

1. $x + x \cdot y$
2. $\overline{(x \cdot (x \to y)) \to y}$
3. $x \cdot ((x \to y) \to y)$

Convert the formulae that are unsatisfiable into conjunctive normal form (either using Tseitin's transformation or the propositional calculus) and construct a resolution refutation proof.

Solution

- satisfiable: 1, 3
- unsatisfiable: 2

$$\overline{(x \cdot (x \to y)) \to y} \equiv \overline{(x \cdot (\overline{x} + y)) + y}$$
$$\equiv (x) \cdot (\overline{x} + y) \cdot (\overline{y})$$

Resolution proof:

$$\text{Res}((\overline{y}), \text{Res}((x), (\overline{x} + y), x), y) \equiv \square$$

Exercise 4 *Construct a resolution refutation graph for the following unsatisfiable formula:*

$$y_1 \cdot y_2 \cdot y_3 \cdot (\overline{y}_1 + x) \cdot (\overline{y}_2 + \overline{x} + z) \cdot (\overline{y}_3 + \overline{z})$$

Solution   The resolution graph for Exercise 4 is shown in Figure 26.

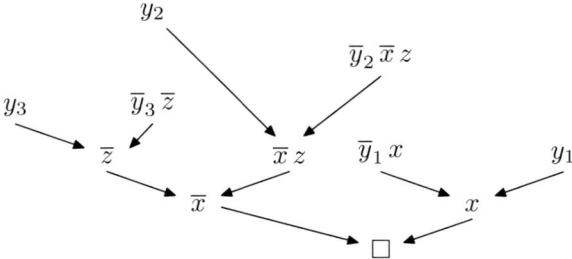

Figure 26. Resolution graph for Exercise 4

Exercise 5 *Apply the rules of the Davis-Putnam procedure (outlined in Section 3.3) to the following formula until you obtain an equi-satisfiable formula that cannot be reduced any further:*

$$y_1 \cdot y_2 \cdot (\overline{y}_1 + x + \overline{z}) \cdot (\overline{y}_2 + \overline{x} + z) \cdot (y_3 + \overline{z}) \cdot y_4$$

Solution   We perform the following steps:

Step	Rule	Formula
1	*1-literal-rule* on y_1	$y_2 \cdot (x + \overline{z}) \cdot (\overline{y}_2 + \overline{x} + z) \cdot (y_3 + \overline{z}) \cdot y_4$
2	*1-literal-rule* on y_2	$(x + \overline{z}) \cdot (\overline{x} + z) \cdot (y_3 + \overline{z}) \cdot y_4$
3	*Affirmative-negative*	$(x + \overline{z}) \cdot (\overline{x} + z)$
4	*Resolution* on x	$(z + \overline{z})$

The resulting formula $(z + \overline{z})$ is a tautology and cannot be eliminated by any of the Davis-Putnam rules. Accordingly, the original formula must be satisfiable.

Exercise 6 *Apply the Davis-Putnam-Logeman-Loveland (DPLL) procedure (described in Section 3.4) to the following formula:*

$$y_1 \cdot y_2 \cdot (\overline{y}_1 + x + z) \cdot (\overline{y}_2 + \overline{x} + z) \cdot (y_3 + \overline{z}) \cdot (\overline{y}_3 + \overline{z})$$

Solution   Table 4 shows one possible scenario. Note that there is no value of x that satisfies the formula. The reader may verify that choosing a decision variable other than x in the third step also yields a contradiction.

Partial Assignment   **Clauses**

$\{y_1 \mapsto 1\}$ $(y_2) (x z) (\overline{y}_2 \overline{x} z) (y_3 \overline{z}) (\overline{y}_3 \overline{z})$

$\{y_1 \mapsto 1, y_2 \mapsto 1\}$ $(x z) (\overline{x} z) (y_3 \overline{z}) (\overline{y}_3 \overline{z})$

No more implications, we guess $x \mapsto 1$

$\{y_1 \mapsto 1, y_2 \mapsto 1, x \mapsto 1\}$ $(z) (y_3 \overline{z}) (\overline{y}_3 \overline{z})$

$\{y_1 \mapsto 1, y_2 \mapsto 1, x \mapsto 1, z \mapsto 1\}$ $(y_3) (\overline{y}_3)$

$\{y_1 \mapsto 1, y_2 \mapsto 1, x \mapsto 1, z \mapsto 1, y_3 \mapsto 1\}$ 0

Contradiction, we have to revert $x \mapsto 1$

$\{y_1 \mapsto 1, y_2 \mapsto 1, x \mapsto 0\}$ $(z) (y_3 \overline{z}) (\overline{y}_3 \overline{z})$

$\{y_1 \mapsto 1, y_2 \mapsto 1, x \mapsto 0, z \mapsto 1\}$ $(y_3) (\overline{y}_3)$

$\{y_1 \mapsto 1, y_2 \mapsto 1, x \mapsto 0, z \mapsto 1, y_3 \mapsto 1\}$ 0

Contradiction, no more decisions to undo

Table 4. Assignment trail for Exercise 6

Exercise 7 *Simulate the* conflict-driven clause learning *algorithm presented in Section 3.5 on the following formula:*

$$\overbrace{(\overline{x} + \overline{y} + \overline{z})}^{C_0} \cdot \overbrace{(\overline{x} + \overline{y} + z)}^{C_1} \cdot \overbrace{(\overline{x} + y + \overline{z})}^{C_2} \cdot \overbrace{(\overline{x} + y + z)}^{C_3} \cdot$$

$$\overbrace{(x + \overline{y} + \overline{z})}^{C_4} \cdot \overbrace{(x + \overline{y} + z)}^{C_5} \cdot \overbrace{(x + y + \overline{z})}^{C_6} \cdot \overbrace{(x + y + z)}^{C_7}$$

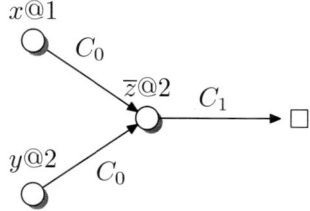

Figure 27. First implication graph arising in Exercise 7

Solution It is obvious that one has to make at least two decisions before one of the clauses becomes unit. If we start with the decisions $x @ 1$ and $y @ 2$, we obtain the implication graph in Figure 27.

By means of resolution (c.f. Section 3.6) we obtain the conflict clause $C_8 \equiv \text{Res}(C_0, C_1, z) \equiv (\bar{x} + \bar{y})$. We revert all decisions up to (but excluding) level 1, which is the second-highest decision level occurring in C_8. The clause C_8 is unit under the assignment $x @ 1$, thus implying the assignment $\bar{y} @ 1$. We obtain the implication graph in Figure 28. Again, there is a conflict.

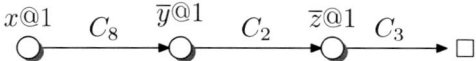

Figure 28. Second implication graph arising in Exercise 7

The resulting conflict clause is $C_9 \equiv \text{Res}(C_8, \text{Res}(C_2, C_3, z), y) \equiv (\bar{x})$, forcing us to revert to decision level zero and set x to 0. Under this assignment, none of the clauses is unit and we have to make a choice for either y or z. If we choose $y @ 1$, the clause C_4 becomes assertive and forces us to assign 0 to z. This assignment, however, is in conflict with C_5, and by means of resolution we obtain the conflict clause $C_{10} \equiv \text{Res}(C_4, C_5, z) \equiv (x + \bar{y})$.

C_{10} in combination with the unit clause C_9 yields $\bar{y} @ 0$. Under this assignment, the clause C_6 is unit, forcing us to assign 0 to z, which conflicts with clause C_7. Note that we obtained this conflict without making any decisions, i.e., we found a conflict at decision level zero. Accordingly, the formula is unsatisfiable.

Exercise 8 *Use the approach described in Section 3.6 to construct a resolution refutation proof for the formula presented in Exercise 7.*

Solution The solution to this exercise follows the steps of the solution to Exercise 7 and is left to the reader.

Exercise 9 *Find an unsatisfiable core of the formula*

$$(y) \cdot (x + \bar{y} + z) \cdot (\bar{x} + z) \cdot (\bar{x} + \bar{y}) \cdot (\bar{z} + \bar{y}).$$

(You are not allowed to provide the set of all clauses as a solution.)
Is your solution minimal?

Solution   The set of clauses

$$\{(y), (x + \overline{y} + z), (\overline{x} + z), (\overline{z} + \overline{y})\}$$

forms a core of the formula in Exercise 9. This can be verified by means of resolution:

$$\text{Res}((y), (x + \overline{y} + z), y) \equiv (x + z)$$
$$\text{Res}((x + z), (\overline{x} + z), x) \equiv (z)$$
$$\text{Res}((z), (\overline{z} + \overline{y}), z) =\equiv (\overline{y})$$
$$\text{Res}((\overline{y}), (y), y) = \square$$

Moreover, the core is minimal, since removing any one of the clauses "breaks" the core. Note that $\{(y), (x + \overline{y} + z), (\overline{x} + \overline{y}), (\overline{z} + \overline{y})\}$ is an alternative minimal solution.

Exercise 10 *Simplify the following formula using the substitution approach described in Section 3.10:*

$$w \cdot (\overline{q} + z) \cdot (\overline{q} + x) \cdot (\overline{z} + \overline{x} + q) \cdot (\overline{p} + \overline{z}) \cdot (\overline{p} + \overline{x}) \cdot (z + x + p) \cdot$$
$$(\overline{p} + u) \cdot (\overline{q} + u) \cdot (\overline{u} + p + q) \cdot (\overline{y} + v) \cdot (\overline{u} + v) \cdot (\overline{v} + y + u) \cdot$$
$$(\overline{x} + w) \cdot (\overline{v} + w) \cdot (\overline{w} + x + v)$$

Solution   Note that we do not know which clauses are "definitional" (i.e., introduce functionally dependent variables). In practice, this information is often not available and inferring it is computationally prohibitively expensive. Therefore we will not attempt to do so. Instead, we start by dividing the clauses into sets according to the positive and negative occurrences of the literals as shown in Figure 29.

Then, for each pair of sets S_ℓ, $S_{\overline{\ell}}$, we derive all possible resolvents and drop the resulting tautologies. If the resulting set of clauses $\text{Res}(S_\ell, S_{\overline{\ell}}, \ell)$ is smaller than $S_\ell \cup S_{\overline{\ell}}$, we replace the clauses $S_\ell \cup S_{\overline{\ell}}$ with $\text{Res}(S_\ell, S_{\overline{\ell}}, \ell)$. Otherwise, we retain the clauses $S_\ell \cup S_{\overline{\ell}}$. The set of resolvents of S_x and $S_{\overline{x}}$ has five elements:

$$\text{Res}(S_x, S_{\overline{x}}, x) \equiv \{(\overline{q} + \overline{p}), (\overline{q} + w), (z + p + w), (\overline{w} + \overline{z} + v + q), (\overline{w} + \overline{p} + v)\}$$

This is one clause less than $S_x \cup S_{\overline{x}}$. Accordingly, replacing the clauses $S_x \cup S_{\overline{x}}$ with the corresponding set of resolvents reduces the size of the formula. This strategy is implemented in the SAT-solver MINISAT [ES04b,EB05].

Exercise 11 *Use the core-guided algorithm presented in Section 4.3.2 to determine the solution of the partial MAX-SAT problem*

$$(\overline{x} + \overline{y}) \cdot (\overline{x} + z) \cdot (\overline{x} + \overline{z}) \cdot (\overline{y} + u) \cdot (\overline{y} + \overline{u}) \cdot (x) \cdot (y) \,,$$

where only the clauses (x) and (y) may be dropped.

$$S_x = \{(\overline{q} + x), (z + x + p), (\overline{w} + x + v)\}$$
$$S_{\overline{x}} = \{(\overline{z} + \overline{x} + q), (\overline{p} + \overline{x}), (\overline{x} + w)\}$$
$$S_y = \{(\overline{v} + y + u)\}$$
$$S_{\overline{y}} = \{(\overline{y} + v)\}$$
$$S_z = \{(\overline{q} + z), (z + x + p)\}$$
$$S_{\overline{z}} = \{(\overline{z} + \overline{x} + q), (\overline{p} + \overline{z})\}$$
$$S_p = \{(z + x + p), (\overline{u} + p + q)\}$$
$$S_{\overline{p}} = \{(\overline{p} + \overline{z}), (\overline{p} + \overline{x}), (\overline{p} + u)\}$$
$$S_q = \{(\overline{z} + \overline{x} + q), (\overline{u} + p + q)\}$$
$$S_{\overline{q}} = \{(\overline{q} + z), (\overline{q} + x), (\overline{q} + u)\}$$
$$S_u = \{(\overline{p} + u), (\overline{v} + y + u), (\overline{q} + u)\}$$
$$S_{\overline{u}} = \{(\overline{u} + p + q), (\overline{u} + v)\}$$
$$S_v = \{(\overline{y} + v), (\overline{u} + v), (\overline{w} + x + v)\}$$
$$S_{\overline{v}} = \{(\overline{v} + y + u), (\overline{v} + w)\}$$
$$S_w = \{(w), (\overline{x} + w), (\overline{v} + w)\}$$
$$S_{\overline{w}} = \{(\overline{w} + x + v)\}$$

Figure 29. Positive and negative occurrences of literals

Solution Assume that the first unsatisfiable core we obtain is $\{(\overline{x} + \overline{y}), (x), (y)\}$. Accordingly, we augment the clauses (x) and (y) with relaxation variables and introduce a cardinality constraint which guarantees that at most one of these clauses is dropped:

$$(\overline{x} + \overline{y}) \cdot (\overline{x} + z) \cdot (\overline{x} + \overline{z}) \cdot (\overline{y} + u) \cdot (\overline{y} + \overline{u}) \cdot (r + x) \cdot (s + y) \cdot \sum (r, s) \leq 1$$

As illustrated in Figure 14, we can encode the constraint $\sum (r, s) \leq 1$ as $(\overline{r} + \overline{s})$, and we obtain the instance

$$(\overline{x} + \overline{y}) \cdot (\overline{x} + z) \cdot (\overline{x} + \overline{z}) \cdot (\overline{y} + u) \cdot (\overline{y} + \overline{u}) \cdot (r + x) \cdot (s + y) \cdot (\overline{r} + \overline{s}),$$

which is still unsatisfiable, since

$$\text{Res}((\overline{x} + z), (\overline{x} + \overline{z}), z) = (\overline{x}),$$
$$\text{Res}((\overline{y} + u), (\overline{y} + \overline{u}), u) = (\overline{y}),$$
$$\text{Res}((r + x), (\overline{r} + \overline{s}), r) = (\overline{s} + x),$$
$$\text{Res}((s + y), (\overline{s} + x), s) = (x + y),$$
$$\text{Res}((\overline{y}), (x + y), y) = (x),$$
$$\text{Res}((\overline{x}), (x), x) = \square$$

Accordingly, we add additional relaxation variables to the clauses $(r + x)$ and $(s + y)$ in the next iteration of the algorithm in Figure 15 and obtain

$$(\overline{x} + \overline{y}) \cdot (\overline{x} + z) \cdot (\overline{x} + \overline{z}) \cdot (\overline{y} + u) \cdot (\overline{y} + \overline{u}) \cdot (t + r + x) \cdot (v + s + y) \cdot \underbrace{(\overline{r} + \overline{s}) \cdot (\overline{t} + \overline{v})}_{\text{cardinality constraints}}$$

It is now possible for the satisfiability solver to relax both clauses (x) and (y) by choosing the assignment $\{t \mapsto 1, r \mapsto 0, v \mapsto 0, s \mapsto 1\}$, for instance. Accordingly, the algorithm in Figure 15 reports that two clauses need to be dropped to make the formula satisfiable.

Exercise 12 *Use the algorithm presented in Section 4.4 to derive all minimal correction sets for the unsatisfiable formula*

$$\overbrace{(x)}^{C_1} \cdot \overbrace{(\overline{x})}^{C_2} \cdot \overbrace{(\overline{x} + y)}^{C_3} \cdot \overbrace{(\overline{y})}^{C_4} \cdot \overbrace{(\overline{x} + z)}^{C_5} \cdot \overbrace{(\overline{z})}^{C_6} .$$

Solution   (This example is presented in [LS08].) Due to the prioritisation of unit clauses, the first unsatisfiable core reported by the satisfiability checker is $UC_1 \equiv \{(x), (\overline{x})\}$. By adding relaxation variables to all clauses of this core and by constraining the respective relaxation literals, we obtain the formula

$$(r_1 + x) \cdot (r_2 + \overline{x}) \cdot (\overline{x} + y) \cdot (\overline{y}) \cdot (\overline{x} + z) \cdot (\overline{z}) \cdot (\overline{r_1} + \overline{r_2})$$

Since dropping the clause $(\overline{x})$ does not yield a satisfiable instance, the ALLSAT procedure returns C_1 as the only MCS of size one. Accordingly, we block the corresponding assignment by adding the blocking clause $(\overline{r_1})$:

$$(r_1 + x) \cdot (r_2 + \overline{x}) \cdot (\overline{x} + y) \cdot (\overline{y}) \cdot (\overline{x} + z) \cdot (\overline{z}) \cdot (\overline{r_1} + \overline{r_2}) \cdot (\overline{r_1})$$

and obtain a new core $\{(\overline{r_1}), (r_1 + x), (\overline{x} + y), (\overline{y})\}$. Accordingly, $UC_2 = \{C_1, C_2\} \cup \{C_1, C_3, C_4\}$, and we obtain the instrumented formula

$$(r_1 + x) \cdot (r_2 + \overline{x}) \cdot (r_3 + \overline{x} + y) \cdot (r_4 + \overline{y}) \cdot (\overline{x} + z) \cdot (\overline{z}) \cdot (\overline{r_1}) \cdot \sum (r_1, r_2, r_3, r_4) \leq 2$$

The ALLSAT algorithm determines all minimal correction sets for this formula. Note that the clause $(\overline{r_1})$ prevents that the algorithm rediscovers the MCS $\{C_1\}$ in this step. Since $\mathrm{Res}((\overline{r_1}), (r_1 + x)) \equiv (x)$, blocking C_1 yields the formula

$$(x) \cdot (r_2 + \overline{x}) \cdot (r_3 + \overline{x} + y) \cdot (r_4 + \overline{y}) \cdot (\overline{x} + z) \cdot (\overline{z}) \cdot \sum (r_1, r_2, r_3, r_4) \leq 2,$$

which is unsatisfiable. We obtain the new core $\{C_1, C_5, C_6\}$ and execute the third iteration of the algorithm with $UC_3 = \{C_1, C_2, C_3, C_4\} \cup \{C_1, C_5, C_6\}$. The corresponding instrumented and constrained version of the original formula is

$$(r_1 + x) \cdot (r_2 + \overline{x}) \cdot (r_3 + \overline{x} + y) \cdot (r_4 + \overline{y}) \cdot (r_5 + \overline{x} + z) \cdot (r_6 + \overline{z}) \cdot$$

$$\sum (r_1, r_2, r_3, r_4, r_5, r_6) \leq 3$$

In this iteration, we obtain the MCSes $\{C_2, C_3, C_5\}$, $\{C_2, C_3, C_6\}$, $\{C_2, C_4, C_5\}$, and $\{C_2, C_3, C_6\}$. Adding the corresponding blocking clauses to INSTRUMENT(F) results in an unsatisfiable instance and the algorithm terminates.

Exercise 13 *Derive all minimal unsatisfiable cores for the formula presented in Exercise 12.*

Solution   The set of MCSes for the formula in Exercise 12 is

$$\{\{C_1\}, \{C_2, C_3, C_5\}, \{C_2, C_3, C_6\}, \{C_2, C_4, C_5\}, \{C_2, C_3, C_6\}\} \ .$$

We construct the corresponding minimal hitting sets as follows:

MCSes(F)	C_1	C_2	C_3	C_4	C_5	C_6
$\{C_1\}$	×					
$\{C_2, C_3, C_5\}$		×	×		×	
$\{C_2, C_3, C_6\}$		×	×			×
$\{C_2, C_4, C_5\}$		×		×	×	
$\{C_2, C_3, C_6\}$		×		×		×

Hitting sets: $\{C_1, C_2\}, \{C_1, C_3, C_4\}, \{C_1, C_5, C_6\}$

References

[AB09]   Sanjeev Arora and Boaz Barak. *Computational Complexity: A Modern Approach*. Cambridge University Press, 1st edition, 2009.

[ABF90]   Miron Abramovici, Melvin A. Breuer, and Arthur D. Friedman. *Digital systems testing and testable design*. Computer Science Press, 1990.

[AKS83]   M. Ajtai, J. Komlós, and E. Szemerédi. An $O(n \log n)$ sorting network. In *ACM Symposium on Theory of Computing (STOC)*, pages 1–9. ACM, 1983.

[BCCZ99]   Armin Biere, Alessandro Cimatti, Edmund M. Clarke, and Yunshan Zhu. Symbolic model checking without BDDs. In *Tools and Algorithms for the Construction and Analysis of Systems (TACAS)*, volume 1579 of *Lecture Notes in Computer Science*, pages 193–207. Springer, 1999.

[BHM+10]   Angelo Brillout, Nannan He, Michele Mazzucchi, Daniel Kroening, Mitra Purandare, Philipp Rümmer, and Georg Weissenbacher. Mutation-based test case generation for Simulink models. In *Formal Methods for Components and Objects (FMCO) 2009*, volume 6286 of *Lecture Notes in Computer Science*, pages 208–227. Springer, 2010.

[BIFH+11]   Omer Bar-Ilan, Oded Fuhrmann, Shlomo Hoory, Ohad Shacham, and Ofer Strichman. Reducing the size of resolution proofs in linear time. *Software Tools for Technology Transfer (STTT)*, 13(3):263–272, 2011.

[Bus98]   Samuel R. Buss. *Handbook of proof theory*. Studies in logic and the foundations of mathematics. Elsevier, 1998.

[CFR+91]   Ron Cytron, Jeanne Ferrante, Barry K. Rosen, Mark N. Wegman, and F. Kenneth Zadeck. Efficiently computing static single assignment form and the control dependence graph. *ACM Transactions on Programming Languages and Systems (TOPLAS)*, 13(4):451–490, 1991.

[CGP99]   Edmund Clarke, Orna Grumberg, and Doron Peled. *Model Checking*. MIT Press, December 1999.

[CKL04]   Edmund M. Clarke, Daniel Kroening, and Flavio Lerda. A tool for checking ANSI-C programs. In *Tools and Algorithms for the Construction and Analysis of Systems (TACAS)*, volume 2988 of *Lecture Notes in Computer Science*, pages 168–176. Springer, 2004.

[Coo71]   Stephen A. Cook. The complexity of theorem-proving procedures. In *ACM Symposium on Theory of Computing (STOC)*, pages 151–158. ACM, 1971.

[CSMSV10]   Yibin Chen, Sean Safarpour, Joao Marques-Silva, and Andreas Veneris. Automated design debugging with maximum satisfiability. *Transactions on CAD of Integrated Circuits and Systems*, 29:1804–1817, 2010.

[CSVMS09]   Yibin Chen, Sean Safarpour, Andreas Veneris, and Joao Marques-Silva. Spatial and temporal design debug using partial MaxSAT. In *Great Lakes Symposium on VLSI*, pages 345–350. ACM, 2009.

[DKW08]   Vijay D'Silva, Daniel Kroening, and Georg Weissenbacher. A survey of automated techniques for formal software verification. *Transactions on Computer-Aided Design of Integrated Circuits and Systems (TCAD)*, 27(7):1165–1178, July 2008.

[DLL62]   Martin Davis, George Logemann, and Donald Loveland. A machine program for theorem-proving. *Communications of the ACM*, 5:394–397, July 1962.

[DP60]   Martin Davis and Hilary Putnam. A computing procedure for quantification theory. *Journal of the ACM*, 7:201–214, July 1960.

[EB05]   Niklas Eén and Armin Biere. Effective preprocessing in SAT through variable and clause elimination. In *Theory and Applications of Satisfiability Testing (SAT)*, volume 3569 of *Lecture Notes in Computer Science*, pages 102–104. Springer, 2005.

[ES04a]   Niklas Eén and Niklas Sörensson. An extensible SAT-solver. In *Theory and Applications of Satisfiability Testing (SAT)*, volume 2919, pages 502–518. Springer, 2004.

[ES04b]   Niklas Eén and Niklas Sörensson. An extensible SAT-solver. In *Theory and Applications of Satisfiability Testing (SAT)*, volume 2919 of *Lecture Notes in Computer Science*, pages 333–336. Springer, 2004.

[FM06]   Zhaohui Fu and Sharad Malik. On solving the partial MAX-SAT problem. In *Theory and Applications of Satisfiability Testing (SAT)*, volume 4121 of *Lecture Notes in Computer Science*, pages 252–265. Springer, 2006.

[FSBD08]   Görschwin Fey, Stefan Staber, Roderick Bloem, and Rolf Drechsler. Automatic fault localization for property checking. *Transactions on CAD of Integrated Circuits and Systems*, 27(6):1138–1149, 2008.

[GN02]   E. Goldberg and Y. Novikov. Berkmin: A fast and robust SAT-solver. In *Design Automation and Test in Europe (DATE)*, pages 142–149. IEEE, 2002.

[GOMS04]   Éric Grégoire, Richard Ostrowski, Bertrand Mazure, and Lakhdar Saïs. Automatic extraction of functional dependencies. In *Theory and Applications of Satisfiability Testing (SAT)*, volume 3542 of *Lecture Notes in Computer Science*. Springer, 2004.

[Har09]   John Harrison. *Handbook of Practical Logic and Automated Reasoning*. Cambridge University Press, 2009.

[HSTV08]   Andreas Holzer, Christian Schallhart, Michael Tautschnig, and Helmut Veith. FShell: Systematic test case generation for dynamic analysis and measurement. In *Computer Aided Verification (CAV)*, volume 5123 of *Lecture Notes in Computer Science*, pages 209–213. Springer, 2008.

[HSTV09]   Andreas Holzer, Christian Schallhart, Michael Tautschnig, and Helmut Veith. Query-driven program testing. In *Verification, Model Checking and Abstract Interpretation (VMCAI)*, volume 5403 of *Lecture Notes in Computer Science*, pages 151–166. Springer, 2009.

[JM11]   Manu Jose and Rupak Majumdar. Cause clue clauses: error localization using maximum satisfiability. In *Programming Language Design and Implementation (PLDI)*, pages 437–446. ACM, 2011.

[JS97]   Roberto J. Bayardo Jr. and Robert Schrag. Using CSP look-back techniques to solve real-world SAT instances. In *Innovative Applications of Artificial Intelligence Conference (AAAI/IAAI)*, pages 203–208, 1997.

[Kar72]   Richard M. Karp. Reducibility among combinatorial problems. *Complexity of Computer Computations*, pages 85–103, 1972.

[Kin70]   James C. King. *A program verifier*. PhD thesis, Carnegie Mellon University, Pittsburgh, PA, USA, 1970.

[Kro67]   M. R. Krom. The decision problem for a class of first-order formulas in which all disjunctions are binary. *Mathematical Logic Quarterly*, 13(1-2):15–20, 1967.

[KS08]   Daniel Kroening and Ofer Strichman. *Decision procedures: An algorithmic point of view*. Texts in Theoretical Computer Science (EATCS). Springer, 2008.

[KSW01]   Joonyoung Kim, Karem Sakallah, and Jesse Whittemore. SATIRE: A new incremental satisfiability engine. In *Design Automation Conference (DAC)*, pages 542–545. IEEE, 2001.

[LS08]   Mark H. Liffiton and Karem A. Sakallah. Algorithms for computing minimal unsatisfiable subsets of constraints. *Journal of Automated Reasoning*, 40(1):1–33, 2008.

[LS09]   Mark H. Liffiton and Karem A. Sakallah. Generalizing core-guided MAX-SAT. In *Theory and Applications of Satisfiability Testing (SAT)*, volume 5584 of *Lecture Notes in Computer Science*, pages 481–494. Springer, 2009.

[McM02]   Kenneth L. McMillan. Applying SAT methods in unbounded symbolic model checking. In *Computer Aided Verification (CAV)*, volume 2404 of *Lecture Notes in Computer Science*, pages 250–264. Springer, 2002.

[McM03]   Kenneth L. McMillan. Interpolation and SAT-based model checking. In *Computer Aided Verification (CAV)*, volume 2725 of *Lecture Notes in Computer Science*, pages 1–13. Springer, 2003.

[MPLMS08]   Paulo J. Matos, Jordi Planes, Florian Letombe, and João Marques-Silva. A MAX-SAT algorithm portfolio. In *European Conference on Artificial Intelligence*, volume 178 of *Frontiers in Artificial Intelligence and Applications*, pages 911–912. IOS Press, 2008.

[MS95]   João Paulo Marques-Silva. *Search algorithms for satisfiability problems in combinational switching circuits.* PhD thesis, University of Michigan, 1995.

[MS99]   João P. Marques-Silva. The impact of branching heuristics in propositional satisfiability algorithms. In *Progress in Artificial Intelligence, (EPIA)*, volume 1695 of *Lecture Notes in Computer Science*, pages 62–74. Springer, 1999.

[MSP08]   João Marques-Silva and Jordi Planes. Algorithms for maximum satisfiability using unsatisfiable cores. In *Design Automation and Test in Europe (DATE)*, pages 408–413. IEEE, 2008.

[MSS96]   João Paulo Marques-Silva and Karem A. Sakallah. GRASP – a new search algorithm for satisfiability. In *International Conference on Computer-aided Design (ICCAD)*, pages 220–227. IEEE, 1996.

[MZ09]   Sharad Malik and Lintao Zhang. Boolean satisfiability from theoretical hardness to practical success. *Communications of the ACM*, 52(8):76–82, 2009.

[MZM$^+$01]   Sharad Malik, Ying Zhao, Conor F. Madigan, Lintao Zhang, and Matthew W. Moskewicz. Chaff: Engineering an efficient SAT solver. *Design Automation Conference (DAC)*, pages 530–535, 2001.

[Par92]   Ian Parberry. The pairwise sorting network. *Parallel Processing Letters*, 2:205–211, 1992.

[Rob65]   J. A. Robinson. A machine-oriented logic based on the resolution principle. *Journal of the ACM*, 12:23–41, January 1965.

[SFBD08]   Andre Sülflow, Görschwin Fey, Roderick Bloem, and Rolf Drechsler. Using unsatisfiable cores to debug multiple design errors. In *Great Lakes Symposium on VLSI*, pages 77–82. ACM, 2008.

[Sha49]   Claude E. Shannon. The synthesis of two-terminal switching circuits. *Bell Systems Technical Journal*, 28:59–98, 1949.

[SMV$^+$07]   Sean Safarpour, Hratch Mangassarian, Andreas G. Veneris, Mark H. Liffiton, and Karem A. Sakallah. Improved design debugging using maximum satisfiability. In *Formal Methods in Computer-Aided Design (FMCAD)*, pages 13–19. IEEE, 2007.

[Str01]   Ofer Strichman. Pruning techniques for the SAT-based bounded model checking problem. In *Correct Hardware Design and Verification Methods (CHARME)*, volume 2144 of *Lecture Notes in Computer Science*, pages 58–70. Springer, 2001.

[Tse83]   G. Tseitin. On the complexity of proofs in poropositional logics. In J. Siekmann and G. Wrightson, editors, *Automation of Reasoning: Classical Papers in Computational Logic 1967–1970*, volume 2. Springer, 1983. Originally published 1970.

[Zha97]   Hantao Zhang. SATO: An efficient propositional prover. In *Conference on Automated Deduction (CADE)*, volume 1249 of *Lecture Notes in Computer Science*, pages 272–275. Springer, 1997.

[Zha03]   Lintao Zhang. *Searching the Truth: Techniques for Satisfiability of Boolean Formulas.* PhD thesis, Princeton University, 2003.

[ZMMM01]   Lintao Zhang, Conor F. Madigan, Matthew W. Moskewicz, and Sharad Malik. Efficient conflict driven learning in boolean satisfiability solver. In *International Conference on Computer-aided Design (ICCAD)*, pages 279–285, 2001.

[ZWM11]   Charlie Shucheng Zhu, Georg Weissenbacher, and Sharad Malik. Post-silicon fault localisation using maximum satisfiability and backbones. In *Formal Methods in Computer-Aided Design (FMCAD)*. IEEE, 2011.

Software Safety and Security
T. Nipkow et al. (Eds.)
IOS Press, 2012
© 2012 The authors and IOS Press. All rights reserved.
doi:10.3233/978-1-61499-028-4-254

Interactive Proof:
Introduction to Isabelle/HOL

Tobias NIPKOW

Technische Universität München

Abstract. This paper introduces interactive theorem proving with the Isabelle/HOL system [3]. The following topics are covered:

- Verified functional programming: The logic HOL contains an ML-style functional programming language. It is shown how to verify functional programs in this language by induction and simplification.
- Predicate logic: Formulas of predicate logic and set theory are introduced, together with methods for proof automation.
- Inductively defined predicates.
- Structured proofs: We introduce the proof language Isar and show how to write structured proofs that are readable by both the machine and the human.

We assume basic familiarity with some functional programming language of the ML or Haskell family, in particular with recursive data types and pattern matching. No specific background in logic is necessary beyond the ability to read predicate logic formulas.

Keywords. Semantics, Theorem Proving, Isabelle.

1. Introduction

Isabelle is a generic system for implementing logical formalisms, and Isabelle/HOL is the specialization of Isabelle for HOL, which abbreviates Higher-Order Logic. We introduce HOL step by step following the equation

$$HOL = \text{Functional Programming} + \text{Logic}.$$

We assume that the reader is familiar with the basic concepts of functional programming and is used to logical and set theoretic notation.

Section §3 introduces HOL as a functional programming language and explains how to write simple inductive proofs of mostly equational properties of recursive functions. Section §4 covers the full logic, sets and automatic proof tools. Section §5 explains inductive definitions. Section §6 introduces Isabelle's full language for writing structured proofs.

2. Basics

2.1. Types, Terms and Formulae

HOL is a typed logic whose type system resembles that of functional programming languages. Thus there are

base types, in particular `bool`, the type of truth values, `nat`, the type of natural numbers, and `int`, the type of integers.
type constructors, in particular `list`, the type of lists, and `set`, the type of sets. Type constructors are written postfix, e.g. `nat list` is the type of lists whose elements are natural numbers.
function types, denoted by ⇒.
type variables, denoted by `'a`, `'b` etc., just like in ML.

Terms are formed as in functional programming by applying functions to arguments. If `f` is a function of type $\tau_1 \Rightarrow \tau_2$ and `t` is a term of type τ_1 then `f t` is a term of type τ_2. We write `t :: τ` to mean that term `t` has type τ.

> There are many predefined infix symbols like + and ≤. The name of the corresponding binary function is `op +`, not just `+`. That is, `x + y` is syntactic sugar for `op + x y`.

HOL also supports some basic constructs from functional programming:

```
(if b then t₁ else t₂)
(let x = t in u)
(case t of pat₁ ⇒ t₁ | ... | patₙ ⇒ tₙ)
```

> The above three constructs must always be enclosed in parentheses if they sit inside other constructs.

Terms may also contain λ-abstractions. For example, $\lambda x. \ x$ is the identity function.

Formulae are terms of type `bool`. There are the basic constants `True` and `False` and the usual logical connectives (in decreasing order of precedence): ¬, ∧, ∨, ⟶.

Equality is available in the form of the infix function = of type `'a ⇒ 'a ⇒ bool`. It also works for formulas, where it means "if and only if".

Quantifiers are written ∀ x. P and ∃ x. P.

Isabelle automatically computes the type of each variable in a term. This is called *type inference*. Despite type inference, it is sometimes necessary to attach explicit *type constraints* (or *type annotations*) to a variable or term. The syntax is `t :: τ` as in `m < (n::nat)`. Type constraints may be needed to disambiguate terms involving overloaded functions such as +, * and ≤.

Finally there are the universal quantifier ⋀ and the implication ⟹. They are part of the Isabelle framework, not the logic HOL. Logically, they agree with their HOL counterparts ∀ and ⟶, but operationally they behave differently. This will become clearer as we go along.

> Right-arrows of all kinds always associate to the right. In particular, $A_1 \Longrightarrow A_2 \Longrightarrow A_3$ means $A_1 \Longrightarrow (A_2 \Longrightarrow A_3)$. The notation ⟦ A_1; ...; A_n ⟧ ⟹ A is short for the iterated implication $A_1 \Longrightarrow ... \Longrightarrow A_n \Longrightarrow A$. Sometimes we also employ inference rule notation: $$\frac{A_1 \quad ... \quad A_n}{A}$$

2.2. Theories

Roughly speaking, a *theory* is a named collection of types, functions, and theorems, much like a module in a programming language. The general format of a theory T is

```
theory T
imports T₁ ... Tₙ
begin
definitions, theorems and proofs
end
```

where $T_1 \ldots T_n$ are the names of existing theories that T is based on. The T_i are the direct *parent theories* of T. Everything defined in the parent theories (and their parents, recursively) is automatically visible. Each theory t must reside in a *theory file* named `T.thy`.

‼ HOL contains a theory `Main`, the union of all the basic predefined theories like arithmetic, lists, sets, etc. Unless you know what you are doing, always include `Main` as a direct or indirect parent of all your theories.

In addition to the theories that come with the Isabelle/HOL distribution (see isabelle.in. tum.de/library/HOL/) there is also the *Archive of Formal Proofs* at afp.sourceforge.net, a growing collection of Isabelle theories that everybody can contribute to.

3. Programming and Proving

This section introduces HOL as a functional programming language and shows how to prove properties of functional programs by induction. Our approach is mostly example-based: We concentrate on examples that cover the typical cases and do not explain the general case if it can be inferred from the examples.

We start by examining the the most important predefined types.

3.1. Types `bool`, `nat` and `list`

3.1.1. Type `bool`

The type of boolean values is a predefined data type

```
datatype bool = True | False
```

with many predefined functions: $\neg$, $\wedge$, $\vee$, $\longrightarrow$ etc. Here is how conjunction could be defined by pattern matching:

```
fun conj :: "bool ⇒ bool ⇒ bool" where
"conj True True = True" |
"conj _ _ = False"
```

Both the data type and function definitions roughly follow the syntax of functional programming languages.

3.1.2. Type nat

Natural numbers are another predefined data type:

```
datatype nat = 0 | Suc nat
```

with many predefined functions: $+$, $*$, $\leq$, etc. And this is how you could define your own addition:

```
fun add :: "nat ⇒ nat ⇒ nat" where
"add 0 n = n" |
"add (Suc m) n = Suc(add m n)"
```

And here is a proof of the fact that $add\ m\ 0 = m$:

```
lemma add_02: "add m 0 = m"
apply(induct m)
apply(auto)
done
```

The **lemma** command starts the proof and gives the lemma a name, add_02. Properties of recursively defined functions need to be established by induction in most cases. Command **apply** $(induct\ m)$ instructs Isabelle to start a proof by induction on m. In response, it will show the following proof state:

```
1. add 0 0 = 0
2. ⋀m. add m 0 = m ⟹ add (Suc m) 0 = Suc m
```

The numbered lines are known as *subgoals*. The first subgoal is the base case, the second one the induction step. The prefix $\bigwedge m$. is Isabelle's way of saying "for an arbitrary but fixed m". The $\Longrightarrow$ separates assumptions from the conclusion. The command **apply** $(auto)$ instructs Isabelle to try and prove all subgoals automatically, essentially by simplifying them. Because both subgoals are easy, Isabelle can do it. The base case $add\ 0\ 0 = 0$ holds by definition of add, and the induction step is almost as simple: $add\ (Suc\ m)\ 0 = Suc(add\ m\ 0) = Suc\ m$ using first the definition of add and then the induction hypothesis. In summary, both proofs rely on simplification with function definitions and the induction hypothesis. The final **done** is like a "QED" (and would fail if there were unproved subgoals). As a result of that final **done**, Isabelle associates the lemma just proved with its name. You can now inspect the lemma with the command

```
thm add_02
```

which displays

```
add ?m 0 = ?m
```

The free variable m has been replaced by the *unknown* $?m$. There is no logical difference between the two but an operational one: unknowns can be instantiated, which is what you want after some lemma has been proved.

‼ Terminology: We use *lemma*, *theorem* and *rule* interchangeably for propositions that have been proved.

‼ Numerals (0, 1, 2, ...) and most of the standard arithmetic operations ($+$, $-$, $*$, $\leq$, $<$ etc)
are overloaded: they are available not just for natural numbers but for other types as well.
For example, given the goal $x + 0 = x$, there is nothing to indicate that you are talking about
natural numbers. Hence Isabelle can only infer that x is of some arbitrary type where 0 and $+$ exist.
As a consequence, you will be unable to prove the goal. To alert you to such pitfalls, Isabelle flags
numerals without a fixed type in its output: $x + (0::'a) = x$. In this particular example, you
need to include an explicit type constraint, for example $x+0 = (x::nat)$. If there is enough
contextual information this may not be necessary: `Suc x = x` automatically implies `x::nat`
because `Suc` is not overloaded.

3.1.3. Type `list`

Although lists are already predefined, we define our own copy just for demonstration
purposes:

```
datatype 'a list = Nil | Cons "'a" "'a list"
```

Similarly for two standard functions, append and reverse:

```
fun app :: "'a list ⇒ 'a list ⇒ 'a list" where
"app Nil ys = ys" |
"app (Cons x xs) ys = Cons x (app xs ys)"

fun rev :: "'a list ⇒ 'a list" where
"rev Nil = Nil" |
"rev (Cons x xs) = app (rev xs) (Cons x Nil)"
```

Command **value** evaluates a term. For example,

```
value "rev(Cons True (Cons False Nil))"
```

yields the result `Cons False (Cons True Nil)`. This works symbolically, too:

```
value "rev(Cons a (Cons b Nil))"
```

yields `Cons b (Cons a Nil)`.

Proofs by induction on lists are essentially proofs over the length of the list, although
the length remains implicit. To prove that some property P holds for all lists xs, i.e.
P xs, you need to prove

1. the base case P `Nil` and
2. the inductive case P `(Cons x xs)` under the assumption P xs, for some arbitrary but fixed xs.

This is often called *structural induction*.

We will now demonstrate the typical proof process, which involves the formulation
and proof of auxiliary lemmas.

3.1.4. Theorem `rev (rev xs) = xs`

Our goal is to show that reversing a list twice produces the original list.

theorem `rev_rev [simp]: "rev(rev xs) = xs"`

Commands **theorem** and **lemma** are interchangeable and merely indicate the importance we attach to a proposition. Via the bracketed attribute `simp` we also tell Isabelle to make the eventual theorem a *simplification rule*: future proofs involving simplification will replace occurrences of `rev (rev xs)` by `xs`. The proof is by induction:

apply `(induct xs)`

As explained above, we obtain two subgoals, namely the base case (`Nil`) and the induction step (`Cons`):

```
1. rev (rev Nil) = Nil
2. ⋀a xs. rev (rev xs) = xs ⟹ rev (rev (Cons a xs)) = Cons a xs
```

Let us try to solve both goals automatically:

apply `(auto)`

Subgoal 1 is proved, and disappears; the simplified version of subgoal 2 becomes the new subgoal 1:

```
1. ⋀a xs.
      rev (rev xs) = xs ⟹
      rev (app (rev xs) (Cons a Nil)) = Cons a xs
```

In order to simplify this subgoal further, a lemma suggests itself.

3.1.5. Lemma `rev (app xs ys) = app (rev ys) (rev xs)`

We insert the following lemma in front of the main theorem:

lemma `rev_app [simp]: "rev(app xs ys) = app (rev ys) (rev xs)"`

There are two variables that we could induct on: `xs` and `ys`. Because `app` is defined by recursion on the first argument, `xs` is the correct one:

apply `(induct xs)`

This time not even the base case is solved automatically:

apply `(auto)`

```
1. rev ys = app (rev ys) Nil
```

Again, we need to abandon this proof attempt and prove another simple lemma first.

3.1.6. *Lemma* `app xs Nil = xs`

We again try the canonical proof procedure:

```
lemma app_Nil2 [simp]: "app xs Nil = xs"
apply(induct xs)
apply(auto)
done
```

Thankfully, this worked. Now we can continue with our stuck proof attempt of the first lemma:

```
lemma rev_app [simp]: "rev(app xs ys) = app (rev ys) (rev xs)"
apply(induct xs)
apply(auto)
```

We find that this time `auto` solves the base case, but the induction step merely simplifies to

```
1. ⋀a xs.
        rev (app xs ys) = app (rev ys) (rev xs) ⟹
        app (app (rev ys) (rev xs)) (Cons a Nil) =
        app (rev ys) (app (rev xs) (Cons a Nil))
```

The the missing lemma is associativity of `app`, which we insert in front of the failed lemma `rev_app`.

3.1.7. *Associativity of* `app`

The canonical proof procedure succeeds without further ado:

```
lemma app_assoc [simp]: "app (app xs ys) zs = app xs (app ys zs)"
apply(induct xs)
apply(auto)
done
```

Finally the proofs of `rev_app` and `rev_rev` succeed, too.

3.1.8. *Predefined lists*

Isabelle's predefined lists are the same as the ones above, but with

- more syntactic sugar:
  * `[]` for `Nil`,
  * `x # xs` for `Cons x xs`,
  * `[x₁, ..., xₙ]` for x_1 `#` ... `#` x_n `#` `[]`, and
  * `xs @ ys` for `app xs ys`,

- and a large library of functions like `length`, `map`, `filter` etc.

3.2. Type and function definitions

3.2.1. Type synonyms

Type synonyms are abbreviations for existing types, for example

type_synonym `string = "char list"`

Type synonyms are expanded after parsing and are not present in internal representation and output. They are mere conveniences for the reader.

3.2.2. Datatypes

The general form of a datatype definition looks like this:

$$\textbf{datatype } ('a_1, \ldots, 'a_n)\, t \;=\; C_1 \; "\tau_{1,1}" \ldots "\tau_{1,n_1}"$$
$$| \quad \ldots$$
$$| \quad C_k \; "\tau_{k,1}" \ldots "\tau_{k,n_k}"$$

The double quotes are not not necessary for simple identifiers like `nat` or `'a`.

This definition introduces the constructors $C_i :: \tau_{i,1} \Rightarrow \cdots \Rightarrow \tau_{i,n_i} \Rightarrow ('a_1, \ldots, 'a_n)\, t$ which obey

- *Distinctness:* $C_i \ldots \neq C_j \ldots$ if $i \neq j$
- *Injectivity:* $(C_i\, x_1 \ldots x_{n_i} = C_i\, y_1 \ldots y_{n_i}) = (x_1 = y_1 \wedge \ldots \wedge x_{n_i} = y_{n_i})$

The datatype also comes with a structural induction rule: to show Px for all x of type $('a_1, \ldots, 'a_n)\, t$, one needs to show $P(C_i\, x_1 \ldots x_{n_i})$ (for each i) assuming $P(x_j)$ for all j where $\tau_{i,j} = ('a_1, \ldots, 'a_n)\, t$. Distinctness and injectivity are applied automatically by `auto` and other proof methods. Induction must be applied explicitly.

Datatypes values can be taken apart with case-expressions, for example

```
(case xs of [] ⇒ 0 | x # _ ⇒ Suc x)
```

just like in functional programming languages. Case expressions must be enclosed in parentheses.

As an example, consider binary trees:

datatype `'a tree = Tip | Node "'a tree" 'a "'a tree"`

with a mirror function:

```
fun mirror :: "'a tree ⇒ 'a tree" where
"mirror Tip = Tip" |
"mirror (Node l a r) = Node (mirror r) a (mirror l)"
```

The following lemma illustrates induction:

```
lemma "mirror(mirror t) = t"
apply (induct t)
```

yields

```
1. mirror (mirror Tip) = Tip
2. ⋀t1 a t2.
      ⟦mirror (mirror t1) = t1; mirror (mirror t2) = t2⟧
      ⟹ mirror (mirror (Node t1 a t2)) = Node t1 a t2
```

The induction step contains two induction hypotheses, one for each subtree. An application of `auto` finishes the proof.

3.2.3. Definitions

Non recursive functions can be defined as in the following example:

definition `sq :: "nat ⇒ nat"` **where**
`"sq n = n*n"`

Such definitions do not allow pattern matching but only `f x₁ ... xₙ = t`, where `f` does not occur in `t`.

3.2.4. Recursive functions

Recursive functions are defined with **fun** by pattern matching over datatype constructors. The order of equations matters. Just as in functional programming languages. However, all HOL functions must be total. This simplifies the logic—terms are always defined—but means that recursive functions must terminate. Otherwise one could define a function `f n = f n + 1` and conclude `0 = 1` by subtracting `f n` on both sides.

   Isabelle automatic termination checker requires that the arguments of recursive calls on the right-hand side must be strictly smaller than the arguments on the left-hand side. In the simplest case, this means that one fixed argument position decreases in size with each recursive call. The size is measured as the number of constructors (excluding 0-ary ones, e.g. `Nil`). Lexicographic combinations are also recognised. In more complicated situations, the user may have to prove termination by hand. For details see [2].

   Functions defined with **fun** come with their own induction schema that mirrors the recursion schema and is derived from the termination order. For example,

fun `div2 :: "nat ⇒ nat"` **where**
`"div2 0 = 0" |`
`"div2 (Suc 0) = Suc 0" |`
`"div2 (Suc(Suc n)) = Suc(div2 n)"`

does not just define `div2` but also proves a customised induction rule:

$$\frac{P\ 0 \qquad P\ (Suc\ 0) \qquad \bigwedge n.\ P\ n \implies P\ (Suc\ (Suc\ n))}{P\ m}$$

This customised induction rule can simplify inductive proofs. For example,

lemma `"div2(n+n) = n"`
apply `(induct n rule: div2.induct)`

yields the 3 subgoals

```
1.  div2 (0 + 0) = 0
2.  div2 (Suc 0 + Suc 0) = Suc 0
3.  ⋀n. div2 (n + n) = n ⟹
           div2 (Suc (Suc n) + Suc (Suc n)) = Suc (Suc n)
```

An application of `auto` finishes the proof. Had we used ordinary structural induction on n, the proof would have needed an additional case distinction in the induction step.

The general case is often called *computation induction*, because the induction follows the (terminating!) computation. For every defining equation

```
f(e) = ... f(r₁) ... f(rₖ) ...
```

where $f(r_i)$, $i=1 \ldots k$, are all the recursive calls, the induction rule `f.induct` contains one premise of the form

```
P(r₁) ⟹ ... ⟹ P(rₖ) ⟹ P(e)
```

If $f :: \tau_1 \Rightarrow \ldots \Rightarrow \tau_n \Rightarrow \tau$ then `f.induct` is applied like this:

apply (induct x_1 ... x_n rule: f.induct)

where typically there is a call $f\ x_1 \ \ldots \ x_n$ in the goal. But note that the induction rule does not mention f at all, except in its name, and is applicable independently of f.

3.3. Induction heuristics

We have already noted that theorems about recursive functions are proved by induction. In case the function has more than one argument, we have followed the following heuristic in the proofs about the append function:

> *Perform induction on argument number i*
> *if the function is defined by recursion on argument number i.*

The key heuristic, and the main point of this section, is to *generalise the goal before induction*. The reason is simple: if the goal is too specific, the induction hypothesis is too weak to allow the induction step to go through. Let us illustrate the idea with an example.

Function `rev` has quadratic worst-case running time because it calls append for each element of the list and append is linear in its first argument. A linear time version of `rev` requires an extra argument where the result is accumulated gradually, using only #:

```
fun itrev :: "'a list ⇒ 'a list ⇒ 'a list" where
"itrev []     ys = ys" |
"itrev (x#xs) ys = itrev xs (x#ys)"
```

The behaviour of `itrev` is simple: it reverses its first argument by stacking its elements onto the second argument, and returning that second argument when the first one becomes empty. Note that `itrev` is tail-recursive: it can be compiled into a loop, no stack is necessary for executing it.

Naturally, we would like to show that `itrev` does indeed reverse its first argument provided the second one is empty:

```
lemma "itrev xs [] = rev xs"
```

There is no choice as to the induction variable:

```
apply (induct xs)
apply (auto)
```

Unfortunately, this attempt does not prove the induction step:

```
1. ⋀a xs. itrev xs [] = rev xs ⟹ itrev xs [a] = rev xs @ [a]
```

The induction hypothesis is too weak. The fixed argument, `[]`, prevents it from rewriting the conclusion. This example suggests a heuristic:

> *Generalise goals for induction by replacing constants by variables.*

Of course one cannot do this naïvely: `itrev xs ys = rev xs` is just not true. The correct generalisation is

```
lemma "itrev xs ys = rev xs @ ys"
```

If `ys` is replaced by `[]`, the right-hand side simplifies to `rev xs`, as required. In this instance it was easy to guess the right generalisation. Other situations can require a good deal of creativity.

Although we now have two variables, only `xs` is suitable for induction, and we repeat our proof attempt. Unfortunately, we are still not there:

```
1. ⋀a xs.
     itrev xs ys = rev xs @ ys ⟹
     itrev xs (a # ys) = rev xs @ a # ys
```

The induction hypothesis is still too weak, but this time it takes no intuition to generalise: the problem is that the `ys` in the induction hypothesis is fixed, but the induction hypothesis needs to be applied with `a # ys` instead of `ys`. Hence we prove the theorem for all `ys` instead of a fixed one. We can instruct induction to perform this generalisation for us by adding `arbitrary: ys`.

```
apply (induct xs arbitrary: ys)
```

The induction hypothesis in the induction step is now universally quantified over `ys`:

```
1. ⋀ys. itrev [] ys = rev [] @ ys
2. ⋀a xs ys.
     (⋀ys. itrev xs ys = rev xs @ ys) ⟹
     itrev (a # xs) ys = rev (a # xs) @ ys
```

Thus the proof succeeds:

```
apply auto
done
```

This leads to another heuristic for generalisation:

> *Generalise induction by generalising all free variables*
> (except the induction variable itself).

Generalisation is best performed with `arbitrary:` $y_1 \ldots y_k$. This heuristic prevents trivial failures like the one above. However, it should not be applied blindly. It is not always required, and the additional quantifiers can complicate matters in some cases. The variables that need to be quantified are typically those that change in recursive calls.

3.4. Simplification

So far we have talked a lot about simplifying terms without explaining the concept. *Simplification* means

- using equations $l = r$ from left to right (only),
- as long as possible.

To emphasise the directionality, equations that have been given the `simp` attribute are called *simplification* rules. Logically, they are still symmetric, but proofs by simplification use them only in the left-to-right direction. The proof tool that performs simplifications is called the *simplifier*. It is the basis of `auto` and other related proof methods.

The idea of simplification is best explained by an example. Given the simplification rules

$$
\begin{aligned}
0\ +\ n &= n & (1) \\
Suc\ m\ +\ n &= Suc\ (m\ +\ n) & (2) \\
(Suc\ m\ \leq\ Suc\ n) &= (m\ \leq\ n) & (3) \\
(0\ \leq\ m) &= True & (4)
\end{aligned}
$$

the formula $0\ +\ Suc\ 0 \leq Suc\ 0\ +\ x$ is simplified to `True` as follows:

$$
\begin{aligned}
(0\ +\ Suc\ 0\ \leq\ Suc\ 0\ +\ x) &\overset{(1)}{=} \\
(Suc\ 0\ \leq\ Suc\ 0\ +\ x) &\overset{(2)}{=} \\
(Suc\ 0\ \leq\ Suc\ (0\ +\ x)) &\overset{(3)}{=} \\
(0\ \leq\ 0\ +\ x) &\overset{(4)}{=} \\
True
\end{aligned}
$$

Simplification is often also called *rewriting* and simplification rules *rewrite rules*.

3.4.1. Simplification rules

The attribute `simp` declares theorems to be simplification rules, which the simplifier will use automatically. In addition, **datatype** and **fun** commands implicitly declare some simplification rules: **datatype** the distinctness and injectivity rules, **fun** the defining equations. Definitions are not declared as simplification rules automatically! Nearly any theorem can become a simplification rule. The simplifier will try to transform it into an equation. For example, the theorem $\neg\ P$ is turned into $P\ =\ False$.

Only equations that really simplify, like `rev (rev xs) = xs` and `xs @ [] = xs`, should be declared as simplification rules. Equations that may be counterproductive as simplification rules should only be used in specific proof steps (see §3.4.4 below). Distributivity laws, for example, alter the structure of terms and can produce an exponential blow-up.

3.4.2. Conditional simplification rules

Simplification rules can be conditional. Before applying such a rule, the simplifier will first try to prove the preconditions, again by simplification. For example, given the simplification rules

```
p 0 = True
p x ⟹ f x = g x,
```

the term `f 0` simplifies to `g 0` but `f 1` does not simplify because `p 1` is not provable.

3.4.3. Termination

Simplification can run forever, for example if both `f x = g x` and `g x = f x` are simplification rules. It is the user's responsibility not to include simplification rules that can lead to nontermination, either on their own or in combination with other simplification rules. The right-hand side of a simplification rule should always be "simpler" than the left-hand side—in some sense. But since termination is undecidable, such a check cannot be automated completely and Isabelle makes little attempt to detect nontermination.

 The case of conditional simplification rules is a bit more complicated. Because the preconditions are proved first, they also need to be simpler than the left-hand side of the conclusion. For example

```
n < m ⟹ (n < Suc m) = True
```

is suitable as a simplification rule: both `n < m` and `True` are simpler than `n < Suc m`. But

```
Suc n < m ⟹ (n < m) = True
```

leads to nontermination: when trying to rewrite `n < m` to `True` one first has to prove `Suc n < m`, which can be rewritten to `True` provided `Suc (Suc n) < m`, *ad infinitum*.

3.4.4. The `simp` proof method

So far we have only used the proof method `auto`. Method `simp` is the key component of `auto`, but `auto` can do much more. In some cases, `auto` is overeager and modifies the proof state too much. In such cases the more predictable `simp` method should be used. Given a goal

```
1. ⟦ P₁; …; Pₘ ⟧ ⟹ C
```

the command

apply (simp add: th₁ … thₙ)

simplifies the assumptions P_i and the conclusion C using

- all simplification rules, including the ones coming from **datatype** and **fun**,
- the additional lemmas th₁ … thₙ, and

- the assumptions.

In addition to or instead of `add` there is also `del` for removing simplification rules temporarily. Both are optional. Method `auto` can be modified similarly:

```
apply (auto simp add: ... simp del: ...)
```

Here the modifiers are `simp add` and `simp del` instead of just `add` and `del` because `auto` does not just perform simplification.

Note that `simp` acts only on subgoal 1, `auto` acts on all subgoals.

3.4.5. Rewriting with definitions

Definitions (**definition**) can be used as simplification rules, but by default they are not: the simplifier does not expand them automatically. Definitions are intended for introducing abstract concepts and not merely as abbreviations. Of course, we need to expand the definition initially, but once we have proved enough abstract properties of the new constant, we can forget its original definition. This style makes proofs more robust: if the definition has to be changed, only the proofs of the abstract properties will be affected.

The definition of a function `f` is a theorem named `f_def` and can be added to a call of `simp` just like any other theorem:

```
apply (simp add: f_def)
```

In particular, let-expressions can be unfolded by making `Let_def` a simplification rule.

3.4.6. Case splitting with `simp`

Goals containing if-expressions are automatically split into two cases by `simp` using the rule

```
P (if A then s else t) = ((A ⟶ P s) ∧ (¬ A ⟶ P t))
```

For example, `simp` can prove

```
(A ∧ B) = (if A then B else False)
```

because both $A \longrightarrow (A \wedge B) = B$ and $\neg A \longrightarrow (A \wedge B) =$ `False` simplify to `True`.

We can split case-expressions similarly. For `nat` the rule looks like this:

```
P (case e of 0 ⇒ a | Suc n ⇒ b n) =
((e = 0 ⟶ P a) ∧ (∀n. e = Suc n ⟶ P (b n)))
```

Case expressions are not split automatically by `simp`, but `simp` can be instructed to do so:

```
apply (simp split: nat.split)
```

splits all case-expressions over natural numbers. For an arbitrary datatype `t` it is `t.split` instead of `nat.split`. Method `auto` can be modified in exactly the same way.

4. Logic and Proof Beyond Equality

4.1. Formulas

The basic syntax of formulas (*form* below) provides the standard logical constructs, in decreasing precedence:

$$form ::= (form) \mid \texttt{True} \mid \texttt{False}$$
$$\mid\ term = term \mid \neg form \mid form \wedge form \mid form \vee form \mid form \longrightarrow form$$
$$\mid\ \forall x.\ form \mid \exists x.\ form$$

‼ Remember that formulas are simply terms of type `bool`. Hence = also works for formulas.
Beware that = has a higher precedence than the other logical operators. Hence $s = t \wedge A$ means $(s = t) \wedge A$. Logical equivalence can also be written with $\longleftrightarrow$ instead of =, where $\longleftrightarrow$ has the same low precedence as $\longrightarrow$.

‼ Quantifiers need to be enclosed in parentheses if they are nested within other constructs (just like `if`, `case` and `let`).

The most frequent logical symbols have the following ASCII representations:

$\forall$	`\<forall>`	`ALL`
$\exists$	`\<exists>`	`EX`
λ	`\<lambda>`	`%`
$\longrightarrow$	`-->`	
$\longleftrightarrow$	`<-->`	
$\wedge$	`/\`	`&`
$\vee$	`\/`	`|`
$\neg$	`\<not>`	`~`
$\neq$	`\<noteq>`	`~=`

The first column shows the symbols, the second column ASCII representations that Isabelle interfaces convert into the corresponding symbol, and the third column shows ASCII representations that stay fixed.

‼ The implication $\Longrightarrow$ is part of the Isabelle framework. It structures theorems and proof states, separating assumptions from conclusion. The implication $\longrightarrow$ is part of the logic HOL and can occur inside the formulas that make up the assumptions and conclusion. Theorems should be of the form $[\![\ A_1;\ \dots;\ A_n\ ]\!] \Longrightarrow A$, not $A_1 \wedge \dots \wedge A_n \longrightarrow A$. Both are logically equivalent but the first one works better when using the theorem in further proofs.

4.2. Sets

Sets are simply predicates, i.e. functions to `bool`:

type_synonym `'a set = "'a ⇒ bool"`

Sets come with the usual notations:

- $\{\}$, $\{e_1, \ldots, e_n\}$, $\{x.\ P\}$
- $e \in A$, $A \subseteq B$
- $A \cup B$, $A \cap B$, $A - B$, $- A$

and much more. Note that set comprehension is written $\{x.\ P\}$ rather than $\{x \mid P\}$ (to emphasise the variable binding nature of the construct). Here are the ASCII representations of the mathematical symbols:

$\in$	\<in>		:
$\subseteq$	\<subseteq>	<=
$\cup$	\<union>	Un
$\cap$	\<inter>	Int

Sets also allow bounded quantifications $\forall x \in A.\ P$ and $\exists x \in A.\ P$.

4.3. Proof automation

So far we have only seen *simp* and *auto*: Both perform rewriting, both can also prove linear arithmetic facts (no multiplication), and *auto* is also able to prove simple logical or set-theoretic goals:

```
lemma "∀x. ∃y. x = y"
by auto

lemma "A ⊆ B ∩ C ⟹ A ⊆ B ∪ C"
by auto
```

where

> **by** *proof-method*

is short for

> **apply** *proof-method*
> **done**

The key characteristics of both *simp* and *auto* are

- They show you were they got stuck, giving you an idea how to continue.
- They perform the obvious steps but are highly incomplete.

A proof method that is still incomplete but tries harder than *auto* is *fastforce*. It either succeeds or fails, it acts on the first subgoal only, and it can be modified just like *auto*, e.g. with *simp add*. Here is a typical example of what *fastforce* can do:

```
lemma "⟦ ∀xs ∈ A. ∃ys. xs = ys @ ys;   us ∈ A ⟧
    ⟹ ∃n. length us = n+n"
by fastforce
```

This lemma is out of reach for *auto* because of the quantifiers. But *fastforce* fails when the quantifier structure becomes more complicated. In that case *blast* is the method of choice. In the following example, T and A are two binary predicates, and it is shown that T is total, A is antisymmetric and T is a subset of A, then A is a subset of T:

lemma
```
  "⟦ ∀x y. T x y ∨ T y x;
     ∀x y. A x y ∧ A y x ⟶ x = y;
     ∀x y. T x y ⟶ A x y ⟧
     ⟹ ∀x y. A x y ⟶ T x y"
```
by *blast*

This is one of the rare cases where a not completely obvious theorem is proved automatically. Method *blast*

- is (in principle) a complete proof procedure for first-order formulas. In practice there is a search bound.
- does no rewriting and knows very little about equality.
- covers logic, sets and relations.
- either succeeds or fails.

Because of its strength in logic and sets and its weakness in equality reasoning, it complements the earlier proof methods.

4.4. Single step proofs

Although automation is nice, it often fails, at least initially, and you need to find out why. When *fastforce* or *blast* simply fail, you have no clue why. At this point, the stepwise application of proof rules may be necessary. For example, if *blast* fails on A $\wedge$ B, you want to attack the two conjuncts A and B separately. This can be achieved by applying *conjunction introduction*

$$\frac{?P \qquad ?Q}{?P \wedge ?Q}\ conjI$$

to the proof state. We will now examine the details of this process.

4.4.1. Instantiating unknowns

We had briefly mentioned earlier that after proving some theorem, Isabelle replaces all free variables x by so called *unknowns* $?x$. We can see this clearly in rule *conjI*. These unknowns can later be instantiated explicitly or implicitly:

- By hand, using *of*. The expression *conjI[of "a=b" "False"]* instantiates the unknowns in *conjI* from left to right with the two formulas $a=b$ and *False*, yielding the rule

$$\frac{a = b \qquad False}{a = b \wedge False}$$

  In general, *th [of string$_1$ ... string$_n$]* instantiates the unknowns in the theorem *th* from left to right with the terms *string$_1$* to *string$_n$*.

- By unification. *Unification* is the process of making two terms syntactically equal by suitable instantiations of unknowns. For example, unifying `?P ∧ ?Q` with `a = b ∧ False` instantiates `?P` with `a = b` and `?Q` with `False`.

We need not instantiate all unknowns. If we want to skip a particular one we can just write `_` instead, for example `conjI[of _ "False"]`. Unknowns can also be instantiated by name, for example `conjI[where ?P = "a=b" and ?Q = "False"]`.

4.4.2. Rule application

Rule application means applying a rule backwards to a proof state. For example, applying rule `conjI` to a proof state

```
1.  ...  ⟹ A ∧ B
```

results in two subgoals, one for each premise of `conjI`:

```
1.  ...  ⟹ A
2.  ...  ⟹ B
```

In general, the application of a rule ⟦ A_1; ...; A_n ⟧ ⟹ A to a subgoal ... ⟹ C proceeds in two steps:

1. Unify A and C, thus instantiating the unknowns in the rule.
2. Replace the subgoal C with n new subgoals A_1 to A_n.

This is the command to apply rule `xyz`:

apply *(rule xyz)*

This is also called *backchaining* with rule `xyz`.

4.4.3. Introduction rules

Conjunction introduction (`conjI`) is one example of a whole class of rules known as *introduction rules*. They explain under which premises some logical construct can be introduced. Here are some further useful introduction rules:

$$\frac{?P \implies ?Q}{?P \longrightarrow ?Q} \; impI \qquad \frac{\bigwedge x. \; ?P \; x}{\forall x. \; ?P \; x} \; allI$$

$$\frac{?P \implies ?Q \quad ?Q \implies ?P}{?P = ?Q} \; iffI$$

These rules are part of the logical system of *natural deduction* (e.g. [1]). Although we intentionally de-emphasise the basic rules of logic in favour of automatic proof methods that allow you to take bigger steps, these rules are helpful in locating where and why automation fails. When applied backwards, these rules decompose the goal:

- `conjI` and `iffI` split the goal into two subgoals,
- `impI` moves a formula (`?P`) into the list of assumptions,
- and `allI` removes a ∀ by turning the quantified variable into a fixed local variable of the subgoal.

Isabelle knows about these and a number of other introduction rules. The command

```
apply rule
```

automatically selects the appropriate rule for the current subgoal.

You can also turn your own theorems into introduction rules by giving them them *intro* attribute, analogous to the *simp* attribute. In that case *blast*, *fastforce* and (to a limited extent) *auto* will automatically backchain with those theorems. The *intro* attribute should be used with care because it increases the search space and can lead to nontermination. Sometimes it is better to use it only in a particular calls of *blast* and friends. For example, *le_trans*, transitivity of $\leq$ on type *nat*, is not an introduction rule by default because of the disastrous effect on the search space, but can be useful in specific situations:

lemma `"⟦ (a::nat) ≤ b; b ≤ c; c ≤ d; d ≤ e ⟧ ⟹ a ≤ e"`
by `(blast intro: le_trans)`

4.4.4. Forward proof

Forward proof means deriving new theorems from old theorems. We have already seen a very simple form of forward proof: the *of* operator for instantiating unknowns in a theorem. The big brother of *of* is *OF* for applying one theorem to others. Given a theorem `A ⟹ B` called `r` and a theorem `A'` called `r'`, the theorem `r[OF r']` is the result of applying `r` to `r'`, where `r` should be viewed as a function taking a theorem `A` and returning `B`. More precisely, `A` and `A'` are unified, thus instantiating the unknowns in `B`, and the result is the instantiated `B`. Of course, unification may also fail.

⚠ Application of rules to other rules operates in the forward direction: from the premises to the conclusion of the rule; application of rules to proof states operates in the backward direction, from the conclusion to the premises.

In general `r` can be of the form `⟦ A₁; ...; Aₙ ⟧ ⟹ A` and there can be multiple argument theorems r_1 to r_m (with $m \leq n$), in which case `r[OF r₁ ... rₘ]` is obtained by unifying and thus proving A_i with r_i, $i = 1...m$. Here is an example, where *refl* is the theorem `?t = ?t`:

thm `conjI[OF refl[of "a"] refl[of "b"]]`

yields the theorem `a = a ∧ b = b`. The command **thm** merely displays the result.

Forward reasoning does also make sense in connection with proof states. Therefore *blast*, *fastforce* and *auto* support a modifier *dest* which instructs the proof method to use certain rules in a forward fashion. If `r` is of the form `A ⟹ B`, the modifier *dest:* `r` allows proof search to reason forward with `r`, i.e. to replace an assumption `A'`, where `A'` unifies with `A`, with the correspondingly instantiated `B`. For example, *Suc_leD* is the theorem `Suc m ≤ n ⟹ m ≤ n`, which works well for forward reasoning:

lemma `"Suc(Suc(Suc a)) ≤ b ⟹ a ≤ b"`
by `(blast dest: Suc_leD)`

In this particular example we could have backchained with *Suc_leD*, too, but because the premise is more complicated than the conclusion this can easily lead to nontermination.

To ease readability we will drop the question marks in front of unknowns from now on.

5. Inductive definitions

Here is a simple example of an inductively defined predicate:

- 0 is even
- If n is even, so is $n + 2$.

The phrase "inductive" implies that these are the only even numbers. In Isabelle you write

```
inductive ev :: "nat ⇒ bool" where
"ev 0" |
"ev n ⟹ ev (n + 2)"
```

To get used to inductive definitions, we will first prove a few properties of `ev` informally before we descend to the Isabelle level.

How do we prove that some number is even, e.g. `ev 4`? Simply by combining the defining rules for `ev`:

```
ev 0 ⟹ ev (0 + 2) ⟹ ev((0 + 2) + 2) = ev 4
```

Showing that all even numbers have some property is more complicated. For example, let us prove that the doubling an even number again yields an even number: `ev m` `⟹ ev (m + m)`. This requires a proof by induction on the length or structure of the derivation of `ev m`.

Base case `ev m` is proved by rule `ev 0`:
```
⟹ m = 0 ⟹ ev (m + m)
```
Induction step `ev m` is proved by rule `ev n ⟹ ev (n + 2)`:
```
⟹ m = n + 2 and by induction hypothesis ev (n + n)
⟹ m + m = (n + 2) + (n + 2) = ((n + n) + 2) + 2
⟹ ev (m + m)
```

What we have just seen is a special case of *rule induction*. Rule induction applies to propositions of this form

```
ev n ⟹ P n
```

That is, we want to prove a property `P n` for all even `n`. But if we assume `ev n`, then there must be some derivation of this assumption using the two defining rules for `ev`. That is, we must prove

Base case `P 0`
Induction step `P n ⟹ P (n + 2)`

The corresponding rule is called `ev.induct` and looks like this:

$$\frac{ev\ n \qquad P\ 0 \qquad \bigwedge n.\ [\![ev\ n;\ P\ n]\!] \implies P\ (n\ +\ 2)}{P\ n}$$

Inductive definitions have the following general form:

```
inductive I :: "τ ⇒ bool" where
```

followed by a sequence of (possibly named) rules of the form

$$\llbracket\ I\ a_1;\ \ldots;\ I\ a_n\ \rrbracket \Longrightarrow I\ a$$

separated by `|`. As usual, n can be 0. The corresponding rule induction principle `I.induct` applies to propositions of the form

$$I\ x \Longrightarrow P\ x$$

Proving such a proposition by rule induction means proving for every rule that P is invariant:

$$\llbracket\ P\ a_1;\ \ldots;\ P\ a_n\ \rrbracket \Longrightarrow P\ a$$

The above format for inductive definitions is simplified in a number of respects. I can have any number of arguments and each rule can have additional premises not involving I, so-called *side conditions*.

6. Isar: A Language for Structured Proofs

Apply-scripts are unreadable and hard to maintain. The language of choice for larger proofs is *Isar*. The two key features of Isar are:

- It is structured, not linear.
- It is readable without running it because you need to state what you are proving at any given point.

Whereas apply-scripts are like assembly language programs, Isar proofs are like structured programs with comments. A typical Isar proof looks like this:

```
proof
    assume "formula₀"
    have "formula₁"    by simp
    ⋮
    have "formulaₙ"    by blast
    show "formulaₙ₊₁"    by ...
qed
```

It proves $formula_0 \Longrightarrow formula_{n+1}$ (provided provided each proof step succeeds). The intermediate **have** statements are merely stepping stones on the way towards the **show** statement that proves the actual goal. In more detail, this is the Isar core syntax:

$$
\begin{array}{rcl}
proof & = & \textbf{by } method \\
 & | & \textbf{proof } [method]\ step^*\ \textbf{qed} \\
\\
step & = & \textbf{fix } variables \\
 & | & \textbf{assume } proposition \\
 & | & [\textbf{from } fact^+]\ (\textbf{have } |\ \textbf{show})\ proposition\ proof
\end{array}
$$

$$proposition \quad = \quad [name{:}] \; \textit{"formula"}$$

$$fact \; = \; name \; | \; \ldots$$

A proof can either be an atomic **by** with a single proof method which must finish off the statement being proved, for example `auto`. Or it can be a **proof–qed** block of multiple steps. Such a block can optionally begin with a proof method that indicates how to start off the proof, e.g. `(induct xs)`.

A step either assumes a proposition or states a proposition together with its proof. The optional **from** clause indicates which facts are to be used in the proof. Intermediate propositions are stated with **have**, the overall goal with **show**. A step can also introduce new local variables with **fix**. Logically, **fix** introduces $\bigwedge$-quantified variables, **assume** introduces the assumption of an implication ($\Longrightarrow$) and **have/show** the conclusion.

Propositions are optionally named formulas. These names can be referred to in later **from** clauses. In the simplest case, a fact is such a name. But facts can also be composed with `OF` and `of` as shown in §4.4.4—hence the ... in the above grammar. Note that assumptions, intermediate **have** statements and global lemmas all have the same status and are thus collectively referred to as *facts*.

Fact names can stand for whole lists of facts. For example, if `f` is defined by command **fun**, `f.simps` refers to the whole list of recursion equations defining `f`. Individual facts can be selected by writing `f.simps(2)`, whole sublists by `f.simps(2-4)`.

6.1. Isar by example

We show a number of proofs of Cantors theorem that a function from a set to its powerset cannot be surjective, illustrating various features of Isar. The constant `surj` is predefined.

```
lemma  "¬ surj(f :: 'a ⇒ 'a set)"
proof
  assume  0: "surj f"
    from 0 have  1: "∀A. ∃a. A = f a" by (simp add: surj_def)
    from 1 have  2: "∃a. {x. x ∉ f x} = f a" by blast
    from 2 show "False" by blast
qed
```

The **proof** command lacks an explicit method how to perform the proof. In such cases Isabelle tries to use some standard introduction rule, in the above case for ¬:

$$\frac{P \Longrightarrow \textit{False}}{\neg \; P}$$

In order to prove ¬ `P`, assume `P` and show `False`. Thus we may assume `surj f`. The proof shows that names of propositions may be (single!) digits—meaningful names are hard to invent and are often not necessary. Both **have** steps are obvious. The second one introduces the diagonal set `{x. x ∉ f x}`, the key idea in the proof. If you wonder why 2 directly implies `False`: from 2 it follows that `(a ∉ f a)` `=` `(a ∈ f a)`.

6.1.1. *this*, *then*, *hence* **and** *thus*

Labels should be avoided. They interrupt the flow of the reader who has to scan the context for the point where the label was introduced. Ideally, the proof is a linear flow, where the output of one step becomes the input of the next step, piping the previously proved fact into the next proof, just like in a UNIX pipe. In such cases the predefined name *this* can be used to refer to the proposition proved in the previous step. This allows us to eliminate all labels from our proof (we suppress the **lemma** statement):

```
proof
  assume "surj f"
  from this have "∃a. {x. x ∉ f x} = f a" by (auto simp: surj_def)
  from this show "False" by blast
qed
```

We have also taken the opportunity to compress the two **have** steps into one.
     To compact the text further, Isar has a few convenient abbreviations:

$$
\begin{array}{rcl}
\textbf{then} & = & \textbf{from } this \\
\textbf{thus} & = & \textbf{then show} \\
\textbf{hence} & = & \textbf{then have}
\end{array}
$$

With the help of these abbreviations the proof becomes

```
proof
  assume "surj f"
  hence "∃a. {x. x ∉ f x} = f a" by (auto simp: surj_def)
  thus "False" by blast
qed
```

There are two further linguistic variations:

$$
\begin{array}{rcl}
(\textbf{have}|\textbf{show}) \; prop \; \textbf{using} \; facts & = & \textbf{from } facts \; (\textbf{have}|\textbf{show}) \; prop \\
\textbf{with} \; facts & = & \textbf{from } facts \; this
\end{array}
$$

The **using** idiom de-emphasises the used facts by moving them behind the proposition.

6.1.2. *Structured lemma statements:* **fixes**, **assumes**, **shows**

Lemmas can also be stated in a more structured fashion. To demonstrate this feature with Cantor's theorem, we rephrase ¬ *surj f* a little:

```
lemma
  fixes f :: "'a ⇒ 'a set"
  assumes s: "surj f"
  shows "False"
```

The optional **fixes** part allows you to state the types of variables up front rather than by decorating one of their occurrences in the formula with a type constraint. The key advantage of the structured format is the **assumes** part that allows you to name each assumption. The **shows** part gives the goal. The actual theorem that will come out of the proof is `surj f ⟹ False`, but during the proof the assumption `surj f` is available under the name `s` like any other fact.

```
proof -
  have "∃ a. {x. x ∉ f x} = f a" using s
    by (auto simp: surj_def)
  thus "False" by blast
qed
```

In the **have** step the assumption `surj f` is now referenced by its name `s`. The duplication of `surj f` in the above proofs (once in the statement of the lemma, once in its proof) has been eliminated.

🔥 Note the dash after the **proof** command. It is the null method that does nothing to the goal. Leaving it out would ask Isabelle to try some suitable introduction rule on the goal `False`— but there is no suitable introduction rule and **proof** would fail.

Stating a lemmas with **assumes-shows** implicitly introduces the name `assms` that stands for the list of all assumptions. You can refer to individual assumptions by `assms(1)`, `assms(2)` etc, thus obviating the need to name them individually.

6.2. Proof patterns

We show a number of important basic proof patterns. Many of them arise from the rules of natural deduction that are applied by **proof** by default. The patterns are phrased in terms of **show** but work for **have** and **lemma**, too.

We start with two forms of *case distinction*: starting from a formula `P` we have the two cases `P` and `¬ P`, and starting from a fact `P ∨ Q` we have the two cases `P` and `Q`:

```
show "R"                      have "P ∨ Q"  ...
proof cases                   then show "R"
  assume "P"                  proof
    :                           assume "P"
                                  :
  show "R"  ...
next                            show "R"  ...
  assume "¬ P"                 next
    :                           assume "Q"
                                  :
  show "R"  ...
qed                             show "R"  ...
                              qed
```

How to prove a logical equivalence:

```
show "P ⟷ Q"
proof
  assume "P"
    :
```

```
  show  "Q"  ...
next
  assume  "Q"

    ⋮

  show  "P"  ...
qed
```

Proofs by contradiction:

```
show  "¬ P"                      show  "P"
proof                            proof (rule ccontr)
  assume  "P"                      assume  "¬P"

    ⋮                                ⋮

  show  "False"  ...               show  "False"  ...
qed                              qed
```

The name `ccontr` stands for "classical contradiction".
     How to prove quantified formulas:

```
show  "∀x. P(x)"                 show  "∃x. P(x)"
proof                            proof
  fix  x
                                   ⋮
    ⋮
                                   show  "P(witness)"  ...
  show  "P(x)"  ...              qed
qed
```

In the proof of ∀x. P(x), the step **fix** x introduces a locale fixed variable x into the
subproof, the proverbial "arbitrary but fixed value". Instead of x we could have chosen
any name in the subproof. In the proof of ∃x. P(x), witness is some arbitrary term
for which we can prove that it satisfies P.
     How to reason forward from ∃x. P(x):

```
have  "∃x. P(x)"  ...
then obtain  x where  p:  "P(x)" by  blast
```

After the **obtain** step, x (we could have chosen any name) is a fixed local variable, and
p is the name of the fact P(x). This pattern works for one or more x. As an example of
the **obtain** command, here is the proof of Cantor's theorem in more detail:

```
lemma  "¬ surj(f :: 'a ⇒ 'a set)"
proof
  assume  "surj f"
  hence    "∃a. {x. x ∉ f x} = f a" by (auto simp: surj_def)
  then obtain  a where    "{x. x ∉ f x} = f a" by  blast
  hence    "a ∉ f a ⟷ a ∈ f a" by  blast
  thus  "False" by  blast
qed
```

How to prove set equality and subset relationship:

```
show "A = B"                    show "A ⊆ B"
proof                          proof
  show "A ⊆ B"  ...              fix x
next                             assume "x ∈ A"
  show "B ⊆ A"  ...              ⋮
qed                              show "x ∈ B"  ...
                               qed
```

6.3. Streamlining proofs

6.3.1. Pattern matching and quotations

In the proof patterns shown above, formulas are often duplicated. This can make the text harder to read, write and maintain. Pattern matching is an abbreviation mechanism to avoid such duplication. Writing

> **show** *formula* (**is** *pattern*)

matches the pattern against the formula, thus instantiating the unknowns in the pattern for later use. As an example, consider the proof pattern for $\longleftrightarrow$:

```
show "formula₁ ⟷ formula₂" (is "?L ⟷ ?R")
proof
  assume "?L"
  ⋮
  show "?R"  ...
next
  assume "?R"
  ⋮
  show "?L"  ...
qed
```

Instead of duplicating $formula_i$ in the text, we introduce the two abbreviations $?L$ and $?R$ by pattern matching. Pattern matching works wherever a formula is stated, in particular with **have** and **lemma**.

The unknown $?thesis$ is implicitly matched against any goal stated by **lemma** or **show**. Here is a typical example:

```
lemma "formula"
proof -
  ⋮
  show ?thesis  ...
qed
```

Unknowns can also be instantiated with **let** commands

> **let** $?t$ = *"some-big-term"*

Later proof steps can refer to $?t$:

have "... ?t ... "

!! Names of facts are introduced with *name* : and refer to proved theorems. Unknowns *?X* refer
•• to terms or formulas.

Although abbreviations shorten the text, the reader needs to remember what they
stand for. Similarly for names of facts. Names like *1*, *2* and *3* are not helpful and should
only be used in short proofs. For longer proof, descriptive names are better. But look at
this example:

have *x_gr_0:* "x > 0"

$\vdots$

from *x_gr_0* ...

The name is longer than the fact it stands for! Short facts do not need names, one can
refer to them easily by quoting them:

have "x > 0"

$\vdots$

from 'x>0' ...

Note that the quotes around *x>0* are *back quotes*. They refer to the fact not by name but
by value.

6.3.2. moreover

Sometimes one needs a number of facts to enable some deduction. Of course one can
name these facts individually, as shown on the right, but one can also combine them with
moreover, as shown on the left:

have "P_1" ...	**have** lab_1: "P_1" ...
moreover have "P_2" ...	**have** lab_2: "P_2" ...
moreover	$\vdots$
$\vdots$	**have** lab_n: "P_n" ...
moreover have "P_n" ...	**from** lab_1 lab_2 ...
ultimately have "P" ...	**have** "P" ...

The **moreover** version is no shorter but expresses the structure more clearly and avoids
new names.

6.3.3. Raw proof blocks

Sometimes one would like to prove some lemma locally with in a proof. A lemma that
shares the current context of assumptions but that has its own assumptions and is gener-
alised over its locally fixed variables at the end. This is what a *raw proof block* does:

```
{ fix x₁ ... xₙ
  assume A₁ ... Aₘ
  ⋮
  have B
}
```

proves $[\![\ A_1; \ \ldots \ ; \ A_m \ ]\!] \implies B$ where all x_i have been replaced by unknowns $?x_i$.

 The conclusion of a raw proof block is *not* indicated by **show** but is simply the final **have**.

As an example we prove a simple fact about divisibility on integers. The definition of *dvd* is *(b dvd a)* = *(∃k. a = b ⋆ k)*.

```
lemma fixes a b :: int assumes "b dvd (a+b)" shows "b dvd a"
proof -
  { fix k assume k: "a+b = b*k"
    have "∃k'. a = b*k'"
    proof
      show "a = b*(k - 1)" using k by (simp add: algebra_simps)
    qed }
  then show ?thesis using assms by (auto simp add: dvd_def)
qed
```

Note that the result of a raw proof block has no name. In this example it was directly piped (via **then**) into the final proof, but it can also be named for later reference: you simply follow the block directly by a **note** command:

```
note name = this
```

This introduces a new name *name* that refers to *this*, the fact just proved, in this case the preceding block. In general, **note** introduces a new name for one or more facts.

6.4. Case distinction and induction

6.4.1. Datatype case distinction

We have seen case distinction on formulas. Now we want to distinguish which form some term takes: is it *0* or of the form *Suc n*, is it *[]* or of the form *x # xs*, etc. Here is a typical example proof by case distinction on the form of *xs*:

```
lemma "length(tl xs) = length xs - 1"
proof (cases xs)
  assume "xs = []"
  thus ?thesis by simp
next
  fix y ys assume "xs = y#ys"
  thus ?thesis by simp
qed
```

Function *tl* ("tail") is defined by *tl []* = *[]* and *tl (x # xs)* = *xs*. Note that the result type of *length* is *nat* and *0 - 1 = 0*.

This proof pattern works for any term *t* whose type is a datatype. The goal has to be proved for each constructor *C*:

```
fix x₁ ... xₙ assume "t = C x₁ ... xₙ"
```

Each case can be written in a more compact form by means of the **case** command:

```
case (C x₁ ... xₙ)
```

This is equivalent to the explicit **fix-assumen** line but also gives the assumption `"t = C x₁ ... xₙ "` a name: `C`, like the constructor. Here is the **case** version of the proof above:

```
proof (cases xs)
  case Nil
  thus ?thesis by simp
next
  case (Cons y ys)
  thus ?thesis by simp
qed
```

Remember that `Nil` and `Cons` are the alphanumeric names for `[]` and `#`. The names of the assumptions are not used because they are directly piped (via **thus**) into the proof of the claim.

6.4.2. Structural induction

We illustrate structural induction with an example based on natural numbers: the sum ($\sum$) of the first n natural numbers (`{0..n::nat}`) is equal to `n * (n + 1) div 2`. Never mind the details, just focus on the pattern:

```
lemma "∑ {0..n::nat} = n*(n+1) div 2" (is "?P n")
proof (induct n)
  show "∑ {0..0::nat} = 0*(0+1) div 2" by simp
next
  fix n assume "∑ {0..n::nat} = n*(n+1) div 2"
  thus "∑ {0..Suc n::nat} = Suc n*(Suc n+1) div 2" by simp
qed
```

Except for the rewrite steps, everything is explicitly given. This makes the proof easily readable, but the duplication means it is tedious to write and maintain. Here is how pattern matching can completely avoid any duplication:

```
lemma "∑ {0..n::nat} = n*(n+1) div 2" (is "?P n")
proof (induct n)
  show "?P 0" by simp
next
  fix n assume "?P n"
  thus "?P (Suc n) " by simp
qed
```

The first line introduces an abbreviation `?P n` for the goal. This make `?P` a function, and pattern matching instantiates `?P` to $\lambda n.\ \sum \{0..n\} = n * (n + 1)\ div\ 2$. Now the proposition to be proved in the base case can be written as `?P 0`, the induction hypothesis as `?P n`, and the conclusion of the induction step as `?P (Suc n)`.

Induction also provides the **case** idiom that abbreviates the **fix-assume** step. The above proof becomes

```
proof (induct n)
```

```
    case  0
    show  ?case by simp
next
    case  (Suc n)
    thus  ?case by simp
qed
```

The unknown *?case* is set in each case to the required claim, i.e. *?P 0* and *?P (Suc n)* in the above proof, without requiring the user to define a *?P*. The general pattern for induction over *nat* is this:

```
show  "P (n) "
proof  (induct n)                          let  ?case =  "P (0) "
    case  0
      ⋮
    show ?case    ...
next
    case (Suc n)                           fix  n assume  Suc:  "P (n) "
      ⋮                                     let  ?case =  "P (Suc n) "
    show ?case    ...
qed
```

On the right side you can see what the **case** command on the left stands for.

In case the goal is an implication, induction does one more thing: the proposition to be proved in each case is not the whole implication but only its conclusion; the premises of the implication are immediately made assumptions of that case. That is, if in the above proof we replace **show** *"P (n) "* by **show** *"A (n) ⟹ P (n) "* then **case** *0* stands for

```
    assume  0:  "A (0) "
    let  ?case =  "P (0) "
```

and **case** *(Suc n)* stands for

```
    fix n
    assume  Suc:     "A (n) ⟹ P (n) "    "A (Suc n) "
    let  ?case =  "P (Suc n) "
```

The list of assumptions *Suc* is actually subdivided into *Suc.hyps*, the induction hypotheses (here *A (n) ⟹ P (n)*) and *Suc.prems*, the premises of the goal being proved (here *A (Suc n)*).

Induction works for any datatype. In general, trying to prove a goal ⟦ A_1 *(x)*; ...; A_k *(x)* ⟧ ⟹ *P (x)* by induction on *x* generates a proof obligation for each constructor *C* of the datatype. The command *case (C x_1 ... x_n)* performs the following steps:

1. **fix** x_1 ... x_n
2. **assume** the induction hypotheses (calling them *C.hyps*) and the premises A_i *(C x_1 ... x_n)* (calling them *C.prems*) and calling the whole list *C*
3. **let** *?case = "P (C x_1 ... x_n) "*

6.4.3. Rule induction

Remember the inductive definition of even numbers in §5:

```
inductive ev :: "nat ⟹ bool" where
ev0: "ev 0" |
evSS: "ev n ⟹ ev(Suc(Suc n))"
```

We had given an informal proof of $ev\ n \implies ev\ (n\ +\ n)$. On the left-hand side is the structured counterpart.

```
lemma "ev n ⟹ ev(n+n)"
proof(induct rule: ev.induct)
  case ev0                              let ?case = "ev(0+0)"
  show ?case
    by(simp add: ev.ev0)
next
  case evSS                            fix n
                                       assume evSS: "ev n" "ev(n+n)"
                                       let ?case =
                                         "ev(Suc(Suc n)+Suc(Suc n))"
  thus ?case
    by(simp add: ev.evSS)
qed
```

The proof resembles structural induction, but the induction rule is given explicitly and the names of the cases are the names of the rules in the inductive definition. On the right-hand side you can see the implicit effect of the two **case** commands. Let us examine the two assumptions named $evSS$: $ev\ n$ is the premise of rule $evSS$, which we may assume because we are in the case where that rule was used; $ev\ (n\ +\ n)$ is the induction hypothesis.

‼ Because each **case** command introduces a list of assumptions named like the case name, which is the name of a rule of the inductive definition, those rules now need to be accessed with a qualified name, here $ev.ev0$ and $ev.evSS$

In the case $evSS$ of the proof above we have pretended that the system fixes a variable n. But unless the user provides the name n, the system will just invent its own name that cannot be referred to. In the above proof, we do not need to refer to it, hence we do not give it a specific name. In case one needs to refer to it one writes

```
    case (evSS m)
```

just like **case** $(Suc\ n)$ in earlier structural inductions. The name m is an arbitrary choice. As a result, case $evSS$ is derived from a renamed version of rule $evSS$: $ev\ m \implies ev\ (m+m)$. Here is an example with an intermediate step that refers to m:

```
lemma "ev n ⟹ ev(n+n)"
proof(induct rule: ev.induct)
  case ev0 show ?case by(simp add: ev.ev0)
next
  case (evSS m)
  have "ev(Suc(Suc(Suc(Suc(m+m)))))"
    using 'ev(m+m)' by(simp add: ev.evSS)
  thus ?case by(simp)
qed
```

In general, let I be an (for simplicity unary) inductively defined predicate and let the rules in the definition of I be called $rule_1, \ldots, rule_n$. A proof by rule induction follows this pattern:

```
show "I x ⟹ P x"
proof (induct rule: I.induct)
   case rule₁
     ⋮
   show ?case  ...
next
⋮
next
   case ruleₙ
     ⋮
   show ?case  ...
qed
```

One may need to provide explicit variable names by writing **case** $(rule_i\ x_1\ \ldots\ x_k)$, thus renaming the first k free variables in rule i to $x_1\ \ldots\ x_k$, going through rule i from left to right.

6.4.4. Assumption naming

In any induction, **case** $name$ sets up a list of assumptions also called $name$, which is subdivided into two parts:

$name.prems$ contains the (suitably instantiated) premises of the statement being proved, i.e. the A_i when proving $[\![\ A_1;\ \ldots;\ A_n\ ]\!] \implies A$;

$name.hyps$ contains all the hypotheses of this case in the induction rule. For structural inductions these are merely the induction hypotheses. For rule inductions these are a mixture of the hypotheses of rule $name$ and the induction hypotheses.

‼ A finer-grained naming policy is offered by method $induction$, which is invoked just like $induct$, but which names the induction hypotheses $name.IH$; for rule inductions, $name.hyps$ contains only the hypotheses of rule $name$, not the induction hypotheses.

More complicated inductive proofs than the ones we have seen so far often need to refer to specific assumptions—just $name$ or even $name.prems$ and $name.IH$ can be too unspecific. This is where the indexing of fact lists comes in handy, e.g. $name.IH(2)$ or $name.prems(1-2)$.

References

[1] M. Huth and M. Ryan. *Logic in Computer Science.* Cambridge University Press, 2004.
[2] A. Krauss. *Defining Recursive Functions in Isabelle/HOL.* http://isabelle.in.tum.de/doc/functions.pdf.
[3] T. Nipkow, L. Paulson, and M. Wenzel. *Isabelle/HOL — A Proof Assistant for Higher-Order Logic,* volume 2283 of *Lect. Notes in Comp. Sci.* Springer-Verlag, 2002.

Software Safety and Security
T. Nipkow et al. (Eds.)
IOS Press, 2012
© *2012 The authors and IOS Press. All rights reserved.*
doi:10.3233/978-1-61499-028-4-286

A Primer on Separation Logic (and Automatic Program Verification and Analysis)

Peter W. O'Hearn [1]

Queen Mary University of London

Abstract. These are the notes to accompany a course at the Marktoberdorf PhD summer school in 2011. The course consists of an introduction to separation logic, with a slant towards its use in automatic program verification and analysis.

Keywords. Program Logic, Automatic Program Verification, Abstract Interpretation, Separation Logic

1. Introduction

Separation logic, first developed in papers by John Reynolds, the author, Hongseok Yang and Samin Ishtiaq, around the turn of the millenium [73,47,61,74], is an extension of Hoare's logic for reasoning about programs that access and mutate data held in computer memory. It is based on the *separating conjunction* $P * Q$, which asserts that P and Q hold for separate portions of memory, and on program-proof rules that exploit separation to provide modular reasoning about programs.

In this course I am going to introduce the basics of separation logic, its semantics, and proof theory, in a way that is oriented towards its use in automatic program-proof tools and abstract interpreters, an area of work which has seen increasing attention in recent years. After the basics, I will describe how the ideas can be used to build a verification or program analysis tool.

The course consists of four lectures:

1. *Basics,* where the fundamental ideas of the logic are presented in a semi-formal style;
2. *Foundations,* where we get into the fomalities, including the semantics of the assertion language and axioms and inference rules for heap-mutating commands, and culminating in an account of the local dynamics which underpin some of the rules in the logic;
3. *Proof Theory and Symbolic Execution,* which describes a way of reasoning about programs by 'executing' programs on formulae rather than concrete states, and which can form the basis for an automatic verifier; and
4. *Program Analysis,* where abstraction is used to infer loop invariants and other annotations, increasing the level of automation.

[1] This work was supported by funding from the Royal Society, the EPSRC and Microsoft Research.

These course notes include two sections based on the first two lectures, followed by a section collecting ideas from the last two lectures. At this stage the notes are incomplete, and they will possibly be improved and extended in the future. I hope, though, that they will still prove useful in giving a flavour of some of the main lines of work, as well as in pointers into the literature. In particular, at the end I give references to current directions being pursued in program analysis.

I should say that, with this slant towards automatic proof and program analysis, there are active ongoing developments related to separation logic in several other directions that I will not be able to cover, particularly in concurrency, data abstraction and refinement, object-oriented languages and scripting languages; a small sample of work in these directions includes [62,64,66,10,81,34,28,38].

2. Basics

In this section I introduce separation logic in a semi-formal way. I am hoping that some of the ideas can strike home and be seen to reflect natural reasoning that programmers might employ, even before we consider formal definitions. Of course, the informal presentation inevitably skates over some issues, issues that could very well lead to unsound conclusions if not treated correctly, and to nail things down we will get to the definitions in the next section.

2.1. The Separating Conjunction.

Consider the following memory structure.

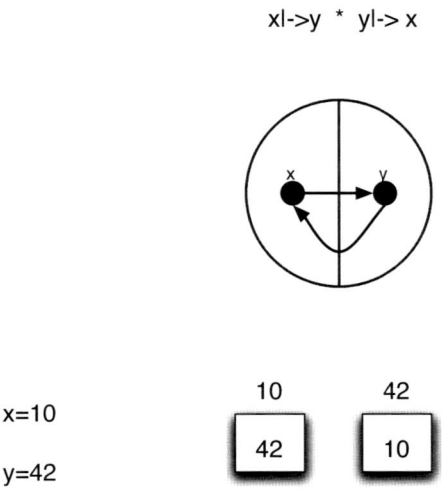

$$xl\text{->}y \ * \ yl\text{->} x$$

x=10

y=42

We read the formula at the top of this figure as 'x points to y, *and separately* y points to x'. Going down the middle of the diagram is a line which represents a heap partitioning: a separating conjunction asks for a partitioning that divides memory into parts satisfying its two conjuncts.

At the bottom of the figure is an example of a concrete memory description that corresponds to the diagram. There, x and y have values 10 and 42 (in the 'environment', or 'register bank'), and 10 and 42 are themselves locations with the indicated contents (in the 'heap', or even 'RAM').

The indicated separating conjunction above is true of the pictured memory because the parts satisfy the corresponding conjuncts. That is, the components

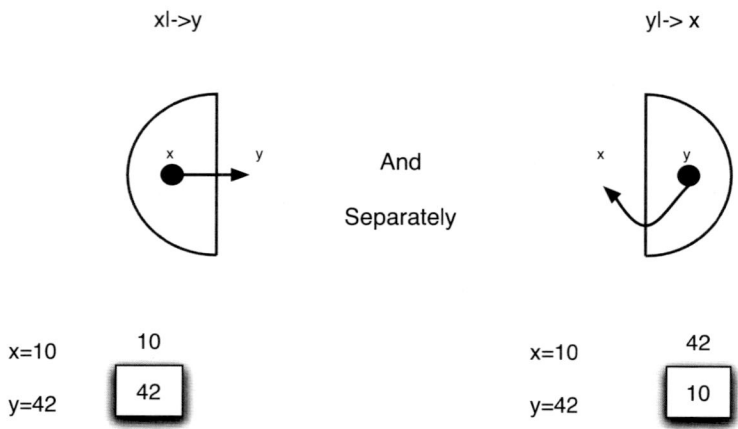

are separate sub-states that satisfy the relevant conjuncts.

It can be confusing to see a diagram like the one on the left where 'x points to y and yet to nothing'. This is disambiguated in the RAM description below the diagram. In the more concrete description x and y denote values (10 and 42), x's value is an allocated memory address which contains y's value, but y's value is not allocated. Notice also that, in comparison to the first diagram, the separating conjunction splits the heap/RAM, but it does *not* split the association of variables to values: heap cells, but not variable associations, are deleted from the original situation to obtain the sub-states. It is usually simplest to think in terms of the picture semantics of separation logic, but when we get formal in the next section we will drop down to the RAM level (as we could always do when pressed).

In general, an assertion P denotes a set of states, and $P * Q$ is true of a state just if its heap/RAM component can be split into two parts, one of which satisfies P and the other of which satisfies Q.

When reasoning about programs that manipulate data structures, one normally wants to use inductively-defined predicates that describe such structures. Here is a definition for a predicate that describes binary trees:

$$tree(E) \iff \text{if } \texttt{isatom?}(E) \text{ then } emp$$
$$\text{else } \exists xy. \, E \mapsto [l: x, r: y] * tree(x) * tree(y)$$

In this definition we assume a boolean expression $\texttt{isatom?}(E)$ which distinguishes atomic values (e.g., characters...) from addressible locations: in the RAM model, we could say that the locations are the non-negative integers and the atoms the negative ones. We have used a record notation $E \mapsto [l: x, r: y]$ for a 'points-to predicate' that describes a single record E that contains x in its l field and y in its r field. Again in the RAM model, this binary points-to can be compiled into the unary one: That is, $E\mapsto[l\colon x, r\colon y]$ could be an abbreviation for $(E\mapsto x) * (E{+}1\mapsto y)$ (Or, you could imagine a model where the heap consists of explicit records with field selection.) The separating conjunction between the $E\mapsto[l\colon x, r\colon y]$ assertion and the two recursive instances of *tree* in the definition ensures that there are no cycles, and the separating conjunction between the two subtrees ensures that we have a tree and not a dag.

The *emp* predicate in the base case of the inductive definition describes the empty heap, the heap with no allocated cells. A consequence of this is that when *tree*(E) holds there are no extra cells, cells in the heap but not in the tree, in a state satisfying the predicate. This is a key specification pattern often employed in separation logic proofs: we use assertions that describe only as much state as is needed, and nothing else.

At this point you might think that I have described an exotic-looking formalism for writing assertions about heaps and you might wonder: why bother? The mere ability to describe heaps in principle is not important in and of itself, and in this separation logic adds nothing significant to traditional predicate logic. It is when we consider the interaction between assertions and operations for mutating memory that the point of the formalism comes out.

2.2. In-place Reasoning

Proving by Executing.   I am going to show you part of a program proof outline in separation logic. It might seem slightly eccentric that I do this before giving you a definition of the logic. My aim is to use a computational reading of the proof steps to motivate the inference rules, rather than starting from them.

Consider the following procedure for disposing the elements in a tree.

```
procedure DispTree(p)
local i, j;
if ¬isatom?(p) then
    i := p→l; j := p→r;
    DispTree(i);
    DispTree(j);
    free(p)
```

This is the expected procedure that walks a tree, recursively disposing left and right subtrees and then the root pointer. It uses a representation of tree nodes as cells containing left and right pointers, with the base case corresponding to atomic, non-pointer values. (See Exercise 2 below for a fuller description.)

The specification of DispTree is just

$$\{\textit{tree}(p)\}\, \texttt{DispTree}(p)\, \{\textit{emp}\}$$

which says that if you have a tree at the beginning then you end up with the empty heap at the end. For this to make sense it is crucial that when *tree*(p) is true of a heap then that heap (or rather the heaplet, a portion of a global heap) contains all and only those cells in the tree. So, the spec talks about as small a portion of the global program state as possible.

The crucial part of the argument for DispTree's correctness, in the then branch, can be pictured with the following annotated program which gives a 'proof by execution' style argument.

$$\{p{\mapsto}[l\colon x, r\colon y] * tree(x) * tree(y)\}$$
$$\quad i := p{\to}l; j := p{\to}r;$$
$$\{p{\mapsto}[l\colon i, r\colon j] * tree(i) * tree(j)\}$$
$$\quad \texttt{DispTree}(i);$$
$$\{p{\mapsto}[l\colon i, r\colon j] * emp * tree(j)\}$$
$$\{p{\mapsto}[l\colon i, r\colon j] * tree(j)\}$$
$$\quad \texttt{DispTree}(j);$$
$$\{p{\mapsto}[l\colon i, r\colon j] * emp\}$$
$$\quad \texttt{free } p$$
$$\{emp\}$$

After we enter the `then` branch of the conditional we know that $\neg\texttt{isatom?}(p)$, so that (according to the inductive definition of the *tree* predicate) p points to left and right subtrees occupying separate storage. Then the roots of the two subtrees are loaded into i and j. The first recursive call operates in-place on the left subtree, removing it. The two consecutive assertions in the middle of the proof are an application of the rule of consequence of Hoare logic. These two assertions are equivalent because *emp* is the unit of $*$. Continuing on, the second call removes the right subtree, and the final instruction frees the root pointer p. The assertions, and their mutations, follow this operational narrative.

I am leading to a more general suggestion: try thinking about reasoning in separation logic as if you are an interpreter. The formulae are like states, *symbolic* states. Execute code forwards, updating formulae in the usual way you do when thinking about in-place update of memory. In-place reasoning works not only for freeing a cell, but for heap mutation and allocation as well. And, it even works for larger-scale operations such as entire procedure calls: we updated the assertions in-place at each of the recursive call sites during this 'proof'.

Exercise 1 *The usual Hoare logic rules for sequencing and consequence are*

$$\frac{\{P\}\, C_1\, \{Q\} \quad \{Q\}\, C_2\, \{R\}}{\{P\}\, C_1; C_2\, \{R\}} \qquad \frac{P \Rightarrow P' \quad \{P'\}\, C\, \{Q'\} \quad Q' \Rightarrow Q}{\{P\}\, C\, \{Q\}}$$

where $\Rightarrow$ refers to implication. Assuming we know how to decide $\Rightarrow$ formulae, convert the annotated program block for the `then` *case above into a proof in the usual logical sense (that is, a tree built from instances of these rules). You can assume that the triples of pre/post for each of the individual statements in the proof outline are given as axioms.*

Local Reasoning and Frame Axioms.   In the steps in the proof outline for $\texttt{DispTree}(p)$ I used the procedure spec as an assumption when reasoning about the recursive calls, as usual when reasoning about recursive procedures in Hoare logic [43]. However, there is an extra ingredient at work. For the second recursive call, for instance, the assertion at the call site does not match the procedure specification's precondition, even after p in the spec is instantiated with j, because the assertion has an extra $*$-conjunct, $p{\mapsto}[l\colon i, r\colon j]$.

> Assertion at call site : $p{\mapsto}[l\colon i, r\colon j] * tree(j)$
> Precondition in spec : $tree(j)$

This extra $*$-conjunct is not touched by the recursive call. It is called a 'frame axiom' in AI. The terminology 'frame axiom' comes from an analogy with animation, where the moving parts of a scene are successively aid over an unchanging frame. Indeed, the fact $p \mapsto [l: i, r: j]$ is left unchanged by the second call. You should be able to pick out the frame in the first call as well.

Thus, there is something slightly awry in this 'proof', unless I tell you more: The mismatch, between the call sites and the procedure precondition, needs to be taken care of if we are really to have a proof of the procedure. One way to resolve the mismatch would be to complicate the specification of the procedure, to talk explicitly about frames in one way or another (see 'back in the day' below). A better approach is to have a generic inference rule, which allows us to avoid mentioning the frames at all in our specifications, but to bring them in when needed. This generic rule is

$$\frac{\{P\} \, C \, \{Q\}}{\{R * P\} \, C \, \{R * Q\}} \quad \text{Frame Rule}$$

and it lets us tack on additional assertions 'for free', as it were. For instance, in the second recursive call the frame axiom R selected is $p \mapsto [l: i, r: j]$ and $\{P\}C\{Q\}$ is a substitution instance of the procedure spec: this captures that the recursive call does not alter the root pointer.

This better way, which avoids talking about frames in specifications, corresponds to programming intuition. When reasoning about a program we should only have to talk about the resources it accesses (its 'footprint'), as all other resources will remain unchanged. This is the *principle of local reasoning* [47,61]. In the specification of DispTree the precondition *tree*(p) describes only those cells touched by the procedure.

Aside: back in the day...   This issue of local reasoning has nothing to do with the 'power' or 'completeness' of a formal method: what is possible to do in principle. It has only to do with the simplicity and directness of the specs and proofs. To see the issue more clearly, consider how we might have written a spec for DispTree(p) in traditional Hoare logic, before we had the frame rule. Here is a beginning attempt:

$$\{tree(p) \wedge \texttt{reach}(p, n)\} \, \texttt{DispTree}(p) \, \{\neg\texttt{allocated}(n)\}$$

assuming that we have defined the predicates that say when p points to a (binary) tree in memory, when n is reachable (following l and r links) from p, and when n is allocated. This spec says that any node n which is in the tree pointed to by p is not allocated on conclusion.

While this specification says part of what we would like to say, it leaves too much unsaid. It does not say what the procedure does to nodes that are not in the tree. As a result, this specification is too weak to use at many call sites. For example, consider the first recursive call, DispTree(i), to dispose the left subtree. If we use the specification (instantiating p by i) as an hypothesis, then we have a problem: the specification does not rule out the possibility that the procedure call alters the right subtree j, perhaps creating a cycle or even disposing some of its nodes. As a consequence, when we come to the second call DispTree(j), we will not know that the required *tree*(j) part of the precondition will hold. So our reasoning will get stuck.

We can fix this 'problem' by making a stronger specification which includes frame axioms.

$$\{tree(p) \wedge \texttt{reach}(p,n) \wedge \neg\textbf{reach}(p,m) \wedge \texttt{allocated}(m) \wedge m.f \ = \ m' \wedge$$
$$\neg\texttt{allocated}(q)\}$$
$$\texttt{DispTree}(p)$$
$$\{\neg\texttt{allocated}(n) \wedge \neg\texttt{reach}(p,m) \wedge \texttt{allocated}(m) \wedge m.f = m' \wedge$$
$$\neg\texttt{allocated}(q)\}$$

The additional parts of the spec say that any allocated cell not reachable from p has the same contents in memory and that any previously unallocated cell remains unallocated. The additional clauses are the frame axioms. (I am assuming that m, m', n and q are auxiliary variables, guaranteed not to be altered. The reason why, say, the predicate $\neg\texttt{allocated}(q)$ could conceivably change, even if q is constant, is that the $\texttt{allocated}$ predicate refers to a behind-the-scenes heap component. f is used in the spec as an arbitrary field name.)

Whether or not this more complicated specification is correct, I think you will agree: it is complicated! I expect that you will agree as well that it is preferable for the frame axioms to be left out of specs, and inferred when needed.

Beyond Shapes. The above shows one inductive definition, for binary trees. The definition is limited in that it does not talk about the contents of a tree. It is the kind of definition often used in automatic shape analysis, as we will describe in Section 4, where avoiding taking about the contents can make it easier to prove entailments or synthesize invariants.

To illustrate the limitation of the definition, suppose that we were to write a procedure to copy a tree rather than delete it. We could give it a specification such as

$$\{tree(p)\} \ q \ := \ \texttt{CopyTree}(p) \ \{tree(p) * tree(q)\}$$

but then this specification would also be satisfied by a procedure that rotates a tree as it copies. A more precise specification would be of the form

$$\{tree(p,\tau)\} \ q \ := \ \texttt{CopyTree}(p) \ \{tree(p,\tau) * tree(q,\tau)\}$$

where $tree(p,\tau)$ is a predicate which says that p points to a data structure in memory representing the *mathematical* tree τ. (I use the term 'mathematical' tree to distinguish if from a representation in the computer memory: the mathematical tree does not contain pointer or other such representation information.)

Exercise 2 *The notion of 'mathematical tree' appropriate to the above inductive definition of the* $\texttt{tree}$ *predicate is that of an s-expression (the terminology comes from Lisp): that is, an atom, or a pair of s-expressions. An s-expression is an element of the least set satisfying the equation*

$$\texttt{Sexp} \ = \ \texttt{Atom} + (\texttt{Sexp} \times \texttt{Sexp})$$

for some set $\texttt{Atom}$ *of atoms, where* $\times$ *and* $+$ *are the cartesian product and disjoint union of sets. Here, then, is the inductive definition of a* $tree(p,\tau)$ *predicate, where* $\tau \in \texttt{Sexp}$:

$$tree(E,\tau) \Longleftrightarrow \text{ if } (\texttt{isatom?}(E) \wedge E = \tau) \text{ then } emp$$
$$\text{else } \exists xy\tau_1\tau_2. \ \tau = \langle\tau_1,\tau_2\rangle \wedge (E\mapsto[l\colon x, r\colon y] * tree(x) * tree(y))$$

Define the `CopyTree` *procedure and give a proof-by-execution style argument for its correctness, where you put assertions (symbolic states) at the appropriate program points. Yes, I am asking you to do a 'proof' in a formalism that has not yet been defined (!), but give it a try.*

2.3. Perspective.

In this section I have attempted to illustrate the following points.

(i) The separating conjunction fits together with inductive definitions in a way that supports natural descriptions of mutable data structures.

(ii) The separating conjunction supports *in-place reasoning*, where a portion of a formula is updated in place when passing from precondition to postcondition, mirroring the operational locality of heap update.

(iii) Frame axioms, which state what does not change, can be avoided when writing specifications.

These points together enable specifications and proofs for pointer programs that are dramatically simpler than was possible previously, in many (not all) cases approaching the simplicity associated with proofs of pure functional programs. (That is, previous approaches excepting the remarkable precursor work of Burstall [15], which provided inspiration for Reynolds's earliest work on separation logic [73]. You can see [12] for references and a good account of work on proving pointer programs before separation logic.)

However, I should stress at once that program proofs do not always go as easily as for `DispTree`. When one considers graph algorithms with significant sharing, or concurrent programs with nontrivial interaction, proofs can become complicated. Neither separation logic nor any other formalism takes programs that are difficult to understand and magically gives them easy proofs.

A more realistic goal is to have *simple proofs for simple programs*. Whether, or to what extent, this might be achieved by any given formalism can only be decided personally by you looking at, or better by doing, proofs of a number of examples.

3. Foundations

Building on the ideas described informally in the previous section, I now give a rigorous treatment of the program logic.

3.1. Semantics of Assertions (the Heaplet Model)

The model has two components, the store and the heap. The store is a finite partial function mapping from variables to integers, and the heap is a finite function from natural numbers to integers.

$$\text{Stores} \triangleq \text{Variables} \rightharpoonup_{fin} \text{Ints} \qquad \text{Heaps} \triangleq \text{Nats} \rightharpoonup_{fin} \text{Ints}$$

($\triangleq$ abbreviates 'is defined to be equal to'.) In logic, what we are calling the store is often called the valuation, and the heap is a possible world. In programming languages, what we are calling the store is also sometimes called the environment (the association of values to variables).

We have standard integer expressions E and boolean expressions B built up from variables and constants. These are heap-independent, so determine denotations

$$[\![E]\!]s \in \texttt{Ints} \qquad [\![B]\!]s \in \{true, false\}$$

where the domain of $s \in \texttt{Stores}$ includes the free variables of E or B. We leave this semantics unspecified.

We use the following notations in the semantics of assertions.

1. $dom(h)$ denotes the domain of definition of a heap $h \in \texttt{Heaps}$, and $dom(s)$ is the domain of $s \in \texttt{Stores}$;
2. $h \# h'$ says that $dom(h) \cap dom(h') = \emptyset$;
3. $h \bullet h'$ denotes the union of functions with disjoint domains, which is undefined if the domains overlap;
4. $(f \mid i \mapsto j)$ is the partial function like f except that i goes to j.

The satisfaction judgement $s, h \models P$ which says that an assertion holds for a given store and heap, assuming that the free variables of P are contained in the domain of s.

$$s, h \models B \qquad \text{iff } [\![B]\!]s = true$$

$$s, h \models E \mapsto F \text{ iff } \{[\![E]\!]s\} = dom(h) \text{ and } h([\![E]\!]s) = [\![F]\!]s$$

$$s, h \models false \qquad \text{never}$$

$$s, h \models P \Rightarrow Q \text{ iff if } s, h \models P \text{ then } s, h \models Q$$

$$s, h \models \forall x.P \quad \text{iff } \forall v \in \texttt{Ints}. [s \mid x \mapsto v], h \models P$$

$$s, h \models emp \qquad \text{iff } h = [\,] \text{ is the empty heap}$$

$$s, h \models P * Q \quad \text{iff } \exists h_0, h_1. \, h_0 \# h_1, \; h_0 * h_1 = h, \; s, h_0 \models P \text{ and } s, h_1 \models Q$$

$$s, h \models P \mathbin{-\!\!*} Q \text{ iff } \forall h'. \text{ if } h' \# h \text{ and } s, h' \models P \text{ then } s, h \bullet h' \models Q$$

The semantics of the connectives ($\Rightarrow$ *false*, $\forall$) gives rise to meanings of other connectives of classical logic ($\exists, \vee, \neg, true$) in the usual way. For example, taking $P \wedge Q$ to be $\neg(P \Rightarrow \neg Q)$, we obtain that $s, h \models P \wedge Q$ has the usual meaning of '$s, h \models P$ and $s, h \models Q$'.

The general logical context of this form of semantics is that it can be seen as a possible world model which combines:

(i) the standard semantics of classical logic ($\Rightarrow$, *false*, $\forall$) in the complete boolean algebra of the power set of heaps; and

(ii) a semantics of 'substructural logic' ($emp, *, \mathbin{-\!\!*}$) in the same power set (which gives us what is known as a residuated commutative monoid, an ordered commutative monoid where $A * (-)$ has a right adjoint $A \mathbin{-\!\!*} (-)$).

The semantics is an instance of the 'resource semantics' of bunched logic devised by David Pym [63,70,69], where one starts from a partial commutative monoid in place of heaps (with • and the empty heap giving partial monoid structure). The resulting mathematical structure on the powerset, of a boolean algebra with an additional commutative residuated monoid structure, is sometimes called a 'boolean BI algebra'. The model of • as heap partitioning, which lies at the basis of separation logic, was discovered by John Reynolds when he first described the separating conjunction [73]. The separating conjunction was connected with Pym's general resource semantics in [47].

Notice that the semantics of $E \hookrightarrow F$ requires that E is the only active address in the current heap. Using $*$ we can build up descriptions of larger heaps. For example, $(10 \mapsto 3) * (11 \mapsto 10)$ describes two adjacent cells whose contents are 3 and 10. We can express an inexact variant of points-to as follows

$$E \hookrightarrow F \;=\; (true * E \mapsto F).$$

Generally, $true * P$ says that P is true of a subheap of the current one. The difference between $\hookrightarrow$ and $\mapsto$ shows up in the presence or absence of projection or Weakening for $*$.

1. $P * (x \mapsto 1) \Rightarrow (x \mapsto 1)$ is not always true.
2. $P * (x \hookrightarrow 1) \Rightarrow (x \hookrightarrow 1)$ is always true.

The different way that the two conjunctions $*$ and $\wedge$ behave is illustrated by the following examples.

1. $(x \mapsto 2) * (x \mapsto 2)$ is unsatisfiable (you can't be in two places at once).
2. $(x \mapsto 2) \wedge (x \mapsto 2)$ is equivalent to $x \mapsto 2$.
3. $(x \mapsto 1) * \neg(x \mapsto 1)$ is satisfiable (thus, we have a kind of 'paraconsistent' logic).
4. $(x \mapsto 1) \wedge \neg(x \mapsto 1)$ is unsatisfiable.

The third example drives home how separation logic assertions do not talk about the global heap: $P * \neg P$ can be consistent because P can hold of one portion of heap and $\neg P$ of another. To understand separation logic assertions you should always think locally: for this you might regard the h component in the semantics of assertions as describing a 'heaplet', a portion of heap, rather than a complete global heap in and of itself.

Exercise 3 *Define $\mapsto$ in terms of $\hookrightarrow$, $\wedge$, $*$, $\neg$ and emp.*

Aside: on $\mapsto$ versus $=$ A frequent source of confusion when first learning separation logic concerns how the $*$ separator splits the heap but not the store, and this translates into confusions reading assertions with $=$ in them. Recall the definitions above

$$s, h \models B \qquad \text{iff } [\![B]\!]s = true$$

$$s, h \models E \mapsto F \text{ iff } \{[\![E]\!]s\} = dom(h) \text{ and } h([\![E]\!]s) = [\![F]\!]s.$$

Notice that the rhs of the clause for $s, h \models B$ does not mention h at all, where for $s, h \models E \mapsto F$ the rhs does contain h. I said I would not give a precise semantics of boolean expressions, but let me consider just one, the expression $x = y$ where x and y are variables:

$$[\![x = y]\!]s \overset{\Delta}{=} (sx = sy).$$

Now, consider the assertion $(x = y) * (x = y)$. Can it ever be true? Well, yes, it is satisfiable, and in fact it has the same meaning as $x = y$ and as $(x = y) \wedge (x = y)$. On the other hand, consider the assertion $(x \mapsto y) * (x \mapsto y)$. Can it ever be true? How about $(x = y) * (x \mapsto y)$? Or $(x = y) \wedge (x \mapsto y)$? Work out the answers to these questions by expanding the semantic definitions.

3.2. Inductive Definitions, Again

Earlier we considered an inductive definition of trees representing s-expressons.

$$tree(E, \tau) \Longleftrightarrow \texttt{if } (\texttt{isatom?}(E) \wedge E = \tau) \texttt{ then } \textit{emp}$$
$$\texttt{else } \exists xy\tau_1\tau_2.\, \tau = \langle \tau_1, \tau_2 \rangle \wedge (E \mapsto [l\colon x, r\colon y] * tree(x) * tree(y))$$

Now we can be more precise about its meaning. The use of if-then-else can be desugared using boolean logic connectives in the usual way. $\texttt{if } B \texttt{ then } P \texttt{ else } Q$ is the same as $(B \wedge P) \vee (\neg B \wedge Q)$ where here B is heap-independent. Therefore, in the inductive definition we can now see that the condition $(\texttt{isatom?}(E) \wedge E = \tau)$ is completely heap-independent, and not affected by $*$: it talks only about values, and not the contents of heap cells.

It is also helpful to ponder the clause

$$\tau = \langle \tau_1, \tau_2 \rangle \wedge (E \mapsto [l\colon x, r\colon y] * tree(x) * tree(y))$$

used in the definition. In fact, we could have rewritten it using $*$ in place of $\wedge$, as

$$(\tau = \langle \tau_1, \tau_2 \rangle \wedge emp) * (E \mapsto [l\colon x, r\colon y] * tree(x) * tree(y)).$$

Here, we have used a general identity

$$B \wedge P \Longleftrightarrow (B \wedge emp) * P$$

which holds whenever B is heap-independent. On the other hand, if we replaced one of the other occurrences of $*$ by $\wedge$, it would more dramatically alter the definition (exercise: by playing with $*$, $\wedge$ and perhaps inserting *true*, can you alter this definition so that it describes dags rather than trees?).

In case you missed it, to be fully formal in the interpretation of this definition we should also extend the store type to be

$$\texttt{Stores} \overset{\Delta}{=} \texttt{Variables} \rightharpoonup_{fin} (\texttt{Ints} + \texttt{Sexp})$$

so that a variable can take on an s-expression as well as an integer value. We could also distinguish s-expression variables τ from program variables x syntactically. (In practice, one would probably want to use a many-sorted rather than one-sorted logic as we are doing in these notes for theoretical simplicity.)

Finally, we can regard $E \mapsto [l\colon x, r\colon y]$ as sugar for $(E \mapsto x) * (E+1 \mapsto y)$ in the RAM model. Note, though, that this low-level desugaring is not part of the essence of separation logic, only this particular model. Other models can be used where heaps are represented by $L \rightharpoonup_{fin} V$ where V might be a structured type to represent records. However, that the RAM model *can* be used is appealing in a foundational way, as we know that programs of all kinds are eventually compiled to such a model (modern concerns with weak memory notwithstanding).

Generally, for any kind of data structure you will want to provide an appropriate predicate definition which will often be inductive. Linked lists are the most basic case, and illustrate some of the issues involved.

When reasoning about imperative data structures, one needs to consider not only complete linked lists (terminated with nil) but also 'partial lists' or linked-list segments. Here is an example of a list segment predicate describing lists from E to F (where F is not allocated).

$$ls(E, F) \Longleftrightarrow \texttt{if } E = F \texttt{ then } emp$$
$$\texttt{else } \exists y.E \mapsto y \; * \; ls(y, F)$$

I am intending that ls is the least predicate satisfying the equation. Mathematically, it can be worked out as the least fixed-point of a monotone function on a certain lattice, by reference to the Tarski fixed-point theorem. (Exercise: what is the lattice and what is the monotone function?) It is possible as well to give an alternate definition whose formalization does not need to talk about lattices: you define a predicate $ls(E, F, n)$ describing a linked list segment from E to F of length n, and then define $ls(E, F)$ to be $\exists n. \, ls(E, F, n)$.

This list segment predicate rules out cycles. However, cycles can be described using two list predicates, or a points-to and a list segment. For example, the following assertion is validated in the pictured model.

$$ls(x, y) \; * \; ls(y, x)$$

These partial lists are sometimes used in the specifications of data structures, such as queues. In other cases, they are needed to state the internal invariants of an algorithm, even when the pre and post of a program use total lists only (total lists $list(E)$ can be regarded as abbreviations for segments $ls(E, nil)$). Here is a program from the SMALL-FOOT tool [7] which exemplifies this point.

```
list_append(x,y) PRE: [list(x) * list(y)] {
  local t;
  if (x == NULL) {
    x = y;
  } else {
    t = x; n = t->tl;
    while (n != NULL) [ls(x,t) * t |->  n * list(n)] {
      t = n;
      n = t->tl;
    }
    t->tl = y;
  } /* ls(x,t) * t |-> y * list(y) */
} POST: [list(x)]
```

This program, which appends two lists by walking down one and then swinging its last pointer to the other, uses a partial list in its loop invariant, even though partial lists are not needed in the overall procedure spec. In proving this program an important point is how one gets from the last statement to the postcondition. A comment near the end of the program shows an assertion describing what is known at that program point, and we need to show that it implies the post to verify the program. That is, we need to show an implication

$$ls(x,t) * t \mapsto y * list(y) \implies list(x).$$

This implication may seem unremarkable, but it is at this point that automatic tools must begin to do something clever. For, consider how you, the human, would convince yourself of the truth of this implication. If it were me, I would look at the semantics and prove this fact by induction on the length of the list from x to t. But if we were to include such reasoning in an automatic tool, we had better try to do so in an inductionless way, else our tool will need to search for induction hypotheses (which is hard to make automatic).

Exercise 4 *There are other definitions of list segments that have been used. Here is one, the 'imprecise list segment'.*

$$ils(E,F) \iff (E = F \land emp)$$
$$\lor \exists y. E \mapsto y * ils(y,F)$$

Q1. *What is a heap that distinguishes $ls(10,10)$ and $ils(10,10)$?*

Q2. *What distinguishes $ls(10,11)$ and $ils(10,11)$?*

Q3. *Prove or disprove the following laws (do your proof by working in the semantics)*

$$ls(x,y) * ls(y,z) \implies ls(x,z) \quad ???$$
$$ils(x,y) * ils(y,z) \implies ils(x,z) ???$$

Q4. *Suppose we want to write a procedure that frees all the cells in a list segment. For which of ils or ls can you do it? If you cannot do it for one of them, why not? That is, we are asking for terminating programs satisfying*

$$\{ls(x,y)\} \; \texttt{delete\_ls}(x,y) \; \{emp\}$$
$$\{ils(x,y)\} \; \texttt{delete\_ils}(x,y) \; \{emp\}$$

(I have not given you the definition of the truth of pre/post specs yet, but you should be able to answer this question anyhow.)

Exercise 5 *Give a definition* $ls(E, F, \sigma)$ *of a predicate describing a linked list from E to F that contains the sequence σ in data fields. Write specification of programs that insert and delete elements from* sorted *linked lists, where σ is sorted according to an ordering. Give at least the loop invariants for these programs (write iterative versions). Attempt a proof-by-execution type argument as well.*

Exercise 6 *The predicate* $tree(E, \tau)$ *we used above considers τ as an s-expression, where the values are only at the leaves of the tree and not at internal nodes. Often, one wants to use a data structure for mathematical trees including data at internal nodes, and one way to describe these is with the set equation*

$$\texttt{Mtree} \;=\; \{nil\} + (\texttt{Mtree} \times \texttt{Atom} \times \texttt{Mtree})$$

In this sort of tree, nil *is the empty tree and the leaves of a non-empty tree are those 3-tuples that have* nil *in their first and third components.*

    Give an inductive definition of a predicate $tree(E, \tau)$, *for $\tau \in$* Mtree. *Hint: use a points-to assertion of the form* $E \mapsto [l\colon x, d\colon y, r\colon z]$ *where d refers to the data, or atom, field. Define the* CopyTree *and* DispTree *procedures for this sort of tree, and give proof-by-execution style arguments for their correctness.*

3.3. Proof Rules for Programs.

The proof rules for procedure calls, sequencing, conditionals and loops are the same as in standard Hoare logic [42,43]. Here I concentrate on the rules for primitive commands for accessing the heap, and the surrounding rules, called the 'structural rules'. (If you are unfamiliar with Hoare logic probably the best way to learn is to go directly to the early sources, such as [42,44,43,37,27], which are pleasantly simple and easy to read.)

    We will use the following abbreviations:

$$
\begin{aligned}
E \mapsto F_0, ..., F_n &\stackrel{\Delta}{=} (E \mapsto F_0) * \cdots * (E + n \mapsto F_n) \\
E \doteq F &\stackrel{\Delta}{=} (E = F) \land emp \\
E \mapsto - &\stackrel{\Delta}{=} \exists y. E \mapsto y \qquad\qquad (y \notin \mathrm{Free}(E))
\end{aligned}
$$

where $\mathrm{Free}(E)$ is the set of free variables in E.

    We have axioms for each of four atomic commands. In the axioms x, m, n are assumed to be distinct variables.

THE SMALL AXIOMS

$$\{E\mapsto-\}\,[E] := F\,\{E\mapsto F\}$$

$$\{E\mapsto-\}\,\texttt{free}(E)\,\{emp\}$$

$$\{x \doteq m\}x := \texttt{cons}(E_1, ..., E_k)\{x\mapsto E_1[m/x], ..., E_k[m/x]\,\}$$

$$\{x \doteq n\}\,x := E\,\{x \doteq (E[n/x])\}$$

$$\{E\mapsto n \wedge x = m\}\,x := [E]\,\{x = n \wedge E[m/x]\mapsto n\}$$

The first small axiom just says that if E points to something beforehand (so it is in the domain of the heaplet), then it points to F afterwards, and it says this for a small portion of the state (heaplet) in which E is the only active cell. This corresponds to the operational idea of $[E] := F$ as a command that stores the value of F at address E in the heap. The other commands have similar explanations. Notice that each axiom mentions only the cells accessed or allocated: the axioms talk only about footprints, and not the entire global program state. We only get fixed-length allocation from $x :=$ $\texttt{cons}(E_1, ..., E_k)$. but it is also possible to axiomatize a command $x := \texttt{alloc}(E)$ that allocates a block of length E.

Notice that our axioms allow us to free any cell that is allocated, even from the middle of a block given by cons. This is different from the situation in the C programming language, where you are only supposed to free an entire block that has been allocated by malloc(). An elegant treatment of this problem has been given using predicate variables in [66].

The assignment statement $x := E$ is for a variable x and heap-independent arithmetic expression E. Thus, this statement accesses and alters the store, but not the heap. It is the assignment statement considered by Hoare in his original system [42]. In contrast, the form $[E] := F$ alters the heap but not the store.

To go along with the small axioms we have additional surrounding rules.

THE STRUCTURAL RULES

Frame Rule

$$\frac{\{P\}C\{Q\}}{\{P * R\}C\{Q * R\}}\ \text{Modifies}(C) \cap \text{Free}(R) = \emptyset$$

Auxiliary Variable Elimination

$$\frac{\{P\}\,C\,\{Q\}}{\{\exists x.P\}\,C\,\{\exists x.Q\}}\ x \notin \text{Free}(C)$$

Variable Substitution

$$\frac{\{P\}\,C\,\{Q\}}{(\{P\}\,C\,\{Q\})[E_1/x_1, ..., E_k/x_k]}\ \begin{array}{l}\{x_1, ..., x_k\} \supseteq \text{Free}(P, C, Q), \text{ and}\\ x_i \in \text{Modifies}(C) \text{ implies}\\ E_i \text{ is a variable not free in any other } E_j\end{array}$$

Rule of Consequence

$$\frac{P' \Rightarrow P \quad \{P\}C\{Q\} \quad Q \Rightarrow Q'}{\{P'\}C\{Q'\}}$$

Modifies(C) here is the set of variables that are assigned to within C. The Modifies set of each of $x := \mathtt{cons}(E_1, ..., E_k)$, $x := E$ and $x := [E]$ is $\{x\}$, while for $\mathtt{free}(E)$ and $[E] := F$ it is empty. Note that the Modifies set only tracks potential alterations to the store, and says nothing about the heap cells that might be modified.

Two of these rules we have already seen: the frame and consequence rules. The others are rules that have been considered in the Hoare logic literature. This collection of axioms and rules is complete in the sense that all true Hoare triples for the basic statements can be derived them (assuming an oracle for implication in the consequence rule). A proof of this fact is contained in Hongseok Yang's thesis [84] (in fact, Yang chose the existential and substitution structural rules precisely in order to make the small axioms complete).

This presentation of the proof system above is from [61]. In his LICS'02 paper [74] Reynolds gives a comprehensive description of a variety of axioms, in local (small) and global and backwards forms, for the various atomic commands. The additional laws are important because one prefers to have derived laws that can be applied at once in common situations without going back to the small axioms every time and invoking the structural rules extensively.

For example, it follows from Yang's results that Hoare's assignment axiom

$$\{P[E/x]\}\, x := E\, \{P\}$$

can be derived, where $x := E$ is the assignment statement that is heap independent. One can also derive Floyd's forwards-running axiom [36]

$$\{P\}\, x := E\, \{\exists x'.\, x = E[x'/x] \wedge P[x'/x]\}$$

where the existentially quantified variable x' (which must be fresh) provides a way to talk about x's value in the pre-state. The symbolic execution rules in SMALLFOOT and related tools use forwards-running rules of this variety (Section 4.2).

As an example derived rule for a heap-accessing command, with the frame rule and auxiliary variable elimination one can obtain an axiom from [73]

$$\{\exists x_1, \cdots, x_n.\, (E \mapsto -) * R\}\, [E] := F\, \{\exists x_1, \cdots, x_n.\, (E \mapsto F) * R\}$$
$$(\text{where } x_1, ..., x_n \notin \mathrm{Free}(E, F).)$$

that will be useful when defining symbolic execution later.

The $-\!\!*$ connective has not often been used in proofs of particular programs (some examples are in [84,66,32]). But it is a handy thing to have when doing metatheoretic reasoning about a system [47,86,67,17]. The de Morgan dual $\neg(P \!-\!\!* \neg Q)$ (called 'septraction' in [81]) has played a central role in the formulation of a logic marrying separation logic and the rely-guarantee method for concurrent programs, and it is used in an automated tool based on the marriage logic [19].

An example metatheoretic use of $-\!\!*$ is in proving completeness results. For example, the following derivation

$$\cfrac{\cfrac{\{E \mapsto -\}\, [E] := F\, \{E \mapsto F\}}{\{(E \mapsto -) * ((E \mapsto F) -\!\!* Q)\}\, [E] := F\, \{(E \mapsto F) * ((E \mapsto F) -\!\!* Q)\}}\ \text{Frame}}{\{(E \mapsto -) * ((E \mapsto F) -\!\!* Q)\}\, [E] := F\, \{Q\}}\ \text{Consequence}$$

gives us general precondition for any postcondition Q, and this is key to showing that the small axiom for mutation is not missing anything.

Exercise 7 *Go back over the proof-by-execution style arguments you gave in the previous exercises, and convince yourself that you can formalize them in the proof system given in this section. You will probably want to use derived laws for each of the basic program statements. In such proofs you get to use the semantics as an oracle when deciding the implication statements in the rule of consequence.*

Exercise 8 *Formulate an operational semantics of $[E] := F$ in terms of stores and heaps. I.e., say when $[E] := F, s, h$ evaluates to s, h'. Don't use separation logic in this formulation.*

For a given set of states Q, say what it means to be the weakest precondition of $[E] := F$ with postcondition Q.

Finally, prove (in math, not in logic) that $(E \mapsto -) * ((E \mapsto F) -\!\!* Q)$ expresses the weakest precondition.

Aside: On Variable Conditions and store-vs-environment. In Section 2 I skated over the issue of Modifies sets, not mentioning them when introducing the frame rule. Conditions involving Modifies sets are inelegant, and are all the more irritating because they arise from a deliberate punning in Hoare logic between store and environment, which is uncommon in programming languages.

At the birth of program semantics, in one of the founding papers of the field, Strachey advised to distinguish the environment (association of variables to values), which can be altered by variable binding in a way that obeys a stack discipline, from the store (association of values to locations), which can be mutated by assignment [78]. Programming languages from C to ML to Java observe Strachey's distinction. The benefit from conflating the ideas is that one gets beautifully simple specifications and proofs of simple example programs in Hoare logic, or in Dijkstra's wp calculus: it leads to neater (shorter) examples to illustrate ideas, so in that sense the pun was worth it. I persist with the pun in these lectures for the same reason. But, researchers are more and more avoiding conflating store and environment in working out their theories, and proof tools for C and Java do not need to worry about Modifies sets. See [65] for further discussion.

3.4. Tight Specifications

The issues related to frame axioms that we discussed in Section 2.2 go a long way back, to the beginning work on logic in AI [57]. Fundamentally, the reason why AI issues are relevant to program logic is just that programmers describe their code in a way that corresponds to a commonsense reading of specifications, where much is left unsaid. Practically, if we do not employ *some kind* of solution to the AI problems, then specifications quickly become extremely complicated [11].

Some people think that the real problem is in a way negative in nature, is to avoid writing nasty frame axioms like we did in the 'back in the day' discussion in Section 2.2. Other people think the problem is just to have succinct specs, however one gets them. I have always thought both of these, succinct specs and avoiding writing frame axioms, should be a consequence of a solution, but are not themselves the problem. My approach to this issue has always been to embrace the 'commonsense reasoning' aspect first, and for this the idea of a 'tight specification' is crucial: the idea is that if you don't say that something changes, then it doesn't. For example, if you say that a robot moves block A from position 1 to position 2, then the commonsense reading is that you are implicitly saying as well that this action does not change the position of a separate block B (unless, perhaps, block B is on top of block A). Programmers' informal descriptions of their code are similar. In the java.util List interface the description of the copy method is just that it 'copies all of the elements from one list into another'. There is no mention of frames in the description: the description carries the understanding that the frame remains unchanged. The need to describe the frames explicitly in some formalisms is just an artefact, which programmers do not find necessary when talking about their code (because of this commonsense reasoning that they employ).

Be that as it may, formalization of the notion of tight specification proved to be surprisingly difficult, and in AI there have been many elaborate theories advanced to try to capture this notion – circumscription, default logic, nonmonotonic logic, and more – far too many to give a proper account of here. Without claiming to be able to solve the general AI problem, this section explains how an old idea in program logic, when connected to the principle of local reasoning (that you only need to talk about the cells a program touches), gives a powerful and yet very simple approach to tight specifications.

The old idea is of *fault-avoiding specifications*. To formulate this, let us suppose that we have a semantics of commands where $C, \sigma \leadsto^* \sigma'$ indicates that there is a terminating computation of command C from state σ to state σ'. In the RAM model σ can be a pair of a store and a heap, but the notion can be formulated at a more general level than this particular model. Additionally, we require a judgement form $C, \sigma \leadsto^*$ fault. In the RAM model, fault can be taken to indicate a memory fault: a dereferencing of a dangling pointer or a double-free. Again, more generally, fault can be used for other sorts of errors.

Here, then, is a fault-avoiding semantics of triples, where for generality we are viewing the preconditions and postconditions as sets of states rather than as formulae written in some particular assertion language.

Faut-Avoiding Partial Correctness

$\{A\} C \{B\}$ holds iff $\forall \sigma \in A$

1. no faults: $C, \sigma \not\leadsto^*$ fault
2. partial correctness: $C, \sigma \leadsto^* \sigma'$ implies $\sigma' \in B$.

The 'no faults' clause is a reasonable thing to have as a way for proven programs to avoid errors, and was used as far back as Hoare and Wirth's axiomatic semantics of Pascal in 1973 [45]. Notice that the small axioms given above are already in a form compatible with the fault-avoiding semantics. For instance, in the axiom

$$\{E \mapsto -\} [E] := F \{E \mapsto F\}$$

the $E \mapsto -$ in the precondition ensures that E is not a dangling pointer, and so $[E] := F$ will not memory fault.

Remarkably, besides ensuring that well-specified programs avoid certain errors, it was realized much later [47] that the fault-avoiding interpretation gives us an approach to tight specifications. The key point is a consequence of the 'no faults' clause: touching any cells not known to be allocated in the precondition falsifies the triple, so *any cells not 'mentioned' (known to be allocated) in the pre will remain unchanged.* To see why, suppose I tell you

$$\{10 \mapsto -\} \, C \, \{10 \mapsto 25\}$$

but I don't tell you what C is. Then I claim C cannot change location 11 if it happens to be allocated in the pre-state (when 10 is also allocated). For, if C changed location 11, it would have to access location 11, and this would lead to `fault` when starting in a state where 10 is allocated and 11 is not. That would falsify the triple (no error clause). As a consequence we obtain that

$$\{10 \mapsto - * 11 \mapsto 4\} \, C \, \{10 \mapsto 25 * 11 \mapsto 4\}$$

should hold.

This reasoning is the basis for the frame rule. But the semantic fact that location 11 doesn't change is completely independent of separation logic. In fact, we could state a similar conclusion without mentioning $*$ at all

$$\{10 \hookrightarrow - \wedge 11 \hookrightarrow 4\} \, C \, \{10 \hookrightarrow 25 \wedge 11 \hookrightarrow 4\}$$

Separation logic, and the frame rule, only give you a *convenient* way to exploit the tightness (that things don't change if you don't mention them) in the fault-avoiding interpretation. This tightness phenomenon is in a sense at a more fundamental level, prior to logic.

It is useful to consider that for this approach to tight specifications to work `fault` does not literally need to indicate memory fault, and it is not necessary to use a low-level memory model. For instance, we can put a notion of 'accesses' or 'ownership' in a model, and then when the program strays beyond what is owned we declare a specification false: then, the same argument as above lets us conclude that certain cells do not change. This is the idea used in implicit dynamic frames [77], and in separation logics for garbage-collected languages like Java where there are no memory faults (e.g., [66]). Alternate approaches may be found in [4,3,49].

I have tried to explain the basis for tight specifications above in a semi-formal way. But, the reader might have noticed that there were some unstated assumptions behind my arguments. One can imagine mathematical relations on states and `fault` that contradict our conclusion that 11 will remain unchanged. One such relation is as follows: if the input heap is a singleton, it sets the contents of the only allocated location to be 25, and otherwise sets all allocated locations in the input heap to have contents 50. This is not a program that you can write in C, but it shows that that there are *locality properties* of the semantics of programs at work behind the tight interpretation of triples, and it is important theoretically to set these conditions down precisely; see [86,18,72].

Exercise 9 *Without saying what the commands C are, and ignoring the store component (i.e., think about heap only), formulate sufficient conditions on the relations $C, \sigma \rightsquigarrow^* \sigma'$ and $C, \sigma \rightsquigarrow^*$ fault which make the frame rule valid according to fault-avoiding partial correctness. Give a proof of the validity of the frame rule from these conditions.*

Are your conditions necessary as well as sufficient?

4. Symbolic Heaps, Symbolic Execution and Abstract Interpretation

In the previous sections I emphasized an informal view of program proof as a form of symbolic execution. That is the view implemented in a number of verification and analysis tools based on separation logic, beginning with SMALLFOOT [7]. In this section I describe the foundations of this approach, and give a short introduction to its extension to program analysis (where abstraction is used to calculate loop invariants).

4.1. Symbolic Heaps

When designing an automatic program verification tool there are almost always compromises to be made, forced by the constraints of recursive undecidability of so many questions about logics and programs. The first tools based on separation logic chose to restrict attention to a certain format of assertions which made three tasks easier than they might otherwise have been: symbolic execution, entailment checking, and frame inference.

  Symbolic heaps [6,30] are formulae of the form

$$\exists \vec{X}.(P_1 \wedge \cdots P_n) \wedge (S_1 * \cdots * S_m)$$

where the P_i and S_j are primitive pure and spatial predicates, and $\vec{X}$ is a vector of logical variables (variables not used in programs). We understand the nullary conjunction of P_i's as *true* and the nullary $*$-conjunction of S_i's as *emp*. The special form of symbolic heaps does not allow, for instance, nesting of $*$ and $\wedge$, or boolean negation $\neg$ around $*$, or the separating implication $-\!*$. This special form was chosen, originally, to match the usage of separation logic in a number of by-hand proofs that had been done. The form does not cover all proofs, such as Yang's proof of the Schorr-Waite algorithm [84], so there are immediately-known limitations.

  The grammar for symbolic heaps can be instantiated with different sets of basic pure and spatial predicates. Pure formulae are heap-independent, and describe properties of variables only, where the spatial formulae specify properties of the heap. One instantiation is as follows

SIMPLE LISTS INSTANTIATION

$$P ::= E{=}E \mid E{\neq}E \mid$$
$$S ::= E{\mapsto}E \mid lsne(E, E) \mid true$$

Expressions E include program variables x, logical variables X, or constants κ (e.g., *nil*). Here, the *points-to* predicate $x{\mapsto}y$ denotes a heap with a single allocated cell at address x with content y, and $lsne(x, y)$ denotes a nonempty list segment from x to y. This is the list segment predicate used in the paper [30] on program analysis, which described the analysis that we call BABY SPACEINVADER (the grown up version is represented in [5,85]). In contrast, the 'possibly empty list segments' predicate *ls* we described before was used in SMALLFOOT. It turns out that there is no one best predicate. In a practical program analysis tool, it is helpful to keep both forms of segment *ls* and *lsne* in the assertion language, even though they can be expressed in terms of one another and disjunction: keeping distinct predicates for empty and nonempty list segments in a language provides a means to help limit the number of disjuncts that need to be considered by the program analysis, a key issue in dealing with state-space explosion [85]. Some tools even prefer the imprecise list segment predicate *ils* from Exercise 4, to make the abstraction or widening step in an abstract interpreter easier to design.

There are many other instantiations that one can consider. One instantiation keeps P the same and replaces simple linked-lists by a higher-order variant which allows lists to be nested [5]. Varieties of trees, possibly with back pointers, have been considered [20]. As have predicates that track arithmetic information or the contents of data structures [8,51,80]. Very complicated abstract domains are needed to cope with the complicated data structures occurring in real-world programs. But in these lectures we will stick with the simple lists, for simplicity of presentation.

CONVENTIONS. We observe the following conventions. In writing a symbolic heap we omit the leading $\exists \vec{X}$, understanding that the logical variables X are implicitly existentially quantified. Also, we overload the $*$ operator, so that it also works for entire symbolic heaps H and not only the components.

$$((P_1 \wedge \cdots P_n) \wedge (S_1 * \cdots * S_m)) * ((P_1' \wedge \cdots P_{n'}') \wedge (S_1' * \cdots * S_{m'}'))$$
$$\triangleq (P_1 \wedge \cdots P_n \wedge P_1' \wedge \cdots P_{n'}') \wedge (S_1 * \cdots * S_m * S_1' * \cdots * S_{m'}')$$

4.2. Symbolic Execution

The symbolic execution semantics $H, A \Longrightarrow H'$ takes a symbolic heap H and an atomic command, and transforms it into an output symbolic heap or `fault`. In these rules we require that the logical variables X, Y be fresh.

SYMBOLIC EXECUTION RULES

$$
\begin{array}{llll}
H & x := E & \Longrightarrow x = E[X/x] \wedge H[X/x] \\
H * E \mapsto F & x := [E] & \Longrightarrow x = F[X/x] \wedge H * E \mapsto F)[X/x] \\
H * E \mapsto F & [E] := G & \Longrightarrow H * E \mapsto G \\
H & x := \mathbf{cons}(-) & \Longrightarrow H[X/x] * x \mapsto X \\
H * E \mapsto F & \mathbf{free}(E) & \Longrightarrow H
\end{array}
$$

With the convention that the logical variables are implicitly existentially quantified, the first rule is just a restating of Floyd's axiom for assignment. The other rules can be obtained from the small axioms of Section 3 by applications of the structural rules.

The rules for $x := [E]$, $[E] := G$ and $[E] := G$ all assume that we have $E \mapsto F$ explicitly in the precondition. In some cases, this knowledge that E points to something will be somewhat less explicit, as in the symbolic heap $E = E' \wedge E' \mapsto F$. Then, a simple amount of logical reasoning can convert this formula to the equivalent form $E = E' \wedge E \mapsto F$, which is now ready for an execution step. In another case, $lsne(E, F)$, we might have to unroll the inductive definition to reveal the $\mapsto$. In general, for any of these heap-accessing forms, we need to massage a symbolic heap to 'make $E \mapsto$ explicit'. Here are sample rules for doing this massaging.

REARRANGEMENT RULES

$$A(E) \quad ::= [E] := G \mid [E] := G \mid [E] := G$$
$$P(E, F) ::= E \mapsto F \mid lsne(E, F)$$

$$\frac{H_0 * P(E, G), \; A(E) \implies H_1}{H_0 * P(F, G), \; A(E) \implies H_1} \quad H_0 \vdash E = F$$

$$\frac{H_0 * E \mapsto X * lsne(X, G), \; A(E) \implies H_1}{H_0 * lsne(E, G), \; A(E) \implies H_1}$$

$$\frac{H_0 * E \mapsto F, \; A(E) \implies H_1}{H_0 * lsne(E, F), \; A(E) \implies H_1}$$

$$\frac{H \nvdash \texttt{Allocated}(E)}{H, \; A(E) \implies \texttt{fault}}$$

In these rules we referred to a notion of entailment $\vdash$ that will be discussed in Section 4.4. $\texttt{Allocated}(E)$ can be represented by the assertion $E \mapsto X * true$ where X is fresh.

[Aside: This rearrangement notion is related to the *partial concretization* operation used in shape analysis [75,76], where one concretizes just enough of an abstract value so that the concrete program semantics can be applied. Rearrangement is also a special case of the concept of frame inference discussed later in Section 4.5.]

It is a good idea, and good for practice, for you to become familiar with the different variations on list segments.

Exercise 10 *Without looking at any of the papers referenced in this section...*

1. *Give an inductive definition of the predicate for necessarily non-empty list segments lsne, corresponding to the rearrangement rules above.*
2. *Give rearrangement rules that would be appropriate for the earlier definition of possibly empty list segments, ls.*
3. *Consider the formulae*

$$ls(x, y) * ls(x, z) \qquad and \qquad lsne(x, y) * lsne(x, z)$$

   Is either formula satisfiable? Might this affect any of the steps in symbolic execution?
4. *(Advanced) Write an inductive definition for a predicate that describes doubly-linked list segments. It should have four arguments. Be careful about the base case.*
   Write rearrangement rules for this doubly-linked list predicate.

4.3. Recipe for Cooking a Verifier

Using symbolic execution, it is possible to construct an automatic verification tool as follows. The input to the tool is a while program with heap-manipulating primitives as in the previous section. The program must be annotated with loop invariants and a precondition and a postcondition. The SMALLFOOT `list_append` program from Section 3.2 is of this form. The usual rules of Hoare logic for loops and conditionals then enable us to chop up the correctness of such a program into a number of questions of the form $\{H\} c_1; ...; c_n \{H'\}$ for atomic commands c_i. If we can verify that each of these straight-line specifications $\{H\} c_1; ...; c_n \{H'\}$ is true then we can conclude that the beginning program satisfies its pre/post spec.

In many verification tools the straightline specs $\{H\} c_1; ...; c_n \{H'\}$ are decided by using a weakest preconditon calculation to obtain a formula $wp(c_1; ...; c_n, H')$ and then asking a theorem prover if $H \Rightarrow wp(c_1; ...; c_n, H')$. Or, a strongest postcondition could be used.

The approach used often in separation logic tools is something like the strongest post calculation, except that lots of subsidiary calls are made to a theorem prover along the way. To decide $\{H\} c_1; ...; c_n \{H'\}$ we first ask the theorem prover if H is inconsistent. If it is, we are done (the spec is true). Second, if $c_1, ..., c_n$ is the empty sequence we ask a prover if $H \vdash H'$. Otherwise, we apply symbolic execution the first statement c_1, and this gives us `fault` or several symbolic heaps (several because there is nondeterminism in rearrangement, and since some basic commands in a real language might have disjunctions in their postconditions. (Why might `malloc()` have a disjunction as its post?). A theorem prover is consulted in the rearrangement phase here. If `fault` resulted from symbolic execution then were are done (the spec is false). If, instead, execution yields several heaps $H_1, ..., H_m$ then we return the conjunction of the smaller questions $\{H_i\} ..; c_n \{H'\}$. This last case essentially relies on the rule

$$\frac{\{P_1\} C \{Q\} \quad \cdots \quad \{P_n\} C \{Q\}}{\{P_1 \vee \cdots \vee P_n\} C \{Q\}}$$

of Hoare logic.

This verification strategy relies on having a theorem prover to answer entailment questions $H \vdash H'$. A straightforward embedding of separation logic into a classical logic, where one writes the semantics in the target logic (e.g., '$\exists \sigma_1 \sigma_2. \sigma = \sigma_1 \bullet \sigma_2...$'), has not yet yielded an effective prover, because it introduces existential quantifiers to give the semantics of $*$. Therefore, proof tools for separation logic has used dedicated proof procedures, built from the proof rules of the logic. (Work is underway on more nuanced interpretations into existing provers that do more than a direct semantic embedding.)

4.4. Proof Procedures for Entailment

An approach to proving symbolic heaps was pioneered by Josh Berdine and Cristiano Calcagno [6]. Their approach revolves around proof rules for abstraction and subtraction. A sample abstraction rule is

$$ls(x, t) * list(t) \vdash list(x)$$

where the subtraction rule is

$$\frac{Q_1 \vdash Q_2}{Q_1 * S \vdash Q_2 * S}$$

Their basic idea is to try to reduce an entailment to an axiom $B \wedge emp \vdash true \wedge emp$ by successively applying abstraction rules, and Subtracting when possible. The basic idea can be appreciated by considering two examples.

First, a successful example:

$\ddot\smile$

$emp \vdash emp$	Axiom!
$list(x) \vdash list(x)$	Subtract
$ls(x,t) * list(t) \vdash list(x)$	Abstract (Inductive)
$ls(x,t) * t{\mapsto}y * list(y) \vdash list(x)$	Abstract (Roll)

The entailment on the bottom is the one we needed to prove at the end of the `list_append` procedure from Section 3.2. The first step, going upward, is a simple rolling up of an inductive definition. The second step is more serious: it is one that we would use induction in the metalanguage to justify. We then get to a position where we can apply the subtraction rule, and this gets us back to a basic axiom.

For an unsuccessful example

$\ddot\frown$

$list(y) \vdash emp$	Junk: Not Axiom!
$list(x) * list(y) \vdash list(x)$	Subtract
$ls(x,t) * t{\mapsto}nil * list(y) \vdash list(x)$	Abstract (Inductive)

The last line is an entailment that SMALLFOOT would attempt to prove if the statement `t->tl = y` at the end of the `list_append` program were replaced by `t->tl = nil`. There we do an abstraction followed by a subtraction and we get to a position where we cannot reduce further. Rightly, we cannot prove this entailment.

The detailed design and theoretical analysis of a proof theory based on these ideas is nontrivial. For the specific case of singly-linked list segments, Berdine and Calcagno were able to formulate a complete and terminating proof theory. There is no space to go into all the details of their theory, but it is worth listing their abstraction rules, presented here as entailments.

Rolling

$$emp \vdash ls(E, E)$$

$$E_1 \neq E_3 \wedge E_1{\mapsto}E_2 * ls(E_2, E_3) \vdash ls(E_1, E_3)$$

Induction Avoidance

$$ls(E_1, E_2) * ls(E_2, nil) \vdash ls(E_1, nil)$$

$$ls(E_1, E_2) * E_2{\mapsto}nil \vdash ls(E_1, nil)$$

$$ls(E_1, E_2) * ls(E_2, E_3) * E_3{\mapsto}E_4 \vdash ls(E_1, E_3) * E_3{\mapsto}E_4$$

$$E_3 \neq E_4 \wedge ls(E_1, E_2) * ls(E_2, E_3) * ls(E_3, E_4)$$
$$\vdash \quad ls(E_1, E_3) * ls(E_3, E_4)$$

The remarkable thing about these abstraction rules is not that they are sound, but in a sense complete: any true fact about list segments and points-to facts that can be expressed in symbolic heap form can be proven using these axioms, without appealing to an explicit induction axiom or rule. The Berdine/Calcagno proof theory works by using these rules on the left (in effect employing a special case of the Cut rule of sequent calculus). It has other rules as well, such as for inferring $x \neq nil$ from $x \mapsto -$: at every stage, their decision procedure records as many pure disequalities as possible on the left, and it substitutes out all equalities, getting to a kind of normal form. It is this normal form that makes the subtraction rule complete (a two-way inference rule).

Note: in this subsection we have gone back to the ls rather than $lsne$ predicate, as Berdine and Calcagno formulated their rules for ls. In fact, it is easier to design a complete proof theory for $lsne$ rather than ls. It is also relatively easy (and was folklore knowledge) to see that entailment for the $lsne$ symbolic heaps can be decided in polytime, but the question for the ls remained open until a recent paper which showed the entailment is indeed in polytime in the original problem [23]. (The reason for subtlety in this question is related to question 3 of Exercise 10; you might go back there and wonder about it.)

I like to call this approach of combining abstraction and subtraction rules the 'crunch, crunch' method. It works by taking a sequent $H \vdash H'$ and applying abstraction and subtraction rules to crunch it down to a smaller size by removing $*$-conjuncts, until you get emp as the spatial part on one side or the other of $\vdash$. If you have emp on only one side, you have a failed proof. If you have other pure facts, of the form $\Pi \wedge emp \vdash \Pi' \wedge emp$ you can then ask a straight classical logic question $\Pi \vdash \Pi'$. The final check, $\Pi \vdash \Pi'$, is a place where one could call an external theorem prover, say for a decidable theory such as linear arithmetic, and that is all the more useful when the pure part can contain a richer variety of assertions than in the simple fragment considered in this section. Indeed, there have been a number of provers for separation logic developed that use variations on this 'crunch, crunch' approach together with an external classical logic solver, including [13,68] and the provers inside VERIFAST [48], JSTAR [31], HIP [60] and SLAYER [9].

4.5. Frame Inference

Entailment is a standard problem for verifiers to face. In work applying separation logic, a pivotal development has been identification of the notion of *frame inference*, which is an extension of the entailment question:

In a frame inference question of the form

$$A \vdash B * \texttt{?frame}$$

the task is, given A and B, to find a formula `?frame` which makes the entailment valid.

Frame inference gives a way to find the 'leftover' portions of heap needed to automatically apply the frame rule in program proofs. This extended entailment capability is used at procedure call sites, where A is an assertion at the call site and B a precondition from a procedure's specification.

A first solution to frame inference was sketched in [6] and implemented in the SMALLFOOT tool. The SMALLFOOT approach works by using information from failed proofs of the standard entailment question $A \vdash B$. Essentially, a failed proof of the form

$$F \vdash emp$$
$$\vdots$$
$$A \vdash B$$

tells us that F is a frame. For, from such a failed proof we can form a proof

$$F \vdash F$$
$$F \vdash emp * F$$
$$\vdots$$
$$A \vdash B * F$$

by tacking $*F$ on the right everywhere in the failed proof. So, the frame inferring procedure is to go upwards using the 'crunch, crunch' proof search method until you can go no further: if your attempted proof is of the form indicated above, it can tell you a frame. (Dealing with multiple branches in proofs requires some more subtlety than this description indicates.)

Frame inference is a workhorse of separation logic verification tools. As you can imagine from the discussion surrounding Disptree in Section 2, it is used at procedure call sites to identify the part of a symbolic heap that is not not touched by a procedure. Interprocedural program analysis tools typically use (often incomplete) implementations of frame inference for reasoning with 'procedure summaries' [39,59]. In SMALLFOOT, proof rules for critical regions in concurrent programs are verified using little phantom procedures (called 'specification statements') with specs of the form $\{emp\} - \{R\}$ and $\{R\} - \{emp\}$ for materializing and annihilating portions of storage protected by a lock. Indeed, if one has a good enough frame inference capacity, then symbolic execution can be seen to be a special case of a more general scheme, where basic commands are treated as specification statements (the small axioms), and frame inference is used in place of the special concept of rearrangement. SMALLFOOT and SPACEINVADER did not follow this idealistic approach, preferring to optimize for the common case of the basic statements, but the more recent JSTAR and SLAYER are examples of tools that call a frame inferring theorem prover at every step of symbolic execution [31,9].

4.6. A Taste of Abstract Interpretation

Beginning in 2006 [30,52], a significant amount of work has been done on the use of separation logic in automatic program analysis. There are a number of academic tools, including SPACEINVADER [5,85], THOR [53], XISA [20], FORRESTER [41], PREDATOR [33], SMALLFOOTRG [19], HEAP-HOP [83] and JSTAR [31], and the industrial tools INFER from Monoidics [16] and SLAYER from Microsoft [9]. The tools in this area are a new breed of *shape analysis*, which attempt to discover the shapes of data structures (e.g., whether a list is cyclic or acyclic) in a program [75]. These tools cannot prove functional correctness, but can be applied to code in the thousands or even millions of LOC [85,17].

The general context for this use of separation logic concerns the relation between program logic and program analysis. It has been known since the work of the Cousots in the 1970s [24,25] that concepts from Hoare logic and static program analysis are related. In principle, static analysis can be used to calculate loop invariants and procedure specifications via fixed-point computations, thereby lessening annotation burden. There is a price to pay in that trying to be completely automatic in this way almost forces one to step away from the ideal of proving full functional correctness.

While the relation between analysis and verification has been long known in principle, the last decade has seen a surge of interest in verification-by-static-analysis, with practical demonstrations of its potential such as in SLAM's application of proof technology to Microsoft device drivers [2] and ASTRÉE's proof of the absence of run-time errors in Airbus code [26]. Separation logic enters the picture because these practical tools for verification-oriented static analysis ignore pointer-based data structures, or use coarse models that are insufficient to prove basic properties of them; e.g., SLAM *assumes* memory safety, and ASTRÉE works only on input programs that do not use dynamic allocation. Similar remarks apply to other tools such as BLAST, Magic and others. Data structures present a significant problem in verification-oriented program analysis, and that is the point that the separation logic program analyses are trying to address.

This section illustrates the ideas in the abstractions used in separation logic program analyzers. To begin, suppose you were to continually symbolically execute a program with a while loop. You collect sets of formulae (abstract states) at program points, and generate new ones by symbolically executing program statements. The immediate problem is that you would go on generating symbolic heaps on loop iterations, and the process could diverge: you would never stop generating new symbolic heaps. The most basic idea of program analysis is to use abstraction, the losing of information, to ensure that such a process terminates.

Consider the following program that creates a linked list of indeterminate length.

$\{Pre : emp\}$
x := *nil*;
while (*nondet*()){
        y := cons(-);
        y→tl := x;
        x := y;
}

Suppose we start symbolically executing the program from pre-state emp. On the first iteration, at the program point immediately inside the loop, we will certainly have that $x = nil \wedge emp$ is true, so let us record this in

Loop Invariant so far (1st iteration)
$x = nil \wedge emp$.

Now, if we go around the loop once more, then it is clear that $x \mapsto nil$ will be true at the same program point, so let us add that to our calculation.

Loop Invariant so far (2nd iteration)
$(x = nil \wedge emp) \vee (x \mapsto nil)$.

At the next step we get

Loop Invariant so far (3rd iteration)

$(x = nil \wedge emp) \vee (x \mapsto nil) \vee (x \mapsto X * X \mapsto nil)$

because we put another element on the front of the list. If we keep going this way, we will get lists of length 3, 4 and so on: infinite regress. However, before we go around the loop again, we might employ abstraction, to conclude that we have a list segment. That is, we use the entailment

$$x \mapsto X * X \mapsto nil \vdash lsne(x, nil)$$

on the third disjunct, giving us

Loop Invariant so far (3rd iteration after abstraction)

$(x = nil \wedge emp) \vee (x \mapsto nil) \vee lsne(x, nil)$

Loss of information has occurred because in the third disjunct we have forgotten that the list from x is of length precisely 2. And, by this step we have taken ourselves to a situation where the assertion describes finitely many heaps (up to isomorphism), to an assertion that describes infinitely many concrete heaps: combining abstraction with symbolic execution allows us to cover a great many more heaps.

Now, if we go around the loop again, we obtain

Loop Invariant so far (4th iteration before abstraction)

$(x = nil \wedge emp) \vee (x \mapsto nil) \vee (x \mapsto X * lsne(X, nil))$

and we can apply a Berdine/Calcagno abstraction rule

$$x \mapsto X * lsne(X, nil) \vdash lsne(x, nil)$$

to obtain

Loop Invariant so far (4th iteration after abstraction)

$(x = nil \wedge emp) \vee (x \mapsto nil) \vee lsne(x, nil)$

Lo and behold, what we have obtained on the 4th iteration after abstraction is the same as the 3rd. We might as well stop now, as further execution of this variety will not give us anything new: we have reached a fixed-point. As it happens, this loop invariant is also the postcondition of the procedure in this example.

In this narrative the human (me) was the abstract interpreter, choosing when and how to do abstraction. To implement a tool we need to make it systematic. In the SPACEINVADER breed of tools, this is done using rewrite rules that correspond to Berdine/Calcagno abstraction rules for entailment described in Section 4.4. The abstract interpreter is sound automatically because applying those rules to simplify formulae is just using the Hoare rule of consequence on the right. The art is in not applying the rules *too often*, which would make one lose too much information, sometimes resulting in `fault` coming out of your abstract interpreter for perfectly safe problems (a 'false alarm').

The way you set up a proof-theoretic abstract interpreter is as follows. In addition to symbolic execution rules, there are abstraction rules which you apply periodically (say, when going through loop iterations); this allows the exection process to saturate (find a fixed-point). Here are some of the rules used in (baby) SPACEINVADER [30].

$$(\rho, \rho' \text{ range over } lsne, \mapsto)$$

$$\exists \vec{X}.H * \rho(x, Y) * \rho'(Y, Z) \longrightarrow \exists \vec{X}.H * lsne(x, Z) \quad \text{where } Y \text{ not free in } H$$

$$\exists \vec{X}.H * \rho(Y, Z) \longrightarrow \exists \vec{X}.H * true \qquad\qquad \text{where } Y \text{ not provably reachable}$$
$$\text{from program vars}$$

The first rule says to forget about the length of uninterrupted list segments, where there are no outside pointers (from H) into the internal point. The abstraction 'gobbles up' logical variables appearing in internal points of lists, by swallowing them into list segments, as long as these internal points are unshared. This is true of either free or bound logical variables. The requirement that they not be shared is an accuracy rather than soundness consideration; we stop the rules from firing too often, so as not to lose too much information.

[A remark on terminology: What I am simply calling the 'abstraction' step is a special case of what is called Widening in the abstract interpretation literature [24], and a direct analogue of the 'canonical abstraction' used in 3-valued shape analysis [76].]

Exercise 11 *Define a program that never faults, but for which the abstract semantics just sketched returns* fault.

Although I have not given a fully formal specification of the abstract interpreter above, thinking about the nature of the list segment predicates and the restricted syntax of symbolic heaps is one way to find such a program (e.g., if the program needs a loop invariant that is not expressible with finitely many symbolic heaps).

This exercise actually concerns a general point in program analysis. If you have a terminating analysis that is trying to solve an undecidable problem, it must necessarily be possible to trick the analysis. Since most interesting questions about programs are undecidable, we must accept that any program analysis for these questions will have an heuristic aspect in its design.

4.7. Contextual Remarks

This specific abstraction idea in the illustration in this section, to forget about the length of uninterrupted list segments, is sometimes called 'the Distefano abstraction': it was defined by Distefano in his PhD thesis [29]. The idea does not depend on separation logic, and similar ideas have been used in other abstract domains, such as based on 3-valued logic [54] or on graphs [55]. Once SMALLFOOT's symbolic execution appeared, it simply was relatively easy to port Distefano's abstraction to separation logic, when defining BABY SPACEINVADER [30]. Around the same time, very similar ideas were independently discovered by Magill et. al. [52].

These first abstract interpreters did not achieve a lot practically, but opened up the possibility of exploring the use of separation logic in program analysis. A growing amount of work has been going forward in a number of directions, an incomplete list of which includes the following, which are good places to start for further reading.

1. The use of the frame rule and frame inference $A \vdash B * ?\texttt{frame}$ in interprocedural analysis [39];

2. The use of abductive inference $A * \,?\texttt{antiframe} \,\vdash\, B$ to approximate footprints, leading to a compositional analysis, and a boost to the level of automation and scalability [17];
3. The use of a higher-order list segment notion to attack complicated data structures in device drivers [5,85];
4. Analyses for concurrent programs [40];
5. Automatic parallelization [71,46];
6. Program-termination proving [8,51,14];
7. Analysis of data structures with sharing [21,50].

This last section has been but a sketch, and I have left out a lot of details. I will possibly extend these notes in future to put more formalities into this last section. For now I just point you to [30] for a mathematically thorough description of one abstract interpreter based on separation logic.

The leading edge, as of 2011, of what can be achieved practically on real-world code by these tools is probably represented by SLAYER [9] and INFER [16], and can be glimpsed by academic papers that fed into them [85,17]. However, there are some areas (sharing, trees) where academic prototypes outperform them precision-wise, and the leading edge in any case is moving quickly at this moment.

I have talked about automatic verification and analysis in these notes, but many of the ideas – such as frame inference, symbolic execution, abstraction/subtraction-based proof theory – are relevant as well in interactive proving. There have been several embeddings of separation logic in higher-order logics used in interactive proof assistants (e.g., [56, 35,82,79,58,1]), where the proof theoretic or symbolic execution rules are derived as lemmas. A recent paper [22] gives a good account of the state of the art and references to the literature, as well as an explanation of expressivity limitations of approaches to program verification based on automatic theorem proving for first-order logic.

It should be mentioned that there is no conflict here of having several logics (separation, first-order, higher-order, etc.): there is no need to search for 'the one true logic'. In particular, even though they can be embedded in foundational higher-order logics, special-purpose formalisms like separation and modal and temporal logics are useful for identifying specification and reasoning idioms that make specifications and proofs easier to find, for either the human or the machine.

References

[1] A.W. Appel. VeriSmall: Verified Smallfoot shape analysis. CPP 2011: First International Conference on Certified Programs and Proofs, 2011.

[2] T. Ball, E. Bounimova, B. Cook, V. Levin, J. Lichtenberg, C. McGarvey, B. Ondrusek, S.K. Rajamani, and A. Ustuner. Thorough static analysis of device drivers. In *Proceedings of the 2006 EuroSys Conference*, pages 73–85, 2006.

[3] A. Banerjee, D.A. Naumann, and S. Rosenberg. Regional logic for local reasoning about global invariants. In *22nd ECOOP, Springer LNCS 5142*, pages 387–411, 2008.

[4] M. Barnett, R. DeLine, M. Fahndrich, K.R.M. Leino, and W. Schulte. Verification of object-oriented programs with invariants. *Journal of Object Technology*, 3(6):27–56, 2004.

[5] J. Berdine, C. Calcagno, B. Cook, D. Distefano, P. O'Hearn, T. Wies, and H. Yang. Shape analysis of composite data structures. *19th CAV, 2007*.

[6]   J. Berdine, C. Calcagno, and P.W. O'Hearn. Symbolic execution with separation logic. In K. Yi, editor, *APLAS 2005*, volume 3780 of *LNCS*, 2005.

[7]   J. Berdine, C. Calcagno, and P.W. O'Hearn. Smallfoot: Automatic modular assertion checking with separation logic. In *4th FMCO*, pp115-137, 2006.

[8]   J. Berdine, B. Cook, D. Distefano, and P. O'Hearn. Automatic termination proofs for programs with shape-shifting heaps. In *18th CAV, Springer LNCS 4144*, pages pp386–400, 2006.

[9]   J. Berdine, B. Cook, and S. Ishtiaq. Slayer: Memory safety for systems-level code. In *23rd CAV, Springer LNCS 6806*, pages 178–183, 2011.

[10] B. Biering, L. Birkedal, and N. Torp-Smith. BI-hyperdoctrines, higher-order separation logic, and abstraction. *ACM TOPLAS*, 5(29), 2007.

[11] A. Borgida, J. Mylopoulos, and R. Reiter. On the frame problem in procedure specifications. *IEEE Transactions of Software Engineering*, 21:809–838, 1995.

[12] R. Bornat. Proving pointer programs in Hoare logic. *Mathematics of Program Construction*, 2000.

[13] M. Botincan, M.J. Parkinson, and W. Schulte. Separation logic verification of C programs with an SMT solver. *Electr. Notes Theor. Comput. Sci.*, 254:5–23, 2009.

[14] J. Brotherston, R. Bornat, and C. Calcagno. Cyclic proofs of program termination in separation logic. In *35th POPL*, pages 101–112, 2008.

[15] R.M. Burstall. Some techniques for proving correctness of programs which alter data structures. *Machine Intelligence*, 7:23–50, 1972.

[16] C. Calcagno and D. Distefano. Infer: An automatic program verifier for memory safety of C programs. In *NASA Formal Methods Symposium, Springer LNCS 6617*, pages 459–465, 2011.

[17] C. Calcagno, D. Distefano, P.W. O'Hearn, and H. Yang. Compositional shape analysis by means of bi-abduction. Journal of the ACM 58(6). (Preliminary version appeared in POPL'09.), 2011.

[18] C. Calcagno, P. O'Hearn, and H. Yang. Local action and abstract separation logic. In *22nd LICS*, pp366-378, 2007.

[19] C. Calcagno, M.J. Parkinson, and V. Vafeiadis. Modular safety checking for fine-grained concurrency. In *14th SAS, Springer LNCS 4634*, pages 233–248, 2007.

[20] B. Chang and X. Rival. Relational inductive shape analysis. In *36th POPL*, pages 247–260. ACM, 2008.

[21] R. Cherini, L. Rearte, and J.O. Blanco. A shape analysis for non-linear data structures. In *17th SAS, Springer LNCS 6337*, pages 201–217, 2010.

[22] A. Chlipala. Mostly-automated verification of low-level programs in computational separation logic. In *32nd PLDI*, pages 234–245, 2011.

[23] B. Cook, C. Haase, J. Ouaknine, M.J. Parkinson, and J. Worrell. Tractable reasoning in a fragment of separation logic. In *22nd CONCUR, Springer LNCS 6901*, pages 235–249, 2011.

[24] P. Cousot and R. Cousot. Abstract interpretation: A unified lattice model for static analysis of programs by construction or approximation of fixpoints. In *4th POPL*, pp238-252, 1977.

[25] P. Cousot and R. Cousot. Systematic design of program analysis frameworks. 6th POPL, pp269-282, 1979.

[26] P. Cousot, R. Cousot, J. Feret, L. Mauborgne, A. Miné, D. Monniaux, and X. Rival. The ASTRÉE analyzer. 14th ESOP, pp21-30, 2005.

[27] E.W. Dijkstra. *A Discipline of Programming*. Prentice Hall, 1976.

[28] T. Dinsdale-Young, P. Gardner, and M.J. Wheelhouse. Abstraction and refinement for local reasoning. In *3rd VSTTE, Springer LNCS 6217*, pages 199–215, 2010.

[29] D. Distefano. *On model checking the dynamics of object-based software: a foundational approach*. PhD thesis, University of Twente, 2003.

[30] D. Distefano, P. O'Hearn, and H. Yang. A local shape analysis based on separation logic. In *12th TACAS*, 2006. pp287-302.

[31] D. Distefano and M. Parkinson. jStar: Towards Practical Verification for Java. In *23rd OOPSLA*, pages 213–226, 2008.

[32] Mike Dodds, Suresh Jagannathan, and Matthew J. Parkinson. Modular reasoning for deterministic parallelism. In *38th POPL*, pages 259–270, 2011.

[33] K. Dudka, P. Peringer, and T. Vojnar. Predator: A practical tool for checking manipulation of dynamic data structures using separation logic. In *23rd CAV, Springer LNCS 6806*, pages 372–378, 2011.

[34] X. Feng, R. Ferreira, and Z. Shao. On the relationship between concurrent separation logic and assume-guarantee reasoning. In *16th ESOP, Springer LNCS 4421*, 2007.

[35]   X. Feng, Z. Shao, Y. Guo, and Y. Dong. Combining domain-specific and foundational logics to verify complete software systems. In *2nd VSTTE, Springer LNCS 5295*, pages 54–69, 2008.

[36]   R.W. Floyd. Assigning meaning to programs. *Proceedings of Symposium on Applied Mathematics, Vol. 19, J.T. Schwartz (Ed.), A.M.S., pp. 19Đ32*, 1967.

[37]   M. Foley and C.A.R. Hoare. Proof of a recursive program: Quicksort. *Computer Journal*, 14:391–395, 1971.

[38]   P. Gardner, S. Maffeis, and G. Smith. Towards a program logic for Javascript. In *40th POPL*. ACM, 2012.

[39]   A. Gotsman, J. Berdine, and B. Cook. Interprocedural shape analysis with separated heap abstractions. In *13th SAS, Springer LNCS 4134*, pages 240–260, 2006.

[40]   A. Gotsman, J. Berdine, B. Cook, and M. Sagiv. Mostly-automated verification of low-level programs in computational separation logic. In *28th PLDI*, pages 266–277, 2007.

[41]   P. Habermehl, L. Holík, A. Rogalewicz, J. Simácek, and T. Vojnar. Forest automata for verification of heap manipulation. In *23rd CAV, Springer LNCS 6806*, 2011.

[42]   C.A.R. Hoare. An axiomatic basis for computer programming. *Comm. ACM*, 12(10):576–580 and 583, 1969.

[43]   C.A.R. Hoare. Procedures and parameters: An axiomatic approach. In E. Engler, editor, *Symposium on the Semantics of Algebraic Languages*, pages 102–116. Springer, 1971. Lecture Notes in Math. 188.

[44]   C.A.R. Hoare. Proof of a Program: FIND. *Comm. ACM*, 14(1):39–45, 1971.

[45]   C.A.R. Hoare and N. Wirth. An axiomatic definition of the programming language Pascal. *Acta Informatica*, 2:335–355, 1973.

[46]   C. Hurlin. Automatic parallelization and optimization of programs by proof rewriting. In *16th SAS, Springer LNCS 5673*, pages 52–68, 2009.

[47]   S. Isthiaq and P. W. O'Hearn. BI as an assertion language for mutable data structures. In *28th POPL*, pages 36–49, 2001.

[48]   B. Jacobs, J. Smans, F. Philippaerts, F. Vogels, W. Penninckx, and F. Piessens. Verifast: A powerful, sound, predictable, fast verifier for C and Java. In *NASA Formal Methods Symposium, Springer LNCS 6617*, pages 41–55, 2011.

[49]   I.T. Kassios. The dynamic frames theory. *Formal Asp. Comput.*, 23(3):267–288, 2011.

[50]   O. Lee, H.Yang, and R. Petersen. Program analysis for overlaid data structures. In *23rd CAV, Springer LNCS 6808*, pages 592–608, 2011.

[51]   S. Magill, J. Berdine, E.M. Clarke, and B. Cook. Arithmetic strengthening for shape analysis. In *14th SAS, Springer LNCS 4634*, pages 419–436, 2007.

[52]   S. Magill, A. Nanevski, E. Clarke, and P. Lee. Inferring invariants in Separation Logic for imperative list-processing programs. *3rd SPACE Workshop*, 2006.

[53]   S. Magill, M.-S. Tsai, P. Lee, and Y.-K. Tsay. THOR: A tool for reasoning about shape and arithmetic. *20th CAV, Springer LNCS 5123*. pp 428-432, 2008.

[54]   R. Manevich, E. Yahav, G. Ramalingam, and M. Sagiv. Predicate abstraction and canonical abstraction for singly-linked lists. In *6th VMCAI*, pages pp181–198, 2005.

[55]   M. Marron, M.V. Hermenegildo, D. Kapur, and D. Stefanovic. Efficient context-sensitive shape analysis with graph based heap models. In *17th CC, Springer LNCS 4959*, pages 245–259, 2008.

[56]   N. Marti and R. Affeldt. A certified verifier for a fragment of separation logic. *Computer Software, 25(3):135-147*, 2008.

[57]   J. McCarthy and P. Hayes. Some philosophical problems from the standpoint of artificial intelligence. *Machine Intelligence*, 4:463–502, 1969.

[58]   A. Nanevski, V. Vafeiadis, and J. Berdine. Structuring the verification of heap-manipulating programs. In *37th POPL*, pages 261–274, 2010.

[59]   H.H. Nguyen and W.-N. Chin. Enhancing program verification with lemmas. *20th CAV, Springer LNCS 5123*. pp 355-369, 2008.

[60]   H.H. Nguyen, C. David, S. Qin, and W.-Ngan Chin. Automated verification of shape and size properties via separation logic. In *8th VMCAI, Springer LNCS 4349*, pages 251–266, 2007.

[61]   P. O'Hearn, J. Reynolds, and H. Yang. Local reasoning about programs that alter data structures. In *15th CSL*, pp1-19, 2001.

[62]   P. W. O'Hearn. Resources, concurrency and local reasoning. *Theoretical Computer Science*, 375(1-3):271–307, 2007. (Preliminary version appeared in CONCUR'04, LNCS 3170, pp49-67).

[63]   P. W. O'Hearn and D. J. Pym. The logic of bunched implications. *Bulletin of Symbolic Logic*, 5(2):215–244, June 99.

[64]   P.W. O'Hearn, H. Yang, and J.C. Reynolds. Separation and information hiding. *ACM TOPLAS*, 31(3), 2009.

[65]   M. Parkinson, R. Bornat, and C. Calcagno. Variables as resource in Hoare logics. In *21st LICS*, 2006.

[66]   M. J. Parkinson. *Local Reasoning for Java*. Ph.D. thesis, University of Cambridge, 2005.

[67]   M.J. Parkinson and A.J. Summers. The relationship between separation logic and implicit dynamic frames. In *20th ESOP, Springer LNCS 6602*, pages 439–458, 2011.

[68]   J. A. Navarro Pérez and A. Rybalchenko. Separation logic + superposition calculus = heap theorem prover. In *32nd PLDI*, pages 556–566, 2011.

[69]   D. Pym, P. O'Hearn, and H. Yang. Possible worlds and resources: the semantics of BI. *Theoretical Computer Science*, 315(1):257–305, 2004.

[70]   D.J. Pym. *The Semantics and Proof Theory of the Logic of Bunched Implications*. Applied Logic Series. Kluwer Academic Publishers, 2002.

[71]   M. Raza, C. Calcagno, and P. Gardner. Automatic parallelization with separation logic. In *18th ESOP, Springer LNCS 5502*, pages 348–362, 2009.

[72]   M. Raza and P. Gardner. Footprints in local reasoning. *Logical Methods in Computer Science*, 5(2), 2009.

[73]   J. C. Reynolds. Intuitionistic reasoning about shared mutable data structure. In Jim Davies, Bill Roscoe, and Jim Woodcock, editors, *Millennial Perspectives in Computer Science*, pages 303–321, Houndsmill, Hampshire, 2000. Palgrave.

[74]   J. C. Reynolds. Separation logic: A logic for shared mutable data structures. In *17th LICS*, pp55-74, 2002.

[75]   M. Sagiv, T. Reps, and R. Wilhelm. Solving shape-analysis problems in languages with destructive updating. *ACM TOPLAS*, 20(1):1–50, 1998.

[76]   M. Sagiv, T. Reps, and R. Wilhelm. Parametric shape analysis via 3-valued logic. *ACM TOPLAS*, 24(3):217–298, 2002.

[77]   J. Smans, B. Jacobs, and F. Piessens. Implicit dynamic frames: Combining dynamic frames and separation logic. In *23rd ECOOP, LNCS 5653*, pages 148–172, 2009.

[78]   C. Strachey. Towards a formal semantics. In T. B. Steel, Jr., editor, *Formal Language Description Languages for Computer Programming, Proceedings of the IFIP Working Conference*, pages 198–220, Baden bei Wien, Austria, September 1964. North-Holland, Amsterdam, 1966.

[79]   T. Tuerk. A formalisation of Smallfoot in HOL. In *TPHOLs, 22nd International Conference, LNCS 5674*, pages 469–484, 2009.

[80]   V. Vafeiadis. Shape-value abstraction for verifying linearizability. In *10th VMCAI, LNCS 5403*, pages 335–348, 2009.

[81]   V. Vafeiadis and M.J. Parkinson. A marriage of rely/guarantee and separation logic. In *18th CONCUR, Springer LNCS 4703*, pages 256–271, 2007.

[82]   C. Varming and L. Birkedal. Higher-order separation logic in Isabelle/HOLCF. *24th MFPS*, 2008.

[83]   J. Villard, É. Lozes, and C. Calcagno. Tracking heaps that hop with Heap-Hop. In *16th TACAS, Springer LNCS 6015*, pages 275–279, 2010.

[84]   H. Yang. *Local Reasoning for Stateful Programs*. Ph.D. thesis, University of Illinois, Urbana-Champaign, 2001.

[85]   H. Yang, O. Lee, J. Berdine, C. Calcagno, B. Cook, D. Distefano, and P. O'Hearn. Scalable shape analysis for systems code. *20th CAV, Springer LNCS 5123*. pp 385-398, 2008.

[86]   H. Yang and P. O'Hearn. A semantic basis for local reasoning. In *5th FOSSACS*, 2002. Springer LNCS 2303 , pp402-416.

Software Safety and Security
T. Nipkow et al. (Eds.)
IOS Press, 2012
© 2012 The authors and IOS Press. All rights reserved.
doi:10.3233/978-1-61499-028-4-319

A Perspective on
Information-Flow Control

Daniel HEDIN [a] and Andrei SABELFELD [a]

[a] *Chalmers University of Technology, Gothenburg, Sweden*

Abstract. Information-flow control tracks how information propagates through the
program during execution to make sure that the program handles the information
securely. Secure information flow is comprised of two related aspects: information confidentiality and information integrity — intuitively pertaining to the reading and writing of the information. The prevailing basic semantic notion of secure information flow is noninterference, demanding independence of public (or,
in the case of integrity, trusted) output from secret (or, in the case of integrity,
untrusted) input. This document gives an account of the state-of-the-art in confidentiality and integrity policies and their enforcement with a systematic formalization of four dominant formulations of noninterference: termination-insensitive,
termination-sensitive, progress-insensitive, and progress-sensitive, cast in the setting of two minimal while languages.

Keywords. Security, confidentiality, integrity, information flow, noninterference.

1. Information-flow control

The control of how information is propagated by computing systems is vital for information security. Historically, *access control* has been the main means of preventing information from being disseminated. As the name indicates, access control verifies that the
program's access rights at the point of access, and either grants or denies the program access. Once the program has been given access to information no further effort is made to
make sure that the program handles the accessed information correctly. However, access
control is inadequate in many situations, since it forces an all-or-nothing choice of either
fully trusting the program not to leak/compromise information or not allowing access to
this information altogether.

Information-flow control tracks how information propagates through the program
during execution to make sure that the program handles the information securely. The
research on secure information flow goes back to the early 70's [35,39], primarily in
the context of military systems. Secure information flow is comprised of two related
aspects: information *confidentiality* and information *integrity* — intuitively pertaining
to the reading and writing of the information. The prevailing basic semantic notion of
secure information flow is *noninterference* [46], demanding independence of public (or,
in the case of integrity, trusted) output from secret (or, in the case of integrity, untrusted)
input. As the field has matured, numerous variations of noninterference [98], as well as
other semantic characterizations have been explored [103].

Recently, information integrity has received attention [55,57,19,4]. Integrity has frequently been seen as the dual of confidentiality [18], though it can be argued that this description might ignore other important facets [19].

One important aspect of integrity lies in its interaction with *declassification* — intentional lowering of security classification of information — in order to prevent the attacker from controlling what information is declassified [77,78].

Below we give an account of the state-of-the-art in confidentiality and integrity policies and enforcement, with a detailed exposition of various formulations of noninterference.

1.1. Attacker model

Information-flow security aims at protecting confidentiality and integrity of information. Traditionally, the attacker model is program-centric; the attacker is assumed to have access to the program source code and to public observable behavior, e.g., public outputs. In addition, it is assumed that the attacker is in control of the public input of the programs.

With the rise of the web as a more general application platform the old program-centric attacker model is no longer adequate. A web application is often a *mashup* (programmableweb.com) of information and services from different distributed sources. In the web setting, a notion of *web attacker* [15] is of interest. The model is built on the assumption of an honest user who runs a trusted browser on a trusted machine and that the attacker is an owner of malicious web sites that the user might be accessing. This implies that the web attacker is unable to mount man-in-the-middle attacks. This is in contrast to the the classical Dolev-Yao attacker where the attacker is able to overhear, intercept and modify messages on the network. Instead, the network capabilities of the web attacker are restricted to the standard network protocols of communication with servers in the domain of attacker's control.

1.2. Policy languages for confidentiality and integrity

Both confidentiality and integrity policies can be staged into two parts. The *policy language* describing the possible classifications of information and how the different classifications relate, i.e., how information from one classification may flow with respect to the other and the *semantic characterization* describing the meaning of the policy language in terms of the semantics of the programming language. The former is predominantly described using a lattice model [38,52] for information classification. Historically, the latter has typically been a variant of noninterference.

Deviating from policy language based on a lattice of security levels is the work by Myers and Liskov on the *Decentralized Label Model* (DLM) [76]. The DLM shares the lattice structure of classifications, but differs in the intentional interpretation of security levels. The security labels of the DLM track information *ownership* and *read rights* — a label $\{A: B\}$ expresses that A owns the data and that B is given read rights to the data.

More fundamentally different is the policy language of FlowLocks [22,23,24]. The core idea is to associate data with a set of clauses of the form $\Sigma \rightarrow A$. The set Σ states the circumstances under which A may view the data.

1.3. Outline and sources

This document is laid out as follows. Section 2 investigates noninterference for confidentiality. In particular, we detail and compare four flavors of noninterference in terms of two small while languages, and discuss their relative merits. The section ends with a discussion on declassification, and the different dimensions of declassification: *what* is declassified, *who* is able to declassify, *where* the declassification occurs and *when* the declassification takes place. Section 3 presents different facets of integrity: integrity *as a dual to confidentiality* and integrity *as program correctness*. The section ends with a discussion on endorsement (the dual to declassification, when integrity is taken to be the dual of confidentiality), and the corresponding interpretation of the four dimensions. Finally, Section 4 discusses different methods for enforcing secure information flow. In particular, dynamic, static and hybrid analyses are contrasted.

   Given the tutorial nature of this document, we borrow some material and exposition from a few sources [103,100,64,19,117]. Yet the systematic formalization of noninterference policies is presented here for the first time. Because this document is more a tutorial than a survey, we discuss a selection of the area's highlights rather than an exhaustive account of all work on the topic.

2. Confidentiality

An important aspect of information-flow security is the preservation of confidentiality of information. In this section we will explore security policies for confidentiality with focus on noninterference. There are various flavors of noninterference offering different levels of assurance depending on the power of the attacker and the features of the underlying programming language. The different variants occur in the literature under a variety of different, sometimes overlapping names. We describe the landscape of noninterference definitions according to the following four dominant axes: termination-insensitive vs. termination-sensitive noninterference and progress-insensitive vs. progress-sensitive noninterference.

2.1. Noninterference

A program may during execution — advertently or inadvertently — leak information. To ensure secure information flow we need to consider *end-to-end* security, which involves not only preventing unauthorized access to information, but also tracking how information is flowing through the program during execution.

2.1.1. Sources of information flow

There are two principal sources of information flow in programs. *Explicit flows* correspond to the direct copying of secrets — when the value of one variable is copied into another. The following code fragment copies the value of a secret (or *high*) variable *h* into a public (or *low*) variable *l*:

```
l = h
```

Implicit flows [39] may arise when the control flow is affected by secret values; any differences in side effects under secret control encode information about the control. Consider, for instance, the following small example where the value of h is copied indirectly into l:

```
l = false; if h then l = true else skip
```

As foreshadowed earlier, the dominant semantic characterization of secure information flow is in terms of *noninterference*. The term noninterference was coined by Goguen and Meseguer [46] but goes back to the notion of *strong dependency* introduced by Cohen [34]. Informally, a program satisfies noninterference if the values of its public outputs do not depend on the values of its secret inputs. Formulated in terms of program executions, if the program is run with different secret inputs, while holding the public values fixed, the public output must not change.

2.1.2. General noninterference

We will show how all four variants of noninterference mentioned above — termination-insensitive, termination-sensitive, progress-insensitive and progress-sensitive noninterference — can be seen as instances of a general schema, which closely follows the intuition that the public output should be independent of the secret input.

Let c range over the commands of some language, and let $\langle c, E \rangle \Downarrow o$ be an *evaluation relation* read c executes in the environment E producing some observable behavior o. Assume further a *low equivalence* relation, $\sim$, on environments that captures that the public parts of the environments are equal, and an *indistinguishability relation*, $\approx$, on behavior that captures the notion of *attacker indistinguishability*, i.e., if $o_1 \approx o_2$ then the attacker is not able to distinguish between o_1 and o_2. In the following, we will use observable behavior of a program and the behavior of a program interchangeably.

A program c satisfies *noninterference*, written $NI(c)$, if, for any two low equivalent environments, a successful run of the program in one of the environments with behavior o_1 guarantees a successful run in the other environment with behavior some o_2 such that the behaviors are indistinguishable.

$$NI(c) = \forall E_1, E_2 \, . \, E_1 \sim E_2 \wedge \langle c, E_1 \rangle \Downarrow o_1 \implies \exists o_2 \, . \, \langle c, E_2 \rangle \Downarrow o_2 \wedge o_1 \approx o_2$$

If we chose the produced behavior to be the public output of the program and chose the indistinguishability relation to be equality, $NI(c)$ captures the intuition of noninterference above precisely, i.e., that the public output should remain equal when run with different secret input while retaining the public input equal.

Below we show how the three parts — 1) low equivalence, 2) the evaluation relation (in particular what is considerer observable behavior), and 3) observational indistinguishability — of this general schema can be concretely instantiated with respect to two different languages with different semantics (one big-step and one small-step) to achieve the four notions of noninterference: termination-insensitive, termination-sensitive, progress-insensitive, and progress-sensitive noninterference.

$$\frac{}{\langle skip, E \rangle \Rightarrow E} \qquad \frac{\langle c_1, E_1 \rangle \Rightarrow E_2 \quad \langle c_2, E_2 \rangle \Rightarrow E_3}{\langle c_1; c_2, E_1 \rangle \Rightarrow E_3}$$

$$\frac{\langle e, E_1 \rangle \Rightarrow true \quad \langle c_1, E_1 \rangle \Rightarrow E_2}{\langle if\ e\ then\ c_1\ else\ c_2, E_1 \rangle \Rightarrow E_2} \qquad \frac{\langle e, E_1 \rangle \Rightarrow false \quad \langle c_2, E_1 \rangle \Rightarrow E_2}{\langle if\ e\ then\ c_1\ else\ c_2, E_1 \rangle \Rightarrow E_2}$$

$$\frac{\langle e, E_1 \rangle \Rightarrow true \quad \langle c, E_1 \rangle \Rightarrow E_2 \quad \langle while\ e\ do\ c\ done, E_2 \rangle \Rightarrow E_3}{\langle while\ e\ do\ c\ done, E_1 \rangle \Rightarrow E_3}$$

$$\frac{\langle e, E \rangle \Rightarrow false}{\langle while\ e\ do\ c\ done, E \rangle \Rightarrow E} \qquad \frac{\langle e, E \rangle \Rightarrow v}{\langle x := e, E \rangle \Rightarrow E[x \mapsto v]}$$

Table 1. Big-step Semantics

2.2. Termination-insensitive vs. termination-sensitive noninterference

To be concrete, we investigate termination-insensitive and termination-sensitive noninterference in terms of a minimal batch-job while language. A batch-job program is a program that starts in an environment and produces a new environment or diverges. The attacker model of the batch-job setting is that the attacker is able to inspect the public part of the final environment.

2.2.1. Batch-job while language

Assume a standard expression, ranged over by e, language consisting of integer and boolean literals, variables, and the standard boolean and arithmetic operators and let the commands, ranged over by c, be built up by skip, sequence, conditional branches, iteration, and assignment.

$$e ::= b \mid n \mid x \mid e_1 \star e_2$$
$$c ::= skip \mid c_1;\ c_2 \mid if\ e\ then\ c_1\ else\ c_2 \mid while\ e\ do\ c\ done \mid x := e$$

Semantics   The batch-job semantics is defined as a big-step operational semantics. Let the values, ranged over by v, be the integers and the booleans, and let the *variable environments*, ranged over by γ, be maps from variable names to values. Let the *environments*, ranged over by E, consist of a single *variable environment* — the section on progress insensitive and progress sensitive noninterference below extends the environments to model input and output. Let $E[x]$ denote looking up variable x in the variable environment of E, and $E[x \mapsto v]$ denote updating variable x with value v in E resulting in a new environment such that $E[x \mapsto v][x] = v$, and $E[x \mapsto v][y] = E[y]$ for $y \neq x$.

Assume an evaluation relation for expressions, $\langle e, E \rangle \Rightarrow v$, read the expression e executes in the environment E yielding the value v, defined structurally as follows.

$$\langle n, E \rangle \Rightarrow n \quad \langle b, E \rangle \Rightarrow b \quad \frac{E[x] = v}{\langle x, E \rangle \Rightarrow v} \quad \frac{\langle e_1, E \rangle \Rightarrow v_1 \quad \langle e_2, E \rangle \Rightarrow v_2}{\langle e_1 \star e_2, E \rangle \Rightarrow v_1 \star v_2}$$

Similarly we define an evaluation relation for commands, $\langle c, E_1 \rangle \Rightarrow E_2$, read the command c executes in environment E_1 and terminates yielding the new environment E_2. The big-step semantics is defined in Table 1.

2.2.2. Security policy language for the batch-job while language

Frequently, the policy language for confidentiality is in terms of a lattice of *security levels* [38,52], where the lattice describes how information may flow between the different levels. For instance, a typical security lattice — and the lattice used in this document — is the two-point lattice described by $H > L$, which introduces two classifications of information — either secret or public — and expresses that secret information must never be considered public, but accepts flows the other way.

Let $\sigma ::= H \mid L$ be security labels corresponding to the security levels and let Γ range over *variable security maps*, maps from variable names to security labels. The intuition is that variables mapped to L should only contain public information, whereas variables mapped to H may contain secrets. In the following, we refer the former as public variables and the latter as secret variables.

In the examples below it is understood that h is a secret variable, and that l is a public variable, i.e., the examples should be read with respect to the following variable security map $\Gamma = \{h \mapsto H, l \mapsto L\}$.

2.2.3. Low equivalence

Based on the variable maps we can define low equivalence of environments structurally by demanding that the parts labeled public by the map are equal. Technically, low equivalence is formulated as a family of relations indexed by variable security maps.

$$\frac{\sigma = L \Longrightarrow v_1 = v_2}{v_1 \sim_\sigma v_2} \qquad \frac{\forall x \in dom(\Gamma) . \gamma_1(x) \sim_{\Gamma(x)} \gamma_2(x)}{\gamma_1 \sim_\Gamma \gamma_2}$$

Two values are low equivalent with respect to public is they are equal; any two values are low equivalent with respect to secret. Two variable environments are low equivalent with respect to a variable map Γ if for all variables in Γ the respective values in the variable environments are low equivalent with respect to the label given by Γ. Thus, two low equivalent variable environments are guaranteed to contain the variables labeled by the variable map, with the additional property that all variables labeled public will contain equal values. Finally, two environments are low equivalent with respect to a variable map if their variable environments are low equivalent with respect to the variabel map.

2.2.4. Termination-insensitive vs. termination-sensitive noninterference

In the batch-job setting it is reasonable to assume an attacker model where the attacker is able to inspect the public parts of the final environment, as indicated by a variable map that maps the variables the attacker can inspect to L.

By letting the final environments of programs be the observable behavior, and let the basis of the indistinguishable relation be low equivalence, we capture the intuition that the public parts of the final environments be independent on secrets. In addition, we let the *divergence* of programs be observable behavior. Making divergence observable behavior is immediate, and does not require explicit modeling of divergence, since, in the semantics of Table 1, failure to execute implies divergence, i.e. a program c diverges in E_1 if $\neg \exists E_2 . \langle c, E_1 \rangle \Rightarrow E_2$.

By letting divergence be an observable behavior, the difference between termination insensitivity and termination sensitivity can be expressed by the indistinguishability relation as shown below.

Let the observable behavior, ranged over by o, be defined by the environments E together with the symbol $\diamond$, which indicates divergence. The evaluation relation for termination-insensitive and termination-sensitive noninterference can be formulated as follows.

$$\frac{\langle c, E_1 \rangle \Rightarrow E_2}{\langle c_1, E_1 \rangle \Downarrow E_2} \qquad \frac{\neg \exists E_2 . \langle c, E_1 \rangle \Rightarrow E_2}{\langle c_1, E_1 \rangle \Downarrow \diamond}$$

If the program terminates the final environment is the observable behavior; otherwise, the program diverges.

Termination-Insensitive noninterference (TINI)   TINI [116,98] demands the following property. For two low equivalent environments, if the program terminates in both producing two new environments, then the environments must be low equivalent. As indicated above, we capture this intuition by letting divergence be indistinguishable from everything else, and two environments be indistinguishable if they are low equivalent.

Two observations are termination-insensitive (TI) indistinguishable if 1) they are low equivalent environments, or 2) either is divergence.

$$\frac{}{\diamond \simeq_{TI} o_2} \qquad \frac{}{o_1 \simeq_{TI} \diamond} \qquad \frac{E_1 \sim_\Gamma E_2}{E_1 \simeq_{TI} E_2}$$

A program c satisfies termination-insensitive noninterference if pairwise execution in low equivalent environments results in TI-indistinguishable behavior, i.e., low equivalent environments in the case both programs terminate.

$$TINI(c) = \forall E_1, E_2 . E_1 \sim_\Gamma E_2 \wedge \langle c, E_1 \rangle \Downarrow o_1 \implies \exists o_2 . \langle c, E_2 \rangle \Downarrow o_2 \wedge o_1 \simeq_{TI} o_2$$

This way, if either of the programs diverges, nothing is demanded, whereas if both programs terminate, we demand that the resulting environments are low equivalent, which corresponds exactly to the description of TINI above.

For batch-job programs this is a perfectly adequate formulation of security; it does not offer complete information security, but is limited to leaking of 1 bit per program run. Consider the following program that loops if the public value l is equal to the secret value h.

```
if (l == h) then while (true) do skip done
```

From the termination behavior of the program an observer can deduce whether $l == h$ or not corresponding to 1 bit of information.

Termination-sensitive noninterference (TSNI)   TSNI [113,98] demands the following property. For two low equivalent environments, if the program terminates in one, then the program must terminate in the other as well and the resulting environments must be low equivalent.

To capture TSNI it suffices to change the indistinguishability relation of TINI in such a way that divergence is not considered indistinguishable from normal termination.

Two environments are termination-sensitive (TS) indistinguishable if 1) they are low equivalent environments, or 2) they are both divergence.

$$\frac{}{\diamond \approx_{TS} \diamond} \qquad \frac{E_1 \sim_\Gamma E_2}{E_1 \approx_{TS} E_2}$$

A program c satisfies termination-insensitive noninterference if pairwise execution in low equivalent environments results in TS-indistinguishable behavior, i.e., both terminate with low equivalent environments, or both diverge.

$$TSNI(c) = \forall E_1, E_2 \, . \, E_1 \sim_\Gamma E_2 \wedge \langle c, E_1 \rangle \Downarrow o_1 \implies \exists o_2 \, . \, \langle c, E_2 \rangle \Downarrow o_2 \wedge o_1 \approx_{TS} o_2$$

2.2.5. Classical formulation of batch-job noninterference

Rather than the formulation above, the classical formulation of batch-job noninterference is in terms of the preservation of low equivalence under execution. For any two low equivalent environments, if the program terminates in both environments then the resulting environments should be low equivalent.

$$TINI_\Gamma(c) = \forall E_{11}, E_{12} \, . \, E_{11} \sim_\Gamma E_{12} \wedge \langle c, E_{11} \rangle \Rightarrow E_{21} \wedge \langle c, E_{12} \rangle \Rightarrow E_{22} \implies E_{21} \sim_\Gamma E_{22}$$

A minor change to the security definition makes it termination sensitive. Instead of demanding that if the program terminates in two low equivalent environments then the resulting environments are low equivalent, we demand that for any low equivalent environments if the program terminates in one, the it must terminate in the other as well, and the resulting environments should be low equivalent.

$$TSNI_\Gamma(c) = \forall E_{11}, E_{12} \, . \, E_{11} \sim_\Gamma E_{12} \wedge$$
$$\langle c, E_{11} \rangle \Rightarrow E_{21} \implies \exists E_{22} \, . \, \langle c, E_{12} \rangle \Rightarrow E_{22} \wedge E_{21} \sim_\Gamma E_{22}$$

It is easy to verify that these definitions are equivalent to the formulations in the previous section.

2.3. From termination to progress

TINI and TSNI are not adequate for programs where the attacker can inspect intermediate steps of the computation, e.g., in the presence of input or output. For such languages TINI and TSNI open up for the entire secret to be leaked instantly. The reason for this is that leaks can be hidden by non-terminating computations. Consider the following program, which is trivially secure with respect to both TINI and TSNI, since it does not terminate for any inputs.

```
output secret on public_channel; while true do skip done
```

Hence, there is need to explicitly model intermediate observations in security definitions for interactive programs. This brings us to progress-insensitive and progress-sensitive noninterference.

2.4. Progress-insensitive vs. progress-sensitive noninterference

We investigate progress-insensitive and progress-sensitive noninterference in terms of a minimal while language with input and output. The assumption is that the attacker is able to inspect the public output of the program.

2.5. While language with input and output

To model input and output, two commands are added to the language: in_σ x which reads a value and stores it in x, and out_σ x which outputs the value of x. The input and output commands are indexed by security labels. The intention is that in_L models sources of public information, whereas in_H models sources of secret information. Similarly, out_L models public sinks, i.e., sinks that the attacker can inspect, and out_H models secret sinks.

$$c ::= skip \mid c_1; \ c_2 \mid if \ e \ then \ c_1 \ else \ c_2 \mid while \ e \ do \ c \ done \mid x := e \mid in_\sigma \ x \mid out_\sigma \ x$$

Semantics   The semantics is defined as a small-step operational semantics, in order to allow for the differentiation between infinitely producing programs and silent divergence. In addition, computation steps that produce attacker observable behavior are decorated with a representation of that behavior — in this case the values output using out_L.

The environments, E, are extended to triples, (γ, ι, ω), where ι, and ω range over pairs of lists of values (one for each security level) representing the available input to the program, and the output of the program, respectively.

Let the pair $\langle c, E \rangle$ of a command and an environment be an *evaluation context*, and let $\dot{v}$ be a decoration, denoting v or nothing. A *terminating* transition, $\langle c, E_1 \rangle \overset{\dot{v}}{\to} E_2$, represents evaluation that terminates in one step and is read the command c terminates in one step when evaluated in environment E_1 yielding environment E_2 and the possible observable behavior $\dot{v}$. A *non-terminating* transition, $\langle c_1, E_1 \rangle \overset{\dot{v}}{\to} \langle c_2, E_2 \rangle$, represents evaluation that does not terminate in one step of evaluation and is read the evaluation context $\langle c_1, E_1 \rangle$ yields in one step of evaluation the new evaluation context $\langle c_2, E_2 \rangle$ and the possible observable behavior $\dot{v}$. The small-step semantics is defined in Table 2, where $(v \cdot \bar{v}_L, \bar{v}_H) \downarrow_L (v, (\bar{v}_L, \bar{v}_H))$, $(\bar{v}_L, v \cdot \bar{v}_H) \downarrow_H (v, (\bar{v}_L, \bar{v}_H))$, $(v, (\bar{v}_L, \bar{v}_H)) \uparrow_L (v \cdot \bar{v}_L, \bar{v}_H)$, and $(v, (\bar{v}_L, \bar{v}_H)) \uparrow_H (\bar{v}_L, v \cdot \bar{v}_H)$ provide shorthand notation for public and secret input and output.

2.5.1. Low equivalence

For values and variable environments the low equivalence relation remains the same as defined for TINI and TSNI above; for environments it must be extended to deal with the input and output lists.

$$\frac{\sigma = L \Longrightarrow v_1 = v_2}{v_1 \sim_\sigma v_2} \qquad \frac{\forall x \in dom(\Gamma) . \gamma_1(x) \sim_{\Gamma(x)} \gamma_2(x)}{\gamma_1 \sim_\Gamma \gamma_2}$$

$$(\bar{v}, \bar{v}_1) \sim (\bar{v}, \bar{v}_2) \qquad \frac{\gamma_1 \sim_\Gamma \gamma_2 \qquad \iota_1 \sim \iota_2 \qquad \omega_1 \sim \omega_2}{(\gamma_1, \iota_1, \omega_1) \sim_\Gamma (\gamma_2, \iota_2, \omega_2)}$$

Two environments are low equivalent given with respect to a variable map if the variable environments are low equivalent with respect to the variable map and the input and output are low equivalent, i.e., that the public input and output lists are equal.

$$\overline{\langle skip, E\rangle \to E}$$

$$\frac{\langle c_1, E_1\rangle \overset{\dot{v}}{\to} \langle c_1', E_2\rangle}{\langle c_1; c_2, E_1\rangle \overset{\dot{v}}{\to} \langle c_1'; c_2, E_2\rangle} \qquad \frac{\langle c_1, E_1\rangle \overset{\dot{v}}{\to} E_2}{\langle c_1; c_2, E_1\rangle \overset{\dot{v}}{\to} \langle c_2, E_2\rangle}$$

$$\frac{\langle e, E\rangle \Rightarrow true}{\langle if\ e\ then\ c_1\ else\ c_2, E\rangle \to \langle c_1, E\rangle} \qquad \frac{\langle e, E\rangle \Rightarrow false}{\langle if\ e\ then\ c_1\ else\ c_2, E\rangle \to \langle c_2, E\rangle}$$

$$\frac{\langle e, E\rangle \Rightarrow true}{\langle while\ e\ do\ c\ done, E\rangle \to \langle c; while\ e\ do\ c\ done, E\rangle}$$

$$\frac{\langle e, E\rangle \Rightarrow false}{\langle while\ e\ do\ c\ done, E\rangle \to E} \qquad \frac{\langle e, E\rangle \Rightarrow v}{\langle x := e, E\rangle \to E[x \to v]}$$

$$\frac{\iota_1 \downarrow_\sigma (v, \iota_2)}{\langle in_\sigma\ x, (\gamma, \iota_1, \omega)\rangle \to (\gamma[x \to v], \iota_2, \omega)}$$

$$\frac{\gamma[x] = v \quad (v, \omega_1) \uparrow_L \omega_2}{\langle out_L\ x, (\gamma, \iota, \omega_1)\rangle \overset{v}{\to} (\gamma, \iota, \omega_2)} \qquad \frac{\gamma[x] = v \quad (v, \omega_1) \uparrow_H \omega_2}{\langle out_H\ x, (\gamma, \iota, \omega_1)\rangle \to (\gamma, \iota, \omega_2)}$$

Table 2. Small-step semantics

Technically, we could remove the demand that the public output lists be equal, since, in the setting below, it is implied by the demand of equality of public observables.

2.5.2. Progress-insensitive vs. progress-sensitive noninterference

Let R range over execution contexts, $\langle c, E\rangle$, and environments, E. We define $\langle c, E\rangle \overset{\dot{v}}{\Rightarrow} R$ to capture evaluation until observable output or termination with or without observable output.

$$\frac{\langle c_1, E_1\rangle \to^* \langle c_2, E_2\rangle \quad \langle c_2, E_2\rangle \overset{v}{\to} R}{\langle c_1, E_1\rangle \overset{v}{\Rightarrow} R} \qquad \frac{\langle c, E_1\rangle \to^* E_2}{\langle c, E_1\rangle \Rightarrow E_2}$$

Let vs range over lists of values with $\cdot$ denoting the cons operation for lists. We extend the above relation to capture evaluation with zero or more observables as follows.

$$\frac{}{\langle c, E\rangle \Rightarrow \langle c, E\rangle} \qquad \frac{\langle c_1, E_1\rangle \overset{v}{\Rightarrow} \langle c_2, E_2\rangle \quad \langle c_1, E_1\rangle \overset{vs}{\Rightarrow} \langle c_2, E_2\rangle}{\langle c_1, E_1\rangle \overset{v\cdot vs}{\Rightarrow} \langle c_2, E_2\rangle}$$

Note that $\neg\exists R, vs\ .\ \langle c, E\rangle \overset{vs}{\Rightarrow} R$ implies that $\langle c, E\rangle$ diverges silently. With this we can formulate the evaluation relation for progress-insensitive and progress-sensitive noninterference.

$$\frac{\langle c, E\rangle \overset{vs}{\Rightarrow} R}{\langle c, E\rangle \Downarrow vs} \qquad \frac{\langle c_1, E_1\rangle \overset{vs}{\Rightarrow} \langle c_2, E_2\rangle \quad \neg\exists R, vs'\ .\ \langle c_2, E_2\rangle \overset{vs'}{\Rightarrow} R}{\langle c, E\rangle \Downarrow vs \cdot \diamond}$$

Progress-insensitive noninterference (PINI)   PINI [3,7,21] demands the following property. For two environments with equal public values, if the program can execute one step producing some observable behavior, then either the program in the other environment diverges silently or produces the same observable behavior. Further, the rest of the two respective executions preserves this stepwise property. This implies that the observable behavior of the program in different low equivalent environments is independent of secrets up to silent divergence.

In the following, let o range over list of values where the last element is allowed to be $\diamond$ to indicate silent divergence. Two lists of observable behavior are progress-insensitive (PI) indistinguishable if 1) they are equal, or 2) one is a divergence terminated prefix of the other.

$$o_1 \simeq_{PI} o_2 \overset{def}{=} o_1 = o_2 \vee (\exists o, o' \,.\, o_1 = o \cdot \diamond \wedge o_2 = o \cdot o') \vee (\exists o, o' \,.\, o_2 = o \cdot \diamond \wedge o_1 = o \cdot o')$$

A program satisfies progress-insensitive noninterference if pairwise execution in low equivalent environments results in PI-indistinguishable behavior, i.e., both executions produce the same output, or both produce the same output up to the point where one diverges.

$$PINI(c) = \forall E_1, E_2 \,.\, E_1 \sim_\Gamma E_2 \wedge \langle c, E_1 \rangle \Downarrow o_1 \implies \exists o_2 \,.\, \langle c, E_2 \rangle \Downarrow o_2 \wedge o_1 \simeq_{PI} o_2$$

Even though progress-insensitive noninterference closes the possibility of leaking the secret in linear time in the size of the secret it is susceptible to the possibility of *enumeration attacks*, where the entire secret is leaked to the attacker. Consider the following program

```
i := 0;
while i < maxNat do
   out_L i;
   if (i == secret) then (while true do skip done)
                    else skip;
   i:=i+1
done
```

Askarov et al. [3] show in the sequential setting that, for uniformly distributed secrets, the advantage of a polynomial-time attacker to learn the secret is negligible in the size of the secret, making PINI appropriate for large uniformly distributed secrets such as cryptographic keys. It is important to note, however, that concurrency empowers such attacks to leak the secret in linear time in the size of the secret.

Progress-sensitive noninterference (PSNI)   Similar to above, demanding that if one execution makes *progress*, i.e., takes one step of execution with observable behavior, then so does the other in addition to the above demands on stepwise matching of the public observables. This corresponds to progress sensitive noninterference, since it forces the progress of the program to be independent of secrets. PSNI subsumes TSNI for interactive programs, since nontermination is formally equal to the absence of progress.

Two sequences of observations are progress-sensitive (PS) indistinguishable if they are equal, i.e., we remove the possibility of one being a divergence terminate prefix of the other, thus demanding that if one diverges then so must the other.

$$o_1 \simeq o_2 \overset{def}{=} o_1 = o_2$$

A program satisfies progress-sensitive noninterference if pairwise execution in low-equivalent environments results in PS-indistinguishable behavior, i.e., they both produce the same sequence of output, before possibly both diverging.

$$PINI(c) = \forall E_1, E_2 \, . \, E_1 \sim_\Gamma E_2 \wedge \langle c, E_1 \rangle \Downarrow o_1 \Longrightarrow \exists o_2 \, . \, \langle c, E_2 \rangle \Downarrow o_2 \wedge o_1 \simeq_{PS} o_2$$

2.6. A note on compositionality and flow sensitivity

Secure composition allows for building secure components by combining secure components, and is important for scalable security analysis regardless of the goal of the analysis, i.e., confidentiality, integrity or otherwise. Compositionality has been an important topic in the context of programming languages [68,104,75,101,97,71] — for instance, type systems are inherently compositional in that programs (statements and expression) are typed by typing the subparts.

However, compositionality is typically not an intrinsic property of security definitions. Rather, compositional security properties that imply the weaker non-compositional security property are frequently formulated to enable proofs of correctness of compositional enforcement methods.

2.6.1. Compositionality of TINI and TSNI

The formulations of *TINI* and *TSNI* above are compositional under the same variable map with respect to sequential composition. We exemplify with the classical formulation of the former.

$$TINI_\Gamma(c_1) \wedge TINI_\Gamma(c_2) \Longrightarrow TINI_\Gamma(c_1; c_2)$$

This fact is easy to see in the classical formulation, which is stated as the preservation of low equivalence of the environments under execution. We must show that $TINI_\Gamma(c_1; c_2)$, i.e

$$TINI_\Gamma(c_1; c_2) = \forall E_{11}, E_{12} \, . \, E_{11} \sim_\Gamma E_{12} \wedge$$
$$\langle c_1; c_2, E_{11} \rangle \Rightarrow E_{21} \wedge \langle c_1; c_2, E_{12} \rangle \Rightarrow E_{22} \Longrightarrow E_{21} \sim_\Gamma E_{22}$$

Thus, assume that (1) $E_{11} \sim_\Gamma E_{12}$, (2) $\langle c_1; c_2, E_{11} \rangle \Rightarrow E_{21}$, and (3) $\langle c_1; c_2, E_{12} \rangle \Rightarrow E_{22}$. From (2) and (3) we have that there exists E'_{11}, and E'_{12} such that (4) $\langle c_1, E_{11} \rangle \Rightarrow E'_{11}$, (5) $\langle c_2, E'_{11} \rangle \Rightarrow E_{21}$, (6) $\langle c_1, E_{12} \rangle \Rightarrow E'_{12}$, and (7) $\langle c_2, E'_{12} \rangle \Rightarrow E_{22}$. From $TINI_\Gamma(c_1)$ together with (1), (4) and (6) we get that (8) $E'_{11} \sim_\Gamma E'_{12}$. Now, $TINI_\Gamma(c_2)$ together with (8), (5) and (7) allows us to conclude.

On the other hand, the formulation of *PINI* and *PSNI* are not compositional, since they offer no guarantees on the produced environments, only on the observable behavior. However, they can both be strengthened to become compositional by making the final environments observable behavior and demanding that they are low analogous to *TINI* and *TSNI*. In the following, let *CompPINI*, and *CompPSNI* denote compositional versions of *PINI* and *PSNI* obtained in this manner, respectively.

2.6.2. Flow sensitivity

Compositionality may come at the price of classifying some secure programs as insecure (from the perspective of attacker observations). Consider, for instance, the following program.

```
out_L 1; l := h
```

While it is secure with respect to *PINI* and *PSNI*, i.e. with respect to attacker observations, when run on its own, it is insecure with respect to *CompPINI* and *CompPSNI*, since the resulting environments are not low equivalent with respect to the initial variable map. Indeed, the program cannot be securely composed with all other programs — for instance, sequential composition of the program with itself would result in an insecure program — it is secure on its own and can be securely composed with any program considering l as secret.

A common way of weakening the demands while retaining compositionality is by allowing the initial and final variable maps to differ. This is known as *flow sensitivity*, since it allows the security map to change with the control flow. For brevity, we exemplify flow sensitivity in terms of the classical formulation of *TINI*; flow-sensitive weakenings of *CompPINI* and *CompPSNI* can be formed in a similar way.

$$TINI_{\Gamma_1,\Gamma_2}(c) = \forall E_{11}, E_{12} . E_{11} \sim_{\Gamma_1} E_{12} \wedge$$

$$\langle c, E_{11}\rangle \Rightarrow E_{21} \wedge \langle c, E_{12}\rangle \Rightarrow E_{22} \Longrightarrow \wedge E_{21} \sim_{\Gamma_2} E_{22}$$

With this formulation of *TSNI* the above example is secure with respect to the initial variable map $\Gamma_1 = \{l \mapsto L, h \mapsto H\}$, and the final variable map $\Gamma_2 = \{l \mapsto H, h \mapsto H\}$. This map also allows for sequential composition with any command secure with respect to Γ_2 as initial variable map. In general, the following holds for sequential composition.

$$TINI_{\Gamma_1,\Gamma_2}(c_1) \wedge TINI_{\Gamma_2,\Gamma_3}(c_2) \Longrightarrow TINI_{\Gamma_1,\Gamma_3}(c_1;c_2)$$

The correctness argument is analogous to the one above.

Further strengthenings of the compositionality result can be obtained. For instance, consider not demanding equality on the intermediate variable map, but rather variable map inclusion $\supseteq$,

$$\Gamma_1 \supseteq \Gamma_2 \Longleftrightarrow \forall x \in dom(\Gamma_2) . \Gamma_1(x) = \Gamma_2(x)$$

where $\Gamma_1 \supseteq \Gamma_2$ should be read as Γ_1 includes Γ_2 in the sense that environments that are low equivalent with respect to Γ_1, are also low equivalent with respect to Γ_2, i.e.,

$$E_1 \sim_{\Gamma_1} E_2 \wedge \Gamma_1 \supseteq \Gamma_2 \Longrightarrow E_1 \sim_{\Gamma_2} E_2$$

With this we can formulate that, for the sequence $c_1;c_2$, the demands by c_2 are included in guarantees of c_1, expressed as follows.

$$TINI_{\Gamma_1,\Gamma_2}(c_1) \wedge \Gamma_2 \supseteq \Gamma_3 \wedge TINI_{\Gamma_3,\Gamma_4}(c_2) \Longrightarrow TINI_{\Gamma_1,\Gamma_4}(c_1;c_2)$$

Again, the correctness argument is analogous.

2.7. Information flow and concurrency

Concurrency poses an important challenge for information flow security. In addition to forcing progress sensitivity, parallel composition of secure programs is not necessarily secure. One reason for this is *internal timing* channels. Consider the following program in which both sub-programs satisfies noninterference, but when run in parallel they leak the secret h to the public variable l.

```
if h {sleep(100)}; l = 1 | sleep(50); l = 0
```

Smith and Volpano [108] investigate a notion of possibilistic noninterference. Possibilistic noninterference states that the possible low outputs of the program should not vary as high inputs are varied. However, possibilistic noninterference is only meaningful for a very restricted set of probabilistic schedulers. Sabelfeld and Sands [104] consider a form of probabilistic noninterference for a language with dynamic thread creation. They show how to define security for a wide class of schedulers, not excluding deterministic schedulers. Mantel and Sabelfeld [70] investigate a timing-sensitive security property for multithreaded programs, later extended to the distributed setting [71]. Sabelfeld [96] considers bisimulation based formulations of confidentiality for multi-threaded programs, focusing on formulations for timing- and probability-sensitive confidentiality. Sabelfeld derives relationships between scheduler specific, scheduler independent and strong confidentiality. Roscoe [87] investigates confidentiality properties in a process-calculus setting. A notion *low-view determinism* is presented, which demands that abstracted publicly observable results are deterministic and, thus, independent of secret inputs.

2.8. Information flow and interactive/reactive programs

Clark and Hunt investigate noninterference for interactive programs [31] and find that for *deterministic* interactive programs attacker *strategies* — functions that produce new input based on the previous communication history [81] — do not have to be employed. Castellani et al. [74] study noninterferences for a class of synchronous reactive programs, introducing a concept of *instant* to handle the absence of signals. Bohannon et al. [21] explore a spectrum of different definitions of secure information flow for reactive programs, in the setting of an event driven sequential language. In continued work, Bohannon and Pierce [20] formalize the core functionality of a Web browser in a model called Featherweight Firefox.

2.9. Erasure

The notion of information erasure is related to information flow. For instance, cryptographic devices might be required to erase secret keys once they are done using them, or an online retailer might be obliged to erase customer data after the transaction is done.

Chong and Myers [27] investigate the semantics of policies for information erasure in the setting of a non-interactive language, but without giving a method of enforcing the policies. Hunt and Sands [50] show that erasure policies can be encoded as flow-sensitive noninterference in the setting of an interactive language, and propose a type system enforcing the policies. Del Tedesco et al. [36] show how ideas from dynamic taint analysis can be used to track sensitive data through a program and provide on-demand erasure.

2.10. Declassification

For many applications a complete separation between secret and public is too restrictive. Consider for instance the login screen of an operating system — when a user tries logging in the response of the system gives away information about the password. If access is refused we know that the attempted password was not the correct one. Even though this gives away partial information about the password, we deem this secure. Another important class of examples is data aggregation. Consider for instance a program that computes average salaries — even though each individual salary may be secret we might want to be able to publish the average.

Clearly, we need a way to *declassify* information, i.e., lowering the security classification of selected information. Sabelfeld and Sands [102] identify four different dimensions of declassification, *what* is declassified, *who* is able to declassify, *where* the declassification occurs and *when* the declassification takes place.

what As illustrated above, it is important to be able to specify what information is declassified, e.g., the four last digits of a credit card number, the average salary. Policies for partial release must guarantee an upper limit on what information is released.

who Another important aspect is who controls the release of information. This pertains to information *integrity* — if the attacker is able to control what information is declassified he might be able to mount a *laundry* attack, i.e., unintended leaks hidden by the systems declassification policy.

where Sabelfeld and Sands identify two principal forms of release locality. Related to the *what* and *when* dimension, the *where* dimension is the most immediate interpretation of where in terms of code locality. The other form is level locality, describing where information may flow relative to the security levels of the system.

when The temporal dimension of declassification pertains to when information is leaked. Sabelfeld and Sands identify three classes of temporal release classifications, *Time-complexity based*, *Probabilistic* and *Relative*. The two former are related. Time-complexity based states that information will not be released until, at the earliest, after a certain time; typically as an asymptotic notion relative to the size of the secret. With probabilistic considerations one can talk about the probability of a leak being very small. The class of relative temporal policies are on the other hand related to program correctness. It controls when declassification can occur relative to other (possibly abstract) events in the system. For example: "downgrading of a software key may occur after confirmation of payment has been received."

Works that address the what *dimension* Lowe [61] investigates a quantifying information flow, where the capacity of channels is formulated in terms of the number of different behaviors of a high level user that can be distinguished by a low level user. Clark et al. [33,32] investigate an information theoretic approach to bounding the interference in a while language with iteration.Sabelfeld and Myers [99] introduce the notion of syntactic escape hatches to delimit the amount of information released. An escape hatch formed by an expression and, semantically, the information allowed to be released is characterized by the expression interpreted in the initial memory. Li and Zdancewic [58] present the concept of relaxed noninterference that mainly addresses the *what* dimension and, to a lesser extent, the *where* dimension. Giacobazzi and Mastroeni [44,45] introduce abstract noninterference, a parameterization of noninterference over an abstract interpretation modeling the power of the attacker. Di Pierro et al. [41] consider a quantitative approach to information flow and declassification in PCCP. Information leakage is allowed via a notion of process similarity, and the quantitative measure is related to the number of statistical tests needed to distinguish between process behaviors.

Works that address the who *dimension*   The *who* dimension of declassification has been investigated in the context of *robustness* [78,4], which controls on whose behalf declassification may occur. Lux and Mantel [62] investigate a bisimulation-based condition that helps expressing who (or, more precisely, what input channels) may affect declassification. Myers and Liskov [76] model ownership in the decentralized label model, where declassification is considered safe if it is performed by the owner of the information.

Works that address the where *dimension*   Matos and Boudol [73] introduce the concept of *non-disclosure* in the setting of concurrent ML. They introduce a local flow policy that allows the computation in the scope of such a declaration to implement information flow according to the local policy. Mantel and Sands [72] investigate the use of *intransitive noninterference* to control where in the classification lattice declassification is allowed — in combination with a syntactic construction for declassification they address both aspects of *where*. Intransitive noninterference [88,85,89,67] allows for policies where information may flow indirectly between two security levels, but not directly.

Works that address the when *dimension*   Time-complexity based information declassification prevents the information from being released until, at the earliest, after a certain time.

Volpano and Smith [115] introduce the notion of relative secrecy. The idea is that the attacker cannot learn the secret in polynomial time. DiPierro et al. [41] consider a purely probabilistic notion of approximate noninterference, where a system is considered secure if the chance of an attacker making distinctions is smaller than some constant ϵ. Chong and Myers [26] investigate security policies, expressed in a logic form, which address when information is released. Recently, Magazinius et al. [64] have proposed support for decentralized policies with possible mutual distrust for tracking information flow in mashups. Their model of *composite delimited release* guarantees that a piece of data may be released only if all origins that own the data agree that it can be released.

Multidimensional declassification   Mantel and Reinhard [69] address the *what* and *where* dimensions of declassification. Their security condition for *where* combines both code locality and where in the lattice — the latter in similar spirit to intransitive noninterference. In addition they provide two different escape hatch based security conditions for *what*. Askarov and Sabelfeld [6] consider the *what* and *where* dimension of information release policies. They present a system based on delimited release which achieves the *where* dimension by using accumulated escape hatches. Banerjee et al. [11] investigate an expressive policy language for *when*, *what* and *where* policies. In addition, Banerjee et al. [13] offer an abstraction based declassification that represents the declassification policy as an abstraction of the secret inputs. A program that satisfies the policy is guaranteed not to expose distinctions within a partition.

Knowledge-based formulations   Recently a knowledge-based formulation has gained popularity, e.g., [42,5,24,22,23,7]. The attacker knowledge given a certain observable behavior is the set of all initial memories that produces the same observable behavior.

Knowledge-based information-flow security supersedes noninterference; both PINI and PSNI have natural interpretations in terms of knowledge. By defining *progress knowledge* — the knowledge the attacker gains by observing progress — PINI can be formulated by demanding that the knowledge of the attacker minus the progress knowledge remains constant under execution. Even easier is PSNI which is achieved by demanding that attacker knowledge does not change during execution. The original work [5] focused on the *where* dimension of declassification but has late been extended to control the *what* dimension by applying the ideas of delimited release.

3. Integrity

Where confidentiality is a relatively well understood concept, what is meant by *integrity* is still partly unexplored. It is clear that there are different *facets* of integrity. Birgirsson et al. [19] identify different facets of integrity.

As Dual to Confidentiality Integrity in the area of information flow often means that trusted output is independent from untrusted input [18]. This is dual to the classical models of confidentiality, where public output is required to be independent from secret input.

As Generalized Invariants and Program Correctness Integrity in the area of access control [105] is concerned with improper/unauthorized data modification. The focus is on preventing data modification operations, when no modification rights are granted to a given principal. Integrity in the context of fault-tolerant systems is concerned with preservation of actual data. For example, a desired property for a file transfer protocol on a lossy channel is that the integrity of a transmitted file is preserved, i.e., the information at both ends of communication must be identical (which can be enforced by detecting and repairing possible file corruption). Integrity in the context of databases often means preservation of some important invariants, such as consistency of data and uniqueness of database keys. The list of different interpretations of integrity can be continued, including rather general notions as integrity as expectation of data quality and integrity as guarantee of accurate data and meaningful data [105,83]. Seeking to clarify the area of integrity policies, Li et al. [55] suggest a classification for data integrity policies into information flow, data invariant and program correctness policies. In a similar spirit, Guttman [47] identifies causality and invariance policies as two major types of data integrity policies. Furthermore, Birgirsson et al. argue that integrity via invariance is itself multi-faceted. For example, the literature (cf. [55]) features formalizations of invariance as predicate preservation (predicate invariance), which is not directly compatible with invariance of memory values (value invariance). Sabelfeld and Myers [98] observe that integrity has an important difference from confidentiality: a computing system can damage integrity without any external interaction, simply by computing data incorrectly. Thus, strong enforcement of integrity requires proving program correctness. Birgirsson et al. generalize the notion of invariants, so that it can describe predicate and value invariance, as well as program correctness.

Dimensions of confidentiality-dual integrity There are many situations where we might wish to upgrade the integrity levels of data. This is known as endorsement. When viewed as dual to confidentiality, the dimensions for declassification can also be applied to endorsement:

What The *what* dimension can be studied with essentially the same semantics and thus deals with what parts of information are endorsed. Interestingly, Li and Zdancewic [57] in a study of the dualization of relaxed noninterference [56], discuss some non-dual aspects of policies, stemming from whether the code itself is trusted or not.

When Temporal endorsement is common in certain scenarios. For example, if you choose to trust some low integrity data only after a digital signature has been verified. Other, complexity-theoretic notions are perhaps less natural in the integrity setting. Although one is able to say that, e.g., "low integrity data remains untrusted in any polynomial time computation", it is less obvious how this kind of property might be useful.

Where Both policy locality and code locality are natural for endorsement. For policy locality we may wish to ensure that untrusted data only becomes trusted by following a particular path (i.e., intransitive noninterference). From the point of view of code locality it is again natural to require that endorsement only takes place at the corresponding points in the program.

Who The *who* dimension is interesting because the notion already embodies a form of integrity. Robust declassification, for example, argues that low integrity data should not effect the decision of what gets declassified [77]. For integrity we might thus define a notion of robust endorsement to mean that the decision to endorse data should not itself be influenced by low integrity data. This approach can benefit from a non-dual treatment of endorsement. Because the potentially dangerous operations like declassification and endorsement are *privileged* operations, it might make sense to apply similar, not dual constrains.

Li et al. [55] discuss unifying policies for confidentiality and integrity in the context of the DLM. They offer a comparison between different models: the binary model, the write model, the trust model and the distrust model. Zdancewic and Myers [118] investigate the interaction between declassification and integrity. They introduce the concept of robust declassification, classification that cannot be influenced by the attacker. The demand is that declassification is only done in high integrity context. This prevents an attacker from laundering information. Myers et al. [77], present a generalization to robust declassification to include endorsement, thus giving a better account for the interaction between confidentiality and integrity. Askarov and Myers [4] introduce a semantic framework for declassification and endorsement. They investigate the power the attacker gains from declassification and introduce novel security conditions for *checked endorsements* and *robust integrity*. Chong and Myers [28] discuss an extension of robustness to systems with mutual distrust and show how the DLM can be used to characterize the power of an arbitrary attacker.

4. Information-flow enforcement

Historically, dynamic techniques are the pioneers of the area of information flow (e.g., [43]). They prevent explicit flows (as in *public* = *secret*) in program runs. In addition, they also address implicit flows (as in if *secret* then *public* = *1*) by enforcing a simple invariant of no public side effects in *secret contexts*, i.e., in the branches of conditionals and loops with secret guards. These techniques, however, come without soundness arguments.

In their seminal work, Denning and Denning [39] suggest a static alternative for information-flow analysis. They argue that static analysis removes runtime overhead for security checks. This analysis prevents both explicit and implicit flows statically. The invariant of no public side effects in secret context is ensured by a syntactic check: no assignments to public variables are allowed in secret contexts. Denning and Denning do not discuss soundness, but Volpano et al. [116] show soundness by proving termination-insensitive noninterference, when they cast Denning and Denning's analysis as a security type system.

Later work is dominated by the use of static techniques for information flow [98]. The common wisdom appears to be that dynamic approaches are not a good match for security since monitoring a single path misses public side effects that could have happened in other paths.

In this light, it might be surprising that it is possible for purely dynamic enforcement to be *as secure as Denning-style static analysis* [100]. The key factor is termination. Denning-style static analysis are typically progress-insensitive (i.e., they ignore leaks via the termination behavior of the program). Thus, they satisfy termination-insensitive noninterference [116], which ignores the channel for signals via the termination of the program. If the monitor, by stopping the underlying program, can introduce nontermination, this feature can be used for collapsing information channels into the progress channel. The implicit-flow channel is one example: stopping the execution at an attempt of a public assignment in secret context is in fact sufficient for termination-sensitive security.

Progress-sensitive noninterference is attractive, but rather difficult to guarantee. Typically, strong restrictions (such as no loops with secret guards [113]) are enforced. Program errors exacerbate the problem. Even in languages like Agda [80], where it is impossible to write nonterminating programs, it is possible to write programs that terminate abnormally: for example, with stack overflow. Generally, abnormal termination due to resource exhaustion, is a channel for leaks that can be hard to counter.

The information flow tools Jif [79], FlowCaml [107] and the SPARK Examiner [14,25] avoid these problems by targeting termination-insensitive noninterference. The price is that the attacker may leak secrets by brute-force attacks via the termination channel. But there is formal assurance that these are the only possible attacks. Askarov et al. [3] show that if a program satisfies progress-insensitive noninterference, then the attacker may not learn the secret in polynomial running time in the size of the secret; and, for uniformly-distributed secrets, the probability of guessing the secret in polynomial running time is negligible. For small secrets this might not be satisfactory, calling for treating large and small secrets differently [37].

4.1. Static vs. dynamic enforcement

Static techniques have benefits of reducing runtime overhead and dynamic techniques have the benefits of permissiveness, which is of particular importance in dynamic applications, where freshly generated code is evaluated. This setting is becoming increasingly more important with the growing use of web browsers as application platforms, since the client side language, JavaScript, is a highly dynamic language.

First, JavaScript is dynamically typed, meaning that type checking is performed at runtime. This allows for a more liberal type system, at the expense of runtime overhead. This also entails that programs may not exhibit static types, which forces dynamic or hybrid analyses.

Second, JavaScript allows the redefinition of functions, methods and prototypes — both user defined and built-in. This presents major challenges for information-flow security, since programs can be included by other programs. Thus, a program cannot assume to run in the standard environment — it may have been included by another program that has modified the standard environment, or it might include other programs that must be prohibited from doing so.

Third, the dynamic code evaluation feature of JavaScript provides a particular challenge. Dynamic code evaluation evaluates a given string using the `eval` function. Static analysis is bound to be conservative when analyzing programs that include `eval`, since the strings to be evaluated are typically not known at the time of analysis.

For example, it is not possible to statically determine if a program using `eval` is secure without being too conservative, since the parameter of `eval` might not be known at the time of analysis or might be subject to change. Moreover, in a heterogeneous environment as the Web, it is also difficult to assume properties about third-party scripts.

Another example to illustrate permissiveness of dynamic techniques is the program `if` $l < 0$ `then` $l = 1$ `else` $l = h$, where l and h are variables that store public and secret values, respectively. Static analysis, as traditional type systems [116], rejects this program as insecure due to the presence of the explicit flow $l = h$. In contrast, some dynamic techniques are able to accept executions of the program when $l < 0$ holds [100]. On the security side, however, both Denning-style analysis and dynamic enforcement have the same guarantees: progress-insensitive noninterference [100].

However, if progress-sensitive noninterference is desired, the absence of side effects of traces not taken becomes, indeed, hard to guarantee dynamically.

4.2. Static analysis

The predominant static technique for enforcing secure information flow statically is the use of type systems, e.g. [82,116,76,48,108,17,114,1,104,119,12,86].

In a security-typed language, the types of program variables and expressions are augmented with annotations that specify policies on the use of the typed data. Denning-style analyses prohibit implicit information flows by keeping track of the security level of the control, frequently known as the security level of the program counter and disallowing public side effects in secret contexts. This enforcement scheme is know as flow-insensitive, since it does not allow the security classification of program locations to vary.

In contrast, Hunt and Sands [49] investigate flow-sensitive type systems for a small while language. The type systems are parameterized over the choice of flow lattice for which the powerset lattice of program variables is shown to provide a principal typing. In addition Hunt and Sands show how to transform any flow-sensitive program into an equivalent program typable in a flow-insensitive type system. The concept of flow-sensitive information-flow security goes back to Banerjee and Amtoft [2], with the enforcement phrased as a Hoare logic rather than a type system.

Statically enforcing confidentiality With respect to practical implementations of information-flow security, Denning-style analyses form the core for information flow tools Jif [79], FlowCaml [107] and the SPARK Examiner [14,25]. Askarov and Sabelfeld [8] present a novel treatment of secure exception handling. They allow secret exceptions to be uncaught given that they always are caught or always uncaught, and show that this is sound with respect to termination insensitive noninterference. Broberg and Sands investigate expressive dynamic information-flow policies — flow-locks — and present a type system for an ML like language [22], subsequently recast using a knowledge based definition [23] and extended to a role-based multi-principal settings [24].

Smith and Volpano [108] show how a strengthening of the type system for sequential programs [116] by disallowing looping on secrets is sufficient for ensuring security under purely nondeterministic schedulers. Sabelfeld [96] proposes a type based analysis for multi-threaded programs in the presence of synchronization. The type system excludes the possibility of synchronizing on secret data — directly or indirectly — in branches of high conditionals. Russo and Sabelfeld [91] present a type system that guarantees security for a wide class of schedulers for languages with dynamic threads. To achieve this the language is augmented with a pair of commands *hide* and *unhide* that move threads between different queues. By disallowing low threads to be scheduled while there are pending high threads internal timing leaks are prevented.

Castellani et al. [74] present a type system guaranteeing noninterference in a simple imperative reactive language. Bohannon et al. [21] explore different definitions of noninterference for reactive programs and define a simple reactive language with an information-flow type system to demonstrate the viability of the approach.

Matos and Boudol [73] introduce a local flow policy that allows the computation in the scope of such to implement information flow according to the local policy and design a type and effect system that enforces this policy. In addition by particularizing the case where the alternatives in a conditional branching both terminate Matos and Boudol show that typing of terminations leaks can be improved. Sabelfeld and Myers [99] introduce the notion of syntactic escape hatches to delimit the amount of information released. An escape hatch is formed by an expression and, semantically, the information allowed to be released is characterized by the expression interpreted in the initial memory. Sabelfeld and Myers present a type system for enforcing delimited release. The type system tracks the variables taking part in declassification and demands that those variables are not the target of update before the declassification statement. Askarov and Sabelfeld [6] extend the notion of delimited release with code locality and present a type system that enforces the new notion by disallowing declassification in secret contexts. Li and Zdancewic [58] present the concept of relaxed noninterference that mainly addresses the *what* dimension and to a lesser extent the *where* dimension enforced via a type system. The soundness theorem of the type system ensures that, if a program is well-typed, then there exists a proof of the security goal for the program. Mantel and Reinhard [69] present a security type system to enforce security with respect to the *what* and *where* dimensions of declassification, where their security condition for *where* combines both code locality and lattice locality.

Statically enforcing integrity   Myers et al. [77] present a generalization to robust declassification to include endorsement, thus giving a better account for the interaction between confidentiality and integrity and present a type based enforcement. The enforcement is based on only high-integrity data being allowed to be declassified and that declassification might only occur in a high-integrity context. Chong and Myers [28] discuss an extension of robustness to systems with mutual distrust and present a type based enforcement. The type system relies on the fact that both the decision to declassify and the information to be declassified are high-integrity and that the decision to endorse information must be of high integrity. Tripp et al. [109] present TAJ, a tool for scalable static taint analysis for Web applications. Being an industrial tool aimed at being able to handle existing complex Web applications no correctness argument is given.

4.3. Dynamic and hybrid analysis

One alternative is purely *dynamic* enforcement (e.g., [43,112,7,100]), that performs dynamic security checks similar to the ones enforced by static analysis. For example, an assignment is allowed by the monitor if the level of the assigned variable is high whenever there is a high variable on the right-hand side of the assignment (tracking explicit flows) or in case the assignment appears inside of a high conditional or while loop (tracking implicit flows). This mechanism dynamically keeps a simple invariant of no assignment to low variables in high context.

As previously noted it has been shown (e.g., [9,100,7,93]) that purely dynamic monitors can enforce the same security property as Denning-style static analysis: termination-insensitive noninterference. In addition, Sabelfeld and Russo [100] prove that sound purely dynamic information-flow enforcement is more permissive than static analysis in the *flow-insensitive* case (where variables are assigned security levels at the beginning of the execution and this assignment is kept unchanged during the execution).

Purely dynamic enforcement   Shroff et al. [106] develop a monitor to track explicit and implicit information flow. The monitor is parameterized over a set of dependencies to track implicit flow. This set can either be computed statically or dynamically at the expense of possibly interfering runs while the monitor collects all dependencies. Russo and Sabelfeld [93] investigate securing timeout instructions in Web applications against internal timing leaks. They propose a monitor using a generalization of security contexts to include time. This way code snippets to be run at time t are run in the associated security context. Askarov and Sabelfeld [7] investigate dynamic tracking of policies for information release, or declassification, for a language with dynamic code evaluation and communication primitives. Russo and Sabelfeld [93] show how to secure programs with timeout instructions using execution monitoring. Furthermore, Russo et al. [94] investigate monitoring information flow in dynamic tree structures. Austin and Flanagan [9] present a dynamic analysis for secure information flow. They apply a no-sensitive-upgrade strategy — on an attempt to assign to a public variable in secret context, the public variable is marked as one that cannot be branched on later in the execution — to avoid the pitfalls of flow-sensitivity and dynamic enforcement. Austin and Flanagan [10] relax the no-sensitive-upgrade strategy to a permissive upgrade, where variables are allowed to be upgraded before the secret context, in which they are assigned to.

Hybrid enforcement Fusion of static and dynamic techniques is becoming increasingly popular [54,106,53,111]. These techniques offer benefits of increasing permissiveness because more information on the actual execution trace is available at runtime, while keeping runtime overhead moderate as some static information can be gathered before the execution. Russo and Sabelfeld [92] show formal underpinnings of the tradeoff between dynamism and permissiveness of flow-sensitive monitors. They also present a general framework for hybrid monitors that is parametric in the monitor's enforcement actions (blocking, outputting default values, and suppressing events). LeGuernic et al. [54] consider a dynamic automaton based monitor for confidentiality. The monitor is a hybrid between dynamic and static enforcement; during execution abstractions of events are sent to the monitor which uses the abstraction to prohibit both explicit and implicit flows. LeGuernic [53] develops a hybrid monitor for concurrent programs. The monitor uses abstractions of program events, e.g., the modified variables of non-taken branches, the set of variables that must be locked for bodies of secret conditionals. Ligatti et al. [60] present a general framework for security policies that can be enforced by monitoring and modifying programs at runtime. They introduce edit automata that enable monitors to stop, suppress, and modify the behavior of programs. Chugh et al. [30] present a hybrid approach to handling dynamic execution. Their approach is staged into two stages. First, the information-flow properties for the available code is examined and a set of residual syntactic checks to be applied to the dynamic code is generated. Once the dynamic code is to be evaluated the residual checks are applied.

Code transformation In addition to execution monitors there exists a line of work that statically or dynamically filters, rewrites or wraps the code to enforce different properties [63]. Devriese and Piessens [40] consider enforcing noninterference by running multiple runs of the program, one for each security level. The idea is that you first perform the public computation, replacing any secret values with dummies. Thereafter you run the secret computation under certain restrictions. For a secure program this preserves the semantics of the original program and enforces noninterference. Phung et al. [84] consider an approach to modifying JavaScript code to become self protecting. The method is lightweight in the sense that it does not rely on browser modifications or runtime rewriting. Magazinius et al. [65] improve on [84] by removing a number of identified vulnerabilities and making the policy language more accessible to the policy writer. Chudnov and Naumann [29] presents a provably correct inlining of a dynamic flow-sensitive monitor. They prove security and transparency by connecting the inlined monitor with a VM monitor, known to have the desired security properties. Magazinius et al. [66] investigate on-the-fly inlining of a dynamic monitor to handle dynamic code evaluation. With respect to concurrency Barthe et al. [16] present a compositional transformation that closes internal timing channels in multithreaded programs with semaphores. Jang et al. [51] consider a rewriting based technique and tool for finding insecure information flow in existing Web applications. The empirical study performed by the authors indicates that steps must be taken to mitigate the privacy threat from covert flows in browsers.

4.4. Libraries

In addition to external information-flow analyses, i.e., analyses implemented outside of the target programming langue, a line of work strives towards achieving similar guarantees by exploiting existing programming language features [95,90,90]. This has the advantage that the existing programming language infrastructure can be used without any modifications.

Conti and Russo [95] show how to provide a taint mode via a library in Python. The library is able to keep track of tainted values for several built-in classes and supports propagation of taint information. The library uses decorators as a noninvasive approach to mark source code with no or minimal modification in the code. A line of work investigates information flow libraries for Haskell. Li and Zdancewic [59] present a library for secure information flow in Haskell, providing a starting point for this line of work. Russo et al. [90] provide a library for secure information flow in Haskell using monads. The library provides combinators for declassification related to the who, when and what dimensions. Tsai, Hughes and Russo[110] present an extension to [59] adding side-effectful computations and threads. DelTedesco et al. [36] implement information erasure as a Python library building on ideas for dynamic taint analysis.

5. Conclusion

We have given an overview of the state-of-the-art in confidentiality and integrity policies and their enforcement. Our presentation of the confidentiality and integrity policies is based on a systematic formalization of four dominant formulations of noninterference: termination-insensitive, termination-sensitive, progress-insensitive, and progress-sensitive, cast in the setting of two minimal while languages. In the account of information-flow enforcement, we have discussed highlights from static, dynamic, and hybrid program analysis for security, as well as security enforcement by libraries.

Acknowledgments

This work was funded by the European Community under the WebSand project and the Swedish research agencies SSF and VR.

References

[1]   J. Agat. Transforming out timing leaks. In *Proc. ACM Symp. on Principles of Programming Languages*, pages 40–53, January 2000.

[2]   Torben Amtoft and Anindya Banerjee. Information flow analysis in logical form. Technical report, George Mason University, 2004.

[3]   A. Askarov, S. Hunt, A. Sabelfeld, and D. Sands. Termination-insensitive noninterference leaks more than just a bit. In *Proc. European Symp. on Research in Computer Security*, volume 5283 of *Lecture Notes in Computer Science*, pages 333–348. Springer-Verlag, October 2008.

[4]   A. Askarov and A. C. Myers. A semantic framework for declassification and endorsement. In *Proc. European Symp. on Programming*, Lecture Notes in Computer Science, March 2010.

[5]   A. Askarov and A. Sabelfeld. Gradual release: Unifying declassification, encryption and key release policies. In *Proc. IEEE Symp. on Security and Privacy*, pages 207–221, May 2007.

[6]   A. Askarov and A. Sabelfeld. Localized delimited release: Combining the what and where dimensions of information release. In *Proc. ACM Workshop on Programming Languages and Analysis for Security (PLAS)*, pages 53–60, June 2007.

[7]   A. Askarov and A. Sabelfeld. Tight enforcement of information-release policies for dynamic languages. In *Proc. IEEE Computer Security Foundations Symposium*, July 2009.

[8]   Aslan Askarov and Andrei Sabelfeld. Catch me if you can: permissive yet secure error handling. In *Proceedings of the ACM SIGPLAN Fourth Workshop on Programming Languages and Analysis for Security*, PLAS '09, pages 45–57, 2009.

[9]   T. H. Austin and C. Flanagan. Efficient purely-dynamic information flow analysis. In *Proc. ACM Workshop on Programming Languages and Analysis for Security (PLAS)*, June 2009.

[10] T. H. Austin and C. Flanagan. Permissive dynamic information flow analysis. In *Proc. ACM Workshop on Programming Languages and Analysis for Security (PLAS)*, June 2010.

[11] A. Banerjee, D. Naumann, and S. Rosenberg. Expressive declassification policies and modular static enforcement. In *Proc. IEEE Symp. on Security and Privacy*, May 2008.

[12] A. Banerjee and D. A. Naumann. Secure information flow and pointer confinement in a Java-like language. In *Proc. IEEE Computer Security Foundations Workshop*, pages 253–267, June 2002.

[13] Anindya Banerjee, Roberto Giacobazzi, and Isabella Mastroeni. What you lose is what you leak: Information leakage in declassification policies. In *Proceedings of the Twenty-Third Conference on Mathematical Foundations of Programming Semantics (MFPS)*, 2007.

[14] J. Barnes and JG Barnes. *High Integrity Software: The SPARK Approach to Safety and Security*. Addison-Wesley Longman Publishing Co., Inc. Boston, MA, USA, 2003.

[15] Adam Barth, Collin Jackson, and John C. Mitchell. Securing frame communication in browsers. In *SS'08: Proceedings of the 17th conference on Security symposium*, pages 17–30, Berkeley, CA, USA, 2008. USENIX Association.

[16] G. Barthe, T. Rezk, A. Russo, and A. Sabelfeld. Security of multithreaded programs by compilation. In *Proc. European Symp. on Research in Computer Security*, volume 4734 of *Lecture Notes in Computer Science*, pages 2–18. Springer-Verlag, September 2007.

[17] G. Barthe and B. Serpette. Partial evaluation and non-interference for object calculi. In *Proc. FLOPS*, volume 1722 of *Lecture Notes in Computer Science*, pages 53–67. Springer-Verlag, November 1999.

[18] K. J. Biba. Integrity considerations for secure computer systems. Technical Report ESD-TR-76-372, USAF Electronic Systems Division, Bedford, MA, April 1977. (Also available through National Technical Information Service, Springfield Va., NTIS AD-A039324.).

[19] A. Birgisson, A. Russo, and A. Sabelfeld. Unifying facets of information integrity. In *Proceedings of the International Conference on Information Systems Security (ICISS)*. Springer-Verlag, 2010.

[20] Aaron Bohannon and Benjamin C. Pierce. Featherweight firefox: Formalizing the core of a web browser. In *Usenix Conference on Web Application Development (WebApps)*, pages 123–134, 2010.

[21] Aaron Bohannon, Benjamin C. Pierce, Vilhelm Sjöberg, Stephanie Weirich, and Steve Zdancewic. Reactive noninterference. In *ACM Conference on Computer and Communications Security*, pages 79–90, November 2009.

[22] N. Broberg and David Sands. Flow locks: Towards a core calculus for dynamic flow policies. In *Programming Languages and Systems. 15th European Symposium on Programming, ESOP 2006*, volume 3924 of *Lecture Notes in Computer Science*, 2006.

[23] Niklas Broberg and David Sands. Flow-sensitive semantics for dynamic information flow policies. In S. Chong and D. Naumann, editors, *ACM SIGPLAN Fourth Workshop on Programming Languages and Analysis for Security (PLAS 2009)*, Dublin, June 15 2009. ACM.

[24] Niklas Broberg and David Sands. Paralocks – role-based information flow control and beyond. In *POPL'10, Proceedings of the 37th Annual ACM SIGACT-SIGPLAN Symposium on Principles of Programming Languages*, 2010.

[25] R. Chapman and A. Hilton. Enforcing security and safety models with an information flow analysis tool. *ACM SIGAda Ada Letters*, 24(4):39–46, 2004.

[26] S. Chong and A. C. Myers. Security policies for downgrading. In *ACM Conference on Computer and Communications Security*, pages 198–209, October 2004.

[27] S. Chong and A. C. Myers. Language-based information erasure. In *Proc. IEEE Computer Security Foundations Workshop*, pages 241–254, June 2005.

[28] S. Chong and A.C. Myers. Decentralized robustness. In *Computer Security Foundations Workshop, 2006. 19th IEEE*, 2006.

[29] A. Chudnov and D. A. Naumann. Information flow monitor inlining. In *Proc. IEEE Computer Security Foundations Symposium*, July 2010.

[30] Ravi Chugh, Jeffrey A. Meister, Ranjit Jhala, and Sorin Lerner. Staged information flow for javascript. *SIGPLAN Not.*, 44:50–62, June 2009.

[31] D. Clark and S. Hunt. Noninterference for deterministic interactive programs. In *Workshop on Formal Aspects in Security and Trust (FAST'08)*, October 2008.

[32] David Clark, Sebastian Hunt, and Pasquale Malacaria. Quantitative information flow, relations and polymorphic types. *Journal of Logic and Computation, Special Issue on Lambda-calculus, type theory and natural language*, 18(2):181–199, 2005.

[33] David Clark, Sebastian Hunt, and Pasquale Malacaria. A static analysis for quantifying information flow in a simple imperative language. *Journal of Computer Security*, 15(3):321–371, 2007.

[34] E. S. Cohen. Information transmission in computational systems. *ACM SIGOPS Operating Systems Review*, 11(5):133–139, 1977.

[35] E. S. Cohen. Information transmission in sequential programs. In R. A. DeMillo, D. P. Dobkin, A. K. Jones, and R. J. Lipton, editors, *Foundations of Secure Computation*, pages 297–335. Academic Press, 1978.

[36] Filippo Del Tedesco, Alejandro Russo, and David Sands. Implementing erasure policies using taint analysis. In Tuomas Aura, editor, *The 15th Nordic Conference in Secure IT Systems*, Lecture Notes in Computer Science. Springer Verlag, October 2010.

[37] D. Demange and David Sands. All Secrets Great and Small. In *Programming Languages and Systems. 18th European Symposium on Programming, ESOP 2009*, number 5502 in Lecture Notes in Computer Science, pages 207–221. Springer Verlag, 2009.

[38] D. E. Denning. A lattice model of secure information flow. *Comm. of the ACM*, 19(5):236–243, May 1976.

[39] D. E. Denning and P. J. Denning. Certification of programs for secure information flow. *Comm. of the ACM*, 20(7):504–513, July 1977.

[40] D. Devriese and F. Piessens. Non-interference through secure multi-execution. In *Proc. IEEE Symp. on Security and Privacy*, May 2010.

[41] A. Di Pierro, C. Hankin, and H. Wiklicky. Approximate non-interference. In *Proc. IEEE Computer Security Foundations Workshop*, pages 1–17, June 2002.

[42] C. Dima, C. Enea, and R. Gramatovici. Nondeterministic nointerference and deducible information flow. Technical Report 2006-01, University of Paris 12, LACL, 2006.

[43] J. S. Fenton. Memoryless subsystems. *Computing J.*, 17(2):143–147, May 1974.

[44] R. Giacobazzi and I. Mastroeni. Abstract non-interference: Parameterizing non-interference by abstract interpretation. In *Proc. ACM Symp. on Principles of Programming Languages*, pages 186–197, January 2004.

[45] R. Giacobazzi and I. Mastroeni. Adjoining declassification and attack models by abstract interpretation. In *Proc. European Symp. on Programming*, volume 3444 of *Lecture Notes in Computer Science*, pages 295–310. Springer-Verlag, April 2005.

[46] J. A. Goguen and J. Meseguer. Security policies and security models. In *Proc. IEEE Symp. on Security and Privacy*, pages 11–20, April 1982.

[47] J. Guttman. Invited tutorial: Integrity. Presentation at the Dagstuhl Seminar on Mobility, Ubiquity and Security, February 2007. http://www.dagstuhl.de/07091/.

[48] N. Heintze and J. G. Riecke. The SLam calculus: programming with secrecy and integrity. In *Proc. ACM Symp. on Principles of Programming Languages*, pages 365–377, January 1998.

[49] S. Hunt and D. Sands. On flow-sensitive security types. In *Proc. ACM Symp. on Principles of Programming Languages*, pages 79–90, 2006.

[50] S. Hunt and David Sands. Just forget it – the semantics and enforcement of information erasure. In *Programming Languages and Systems. 17th European Symposium on Programming, ESOP 2008*, number 4960 in Lecture Notes in Computer Science, pages 239–253, 2008.

[51] Dongseok Jang, Ranjit Jhala, Sorin Lerner, and Hovav Shacham. An empirical study of privacy-violating information flows in javascript web applications. In *Proceedings of the 17th ACM conference on Computer and communications security*, CCS '10, pages 270–283, New York, NY, USA, 2010. ACM.

[52] J. Landauer and T. Redmond. A lattice of information. In *Proc. IEEE Computer Security Foundations Workshop*, pages 65–70, June 1993.

[53] Gurvan Le Guernic. Automaton-based confidentiality monitoring of concurrent programs. In *Proc. IEEE Computer Security Foundations Symposium*, pages 218–232, July 2007.

[54] Gurvan Le Guernic, Anindya Banerjee, Thomas Jensen, and David Schmidt. Automata-based confidentiality monitoring. In *Proc. Asian Computing Science Conference (ASIAN'06)*, volume 4435 of *Lecture Notes in Computer Science*. Springer-Verlag, 2006. To appear.

[55] P. Li, Y. Mao, and S. Zdancewic. Information integrity policies. In *Workshop on Formal Aspects in Security and Trust (FAST'03)*, 2003.

[56] P. Li and S. Zdancewic. Downgrading policies and relaxed noninterference. In *Proc. ACM Symp. on Principles of Programming Languages*, pages 158–170, January 2005.

[57] P. Li and S. Zdancewic. Unifying confidentiality and integrity in downgrading policies. In *Workshop on Foundations of Computer Security*, pages 45–54, June 2005.

[58] Peng Li and Steve Zdancewic. Downgrading policies and relaxed noninterference. *SIGPLAN Not*, pages 158–170, 2005.

[59] Peng Li and Steve Zdancewic. Encoding information flow in haskell. *Computer Security Foundations Workshop, IEEE*, 0:16, 2006.

[60] Jay Ligatti, Lujo Bauer, and David Walker. Edit automata: Enforcement mechanisms for run-time security policies. *International Journal of Information Security*, 4:2–16, 2005.

[61] G. Lowe. Quantifying information flow. In *Proc. IEEE Computer Security Foundations Workshop*, pages 18–31, June 2002.

[62] A. Lux and H. Mantel. Who can declassify? In *Workshop on Formal Aspects in Security and Trust (FAST'08)*, volume 5491 of *Lecture Notes in Computer Science*, pages 35–49. Springer-Verlag, 2009.

[63] S. Maffeis, J.C. Mitchell, and A. Taly. Isolating javascript with filters, rewriting, and wrappers. In *Proc of ESORICS'09*. Lecture Notes in Computer Science, 2009.

[64] J. Magazinius, A. Askarov, and A. Sabelfeld. A lattice-based approach to mashup security. In *Proc. ACM Symposium on Information, Computer and Communications Security (ASIACCS)*, April 2010.

[65] J. Magazinius, P. Phung, and D. Sands. Safe wrappers and sane policies for self protecting javascript. In *15th Nordic Conference on Secure IT Systems*, 2010.

[66] J. Magazinius, A. Russo, and A. Sabelfeld. On-the-fly inlining of dynamic security monitors. In *Proceedings of the IFIP International Information Security Conference (SEC)*, September 2010.

[67] H. Mantel. Information flow control and applications—Bridging a gap. In *Proc. Formal Methods Europe*, volume 2021 of *Lecture Notes in Computer Science*, pages 153–172. Springer-Verlag, March 2001.

[68] H. Mantel. On the composition of secure systems. In *Proc. IEEE Symp. on Security and Privacy*, pages 81–94, May 2002.

[69] H. Mantel and A. Reinhard. Controlling the what and where of declassification in language-based security. In *Proc. European Symp. on Programming*, volume 4421 of *Lecture Notes in Computer Science*, pages 141–156. Springer-Verlag, March 2007.

[70] H. Mantel and A. Sabelfeld. A generic approach to the security of multi-threaded programs. In *Proc. IEEE Computer Security Foundations Workshop*, pages 126–142, June 2001.

[71] H. Mantel and A. Sabelfeld. A unifying approach to the security of distributed and multi-threaded programs. *J. Computer Security*, 11(4):615–676, September 2003.

[72] H. Mantel and D. Sands. Controlled downgrading based on intransitive (non)interference. In *Proc. Asian Symp. on Programming Languages and Systems*, volume 3302 of *Lecture Notes in Computer Science*, pages 129–145. Springer-Verlag, November 2004.

[73] Ana Almeida Matos and Gerard Boudol. On declassification and the non-disclosure policy. *Computer Security Foundations Workshop, IEEE*, 0:226–240, 2005.

[74] Ana Almeida Matos, Gérard Boudol, and Ilaria Castellani. Typing noninterference for reactive programs. *Journal of Logic and Algebraic Programming*, 72(2):124 – 156, 2007. Programming Language Interference and Dependence.

[75] J. McLean. A general theory of composition for trace sets closed under selective interleaving functions. In *Proc. IEEE Symp. on Security and Privacy*, pages 79–93, May 1994.

[76] A. C. Myers and B. Liskov. A decentralized model for information flow control. In *Proc. ACM Symp. on Operating System Principles*, pages 129–142, October 1997.

[77] A. C. Myers, A. Sabelfeld, and S. Zdancewic. Enforcing robust declassification. In *Proc. IEEE Computer Security Foundations Workshop*, pages 172–186, June 2004.

[78] A. C. Myers, A. Sabelfeld, and S. Zdancewic. Enforcing robust declassification and qualified robustness. *J. Computer Security*, 14(2):157–196, May 2006.

[79] A. C. Myers, L. Zheng, S. Zdancewic, S. Chong, and N. Nystrom. Jif: Java information flow. Software release. Located at http://www.cs.cornell.edu/jif, July 2001–2006.

[80] Ulf Norell. *Towards a practical programming language based on dependent type theory*. PhD thesis, Department of Computer Science and Engineering, Chalmers University of Technology, SE-412 96 Göteborg, Sweden, September 2007.

[81] K. O'Neill, M. Clarkson, and S. Chong. Information-flow security for interactive programs. In *Proc. IEEE Computer Security Foundations Workshop*, pages 190–201, July 2006.

[82] P. Ørbæk and J. Palsberg. Trust in the λ-calculus. *J. Functional Programming*, 7(6):557–591, 1997.

[83] Charles P. Pfleeger and Shari Lawrence Pfleeger. *Security in Computing (4th Edition)*. Prentice Hall, 2006.

[84] Phu H. Phung, David Sands, and Andrey Chudnov. Lightweight self-protecting javascript. In *ASIACCS '09: Proceedings of the 4th International Symposium on Information, Computer, and Communications Security*, pages 47–60, New York, NY, USA, 2009. ACM.

[85] S. Pinsky. Absorbing covers and intransitive non-interference. In *Proc. IEEE Symp. on Security and Privacy*, pages 102–113, May 1995.

[86] F. Pottier and V. Simonet. Information flow inference for ML. *ACM TOPLAS*, 25(1):117–158, January 2003.

[87] A. W. Roscoe. CSP and determinism in security modeling. In *Proc. IEEE Symp. on Security and Privacy*, pages 114–127, May 1995.

[88] A. W. Roscoe and M. H. Goldsmith. What is intransitive noninterference? In *Proc. IEEE Computer Security Foundations Workshop*, pages 228–238, June 1999.

[89] J. M. Rushby. Noninterference, transitivity, and channel-control security policies. Technical Report CSL-92-02, SRI International, 1992.

[90] A. Russo, K. Claessen, and J. Hughes. A library for light-weight information-flow security in Haskell. In *Haskell '08: Proceedings of the first ACM SIGPLAN symposium on Haskell*, pages 13–24. ACM, 2008.

[91] A. Russo and A. Sabelfeld. Securing interaction between threads and the scheduler. In *Proc. IEEE Computer Security Foundations Workshop*, pages 177–189, July 2006.

[92] A. Russo and A. Sabelfeld. Dynamic vs. static flow-sensitive security analysis, April 2009. Draft.

[93] A. Russo and A. Sabelfeld. Securing timeout instructions in web applications. In *Proc. IEEE Computer Security Foundations Symposium*, July 2009.

[94] A. Russo, A. Sabelfeld, and A. Chudnov. Tracking information flow in dynamic tree structures. In *Proc. European Symp. on Research in Computer Security*, Lecture Notes in Computer Science. Springer-Verlag, September 2009.

[95] Alejandro Russo and Juan José Conti. A taint mode for python via a library. In *OWASP AppSec Research*, 2010.

[96] A. Sabelfeld. The impact of synchronisation on secure information flow in concurrent programs. In *Proc. Andrei Ershov International Conference on Perspectives of System Informatics*, volume 2244 of *Lecture Notes in Computer Science*, pages 225–239. Springer-Verlag, July 2001.

[97] A. Sabelfeld and H. Mantel. Static confidentiality enforcement for distributed programs. In *Proc. Symp. on Static Analysis*, volume 2477 of *Lecture Notes in Computer Science*, pages 376–394. Springer-Verlag, September 2002.

[98] A. Sabelfeld and A. C. Myers. Language-based information-flow security. *IEEE J. Selected Areas in Communications*, 21(1):5–19, January 2003.

[99] A. Sabelfeld and A. C. Myers. A model for delimited information release. In *Proc. International Symp. on Software Security (ISSS'03)*, volume 3233 of *Lecture Notes in Computer Science*, pages 174–191. Springer-Verlag, October 2004.

[100] A. Sabelfeld and A. Russo. From dynamic to static and back: Riding the roller coaster of information-flow control research. In *Proc. Andrei Ershov International Conference on Perspectives of System Informatics*, Lecture Notes in Computer Science. Springer-Verlag, June 2009.

[101] A. Sabelfeld and D. Sands. A per model of secure information flow in sequential programs. *Higher Order and Symbolic Computation*, 14(1):59–91, March 2001.

[102] A. Sabelfeld and D. Sands. Dimensions and principles of declassification. In *Proc. IEEE Computer Security Foundations Workshop*, pages 255–269, June 2005.

[103] A. Sabelfeld and D. Sands. Declassification: Dimensions and principles. *J. Computer Security*, January 2009.

[104] Andrei Sabelfeld and David Sands. Probabilistic noninterference for multi-threaded programs. In *Proceedings of the 13th IEEE Computer Security Foundations Workshop*, pages 200–214, Cambridge, England, July 2000. IEEE Computer Society Press.

[105] Ravi S. Sandhu. On five definitions of data integrity, 1993.

[106] P. Shroff, S. Smith, and M. Thober. Dynamic dependency monitoring to secure information flow. In *Proc. IEEE Computer Security Foundations Symposium*, pages 203–217, July 2007.

[107] V. Simonet. The Flow Caml system. Software release. Located at http://cristal.inria.fr/~simonet /soft/flowcaml/, July 2003.

[108] G. Smith and D. Volpano. Secure information flow in a multi-threaded imperative language. In *Proc. ACM Symp. on Principles of Programming Languages*, pages 355–364, January 1998.

[109] Omer Tripp, Marco Pistoia, Stephen J. Fink, Manu Sridharan, and Omri Weisman. TAJ: Effective Taint Analysis for Java. In *ACM SIGPLAN 2009 Conference on Programming Language Design and Implementation (PLDI 2009)*, June 2009.

[110] Ta Chung Tsai, A. Russo, and J. Hughes. A library for secure multi-threaded information flow in Haskell. In *Proc. of the 20th IEEE Computer Security Foundations Symposium*, July 2007.

[111] P. Vogt, F. Nentwich, N. Jovanovic, E. Kirda, C. Kruegel, and G. Vigna. Cross-site scripting prevention with dynamic data tainting and static analysis. In *Proc. Network and Distributed System Security Symposium*, February 2007.

[112] D. Volpano. Safety versus secrecy. In *Proc. Symp. on Static Analysis*, volume 1694 of *Lecture Notes in Computer Science*, pages 303–311. Springer-Verlag, September 1999.

[113] D. Volpano and G. Smith. Eliminating covert flows with minimum typings. *Proc. IEEE Computer Security Foundations Workshop*, pages 156–168, June 1997.

[114] D. Volpano and G. Smith. Probabilistic noninterference in a concurrent language. *J. Computer Security*, 7(2–3):231–253, November 1999.

[115] D. Volpano and G. Smith. Verifying secrets and relative secrecy. In *Proc. ACM Symp. on Principles of Programming Languages*, pages 268–276, January 2000.

[116] D. Volpano, G. Smith, and C. Irvine. A sound type system for secure flow analysis. *J. Computer Security*, 4(3):167–187, 1996.

[117] WebSand. Deliverable 1.1: Consolidation of state-of-the-art. January 2011.

[118] S. Zdancewic and A. C. Myers. Robust declassification. In *Proc. IEEE Computer Security Foundations Workshop*, pages 15–23, June 2001.

[119] S. Zdancewic and A. C. Myers. Secure information flow and CPS. In *Proc. European Symp. on Programming*, volume 2028 of *Lecture Notes in Computer Science*, pages 46–61. Springer-Verlag, April 2001.

Software Safety and Security
T. Nipkow et al. (Eds.)
IOS Press, 2012
© *2012 The authors and IOS Press. All rights reserved.*
doi:10.3233/978-1-61499-028-4-348

Precise Program Analysis through Strategy Iteration and Optimization

Thomas Martin GAWLITZA [a]   Helmut SEIDL [b,1]

[a] *The University of Sydney, Australia,* `gawlitza@it.usyd.edu.au`
[b] *Technische Universität München, Germany,* `seidl@in.tum.de`

Abstract. We present a practical algorithm for computing least solutions of systems of (fixpoint-)equations over the integers with, besides other monotone operators, addition, multiplication by positive constants, maximum, and minimum. The algorithm is based on max-strategy iteration. Its worst-case running-time (w.r.t. a uniform cost measure) is independent of the sizes of occurring numbers. We apply this algorithm to the problem of computing the abstract semantics of programs over integer intervals as well as over integer zones.

Keywords. static program analysis, abstract interpretation, fixpoint equation systems, strategy improvement algorithms, intervals, octogons, template constraints, Bellman-Ford algorithm, linear programming

1. Introduction

This article does not contain original material. It is based on the article *Abstract Interpretation over Zones without Widening* by Gawlitza and Seidl [18]. It provides additional material on the first part of the tutorial held by the second author at MOD'2011 on *Precise Program Analysis through Strategy Iteration and Mathematical Programming* which reviews techniques for inferring precise numerical invariants for variables. While the first part of the tutorial concentrated on techniques for integer variables, the second part was concerned with numerical invariants over the rationals or reals. It provided an in-depth comparison of two different approaches which both are based on strategy iteration. The first approach has been suggested by Gaubert, Goubault, Taly, and Zennou [14] and later Adjé, Gaubert, and Goubault [1] (quoted as the *max-strategy approach*), while the second is ours from [15, 20, 21] (quoted as the *min-strategy approach*). This comparison is not included here, as it can be found in [19].

In this article, we concentrate on techniques for integers. Tight bounds on the possible values of integer variables are crucial when memory errors at array indexing are to be excluded. Just to name one further prominent application, such bounds are also crucial for inferring worst-case execution times [34]. Various extensions of interval analysis have been considered which also infer nontrivial relationships between integer variables. Beyond upper and lower bounds on the values of variables, the abstract domain of *zones*

---

[1]Corresponding Author: Helmut Seidl, Fakulät für Informatik, TU München, Boltzmannstr. 3, 85648 Garching, Germany

allows to express bounds on the *differences* between the values of two variables. This domain has been introduced by Dor et al. [12] for the analysis of string manipulating C functions and has later been refined by Miné [27]. Bounds on variable differences, however, have earlier been widely used by the model-checking community [26, 36]. A dedicated representation for zones, called *difference bound matrices*, as well as various operators on these for model-checking timed automata were introduced by Larsen et al. [26], and Yovine [36]. Later, this domain has been generalized to *octagons* which additionally track bounds on the *sums* of the values of two variables [28]. All of these domains are special instances of *template polyhedra* as studied by Sankaranarayanan et al. [31].

The approach of inferring invariants by means of abstract interpretation first translates the program into a set of constraints over an abstract lattice of possible invariants. The least solution of this constraint system represents the abstract semantics of the program, i.e., the most precise invariants which the analysis can infer. The most immediate idea for determining this least solution is to use some variant of Kleene fixpoint iteration which, starting from the least value of the abstract domain, repeatedly re-evaluates constraints until no further contribution to the values of unknowns is found. Already interval analysis, however, relies on lattices with *infinite* strictly ascending chains. For such lattices, a Kleene fixpoint iteration may not terminate and thus fail to determine the least solution. In order to enforce termination, Cousot and Cousot proposed a *widening* iteration which returns *some*, perhaps very imprecise solution, which subsequently is improved by a *narrowing* iteration [11]. For the specific case of zones, widening and narrowing operators have been introduced by Miné [27]. Since widening trades termination of the fixpoint iteration against precision, widening/narrowing-based techniques may not succeed in computing the least solution, i.e., they may not succeed in computing the most precise invariant that is expressible in the abstract domain.

This was more or less state of the art until Costan, Gaubert, Goubault, Martel, and Putot [8] proposed an alternative technique for computing solutions to constraint systems over integer intervals. They considered the problem of computing least solutions to constraint systems of integer intervals as a two-players zero-sum game where one player (the maximizer) aims at maximizing and his opponent (the minimizer) aims at minimizing the values of the variables. Then, they apply (min-)strategy iteration to find a small solution to the constraints, i.e., they try to improve the strategy for the minimizer step by step. While this approach still may not result in the least solution, it at least avoids the crude overapproximation through widening.

Strategy iteration in itself is not new. Strategy iteration was introduced by Howard [23] for solving one-player games. Hoffman and Karp [22] used the idea for solving certain *two-players games*. A strategy improvement algorithm performs two basic steps that are to be alternated: each strategy has to be *evaluated* and based on the result of this evaluation it has to be *improved* (if possible). These steps are repeated until stabilization, i.e., until no further improvement is possible. In the context of program analysis through abstract interpretation, Gaubert, Goubault, Taly, and Zennou [14] generalized the idea of Costan, Gaubert, Goubault, Martel, and Putot [8] and applied it to *zones, octagons*, and, more generally, arbitrary *template polyhedra*. In contrast to the interval domain, these domains are *relational*, i.e., they are able to express relations between the values of different variables. Their method applies linear programming to perform a strategy improvement step, i.e., to evaluate and improve a given strategy for the minimizer. It returns quite precise solutions which, however, are not guaranteed to be minimal.

The article [18], which we follow here, elaborates the techniques for analyzing values of integer variables which we have developed in [16, 17]. In these articles, we have proposed a max-strategy iteration which is guaranteed to terminate with the least solution. Our approach differs from the approach proposed by Costan et al. [8], Gaubert et al. [14] in that we improve the strategy for the maximizer instead of the strategy for the minimizer. Each strategy for the maximizer is evaluated using a generalization of the Bellman-Ford algorithm. Our approach finally allows to compute the abstract semantics of programs over integer intervals. We later extended this approach to tackle the problem of computing the abstract semantics over zones, octagons or template polyhedra [15, 21]. The latter methods, however, use exact rational arithmetic and apply linear programming to evaluate the strategies for the maximizer.

Although fast implementations of linear programming are available, no *strongly* polynomial algorithm is known. Therefore, it is not clear how well algorithms that rely on linear programming may scale to larger inputs — in particular, when exact rational arithmetic is applied. In this article, we show that if we are only interested in integer zones, then full-fletched linear programming is not necessary to evaluate a strategy for the maximizer. Instead, an algorithm can be constructed which is based on the Bellman-Ford algorithm extended with subroutine calls to solve minimum cost flow problems [30]. For the latter problem various strongly polynomial algorithms have been devised (see e.g. Ahuja et al. [2] for a recent overview).

2. The Framework

Notations The transpose of a matrix A is denoted by $A^\top$. The i-th row (resp. j-th column) of a matrix A is denoted by $A_i.$ (resp. $A_{.j}$). Accordingly, $A_{i.j}$ denotes the entry in the i-th row and the j-th column. This notation is also used for vectors and functions $f : X \to Y^k$, i.e., $f_i.(x) = (f(x))_i.$ for all $x \in X$ and all $i \in \{1, \ldots, k\}$.

2.1. Programs and their Collecting Semantics

For this overview, a *program* is given by a *control flow graph* $G = (N, E, \mathbf{st})$ that consists of a finite set N of *control points*, a finite set $E \subseteq N \times \mathbf{Stmt} \times N$ of *(control flow) edges* and a special *start control point* $\mathbf{st} \in N$. $\mathbf{Stmt}$ is a set of statements. We assume that the program G uses $n \in \mathbb{N}\setminus\{0\}$ variables that take values from $\mathbb{Z}$. We fix a so-called *template constraint matrix* $T \in \{-1, 0, 1\}^{m \times n}$. Each row of the template constraint matrix represents a template (here: a linear function). We restrict ourselves to the case where we can only talk about upper and lower bounds for program variables and upper bounds for the differences of program variables. That is, we assume that each row of T contains at most one 1 and at most one -1. For simplicity, we further assume w.l.o.g. that each row of T contains at least one non-zero entry.

Example 1 *For $n = 2$ we might, for instance, choose*

$$T = \begin{pmatrix} 1 & 0 \\ 0 & 1 \\ -1 & 1 \end{pmatrix}. \tag{1}$$

Figure 1. A simple program

This template constraint matrix allows us to reason about upper bounds on the program variables $\mathbf{x}_1$ and $\mathbf{x}_2$, as well as upper bounds on the difference $\mathbf{x}_2 - \mathbf{x}_1$. ☐

We assume that each statement $s \in \mathbf{Stmt}$ is of the form

$$T\mathbf{x} \leq c; \mathbf{x} := A\mathbf{x} + b, \tag{2}$$

where $c \in \mathbb{Z}^m$, $A \in \mathbb{Z}^{n \times n}$, and $b \in \mathbb{Z}^n$ (recall that T is the template constraint matrix we have fixed beforehand). Hence, a statement combines a guard ($T\mathbf{x} \leq c$) with an assignment ($\mathbf{x} := A\mathbf{x}+b$). The collecting semantics $[\![T\mathbf{x} \leq c; \mathbf{x} := A\mathbf{x}+b]\!] : 2^{\mathbb{Z}^n} \to 2^{\mathbb{Z}^n}$ of the statement $T\mathbf{x} \leq c; \mathbf{x} := A\mathbf{x} + b$ is defined by

$$[\![T\mathbf{x} \leq c; \mathbf{x} := A\mathbf{x} + b]\!]X = \{Ax + b \mid x \in X,\ Tx \leq c\} \quad \text{for all } X \subseteq \mathbb{Z}^n. \tag{3}$$

In order to model user inputs we could additionally allow non-deterministic assignments, i.e., statements of the form $\mathbf{x}_i := ?$, where the collecting semantics $[\![\mathbf{x}_i := ?]\!] : 2^{\mathbb{Z}^n} \to 2^{\mathbb{Z}^n}$ of $\mathbf{x}_i := ?$ is defined by $[\![\mathbf{x}_i := ?]\!]X = \{(x_1, \ldots, x_{i-1}, y, x_{i+1}, \ldots, x_n)^\top \mid (x_1, \ldots, x_n)^\top \in X,\ y \in \mathbb{Z}\}$ for all $X \subseteq \mathbb{Z}^n$. However, we abandon this, because these statements can be simulated by introducing new program variables or additional loops.

The collecting semantics V of a non-deterministic program G finally associates a set of vectors from $\mathbb{Z}^n$ to each control point $v \in N$. It is defined as the least solution of the following constraint system:

$$\mathbf{V}[\mathbf{st}] \supseteq \mathbb{Z}^n \tag{4}$$

$$\mathbf{V}[v] \supseteq [\![s]\!](\mathbf{V}[u]) \quad \text{for each control-flow edge } (u, s, v) \in E \tag{5}$$

The unknowns $\mathbf{V}[v]$, $v \in N$ take values in $2^{\mathbb{Z}^n}$. We denote the components of the collecting semantics V by $V[v]$ for $v \in N$.

Example 2 *Figure 1 shows a program G with the two integer variables $\mathbf{x}_1$ and $\mathbf{x}_2$. The collecting semantics V of G is given by $V[\mathbf{st}] = \mathbb{Z}^2$, and $V[1] = \{(0, 1), (2, 3), (4, 5), (6, 7), (8, 9), (10, 11)\}$.* ☐

3. Abstract Interpretation over Intervals and Zones

Our goal is to perform static program analysis by abstract interpretation over integer intervals as studied by Cousot and Cousot [9, 10]. That is, for each program point, we aim at computing small upper bounds for expressions of the form $\mathbf{x}$ and $-\mathbf{x}$, where $\mathbf{x}$ is a program variable. We then extend this to work over the abstract domain of integer zones (cf. Miné [27]). That is, we additionally aim at computing small upper bounds for expressions of the form $\mathbf{x} - \mathbf{y}$, where $\mathbf{x}$ and $\mathbf{y}$ are program variables.

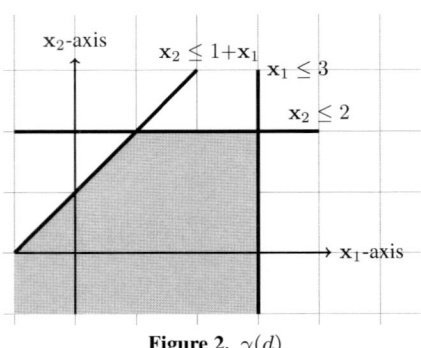

Figure 2. $\gamma(d)$

3.1. The Program's Abstract Semantics

We use the abstract domain of integer zones to define the program's abstract semantics. In this article we restrict ourselves to the integer zones that can be expressed through the template constraint matrix T. Let $\overline{\mathbb{Z}}$ denote the lattice of all integers extended with a least element $-\infty$ and a greatest element ∞. Note that $\overline{\mathbb{Z}}$ then becomes a *complete* lattice. In consequence, $\overline{\mathbb{Z}}^n$ together with the component-wise extension of the ordering on $\overline{\mathbb{Z}}$ also forms a complete lattice. For convenience, we denote least upper bounds and greatest lower bounds on $\overline{\mathbb{Z}}$ and on $\overline{\mathbb{Z}}^n$ by $\vee$ and $\wedge$, respectively. That is, for all $x, y \in \overline{\mathbb{Z}}$, $x \wedge y$ denotes the minimum of x and y, because $\overline{\mathbb{Z}}$ is linearly ordered. For all $x, y \in \overline{\mathbb{Z}}^n$, $x \wedge y$ is given by $(x \wedge y)_{i.} = x_{i.} \wedge y_{i.}$ for all $i \in \{1, \ldots, n\}$. The abstract elements are vectors from $\overline{\mathbb{Z}}^m$. They are interpreted w.r.t. the template constraint matrix T. That is, the *concretization* $\gamma : \overline{\mathbb{Z}}^m \to 2^{\mathbb{Z}^n}$ and the *abstraction* $\alpha : 2^{\mathbb{Z}^n} \to \overline{\mathbb{Z}}^m$ are defined by

$$\gamma(d) := \{x \in \mathbb{Z}^n \mid Tx \leq d\} \qquad \text{for all } d \in \overline{\mathbb{Z}}^m, \text{ and} \qquad (6)$$

$$\alpha(X) := \min \{d \in \overline{\mathbb{Z}}^m \mid \gamma(d) \supseteq X\} \qquad \text{for all } X \subseteq \mathbb{Z}^n. \qquad (7)$$

Each abstract value $d \in \overline{\mathbb{Z}}^m$ represents the set $\gamma(d)$ of concrete values. The abstraction α and the concretization γ form a *Galois connection* (see e.g. Sankaranarayanan et al. [31]). Recall that the template constraint matrix T is an element of the set $\{-1, 0, 1\}^{m \times n}$ and each row contains at most one -1 and at most one 1.

Example 3 *Figure 2 shows $\gamma(d)$ for $d = (3, 2, 1)^\top$, where T is defined as in Example 1.*
$\square$

The *abstract semantics* $[\![s]\!]^\sharp : \overline{\mathbb{Z}}^m \to \overline{\mathbb{Z}}^m$ of a statement $s \in \mathbf{Stmt}$ is defined by $[\![s]\!]^\sharp := \alpha \circ [\![s]\!] \circ \gamma$. Hence, we are concerned with best abstract transformers (cf. Cousot and Cousot [10]). The abstract semantics $V^\sharp$ of a program G is then defined as the least solution of the following constraint system:

$$\mathbf{V}^\sharp[\mathbf{st}] \geq \alpha(\mathbb{Z}^n) \qquad (8)$$

$$\mathbf{V}^\sharp[v] \geq [\![s]\!]^\sharp(\mathbf{V}^\sharp[u]) \qquad \text{for each control-flow edge } (u, s, v) \in E \qquad (9)$$

Here, the variables $\mathbf{V}^\sharp[v]$, $v \in N$ take values in $\overline{\mathbb{Z}}^m$. We denote the components of the abstract semantics $V^\sharp$ by $V^\sharp[v]$ for all $v \in N$. The abstract semantics $V^\sharp$ safely over-approximates the collection semantics V, i.e., $\gamma(V^\sharp[v]) \supseteq V[v]$ for all $v \in N$.

3.2. Intervals

In this subsection, we only consider the abstract domain of integer intervals. This case is obtained from the general case, if the matrix T provides rows with single non-zero entries 1 or -1 only. Let us for simplicity assume that the row $T_{i\cdot}$ contains a 1 in column i and the row $T_{n+i\cdot}$ contains a -1 in column i. Hence, $T \in \mathbb{Z}^{2n \times n}$. Assume that $d = (d_1, \ldots, d_{2n})^\top \in \overline{\mathbb{Z}}^{2n}$ is an abstract value. Then, for all $i \in \{1, \ldots, n\}$, the entries d_i and d_{n+i} provide upper and *negated* lower bounds for the possible values of the program variable $\mathbf{x}_i$. The concretization $\gamma(d)$ of d is non-empty iff the interval $[-d_{n+i}, d_i]$ is non-empty for all i, i.e., $d_i + d_{n+i} \geq 0$ for all i.

Now consider a statement $s = (T\mathbf{x} \leq c; \mathbf{x}:=A\mathbf{x} + b)$ and let $d \in \overline{\mathbb{Z}}^{2n}$ denote an abstract value. If $\gamma(d \wedge c) = \emptyset$, then $[\![s]\!]^\sharp(d) = (-\infty, \ldots, -\infty)^\top$ (recall that $d \wedge c$ denotes the greatest lower bound of the vectors c and d). In order to deal with the other cases, we define matrices $A^+, A^- \in \mathbb{Z}^{n \times n}$ by:

$$A^+_{i\cdot j} := A_{i\cdot j} \vee 0 \qquad A^-_{i\cdot j} := -A_{i\cdot j} \vee 0 \qquad \text{for all } i, j \in \{1, \ldots, n\} \qquad (10)$$

Thus, the matrix A^+ collects the positive entries of A whereas the matrix A^- collects the negated negative entries of A. The other entries are set to 0. We have $A = A^+ - A^-$. Finally, we set

$$A^\pm := \begin{pmatrix} A^+ & A^- \\ A^- & A^+ \end{pmatrix}, \text{ and } \qquad b^\pm := \begin{pmatrix} b \\ -b \end{pmatrix}. \qquad (11)$$

Then

$$\alpha(\{A\mathbf{x} + b\}) = A^\pm \begin{pmatrix} x \\ -x \end{pmatrix} + b^\pm \qquad \text{for all } x \in \mathbb{Z}^n. \qquad (12)$$

We now develop an explicit representation of the best abstract transformer. That is, we verify the following equality under the assumption that $\gamma(c \wedge d) \neq \emptyset$ holds:

$$[\![s]\!]^\sharp(d) = \alpha([\![s]\!](\gamma(d)))$$

$$= \bigvee \{\alpha(\{A\mathbf{x} + b\}) \mid T\mathbf{x} \leq c, \, x \in \gamma(d)\}$$

$$= \bigvee \left\{ \alpha(\{A\mathbf{x} + b\}) \mid \begin{pmatrix} x \\ -x \end{pmatrix} \leq c, \, \begin{pmatrix} x \\ -x \end{pmatrix} \leq d \right\}$$

$$= \bigvee \left\{ A^\pm \begin{pmatrix} x \\ -x \end{pmatrix} + b^\pm \mid \begin{pmatrix} x \\ -x \end{pmatrix} \leq c \wedge d \right\} \qquad \text{(because of (12))}$$

$$= A^\pm (c \wedge d) + b^\pm \qquad \text{(because } A^\pm \text{ is monotone)}$$

The last equation holds, since the matrix $A^\pm$ contains non-negative entries only, which implies that the linear operator $A^\pm$ is monotone.

In order to practically determine the abstract semantics w.r.t. the interval domain, we decompose the constraint system for the abstract semantics into a constraint system over the integers alone. For that, we introduce unknowns $\mathbf{x}_{v,i}$ for every program point

$v \in N$ and $i \in \{1, \ldots, 2n\}$. The unknown $\mathbf{x}_{v,i}$ stands for the i-th component of the vector $\mathbf{V}^\sharp[v]$. Accordingly, each unknown takes values in $\overline{\mathbb{Z}}$. Each constraint $\mathbf{V}^\sharp[v] \geq [\![s]\!]^\sharp (\mathbf{V}^\sharp[u])$ and each $i \in \{1, \ldots, 2n\}$ gives rise to the following constraint:

$$\mathbf{x}_{v,i} \geq ((\mathbf{x}_{u,1} \wedge c_{1\cdot}) + (\mathbf{x}_{u,n+1} \wedge c_{n+1\cdot})) \geq 0? \tag{13}$$

$$\cdots \tag{14}$$

$$((\mathbf{x}_{u,n} \wedge c_{n\cdot}) + (\mathbf{x}_{u,n+n} \wedge c_{n+n\cdot})) \geq 0? \tag{15}$$

$$A_{i\cdot 1}^{\pm}(\mathbf{x}_{u,1} \wedge c_{1\cdot}) + \cdots + A_{i\cdot 2n}^{\pm}(\mathbf{x}_{u,2n} \wedge c_{2n\cdot}) + b_{i\cdot}^{\pm} \tag{16}$$

Here, for all $a, b \in \overline{\mathbb{Z}}$, a test $a \geq 0 ? b$ evaluates to b if $a \geq 0$ and to $-\infty$ otherwise. Thus, the tests at the beginning of the right-hand sides ensure that the right-hand sides only evaluate to a value greater than $-\infty$ if the guard $T\mathbf{x} \leq c$ can be fulfilled.

Let $\rho^\sharp$ denote the least solution of the resulting constraint system. That is, $\rho^\sharp$ is a function that maps all variables to values from $\overline{\mathbb{Z}}$ such that all constraints of the resulting constraint system are solved. Then, by construction, we have $V_{i\cdot}^\sharp[v] = \rho^\sharp(\mathbf{x}_{v,i})$ for all program points $v \in N$ and all $i \in \{1, \ldots, 2n\}$.

Different right-hand sides of the resulting constraint system for the same unknown $\mathbf{x}_{v,i}$ may be combined into one by means of the maximum operator $\vee$. As a result, we obtain a system of *equations* over the integers $\overline{\mathbb{Z}}$ where right-hand sides are built up from constants and unknowns by means of the operators $\vee, \wedge, +$, multiplication with non-negative constants and the operator $\geq 0?$. Such equations are called *extended* integer equations in section 9. We obtain:

Theorem 1 (Interval Analysis) *The abstract semantics $V^\sharp$ of a program G w.r.t. the interval domain can be characterized as the least solution of a system of extended integer equations, which can be constructed from G in polynomial time.* ☐

Thus, performing interval analysis boils down to computing some (hopefully the least) solution to a system of extended integer equations. We tackle the latter problem in the remainder of this article.

4. Basics / Notations

We start by introducing some notations. For two functions $f : X \to Y$ and $g : X' \to Y$, the function $f \oplus g : (X \cup X') \to Y$ is defined by

$$(f \oplus g)(x) = \begin{cases} g(x) & \text{if } x \in X' \\ f(x) & \text{if } x \in X \setminus X' \end{cases} \qquad \text{for all } x \in X \cup X'. \tag{17}$$

We use a uniform cost measure where we count arithmetic operations and memory accesses for $\mathcal{O}(1)$. The size of a data structure S in the uniform cost measure will be denoted by $\|S\|$. An algorithm is called *uniform* iff its running time w.r.t. the uniform cost measure only depends on the size of the input in the uniform cost measure, i.e., the running time does not depend on the sizes of the occurring numbers.

4.1. Monotone Self-Maps on Complete Lattices

Let $\mathbb{D}$ be a partially ordered set (partially ordered by $\leq$). For $x \in \mathbb{D}$, we set $\mathbb{D}_{\geq x} := \{y \in \mathbb{D} \mid y \geq x\}$ and $\mathbb{D}_{\leq x} := \{y \in \mathbb{D} \mid y \leq x\}$. As usual, for $x, y \in \mathbb{D}$, we write $x < y$ iff $x \leq y$ and $x \neq y$. We denote the *least upper bound* and the *greatest lower bound* of a set X by $\bigvee X$ and $\bigwedge X$, respectively. $\mathbb{D}$ is called a *complete lattice* iff $\bigvee X$ and $\bigwedge X$ exist for all $X \subseteq \mathbb{D}$. The least element $\bigvee \emptyset$ (resp. the greatest element $\bigwedge \emptyset$) is denoted by $\bot$ (resp. $\top$). We define the binary operators $\vee$ and $\wedge$ by

$$x \vee y := \bigvee\{x, y\}, \text{ and} \qquad\qquad x \wedge y := \bigwedge\{x, y\} \qquad (18)$$

for all $x, y \in \mathbb{D}$, respectively. For $\square \in \{\vee, \wedge\}$, we will also consider $x_1 \square \cdots \square x_k$ as the application of a k-ary operator. This will cause no problems, since the binary operators $\vee$ and $\wedge$ are associative. In order to simplify notations, we assume that $\wedge$ binds tighter than $\vee$, i.e., $x \wedge y \vee z = (x \wedge y) \vee z$ holds for all $x, y, z \in \mathbb{D}$.

Let $f : \mathbb{D} \to \mathbb{D}$ be a self-map. An element $x \in \mathbb{D}$ is called a fixpoint (resp. pre-fixpoint, resp. post-fixpoint) iff $x = f(x)$ (resp. $x \leq f(x)$, resp. $x \geq f(x)$). The set of all fixpoints (resp. pre-fixpoints, resp. post-fixpoints) of f is denoted by $\mathbf{Fix}(f)$ (resp. $\mathbf{PreFix}(f)$, resp. $\mathbf{PostFix}(f)$). The least fixpoint (resp. the greatest fixpoint) of f is denoted by μf (resp. νf), provided that it exists. For $x \in \mathbb{D}$, $\mu_{\geq x} f$ (resp. $\nu_{\leq x} f$) denotes the least (resp. greatest) element from $\mathbb{D}_{\geq x} \cap \mathbf{Fix}(f)$ (resp. $\mathbb{D}_{\leq x} \cap \mathbf{Fix}(f)$), provided that it exists.

A map f is called monotone iff $x \leq y$ implies $f(x) \leq f(y)$ for all x, y. The existence of least and greatest fixpoints of monotone self-maps on complete lattices is ensured by the Knaster-Tarski fixpoint theorem [33]: Every monotone self-map f on a complete lattice has a least fixpoint μf and a greatest fixpoint νf. Furthermore, $\mu f = \bigwedge \mathbf{PostFix}(f)$, and $\nu f = \bigvee \mathbf{PreFix}(f)$.

Let f be a monotone self-map on a complete lattice $\mathbb{D}$. Let $x \in \mathbf{PreFix}(f)$. Then $\mathbb{D}_{\geq x}$ is also a complete lattice and the restriction of f to $\mathbb{D}_{\geq x}$ is a self-map on $\mathbb{D}_{\geq x}$. Thus, the Knaster-Tarski fixpoint theorem implies that $\mu_{\geq x} f$ exists. Dually, if $x \in \mathbf{PostFix}(f)$, then $\nu_{\leq x} f$ exists.

Let $\mathbf{X}$ be a set of variables. The set $\mathbf{X} \to \mathbb{D}$ of all *variable assignments* is partially ordered by the point-wise extension of $\leq$ which we, for simplicity, again denote by $\leq$. If $\mathbb{D}$ is a complete lattice, then $\mathbf{X} \to \mathbb{D}$ is also a complete lattice. For $d \in \mathbb{D}$, $\underline{d}$ denotes the variable assignment $\{\mathbf{x} \mapsto d \mid \mathbf{x} \in \mathbf{X}\}$.

4.2. Systems of Monotone Equations

Assume that a fixed set $\mathbf{X}$ of variables and a partially ordered set $\mathbb{D}$ (for instance $\overline{\mathbb{Z}}$) are given. We consider (fixpoint-)equations of the form $\mathbf{x} = e$, where $\mathbf{x} \in \mathbf{X}$ is a variable that takes values in $\mathbb{D}$ and e is an expression over $\mathbb{D}$. A *system* $\mathcal{E}$ of (fixpoint-)equations is a finite set $\{\mathbf{x}_1 = e_1, \ldots, \mathbf{x}_n = e_n\}$ of equations, where $\mathbf{x}_1, \ldots, \mathbf{x}_n$ are pairwise distinct variables. We denote the set $\{\mathbf{x}_1, \ldots, \mathbf{x}_n\}$ of variables occurring in $\mathcal{E}$ by $\mathbf{X}_\mathcal{E}$. We drop the subscript, whenever it is clear from the context. The set of subexpressions occurring in the right-hand sides of $\mathcal{E}$ is denoted by $\mathcal{S}(\mathcal{E})$. The set of variables occurring in the right-hand sides of $\mathcal{E}$ is denoted by $\mathbf{Vars}(\mathcal{E})$. For $\mathbf{X}' \subseteq \mathbf{X}$, we set $\mathcal{E} \oplus \{\mathbf{x} = e_\mathbf{x} \mid \mathbf{x} \in \mathbf{X}'\} := \{\mathbf{x} = e \in \mathcal{E} \mid \mathbf{x} \notin \mathbf{X}'\} \cup \{\mathbf{x} = e_\mathbf{x} \mid \mathbf{x} \in \mathbf{X}'\}$.

For an expression e, we write $e[e_\mathbf{x}/\mathbf{x}]_{\mathbf{x}\in\mathbf{X}'}$ for the expression which is obtained from e by simultaneously substituting all occurrences of the variable $\mathbf{x}$ with the expression $e_\mathbf{x}$ for all variables $\mathbf{x} \in \mathbf{X}'$. We set $\mathcal{E}[e_\mathbf{x}/\mathbf{x}]_{\mathbf{x}\in\mathbf{X}'} := \{\mathbf{x} = e[e_\mathbf{x}/\mathbf{x}]_{\mathbf{x}\in\mathbf{X}'} \mid \mathbf{x} = e \in \mathcal{E}\}$.

For a variable assignment $\rho : \mathbf{X} \to \mathbb{D}$, e is mapped to a value $[\![e]\!]\rho$ by

$$[\![\mathbf{x}]\!]\rho := \rho(\mathbf{x}), \quad \text{and} \quad [\![f(e_1,\ldots,e_k)]\!]\rho := f([\![e_1]\!]\rho,\ldots,[\![e_k]\!]\rho), \tag{19}$$

where $\mathbf{x} \in \mathbf{X}$, f is a k-ary operator, for instance $+$, and $e_1,\ldots,e_k$ are expressions. Let $\mathcal{E}$ be a system of (fixpoint-)equations. We define the unary operator $[\![\mathcal{E}]\!]$ on $\mathbf{X} \to \mathbb{D}$ by setting

$$([\![\mathcal{E}]\!]\rho)(\mathbf{x}) := [\![e]\!]\rho \qquad \text{for all equations } \mathbf{x} = e \text{ of } \mathcal{E}. \tag{20}$$

A solution of $\mathcal{E}$ is a variable assignment ρ such that $\rho = [\![\mathcal{E}]\!]\rho$. The set of solutions is denoted by $\mathbf{Sol}(\mathcal{E})$. A pre-solution (resp. post-solution) of $\mathcal{E}$ is a variable assignment ρ such that $\rho \leq [\![\mathcal{E}]\!]\rho$ (resp. $\rho \geq [\![\mathcal{E}]\!]\rho$). The set of pre-solutions (resp. the set of post-solutions) is denoted by $\mathbf{PreSol}(\mathcal{E})$ (resp. $\mathbf{PostSol}(\mathcal{E})$). The least solution (resp. the greatest solution) of a system $\mathcal{E}$ of equations is denoted by $\mu[\![\mathcal{E}]\!]$ (resp. $\nu[\![\mathcal{E}]\!]$), provided that it exists. For a pre-solution ρ (resp. for a post-solution ρ), $\mu_{\geq\rho}[\![\mathcal{E}]\!]$ (resp. $\nu_{\leq\rho}[\![\mathcal{E}]\!]$) denotes the least solution that is greater than or equal to ρ (resp. the greatest solution that is less than or equal to ρ).

An expression e (resp. an equation $\mathbf{x} = e$) is called *monotone* iff all operators occurring in e are monotone. An expression e or an equation $\mathbf{x} = e$ is called *disjunctive* (resp. *conjunctive*) iff e does not contain $\wedge$-operators (resp. $\vee$-operators). An expression e or an equation $\mathbf{x} = e$ is called *basic* iff e does neither contain $\wedge$- nor $\vee$-operators.

In our setting, the Knaster-Tarski fixpoint theorem can be stated as follows: every system $\mathcal{E}$ of monotone equations over a complete lattice has a least solution $\mu[\![\mathcal{E}]\!]$ and a greatest solution $\nu[\![\mathcal{E}]\!]$. Furthermore, $\mu[\![\mathcal{E}]\!] = \bigwedge \mathbf{PostSol}(\mathcal{E})$, and $\nu[\![\mathcal{E}]\!] = \bigvee \mathbf{PreSol}(\mathcal{E})$.

5. Systems of Integer Equations

In this section, we introduce the class of fixpoint equation systems we will focus on in the remainder of this article. We moreover study elementary properties of these equation systems and the operators that are allowed in right-hand sides.

5.1. Operators on $\overline{\mathbb{Z}}$

On $\overline{\mathbb{Z}}$ we consider two additions, $+^{-\infty}$ and $+^{\infty}$, which are dual to each other. Both coincide on $\mathbb{Z}$ with the usual addition. The operator $+^{-\infty}$ preserves $-\infty$, whereas the operator $+^{\infty}$ preserves ∞:

$$x +^{-\infty} y := \begin{cases} -\infty & \text{if } -\infty \in \{x,y\} \\ \infty & \text{if } -\infty \notin \{x,y\} \text{ and } \infty \in \{x,y\} \\ x + y & \text{if } x, y \in \mathbb{Z} \end{cases} \qquad \text{for all } x, y \in \overline{\mathbb{Z}} \tag{21}$$

$$x +^\infty y := \begin{cases} \infty & \text{if } \infty \in \{x, y\} \\ -\infty & \text{if } \infty \notin \{x, y\} \text{ and } -\infty \in \{x, y\} \\ x + y & \text{if } x, y \in \mathbb{Z} \end{cases} \quad \text{for all } x, y \in \overline{\mathbb{Z}}. \quad (22)$$

We have $x +^{-\infty} y = x +^\infty y$, whenever $(x, y) \notin \{(-\infty, \infty), (\infty, -\infty)\}$. In particular, both operators $+^{-\infty}$ and $+^\infty$ behave equal, if one argument is from $\mathbb{Z}$. In our applications, we mostly use the operator $+^{-\infty}$. Therefore, in the following we also denote the operator $+^{-\infty}$ simply by $+$. We extend the multiplication on $\mathbb{Z}$ as usual, i.e.,

$$x \cdot \infty = \infty \cdot x = \infty, \quad x \cdot -\infty = -\infty \cdot x = -\infty \qquad \text{for } x > 0 \quad (23)$$

$$x \cdot \infty = \infty \cdot x = -\infty, \quad x \cdot -\infty = -\infty \cdot x = \infty \qquad \text{for } x < 0 \quad (24)$$

$$0 \cdot \infty = \infty \cdot 0 = 0 \cdot -\infty = -\infty \cdot 0 = 0. \quad (25)$$

Observe that the multiplication $\cdot$ on $\overline{\mathbb{Z}}$ is not monotone, since for instance $(-1, 0) \leq (-1, 1)$ and $-1 \cdot 0 = 0 \not\leq -1 = -1 \cdot 1$. For $c \in \overline{\mathbb{Z}}$, we denote the unary operator that assigns $c + x$ (resp. $c \cdot x$) to each $x \in \overline{\mathbb{Z}}$ by $c+$ (resp. $c\cdot$). The operator $c\cdot$ is monotone, whenever c is positive. For simplicity, we make the following agreements: The operator $c\cdot$ binds tighter than the operators $+^{-\infty}$ and $+^\infty$. These operators bind tighter than $\wedge$, which binds tighter than $\vee$. All operators are left-associative.

5.2. Expansivity

In this article, we are in particular interested in expressions e for which the evaluation function $\llbracket e \rrbracket$ is *expansive* (see below) in all variables occurring in e. Informally, this means that the value of an expression e increases (resp. decreases) by at least δ, whenever the value of a variable increases (resp. decreases) by δ.

Let X be a set and $f : (X \to \overline{\mathbb{Z}}) \to \overline{\mathbb{Z}}$ be a mapping. The mapping f is called *upward-expansive in $X' \subseteq X$* iff

$$f(\rho \oplus \{x \mapsto \rho(x) + \delta\}) \geq f(\rho) + \delta \qquad \text{for all } x \in X', \ \rho : X \to \overline{\mathbb{Z}}, \ \delta \in \mathbb{N}. \quad (26)$$

Dually, f is called *downward-expansive in $X' \subseteq X$* iff

$$f(\rho \oplus \{x \mapsto \rho(x) - \delta\}) \leq f(\rho) - \delta \qquad \text{for all } x \in X', \ \rho : X \to \overline{\mathbb{Z}}, \ \delta \in \mathbb{N}. \quad (27)$$

The mapping f is called *expansive in $X' \subseteq X$* iff it is upward- and downward-expansive in $X' \subseteq X$. It is simply called *upward-expansive* (resp. *downward-expansive*, resp. *expansive*) iff it is upward-expansive in X (resp. downward-expansive in X, resp. expansive in X). Since $\overline{\mathbb{Z}}^n$ can be identified with the set $\overline{\mathbb{Z}}^{\{1,\dots,n\}} = \{1, \dots, n\} \to \overline{\mathbb{Z}}$ of all functions from $\{1, \dots, n\}$ to $\overline{\mathbb{Z}}$, the above definitions also apply to operators.

Lemma 1 *If all operators that occur in an expression e are expansive (respectively upward-expansive, respectively downward-expansive), then the evaluation function $\llbracket e \rrbracket$ of e is expansive (respectively upward-expansive, respectively downward-expansive) in* **Vars**(e). ☐

In the remainder of this article we are in particular interested in operators that are monotone and expansive. The operators $+^{-\infty}, +^\infty$, $c+$ ($c \in \mathbb{Z}$), and $c\cdot$ ($c \in \mathbb{N}\backslash\{0\}$), are important examples for operators that are monotone and expansive.

5.3. Systems of Integer Equations

Let $\mathbf{X}$ be a set of variables and $\mathcal{F}$ be a set of operators. We denote the set of all expressions that can be built up using variables from $\mathbf{X}$ and operators from $\mathcal{F}$ by $\mathbf{E}(\mathcal{F}, \mathbf{X})$. Moreover, we identify constants with nullary operators. For instance, we have $\mathbf{x} + 2 \in \mathbf{E}(\overline{\mathbb{Z}} \cup \{+\}, \{\mathbf{x}\})$. An expression from $\mathbf{E}(\mathcal{F}, \mathbf{X})$ is called a $\mathbf{E}(\mathcal{F}, \mathbf{X})$-expression. An equation $\mathbf{x} = e$ is called a $\mathbf{E}(\mathcal{F}, \mathbf{X})$-equation iff $\mathbf{x} \in \mathbf{X}$ and $e \in \mathbf{E}(\mathcal{F}, \mathbf{X})$. We define the sets $\mathcal{F}$, $\mathcal{F}^l$ and $\mathcal{F}^s$ of operators as follows:

$$\mathcal{F} := \{\wedge, \vee\} \cup \{f : \overline{\mathbb{Z}}^k \to \overline{\mathbb{Z}} \mid f \text{ is monotone and expansive}\} \tag{28}$$

$$\mathcal{F}^l := \{\wedge, \vee, +^{-\infty}, +^{\infty}\} \cup \{c \cdot \mid c \in \mathbb{N}\backslash\{0\}\} \tag{29}$$

$$\mathcal{F}^s := \{\wedge, \vee\} \cup \{c + \mid c \in \mathbb{Z}\} \tag{30}$$

Let $\mathbf{X}$ be a set of variables. An $\mathbf{E}(\overline{\mathbb{Z}} \cup \mathcal{F}, \mathbf{X})$-expression is called *integer expression*, an $\mathbf{E}(\overline{\mathbb{Z}} \cup \mathcal{F}, \mathbf{X})$-equation is called *integer equation*, and an $\mathbf{E}(\overline{\mathbb{Z}} \cup \mathcal{F}^l, \mathbf{X})$-expression is called *linear integer equation*. Accordingly, an $\mathbf{E}(\overline{\mathbb{Z}} \cup \mathcal{F}^l, \mathbf{X})$-equation is called *linear integer equation*, an $\mathbf{E}(\overline{\mathbb{Z}} \cup \mathcal{F}^s, \mathbf{X})$-expression is called *simple integer expression*, and an $\mathbf{E}(\overline{\mathbb{Z}} \cup \mathcal{F}^s, \mathbf{X})$-equation is called *simple integer equation*.

Every system of *simple* integer equations can be identified with a system of *linear* integer equations. The Knaster-Tarski fixpoint theorem implies that every system of integer equations has a least and a greatest solution.

Example 4 *The system* $\mathcal{E} = \{\mathbf{x}_1 = (\mathbf{x}_2 \vee \mathbf{x}_1 + 1) \wedge 100,\ \mathbf{x}_2 = 0\}$ *is a system of simple integer equations. The least solution is* $\mu[\![\mathcal{E}]\!] = \{\mathbf{x}_1 \mapsto 100,\ \mathbf{x}_2 \mapsto 0\}$. □

As the following example shows, Kleene fixpoint iteration is not an effective method for computing least solutions of systems of integer equations.

Example 5 (Kleene Fixpoint Iteration) *The least solution of the system* $\mathcal{E} = \{\mathbf{x} = 1 \vee \mathbf{x} + 1\}$ *of simple integer equations is* $\mu[\![\mathcal{E}]\!] = \{\mathbf{x} \mapsto \infty\}$. *For* $i \geq 1$, *the* i-th *Kleene approximate is* $[\![\mathcal{E}]\!]^i(-\infty) = \{\mathbf{x} \mapsto i\} < \{\mathbf{x} \mapsto \infty\}$. *Thus, there does not exists an* $i \in \mathbb{N}$ *such that* $[\![\mathcal{E}]\!]^i(-\infty) = \mu[\![\mathcal{E}]\!]$. □

For every system $\mathcal{E}$ of *linear* integer equations, we can compute bounds for the finite values of the least solution. That is, we can (even in polynomial time) compute some $B(\mathcal{E}) \in \mathbb{N}$ such that $|\mu[\![\mathcal{E}]\!](\mathbf{x})| \leq B(\mathcal{E})$ for every variable $\mathbf{x} \in \mathbf{X}$ with $\mu[\![\mathcal{E}]\!](\mathbf{x}) \in \mathbb{Z}$. We can then compute the least solution using a modified Kleene fixpoint iteration that sets the value of a variable to ∞ as soon as it is known to be greater then $B(\mathcal{E})$. However, the number of iterations then depends on the sizes of the constants that occur in the equation system, i.e., this method is *not* uniform.

5.4. Duality

Since $-(-x) = x$, $-(x \vee y) = -x \wedge -y$ and $-(x \wedge y) = -x \vee -y$ for all $x, y \in \overline{\mathbb{Z}}$, the unary minus $- : \overline{\mathbb{Z}} \to \overline{\mathbb{Z}}$ is a negation. The *dual* f^δ of a k-ary operator f on $\overline{\mathbb{Z}}$ is defined by $f^\delta(x_1, \ldots, x_k) := -f(-x_1, \ldots, -x_k)$ for all $x_1, \ldots, x_k \in \overline{\mathbb{Z}}$. The operators $\vee$ and $\wedge$ are dual to each other, $+^{-\infty}$ and $+^{\infty}$ are dual to each other, and $c \cdot$ ($c \in \mathbb{N}_{>0}$)

is self-dual, i.e., $c\cdot$ is the dual of $c\cdot$. The dual e^δ of an integer expression e is inductively defined by $\mathbf{x}^\delta := \mathbf{x}$, and $f(e_1, \ldots, e_k) := f^\delta(e_1^\delta, \ldots, e_k^\delta)$, where $\mathbf{x}$ is a variable, f is a k-ary operator, and $e_1, \ldots, e_k$ are integer expressions. Finally, the dual $\mathcal{E}^\delta$ of a system $\mathcal{E}$ of integer equations is defined by $\mathcal{E}^\delta := \{\mathbf{x} = e^\delta \mid \mathbf{x} = e \in \mathcal{E}\}$.

The class of systems of integer equations (resp. linear integer equations, resp. simple integer equations) is closed under dualization. Moreover, we have $\nu[\![\mathcal{E}]\!] = -\mu[\![\mathcal{E}^\delta]\!]$ for every system $\mathcal{E}$ of integer equations.

Example 6 *The dual $\mathcal{E}^\delta$ of the system $\mathcal{E} = \{\mathbf{x}_1 = (2 \cdot \mathbf{x}_1 \wedge 100) \vee 1\}$ of linear integer equations is $\mathcal{E}^\delta = \{\mathbf{x}_1 = (2 \cdot \mathbf{x}_1 \vee -100) \wedge -1\}$. Indeed, we have*

$$\mu[\![\mathcal{E}]\!] = \{\mathbf{x}_1 \mapsto 100\} = -\{\mathbf{x}_1 \mapsto -100\} = -\nu[\![\mathcal{E}^\delta]\!]. \quad \square \tag{31}$$

5.5. Strategies

A $\vee$-*strategy* σ (resp. $\wedge$-*strategy* π) for a system $\mathcal{E}$ of equations is a function that maps every expression $e_1 \vee \cdots \vee e_k$ (resp. $e_1 \wedge \cdots \wedge e_k$) occurring in $\mathcal{E}$ to one of the immediate subexpressions e_j, $j \in \{1, \ldots, k\}$. We denote the set of all $\vee$-strategies (resp. $\wedge$-strategies) for $\mathcal{E}$ by $\Sigma_\mathcal{E}$ (resp. $\Pi_\mathcal{E}$). We drop subscripts, whenever they are clear from the context. For all $\vee$-strategies $\sigma \in \Sigma$, the expression $e\sigma$ is inductively defined by

$$(e_1 \vee \cdots \vee e_k)\sigma := (\sigma(e_1 \vee \cdots \vee e_k))\sigma, \tag{32}$$

$$(f(e_1, \ldots, e_k))\sigma := f(e_1\sigma, \ldots, e_k\sigma), \tag{33}$$

where $f \neq \vee$ is some operator. Finally, we set

$$\mathcal{E}(\sigma) := \{\mathbf{x} = e\sigma \mid \mathbf{x} = e \in \mathcal{E}\}. \tag{34}$$

The definitions of $e\pi$ and $\mathcal{E}(\pi)$ for a $\wedge$-strategy π are dual.

There exists a $\wedge$-strategy π for every system $\mathcal{E}$ of integer equations such that $\mu[\![\mathcal{E}(\pi)]\!] = \mu[\![\mathcal{E}]\!]$. However, an analogous statement does not hold for $\vee$-strategies, i.e., there does not always exist a $\vee$-strategy σ for $\mathcal{E}$ such that $\mu[\![\mathcal{E}(\sigma)]\!] = \mu[\![\mathcal{E}]\!]$ — even if we restrict ourselves to systems of *simple* integer equations.

Example 7 *We consider the system $\mathcal{E} = \{\mathbf{x}_1 = \mathbf{x}_1 + 1 \vee 0\}$ of simple integer equations. Let $\sigma_1 := \{\mathbf{x}_1 + 1 \vee 0 \mapsto \mathbf{x}_1 + 1\}$ and $\sigma_2 := \{\mathbf{x}_1 + 1 \vee 0 \mapsto 0\}$ be the $\vee$-strategies for $\mathcal{E}$, i.e., we have $\Sigma = \{\sigma_1, \sigma_2\}$. We have*

$$\mu[\![\mathcal{E}(\sigma_1)]\!] = \{\mathbf{x}_1 \mapsto -\infty\} \neq \mu[\![\mathcal{E}]\!] = \{\mathbf{x}_1 \mapsto \infty\} \neq \{\mathbf{x}_1 \mapsto 0\} = \mu[\![\mathcal{E}(\sigma_2)]\!]. \tag{35}$$

Thus, there does not exist a $\vee$-strategy σ for $\mathcal{E}$ such that $\mu[\![\mathcal{E}(\sigma)]\!] = \mu[\![\mathcal{E}]\!]$. $\quad \square$

Because of duality, the existence of a $\wedge$-strategy π for $\mathcal{E}$ such that $\nu[\![\mathcal{E}(\pi)]\!] = \nu[\![\mathcal{E}]\!]$ is also not ensured in general.

6. Adaption of the Bellman-Ford Algorithm

In this section we present an adaption of the Bellman-Ford algorithm. Later, we will use this algorithm for computing *least solutions* of systems of *disjunctive* integer equations, or dually for computing *greatest solutions* of systems of *conjunctive* integer equations. Recall that an equation $x = e$ is called disjunctive (resp. conjunctive) iff the right-hand side e does not contain the operator $\wedge$ (resp. the operator $\vee$). The Bellman-Ford algorithm is a graph algorithm for solving the *single source shortest path problem* for edge-weighted directed graphs (see e.g. Cormen et al. [7]). An edge-weighted directed graph together with a source can be represented by a system of *conjunctive* simple integer equations whose greatest solution corresponds to the solution of the *single source shortest path problem*.

The adaption of the Bellman-Ford algorithm we present in this section can be applied to compute least solutions of systems of disjunctive integer equations. However, in order to simplify the argumentations, we consider a more general class of equations, which we will call *BF-eqautions*.

Let X be a set. A monotone function $f : (X \to \overline{\mathbb{Z}}) \to \overline{\mathbb{Z}}$ is called *Bellman-Ford function* (*BF-function* for short) iff the following holds for all $\rho, \rho' : X \to \overline{\mathbb{Z}}$ with $\rho' \geq \rho$: If $f(\rho') > f(\rho)$, then there exists some $x \in X$ and some $\delta \in \overline{\mathbb{Z}} \setminus \{-\infty\}$ such that the following properties are fulfilled:

1. $\rho'(x) > \rho(x)$.
2. $f(\rho') = \rho'(x) + \delta$.
3. $f(\rho'') \geq \rho''(x) + \delta$ for all $\rho'' \geq \rho'$.

Such an x is called *relevant for the statement* $f(\rho') > f(\rho)$.

The above definition also makes sense in its dual form. Using the dual form it is possible to compute greatest solutions of systems of conjunctive integer equations directly. We will not discuss these aspects in detail. Instead we will compute greatest solutions of systems of conjunctive integer equations by using duality as discussed in Subsection 5.4.

The above definition can also be applied to k-ary operators, since the set $\overline{\mathbb{Z}}^k$ can be identified with the set $\overline{\mathbb{Z}}^{\{1,\dots,k\}} = \{1,\dots,k\} \to \overline{\mathbb{Z}}$ of all functions from $\{1,\dots,k\}$ to $\overline{\mathbb{Z}}$. Every nullary operator is a BF-operator. Moreover, all operators that occur in systems of disjunctive integer equations are BF-operators:

Lemma 2 *The operator $\vee$ and all operators that are monotone and upward-expansive are BF-operators.* $\square$

An expression e (resp. an equation $x = e$) is called *BF-expression* (resp. *BF-equation*) iff all operators occurring in e are BF-operators. Since the set of BF-functions is closed under composition, $[\![e]\!]$ is a BF-function for all BF-expressions e.

The most important step for the adaption of the Bellman-Ford algorithm consists in showing that, for a system $\mathcal{E}$ of BF-equations with n variables, the value $\mu[\![\mathcal{E}]\!](x)$ for a variable x, whose value changes after the n-th Kleene iteration, must be ∞:

Lemma 3 *Let $\mathcal{E}$ be a system of BF-equations with n variables. Let $\rho^{(i)} := [\![\mathcal{E}]\!]^i(-\infty)$ for all $i \in \mathbb{N}$. The following holds for every variable $x \in X$: If there exists some $k > n$ with $\rho^{(k)}(x) > \rho^{(n)}(x)$, then $\mu[\![\mathcal{E}]\!](x) = \infty$.*

Proof. See Appendix B. The proof is based on a pumping lemma argument. If there exists some $k > n$ with $\rho^{(k)}(\mathbf{x}) > \rho^{(n)}(\mathbf{x})$, then there exists some cyclic dependency with a positive weight that can be iterated. $\qquad\square$

As a corollary of Lemma 3 we get the following theorem which enables us to use more sophisticated fixpoint iteration schemas, whenever the least solution does not contain the value ∞.

Theorem 2 *Let $\mathcal{E}$ be a system of BF-equations with n variables. Assume further that $\mu[\![\mathcal{E}]\!] \lhd \infty$. Then $\mu[\![\mathcal{E}]\!] = [\![\mathcal{E}]\!]^n(-\infty)$.*

Proof. Let $\rho^{(i)} := [\![\mathcal{E}]\!]^i(-\infty)$ for all $i \in \mathbb{N}$ and $\rho^* := \mu[\![\mathcal{E}]\!]$. For the sake of contradiction assume $\rho^* \neq \rho^{(n)}$. Then $\rho^* > \rho^{(n)}$. In particular $\rho^{(n)} \notin \mathbf{Sol}(\mathcal{E})$. Thus, there exists a variable $\mathbf{x} \in \mathbf{X}$ with $\rho^{(n+1)}(\mathbf{x}) > \rho^{(n)}(\mathbf{x})$. Using Lemma 3 we get $\rho^*(\mathbf{x}) = \infty$ — contradiction to the assumption that $\rho^*(\mathbf{x}) < \infty$. $\qquad\square$

In our applications, the pre-conditions of Theorem 2 are mostly fulfilled. Since then the Kleene fixpoint iteration always terminates, it is also possible to use fixpoint iteration schemes that perform their evaluations according to the variable dependencies, e.g. Charlier and Hentenryck [5, 6], Fecht and Seidl [13], Kildall [25]. Although these methods are not an improvement for the worst case, in practice theses methods are mostly vastly superior to the Kleene fixpoint iteration.

We are now prepared to present the main result of this section which states that the least solution of a system $\mathcal{E}$ of BF-equations can be computed using the following adaption of the Bellman-Ford algorithm:

Algorithm 1 Adaption of the Bellman-Ford Algorithm

Input: A system $\mathcal{E}$ of BF-equations with n variables
Output: The least solution $\mu[\![\mathcal{E}]\!]$ of $\mathcal{E}$

$\rho \leftarrow -\infty$
for $i = 1$ **to** n **do** $\rho \leftarrow [\![\mathcal{E}]\!]\rho$

$\rho \leftarrow \rho'$ where $\rho'(\mathbf{x}) = \begin{cases} \rho(\mathbf{x}) & \text{if } ([\![\mathcal{E}]\!]\rho)(\mathbf{x}) \leq \rho(\mathbf{x}) \\ \infty & \text{if } ([\![\mathcal{E}]\!]\rho)(\mathbf{x}) > \rho(\mathbf{x}) \end{cases}$ for all $\mathbf{x} \in \mathbf{X}$

for $i = 1$ **to** $n - 1$ **do** $\rho \leftarrow \rho \vee [\![\mathcal{E}]\!]\rho$

return ρ

The first loop of the algorithm performs n least fixpoint iteration steps. It then sets the values of variables that are not stable to ∞. The second loop propagates the value ∞.

Theorem 3 (Adaption of the Bellman-Ford Algorithm) *Let $\mathcal{E}$ be a system of BF-equations (for instance a system of disjunctive integer equations) with n variables. The least solution $\mu[\![\mathcal{E}]\!]$ of $\mathcal{E}$ can be computed using the adaption of the Bellman-Ford algorithm (Algorithm 1). The algorithm performs $2n$ evaluations of the operator $[\![\mathcal{E}]\!]$.*

Proof. See Appendix B. $\qquad\square$

Example 8 *We use Algorithm 1 to compute the least solution of the system*

$$\mathcal{E} = \{\mathbf{x} = 1, \ \mathbf{y} = \mathbf{y} + \mathbf{x} \vee -10, \ \mathbf{z} = \mathbf{x} \cdot^+ \mathbf{y}\} \tag{36}$$

of disjunctive integer equations, where the monotone and expansive operator $\cdot^+$ is defined by

$$x \cdot^+ y := \begin{cases} x \cdot y & \text{if } x, y > 0 \\ -\infty & \text{if } x \leq 0 \text{ or } y \leq 0 \end{cases} \qquad \text{for all } x, y \in \mathbb{Z}. \tag{37}$$

After the execution of the first for-loop we obtain the pre-solution

$$\rho_0 := [\![\mathcal{E}]\!]^3(\underline{-\infty}) = [\![\mathcal{E}]\!]^2 \{\mathbf{x} \mapsto 1, \ \mathbf{y} \mapsto -10, \ \mathbf{z} \mapsto -\infty\} \tag{38}$$

$$= [\![\mathcal{E}]\!] \{\mathbf{x} \mapsto 1, \ \mathbf{y} \mapsto -9, \ \mathbf{z} \mapsto -\infty\} = \{\mathbf{x} \mapsto 1, \ \mathbf{y} \mapsto -8, \ \mathbf{z} \mapsto -\infty\}. \tag{39}$$

Since $([\![\mathcal{E}]\!]\rho_0)(\mathbf{y}) = -7 > \rho_0(\mathbf{y}) = -8$ holds, it follows $\mu[\![\mathcal{E}]\!](\mathbf{y}) = \infty$. The value of the variable $\mathbf{y}$ is thus set to ∞, i.e.,

$$\rho_1 := \{\mathbf{x} \mapsto 1, \ \mathbf{y} \mapsto \infty, \ \mathbf{z} \mapsto -\infty\} \tag{40}$$

is the value of the program variable ρ before the first execution of the body of the second for-loop. After the first execution of the body of the second for-loop we obtain

$$\rho_2 := \rho_1 \vee [\![\mathcal{E}]\!]\rho_1 = \{\mathbf{x} \mapsto 1, \ \mathbf{y} \mapsto \infty, \ \mathbf{z} \mapsto \infty\}. \tag{41}$$

After the second and last execution of the body of the second for-loop we finally obtain

$$\mu[\![\mathcal{E}]\!] = \rho_3 := \rho_2 \vee [\![\mathcal{E}]\!]\rho_2 = \{\mathbf{x} \mapsto 1, \ \mathbf{y} \mapsto \infty, \ \mathbf{z} \mapsto \infty\}. \ \square \tag{42}$$

7. The Min-Strategy Improvement Algorithm

The first algorithm for solving equation systems over intervals by means of strategy iteration has been proposed by Costan, Gaubert, Goubault, Martel, and Putot [8] (the first instance of the *min-strategy* approach). Applied to solving systems of integer equations, their idea is to compute a sequence of upper approximations to the least solution by means of least solutions to systems of *disjunctive* integer equations. Each such disjunctive equation system is obtained by substituting every $\wedge$-expression $e_1 \wedge e_2$ occurring in the right-hand sides by one of its arguments e_1 or e_2. Consider, e.g., the system

$$\mathcal{E} = \{\mathbf{x}_1 = 2 \cdot \mathbf{x}_2 \wedge 10, \ \mathbf{x}_2 = \mathbf{x}_1 \vee 0\}$$

of integer equations. One substitution may replace the $\wedge$-expression $2 \cdot \mathbf{x}_2 \wedge 10$ with the constant 10. The resulting system of equations is:

$$\mathcal{E}_1 = \{\mathbf{x}_1 = 10, \ \mathbf{x}_2 = \mathbf{x}_1 \vee 0\}$$

Since it contains no $\wedge$ operator, this system of equations can be solved by the generalized Bellman-Ford algorithm (see Section 6).

Since minimum expressions are replaced by expressions, which result in possibly larger values, the least solution of the disjunctive system resulting from the substituion, will always be an upper approximation to the least solution of the original system of equations. In the example, we obtain:

$$\rho_1 = \{\mathbf{x}_1 \mapsto 10, \ \mathbf{x}_2 \mapsto 10\}$$

In this case, ρ_1 is a solution of the original system $\mathcal{E}$ as well. If this is not the case, the first selection of arguments of minimum subexpressions can be improved. Let us call one such selection a $\wedge$-*strategy*. Let π be a $\wedge$-strategy where the least solution ρ_π of the corresponding disjunctive equation system is not a solution of the original system $\mathcal{E}$. The algorithm then improves the strategy π by updating its values for those minimum subexpressions $e_1 \wedge e_2$ where, w.r.t. the variable assignment ρ_π, $\pi(e_1 \wedge e_2)$ evaluates to a larger value than $e_1 \wedge e_2$ itself. For the improved strategy, again the corresponding disjunctive system is extracted from $\mathcal{E}$ and so on.

Iteration over $\wedge$-strategies will terminate with some solution, in the worst case, after cycling through all $\wedge$-strategies. Two remarks are important. First, if one is interested in sound overapproximations of the least solution only, $\wedge$-strategy iteration may be stopped after *any* number of iterations. However, even if $\wedge$-strategy iteration terminates, it still may be the case that the iteration has not reached the *least* solution, but just *some* solution. This is the case for the example. Here, although the algorithm terminates with the solution ρ_1, the least solution is given by:

$$\rho^* := \{\mathbf{x}_1 \mapsto 0, \ \mathbf{x}_2 \mapsto 0\}$$

In this article, we will not elaborate on the details of $\wedge$-strategy iteration. Instead, we consider a strategy iteration approach that is based on selection at $\vee$-*operators* as proposed by Gawlitza and Seidl [16, 17] (the *max-strategy* approach). This approach allows to compute least solutions.

8. The Max-Strategy Improvement Algorithm

In this section, we present and discuss our max-strategy improvement algorithm. Our goal is to compute least solutions of systems of monotone equations over a complete *linearly* ordered set. We afterwards specialize the algorithm in order to compute least solutions of systems of integer equations.

8.1. The General Framework

Our algorithm iterates over $\vee$-strategies. It maintains a current $\vee$-strategy and a current *approximate* to the least solution. A so called $\vee$-*strategy improvement operator* is used to determine a next, improved $\vee$-strategy. Whether or not a $\vee$-strategy represents an *improvement* may depend on the current approximate. It can indeed be the case that a switch from one $\vee$-strategy to another $\vee$-strategy is only then *profitable*, when it is known that the least solution is of a certain size. Hence, we talk about an *improvement* of a ∨-strategy w.r.t. an approximate:

Let $\mathcal{E}$ be a system of monotone equations over a complete linearly ordered set. Let σ be a ∨-strategy for $\mathcal{E}$ and ρ be a pre-solution of $\mathcal{E}(\sigma)$. The ∨-strategy σ' is called an *improvement of σ w.r.t. ρ* iff the following conditions are fulfilled:

1. If $\rho \notin \mathbf{Sol}(\mathcal{E})$, then $[\![\mathcal{E}(\sigma')]\!]\rho > \rho$.
2. For all ∨-expressions $e \in \mathcal{S}_\vee(\mathcal{E})$ the following holds: If $\sigma'(e) \neq \sigma(e)$, then $[\![e\sigma']\!]\rho > [\![e\sigma]\!]\rho$.

A function $P_\vee$ which assigns an improvement of σ w.r.t. ρ to every pair (σ, ρ) is called a *∨-strategy improvement operator for $\mathcal{E}$*. An *improvement of a ∧-strategy π w.r.t. a post-solution of $\mathcal{E}(\pi)$* and a *∧-strategy improvement operator for $\mathcal{E}$* are defined dually.

The first condition ensures a progress in the case that ρ is not yet a solution. The second condition ensures that the ∨-strategy σ may only modified in such a way that every modification ensures a local progress that is *strict*. This will later be important in order to ensure that the ∨-strategy improvement algorithm stays in a *feasible area*. We illustrate the definitions by an example:

Example 9 (Improvement of a ∨-Strategy) *We consider the system*

$$\mathcal{E} = \{\mathbf{x} = (2 \cdot \mathbf{x} \wedge 10) \vee 1 \vee -\infty\}$$

of linear integer equations. The mapping $\sigma := \{(2 \cdot \mathbf{x} \wedge 10) \vee 1 \vee -\infty \mapsto 1\}$ is a ∨-strategy for $\mathcal{E}$ and $\rho := \{\mathbf{x} \mapsto 1\}$ is a pre-solution (even a solution) of $\mathcal{E}(\sigma) = \{\mathbf{x} = 1\}$. However, the variable assignment ρ is not a solution of $\mathcal{E}$. An improvement of σ w.r.t. ρ is the ∨-strategy $\sigma' = \{(2 \cdot \mathbf{x} \wedge 10) \vee 1 \vee -\infty \mapsto (2 \cdot \mathbf{x} \wedge 10)\}$, since $[\![\mathcal{E}(\sigma')]\!]\rho = \{\mathbf{x} \mapsto 2\} > \rho$ and $[\![((2 \cdot \mathbf{x} \wedge 10) \vee 1 \vee -\infty)\sigma']\!]\rho = 2 > 1 = [\![((2 \cdot \mathbf{x} \wedge 10) \vee 1 \vee -\infty)\sigma]\!]\rho$. The ∨-strategy σ' is the only improvement of σ w.r.t. ρ. □

An improvement σ' of a ∨-strategy σ w.r.t. a pre-solution ρ of $\mathcal{E}(\sigma)$ is, locally at the approximate ρ, at least as good as the ∨-strategy σ. That is, if σ' is an *improvement of σ w.r.t. ρ*, then $[\![\mathcal{E}(\sigma')]\!]\rho \geq [\![\mathcal{E}(\sigma)]\!]\rho$. We in particular have $\rho \in \mathbf{PreSol}(\mathcal{E}(\sigma'))$. A dual statement holds for ∧-strategies.

In many cases, there exist several, different improvements of a ∨-strategy σ w.r.t. a pre-solution ρ of $\mathcal{E}(\sigma)$. Accordingly, there exist several, different possibilities for defining a ∨-strategy improvement operator. Under the assumption that the operator ∨ is only used in its binary version, one possibility is known as *all profitable switches* (see e.g. Björklund et al. [3], Bjorklund et al. [4]). Carried over to the case considered here, this means that the ∨-strategy σ will be modified at any ∨-expression $e_1 \vee e_2$ with $[\![e_1 \vee e_2]\!]\rho > [\![\sigma(e_1 \vee e_2)]\!]\rho$. According to the definition, the selection must be preserved at the other ∨-expressions. If ∨ is not only used in its binary version, we can think of $\sigma' = P_\vee^{\mathrm{eager}}(\sigma, \rho)$ as some arbitrary improvement of σ w.r.t. ρ that satisfies $[\![\mathcal{E}(\sigma')]\!]\rho = [\![\mathcal{E}]\!]\rho$. One consequence is that a ∨-strategy iteration based on the ∨-strategy improvement operator $P_\vee^{\mathrm{eager}}$ converges at least as fast as a Kleene fixpoint iteration. Note that $\sigma' = P_\vee^{\mathrm{eager}}(\sigma, \rho)$ is not necessarily uniquely determined.

Example 10 (The ∨-Strategy Improvement Operator $P_\vee^{\text{eager}}$) *The function*

$$\sigma = \{10 \vee \mathbf{x}_1 \mapsto \mathbf{x}_1, \ \mathbf{x}_2 + 1 \vee \mathbf{x}_1 \mapsto \mathbf{x}_2 + 1\} \tag{43}$$

is a ∨-strategy for the system

$$\mathcal{E} = \{\mathbf{x}_1 = 10 \vee \mathbf{x}_1, \ \mathbf{x}_2 = \mathbf{x}_2 + 1 \vee \mathbf{x}_1\} \tag{44}$$

of simple integer equations. The variable assignment $\rho = \{\mathbf{x}_1 \mapsto 0, \ \mathbf{x}_2 \mapsto -\infty\}$ is a pre-solution of $\mathcal{E}(\sigma) = \{\mathbf{x}_1 = \mathbf{x}_1, \mathbf{x}_1 = \mathbf{x}_2 + 1\}$. We have

$$\sigma' := P_\vee^{\text{eager}}(\sigma, \rho) = \{10 \vee \mathbf{x}_1 \mapsto 10, \ \mathbf{x}_2 + 1 \vee \mathbf{x}_1 \mapsto \mathbf{x}_1\} \tag{45}$$

and thus $\mathcal{E}(\sigma') = \{\mathbf{x}_1 = 10, \ \mathbf{x}_2 = \mathbf{x}_1\}$. In this example, the ∨-strategy σ' is not the only improvement of σ w.r.t. ρ. The ∨-strategies

$$\sigma_1 = \{10 \vee \mathbf{x}_1 \mapsto 10, \ \mathbf{x}_2 + 1 \vee \mathbf{x}_1 \mapsto \mathbf{x}_2 + 1\}, \text{ and} \tag{46}$$

$$\sigma_2 = \{10 \vee \mathbf{x}_1 \mapsto \mathbf{x}_1, \ \mathbf{x}_2 + 1 \vee \mathbf{x}_1 \mapsto \mathbf{x}_1\} \tag{47}$$

are also improvements of σ w.r.t. ρ. However,

$$[\![\mathcal{E}]\!]\rho = [\![\mathcal{E}(\sigma')]\!]\rho > [\![\mathcal{E}(\sigma_1)]\!]\rho, [\![\mathcal{E}(\sigma_2)]\!]\rho > [\![\mathcal{E}(\sigma)]\!]\rho. \tag{48}$$

Thus, locally at ρ, σ' is the best possible improvement. □

We can now formulate the ∨-strategy improvement algorithm for computing least solutions of systems of monotone equations over complete linearly ordered sets. This algorithm is parameterized with a ∨-strategy improvement operator $P_\vee$. The input is a system $\mathcal{E}$ of monotone equations over a complete linearly ordered set, a ∨-strategy σ_{init} for $\mathcal{E}$, and a pre-solution ρ_{init} of $\mathcal{E}(\sigma_{\text{init}})$. In order to compute the *least* and not some *arbitrary* solution, we additionally require that $\rho_{\text{init}} \leq \mu[\![\mathcal{E}]\!]$ holds. The algorithm maintains a *current* ∨-strategy σ and a *current* approximate ρ to the least solution $\mu[\![\mathcal{E}]\!]$. During the computation, the current approximate ρ remains smaller than or equal to the least solution $\mu[\![\mathcal{E}]\!]$. Furthermore, ρ will grow in each iteration until the least solution of $\mathcal{E}$ is found. In each iteration we compute an improvement σ' of the current ∨-strategy σ w.r.t. ρ using the ∨-strategy improvement operator $P_\vee$, provided that ρ does not solve $\mathcal{E}$. The improvement σ' will be the new current ∨-strategy σ for the next iteration. Then, we will consider the system $\mathcal{E}(\sigma)$ of conjunctive monotone equations for which ρ is a pre-solution. The next current approximate ρ is then the least solution of $\mathcal{E}(\sigma)$ that is greater than or equal to ρ:

Algorithm 2 The $\vee$-Strategy Improvement Algorithm

Parameter : A $\vee$-strategy improvement operator $P_\vee$

$$\text{Input} \quad : \begin{cases} \text{A system } \mathcal{E} \text{ of monotone equations over a complete linearly ordered set} \\ \text{A } \vee\text{-strategy } \sigma_{\text{init}} \text{ for } \mathcal{E} \\ \text{A pre-solution } \rho_{\text{init}} \text{ of } \mathcal{E}(\sigma_{\text{init}}) \text{ with } \rho_{\text{init}} \leq \mu[\![\mathcal{E}]\!] \end{cases}$$

Output   : The least solution $\mu[\![\mathcal{E}]\!]$ of $\mathcal{E}$

$\sigma \leftarrow \sigma_{\text{init}}$
$\rho \leftarrow \rho_{\text{init}}$
while $(\rho \notin \mathbf{Sol}(\mathcal{E}))$ {
    $\sigma \leftarrow P_\vee(\sigma, \rho)$
    $\rho \leftarrow \mu_{\geq \rho}[\![\mathcal{E}(\sigma)]\!]$
}
return ρ

In order to execute the $\vee$-strategy improvement algorithm (Algorithm 2), we need a method for computing $\mu_{\geq \rho}[\![\mathcal{E}(\sigma)]\!]$ for the $\vee$-strategies σ and the approximates ρ that occur during the execution. Which method we have to use for that purpose depends on the class of systems of monotone equations under consideration. So far, we have:

Lemma 4 *Let $\mathcal{E}$ be a system of monotone equations over a complete linearly ordered set. For $i \in \mathbb{N}$, let ρ_i be the value of the program variable ρ and σ_i be the value of the program variable σ in the $\vee$-strategy improvement algorithm (Algorithm 2) after the i-th evaluation of the loop-body. The following statements hold for all $i \in \mathbb{N}$: (1) $\rho_i \leq \mu[\![\mathcal{E}]\!]$. (2) $\rho_i \in \mathbf{PreSol}(\mathcal{E}(\sigma_{i+1}))$. (3) If $\rho_i < \mu[\![\mathcal{E}]\!]$, then $\rho_{i+1} > \rho_i$. (4) If $\rho_i = \mu[\![\mathcal{E}]\!]$, then $\rho_{i+1} = \rho_i$.* □

As an immediate consequence of Lemma 4, we obtain:

Lemma 5 *Whenever the $\vee$-strategy improvement algorithm (Algorithm 2) terminates, it returns the least solution $\mu[\![\mathcal{E}]\!]$ of $\mathcal{E}$.* □

If we use the $\vee$-strategy improvement operator $P_\vee^{\text{eager}}$, then the i-th approximate ρ_i is greater than or equal to the i-th Kleene approximate $[\![\mathcal{E}]\!]^i(\bot)$.

Example 11 (A Run of the $\vee$-Strategy Improvement Algorithm) *Let us compute the least solution of the system*

$$\mathcal{E} = \{\mathbf{x}_1 = 0 \vee \mathbf{x}_1 + \mathbf{x}_2 - 4, \ \mathbf{x}_2 = -10 \vee ((\mathbf{x}_1 + 1 \vee 2 \cdot \mathbf{x}_2) \wedge 5)\} \qquad (49)$$

of linear integer equations using our $\vee$-strategy improvement algorithm. We will use the $\vee$-strategy improvement operator $P_\vee^{\text{eager}}$. Assume that the first $\vee$-strategy σ_{init} leads to the system

$$\mathcal{E}(\sigma_{\text{init}}) = \{\mathbf{x}_1 = 0, \ \mathbf{x}_2 = -10\}. \qquad (50)$$

The variable assignment $\rho_{\text{init}} = \{\mathbf{x}_1 \mapsto 0, \mathbf{x}_2 \mapsto -10\}$ *is a pre-solution (even a solution) of* $\mathcal{E}(\sigma_{\text{init}})$. *The first application of* $P_\vee^{\text{eager}}$ *leads to the* $\vee$-*strategy* $\sigma_1 := P_\vee^{\text{eager}}(\sigma_{\text{init}}, \rho_{\text{init}})$ *with*

$$\mathcal{E}(\sigma_1) = \{\mathbf{x}_1 = 0, \mathbf{x}_2 = \mathbf{x}_1 + 1 \wedge 5\}. \tag{51}$$

In the next step, we get $\rho_1 := \mu_{\geq \rho_{\text{init}}}[\![\mathcal{E}(\sigma_1)]\!] = \{\mathbf{x}_1 \mapsto 0, \mathbf{x}_2 \mapsto 1\}$. *Within the next iteration, we obtain the* $\vee$-*strategy* $\sigma_2 := P_\vee^{\text{eager}}(\sigma_1, \rho_1)$ *with*

$$\mathcal{E}(\sigma_2) = \{\mathbf{x}_1 = 0, \mathbf{x}_2 = 2 \cdot \mathbf{x}_2 \wedge 5\}. \tag{52}$$

Therefore, we obtain $\rho_2 := \mu_{\geq \rho_1}[\![\mathcal{E}(\sigma_2)]\!] = \{\mathbf{x}_1 \mapsto 0, \mathbf{x}_2 \mapsto 5\}$. *In the last iteration, we finally obtain* $\sigma_3 := P_\vee^{\text{eager}}(\sigma_2, \rho_2)$, *which leads to the system*

$$\mathcal{E}(\sigma_3) = \{\mathbf{x}_1 = \mathbf{x}_1 + \mathbf{x}_2 - 4, \mathbf{x}_2 = 2 \cdot \mathbf{x}_2 \wedge 5\}. \tag{53}$$

Hence, $\rho_3 := \mu_{\geq \rho_2}[\![\mathcal{E}(\sigma_3)]\!] = \{\mathbf{x}_1 \mapsto \infty, \mathbf{x}_2 \mapsto 5\}$. *Since* ρ_3 *is a solution of* $\mathcal{E}$, *the algorithm terminates and returns* $\mu[\![\mathcal{E}]\!] = \rho_3$. $\square$

It remains to explain how to compute $\mu_{\geq \rho}[\![\mathcal{E}(\sigma)]\!]$ for the $\vee$-strategies σ and the approximates ρ that occur during the execution of our $\vee$-strategy improvement algorithm. How this can be done depends on the properties of the systems of equations under consideration.

Similar to the well-known simplex algorithm for linear programming our $\vee$-strategy improvement algorithm must be started in a *feasible area*. It then stays in the feasible area.

8.2. Feasibility

In this subsection, we define our notion of *feasibility*. In order to do so, we first define *derived equations* for systems of basic integer equations as follows:

Let $\mathcal{E}$ be a system of basic integer equations and ρ be a pre-solution of $\mathcal{E}$. The set $\mathcal{D}_\rho(\mathcal{E})$ of all w.r.t. ρ *derived equations of* $\mathcal{E}$ is the smallest set of basic integer equations such that the following statements hold:

1. If $\mathbf{x} = e \in \mathcal{E}$ with $-\infty < \rho(\mathbf{x}) = [\![e]\!]\rho < \infty$, then $\mathbf{x} = e \in \mathcal{D}_\rho(\mathcal{E})$.
2. If $\mathbf{x} = e[\mathbf{x}'] \in \mathcal{D}_\rho(\mathcal{E})$ and $\mathbf{x}' = e' \in \mathcal{D}_\rho(\mathcal{E})$, then $\mathbf{x} = e[e'] \in \mathcal{D}_\rho(\mathcal{E})$.

In the above definition $e[\mathbf{x}']$ denotes an expression which contains the variable $\mathbf{x}'$ at the position denoted by $e[]$. $e[]$ itself is a *single hole context*. The expression $e[e']$ finally denotes the expression which contains the expression e' instead of the variable $\mathbf{x}'$ at the position denoted by $e[]$.

Example 12 (Derived Equations) *The set* $\mathcal{D}_\rho(\mathcal{E})$ *of all w.r.t.* $\rho = \{\mathbf{x}_1 \mapsto 1\}$ *derived equations of the system* $\mathcal{E} = \{\mathbf{x}_1 = 2 \cdot \mathbf{x}_1\}$ *of basic integer equations is* $\mathcal{D}_\rho(\mathcal{E}) = \emptyset$, *because* $1 = \rho(\mathbf{x}_1) < [\![2 \cdot \mathbf{x}_1]\!]\rho = 2$. $\square$

We are now prepared to define our notion of *feasibility*: A pre-solution ρ of a system $\mathcal{E}$ of basic integer equations is called $(\mathcal{E}\text{-})$*feasible* iff the following statements are fulfilled:

1. There does not exist an equation $\mathbf{x} = e$ in $\mathcal{E}$ with $[\![e]\!]\rho = -\infty$ and $e \neq -\infty$.
2. There does not exist a derived equation $\mathbf{x} = e \in \mathcal{D}_\rho(\mathcal{E})$ with $\mathbf{x} \in \mathbf{Vars}(e)$.

A pre-solution ρ of a system $\mathcal{E}$ of conjunctive integer equations is called *($\mathcal{E}$-)feasible* iff it is $\mathcal{E}(\pi)$-feasible for all $\pi \in \Pi$. A system of conjunctive integer equations is called *feasible* iff it has a feasible pre-solution.

Example 13 (Feasibility) *We consider the system $\mathcal{E} = \{\mathbf{x}_1 = 2 \cdot \mathbf{x}_1 \wedge 10\}$ of conjunctive linear integer equations. Let $\pi_1 := \{2 \cdot \mathbf{x}_1 \wedge 10 \mapsto 2 \cdot \mathbf{x}_1\}$ and $\pi_2 := \{2 \cdot \mathbf{x}_1 \wedge 10 \mapsto 10\}$ be the $\wedge$-strategies for $\mathcal{E}$. The solution $\rho_0 := \{\mathbf{x}_1 \mapsto 0\}$ of $\mathcal{E}$ is not feasible, since $\mathbf{x}_1 = 2 \cdot \mathbf{x}_1 \in \mathcal{D}_{\rho_0}(\mathcal{E}(\pi_1))$ and thus ρ_0 is not $\mathcal{E}(\pi_1)$-feasible. The pre-solution $\rho_1 := \{\mathbf{x}_1 \mapsto 1\}$ of $\mathcal{E}$ is $\mathcal{E}$-feasible, since $\mathcal{D}_{\rho_1}(\mathcal{E}(\pi_1)) = \mathcal{D}_{\rho_1}(\mathcal{E}(\pi_2)) = \emptyset$. The greatest solution $\rho_2 := \{\mathbf{x}_1 \mapsto 10\}$ of $\mathcal{E}$ is also $\mathcal{E}$-feasible, since $\mathcal{D}_{\rho_2}(\mathcal{E}(\pi_1)) = \emptyset$ and $\mathcal{D}_{\rho_2}(\mathcal{E}(\pi_2)) = \{\mathbf{x} = 10\}$.* □

The set of feasible pre-solutions is upward closed in the following sense:

Lemma 6 *Let $\mathcal{E}$ be a system of conjunctive integer equations and ρ be a feasible pre-solution of $\mathcal{E}$. Every pre-solution ρ' of $\mathcal{E}$ with $\rho' \geq \rho$ is feasible.*

Proof. See Appendix C. □

Since the greatest solution $\nu[\![\mathcal{E}]\!]$ of a system $\mathcal{E}$ of conjunctive integer equations (by the Knaster-Tarski fixpoint theorem) is greater than or equal to any pre-solution of $\mathcal{E}$, we can in particular conclude (using Lemma 6) that the greatest solution $\nu[\![\mathcal{E}]\!]$ is feasible, whenever $\mathcal{E}$ is feasible. In the next step, we show that every *feasible* system $\mathcal{E}$ of conjunctive integer equations has exactly one *feasible solution*. Thus, this solution must be the greatest solution $\nu[\![\mathcal{E}]\!]$ of $\mathcal{E}$.

Lemma 7 *Let $\mathcal{E}$ be a system of basic integer equations and ρ be a feasible solution of $\mathcal{E}$. Then $\rho = \nu[\![\mathcal{E}]\!]$.*

Proof. We do induction on $\mathbf{Vars}(\mathcal{E})$. If $\mathbf{Vars}(\mathcal{E}) = \emptyset$, then the statement is fulfilled, since $\mathcal{E}$ has exactly one solution and this solution is feasible. Thus, we assume that $\mathbf{Vars}(\mathcal{E}) \neq \emptyset$. Let $\mathbf{x} \in \mathbf{Vars}(\mathcal{E})$ and $\mathbf{x} = e \in \mathcal{E}$ be the equations for the variable $\mathbf{x}$.

Case 1: $\mathbf{x} \notin \mathbf{Vars}(e)$. Let $\mathcal{E}' := \mathcal{E}[e/\mathbf{x}]$. Since $\mathcal{D}_\rho(\mathcal{E}') \subseteq \mathcal{D}_\rho(\mathcal{E})$, ρ is a feasible solution of $\mathcal{E}'$. Since $\mathbf{Vars}(\mathcal{E}') \subset \mathbf{Vars}(\mathcal{E})$, it follows $\rho = \nu[\![\mathcal{E}']\!]$ using the induction hypothesis. In order to show $\rho = \nu[\![\mathcal{E}]\!]$, let $\rho' \in \mathbf{Sol}(\mathcal{E})$. Then $\rho' \in \mathbf{Sol}(\mathcal{E}')$. Hence, we obtain $\rho' \leq \nu[\![\mathcal{E}']\!] = \rho$.

Case 2: $\mathbf{x} \in \mathbf{Vars}(e)$. Since ρ is a feasible solution of $\mathcal{E}$, we have $\rho(\mathbf{x}) = \infty$. Let $\mathcal{E}' := (\mathcal{E} \oplus \{\mathbf{x} = \infty\})[\infty/\mathbf{x}]$. Since $\mathcal{D}_\rho(\mathcal{E}') \subseteq \mathcal{D}_\rho(\mathcal{E})$, ρ is a feasible solution of $\mathcal{E}'$. Since $\mathbf{Vars}(\mathcal{E}') \subset \mathbf{Vars}(\mathcal{E})$, we get $\rho = \nu[\![\mathcal{E}']\!]$ using the induction hypothesis. In order to show $\rho = \nu[\![\mathcal{E}]\!]$, let $\rho' \in \mathbf{Sol}(\mathcal{E})$. Thus, $\rho' \in \mathbf{PreSol}(\mathcal{E}')$. Hence, $\rho' \leq \nu[\![\mathcal{E}']\!] = \rho$. □

We now generalize the statement of Lemma 7:

Theorem 4 (Uniqueness of Feasible Solutions) *Let $\mathcal{E}$ be a system of conjunctive integer equations and ρ be a feasible solution of $\mathcal{E}$. Then $\rho = \nu[\![\mathcal{E}]\!]$.*

Proof. There exists a $\wedge$-strategy $\pi \in \Pi$ for $\mathcal{E}$ such that $[\![\mathcal{E}(\pi)]\!]\rho = [\![\mathcal{E}]\!]\rho = \rho$. Hence, $\rho \in \mathbf{Sol}(\mathcal{E}(\pi))$ and ρ is by definition a feasible solution of $\mathcal{E}(\pi)$. By Lemma 7, we get $\rho = \nu[\![\mathcal{E}(\pi)]\!]$. Since by the Knaster-Tarski fixpoint theorem $\nu[\![\mathcal{E}(\pi)]\!] \geq \nu[\![\mathcal{E}]\!]$ and ρ is a solution of $\mathcal{E}$, we get $\rho = \nu[\![\mathcal{E}]\!]$. □

By Theorem 4, *the* (uniquely determined) feasible solution of a feasible system $\mathcal{E}$ of conjunctive integer equations is the greatest solution $\nu[\![\mathcal{E}]\!]$ of $\mathcal{E}$. Thus, we can compute it through our adaption of the Bellman-Ford algorithm (see Theorem 3).

In order to show that our $\vee$-strategy improvement algorithm stays in the feasible area, it remains to show that every $\vee$-strategy improvement step preserves feasibility:

Lemma 8 ($\vee$-Strategy Improvement Steps Preserve Feasibility) *Let $\mathcal{E}$ be a system of integer equations, $\sigma \in \Sigma$ a $\vee$-strategy for $\mathcal{E}$ and ρ be a feasible pre-solution of $\mathcal{E}(\sigma)$. Let σ' be an improvement of σ w.r.t. ρ. Then ρ is also a feasible pre-solution of $\mathcal{E}(\sigma')$.*

Proof. See Appendix C. □

It remains to show how we can benefit from the above result in order to compute $\mu_{\geq\rho}[\![\mathcal{E}(\sigma)]\!]$ within the $\vee$-strategy improvement algorithm. For that, let $\mathcal{E}$ be a system of integer equations. Assume that σ_{init} is a $\vee$-strategy for $\mathcal{E}$ and ρ_{init} is a *feasible* pre-solution of $\mathcal{E}(\sigma_{\text{init}})$ with $\rho_{\text{init}} \leq \mu[\![\mathcal{E}]\!]$. For $i \in \mathbb{N}$, let σ_i and ρ_i denote the values of the program variables σ and ρ after the i-th evaluation of the body of the loop in the $\vee$-strategy improvement algorithm (Algorithm 2). We get:

Lemma 9 *For all $i \in \mathbb{N}$, ρ_i is a feasible pre-solution of $\mathcal{E}(\sigma_{i+1})$. Moreover, $\rho_{i+1} = \nu[\![\mathcal{E}(\sigma_{i+1})]\!]$.* □

It remains to show that the $\vee$-strategy improvement algorithm terminates at the latest after considering all $\vee$-strategies $\sigma \in \Sigma$ for $\mathcal{E}$. For the sake of contradiction assume that this is not the case, i.e., assume that $\rho_{|\Sigma|} \notin \mathbf{Sol}(\mathcal{E})$. By Lemma 4, we get

$$\rho_{i+1} > \rho_i \text{ for all } i \in \{0, \ldots, |\Sigma|\}. \tag{54}$$

Using the pigeonhole principle, we get that there exists a $\vee$-strategy $\sigma \in \Sigma$ which occurs twice in the sequence $\sigma_1, \ldots, \sigma_{|\Sigma|+1}$, i.e., there exist $k_1, k_2 \in \{1, \ldots, |\Sigma|+1\}$ with $k_1 < k_2$ and $\sigma_{k_1} = \sigma_{k_2}$. Using Lemma 9 we finally get $\rho_{k_1} = \nu[\![\mathcal{E}(\sigma_{k_1})]\!] = \nu[\![\mathcal{E}(\sigma_{k_2})]\!] = \rho_{k_2}$. This is in contradiction to (54).

The number $|\Sigma|$ of all $\vee$-strategies is exponential in the number of $\vee$-expressions. Whether or not there exist systems of linear integer equations, for which, when we use the $\vee$-strategy improvement operator $P_{\vee}^{\text{eager}}$, we in fact have to do exponentially many $\vee$-strategy improvement steps for computing least solutions, is not known.

It remains to estimate the worst case running time of the loop-body w.r.t. the uniform cost measure. Since, by Lemma 9, $\rho_{i+1} = \nu[\![\mathcal{E}(\sigma_{i+1})]\!]$ for all $i \in \mathbb{N}$, we have to compute the greatest solution of a system of conjunctive integer equations. By Theorem 3, this can be done through our adaption of the Bellman-Ford algorithm. In practice we can compute

ρ_{i+1} more efficiently. Since $\mathcal{E}(\sigma_{i+1})$ is feasible, the greatest solution $\rho_{i+1} = \nu[\![\mathcal{E}(\sigma_{i+1})]\!]$ of $\mathcal{E}(\sigma_{i+1})$ is, because of Theorem 2, the $|\mathbf{X}|$-th Kleene approximate. Therefore, we can compute it using an *arbitrary* generic fixpoint algorithm. Algorithms that take variable dependencies into account [5, 6, 13, 25] have proven themselves good. Summarizing, we have shown the following result:

Theorem 5 *Let $\mathcal{E}$ be a system of integer equations. Let σ_{init} be a $\vee$-strategy for $\mathcal{E}$ and ρ_{init} be a feasible pre-solution of $\mathcal{E}(\sigma_{\text{init}})$ with $\rho_{\text{init}} \le \mu[\![\mathcal{E}]\!]$. The $\vee$-strategy improvement algorithm (Algorithm 2) computes the least solution $\mu[\![\mathcal{E}]\!]$ of $\mathcal{E}$. At most $|\Sigma|$ $\vee$-strategy improvement steps are performed. Each $\vee$-strategy improvement step can be carried out by performing a greatest fixpoint iteration that terminates after at most $|\mathbf{X}|$ steps.*   □

8.3. Determining a Feasible $\vee$-Strategy

Until now, we have assumed that σ_{init} is a $\vee$-strategy for $\mathcal{E}$ and ρ_{init} is a *feasible* pre-solution of $\mathcal{E}(\sigma_{\text{init}})$ with $\rho_{\text{init}} \le \mu[\![\mathcal{E}]\!]$. We are now going to explain how to abandon this precondition. For a system $\mathcal{E}$ of integer equations, we set

$$\mathcal{E} \vee -\infty := \{\mathbf{x} = e \vee -\infty \mid \mathbf{x} = e \in \mathcal{E}\}.$$

Obviously, $\mathcal{E}$ and $\mathcal{E} \vee -\infty$ have the same least solution, i.e., we have $\mu[\![\mathcal{E} \vee -\infty]\!] = \mu[\![\mathcal{E}]\!]$. Thus we can solve the system $\mathcal{E} \vee -\infty$ instead of the system $\mathcal{E}$. The advantage of considering $\mathcal{E} \vee -\infty$ instead of $\mathcal{E}$ is that $-\infty$ is a feasible pre-solution of $(\mathcal{E} \vee -\infty)(\sigma_{-\infty})$. Here, the $\vee$-strategy $\sigma_{-\infty}$ is an arbitrary $\vee$-strategy for $\mathcal{E} \vee -\infty$ that assigns the expression $-\infty$ to every expression $e \vee -\infty$, i.e., $\sigma_{-\infty}(e \vee -\infty) = -\infty$ holds for all equations $\mathbf{x} = e$ of $\mathcal{E}$. Hence, Algorithm 2 can be started with $\sigma_{\text{init}} := \sigma_{-\infty}$ and $\rho_{\text{init}} := -\infty$ for computing $\mu[\![\mathcal{E} \vee -\infty]\!] = \mu[\![\mathcal{E}]\!]$.

For the complexity estimation it is important to note that, since $\mathcal{E} \vee -\infty$ is considered instead of $\mathcal{E}$, the number of $\vee$-expressions increases by the number $|\mathbf{X}|$ of variables of $\mathcal{E}$. Thus, we have $|\Sigma_{\mathcal{E} \vee -\infty}| = 2^{|\mathbf{X}|} \cdot |\Sigma_{\mathcal{E}}|$. However, all right-hand sides of $\mathcal{E} \vee -\infty$ are of the form $e \vee -\infty$. It can be shown that $\sigma_j(e \vee -\infty) = e$ holds for all $j \ge i$, if $\sigma_i(e \vee -\infty) = e$ holds for $i \in \mathbb{N}$. In consequence, we need at most $|\mathbf{X}| \cdot |\Sigma_{\mathcal{E}}|$ $\vee$-strategy improvement steps. Summarizing, we have shown the following main result:

Theorem 6 *Let $\mathcal{E}$ be a system of integer equations. The least solution $\mu[\![\mathcal{E}]\!]$ of $\mathcal{E}$ can be computed using the $\vee$-strategy improvement algorithm (Algorithm 2). At most $|\mathbf{X}| \cdot |\Sigma|$ $\vee$-strategy improvement steps are performed. Each $\vee$-strategy improvement step can be carried out by performing a greatest fixpoint iteration that terminates after at most $|\mathbf{X}|$ steps.*

Proof.   See Appendix C.   □

9. Systems of Extended Integer Equations

In this section, we extend the applicability of our $\vee$-strategy improvement algorithm by allowing operators that are not expansive but at least equivalent to expansive operators on the regions where they evaluate to a value greater than $-\infty$.

An operator $f : (X \to \overline{\mathbb{Z}}) \to \overline{\mathbb{Z}}$ is called *quasi-expansive* iff there exists some $X' \subseteq X$ and some expansive operator $f^{>-\infty} : (X' \to \overline{\mathbb{Z}}) \to \overline{\mathbb{Z}}$ such that $f(\rho) = f^{>-\infty}(\rho|_{X'})$ for all $\rho : X \to \overline{\mathbb{Z}}$ with $f(\rho) > -\infty$.

The binary operators ; and $\geq z?$ (for $z \in \overline{\mathbb{Z}}$) that are defined by

$$x; y := \begin{cases} -\infty & \text{if } x = -\infty \\ y & \text{otherwise} \end{cases}, \quad x, y \in \overline{\mathbb{Z}}, \text{ and} \tag{55}$$

$$x \geq z? \, y := \begin{cases} -\infty & \text{if } x < z \\ y & \text{otherwise} \end{cases}, \quad x, y, z \in \overline{\mathbb{Z}} \tag{56}$$

are important instances of monotone and quasi-expansive. However, they are not expansive. Thus, they are not allowed to occur within systems of integer equations.

Every expansive function is quasi-expansive, but not vice-versa. We extend integer expressions (resp. integer equations) to *extended integer expressions* (resp. *extended integer equations*) by allowing monotone and quasi-expansive operators instead of monotone and expansive operators.

We now show that our $\vee$-strategy improvement algorithm is also capable of solving systems of *extended* integer equations. For that, we define the transformation $[\cdot]^{>-\infty}$ as follows:

$$[-\infty]^{>-\infty} := -\infty \tag{57}$$

$$[\mathbf{x}]^{>-\infty} := \mathbf{x} \tag{58}$$

$$[f(e_1, \ldots, e_k)]^{>-\infty} := f^{>-\infty}([e_1]^{>-\infty}, \ldots, [e_k]^{>-\infty}) \tag{59}$$

$$[e_1 \wedge \cdots \wedge e_k]^{>-\infty} := [e_1]^{>-\infty} \wedge \cdots \wedge [e_k]^{>-\infty} \tag{60}$$

Here, $\mathbf{x}$ is a variable, $f \notin \{-\infty, \wedge\}$ is a k-ary operator (recall that constants are nullary operators), and $e_1, e_2, \ldots, e_k$ are conjunctive extended integer expressions. If e is a conjunctive extended integer expression, then $[e]^{>-\infty}$ is a conjunctive integer expression. Finally, we set

$$[\mathcal{E}]^{>-\infty} := \{\mathbf{x} = [e]^{>-\infty} \mid \mathbf{x} = e \in \mathcal{E}\} \tag{61}$$

for every system $\mathcal{E}$ of conjunctive extended integer equations. $[\mathcal{E}]^{>-\infty}$ is then a system of conjunctive integer equations. Using the results of Section 8, we can straightforwardly prove the following statement:

Lemma 10 *Assume that each equation of the system $\mathcal{E}$ of extended integer equations is of the form $\mathbf{x} = -\infty \vee e$ and that the $\vee$-strategy σ_{init} maps every right-hand side to $-\infty$. For $i \in \mathbb{N}$, let σ_i and ρ_i denote the values of the program variables σ and ρ after the i-th evaluation of the body of the loop of the $\vee$-strategy improvement algorithm (Algorithm 2).*

For all $i \in \mathbb{N}$, $\mu_{\geq \rho_i}[\![\mathcal{E}(\sigma_{i+1})]\!] = \mu_{\geq \rho_i}[\![[\mathcal{E}(\sigma_{i+1})]^{>-\infty}]\!]$ and ρ_i is a feasible pre-solution of $[\mathcal{E}(\sigma_{i+1})]^{>-\infty}$. Thus,

$$\rho_{i+1} = \mu_{\geq \rho_i}[\![\mathcal{E}(\sigma_{i+1})]\!] = \nu[\![[\mathcal{E}(\sigma_{i+1})]^{>-\infty}]\!] = \nu[\![\mathcal{E}(\sigma_{i+1})]\!] \qquad (62)$$

for all $i \in \mathbb{N}$. □

Because of Lemma 10, we can, for all $i \in \mathbb{N}$, compute ρ_{i+1} by performing a greatest fixpoint computation on $[\![\mathcal{E}(\sigma_{i+1})]\!]$ which terminates at the latest after $|\mathbf{X}|$ fixpoint iteration steps, i.e., $\rho_{i+1} = \nu[\![\mathcal{E}(\sigma_{i+1})]\!] = [\![\mathcal{E}(\sigma_{i+1})]\!]^{|\mathbf{X}|}(\infty)$. Hence, we have shown the following theorem:

Theorem 7 *Let $\mathcal{E}$ be a system of extended integer equations. The least solution $\mu[\![\mathcal{E}]\!]$ of $\mathcal{E}$ can be computed through our $\vee$-strategy improvement algorithm (Algorithm 2). At most $|\mathbf{X}| \cdot |\Sigma|$ $\vee$-strategy improvement steps are performed. Each $\vee$-strategy improvement step can be carried out by performing a greatest fixpoint iteration that terminates after at most $|\mathbf{X}|$ steps.* □

Example 14 *Let us compute the least solution $\mu[\![\mathcal{E}]\!]$ of the system*

$$\mathcal{E} = \{\mathbf{x} = -\infty \vee 0 \vee \mathbf{x} + \mathbf{y}, \ \mathbf{y} = -\infty \vee \mathbf{x}; 1\} \qquad (63)$$

of extended integer equations. For $i \in \mathbb{N}$, let σ_i and ρ_i denote the values of the program variables σ and ρ after the i-th evaluation of the body of the loop in the $\vee$-strategy improvement algorithm (Algorithm 2). We get

$$\mathcal{E}(\sigma_0) = \{\mathbf{x} = -\infty, \ \mathbf{y} = -\infty\} \qquad \mathcal{E}(\sigma_1) = \{\mathbf{x} = 0, \ \mathbf{y} = -\infty\} \qquad (64)$$
$$\mathcal{E}(\sigma_2) = \{\mathbf{x} = 0, \ \mathbf{y} = \mathbf{x}; 1\} \qquad \mathcal{E}(\sigma_3) = \{\mathbf{x} = \mathbf{x} + \mathbf{y}, \ \mathbf{y} = \mathbf{x}; 1\} \qquad (65)$$

Since $\rho_3 = \nu[\![\mathcal{E}(\sigma_3)]\!] = [\![\mathcal{E}(\sigma_3)]\!]^2 \infty = \{\mathbf{x} \mapsto \infty, \ \mathbf{y} \mapsto 1\}$ solves $\mathcal{E}$, we finally get $\mu[\![\mathcal{E}]\!] = \{\mathbf{x} \mapsto \infty, \ \mathbf{y} \mapsto 1\}$. □

10. Application to Interval Analysis and the Extension to Zones

In the last sections, we developed an algorithm based on $\vee$-strategy iteration which is able to compute the least solution of extended integer equations (Theorem 7). In Theorem 1, we have seen that the abstract semantics of a program can be compiled into a system of extended integer equations. Accordingly, we obtain:

Theorem 8 (Interval Analysis) *The abstract semantics $V^\sharp$ of G w.r.t. the interval domain can be computed using our $\vee$-strategy improvement algorithm. The number of $\vee$-strategy improvement steps is bounded by $2n \cdot |N| \cdot \prod_{v \in N}(\max\ \{1, \ \mathrm{indeg}(v)\})^{2n}$. Each $\vee$-strategy improvement step can be performed in strongly polynomial time. More precisely: the algorithm performs at most $\mathcal{O}(|N|^2 \cdot n^3)$ arithmetic operations for each $\vee$-strategy improvement step.* □

Instead of proving Theorem 8 for intervals, we turn to a treatment of the more general domain of integer zones. Analogously as for intervals, we aim at reducing the computation of the abstract semantics over integer zones to computing the least solution of a suitable system of extended integer constraints. In presence of bounds to variable differences, however, the abstract transformers for program statements are more involved. In Subsection 10.2, we show that these can be reduced to solving (uncapacited) minimum cost flow problems. This reduction allows us to use our $\vee$-strategy improvement algorithm developed in Sections 8 and 9 to compute the abstract semantics $V^{\sharp}$ of a program G over integer zones efficiently. The resulting algorithm is uniform, i.e., its running-time is independent of the sizes of involved numbers, since minimum cost flow problems can be solved in strongly polynomial time [30].

10.1. Minimum Cost Flow Problems

A *(uncapacitated) minimum cost flow problem* is a linear programming problem of the form

$$z = \inf \{c^{\top}x \mid x \in \mathbb{R}_{\geq 0}^{n}, \ Ax = b\} \tag{66}$$

where the following conditions are fulfilled: (1) $c \in \mathbb{Z}^{n}$. (2) $b \in \mathbb{Z}^{m}$ with $\sum_{i=1}^{m} b_{i\cdot} = 0$. (3) $A \in \{-1, 0, 1\}^{m \times n}$, where each column $A_{\cdot j}$ contains exactly one -1 and exactly one 1. All other entries of $A_{\cdot j}$ are 0.

The above linear programming problem represents a directed graph (the matrix A) together with a function that assigns supplies (the $b_{i\cdot}$'s) to nodes and a function that assigns costs (the $c_{j\cdot}$'s) to edges. Each $i \in \{1, \ldots, m\}$ represents a node that supplies $b_{i\cdot}$ packages (per time unit). A negative supply is a demand. Each $j \in \{1, \ldots, n\}$ represents an edge. A transmission of one package (per time unit) over this edge induces the cost $c_{j\cdot}$ (per time unit). The source (resp. target) of the edge j is k iff $A_{k\cdot j} = 1$ (resp. $A_{k\cdot j} = -1$). Note that each edge j has exactly one source and one target.

Each $x \in \mathbb{R}_{\geq 0}^{n}$ represents a *flow*, where $x_{j\cdot}$ is the number of packages (per time unit) transmitted over the edge j. A flow $x \in \mathbb{R}_{\geq 0}^{n}$ is called a *feasible flow* iff $Ax = b$, i.e., all supplies and all demands are fulfilled. The value $c^{\top}x$ is the cost (per time unit) of the flow x. The minimum cost flow problem is called *infeasible* iff there does not exists a feasible flow. If this is the case, then $z = \infty$. Another corner case is that the problem is unbounded, i.e., for every $z' \in \mathbb{Z}$, there exists some feasible flow x such that $c^{\top}x \leq z'$. If this is the case, then the problem is called *unbounded* and $z = -\infty$. If the problem is feasible and bounded, then $z \in \mathbb{Z}$ and moreover there exists a feasible flow $x \in \mathbb{R}_{\geq 0}^{n}$ such that $c^{\top}x = z$ and all entries of x are integral, i.e., natural numbers.

Since every minimum cost flow problem is a linear programming problem, it can be solved in polynomial time through interior point methods (see e.g. Karmarkar [24], Schrijver [32], Wright [35]). However, the worst-case running-times of these algorithms depend on the sizes of the numbers occurring in the input. In this context this is called a *weak* polynomial-time algorithm. Whether or not there exist *strongly* polynomial-time algorithms for linear programming is a long outstanding question. A strongly polynomial time algorithm is an algorithm where (1) the number of arithmetic operations is bounded by a polynomial that does not depend and the sizes of the occurring numbers (i.e., the polynomial only depends on the number of nodes m and the number of edges n) and (2) each arithmetic operation can be performed in polynomial time. For the special case of minimum cost flow problems there exist several algorithms that make use of the special structure of these linear programming problems. In contrast to the general case, there indeed exist strongly polynomial algorithms [30]. The enhanced capacity scaling algorithm of Orlin [30], for instance, requires $\mathcal{O}(m \cdot \log m \cdot (n + m \cdot \log m))$ arithmetic operations. For more information regarding minimum cost flow problems, we refer to Ahuja et al. [2]. In order to simplify notations, we denote the number of arithmetic operations required for solving a minimum cost flow problem with m nodes and n edges by $\mathsf{MCF}(m, n)$.

10.2. Computing $[\![s]\!]^{\sharp}(d)$

In this subsection, we aim at computing $[\![s]\!]^{\sharp}(d)$ for a given statement s and a given abstract value $d \in \overline{\mathbb{Z}}^{m}$. For $k \in \{1, \ldots, m\}$, we are hence interested in computing the k-th component of $[\![T\mathbf{x} \leq c; \mathbf{x} := A\mathbf{x} + b]\!]^{\sharp}(d)$, i.e., we aim at computing the value

$$z := [\![T\mathbf{x} \leq c; \mathbf{x} := A\mathbf{x} + b]\!]^{\sharp}_{k\cdot}(d) \tag{67}$$

We get:

$$z = \sup \{T_{k\cdot}(Ax + b) \mid x \in \mathbb{Z}^{n},\ Tx \leq (c \wedge d)\} \tag{68}$$

$$= T_{k\cdot}b + \sup \{T_{k\cdot}Ax \mid x \in \mathbb{Z}^{n},\ Tx \leq (c \wedge d)\} \tag{69}$$

$$= T_{k\cdot}b + \sup \{T_{k\cdot}Ax \mid x \in \mathbb{R}^{n},\ Tx \leq (c \wedge d)\} \tag{70}$$

The last equality holds, because the matrix T is totally unimodular (this implies that all optimal solutions of the linear programming problem (70) are integral). Observe that $z > -\infty$ iff $\{x \in \mathbb{R}^{n} \mid Tx \leq (c \wedge d)\} \neq \emptyset$. Whether or not $\{x \in \mathbb{R}^{n} \mid Tx \leq (c \wedge d)\} \neq \emptyset$ holds can be determined in strongly polynomial time (using e.g. the Floyd–Warshall algorithm (cf. e.g. Miné [27])). Therefore, we from now on assume that $z > -\infty$, i.e., the linear programming problem is feasible. Hence, the strong duality theorem for linear programming can be applied. We get

$$z = T_{k\cdot}b + \inf \{(c \wedge d)^{\top}y \mid y \in \mathbb{R}^{m}_{\geq 0},\ T^{\top}y = (T_{k\cdot}A)^{\top}\}. \tag{71}$$

Our goal is to compute z by solving a minimum cost flow problem. Each row of T and thus each column of $T^{\top}$ has at most two non-zero entries. These entries are distinct and in the set $\{-1, 1\}$. Therefore, each column of the matrix

$$B := \begin{pmatrix} T^{\top} \\ -(1, \ldots, 1)\, T^{\top} \end{pmatrix} \tag{72}$$

contains exactly one -1 and exactly one 1. All other entries are 0. Further, for

$$g := \begin{pmatrix} (T_{k\cdot}A)^{\top} \\ -(1, \ldots, 1)\, (T_{k\cdot}A)^{\top} \end{pmatrix}, \tag{73}$$

we have $\sum_{i=1}^{m} g_{i\cdot} = 0$. If we now replace $T^{\top}$ by B and $(T_{k\cdot}A)^{\top}$ by g, then we do not modify the feasible space of the linear programming problem, i.e., $T^{\top}y = (T_{k\cdot}A)^{\top}$ iff $By = g$ for all $y \in \mathbb{R}_{\geq 0}^{m}$. Therefore, we are now faced with the problem of computing

$$z = T_{k\cdot}b + \inf\{(c \wedge d)^{\top}y \mid y \in \mathbb{R}_{\geq 0}^{m}, \ By = g\}. \tag{74}$$

This is a minimum cost flow problem (cf. Subsection 10.1). Note that, for some edges j, the cost $(c \wedge d)_{j\cdot}$ might be ∞. If this is the case, then we remove these edges from the minimum cost flow problem, since these edges will never be used by an optimal flow. We get:

Lemma 11 *Let $d \in \overline{\mathbb{Z}}^{m}$ be an abstract value and $k \in \{1, \ldots, m\}$. Then:*

1. *$[\![Tx \leq c; x := Ax + b]\!]_{k\cdot}^{\sharp}(d)$ can be computed in strongly polynomial time through a polynomial-time reduction to a minimum cost flow problem.*
2. *There exists some finite set $M \subseteq \mathbb{N}^{m}$ such that*

$$[\![Tx \leq c; x := Ax + b]\!]_{k\cdot}^{\sharp}(d) = T_{k\cdot}b + \min\{a^{\top}(c \wedge d) \mid a \in M\} \tag{75}$$

for all $d \in \overline{\mathbb{Z}}^{m}$ with $[\![Tx \leq c; x := Ax + b]\!]_{k\cdot}^{\sharp}(d) > -\infty$.

Proof. The first statement is already shown. The second statement follows from the fact that all edges of the convex polyhedron $\{y \in \mathbb{R}_{\geq 0}^{m} \mid By = g\}$ (with B and g as in (74)) are from $\mathbb{N}^{m}$. This is a consequence of the fact that B is totally unimodular. □

Part 2 of Lemma 11 states that the operator $[\![s]\!]_{k\cdot}^{\sharp}$ is a conjunctive extended integer expression. Hence, we can use it within our $\vee$-strategy improvement algorithm (cf. Section 9).

10.3. Computing the Abstract Semantics of a Program through $\vee$-Strategy Iteration

In order to compute the abstract semantics $V^{\sharp}$, we construct a system $\mathcal{C}$ of inequalities as follows: For each $k \in \{1, \ldots, m\}$, we add the inequality

$$\mathbf{x}_{\mathsf{st},k} \geq \infty \tag{76}$$

These inequalities correspond to inequality (8). For each control-flow edge $(u, s, v) \in E$ and each $k \in \{1, \ldots, m\}$, we add the inequality

$$\mathbf{x}_{v,k} \geq [\![s]\!]_{k\cdot}^{\sharp}(\mathbf{x}_{u,1}, \ldots, \mathbf{x}_{u,m}) \tag{77}$$

These inequalities correspond to inequality (9). The Knaster-Tarski fixpoint theorem implies that $\mathcal{E} := \{\mathbf{x} = \bigvee_{\mathbf{x} \geq e \text{ is an inequality from } \mathcal{C}} e \mid \mathbf{x} \text{ is a variable of } \mathcal{C}\}$ has the same least solution as $\mathcal{C}$. By construction, we get:

Lemma 12 $(V^{\sharp}[v])_{i\cdot} = (\mu[\![\mathcal{E}]\!])(\mathbf{x}_{v,i})$ *for all $v \in N$ and all $i \in \{1, \ldots, m\}$.* □

Since $\mathcal{E}$ is a system of extended integer equations, we can apply our $\vee$-strategy improvement algorithm. The equation system $\mathcal{E}$ has $|N| \cdot m$ variables. Each expression $[\![s]\!]_{k.}^{\sharp}(\mathbf{x}_{u,1}, \ldots, \mathbf{x}_{u,m})$ can be evaluated in strongly polynomial time using $\mathsf{MCF}(n + 1, m)$ operations. Therefore, we finally get the following main result:

Theorem 9 *The abstract semantics $V^{\sharp}$ of G w.r.t. the integer zone template constraint matrix $T \in \mathbb{Z}^{m \times n}$ can be computed through our $\vee$-strategy improvement algorithm. The number of $\vee$-strategy improvement steps is bounded by $m \cdot |N| \cdot \prod_{v \in N}(\max \{1, \mathrm{indeg}(v)\})^m$. Each $\vee$-strategy improvement step can be performed in strongly polynomial time. More precisely: the algorithm performs at most $\mathcal{O}(|N|^2 \cdot m^2 \cdot \mathsf{MCF}(n+1, m))$ arithmetic operations for each $\vee$-strategy improvement step.* $\square$

Example 15 *We continue Examples 1 and 2. In order to determine the abstract semantics $V^{\sharp}$ of the program G, we have to compute the least solution of the following system of inequalities:*

$$\mathbf{x}_{\mathsf{st},i} \geq \infty \qquad\qquad i = 1, 2, 3 \quad (78)$$

$$\mathbf{x}_{1,i} \geq [\![(x_1, x_2) := (0, 1)]\!]_{i.}^{\sharp}(\mathbf{x}_{\mathsf{st},i}, \mathbf{x}_{\mathsf{st},2}, \mathbf{x}_{\mathsf{st},3}) \qquad\qquad i = 1, 2, 3 \quad (79)$$

$$\mathbf{x}_{1,i} \geq [\![x_1 \leq 8; (x_1, x_2) := (x_1 + 2, x_2 + 2)]\!]_{i.}^{\sharp}(\mathbf{x}_{1,1}, \mathbf{x}_{1,2}, \mathbf{x}_{1,3}) \quad i = 1, 2, 3 \quad (80)$$

For simplicity, we replace the variables $\mathbf{x}_{\mathsf{st},i}$ ($i = 1, 2, 3$) by their values. Since $[\![(x_1, x_2) := (0, 1)]\!]_{1.}^{\sharp}(\infty, \infty, \infty) = 0$, $[\![(x_1, x_2) := (0, 1)]\!]_{2.}^{\sharp}(\infty, \infty, \infty) = 1$, and $[\![(x_1, x_2) := (0, 1)]\!]_{3.}^{\sharp}(\infty, \infty, \infty) = 1$, we have to compute the least solution of the following system $\mathcal{E}$ of extended integer equations:

$$\mathbf{x}_{1,1} = -\infty \vee 0 \vee [\![x_1 \leq 8; (x_1, x_2) := (x_1 + 2, x_2 + 2)]\!]_{1.}^{\sharp}(\mathbf{x}_{1,1}, \mathbf{x}_{1,2}, \mathbf{x}_{1,3}) \quad (81)$$

$$\mathbf{x}_{1,2} = -\infty \vee 1 \vee [\![x_1 \leq 8; (x_1, x_2) := (x_1 + 2, x_2 + 2)]\!]_{2.}^{\sharp}(\mathbf{x}_{1,1}, \mathbf{x}_{1,2}, \mathbf{x}_{1,3}) \quad (82)$$

$$\mathbf{x}_{1,3} = -\infty \vee 1 \vee [\![x_1 \leq 8; (x_1, x_2) := (x_1 + 2, x_2 + 2)]\!]_{3.}^{\sharp}(\mathbf{x}_{1,1}, \mathbf{x}_{1,2}, \mathbf{x}_{1,3}) \quad (83)$$

Our $\vee$-strategy improvement algorithm starts with the $\vee$-strategy σ_0 that corresponds to the following system $\mathcal{E}(\sigma_0)$ of conjunctive extended integer equations:

$$\mathbf{x}_{1,1} = -\infty \qquad\qquad \mathbf{x}_{1,2} = -\infty \qquad\qquad \mathbf{x}_{1,3} = -\infty \qquad (84)$$

The first $\vee$-strategy improvement step can, for instance, result in the $\vee$-strategy σ_1 that corresponds to the following system $\mathcal{E}(\sigma_1)$ of conjunctive extended integer equations:

$$\mathbf{x}_{1,1} = 0 \qquad\qquad \mathbf{x}_{1,2} = 1 \qquad\qquad \mathbf{x}_{1,3} = 1 \qquad (85)$$

The second $\vee$-strategy improvement step can, for instance, result in the $\vee$-strategy σ_2 that corresponds to the following system $\mathcal{E}(\sigma_2)$ of conjunctive extended integer equations:

$$\mathbf{x}_{1,1} = [\![x_1 \leq 8; (x_1, x_2) := (x_1 + 2, x_2 + 2)]\!]_{1.}^{\sharp}(\mathbf{x}_{1,1}, \mathbf{x}_{1,2}, \mathbf{x}_{1,3}) \quad (86)$$

$$\mathbf{x}_{1,2} = [\![x_1 \leq 8; (x_1, x_2) := (x_1 + 2, x_2 + 2)]\!]_{2.}^{\sharp}(\mathbf{x}_{1,1}, \mathbf{x}_{1,2}, \mathbf{x}_{1,3}) \quad (87)$$

$$\mathbf{x}_{1,3} = 1 \tag{88}$$

We can switch to this $\vee$-strategy, since

$$[\![x_1 \le 8; (x_1, x_2) := (x_1 + 2, x_2 + 2)]\!]_1^\sharp.(0, 1, 1) = 2 > 0 \tag{89}$$

$$[\![x_1 \le 8; (x_1, x_2) := (x_1 + 2, x_2 + 2)]\!]_2^\sharp.(0, 1, 1) = 3 > 1 \tag{90}$$

$$[\![x_1 \le 8; (x_1, x_2) := (x_1 + 2, x_2 + 2)]\!]_3^\sharp.(0, 1, 1) = 1 \tag{91}$$

We now have to compute the greatest solution $\nu[\![\mathcal{E}(\sigma_2)]\!]$ of $\mathcal{E}(\sigma_2)$. From the results of Section 8 and 9, we know that this can be done by a greatest fixpoint iteration that reaches the greatest fixpoint at the latest after 3 iterations, i.e., $[\![\mathcal{E}(\sigma_2)]\!]^3(\infty)$ is the greatest fixpoint. Because of Lemma 11, we can perform each iteration in strongly polynomial time through a reduction to minimum cost flow problems. The following table illustrates the greatest fixpoint iteration:

$$
\begin{array}{c||c|c|c|c}
 & 0 & 1 & 2 & 3 \\
\hline
\mathbf{x}_{1,1} & \infty & 10 & 10 & 10 \\
\mathbf{x}_{1,2} & \infty & \infty & 11 & 11 \\
\mathbf{x}_{1,3} & \infty & 1 & 1 & 1
\end{array}
\tag{92}
$$

Observe that $\nu[\![\mathcal{E}(\sigma_2)]\!] = \{\mathbf{x}_{1,1} \mapsto 10, \mathbf{x}_{1,2} \mapsto 11, \mathbf{x}_{1,3} \mapsto 1\}$ is a solution of $\mathcal{E}$ and hence the least solution of $\mathcal{E}$. Therefore, $V^\sharp[\mathbf{st}] = (\infty, \infty, \infty)$, and $V^\sharp[1] = (10, 11, 1)$. That is, 10 is an upper bound on the value for the variable x_1 at program point 1, 11 is an upper bound on the value for the variable x_2 at program point 1, and 1 is an upper bound on the difference $x_2 - x_1$ at program point 1. Observe that the obtained result cannot be established if we use intervals as the abstract domain. □

11. Conclusion

We presented a practical algorithm for computing least solutions of systems of (extended) integer equations. This algorithm is based on iteration over $\vee$-strategies. While the required number of arithmetic operations is independent of the sizes of occurring numbers, the practical complexity crucially depends on the number of strategies encountered during iteration. We indicated how this algorithm can be applied to perform precise interval analysis. We further indicated how this algorithm can also be applied to perform precise program analysis based on integer zones. For that analysis, we provided that the basic step, the application of the best abstract transformer corresponding to guards and assignments, can be implemented by a reduction to a minimum cost network flow problem, for which fast strongly polynomial algorithms exist.

Acknowledgement   We thank Riko Jakob from the Technical University of Munich for the reduction to minimum cost flow problems.

References

[1] A. Adjé, S. Gaubert, and E. Goubault. Coupling policy iteration with semi-definite relaxation to compute accurate numerical invariants in static analysis. In A. D. Gordon, editor, *ESOP*, volume 6012 of *Lecture Notes in Computer Science*, pages 23–42. Springer, 2010. ISBN 978-3-642-11956-9.

[2] R. K. Ahuja, T. L. Magnati, and J. B. Orlin. *Network Flows*. Prentice Hall, 1993.

[3] H. Björklund, S. Sandberg, and S. Vorobyov. Optimization on completely unimodal hypercubes. Technichal report 2002-18, Department of Information Technology, Uppsala University, 2002.

[4] H. Bjorklund, S. Sandberg, and S. Vorobyov. Complexity of Model Checking by Iterative Improvement: the Pseudo-Boolean Framework . In *Proc. 5th Int. Andrei Ershov Memorial Conf. Perspectives of System Informatics*, pages 381–394. LNCS 2890, Springer, 2003.

[5] B. L. Charlier and P. V. Hentenryck. A Universal Top-Down Fixpoint Algorithm. Technical Report CS-92-25, Brown University, Providence, RI 02912, 1992.

[6] B. L. Charlier and P. V. Hentenryck. Experimental Evaluation of a Generic Abstract Interpretation Algorithm for Prolog. *ACM Transactions of Programming Languages and Systems (TOPLAS)*, 16(1):35–101, 1994.

[7] T. H. Cormen, C. E. Leiserson, R. L. Rivest, and C. Stein. *Introduction to Algorithms, Second Edition*. The MIT Press and McGraw-Hill Book Company, 2001. ISBN 0-262-03293-7, 0-07-013151-1.

[8] A. Costan, S. Gaubert, E. Goubault, M. Martel, and S. Putot. A Policy Iteration Algorithm for Computing Fixed Points in Static Analysis of Programs. In *Computer Aided Verification, 17th Int. Conf. (CAV)*, pages 462–475. LNCS 3576, Springer Verlag, 2005.

[9] P. Cousot and R. Cousot. Abstract interpretation: A unified lattice model for static analysis of programs by construction or approximation of fixpoints. In *POPL*, pages 238–252, 1977.

[10] P. Cousot and R. Cousot. Systematic Design of Program Analysis Frameworks. In *6th ACM Symp. on Principles of Programming Languages (POPL)*, pages 238–352, 1979.

[11] P. Cousot and R. Cousot. Comparison of the Galois Connection and Widening/Narrowing Approaches to Abstract Interpretation. JTASPEFL '91, Bordeaux. *BIGRE*, 74:107–110, Oct. 1991.

[12] N. Dor, M. Rodeh, and M. Sagiv. Cleanness Checking of String Manipulations in C Programs via Integer Analysis. In *8th Int. Static Analysis Symposium (SAS'01)*, pages 194–212. LNCS 2126, Springer Verlag, 2001.

[13] C. Fecht and H. Seidl. A Faster Solver for General Systems of Equations. *Science of Computer Programming (SCP)*, 35(2):137–161, 1999.

[14] S. Gaubert, E. Goubault, A. Taly, and S. Zennou. Static analysis by policy iteration on relational domains. In Nicola [29], pages 237–252. ISBN 978-3-540-71314-2.

[15] T. Gawlitza and H. Seidl. Precise relational invariants through strategy iteration. In J. Duparc and T. A. Henzinger, editors, *CSL*, volume 4646 of *Lecture Notes in Computer Science*, pages 23–40. Springer, 2007. ISBN 978-3-540-74914-1.

[16] T. Gawlitza and H. Seidl. Precise fixpoint computation through strategy iteration. In Nicola [29], pages 300–315. ISBN 978-3-540-71314-2.

[17] T. Gawlitza and H. Seidl. Precise interval analysis vs. parity games. In J. Cuéllar, T. S. E. Maibaum, and K. Sere, editors, *FM*, volume 5014 of *Lecture Notes in Computer Science*, pages 342–357. Springer, 2008. ISBN 978-3-540-68235-6.

[18] T. Gawlitza and H. Seidl. Abstract interpretation over zones without widening. In *Easychair Proceedings*, 2012. To appear.

[19] T. Gawlitza, H. Seidl, A. Adje, S. Gaubert, and E. Goubault. Abstract interpretation meets convex optimization. *Journal of Symbolic Computation (JSC)*, 2011. To appear.

[20] T. M. Gawlitza and H. Seidl. Computing relaxed abstract semantics w.r.t. quadratic zones precisely. In R. Cousot and M. Martel, editors, *SAS*, volume 6337 of *Lecture Notes in Computer Science*, pages 271–286. Springer, 2010. ISBN 978-3-642-15768-4.

[21] T. M. Gawlitza and H. Seidl. Solving systems of rational equations through strategy iteration. *ACM Trans. Program. Lang. Syst.*, 33(3):11, 2011.

[22] A. Hoffman and R. Karp. On Nonterminating Stochastic Games. *Management Sci.*, 12:359–370, 1966.

[23] R. Howard. *Dynamic Programming and Markov Processes*. Wiley, New York, 1960.

[24] N. Karmarkar. A new polynomial-time algorithm for linear programming. *Combinatorica*, 4(4):373–396, 1984.

[25] G. A. Kildall. A unified approach to global program optimization. In *POPL*, pages 194–206, 1973.

[26] K. G. Larsen, F. Larsson, P. Pettersson, and W. Yi. Efficient verification of real-time systems: compact data structure and state-space reduction. In *IEEE Real-Time Systems Symposium*, pages 14–24. IEEE Computer Society, 1997.

[27] A. Miné. A new numerical abstract domain based on difference-bound matrices. In O. Danvy and A. Filinski, editors, *PADO*, volume 2053 of *Lecture Notes in Computer Science*, pages 155–172. Springer, 2001. ISBN 3-540-42068-1.

[28] A. Miné. The octagon abstract domain. In *WCRE*, pages 310–, 2001.

[29] R. D. Nicola, editor. *Programming Languages and Systems, 16th European Symposium on Programming, ESOP 2007, Held as Part of the Joint European Conferences on Theory and Practics of Software, ETAPS 2007, Braga, Portugal, March 24 - April 1, 2007, Proceedings*, volume 4421 of *Lecture Notes in Computer Science*, 2007. Springer. ISBN 978-3-540-71314-2.

[30] J. B. Orlin. A faster strongly polynominal minimum cost flow algorithm. In *STOC*, pages 377–387. ACM, 1988.

[31] S. Sankaranarayanan, H. B. Sipma, and Z. Manna. Scalable analysis of linear systems using mathematical programming. In R. Cousot, editor, *VMCAI*, volume 3385 of *Lecture Notes in Computer Science*, pages 25–41. Springer, 2005. ISBN 3-540-24297-X.

[32] A. Schrijver. *Theory of Linear and Integer Programming*. Wiley, 1986.

[33] A. Tarski. A lattice-theoretical fixpoint theorem and its appications. *Pac. J. Math.*, 5:285–309, 1955.

[34] R. Wilhelm, J. Engblom, A. Ermedahl, N. Holsti, S. Thesing, D. B. Whalley, G. Bernat, C. Ferdinand, R. Heckmann, T. Mitra, F. Mueller, I. Puaut, P. P. Puschner, J. Staschulat, and P. Stenström. The worst-case execution-time problem - overview of methods and survey of tools. *ACM Trans. Embedded Comput. Syst.*, 7(3), 2008.

[35] S. J. Wright. *Primal-Dual Interior-Point Methods*. Philadelphia, PA, U.S.A., 1997.

[36] S. Yovine. Model checking timed automata. In G. Rozenberg and F. W. Vaandrager, editors, *European Educational Forum: School on Embedded Systems*, volume 1494 of *Lecture Notes in Computer Science*, pages 114–152. Springer, 1996. ISBN 3-540-65193-4.

A. Additional Lemmata

Lemma 13 *Let $f : (X \to \mathbb{Z}) \to \mathbb{Z}$ be a BF-function. For all $\rho : X \to \overline{\mathbb{Z}}$ and all $X' \subseteq X$ we have: $f(\rho \oplus \{x \mapsto \infty \mid x \in X'\}) > f(\rho)$ implies $f(\rho \oplus \{x \mapsto \infty \mid x \in X'\}) = \infty$.*
$\square$

B. Omitted Proofs: Section 6

Proof. [of Lemma 2] First of all we consider the operator $\vee$. Let $x = (x_1, x_2)$, $y = (y_1, y_2)$, $y \geq x$, and $y_1 \vee y_2 > x_1 \vee x_2$. We assume w.l.o.g. that $y_1 \geq y_2$ holds. Let $\delta := 0$. Then, we get (a) $y_1 > x_1$, (b) $y_1 \vee y_2 = y_1 + \delta$, and (c) $z_1 \vee z_2 \geq z_1 + \delta$ for all $(z_1, z_2) \geq y$.

We now consider an arbitrary monotone and upward-expansive operator $f : (X \to \overline{\mathbb{Z}}) \to \overline{\mathbb{Z}}$. Let $\rho' \geq \rho$, $f(\rho') > f(\rho)$, $x \in X$ with $\rho'(x) > \rho(x)$, and $\delta := f(\rho') - \rho'(x)$. Here, we assume that $\rho'(x) < \infty$ (otherwise it is trivial, since $\rho'(x) = \infty$ implies $f(\rho') = \infty$). Requirement (a) and (b) hold be definition. In order to prove requirement (c), let $\rho'' \geq \rho'$. We get:

$$f(\rho'') \geq f(\rho' \oplus \{x \mapsto \rho''(x)\}) \qquad \text{(Monotonicity)}$$
$$\geq f(\rho') + \rho''(x) - \rho'(x) \qquad \text{(Upward-expansivity)}$$
$$= \rho''(x) + \delta$$

This completes the proof. $\square$

Proof. [of Lemma 3] Let $e_{\mathbf{x}}$ denote the right hand-side of the equation for $\mathbf{x}$ in $\mathcal{E}$, i.e., $\mathbf{x} = e_{\mathbf{x}} \in \mathcal{E}$ holds for all $\mathbf{x} \in \mathbf{X}$. Within this proof, for some $i \geq 2$ and some variable $\mathbf{x}' \in \mathbf{X}$, a variable $\mathbf{x}$ is called *relevant for* $\rho^{(i)}(\mathbf{x}') > \rho^{(i-1)}(\mathbf{x}')$ iff $\mathbf{x}$ is relevant for $[\![e_{\mathbf{x}'}]\!]\rho^{(i-1)} > [\![e_{\mathbf{x}'}]\!]\rho^{(i-2)}$. Since $[\![e_{\mathbf{x}'}]\!]$ is a BF-function, there always exists some variable $\mathbf{x}$ that is relevant for $\rho^{(i)}(\mathbf{x}') > \rho^{(i-1)}(\mathbf{x}')$.

Note that $\rho^{(i)} \leq \rho^* := \mu[\![\mathcal{E}]\!]$ for all $i \in \mathbb{N}$, since $[\![\mathcal{E}]\!]$ is monotone. Let $\mathbf{x} \in \mathbf{X}$ and $k > n$ with $\rho^{(k)}(\mathbf{x}) > \rho^{(n)}(\mathbf{x})$. Furthermore, assume w.l.o.g. that $\rho^{(k)}(\mathbf{x}) > \rho^{(k-1)}(\mathbf{x})$. If $\rho^{(k)}(\mathbf{x}) = \infty$, then we directly obtain $\rho^*(\mathbf{x}) = \infty$. Therefore, we assume $\rho^{(k)}(\mathbf{x}) < \infty$.

Auxiliary Lemma 1 *There exist variables $\mathbf{x}_1, \ldots, \mathbf{x}_k \in \mathbf{X}$ such that the following conditions are fulfilled:*

1. $\mathbf{x}_k = \mathbf{x}$.
2. $\rho^{(i)}(\mathbf{x}_i) > \rho^{(i-1)}(\mathbf{x}_i)$ for all $i \in \{1, \ldots, k\}$.
3. $\mathbf{x}_{i-1}$ is relevant for $\rho^{(i)}(\mathbf{x}_i) > \rho^{(i-1)}(\mathbf{x}_i)$ for all $i \in \{2, \ldots, k\}$.

Proof. The statement can be shown by backward induction using the fact that $\mathcal{E}$ is a system of BF-equations. $\square$

Auxiliary Lemma 2 *Let $i_1, i_2 \in \{1, \ldots, k\}$ with $i_1 \leq i_2$ and $\delta := \rho^{(i_2)}(\mathbf{x}_{i_2}) - \rho^{(i_1)}(\mathbf{x}_{i_1})$. Then $([\![\mathcal{E}]\!]^{i_2 - i_1} \rho)(\mathbf{x}_{i_2}) \geq \rho(\mathbf{x}_{i_1}) + \delta$ for all $\rho \geq \rho^{(i_1)}$.*

Proof. Let $\rho \geq \rho^{(i_1)}$. We do induction on $i_2 - i_1$. The statement is obviously fulfilled for $i_2 - i_1 = 0$. Therefore, assume $i_2 - i_1 > 0$. From the induction hypothesis we get $(\llbracket\mathcal{E}\rrbracket^{i_2-1-i_1}\rho)(\mathbf{x}_{i_2-1}) \geq \rho(\mathbf{x}_{i_1}) + \delta'$, where $\delta' := \rho^{(i_2-1)}(\mathbf{x}_{i_2-1}) - \rho^{(i_1)}(\mathbf{x}_{i_1})$. We have $\rho^{(i_2)}(\mathbf{x}_{i_2}) = \llbracket e_{\mathbf{x}_{i_2}}\rrbracket\rho^{(i_2-1)}$ and, by Auxiliary Lemma 1, $\mathbf{x}_{i_2-1}$ is relevant for $\rho^{(i_2)}(\mathbf{x}_{i_2}) > \rho^{(i_2-1)}(\mathbf{x}_{i_2})$. Let $\delta'' := \rho^{(i_2)}(\mathbf{x}_{i_2}) - \rho^{(i_2-1)}(\mathbf{x}_{i_2-1})$ and $\delta := \delta' + \delta'' = \rho^{(i_2)}(\mathbf{x}_{i_2}) - \rho^{(i_1)}(\mathbf{x}_{i_1})$. Thus, we get:

$$(\llbracket\mathcal{E}\rrbracket^{i_2-i_1}\rho)(\mathbf{x}_{i_2}) = (\llbracket\mathcal{E}\rrbracket(\llbracket\mathcal{E}\rrbracket^{i_2-1-i_1}\rho))(\mathbf{x}_{i_2}) = \llbracket e_{\mathbf{x}_{i_2}}\rrbracket(\llbracket\mathcal{E}\rrbracket^{i_2-1-i_1}\rho)$$

$$\geq (\llbracket\mathcal{E}\rrbracket^{i_2-1-i_1}\rho)(\mathbf{x}_{i_2-1}) + \delta'' \geq \rho(\mathbf{x}_{i_1}) + \delta' + \delta'' = \rho(\mathbf{x}_{i_1}) + \delta$$

This completes the proof of auxiliary lemma 2.   □

Since $k > n$, by the pigeon-hole principle, there exist $k_1, k_2 \in \mathbb{N}$ with $1 \leq k_1 < k_2 \leq k$ such that $\mathbf{y} := \mathbf{x}_{k_2} = \mathbf{x}_{k_1}$. Let $\delta := \rho^{(k_2)}(\mathbf{y}) - \rho^{(k_1)}(\mathbf{y})$. Since $\rho^{(k_2)}(\mathbf{y}) > \rho^{(k_1)}(\mathbf{y})$, we have $\delta = \rho^{(k_2)}(\mathbf{y}) - \rho^{(k_1)}(\mathbf{y}) > 0$.

Next, we show $\rho^*(\mathbf{y}) = \infty$. For the sake of contradiction assume $\rho^*(\mathbf{y}) < \infty$. Since $\rho^* \geq \rho^{(k_1)}$ holds, $(\llbracket\mathcal{E}\rrbracket^{k_2-k_1}\rho^*)(\mathbf{y}) \geq \rho^*(\mathbf{y}) + \delta > \rho^*(\mathbf{y})$ holds by Auxiliary Lemma 2 — contradiction to $\rho^* \in \mathbf{Sol}(\mathcal{E})$. Thus, we have $\rho^*(\mathbf{y}) = \infty$. It remains to show $\rho^*(\mathbf{x}) = \infty$. Since $\rho^* \in \mathbf{Sol}(\mathcal{E})$, we have $\rho^*(\mathbf{x}) = (\llbracket\mathcal{E}\rrbracket^{k-k_2}\rho^*)(\mathbf{x}) \geq \rho^*(\mathbf{y}) + (\rho^{(k)}(\mathbf{x}) - \rho^{(k_2)}(\mathbf{y})) = \infty$, because of Auxiliary Lemma 2.   □

Proof. [of Theorem 3] Let ρ_0 be the value of the program variable ρ after the execution of the first for-loop, i.e., we have $\rho_0 = \llbracket\mathcal{E}\rrbracket^n(-\infty)$. We denote the value of the program variable ρ immediate before the execution of the second for-loop by ρ_1. For $i = 2, \ldots, n$, we denote the value of the program variable ρ after the $(i-1)$-th execution of the loop-body of the second for-loop by ρ_i.

Let $\rho^* \in \mathbf{PostSol}(\mathcal{E})$. Since $\llbracket\mathcal{E}\rrbracket$ is monotone, we have $\rho_0 \leq \rho^*$. Firstly, we show that $\rho_i \leq \rho^*$ holds for all $i = 1, \ldots, n$. By Lemma 3, $\rho^*(\mathbf{x}) = \infty$, whenever $(\llbracket\mathcal{E}\rrbracket\rho_0)(\mathbf{x}) > \rho_0(\mathbf{x})$. Hence, we have $\rho_1 \leq \rho^*$, i.e., the statement holds for $i = 1$. Assume that the statement holds for $i \in \{1, \ldots, n-1\}$, i.e., $\rho_i \leq \rho^*$. Since $\llbracket\mathcal{E}\rrbracket$ is monotone, we have $\rho_{i+1} = \rho_i \vee \llbracket\mathcal{E}\rrbracket\rho_i \leq \rho_i \vee \llbracket\mathcal{E}\rrbracket\rho^* \leq \rho^*$. Thus, we have shown that $\rho_i \leq \rho^*$ for all $i = 1, \ldots, n$.

Finally, we show that $\rho_n \in \mathbf{PostSol}(\mathcal{E})$. For $i = 0, \ldots, n$, let $\mathbf{X}_i^\infty := \{\mathbf{x} \in \mathbf{X} \mid \rho_i(\mathbf{x}) = \infty\}$. By construction we have $\rho_1 = \rho_0 \oplus \{\mathbf{x} \mapsto \infty \mid \mathbf{X}_1^\infty \setminus \mathbf{X}_0^\infty\}$. By induction we show that $\rho_i = \rho_{i-1} \oplus \{\mathbf{x} \mapsto \infty \mid \mathbf{x} \in \mathbf{X}_i^\infty \setminus \mathbf{X}_{i-1}^\infty\}$ for all $i \in \{2, \ldots, n\}$. Because of Lemma 13, the following holds for $i = 2$ and every equations $\mathbf{x} = e \in \mathcal{E}$:

$$\rho_i(\mathbf{x}) = \rho_2(\mathbf{x}) = \rho_1(\mathbf{x}) \vee \llbracket e\rrbracket\rho_1 = \rho_1(\mathbf{x}) \vee \begin{cases} \infty & \text{if } \llbracket e\rrbracket\rho_1 > \llbracket e\rrbracket\rho_0 \\ \llbracket e\rrbracket\rho_0 & \text{if } \llbracket e\rrbracket\rho_1 \leq \llbracket e\rrbracket\rho_0 \end{cases}$$

$$= \begin{cases} \infty & \text{if } \llbracket e\rrbracket\rho_1 > \llbracket e\rrbracket\rho_0 \\ \rho_1(\mathbf{x}) & \text{if } \llbracket e\rrbracket\rho_1 \leq \llbracket e\rrbracket\rho_0 \end{cases}$$

Let $i > 2$ and assume that the statement holds for $i - 1$. Since $\llbracket e\rrbracket$ is a BF-function, the following holds for every equation $\mathbf{x} = e \in \mathcal{E}$:

$$\rho_i(\mathbf{x}) = \rho_{i-1}(\mathbf{x}) \vee \llbracket e\rrbracket\rho_{i-1} = \rho_{i-1}(\mathbf{x}) \vee \begin{cases} \infty & \text{if } \llbracket e\rrbracket\rho_{i-1} > \llbracket e\rrbracket\rho_{i-2} \\ \llbracket e\rrbracket\rho_{i-2} & \text{if } \llbracket e\rrbracket\rho_{i-1} \leq \llbracket e\rrbracket\rho_{i-2} \end{cases}$$

$$= \begin{cases} \infty & \text{if } \llbracket e \rrbracket \rho_{i-1} > \llbracket e \rrbracket \rho_{i-2} \\ \rho_{i-1}(\mathbf{x}) & \text{if } \llbracket e \rrbracket \rho_{i-1} \leq \llbracket e \rrbracket \rho_{i-2} \end{cases}$$

Thus, $\rho_i = \rho_{i-1} \oplus \{\mathbf{x} \mapsto \infty \mid \mathbf{x} \in \mathbf{X}_i^\infty \setminus \mathbf{X}_{i-1}^\infty\}$ for all $i \in \{1, \ldots, n\}$. Thus, for all $i = 1, \ldots, n$, either $\mathbf{X}_i^\infty \supset \mathbf{X}_{i-1}^\infty$ or $\rho_i = \rho_{i-1}$. If there exists some $i = 1, \ldots, n-1$ with $\rho_i = \rho_{i-1}$, then the statement is proven, since then $\llbracket \mathcal{E} \rrbracket \rho_{i-1} \leq \rho_{i-1}$ and thus $\rho_n = \rho_{i-1} \in \mathbf{PostSol}(\mathcal{E})$. Otherwise, i.e., if $\rho_i > \rho_{i-1}$ for all $i \in \{1, \ldots, n\}$, then $\mathbf{X}_i^\infty \supset \mathbf{X}_{i-1}^\infty$ for all $i \in \{1, \ldots, n\}$. Therefore, we get $\rho_n = \infty$. Thus, we have shown, that $\rho_n \in \mathbf{PostSol}(\mathcal{E})$.

We have $\rho^* \geq \rho_n \in \mathbf{PostSol}(\mathcal{E})$ for all $\rho^* \in \mathbf{PostSol}(\mathcal{E})$, i.e., ρ_n is the least post-solution. Thus, ρ_n is also the least solution of $\mathcal{E}$. $\qquad \square$

C. Omitted Proofs: Section 8

Proof. [of Lemma 6] We only have to consider the case that $\mathcal{E}$ is a system of basic integer equations. Thus, let $\mathcal{E}$ be a system of basic integer equations. For a pre-solution ρ'' of $\mathcal{E}$, let $M_{\rho''}$ be the smallest set of of equations of the form $\mathbf{x} = e$ with the following properties:

1. If $\mathbf{x} = e \in \mathcal{E}$ with $\rho''(\mathbf{x}) < \llbracket e \rrbracket \rho'' < \infty$, then $\mathbf{x} = e \in M_{\rho''}$.
2. If $(\mathbf{x} = e[\mathbf{x}'], \mathbf{x}' = e') \in M_{\rho''} \times M_{\rho''} \cup M_{\rho''} \times \mathcal{D}_{\rho''}(\mathcal{E}) \cup \mathcal{D}_{\rho''}(\mathcal{E}) \times M_{\rho''}$, then $\mathbf{x} = e[e'] \in M_{\rho''}$.

Because of expansivity $\rho''(\mathbf{x}) < \llbracket e \rrbracket \rho'' < \infty$ holds for all $\mathbf{x} = e \in M_{\rho''}$ and all pre-solutions ρ'' of $\mathcal{E}$. Furthermore, $M_\rho \cup \mathcal{D}_\rho(\mathcal{E}) \supseteq M_{\rho'} \cup \mathcal{D}_{\rho'}(\mathcal{E})$, because of the feasibility of ρ.

We show that ρ' is feasible. For the sake of contradiction we assume that ρ' is not feasible. Thus, there exists some $\mathbf{x} = e \in \mathcal{D}_{\rho'}(\mathcal{E})$ with $\mathbf{x} \in \mathbf{Vars}(e)$. By definition, we have $-\infty < \rho'(\mathbf{x}) = \llbracket e \rrbracket \rho' < \infty$. Since $\llbracket e \rrbracket$ is monotone and by Lemma 1 expansive, we have $\rho(\mathbf{x}) \geq \llbracket e \rrbracket (\rho' \oplus \{\mathbf{x} \mapsto \rho(\mathbf{x})\}) \geq \llbracket e \rrbracket \rho$. Since $\mathbf{x} = e \in \mathcal{D}_{\rho'}(\mathcal{E}) \subseteq M_\rho \cup \mathcal{D}_\rho(\mathcal{E})$, we get $\rho(\mathbf{x}) \leq \llbracket e \rrbracket \rho$. We get $\rho(\mathbf{x}) = \llbracket e \rrbracket \rho$. Therefore, $\mathbf{x} = e \in \mathcal{D}_\rho(\mathcal{E})$. This contradicts the assumption that ρ is feasible. $\qquad \square$

Proof. [of Lemma 8] For the sake of contradiction assume that ρ is not $\mathcal{E}(\sigma')$-feasible. Hence, there exists a $\pi' \in \Pi_{\mathcal{E}(\sigma')}$ such that ρ is not $\mathcal{E}(\sigma')(\pi')$-feasible. Thus, there exists an equation $\bar{\mathbf{x}} = \bar{e} \in \mathcal{D}_\rho(\mathcal{E}(\sigma')(\pi'))$ with $\bar{\mathbf{x}} \in \mathbf{Vars}(\bar{e})$. For all expressions $e \in \mathcal{S}(\mathcal{E})$, the following holds: If $\infty > \llbracket e\sigma' \pi' \rrbracket \rho = \llbracket e\sigma \rrbracket \rho > -\infty$ holds, then there exists a $\wedge$-strategy $\pi \in \Pi_{\mathcal{E}(\sigma)}$, such that $e\sigma' \pi' = e\sigma \pi$ holds. This holds, because, by Lemma 1, $\llbracket e \rrbracket$ is expansive in $\mathbf{Vars}(e)$ for every basic integer expression and because σ' is an improvement of σ w.r.t. ρ and thus we have $\llbracket e\sigma' \rrbracket \rho > \llbracket e\sigma \rrbracket \rho$ for all $e \in \mathcal{S}_\vee(\mathcal{E})$ with $\sigma'(e) \neq \sigma(e)$. From this it in particular follows the validity of the following statement: If $\infty > \llbracket e\sigma' \pi' \rrbracket \rho = \llbracket e\sigma \rrbracket \rho = \rho(\mathbf{x}) > -\infty$ for an equation $\mathbf{x} = e \in \mathcal{E}$, then there exists a $\wedge$-strategy π for $\mathcal{E}(\sigma)$ such that $e\sigma' \pi' = e\sigma \pi$. Thus, we can construct a $\wedge$-strategy π for $\mathcal{E}(\sigma)$ such that $e\sigma' \pi' = e\sigma \pi$ for all equations $\mathbf{x} = e \in \mathcal{E}$ with $\infty > \llbracket e\sigma' \pi' \rrbracket \rho = \rho(\mathbf{x}) > -\infty$. Let π be such a $\wedge$-strategy for $\mathcal{E}(\sigma)$. We in particular also get

$\bar{\mathbf{x}} = \bar{e} \in \mathcal{D}_\rho(\mathcal{E}(\sigma)(\pi))$. This is a contradiction, since ρ is $\mathcal{E}(\sigma)$-feasible and thus also $\mathcal{E}(\sigma)(\pi)$-feasible. □

Proof. [of Theorem 6] We show that at most $|\mathbf{X}| \cdot |\Sigma|$ $\vee$-strategy improvement steps are preformed. As input we have the system $\mathcal{E}\vee -\infty$, a $\vee$-strategy σ_{init} with $\sigma_{\text{init}}(e\vee -\infty) = -\infty$ for all $\mathbf{x} = e \in \mathcal{E}$ and the variable assignment $\rho_{\text{init}} = \underline{-\infty}$. For $i \in \mathbb{N}$, let σ_i and ρ_i be the values of the program variables σ and ρ after the i-th execution of the loop-body, respectively.

For the sake of contradiction assume that $\rho_{|\mathbf{X}|\cdot|\Sigma|} \neq \mu[\![\mathcal{E}]\!]$ holds. Thus, we have $\rho_0 < \cdots < \rho_{|\mathbf{X}|\cdot|\Sigma|+1}$. From $\sigma_i(e\vee -\infty) = e$ we get $\sigma_j(e\vee -\infty) = e$ for all $j \geq i \in \mathbb{N}$. Hence, at most $|\mathbf{X}| \cdot |\Sigma|$ different $\vee$-strategies occur in the sequence $\sigma_1, \ldots, \sigma_{|\mathbf{X}|\cdot|\Sigma|+1}$. Because of the pigeon-hole principle, there exists a $\vee$-strategy σ that occurs twice in the sequence $\sigma_1, \ldots, \sigma_{|\mathbf{X}|\cdot|\Sigma|+1}$, i.e., there exist $i_1, i_2 \in \{1, \ldots, |\mathbf{X}| \cdot |\Sigma| + 1\}$ with $i_1 < i_2$ and $\sigma_{i_1} = \sigma_{i_2}$. Thus, we have $\rho_{i_1} = \nu[\![\mathcal{E}(\sigma_{i_1})]\!] = \nu[\![\mathcal{E}(\sigma_{i_2})]\!] = \rho_{i_2}$. This contradicts the fact that $\rho_{i_1} < \rho_{i_2}$ holds. □

Software Safety and Security
T. Nipkow et al. (Eds.)
IOS Press, 2012

Subject Index

Software Safety and Security
T. Nipkow et al. (Eds.)
IOS Press, 2012

Author Index